2

AVIATION DISASTERS

The World's Major Civil Airliner Crashes since 1950

FOURTH EDITION

DAVID GERO

PATRICK STEPHENS LIMITED
AN IMPRINT OF HAYNES PUBLISHING

First published in the United Kingdom in 1993 by
Patrick Stephens Limited

British Library Cataloguing in Publication Data
A catalogue record for this book is available from the British Library.

ISBN 0-7509-3146-9

Patrick Stephens is an imprint of
Haynes Publishing, Sparkford.

Tel: 01963 440635 Fax: 01963 440001
Int. tel: +44 1963 440635 Int. Fax: +44 1963 440001

Email: sales@haynes-manuals.co.uk
Web site: http://www.haynes.com

Printed and bound in Great Britain by
J.H. Haynes & Co. Ltd, Sparkford

CONTENTS

INTRODUCTION

When *Aviation Disasters* was first published nearly a decade and a half ago, it was unique in the world of trade books, a reference publication dedicated to the subject of air calamities. In the years since, numerous books on the subject have come out, and they have been joined by several air crash websites on the worldwide Internet. I would like to think that *Aviation Disasters* started or at least helped to spark interest in this field of research.

This latest edition is essentially a new book. Not only does it include events occurring in the young twenty-first century, but it also updates information on disasters recounted in earlier versions. I'm happy to see more nations and investigative agencies becoming willing to share accident information. When I began my research for the first edition, censorship was still a major issue; the second in fact offered the first in-depth coverage on disasters that had occurred, but generally not been reported, in the former Soviet Union and its Eastern Bloc allies. The availability of material has helped to make this fourth edition of *Aviation Disasters* the most comprehensive ever.

Since the beginning of 1950, the airlines of the world have suffered well over 1,000 significant mishaps, i.e. those involving fatalities and/or the destruction of an aircraft. Since the task of presenting all of these in any detail would be beyond the scope of a single book, I have concentrated on those most serious catastrophes. The primary criterion for entry into this volume is severity in terms of lives lost. I have included accounts on every known accident occurring on a passenger flight with at least 80 fatalities, and every one involving an air carrier of the industrialised world resulting in at least 60 deaths. Additionally, I have included accounts on other incidents that may

be less serious in terms of casualties but are of some historic value. Every type of calamity is included, whether it be the result of crew error, bad weather, technical failure or hostile action (the latter referring to both sabotage and aircraft attacked from the ground, sea or air).

Readers may observe that *Aviation Disasters* is biased, both in the number of accounts and in their length and coverage, towards operators in Western Europe, North America, Oceania and Japan. This should not be construed as meaning that these nations have inferior safety records (just the opposite, in fact, they are the safest), but rather can be explained by their greater volume of air traffic coupled with their willingness to share accident information (which probably accounts for their superior records).

Whenever possible, I have endeavoured to obtain information from 'official' sources. Generally, civil air mishaps are investigated by government bodies, such as the National Transportation Safety Board (NTSB) in the US and the Air Accidents Investigation Branch (AIB) in the UK, which publish accident reports or summary briefs. Recommendations coming therefrom are then implemented by government regulatory bodies, the best known of which are the US Federal Aviation Administration (FAA) and the British Civil Aviation Authority (CAA). I have also relied heavily on the aviation media, whose writers are more knowledgeable on the subject than most journalists, and which will normally guarantee greater accuracy. I must also give praise to the many international airlines that offered assistance, and wish further to credit the aforementioned Internet which has greatly improved access to accident information. (I might note that the Internet works both ways, however; it's interesting to see how certain websites have lifted information from my books, sometimes giving me credit, sometimes not.)

In writing this book, I have gone to great lengths in providing specific details of individual mishaps, even to the point of listing the specific model of a certain type of aircraft and its serial number, and the local time of occurrence. Each account is literally a 'mini-volume' of the incident, making the book easy reference for those seeking information on a particular disaster. It was a very challenging project!

Although my name appears on its cover, this latest *Aviation Disasters* was the result of the work of many individuals – information and photographic researchers, translators, technical advisers and even readers who have offered opinions and corrective assistance. As stated in the very first edition, I hope new and returning readers will find it interesting and enlightening.

David Gero
San Gabriel, California

ACKNOWLEDGEMENTS

The author would like to thank the following organisations and individuals for their help in the preparation of this book:

Airbus Industrie; Air Accidents Investigation Branch (UK); Air Canada Flight Safety Division. Contact: J.A. Mitchell; Airclaims Ltd. Contact: Paul Hayes; Airclaims CIS. Contact: Elena Kuznetsova; Danish Aircraft Accident Investigation. Contact: Niels Jaksobsen; Norwegian Aircraft Accident Investigation Board. Contacts: T.B. Kirkvaag, Ragnar Rygnestad; Air France Office of Public Affairs. Contact: Gail Muntner; Mete Akkaya, Turkish Representative to the ICAO; Alitalia; All Nippon Airways Safety Promotion Committee. Contacts: Yoshi Funatsu, Hiroshi Sakabe; Argentine Air Force. Contacts: Guillermo Raul Barreira, Mario Santamaria; Belgian World Airlines (SABENA). Contact: J. Deschutter; Arif Boediman, Indonesian Representative to the ICAO; Boeing Canada de Havilland. Contact: Colin Fisher; British Airways Air Safety Branch. Contacts: Roy Lomas, C.N. Hall; Australian Bureau of Air Safety Investigation. Contacts: W.G. Duffy, F. St. G. Hornblower, D.J. Nicholas, R.J. Sibbison; Canadian Airlines International Ltd. Contact: P.G. Howe; Canadian Aviation Safety Board. Contacts: Nicole Brind'Amour, Manon Ouimet van Riel, Joyce Pedley; Centro de Investigacao e Prevencao de Acidentes Aeronauticos (Brazil). Contacts: Osmar Nascimento Amorim, Renato Tristao de Menezes, Paulo Fernando Peralta, Carlos Machado Vallim, Paulo C.F. Viana; Civil Aviation Authority (UK); Civil Aviation Department (Hong Kong). Contact: Y.S. Fong; Departamento Administrativo de Aeonautica Civil (Colombia). Contacts: Carlos German Barrero Fandino, William Mejia Restrepo; Department of Civil Aviation (Malta). Contact: C.D. Caruana; Department of Civil Aviation (Pakistan).

Contact: Patrick Callaghan; Department of Transport (South Africa). Contact: Barend P.K. Jordaan; Department of Transport and Power (Ireland). Contacts: G. Guihen, J. McStay; Dirección General de Aeronáutica Civil (Mexico). Contact: Carlos Moran Moguel; Direcçao-Geral Da Aviaçao Civil (Portugal). Contact: Jose Camilo Pastor; Direction des Journaux Officiels (France). Contacts: Jeannine Valin, Monique Masson; Director General Of Civil Aviation (India). Contact: B.R. Chopra; Directorate of Civil Aviation (Iceland); Ecuadorean Dirección General de Aviacion Civil. Contact: Edmundo Baquero M; Embassy of South Africa to the US. Contact: Neville C. Parkins; Embassy of the US to Peru. Contact: David Stebbing; Embassy of the US to Venezuela. Contact: Hans Mueller; Federal Aircraft Accident Investigation Bureau (Switzerland). Contacts: Erich Keller, A.D. Salzmann; Federal Ministry of Transport (Germany). Contact: I.A. Kramer; Hellenic Republic Ministry of Communications, Civil Aviation Authority (Greece). Contacts: G. Fotiades, K. Mavrogenis, G. Tzouvalis; Inspection Generale de l'Aviation Civile et de la Meteorologie (France). Contacts: Robert Davidson, M. Dulac; International Civil Aviation Organisation (ICAO). Contacts: Tracey Martineau, Germaine Zaloum; Japan Aeronautical Engineers' Association; Japan Airlines. Contacts: M. Osaki, Geoffrey Tudor; Japan Air System. Contact: H. Kanai; KLM Royal Dutch Airlines. Contact: Peter Offerman; Nick Komons, Historian, Federal Aviation Administration (US); Lauda Air. Contact: Ronald Kraftner; Library of Congress (US); Lockheed; Lufthansa German Airlines. Contact: Norbert Wagner; Ministere des Communications Administration de l'Aeronautique (Belgium). Contact: J. Van Laer; Ministerio de Transportes, Turismo y Comunicaciones (Spain).

Contact: Jose Bellido Grela; Ministerio de Transportes y Comunicaciones (Peru). Contact: Luis Bouroncle Loayza; Ministry of Defence (UK). Contacts: Les Howard, Eric Munday; Ministry of Transport (Israel). Contact: Giora Chalamish; Ministry of Transport (Japan); Ministry of Transport and Public Works (The Netherlands). Contact: F.A. van Reijsen; Ministry of Transportation and Communications Bureau (Philippines). Contact: M.S. Talento, Jr; National Archives (US). Contacts: Vernon Brooks, Janet Kennelly, Jane Lange, A'Donna Thomas, Jessie White; National Board of Aviation (Finland). Contacts: Seppo Hamalainen, Jorma Kivinen; National Transportation Safety Board (US). Contact: Susan Stevenson; Nordic Delegation to the ICAO. Contact: O. Mydland; Office of Air Accidents Investigation (New Zealand). Contacts: L.J. Banfield, L.F. Blewett, Ron Chippindale; Philippine Airlines. Contact: Enrique Santos; Public Archives of Canada. Contact: Glenn Wright; Qantas Airways. Contact: John J. White; Scandinavian Airlines System (SAS). Contact: Gunnel Thorne; Singapore Ministry of Transport. Contact: Ong Yunn Shing; Swedish Civil Aviation Administration. Contacts: Klas Bask, Roland Nilsson; Swissair FAH Historical Society; US Air Force Historical Research Center. Contact: Lt Col Alan Clair; US Air Force Inspection and Safety Center. Contacts: John J. Clark Jr, Vincent Murone; US Department of Defense; Venezolana Internacional de Aviacion SA (VIASA). Contact: Capt Eduardo Nieto Willett.

Special thanks to: Monique Bouscarle, Inspection Generale de l'Aviation Civile et de la Meteorologie (France); Loyita Worley, Civil Aviation Authority (UK); and the entire staff at the Los Angeles Regional Office of the National Transportation Safety Board (US).

Research services were provided by: ARIOMA Editorial Services (Moira and Patrick Smith); Jacques Clairoux; Alan Cooper; Diane Hamilton; Historial Newspaper Service (John Frost); Ronan Hubert; Sarah Molumby; Kathryn Powers; Graham K. Salt; A. Spanier; Task Force Pro Libra Ltd (Susan Hill, Anne Williams); and Hilary Thomas.

Translation services were provided by: Raymundo Aguirre; Agnes Allard; Lupe Anaya; Victoria Aranda; Ramona Barranco; Robert Beck; Berlitz Translation Services; Else Bokkers; Alice Bonnefoi; Martin Bredboell; Richard Brome; Jim Buendia; Dale Carter; Luca Cortelezzi; Vivian Curtis; Francisco Fan; Iris Fiorito, Fliteline Language Services; Mitsuko Fujiwara; Guillaume Gavillet; Patrick Germain; Francoise Gerardin; Luis Gonzalez; David Green; Boris Hasselblatt; Inge Hochner; Vanna Hungerford; Kayo Ide; Milena Kaylin; Noriyuki Kawabata; Yan Kuhn; Giancarlo Losi; Marci Moody; David Newton; Masako Ohnuki; Delores Pedro; Poly-Languages Institute; Julio Puchalt; Liselotte Runde; Millicent Sharma; Monique Swadowski; Delfina Vadi; Natalie Vetchinne; Ruth Quirk Von Woo; Marie-Antoinette Zrimc.

Publications consulted included the following: *Aeroplane and Commercial Aviation News* magazine; *Aircraft Accident Digest* (International Civil Aviation Organisation (ICAO)); *Air Disasters* by Stanley Stewart (Ian Allan Ltd, 1986); *Airliner Production Lists* by Tony Eastwood and John Roach (The Aviation Hobby Shop); *Anvil of the Gods* by Fred McClement (J.B. Lippincott Co, 1964); *Aviation/Space Dictionary* by Ernest J. Gentle and Lawrence W. Reithmaier (Aero Publishers Inc, 1980); *Aviation Week and Space Technology* magazine; *Crash* by Rob and Sarah Elder (Atheneum Publishers, 1977); *Daily Express* newspaper; *Daily Mirror* newspaper; *Destination Disaster* by Paul Eddy, Bruce Page and Elaine Potter (Times Newspapers, 1976); *Flight International* magazine; *Hostile Actions Against Civil Aviation* (Air Incident Research); *It Doesn't Matter Where You Sit* by Fred McClement (Holt, Rinehart and Winston, 1969); *Jane's Aerospace Dictionary* by Bill Gunston (Jane's Publishing Co Ltd, 1986); *Jane's All The World's Aircraft* (Jane's Information Group); *Jet Airliner Checklist* by Paul Rainford (Executive Aircraft Historians, 1988); *KE 007: A Conspiracy of Circumstance* by Murray Sayle (in the New York Times Review of Books, 25 April 1985); *La Opinion* newspaper; *Lloyd's List* newspaper; *Los Angeles Times* newspaper; *Loud and Clear* by Robert J. Serling (Dell Publishing Co, 1970); *Newsweek* magazine; *New York Times* newspaper; *Paris Match* magazine; *Proceedings* magazine, September 1989 (US Naval Institute); *Prop Airliner Checklist* by Tony Hyatt (Executive Aircraft Historians, 1988); *Reader's Digest* magazine, February 1973: article entitled 'Nightmare in the Jungle'; *Recovered Mail* by Henri L. Nierinck (R-Editions, 1980); *Shootdown* by

Richard W. Johnson (Viking Penguin Inc, 1986); *Skin Diver* magazine, May 1975: article entitled 'Wings of Death', excerpted from Dr Joseph B. MacInnis's book *The Underwater Man*; *Soviet Airliners* by Peter Hillman (Executive Aircraft Historians, 1989); *Time* magazine; *The Times Atlas of the World*; *The Times* (of London) newspaper; *The World Book Encyclopaedia* (Field Enterprises Corp); *World Airline Accident Summary* (Civil Aviation Authority (CAA)); and *World Commercial Aircraft Accidents* by Chris Kimura.

Other sources of information include the following: *Tracking the Pan Am Bombers*, an edition of the *Frontline* television series, produced by the Public Broadcasting System (PBS), and Crewmembers International Internet site.

The following accident accounts are copyrighted by Airclaims CIS, Moscow, Russian Federation: Aeroflot Tu-104 (15 August 1958); Tu-104 (17 October 1958); Tu-104 (30 June 1962); An-10 (28 July 1962); Tu-104 (2 September 1962); Il-18 (2 September 1964); Il-18 (16 November 1967); Il-18 (29 February 1968); Il-18 (6 February 1970); Tu-104 (25 July 1971); An-10 (18 May 1972); Il-18 (31 August 1972); Il-18 (1 October 1972); Il-62 (13 October 1972); Tu-104 (30 September 1973); Tu-104 (13 October 1973); Il-18 (27 April 1974); Il-18 (6 March 1976); Tu-104 (13 January 1977); Tu-134 collision (11 August 1979); Tu-154 (8 July 1980); Tu-154 (16 November 1981); Yak-42 (28 June 1982); Il-62 (6 July 1982); Tu-134 (30 August 1983); Tu-154 (11 October 1984); Tu-154 (23 December 1984); Tu-134/An-26 collision (3 May 1985); Tu-154 (10 July 1985); Tu-134 (27 August 1992); Yak-40 (28 August 1993); Tu-154 (3 January 1994); A310 (22 March 1994); Aviaimpex Yak-42D (20 November 1993); Far East Aviation Tu-154 (8 December 1995); African Air An-32 (8 January 1996); Saudi Arabian Airlines Boeing 747/Air Kazakhstan Il-76 (12 November 1996); Tu-154 (15 December 1997); and Vladivostok Air Tu-154 (4 July 2001).

PICTURE SOURCES

Aeroflot; Air Britain Historians Ltd. Contact: Glyn Ramsden; Airbus Industrie. Contact: Sean Lee; Aircraft Photographic; All Nippon Airways Public Relations Section; American Airlines; AP Images. Contact: Yvette Reyes; Aviation Photo News; The Bettmann Archive; Black Star. Contacts: Cheryl Himmelstein, Judith Wolf; Boeing Commercial Airplane Group. Contact: Danielle Gerrard; British Aerospace. Contacts: Mike Brown, P.N.P. Smith; Corbis Inc. Contact: Michelle Piatkowski; Eastern Airlines; Fokker BV. Contact: Leo J.N. Steijn; Gamma Liaison. Contacts: Jennifer Coley, Grace How; General Dynamics; General Microfilm; Douglas Green; Liaison Agency; Los Angeles Times; Lux Photographic Services; Magnum Photos; McDonnell Douglas. Contact: Harry Gann; Adrian Meredith Photography; Pan American World Airways; 'PA' News; Popperfoto/Uniphoto Press International. Contacts: Ian Blackwell, Toyoo Ohta; Programmed Communications Ltd. Contact: Sheila Hamilton; Sikorsky Aircraft; Sygma. Contact: Claire Gouldstone; Trans World Airlines; United Airlines; Avions de Transport Regional and videographer Evan Fairbanks.

THE 1950S

Commercial aviation truly came of age in the 1950s. The air travel boom that had begun shortly after the Second World War, introducing to the average person that which previously had been available only to those wealthy and daring enough to step on to an aeroplane, was in full swing. More flights were available to more destinations, with airliners carrying more passengers at greater speeds and higher levels of safety and comfort than ever before.

A number of larger and higher-performance aircraft saw their first passenger service in the 1950s. These included the Douglas DC-7 and Lockheed Super Constellation, which represented the peak in piston-engine transport development. In 1952 the de Havilland Comet introduced the first jet passenger service. The aircraft had to be withdrawn from use only two years later due to a serious structural deficiency, but the new refined Comet would return in 1958, providing the first jet airliner service across the Atlantic. It was joined by such jets as the French Caravelle and US Boeing 707; the latter would serve for many years as the backbone of long-haul air transport. Also introduced durng this period were several models of propeller/turbine aircraft, or turboprops, including the Vickers Viscount, Bristol Britannia and Lockheed Electra.

One of the most notable safety advances coming into operation in the 1950s was airborne weather radar. But of course the increased passenger-carrying capability of an aircraft would mean more casualties in the event of a crash, and, indeed, in 1956 commercial aviation suffered its first disaster to claim more than 100 lives when two transports collided over the Grand Canyon. Concern over air traffic control would cloud the industry throughout the latter half of the decade and into the 1960s.

Date: 12 March 1950 (*c*. 14:50)
Location: Near Sigginstone, South Glamorgan, Wales
Operator: Fairflight Ltd (UK)
Aircraft type: Avro 689 Tudor V (*G-AKBY*)

The airliner was on a charter service, carrying Welsh rugby fans home from Dublin, Ireland, where they had watched their team defeat the Irish in an international match. During its approach to land on Runway 28 at Llandow Airport, located some 15 miles (25 km) west-south-west of Cardiff, the four-engine transport assumed a glide path that gave eyewitnesses the impression that it would touch the ground prematurely.

While at an approximate height of 100 to 150 ft (30–50 m), a small increase in power was noted, which slightly reduced the aircraft's descent rate. This was followed by the sudden application of full power and, concurrently, by its nose pitching up. Climbing to about 300 ft (100 m), the Tudor stalled, then plunged into a field some 2,500 ft (750 m) from the threshold of the runway at a steep angle and on its right side, and with its undercarriage and flaps extended. There was evidence that the ignition had been switched off before impact, which may have accounted for the absence of a post-crash fire. All but three passengers among the 83 persons aboard were killed, including the entire crew of five; the survivors suffered injuries. The weather on this Sunday afternoon was good, with a visibility of 15 miles (*c*. 25 km) and westerly winds blowing at 10 to 15 knots.

An investigative court found that due to an inadequate amount of baggage placed forward in relationship to the passenger load, the aircraft's centre of gravity was at least 9 ft (2.7 m) aft of the specified limit. This probably resulted in insufficient

An Avro 689 Tudor, representative of the large piston-engine transports used by Western carriers in the 1950s and the type involved in the disaster in Wales. *(BAe Systems)*

elevator control remaining to counteract the rise of the nose upon the application of full power at a velocity that, while well above the stalling speed, was low enough to create a condition of acute instability. The court also regarded as unsatisfactory the loading instructions pertaining to the Tudor V, which did not contain adequate directions in determining how passengers and their luggage should be distributed. It said that the system then in use placed an unduly heavy burden of responsibility on the pilot.

For the trip to and from Dublin, there had been an alteration in the seating arrangement of the aircraft to allow for six more passengers than the maximum permissible, and this had required amending its certificate of airworthiness. However, the loading of the transport was not in compliance with the provisions of this amendment. For its violation, Fairflight was fined £50, plus an additional £150 to cover court costs.

The court recommended that whenever an aircraft's seating arrangements were to be changed, a new 'daily certificate' and 'technical log' should be prepared, and that it should be the function of the maintenance engineer responsible for the alterations to record in these documents the relevant information for reference by the pilot, with a provision for cross-checks.

Date: 24 June 1950 (*c.* 00:25)
Location: Lake Michigan, US
Operator: Northwest Airlines (US)
Aircraft type: Douglas DC-4 (*N95425*)

Operating as Flight 2501, the aircraft crashed into the great lake some 20 miles (30 km) north-north-west of Benton Harbor, Michigan, while en route from New York, New York, to Minneapolis, Minnesota, the first segment of a domestic transcontinental service destined for Seattle, Washington. All 58 persons aboard (55 passengers and three crew members) perished.

The DC-4 was last reported cruising in the early morning darkness at 3,500 ft (*c.* 1,050 m) after a request for descent to 2,500 ft (*c.* 750 m), which the crew made for no reason, had been denied due to conflicting air traffic in the area.

Subsequently recovered from the surface of the water were such light debris as cabin furnishings and personal effects. The bottom of the lake was 150 ft (*c.* 50 m) below the surface and covered by a layer of silt and mud estimated to be 30 to 40 ft (*c.* 10–12 m) thick, and despite a search using divers and sonar equipment, the main wreckage could not be located.

It was known that the disaster occurred shortly after the aircraft entered the area of severe turbulence associated with thunderstorm activity, which probably resulted in either structural failure or a loss of control, but there was insufficient evidence to determine which one of these possibilities actually caused the crash.

The forecast of a squall line in the area had been issued 1 hour 40 minutes before the accident, but this information was not made available to the flight.

Date: 31 August 1950 (*c.* 02:00)
Location: Near Wadi Natrun, Egypt
Operator: Trans World Airlines (TWA) (US)
Aircraft type: Lockheed 749A Constellation (*N6004C*)

Flight 903 took off from Farouk Airport, serving Cairo, bound for Rome, Italy, one segment of a service originating at Bombay, India, with an ultimate destination of New York City. About 20 minutes later ground witnesses observed the aircraft to be on fire. Subsequently it crashed and burned some 65 miles (105 km) north-west of the capital city, and all 55 persons aboard (48 passengers and a crew of seven) were killed.

The accident was attributed to the failure of the rear master rod bearing in the Constellation's No. 3 power plant, which caused the rear crankpin to overheat and collapse. This condition allowed the piston strokes to increase until the pistons began to strike the valves and cylinder heads. All the rear articulated and rear master rods then failed and sliced through the walls of the rear row of cylinders, tearing away a section of the crankcase. In turn, the fire seal was distorted and displaced. The general breakage was so widespread that oil lines were severed, and the release of the inflammable fluid and its fumes led to the fire.

Intensifying after the aircraft had turned back towards Cairo, the blaze ultimately melted the adjoining dural structure rearward of the firewall, causing the involved engine (whose propeller had been feathered) to fall free. Numerous other parts also separated as the fire burned through the top skin of the starboard wing.

Unable to reach the airport, the crew apparently attempted a forced landing on a desert plain in the early morning darkness, and while still under control the Constellation struck the ground in a

The crash of the Fairflight Tudor V nearly tripled the death toll of the worst previous British civil aviation disaster. (*ClassicStock*)

A Trans World Airlines
Lockheed 749A
Constellation, identical to
the aircraft that crashed
in the Egyptian desert.
(Trans World Airlines)

slight nose and right wing-low attitude, with its undercarriage and flaps retracted.

There was a distinct possibility that sludge that had built up within the crankpins had broken away and obstructed the flow of oil, resulting in the master rod bearing failure. Because of this accident and other master rod bearing failures in the same model of Wright engine, several corrective measures were taken. These included more frequent oil changes, improved oil screens and the development of a crankpin plug to reduce sludge accumulation.

Date: 13 November 1950 (*c.* 18:00)
Location: Near Corps, Rhône-Alps, France
Operator: Curtiss-Reid Flying Services Ltd (Canada)
Aircraft type: Douglas DC-4 (*CF-EDN*)

The airliner was on a charter service from Rome, Italy, to Montreal, Canada, with a planned stop at Paris, France, when it struck de l'Obiou Peak, in the Devoluy range of the Alps, some 30 miles (50 km) south of Grenoble. All 58 persons aboard perished, including seven crew members; its passengers were Catholics returning home from a pilgrimage to the Vatican.

At the time of its crash at an elevation of 9,000 ft (*c.* 2,700 m), *CF-EDN* had been approximately 55 miles (90 km) to the east of, but flying at the altitude selected for, the normal route. Although the aircraft disintegrated in a flash fire on impact, there was no sustained blaze. The accident occurred in darkness and, reportedly, cloudy weather conditions.

Factoring in the error of navigation was the apparent misidentification of landmarks, including the town of Gap for Montelimar. The pilot probably realised the deviation and was attempting to take corrective action when the DC-4 hit the mountain.

Date: 30 June 1951 (*c.* 02:00)
Location: Near Fort Collins, Colorado, US
Operator: United Air Lines (US)
Aircraft type: Douglas DC-6 (*N37543*)

All 50 persons aboard (45 passengers and a crew of five) perished when the aircraft, designated as Flight 610, crashed some 50 miles (80 km) north-north-west of Denver, where it was to have landed during a domestic transcontinental service from San Francisco, California, to Chicago, Illinois, its last scheduled stop having been at Salt Lake City, Utah.

Following passage of the Cheyenne radio range station, the DC-6 was to have turned right and headed south towards Denver. Instead, the turn was well in excess of 90 degrees, which placed it on a south-south-westerly heading. Flying in darkness, the cleanly configured aircraft continued in this direction until it struck cloud-obscured Crystal Mountain, at an approximate elevation of 8,500 ft (2,600 m), disintegrating on impact. Despite some localised fires, there was no major post-crash blaze.

It could not be determined why the flight had not followed the prescribed airway. One plausible theory was that the captain had depressed the wrong toggle switches on the aircraft's audio selector control panel (this could have happened in the darkened cockpit, especially considering that the switches were not obvious and were usually activated by feel). As a result, he may have silenced the signals of the Denver low-frequency radio range, whose beam demarcated the proper track, but allowed receipt of the Denver visual aural range (VAR) signals. This radio range, which would only have been used by the crew to determine at what point the turn should be initiated, ran roughly parallel to the low-frequency range, and its signals were such that they would be difficult to differ-entiate.

It was also considered possible that the pilot had tuned his automatic direction finder (ADF) in such a way that it had been affected by the radio range station at Fort Bridger, Wyoming.

The US Civil Aeronautics Administration (CAA) later took action to eliminate confusion between the Denver and VAR ranges. Meanwhile, the carrier modified its audio selector panels to prevent a possible mistake in switch selection, and also implemented a programme with a particular emphasis on route training and equipment qualification for its crews.

Date: 24 August 1951 (*c*. 05:30)
Location: Near Union City, California, US
Operator: United Air Lines (US)
Aircraft type: Douglas DC-6B (*N37550*)

Flight 615 had been cleared for a straight-in landing approach to Oakland Municipal Airport, a scheduled stop during a domestic transcontinental service destined for nearby San Francisco, which originated at Boston, Massachusetts. Descending in twilight through a broken layer of stratus clouds, with a base of about 1,500 ft (500 m), and in patches of fog that obscured the terrain, the aircraft crashed some 15 miles (25 km) south-east of the airport. All 50 persons aboard (44 passengers and six crew members) perished in the disaster.

Although the DC-6B was to have proceeded along the Oakland radio range course, neither of its two low-frequency receivers were tuned to the station. Instead, the captain had deviated from the prescribed instrument procedures, and may have attempted to fly by visual reference, using the first officer's automatic direction finder (ADF) to

A United Air Lines DC-6B, the type that crashed during a landing attempt at Oakland Airport. *(McDonnell Douglas)*

maintain the proper course. As a result the flight was approximately 3 miles (5 km) to the right of the on-course beam and well below the minimum prescribed altitude of 3,500 ft (c. 1,050 m).

Its main undercarriage down and flaps either retracted or partially extended, the aircraft struck a hill at an elevation of about 1,000 ft (300 m), or less than 30 ft (10 m) below its crest, while on a north-westerly heading and at a ground speed of between 225 and 240 mph (c. 360–385 kmh), then disintegrated in a fiery explosion.

Subsequently, the carrier enacted a requirement that crews operate under instrument flight rules (IFR) when above an overcast, to assure adherence to minimum altitudes.

Date: 16 December 1951 (c. 15:10)
Location: Elizabeth, New Jersey, US
Operator: Miami Airline Inc (US)
Aircraft type: Curtiss Wright C-46F (*N1678M*)

The twin-engine transport had just taken off from Newark Airport on a non-scheduled domestic service to Tampa, Florida, when control tower personnel noticed smoke emanating from its right side. Although the tower controller cleared the crew for an immediate landing, the message was not acknowledged. At about the same time another ground witness, a Miami Airline captain, also observed *N1678M* trailing smoke. Believing that the source of the smoke was an overheated right brake, he telephoned the control tower, suggesting that the crew be instructed to extend the gear. The pilots, unfortunately, followed his advice.

Trailing smoke from its right engine, the Miami Airline C-46F is photographed shortly before it crashed at Elizabeth, New Jersey, US. *(CORBIS)*

Minutes later, the C-46 began a gradual descending left turn, its starboard propeller still windmilling. Suddenly its port wing dropped, and the airliner struck the roof of a house and a building, then crashed in the Elizabeth River. The wreckage, which had come to rest largely inverted in the shallow water, then erupted into flames. All 56 persons aboard were killed, including a regular crew of three and an off-duty airline employee riding as a passenger, who was not on the manifest. Additionally, one person on the ground was seriously injured.

The accident was ascribed to faulty maintenance procedures by the airline. Examination of the right power plant revealed that the 15 hold-down studs on the No. 10 cylinder had failed from fatigue due to improper installation of their securing nuts. This caused the cylinder to separate completely from the crankcase during or shortly after take-off.

The fire that erupted in the base of the failed cylinder could have resulted from several sources of ignition, including a continuous egress of both liquid and atomised lubricating oil, a connection rod that had broken and was flailing, or from opened exhaust or inlet ducts. Activation of the fire-extinguishing system failed to check the blaze, and it ultimately burned through lines carrying fuel, oil and hydraulic fluid, and through the closed doors of the right wheel well. And when the undercarriage was lowered, the flames were allowed freer entry into this compartment, causing even more damage. The gear extention would also have increased drag, and this, coupled with the power loss, the inability of the crew to feather the right propeller (probably because the fire had destroyed an electrical or oil line) and the fact that the transport was loaded by nearly 120 lb (c. 55 kg) above its maximum allowable gross weight, caused a stall at a height of about 200 ft (60 m), which led to the crash.

Numerous violations by the carrier over a period of 3½ years, most involving the overloading of aircraft, were noted in the investigative report of the US Civil Aeronautics Board (CAB). Additionally, inadequacies were identified in the method by which the airline trained its pilots in the area of emergency procedures, and this could have had a bearing on what appeared to be a delay in such action being taken by the crew of *N1678M*.

A completely redesigned nacelle, which incorporated new fire protection devices, would later be developed by a private company for use on the C-46.

A Pan American World Airways Douglas DC-4, identical to the aircraft that ditched off northern Puerto Rico, with a loss of 52 lives. *(Pan American World Airways)*

Date: 11 April 1952 (*c.* 12:20)
Location: North of San Juan, Puerto Rico
Operator: Pan American World Airways (US)
Aircraft type: Douglas DC-4 (*N88899*)

Operating as Flight 526A, the airliner took off from Isle Grande Airport, serving San Juan, bound for New York City. Shortly afterwards, the crew noticed a loss of pressure and an increase in temperature in the oil of the No. 3 power plant; after turning back, they feathered the corresponding propeller. The No. 4 engine then began to run rough when power was increased. Minutes later the DC-4 crash-landed in the Atlantic Ocean, some 5 miles (10 km) off the northern coast of the island, its undercarriage and flaps having been extended beforehand. The ditching took place in turbulent seas, and the transport, its empennage having broken off in the impact, remained afloat for only about 3 minutes. Among the 69 persons aboard, 52 passengers lost their lives; the five crew members were among the 17 survivors rescued. Only 13 bodies were found, and the aircraft sank in water approximately 2,000 ft (600 m) deep and could not be recovered.

Maintenance personnel reported finding aluminium shavings in the oil sump and screen and the nose section housing of the No. 3 engine the previous day. Though mechanics changed the nose section, this alone was not in accordance with prescribed procedures under the circumstances.

This led the US Civil Aeronautics Board (CAB) to conclude that *N88899* was not airworthy upon its departure from San Juan. The accident was therefore attributed to inadequate maintenance by the airline, and to the actions of the pilot.

It was ruled that the captain's persistence in attempting to re-establish a climb without using all available power after a critical loss of power in the No. 4 engine resulted in a nose-high attitude, a progressive loss of air speed and a settling of the aircraft at too low an altitude to effect recovery.

An additional factor that might have reduced the survivability of the disaster was the failure of the flight crew to warn the cabin attendants of the situation, which prevented them from preparing the passengers for the water landing. Furthermore, the life rafts were all stowed in a single compartment, and only one could be launched after the ditching.

Today's routine procedure of briefing passengers before extended over-water flights as to the location and use of flotation equipment and emergency exits was an outcome of this tragedy.

Date: 29 April 1952 (*c.* 03:40)
Location: Central Brazil
Operator: Pan American World Airways (US)
Aircraft type: Boeing 377 Stratocruiser (*N1039V*)

In the last message received from Flight 202, the airliner was reportedly at an altitude of 14,500 ft (*c.* 4,400 m) in visual flight rules (VFR) conditions, with an estimation that it would be abeam of the Carolina check point in 90 minutes. But there was no further communication with *N1039V*.

Two days later the burned wreckage of the Stratocruiser was found scattered for nearly 1 mile (1.5 km) and lying inverted in a tropical forest area in the south-eastern corner of Para state, some 1,000 miles (1,600 km) north-north-west of Rio de Janeiro, where it had last stopped before proceeding on to Port-of-Spain, Trinidad, one segment of a service originating at Buenos Aires, Argentina, with an ultimate destination of New York City. All 50 persons aboard (41 passengers and a crew of nine) perished in the crash.

It was apparent that the aircraft had disintegrated in flight, while cruising in pre-dawn darkness on an approximate heading of 340 degrees, and that the sequence of events began with the separation of its No. 2 engine/propeller assembly due to highly unbalanced forces. Then, possibly because of severe buffeting, there was a partial failure of the left horizontal stabiliser. Examination of the debris indicated that the outer portion of the stabiliser continued to hang on, oscillating in such a manner as to cause the elevators to snap upward, placing a very high down-load on the tail surfaces. This would in turn have caused a considerable increase in lift on the

wings, a sufficient force to break the left one in an upward direction, just beyond the missing inboard power plant. The resulting nose-down pitching motion attributed to the loss of the wing coupled with the existing down-load on the horizontal tail surfaces would likely have caused the empennage to break off in a downward direction, which must have been almost simultaneous with the wing failure. Both the left wing and the tail assembly were found a distance from the main wreckage, confirming that these components had separated before the impact with the ground.

Since it could not be located, there was no way of knowing exactly what happened to the No. 2 engine. However, in other accidents involving the same type of aircraft, such separations were precipitated by the failure of a propeller blade, with the resulting imbalance generating destructive forces. As noted in the investigative report, the type of propeller with which the Boeing 377 was equipped had been known to experience fatigue failure after suffering comparatively minor damage.

Three years later, and following the loss of another Stratocruiser and four lives under similar circumstances, the US Civil Aeronautics Administration (CAA) issued an advisory that operators of the type replace the hollow steel propeller blades then in use with solid metal ones. Another preventative measure was the development of propeller blade imbalance detectors, the use of which became a CAA requirement, also in 1955.

The wreckage of the Pan American World Airways Boeing 377 Stratocruiser rests in the Brazilian jungle after an in-flight break-up. *(CORBIS)*

Date: 2 May 1953 (*c.* 16:35)
Location: Near Jagalogori, West Bengal, India
Operator: British Overseas Airways Corporation (BOAC)
Aircraft type: de Havilland Comet 1 (*G-ALYV*)

Exactly one year after the inauguration of the Comet into regular service, this particular one became the first jet airliner to crash fatally during a scheduled passenger operation.

Flight 783/057 had taken off from Dum-Dum Airport, serving Calcutta, bound for Delhi, one segment of a service originating at Singapore, with an ultimate destination of London. Only 6 minutes later it plunged to earth in flames some 30 miles (50 km) north-west of Calcutta. All 43 persons aboard (37 passengers and six crew members) perished.

The accident occurred during a violent thunderstorm, with heavy rain and high winds. Wreckage was scattered over flat terrain for a distance of about 5 miles (10 km), indicating that the Comet had come apart in the air. The structural failure was believed to have resulted from stresses that exceeded its designed limits, due either to an encounter with severe gusts, or to over-controlling or a loss of control by the crew. However, both the carrier and the manufacturer doubted the latter theory.

A study of the wreckage strongly suggested the failure of both elevator spars caused by a heavy down-load that may have been associated with a pull-up manoeuvre after the aircraft had encountered a sudden down draught. This was followed by the failure of both wings, which could have then struck the tailplane, shearing off the vertical stabiliser. Fire erupted after the wings snapped.

The Comet was upset at an estimated height of 7,000 ft (c. 2,000 m), while climbing to its cruising altitude.

Date: 12 July 1953 (c. 20:40)
Location: North Pacific Ocean
Operator: Transocean Air Lines (US)
Aircraft type: Douglas DC-6A (N9086)

The transport crashed in darkness approximately 350 miles (550 km) east of Wake Island, from where it had taken off less than 2 hours earlier, bound for Honolulu, Hawaii, one segment of a non-scheduled service from Guam to Oakland, California, US. Searchers later found a small amount of debris and 14 bodies, but there were no survivors among the 58 persons aboard (50 passengers and a crew of eight).

According to its last message, the aircraft was cruising between cloud layers at 15,000 ft (c. 5,000 m). There were indications of thunderstorm activity, containing moderate to heavy turbulence, in the area along the route taken.

Due to insufficient evidence, the cause of the disaster could not be determined. Had there been a mechanical or structural failure, the occurrence must have been sudden. As concluded from the examination of the recovered victims and wreckage, the impact with the water was at a high velocity, which would point to a loss of control by the pilots.

There was no evidence of either sabotage or in-flight fire.

The BOAC disaster in India occurred one year to the day after the de Havilland Comet 1 inaugurated the world's first commercial jet passenger service.
(British Airways)

Date: 10 January 1954 (c. 11:00)
Location: Tyrrhenian Sea
Operator: British Overseas Airways Corporation (BOAC)
Aircraft type: de Havilland Comet 1 (G-ALYP)

The same aircraft that had inaugurated the world's first jet passenger service, in May 1952, took off on this Sunday morning from Rome as Flight 781, on the final leg of a Singapore to London international trip. About 30 minutes later, while at an estimated height of 27,000 ft (c. 8,200 m) and climbing in good weather conditions to its cruising altitude, the Comet disintegrated. Its flaming wreckage then plummeted into the sea, in an area where the water ranged from 300 to 500 ft (c. 100–150 m) deep, some 15 miles (25 km) south of the Italian island of Elba. All 35 persons aboard (29 passengers and a crew of six) were killed.

Searchers recovered the bodies of 15 victims and, eventually, approximately 70 per cent of the wreckage. Through the assistance of the Royal Aircraft Establishment (RAE), a court of inquiry was able to conclude that the accident resulted from structural failure of the aircraft's pressure cabin brought about by metal fatigue. Examination revealed cracks in the reinforcing plates of the ports, or 'windows', containing the automatic direction finder (ADF) aerials and located atop the fuselage. The initial failure was followed by a more general break-up of the jet.

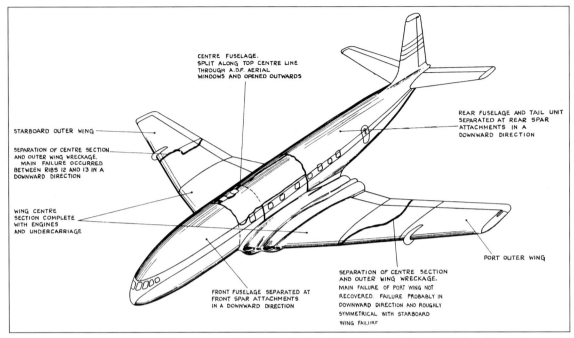

A diagram showing the main failure areas of G-ALYP, the first of two Comets that crashed in the Tyrrhenian Sea in 1954 due to structural break-up. *(Ministry of Transport and Civil Aviation)*

The black streak in the centre of the picture marks the crash site of the United Air Lines DC-4 on Medicine Bow Peak. *(AP Images)*

As designed, the pressure cabin of the Comet was unable to withstand repeated pressurisation.

Date: 8 April 1954 (*c.* 20:10)
Location: Tyrrhenian Sea
Operator: South African Airways
Aircraft type: de Havilland Comet 1 (*G-ALYY*)

The accident that brought a temporary end to the commercial jet era involved Flight 201, which was en route from Rome to Cairo, Egypt, one segment of an international service originating at London, with an ultimate destination of Johannesburg, South Africa.

Leased from British Overseas Airways Corporation (BOAC), *G-ALYY* disintegrated while flying in darkness and good meteorological conditions at or near an altitude of 35,000 ft (*c.* 10,700 m), then crashed about 70 miles (110 km) south of Naples, Italy. All 21 persons aboard (14 passengers and a crew of seven) were killed. Searchers recovered six bodies and some debris, but most of the wreckage was lost in water more than 2,500 ft (750 m) deep. As a result, a court of inquiry was unable to determine the cause of the tragedy. But evidence pointed to a structural failure in the same vein as what happened to the Comet off Elba three months earlier (see separate entry, 10 January 1954).

Although the Comet 1 was immediately withdrawn from service, the de Havilland jet airliner would fly again, in a newer form. Featuring a longer fuselage and distinctive round windows, the Comet IV would in fact launch the first jet passenger service across the Atlantic Ocean, in October 1958. The lessons learned from the failure of its predecessor would also be incorporated by manufacturers around the world, leading to 'fail-safe' structural design in the development and construction of commercial aircraft.

Date: 6 October 1955 (*c.* 07:25)
Location: Near Centennial, Wyoming, US
Operator: United Air Lines (US)
Aircraft type: Douglas DC-4 (*N30062*)

All 66 persons aboard (63 passengers and a crew of three) perished when the aircraft crashed into Medicine Bow Peak, some 30 miles (50 km) west of Laramie.

Designated as Flight 409, the DC-4 had taken off earlier from Denver, Colorado, bound for Salt Lake City, Utah, one segment of a domestic trans-continental service originating at New York, New York, with an ultimate destination of San Francisco, California. It was some 20 miles (30 km) to the west of the prescribed course and on a north-westerly heading when it struck a sheer rock wall at an approximate elevation of 11,500 ft (3,500 m), or only about 60 ft (20 m) below its crest. The transport disintegrated on impact, and most of the wreckage and bodies tumbled down the mountain, coming to rest at the bottom of the cliff.

The meteorological conditions in the area at the time consisted of a broken overcast, with the clouds covering the tops of the mountains, and isolated snow showers.

In its investigation, the US Civil Aeronautics Board (CAB) could find no evidence of mechanical failure in the aircraft, and considered it doubtful, due to the captain's familiarity with the route and the facilities available and comparatively good visibility along it, that the disaster could have resulted from a navigational error. Not completely ruled out was the possibility that the two pilots had been physically incapacitated, possibly by poisonous gases emitted by a malfunctioning cockpit heater.

However, there were other indications, including witness accounts, that the DC-4 had been under control prior to the crash.

The CAB found it difficult to accept that the captain had attempted a short-cut over the high terrain, especially considering the weather, the lack of cabin pressurisation in the aircraft, and the fact that the time saved by such action would have been inconsequential. It therefore had to conclude that the deviation was intentional on the part of the pilot, for reasons unknown.

Date: 18 February 1956 (*c.* 13:20)
Location: Near Zurrieq, Malta
Operator: Scottish Airlines (UK)
Aircraft type: Avro York (*G-ANSY*)

Operating under contract to the (British) Air Ministry and carrying 45 service personnel as passengers and five civilian crew members, the four-engine transport took off from Luqa Airport, Malta, bound for England. Its undercarriage retracted normally, but around this time smoke was seen emanating from its left outbound power plant. Instead of turning right as instructed, the York appeared to drift to the left. Shortly afterwards it banked steeply to port, then plummeted almost vertically into the cliffs along the southern coast of the Mediterranean island, exploding on impact. All 50 persons aboard were killed.

Evidence indicated that the No. 1 engine had malfunctioned, stemming from the failure of its boost enrichment capsule, which was found to have two cracks in the second convolution from the top, associated with corrosion and normal stresses. The resulting weak fuel mixture caused the flame traps to become incandescent, and this condition was responsible for a series of backfires. Ultimately the heat generated by the continuous burning in the induction system resulted in the disintegration of the supercharger rotor, leading to the complete failure of the power plant.

The initiating factor, the loss of power, alone should not have caused the accident. Instead, the crash was attributed to the mechanical malfunction in combination with a judgement error on the part of the pilot, who did not stop the leftward swing of the aircraft using the rudder, did not correct its nose-high attitude, and failed to feather the No. 1 propeller in order to reduce drag. Also, the full

An Avro York, shown in the livery of another airline but the type operated by Scottish Airlines that crashed on Malta. *(British Airways)*

retraction of the aircraft's flaps increased the stalling speed of the York. These omissions led to a loss of air speed and consequent loss of directional control.

Better pilot training for emergency conditions and an improved boost enrichment capsule, with a spring-balance safety device, were among the recommendations made by the court of inquiry in the wake of the disaster.

Date: 20 June 1956 (*c.* 00:30)
Location: Off New Jersey, US
Operator: Linea Aeropostal Venezolana
Aircraft type: Lockheed 1049E Super Constellation (YV-C-AMS)

Trouble was first reported about 1 hour 20 minutes after Flight 253 had taken off from New York International Airport, on an international service to Caracas, Venezuela. The pilot radioed that its No. 2 propeller was overspeeding and could not be feathered. Turning back towards its point of departure, the Super Constellation was soon joined by a US Coast Guard aircraft to provide an escort.

Shortly after the flight reported sighting New York City in the early morning darkness, the dumping of fuel was begun in preparation for landing. Moments later, however, the transport caught fire and made a sharp turn to the right. Upon completion of this turn, a quivering, incandescent mass separated from its port side. The airliner then started to climb while veering left, during which time three more incandescent masses were seen to break away. At the top of its climb, and while in a vertical attitude at an approximate height of 9,000 ft (2,700 m), the Super Constellation broke apart, then plunged into the Atlantic Ocean in flames some 30 miles (50 km) east of Asbury Park. All 74 persons aboard (64 passengers and a crew of 10) were killed. Searchers recovered little wreckage and only a few bodies from the water, which was about 100 ft (30 m) deep at the crash site.

Although the reason for the disaster could not be determined with absolute certainty, it was assumed that the vibration resulting from the uncontrollable propeller caused one of the inside wing attachments to loosen or break somewhere between the fuel tank and the dump chute, at the symmetrical point of the oscillation.

Three years later a requirement went into effect mandating propeller pitch locks on piston-engine transport aircraft, devices designed to prevent the type of overspeeding that proved disastrous to *YV-C-AMS*.

Following the collision, the TWA aircraft fell into the canyon near the Colorado River (lower arrow), while the United transport crashed atop Chuar Butte about 1 mile (1.5 km) away. *(ClassicStock)*

reference point, an imaginary line demarcated by two navigational aids that stretched north-westwards from Winslow, Arizona, into southern Utah, at the same time, 11:31. There would be no further communication with either aircraft until a frantic message was transmitted from the DC-7 about half an hour later. Sent by the first officer, it was later deciphered to be 'Salt Lake . . . seven eighteen . . . we are going in!'

The fragmented, burned wreckage of the two transports was found the following day on the west side of the canyon, near the confluence of the Colorado and Little Colorado Rivers. All 128 persons aboard both aircraft perished in the tragedy. Investigation by the US Civil Aeronautics Board (CAB), which included a detailed examination of the debris, confirmed that a mid-air crash had taken place.

The collision was believed to have occurred at or near 21,000 ft, probably in a clear area, despite the presence of nearby thunderhead build-ups. At the time of impact, the angle of the two aircraft relative to each other was approximately 25 degrees. Initial contact appeared to have been between the DC-7's

left aileron tip and the centre vertical tail fin of the Super Constellation. Instantly thereafter, the lower surface of the former's left wing struck the upper aft fuselage section of the latter. During this time the No. 1 propeller of the DC-7 inflicted a series of cuts in the aft baggage compartment of the other aircraft. This entire sequence must have taken place in less than half a second.

At the moment they collided, the DC-7 was rolled about 20 degrees right wing-down in relation to the Super Constellation, with its wing above the latter's fuselage and its nose lower than that of the other. This attitude might indicate the initiation of evasive action by one or both, but this could not be proved.

Following the collision, the TWA transport, its empennage having been severed (which would have caused an explosive cabin decompression), pitched down and plummeted, in an inverted attitude, into a draw on the north-east slope of Temple Butte. The United aircraft, meanwhile, which was missing about 20 ft (6 m) of its left outer wing, fell less steeply, probably on a turning path, and crashed near the top of Chuar Butte, approximately 1 mile

(1.5 km) north-east of the TWA impact site, scattering wreckage and victims down the precipitous, inaccessible terrain.

It could not be determined with certainty why the pilots failed to see each other's aircraft in time to prevent the accident (this was particularly relevant with regard to the United crew, who, studies showed, could have seen the Super Constellation up to 2 minutes before the accident, depending on the circumstances). Evidence suggested that it was due to intervening clouds restricting visibility before they reached the clear area; cockpit visibility limitations; preoccupation with normal duties or with unrelated activities, such as trying to give the passengers a more scenic view of the canyon; physiological limits to human vision; or to a combination of these factors. Also significant was the lack of traffic advisory information provided to either crew due to inadequate facilities and an insufficient workforce.

During a CAB public hearing, air traffic control personnel were questioned as to whether such advisories should have been given to the flights, especially considering that both were known to have been at the same altitude and estimating that they would reach the Painted Desert position at the same time. The controller directly involved explained that he had no way of knowing exactly where the aircraft would cross the line, which was nearly 175 miles (280 km) long. He further stated

that since both were then in uncontrolled airspace, their crews would have been operating under the 'see-and-be-seen' guidelines associated with visual flight rules (VFR) procedures.

One of the mysteries of the disaster was that both flights had estimated that they would reach the Painted Desert at almost the same moment the collision took place, which was some 3 minutes flying time from that point.

A number of improvements came out of this tragedy, with increased funding by the government for air navigational facilities and a modernisation of the nation's air traffic control system. Procedural changes included greater adherence in air carrier operations to prescribed routes and assigned flight levels. Nevertheless, the collision menace would continue to plague US aviation for the next half-decade, culminating in a catastrophe over New York City involving, ironically, United Air Lines and TWA (see separate entry, 16 December 1960).

Date: 9 December 1956 (*c*. 19:15)
Location: Near Hope, British Columbia, Canada
Operator: Trans-Canada Air Lines
Aircraft type: Canadair DC-4M-2 North Star (*CF-TFD*)

Flight 810–9 departed from Vancouver, en route to Calgary, Alberta, the first segment of a domestic service with an ultimate destination of Montreal,

A Trans-Canada Air Lines Canadair North Star, the type that crashed in British Columbia with a loss of 62 lives. *(Programmed Communications Ltd)*

Quebec. Some 50 minutes later, the pilot reported a fire in the No. 2 power plant, which had been shut down, and that he was turning back. In the last radio transmission from the aircraft, clearance for descent to 8,000 ft (c. 2,500 m) was acknowledged.

Despite an extensive search, no trace of the North Star was found until May 1957, when a small group of mountaineers came upon it, quite by accident, on Mt Sleese, some 50 miles (80 km) east of Vancouver. The transport had slammed into a sheer granite wall at an approximate elevation of 7,500 ft (2,300 m) and disintegrated. It was apparent that all 62 persons on board (59 passengers and three crew members) had perished in the crash. Debris was scattered across, and more than 2,000 ft (600 m) down, the mountain. Due to the poor accessibility of the terrain, the wreckage and remains of the victims could not be recovered.

The disaster occurred in darkness and the weather in the area at the time was bad, with broken cloud layers at various altitudes, rain showers, severe turbulence, icing conditions and winds ranging from 65 to 85 knots.

According to the board of inquiry report, there was a high probability that while flying under the power of three engines, the aircraft had encountered severe icing, turbulence or some other difficulty, or a combination of adverse factors, whose sudden or dire nature was such that the crew were unable to maintain control or even send a distress message. It could not be determined why the North Star was approximately 12 miles (20 km) south of the assigned airway at the time of impact.

One of the recommendations made by the board was to encourage pilots to dump fuel in order to regain or maintain the performance of an aircraft after the loss of engine power.

Date: 14 March 1957 (13:46)
Location: Wythenshawe, Cheshire, England
Operator: British European Airways (BEA)
Aircraft type: Vickers Viscount 701 (*G-ALWE*)

The first fatal crash of a turboprop airliner engaged in a regular passenger operation involved Flight 411, which was about to complete a service from Amsterdam, The Netherlands. During the final, visual phase of an attempted landing at Manchester's Ringway Airport, after a ground-controlled approach (GCA) radar-monitored let-down through a broken layer of clouds, the Viscount suddenly commenced a steep right turn and plunged into a residential area, killing all 20 persons aboard (15 passengers and a crew of five) and two others on the ground (a woman and her infant son). Initial contact was with its starboard

The first turboprop airliner to provide a regular service suffered its first fatal crash on a passenger flight when a British European Airways Viscount 701 plunged into a residential area near Manchester airport. *(BAe Systems)*

wing-tip approximately half a mile (0.8 km) from the threshold of the runway and some 500 ft (150 m) to the right of its extended centreline, and the aircraft then struck the houses and burst into flames. Two residences were destroyed.

Investigation revealed that an improperly machined and seated lug in a starboard wing-flap unit had broken prior to the accident, and the corresponding botl, which was fatigued, then failed under the normal aerodynamic stresses. This caused the two inboard sections of the flap, which had been extended in preparation for landing, to move away from and then rise above the trailing edge of the wing. The wing then dropped, resulting in the sharp bank to the right. Evidence also suggested that the gust lock control wire had been displaced, which would have jammed the aileron and kept the crew from regaining control.

Subsequently, Vickers initiated a modification programme to prevent a recurrence of what happened to *G-ALWE*. Reinforcing gussets and angle plates were added to the lower part of the flap units on the Viscount, and a fishplate added to the outside of the wing surface. As a further safeguard should a unit become detached, the manufacturer also introduced a method of examining the bolts in an aircraft that took tension loads or those that fitted into holes reamed out on assembly.

Date: 16 July 1957 (03:36)
Location: Off Biak Island, Netherlands New Guinea
Operator: KLM Royal Dutch Airlines
Aircraft type: Lockheed 1049E Super Constellation (*PH-LKT*)

No reason was given by the pilot for his request to make a low pass over the Mokmer airport, from where the aircraft, operating as Flight 844, had taken off a few minutes earlier. He did, however, announce over the public address system his intention to give everyone a final glimpse of the island before proceeding on to Manila, Philippines, the first en route stop of a service with an ultimate destination of Amsterdam.

Granted permission, the Super Constellation began its approach from the east, gradually descending over the sea. At a point approximately half a mile (0.8 km) from the shore it crashed, burst into flames, broke apart and sank. Only 10 passengers survived,

rescued by native boats. The other 58 persons aboard, including all nine crew members, were killed. Efforts to recover the wreckage from the water, which was some 800 ft (250 m) deep, were unsuccessful.

An investigative board was only able to conclude that the disaster resulted from either pilot error or technical failure. There was, of course, the possibility that both factors had come into play. As noted in the accident report, in the dark, moonlit conditions, the pilot might have misjudged his height over the sea, especially considering that he would have lost sight of the runway lights once the aircraft was below an altitude of about 200 ft (60 m), owing to trees and other obstacles. Reports of an in-flight fire by some ground witnesses could not be confirmed.

The board recommended against low runs in commercial air carrier services.

Date: 11 August 1957 (*c.* 14:15)
Location: Near Issoudun, Quebec, Canada
Operator: Maritime Central Airways (Canada)
Aircraft type: Douglas DC-4 (*CF-MCF*)

The transport was on a transatlantic charter service from London to Toronto, Ontario, its passengers, British veterans from the Second World War, returning home after visiting their native land with their families. Two en route refuelling stops were planned, at Keflavik, Iceland, where it landed, and at Goose Bay, Newfoundland, which the pilot elected to fly past.

Flying at an altitude of 6,000 ft (*c.* 1,800 m), the aircraft entered a thunderstorm in which heavy rain and strong, gusty winds were reported. Subsequently it plunged to earth almost vertically at a speed calculated to be in excess of 230 mph (370 kmh), bursting into flames on impact. All 79 persons aboard, including a crew of six, perished. A crater marked the crash site, some 15 miles (25 km) south-south-west of the city of Quebec.

Although there was no way of knowing exactly what events had taken place, an investigative board ascribed the disaster to an encounter with severe turbulence that ultimately led to a loss of control. One possibility was that the aircraft had assumed a nose-high attitude due to the turbulent conditions, which, coupled with the fact that the fuel tanks were only partially filled, allowed air to be drawn into the engines, causing a loss of power in one or more of them. Advancing the throttles, a pilot's natural reaction to such a situation, could have caused the propellers to overspeed once power was restored and, in turn, the crew to lose control.

It was also plausible that the same extreme attitude had led to a stall. The pilots might have countered by altering engine power settings to maintain air speed and altitude. A violent nose-down pitch of the transport at the time of recovery from the stall, with a resultant increase in air speed, and a sudden application of power could also cause the propellers to overspeed to the point where they could not be controlled by their governors. Recovery from this condition, especially in heavy turbulence, would have been unlikely.

The fact that the aircraft's centre of gravity was believed to have been at or slightly beyond the aft limit would have aggravated the situation in either case.

No weather bulletin had been issued regarding the storm activity west of Quebec, and the crew could have unwittingly flown into the cumulonimbus. On the other hand, being low on fuel due to his earlier decision not to land at Goose Bay, the pilot could have elected to penetrate rather than circumnavigate what might have appeared as a minor build-up of clouds. The pilots had been on duty for nearly 20 hours, and the resulting fatigue would have adversely affected their ability to cope with such a situation.

Searchers sift through the shattered remains of the Maritime Central Airways DC-4 that crashed in Quebec. (National Archives of Canada)

One of the safety recommendations made in the investigative report was to establish a Canadian national standard of on-duty time limitations for flight crews. This policy would later be adopted, as it had already been in some other countries, in order to reduce the risk of fatigue.

Date: 8 November 1957 (c. 16:30)
Location: North Pacific Ocean
Operator: Pan American World Airways (US)
Aircraft type: Boeing 377 Stratocruiser (N90944)

Designated as Flight 7 and carrying 44 persons (36 passengers and a crew of eight), the airliner had taken off from San Francisco, California, US, bound for Honolulu, Hawaii, its first scheduled stop during an around-the-world service. In its last position report, sent when it was slightly beyond the midway point between the two cities and cruising at an altitude of 10,000 ft (c. 3,000 m), there were no indications of any abnormalities, but nothing further was heard from the Stratocruiser.

About a week later, searchers recovered a small amount of debris, including cabin furnishings and packets of mail, and 19 bodies floating some 940 miles (1,510 km) north-east of Honolulu and approximately 90 miles (145 km) north of the flight's intended track. There were no survivors from the disaster, which was never explained due to a lack of tangible evidence.

Among the victims, about half probably died from drowning; most were wearing life preservers, indicating that preparations for a ditching had been made. A forced landing in the ocean may actually have been attempted, but with the aircraft breaking up on impact. It was determined that a post-crash fire on the surface of the water had taken place.

There was no evidence of an explosion or major in-flight fire. However, a localised blaze in the fuselage or in a power plant may have occurred. With regard to the latter, the fire may have been in conjunction with the break-up or separation of the engine, as had been noted in previous Boeing 377 accidents. This would also be expected to cause difficulty in maintaining directional control, which could explain why the aircraft was so far off the normal course. But there was no absolute proof of such a mechanical failure. The weather was not considered a factor.

Date: 21 April 1958 (*c.* 08:30)
Location: Near Sloan, Nevada, US
First aircraft
Operator: United Air Lines (US)
Type: Douglas DC-7 (*N6328C*)
Second aircraft
Operator: US Air Force
Type: North American F-100F Super Sabre (*56–3755A*)

This disaster occurred suddenly in the clear morning sky when the airliner and jet fighter collided at a height of 21,000 ft (6,400 m), approximately 10 miles (15 km) south-west of Las Vegas, and both then plummeted into the desert below and exploded. All 47 persons aboard the DC-7 (42 passengers and five crew members) and both pilots of the F-100 (a trainee and his instructor) perished.

Operating as Flight 736, the commercial transport was en route from Los Angeles, California, to Denver, Colorado, the first segment of a domestic trans-continental service with the ultimate destination of New York City, and had been cruising along a designated airway in a north-north-easterly direction under instrument flight rules (IFR) procedures. The military aircraft was on an instrument training mission being conducted under visual flight rules (VFR), and descending from 28,000 ft (*c.* 8,500 m) while on a south-easterly heading.

The fighter had initiated an evasive manoeuvre and the airliner probably began one just before the collision, and the former was banking to the left at the time of impact. Its right wing slashed into the right outer wing of the DC-7, shearing off these sections from both aircraft. Both crews were able to transmit 'Mayday' distress messages during their fall to earth, and the instructor pilot in the front seat of the F-100 ejected at a low altitude before the jet crashed.

Despite a visibility of more than 35 miles (55 km) in the area, the high rate of the nearly head-on closure, calculated to have been about 765 mph (1,230 kmh), together with human and cockpit limitations, precluded the ability of either crew to avoid the accident through visual separation. An additional factor was the failure of both the US Civil Aeronautics Administration (CAA) and the US Air Force to reduce the collision danger, especially considering that training operations out of Nellis Air Force Base were being conducted largely within the confines of several airways, and that numerous

A Pan American World Airways Boeing 377 Stratocruiser, the type that crashed under mysterious circumstances in the North Pacific Ocean. *(Pan American World Airways)*

close encounters with military jets had been reported by airline crews for more than a year before the tragedy.

Subsequent procedural changes by civilian and military authorities would help lessen the chance of a similar disaster, at least in this particular region.

Date: 18 May 1958 (*c.* 04:30)
Location: Near Casablanca, Morocco
Operator: Belgian World Airlines (SABENA)
Aircraft type: Douglas DC-7C (*OO-SFA*)

Trouble developed in the aircraft's No. 1 engine as the DC-7C was en route from Lisbon, Portugal, to Léopoldville, in the Belgian Congo (Zaire), the second segment of a scheduled service originating at Brussels, Belgium. Due to a reported vibration, the power plant was shut down and the flight diverted for a precautionary landing at Cazes Airport.

An approach was begun to Runway 21 in pre-dawn darkness, but at a point some 1,500 ft (500 m) beyond its threshold and with the transport less than 15 ft (5 m) above the ground, the pilot initiated an overshoot. This action, which probably resulted from an encounter with conditions of reduced visibility on account of patchy fog, reflected an error in judgement on his part, since the aircraft was neither properly configured nor flying at a sufficient speed to carry out such a manoeuvre. Safe operating procedures would have dictated that power be applied gradually, air speed be increased to assure that control be maintained, and flaps be retracted to the take-off position in the event of a baulked landing.

Following the application of full power on the three remaining engines, the DC-7C stalled at an approximate height of 80 ft (25 m), clipped a small building, then struck a hangar while in a steep nose-down and sharp left-banking attitude. The aircraft immediately burst into flames, its undercarriage retracted but flaps fully extended at impact. The accident claimed the lives of 65 persons aboard, including the entire crew of nine. Four passengers survived.

Examination revealed pre-crash damage to a cylinder in the power plant that was feathered, probably caused by a loosening of the exhaust valve regulating screw leading to overheating around the valve and its seat, to the point that the metal actually melted. Though this technical fault necessitated the forced landing, it was not blamed for the subsequent disaster.

Date: 14 August 1958 (*c.* 03:45)
Location: North Atlantic Ocean
Operator: KLM Royal Dutch Airlines
Aircraft type: Lockheed 1049H Super Constellation (*PH-LKM*)

Designated as Flight 607E, the aircraft had taken off from Shannon Airport, Ireland, bound for Gander, Newfoundland, Canada, its next scheduled stop during a transatlantic service from Amsterdam to New York City. Not more than 10 minutes after its last radio transmission, which was normal, the Super Constellation plunged into the sea some 100 miles (150 km) off the Irish coast and approximately due west of Galway Bay. All 99 persons aboard (91 passengers and eight crew members) perished.

The transport had been climbing to its cruising altitude and was presumed to have reached a height of about 13,000 ft (4,000 m) just before the catastrophe took place, in pre-dawn darkness. A small amount of debris was later recovered, including parts from the cabin and cockpit and the undercarriage wheels, as were the remains of 34 victims. The depth of the ocean in the area and the fact that the exact location was not known precluded any attempt to salvage the main wreckage.

On the available evidence, an investigative board was unable to establish with certainty the cause of the disaster. However, it regarded with 'a high degree of probability' that the crash resulted from overspeeding of an outer propeller.

According to this hypothesis, the sequence of events would have begun with a fracture in one of the driving gears of a power plant blower, occurring when the supercharger was accelerated; the engines with which *PH-LKM* was equipped were known to be susceptible to such failures. A fracture would

This crash of a SABENA DC-7C into an airport hangar near Casablanca claimed the lives of 65 persons aboard the airliner. *(AP Images)*

An Aeroflot Tupolev Tu-104A jet airliner, two of which were involved in remarkably similar accidents during a two-month period in 1958. *(Aviation Photo News)*

release metal particles into the oil system, which would in turn clog a valve in the propeller governor and prevent its proper operation. Under the circumstances, it would not be possible to shut off the oil supply to the pitch mechanisms of the individual blades. The crew would thus be unable to feather the propeller, even by stopping the flow of fuel. This condition might provoke a flight disturbance that could only be corrected by the prompt and powerful handling of the aileron and rudder controls, and ultimately result in an uncontrolled descent.

In the short period of time in which the malfunction probably occurred, the pilots might not have been able to recognise the situation soon enough to restore control. For that reason, the board had no cause to suspect incorrect action by the crew in response to the emergency nor any neglect on the part of maintenance personnel. It also expressed satisfaction that the propeller governors of the type used by KLM had been fitted with a device designed to improve the reliability of the feathering mechanism subsequent to the crash of *PH-LKM*.

The weather in the area at the time of the accident was good and was thus not considered a contributing factor.

Date: 15 August 1958 (time unknown)
Location: Near Chita, Russian Soviet Federative Socialist Republic, USSR
Operator: Aeroflot (USSR)
Aircraft type: Tupolev Tu-104A (*SSSR-42349*)

All 64 persons aboard (54 passengers and a crew of 10) perished when the jet airliner crashed during a scheduled domestic service from Moscow to Khabarovsk.

The accident occurred at night and in instrument meteorological conditions, shortly after the aircraft had been cleared by the flight manager on the ground to fly over an area of thunderstorm activity. Climbing to about 40,000 ft (12,000 m) above the ground, which was in excess of its operational ceiling when considering its weight, the Tu-104 then encountered a vertical airflow associated with the storm, causing it to assume an extreme nose-high attitude, with the result that it lost longitudinal stability. The aircraft stalled and plummeted to earth, the pilots unable to effect recovery due to a lack of bank angle and pitch indication in the cockpit, this because the artificial horizon did not function at high angles of attack.

Date: 17 October 1958 (time unknown)
Location: Near Kanash, Russian Soviet Federative Socialist Republic, USSR
Operator: Aeroflot (USSR)
Aircraft type: Tupolev Tu-104A (*SSSR-42362*)

The jet airliner had been en route from Omsk to Moscow, the domestic segment of a scheduled international service originating at Peking, China, before it crashed some 400 miles (650 km) east of the Soviet capital, and all 80 persons aboard (71 passengers and a crew of nine) perished.

Flying at night and in instrument meteorological conditions at about 36,000 ft (11,000 m), the flight had been instructed by the ground manager to proceed to an alternative airport due to deteriorating weather at its original destination.

The crash of the American Airlines Electra, serial number N6101A, came less than a month after the type had entered regular service. *(American Airlines)*

During a climbing turn, the jet encountered severe turbulence associated with a thunderstorm, assuming an extreme nose-high attitude to the point of a longitudinal upset. It then stalled, plunged to the ground and caught fire. As in the above-mentioned incident, recovery was not possible due to a lack of bank and pitch indications in the cockpit, the artificial horizon not functioning when at high angles of attack.

One remarkable aspect of this disaster was the action of the captain, who described everything as it happened as he attempted to recover from the uncontrolled descent, ending the radio transmission with words of farewell. The information he provided proved useful in identifying the cause of this and the Tu-104 crash two months earlier, leading to design changes. The aircraft was found to have a very slow and limited response when in manual control, and its autopilot did not function efficiently in controlling bank at high altitude. Besides structural modification of the stabiliser, additional attitude instruments were installed to supplement the single artificial horizon then in use.

Date: 3 February 1959 (23:55)
Location: New York, New York, US
Operator: American Airlines (US)
Aircraft type: Lockheed 188A Electra (*N6101A*)

Flight 320 had been cleared for a back-course instrument landing system (ILS) approach to Runway 22 at La Guardia Airport, at the end of a domestic service from Chicago, Illinois. However, during the attempt to land, in darkness and adverse meteorological conditions, the four-engine turboprop descended below the minimum altitude and ultimately crashed in the East River off Rikers Island, approximately 1 mile (1.5 km) from the runway threshold and some 600 ft (180 m) to the right of its extended centreline. The accident killed 65 of the persons aboard, including the captain and a stewardess. Five passengers, the first and second officers and the other stewardess survived with various injuries.

This was a disaster in which the combined effects of several interrelated factors came into play. Primarily the crash was believed to have resulted from the failure of the crew to monitor properly essential instruments for determining attitude and height due to preoccupation with particular aspects of the aircraft and its environment. The contributing elements were cumulative.

Though highly experienced, none of the three flight crewmen had served much time in the Electra, whose instrumentation differed from that found in the piston-engined transports with which they were familiar. Specifically, its altimeters had a window through which 1,000 ft levels were given in single digits, with a triangular-shaped index on each side. Conceivably, the index on the left could have been mistaken for the 1,000 ft pointer used on earlier altimeters, giving the impression that it was indicating a height of 2,500 ft. Similarly, the index on the right could have been mistaken for the 100 ft pointer. Additionally, its vertical speed indicator (VSI) was more sensitive, giving a reading that more closely represented the actual performance of the aircraft. An indication that should alarm a pilot probably would not have evoked the same response with an earlier design of VSI. In this case, the difference could have led to an excessive descent rate during the approach.

A post-crash examination of the instruments also revealed that the captain's altimeter had been incorrectly set. The resulting indication could have been as much as 125 ft (*c.* 40 m) too high, which would have been significant during a landing.

The captain was also criticised for a faulty approach technique, which utilised the heading mode of the autopilot until the final seconds of the flight, contrary to the operating manual. Records in fact showed that despite more than 28,000 hours of flying time, the pilot had never before executed a back course ILS approach at La Guardia Airport in instrument conditions.

The weather was regarded as an additional contributing factor, with a ceiling of only 300–400 ft (*c.* 100–120 m), a visibility of 2 miles (*c.* 3 km) in light rain and fog, and a 6-knot wind from a south-south-westerly direction. Under the circumstances, and especially considering the sparsity of lights in the approach area, it was quite possible that the crew had been deceived by a sensory illusion that created a false impression regarding the height and attitude of the aircraft.

But while the captain may have erred, the first officer could still have prevented the accident, according to the US Civil Aeronautics Board (CAB) report, by following the prescribed procedures and being fully alert and attentive to all his cockpit duties. It was likely that he was paying close attention to the apparent difficulties of the pilot in maintaining the localiser path, to the point that he failed to call out altitude and air speed indications below 600 ft, as required. Just before impact, the co-pilot was probably anticipating breaking out of the overcast and, having seen lights on the ground or water, concentrating on making visual identification of the airport, and thus not monitoring the instruments.

The Electra struck the water while in a shallow descent at a ground speed of about 150 mph (250 kmh); with its undercarriage and flaps extended, it then broke apart and sank in water some 30 ft (10 m) deep. More than 90 per cent of its wreckage was subsequently recovered, as were the bodies of all but two of the victims; death was attributed to both trauma and drowning. The eight survivors owe their lives to a tugboat that happened to be in the area at the time and rescued them from the river.

Landing restrictions imposed by the US Federal Aviation Agency (FAA) in the wake of the accident were lifted following replacement of drum/pointer altimeters in the Electra fleet with the then-standard 'three-pointer' units. Also, a CAB

The empennage and rear fuselage section of the Electra is raised from the East River following the accident that claimed 65 lives. (*CORBIS*)

A Trans World Airlines Lockheed 1649A Starliner, the type that crashed in Italy after a mid-air explosion. *(Trans World Airlines)*

recommendation for flight data recorders on turboprop airliners, as on pure jets, would later become standard throughout the industry.

Date: 26 June 1959 (*c.* 17:35)
Location: Near Varese, Lombardy, Italy
Operator: Trans World Airlines (TWA) (US)
Aircraft type: Lockheed 1649A Starliner (*N7313C*)

Operating as Flight 891 and on a service originating at Athens, Greece, with an ultimate destination of Chicago, Illinois, US, the aircraft was at an approximate height of 11,000 ft (3,400 m) and climbing when an explosion shattered its right wing. The Starliner then plummeted into a field some 20 miles (30 km) north-west of Milan and burst into flames, the crash occurring about 15 minutes after it had taken off from that city's Malpensa Airport, bound for Paris, France. All 68 persons aboard (59 passengers and nine crew members) perished.

The late afternoon disaster occurred during a light rain and low overcast, with a ceiling of around 2,000 ft (600 m), and a visibility of approximately 2 miles (3 km). There was also thunderstorm activity in the area.

An investigative board examined several possible reasons for the tragedy, but discarded most of them, including metal fatigue, structural failure due to turbulence, and sabotage. Not completely ruled out, however, was that the maximum speed of the aircraft had been exceeded during an uncontrolled descent.

In the absence of concrete evidence the theory considered most plausible was the ignition of gasoline vapours emanating from one or both of the No. 7 fuel tank vent pipes as a consequence of static electricity discharges, or streamer corona, which developed in these outlets. This would have led to the explosion of the vapours in that tank, followed by an excess of pressure or another explosion in the adjacent fuel tank, No. 6.

Tests proved such a scenario to be within the realm of possibility under certain atmospheric conditions, and only when the aircraft was ascending; in addition, the weather at the time of the accident was conducive to this phenomenon, with frequent electrical discharges. Static discharges could have occurred had the Starliner been struck anywhere by lightning, or had it flown through clouds that were electrically charged.

Following the explosion in the wing of *N7313C*, which took place near its No. 3 nacelle, aerodynamic forces caused the separation of its tail assembly.

Research begun in the wake of this disaster on the potential threat to aircraft posed by electrical discharges was under way when lightning destroyed a commercial jet in 1963 (see separate entry, 8 December 1963).

THE 1960S

The term 'jet set' became part of our vernacular during the 1960s, and no wonder, considering the tremendous effect on business and pleasure travel brought about by jet aircraft, the popularity of which contributed to a soar in passenger traffic.

Half-way through the decade a new generation of short-haul aircraft, such as the Boeing 727, Douglas DC-9 and Hawker Siddeley Trident, would for the first time bring jet passenger service to smaller communities and airports. This was also the era of the VC-10, which would be the pride of the British commercial aviation industry until the coming of supersonic air travel in the 1970s. By the late 1960s many major airlines had retired their last propeller-driven transports and were boasting of 'all-jet' fleets.

The reliability and durability of jet aircraft were credited with continued improvement in the industry's safety record during this period. But while the number of accidents in relation to the number of flights decreased, greater passenger capacity increased the potential for a major disaster. Before 1960 there had been but one airline crash to claim more than 100 lives; by the beginning of 1970 that figure had risen to 18.

However, despite the potential for even more serious disasters with the advent in the late 1960s of aircraft capable of carrying more than 200 passengers, the record death toll of 134 set in the collision over New York City would not be exceeded until the last year of the decade.

Date: 18 January 1960 (c. 22:20)
Location: Near Charles City, Virginia, US
Operator: Capital Airlines (US)
Aircraft type: Vickers Viscount 745D (N7462)

The four-engine turboprop crashed and burned in a wooded area some 30 miles (50 km) south-east of Richmond, Virginia, killing all 50 persons aboard (46 passengers and a crew of four). It was dark at the time, and the local weather consisted of light, scattered showers and patchy fog. Designated as Flight 20, the aircraft had stopped at Washington, DC, during a domestic service from Chicago, Illinois, to Norfolk, Virginia. Cruising at 8,000 ft (c. 2,500 m), it would have encountered conditions conducive to icing, i.e. sub-zero temperatures, clouds and rain. It was believed that the crew delayed arming the power plant ice-protection systems, leading to the failure of at least two engines. The others must have flamed out after a descent to a lower altitude was initiated, either from the ingestion of melted ice or because the anti-icing system had been left on in the warmer air. Under the circumstances, all four propellers would have autofeathered.

The Viscount was apparently put into a dive in an attempt to drive the propellers out of their feathered positions, while, simultaneously, the crew tried to restart the engines. Successful relights were either interrupted by autofeathering action due to the premature advancing of the power levers prior to complete restart, or prevented by insufficient battery electrical energy associated with the loss of engine rotation.

In the final seconds of the flight, the crew managed to restart engine No. 4, but the application of full power created an asymmetrical control difficulty, causing the aircraft to make two left-hand circles, as confirmed by witnesses. The No. 3 must also have been relit just prior to impact. It was possible that the pilots saw the ground and initiated a pull-up before the turboprop slammed to earth in a nearly level attitude, with no forward velocity.

The reason for the delay in activating the ice-protection systems may have been due to the captain's lack of knowledge that they must be

Tree trunks piercing the wings and fuselage indicate an impact with no forward velocity in the crash of this Capital Airlines Viscount. *(AP Images)*

switched on below a specified temperature; late anticipation of ice accretion; variations in temperature instrument indications; or to a combination of these factors.

As a result of this accident, the airline dropped the phrase 'descend to a warmer climate for relight' from its emergency checklist and instructed its Viscount pilots that engine restart could be accomplished at any height providing that the correct drill was followed.

Date: 17 March 1960 (15:25)
Location: Near Cannelton, Indiana, US
Operator: Northwest Airlines (US)
Aircraft type: Lockheed 188C Electra (*N121US*)

Following a scheduled stop at Chicago, Illinois, Flight 710 took off for Miami, Florida, on the second leg of a domestic service originating at Minneapolis, Minnesota. Less than an hour later, while cruising at an altitude of 18,000 ft (c. 5,500 m), the Electra suffered catastrophic structural failure. Its entire right wing and a large portion of its left having separated, the fuselage of the aircraft

plummeted almost vertically into a field at a speed in excess of 600 mph (965 kmh). All 63 persons aboard (57 passengers and six crew members) perished. A crater measuring 40 ft (12 m) across at its widest point and approximately 10 ft (3 m) deep marked the crash site, some 10 miles (15 km) south-east of Tell City and just north of the Ohio River. Most of the wreckage and the remains of the victims lay buried and were recovered during the subsequent excavation of the crater. The right wing was found more than 2 miles (3 km) from the main wreckage, confirming that an in-flight break-up of the four-engine turboprop had taken place.

An intensive investigation prompted by this and a similar Electra accident six months earlier, which included both flight and ground testing, revealed that the two tragedies had apparently resulted from uncontrolled propeller oscillation, also known as 'whirl mode'. In the case of *N121US*, the propeller wobble was transferred to the outboard nacelles, whose oscillations induced flutter in the wings to the point of overstress. The initial failure was in the right wing, which folded rearward.

Prior damage was, however, considered a prerequisite for undampened 'whirl mode' to reach a destructive level, and the source of the damage to this particular aircraft may have been a hard landing at Chicago's Midway Airport, occurring about 90 minutes before the crash, which was reported by some of the passengers who disembarked there. An encounter with severe clear air turbulence, which had been noted by other pilots flying in the area around the time of the disaster, probably contributed to the start of the flutter.

As a result of the findings into this and the first crash, every Electra in service was modified. Nacelle-wing improvements included the installation of additional support features and the replacement of existing structures with heavier materials. During the modification process, which took some three weeks per aircraft, about half the Electra fleet remained airborne, but with speed and other operating restrictions. These were lifted following completion of the programme in July 1961.

A crater marks the crash site of the Northwest Airlines Electra that lost a wing over Indiana. *(AP Images)*

The first fatal crash of a commercial helicopter on a regular passenger service involved a Chicago Helicopter Airways Sikorsky S-58 on an intra-urban flight. *(Sikorsky)*

Date: 27 July 1960 (22:38)
Location: Forest Park, Illinois, US
Operator: Chicago Helicopter Airways (US)
Aircraft type: Sikorsky S-58C (*N879*)

The first fatal crash of a commercial helicopter engaged in a regular passenger operation occurred during a commuter service between Chicago's two air carrier airports, from Midway to O'Hare International.

Flight 698 was cruising at its assigned height of 1,500 ft (*c.* 500 m) when one of its four main rotor blades snapped, breaking about 8 ft (2.5 m) from the root. After it had descended to a lower altitude, its tail rotor and cone separated due to vibrations generated by the imbalance of the main rotor assembly, attributed to the loss of the blade, and the aircraft then crashed in a cemetery and burst into flames, killing all 13 persons aboard (11 passengers and two pilots). The accident took place in darkness and clear weather conditions on the outskirts of Chicago, approximately half-way between the two airports.

The failure of the main blade was initiated by a fatigue fracture, which had apparently developed in the 68 hours of flying since its last inspection. A subsequent directive issued by the US Federal Aviation Agency (FAA) elaborated on inspection requirements for main rotor blades and limited their service life to 1,000 hours.

Date: 29 August 1960 (*c*. 06:50)
Location: Off Dakar, Senegal
Operator: Air France
Aircraft type: Lockheed 1049G Super Constellation (*F-BHBC*)

Operating as Flight 343, the airliner was to have landed at Yoff Airport, serving Dakar, a scheduled stop during a service originating at Paris, France, with an ultimate destination of Abidjan, in the Ivory Coast. Following an unsuccessful approach, it began a second attempt, flying over the airport towards the west. A few minutes later, and after reporting 'downwind' while at a height of 1,000 ft (*c*. 300 m), the Super Constellation crashed in the Atlantic Ocean approximately 1 mile (1.5 km) from the shore, in the midst of a rain squall. All 63 persons aboard (55 passengers and a crew of eight) perished.

The disaster occurred shortly before sunrise and in meteorological conditions that also consisted of a low overcast, with 7/8 cloud coverage at 2,000–3,000 ft (*c*. 600–1,000 m), and a visibility that varied from one minute to the next. There was also thunderstorm activity in the area.

Its undercarriage and flaps extended, the aircraft was believed to have struck the surface of the sea at a relatively steep angle and while probably banked to the right. Most of the victims' bodies were recovered, but salvage operations yielded only about 20 per cent of the wreckage from the water, which was some 130 ft (40 m) deep.

Although the cause could not be determined, it was considered possible that the crash resulted from structural failure or a loss of control due to turbulence; sensory illusion; distraction of the flight crew, which could have been associated with a lightning strike; inaccuracy of an air speed indicator or altimeter; or faulty reading of the latter instrument.

Date: 19 September 1960 (*c*. 06:00)
Location: Guam, Mariana Islands
Operator: World Airways (US)
Aircraft type: Douglas DC-6AB (*N90779*)

The airliner, which was being flown under contract to the US Military Air Transport Service (MATS) and was carrying as passengers American service personnel and some dependants, had landed at Agana Naval Air Station during a transoceanic service from the Philippines to Travis Air Force Base, California, US. It departed before dawn, bound for Wake Island, its next en route stop.

Less than a minute after its take-off from Runway 06L, the transport crashed on Mt Barrigada, about 2 miles (3 km) east of the air base and some 5 miles (10 km) east-north-east of the island's capital city, bursting into flames on impact. Killed in the accident were 80 of the 94 persons aboard, including seven crew members; the navigator was among the injured survivors. The casualties were more attributable to the effects of the fire than the crash itself.

Its undercarriage and flaps having been retracted, the aircraft was in a slight right bank but practically level longitudinally when it initially struck trees at an approximate elevation of 600 ft (180 m), or slightly less than 100 ft (30 m) below the summit of the peak.

The pilot had failed to comply with the published departure procedures applicable to the runway used by initiating a right turn before attaining an altitude of 1,000 ft (*c*. 300 m). Despite the visual flight rules (VFR) conditions existing at the time, with scattered clouds at 1,400 ft (*c*. 430 m), a high overcast and a visibility of about 15 miles (25 km), it was doubtful whether in the darkness and haze the crew could have seen the single flashing red beacon atop the mountain, the only visual warning of the obstacle.

As a safety measure, the minimum height requirement was later included in the air traffic control departure information.

Date: 4 October 1960 (17:40)
Location: Boston, Massachusetts, US
Operator: Eastern Air Lines (US)
Aircraft type: Lockheed 188A Electra (*N5533*)

Designated as Flight 375, the turboprop crashed in Winthrop Bay about a minute after taking off from Runway 05 at Boston's Logan International Airport, killing 62 persons aboard (59 passengers and the three members of the flight crew). The 10 injured survivors included both stewardesses.

Bound for Philadelphia, Pennsylvania, the aircraft's first scheduled stop during a domestic service with an ultimate destination of Atlanta, Georgia, it had just become airborne when it struck a flock of starlings, and a large number of the birds were ingested into three of its four engines. The

No. 1 was shut down when its propeller auto-feathered, No. 2 flamed out completely and No. 4 experienced a partial loss of power. This asymmetrical power condition, which was aggravated by the recovery of full power to the No. 4 engine before the No. 2 relit, resulted in a yaw to the left. Meanwhile, the overall power loss caused the transport to decelerate. The Electra then stalled during a skidding left turn while continuing to yaw, and after its port wing dropped and nose pitched up, it rolled left into a spin and plummeted almost vertically into the shallow water of the Boston Harbour inlet, some 500 ft (150 m) from the shore, its undercarriage retracted and flaps extended at impact. The meteorological conditions at the time, consisting of scattered clouds and a visibility of 15 miles (c. 25 km), were not considered a factor in the crash.

The only means of regaining control and air speed before the spin would have been to intentionally reduce power and lower the nose, but the low altitude of the aircraft, which at that point was less than 150 ft (50 m), precluded any such recovery action by the pilots.

As a result of this accident, the US Federal Aviation Agency (FAA) initiated a research programme aimed at improving the tolerance of turbine engines to bird ingestion.

Date: 16 December 1960 (c. 10:30)
Location: New York, New York, US
First aircraft
Operator: United Air Lines (US)
Type: Douglas DC-8 Series 11 (N8013U)
Second aircraft
Operator: Trans World Airlines (TWA) (US)
Type: Lockheed 1049 Super Constellation (N6907C)

The same two carriers involved in the 1956 Grand Canyon disaster (see separate entry, 30 June 1956) were the principals in this mid-air crash, which exhibited some other amazing similarities. One of the aircraft was of the identical make and model in both cases, while the other was produced by the same manufacturer and only one generation apart. In addition, the combined death toll of those aboard the two transports was the same in each accident.

There were also some significant differences, most notably that this time both aircraft were operating in accordance with instrument flight rules (IFR) and, presumably, under the watchful eye of ground radar. This collision was tragic proof that, despite procedural changes and technological advances since the first accident, serious inadequacies still existed in the US air traffic control (ATC) system.

A United Air Lines DC-8, the type that collided with a Trans World Airlines Super Constellation over New York City, became the first US commercial jet to crash fatally during a passenger service. *(United Air Lines)*

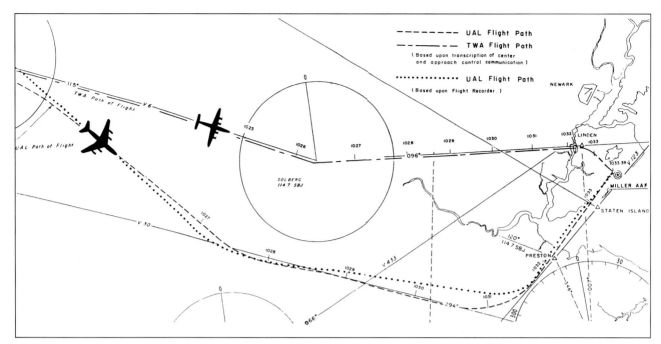

The courses of the United and TWA flights leading up to the collision over Staten Island. *(Civil Aeronautics Board)*

United Flight 826 had originated at Chicago, Illinois, bound for New York International Airport, with the DC-8 jet carrying 77 passengers and seven crew members. TWA Flight 266 was also on a domestic service, from Dayton and Columbus, Ohio, and was scheduled to land at New York's other major airport, La Guardia. Aboard the piston-engine Super Constellation were 39 passengers plus a crew of five. The weather over the city on this Friday morning was overcast, with a ceiling of about 5,000 ft (1,500 m), accompanied by fog and snow or sleet, conditions that were not conducive to visual flight rules (VFR) operations.

Following its passage of Allentown, Pennsylvania, and just before beginning its descent from 25,000 ft (c. 7,500 m), the DC-8 was assigned a shortened route. This new clearance, which would in fact be regarded as a contributing factor in the subsequent collision, reduced its distance by some 12 miles (20 km) to the Preston Intersection, a position defined by two radials from two different very-high-frequency omnidirectional range (VOR) stations, where the aircraft should have entered a 'racetrack' holding pattern to await landing instructions.

Unbeknown to the New York centre, one of the DC-8's two VOR receivers was inoperative. As a result, the crew would have to establish a holding fix by tuning the single receiver from one station to the other, a time-consuming process; and with the shortened clearance, the pilots would have less time

to accomplish this task. In the final seconds before the accident, the centre advised the crew that radar service was terminated, and that they should contact Idlewild Approach Control. There was, however, no actual 'hand-off' from one control facility to the other. The last message from the jet, directed to approach control, was 'Approaching Preston at five thousand'.

Simultaneous with these events, the Super Constellation was descending in preparation for its own landing. The transport was receiving radar vectors from La Guardia Approach Control, and had last been instructed to make a left turn and assume a heading of 130 degrees. After noticing an unidentified blip on his radarscope, the controller advised the TWA flight that it appeared to be jet traffic 'off your right, now three o'clock at one mile, north-eastbound'. The two targets then merged.

The aircraft collided at 10:33 while in the clouds at an approximate altitude of 5,000 ft (1,500 m), almost directly over Miller Army Air Field, located in New Dorp, on Staten Island. Flying along Airway V123 at a ground speed of about 380 mph (610 kmh), an excessive velocity that also contributed to the accident, the DC-8 overtook the Super Constellation from behind and to the latter's right side, striking the top of its fuselage at an angle of about 110 degrees. Cabin insulation and human remains were later found in the DC-8's right outboard engine, a grim reminder of how it must have sliced into the passenger compartment. At the time of impact, the jet was in a nearly straight and level attitude, the propeller transport banking to the left.

The Super Constellation broke into three main sections and plummeted to earth in flames, crashing at the airfield. Scattered among its debris were pieces of the DC-8, including the No. 4 power plant and starboard wing outboard of the engine. Following the collision, the jet continued in a north-easterly direction for another 8.5 miles (c. 13.5 km) before it plunged into the Park Slope section of Brooklyn and exploded in flames, its empennage coming to rest at the intersection of Sterling Place and Seventh Avenue.

Three occupants were removed alive from the wreckage of the Super Constellation, but died shortly afterwards. One passenger on the jet, an 11-year-old boy riding in the aft part of its cabin, was thrown into a snowbank and miraculously lived through the crash with severe burns and other injuries, only to succumb in hospital the following day, leaving no survivors from either aircraft. The final toll was 134 persons killed, including six on the ground in Brooklyn, where six others were injured. There was considerable damage in the area where the DC-8 crashed; the impact and resulting fires destroyed 10 tenements, some shops and a church.

Due to an apparent navigational error by its crew, the jet had proceeded beyond its clearance limit and the confines of the airspace allocated to the flight. It was probably more than coincidental that the distance it had travelled beyond its intended holding position and the point of the collision equalled the length of the shortcut. In its investigative report, the US Civil Aeronautics Board (CAB) concluded that the pilots did not take note of the change in time and distance associated with the new clearance.

There were indications that, in lieu of a second VOR unit, the crew had used their automatic direction finding (ADF) equipment to take cross-bearings. This would have required rapid mental calculation, and the display could easily have been misinterpreted. Had the No. 1 ADF receiver been tuned to the Scotland low-frequency radio beacon, the captain, when transitioning to it, may have confused this instrument with the VOR. (The pictorial display of the ADF at the location of the collision would under the circumstances resemble the VOR when it was tuned to the appropriate station.) Thus, when the

flight reported that it was approaching Preston, it was already well beyond that point.

But the United crew were not alone in their culpability, because the CAB further determined that the New York control centre did not adequately monitor the aircraft, and the controller failed to observe it proceed through the Preston intersection. When he reported radar service as being terminated, the jet was nearly 10 miles (15 km) beyond its clearance limit.

This accident brought about a major revitalisation of the nation's ATC system. Most significant was the development of the system of 'positive control'. Under this principle, radar control would be exerted over all aircraft flying above 24,000 ft (c. 7,300 m), and positive control would extend down to 8,000 ft (c. 2,500 m) on high-density airways, and to most airline operations (all that employed jets). A new speed limit below 10,000 ft (c. 3,000 m) and within 30 nautical miles (55 km) of the destination airport was also imposed, as were strict guidelines in the transferral of flights from one control facility to another.

A scene of devastation is left by the crash of the United Air Lines jet in Brooklyn, where six persons lost their lives in addition to the 128 aboard the two aircraft. *(CORBIS)*

Additionally, the installation of two devices would be required on all aircraft weighing more than 12,500 lb (5,670 kg) that operated in US airspace. The first of these was the transponder, which would help identify the aircraft's target on radar. The second was distance-measuring equipment (DME), designed to assist pilots in determining their exact position by calculating the mileage between navigational facilities. Later refinements included three-dimensional radar and alphanumeric displays for easy identification of the radar blip.

The system is far from foolproof, however, and lapses still occur periodically. But one of the primary objectives of the positive control system, i.e. to provide separation of air carrier flights, has worked exceedingly well. In fact, not since 1960 has a castastrophic mid-air collision between two large commercial aircraft occurred anywhere over the United States.

Date: 15 February 1961 (10:05)
Location: Near Brussels, Belgium
Operator: Belgian World Airlines (SABENA)
Aircraft type: Boeing 707-329 (*OO-SJB*)

Among the passengers who boarded Flight 548 at New York International Airport were the 18 members of the US figure skating team, including the coach, on their way to a world meet in Prague, Czechoslovakia. Following the 8½ hour transatlantic trip, the 707 began its approach to land at Brussels National Airport.

Everything seemed normal, but as the aircraft was about to touch down on Runway 20, engine power increased and its undercarriage and flaps were then retracted in what appeared to be an overshoot manoeuvre. Climbing to an estimated height of 1,500 ft (*c.* 500 m), the 707 completed three left-hand circles while ascending and descending as thrust was both increased and decreased. During this period of time its attitude became generally steeper until finally, while in a near-vertical left bank, the jetliner nosed down and crashed in a field approximately 1 mile (1.5 km) from the runway threshold, near Heist-op-den-Berg, a village located in the province of Antwerpen some 20 miles (30 km) north-east of the capital city, bursting into flames on impact. All 72 persons aboard, including 11 crew members, perished. A

farmer on the ground was also killed and a second seriously injured.

The airport weather at the time, which was not considered a factor, consisted of a high overcast and a visibility of about 2 miles (3 km).

A Belgian investigative commission concluded that the accident was probably related to the material failure of the aircraft's flying controls. Two hypotheses were considered possible: either the jamming of the outboard ailerons near the neutral position, or the unwanted extension of the spoilers; although it could not be corroborated, available evidence pointed to the latter.

Examination of the wreckage revealed that the sheer rivets in the follow-up mechanism between all four spoilers and their hydraulic valves were broken. Had these rivets been sheared in flight, the spoilers could have either gone into a fully extended position or retracted with only a minimal amount of aileron movement. Ultimately this could lead to the asymmetrical deployment of the spoilers, causing severe lateral instability. In this case, the right inboard spoiler was extended at the time of the crash, and the left inboard one probably retracted. The position of either outboard spoiler could not be determined.

There were indications that the crew had tried to bypass the spoilers. However, the left outboard bypass valve was not functioning properly and remained jammed in the open position, which would have prevented such action. In such an event the only recourse would have been to suppress the hydraulic pressure pumps, but there would have been little time to accomplish this. Moreover, the pilots would have difficulty identifying the problem, especially considering that the spoilers were not visible from the cockpit.

Representing the nation of manufacture, the US Federal Aviation Agency (FAA) doubted the Belgian theory, maintaining that *OO-SJB* should have been controllable even with an outboard spoiler fully extended. It suspected that a malfunction in the stabiliser adjusting mechanism had caused the accident.

The recommended modifications to the 707 included in service bulletins sent out by Boeing and SABENA, involved the spoiler follow-up crank shear joint and the outboard spoiler shut-off valve, replacement of the control wheel stabiliser switch, and the installation of a supplementary brake for

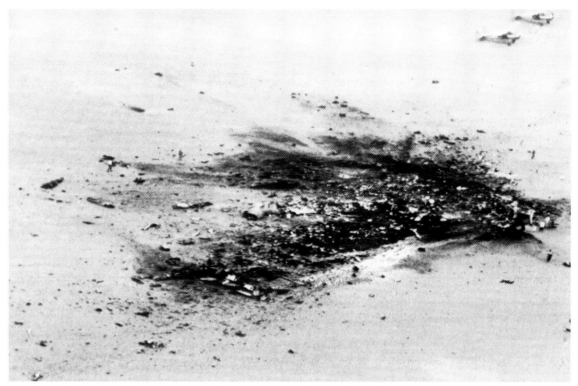

The charred remains of the Air France Starliner are scattered across the Sahara Desert after an in-flight break-up believed to have been caused by a bomb. *(AP Images)*

the stabiliser trim actuator. The commission also suggested the introduction of a spoiler position indicator.

Date: 10 May 1961 (*c*. 02:30)
Location: Eastern Algeria
Operator: Air France
Aircraft type: Lockheed 1649A Starliner (*F-BHBM*)

Operating as Flight 406, the airliner crashed and burned in the Sahara Desert while en route from Fort-Lamy (Ndjamena), Chad, to Marseilles, France, one segment of a service originating at Brazzaville, Congo, with an ultimate destination of Paris. All 78 persons aboard (69 passengers and a crew of nine) perished.

Cruising in early morning darkness and clear weather conditions, the Starliner broke up at an approximate altitude of 20,000 ft (6,000 m) before it plunged to earth some 30 miles (50 km) south-west of Ghadamis, Libya. Its empennage and other components were reportedly found about 1 mile (1.5 km) from the main wreckage site.

The most probable cause of the catastrophe was sabotage with nitrocellulose explosive.

Date: 30 May 1961 (*c*. 01:20)
Location: Near Lisbon, Portugal
Operator: KLM Royal Dutch Airlines
Aircraft type: Douglas DC-8 Series 53 (*PH-DCL*)

Designated as Flight 897, the jetliner was being operated by the Dutch carrier for the Venezuelan airline VIASA on a service from Rome, Italy, to Caracas, Venezuela, with three en route stops. Only about 5 minutes after it had taken off from Lisbon airport, the DC-8 plunged into the Atlantic Ocean south of the Tagus River estuary, and all 61 persons aboard (47 passengers and 14 crew members) perished.

The crash took place in darkness, and the meteorological conditions in the area probably consisted of light rain, light to moderate turbulence, a 20-knot wind out of the west, a visibility of around 5 miles (10 km) and a low overcast, with 4/8 stratocumulus clouds at about 2,000 ft (600 m) and solid altostratus.

Located on the ocean floor some 2 miles (3 km) off shore and at a depth of approximately 100 ft (30 m), about 75 per cent of the wreckage was subsequently recovered. Evidence indicated that the aircraft, which was last reported climbing through

6,000 ft (c. 1,800 m), struck the surface of the water at a speed in excess of 500 mph (800 kmh), and while in a slight descent and banked to the right.

There was no evidence of any pre-impact defects or malfunctions, though they could not be definitely excluded. Nor could the possibility, though remote, of sabotage or some other malicious act. There were indications that the jetliner went into a spiral dive from a steep left-banking attitude, possibly due to crew inattentiveness or because one or both pilots were misled by the failure of an artificial horizon or some other vital flight instrument, in either case resulting in a loss of control. The attitude of the DC-8 at the moment of impact pointed to over-correction during the attempt to level off, but the loss of altitude must have been too rapid for the crew to effect recovery.

The investigative board recommended the installation in commercial aircraft of a third, independent horizon that could be referred to in the event of a malfunction in either or both of the captain's and first officer's instruments, a safety feature that would come into use some years later.

Date: 1 September 1961 (c. 02:05)
Location: Near Hinsdale, Illinois, US
Operator: Trans World Airlines (TWA) (US)
Aircraft type: Lockheed 049 Constellation (N86511)

Operating as Flight 529, the transport crashed and disintegrated in a fiery explosion some 10 miles (15 km) west of Chicago's Midway Airport, from where it had taken off only 5 minutes earlier, bound for Las Vegas, Nevada, one segment of a domestic transcontinental service originating at Boston, Massachusetts, with an ultimate destination of San Francisco, California. All 78 persons aboard (73 passengers and a crew of five) perished.

The Constellation had been flying on a westerly course in early morning darkness and good weather conditions, which at the airport consisted of a high overcast and a visibility of 3 miles (c. 5 km), before it plunged into a cornfield in a nose-down attitude and while banked slightly to the left, its undercarriage and flaps retracted at the moment of impact. A portion of its horizontal stabiliser to which the right vertical fin was attached had separated in flight.

Examination of the wreckage revealed that a $\frac{7}{16}$ in nickel steel bolt was missing from the parallelogram linkage of the aircraft's elevator boost system, and

the US Civil Aeronautics Board (CAB) concluded that it must have fallen out prior to the crash. This would have caused the elevator to move to its full upward position, creating a stall. In response to the violent pitch-up, one or both pilots could have been expected to apply forward pressure to the control column, but this action would also make it difficult, if not impossible, to move the handle in order to shift the elevator system to manual operation, which would be the only way of overcoming the situation. Under the circumstances, the crew were unable to maintain control. The pre-impact empennage damage was the apparent result of the accelerated stall vibrations.

Though the theory could not be substantiated, the almost probable reason for the bolt's loss was that it had not been properly secured during the replacement of the parallelogram assembly, which had taken place some 10 months earlier. Over a period of time the nut had backed off until the bolt finally came out on the fatal flight.

Citing the 'excellent service history' of the Constellation, the US Federal Aviation Agency (FAA) rejected the recommendations of the CAB for modifications in the aircraft's elevator boost system that it made in the light of this accident.

Date: 10 September 1961 (c. 03:55)
Location: Near Limerick, Ireland
Operator President Airlines (US)
Aircraft type: Douglas DC-6B (N90773)

The aircraft was on a charter service from Düsseldorf, (West) Germany, to Chicago, Illinois, US, with two en route stops. Aboard were European passengers, mostly Germans, plus six crew members, all Americans. Shortly after it had taken off from Runway 24 at Shannon Airport, Ireland, in pre-dawn darkness and during a fog, bound for Gander, Newfoundland, Canada, the DC-6B plunged into the estuary of the River Shannon. Cleared for a right turn, the transport had instead turned to the left, and was in a bank of at least 90 degrees when it crashed in the shallow water approximately 1 mile (1.5 km) from the end of the runway.

The bodies of 84 persons were subsequently recovered, one more than listed on the manifest, and there were no survivors (one passenger was found alive in the wreckage but later died in hospital).

The plunge of this President Airlines DC-6B into the estuary of Ireland's River Shannon occurred moments after the transport had taken off. *(CORBIS)*

The disaster probably resulted from the failure of the captain to maintain control, either due to a defective artificial horizon or a fault in the aircraft's right-hand aileron tabs. Contributing factors may have been the unfavourable meteorological conditions, which at the time of take-off were below the minima authorised by the carrier, and possible crew fatigue.

Date: 12 September 1961 (21:09)
Location: Near Rabat, Morocco
Operator: Air France
Aircraft type: Sud-Aviation Caravelle III (*F-BJTB*)

Designated as Flight 2005, the jet airliner crashed and burned while attempting to land at Sale Airport, which also serves Rabat, a scheduled stop during a service from Paris to Casablanca, Morocco, and all 77 persons aboard (71 passengers and a crew of six) were killed.

Immediately after the pilot had reported his intention to break through a thick, low fog over the non-directional beacon (NDB), the control tower replied that the navigational facility was not in line with the runway, but the flight did not acknowledge the message. Its undercarriage down and flaps partially extended, the Caravelle struck the ground in a slight nose-down attitude and while probably banked gently to the left. Bouncing twice, it finally slammed into the side of a gorge and broke apart

some 5 miles (10 km) from the threshold of Runway 04 and approximately 1 mile (1.5 km) to the left of its extended centreline. It was dark at the time, and the airport weather consisted of a solid overcast at about 100 ft (30 m) and a horizontal visibility of around 1,500 ft (500 m).

Material failure appeared unlikely, and both altimeters were found to have been correctly set. Therefore, the hypothesis considered more probable than any other as causing the accident was an altimeter misreading of 1,000 ft. The error could have been made at the beginning of the descent, then, retaining it, the pilot may have given his full attention to the pointer in order to bring the aircraft to what he believed was the minimum authorised height. As noted in the investigative report, the reading of the Kollsman window altimeter, with which *F-BJTB* was equipped, could be subject to misinterpretation.

Date: 8 November 1961 (*c.* 21:30)
Location: Near Richmond, Virginia, US
Operator: Imperial Airlines (US)
Aircraft type: Lockheed 049E Constellation (*N2737A*)

The four-engine transport was being flown under a US military contract, carrying 74 army recruits on their way to Fort Jackson, near Columbia, South Carolina, plus five civilian crew members, the latter

An American Airlines Boeing 707-123B, identical to the aircraft that crashed after take-off from New York International Airport. *(American Airlines)*

including a student flight engineer in addition to the regular one. Both pilots were qualified captains. Having boarded passengers at Newark, New Jersey, Wilkes Barre, Pennsylvania, and Baltimore, Maryland, the Constellation proceeded towards its ultimate destination.

As the aircraft took off from Baltimore, a momentary fluctuation was noted in the fuel pressure of its No. 3 power plant, probably due to the failure of its fuel boost pump, which may have been fitted with the wrong kind of electrical brush (as, it turns out, was the No. 2). In response, the student engineer opened both the No. 3 and No. 4 cross-feed valves; but because of the inoperative boost pump, the higher pressure in the cross-feed manifold supplied by the operating pump held closed a check valve between the manifold and the No. 3 fuel tank. Fuelling both starboard engines, the gasoline supply in the No. 4 tank was soon exhausted, causing both power plants to fail.

Immediately taking over, the regular flight engineer then committed a procedural error by leaving on the No. 4 boost pump, which allowed air to be drawn into the fuel supply lines of both the No. 3 and No. 4 engines, thus preventing either from being restarted. The corresponding

propellers were feathered, and the crew elected to land at Byrd Field, located just outside the Richmond suburb of Sandston.

During the approach to Runway 33, the captain acting as co-pilot inexplicably switched to Runway 02. However, the landing had to be abandoned altogether when the undercarriage would not extend, this because of the crew's failure to activate a crossover valve that would have permitted the use of hydraulic pressure from the No. 1 and No. 2 engines to assume the function normally borne by the two right-hand ones.

As the transport circled the airport in an anticlockwise direction, this time to land on Runway 33, its banking angle was steepened to the point where it resulted in a loss of air speed and, in turn, altitude. Responding to the higher sink rate, brought about by the poorly executed go-around manoeuvre, the crew applied full power to the two port engines, but under the strain of the overboosting, the No. 1 quickly failed. Unable to maintain height on only one power plant, the Constellation, which had flown about half a mile (0.8 km) beyond the extended centreline of the runway, finally crashed approximately 1 mile (1.5 km) from its threshold. A sharp pull-up was made just before the aircraft slammed into a wooded area and erupted into flames, its main undercarriage down on impact but nose gear still retracted.

Although the crash itself was totally survivable, the post-impact fire – specifically, the effects of carbon monoxide poisoning – resulted in 77 fatalities. Only the pilot-in-command and the regular flight engineer, both of whom were injured, survived. It was dark at the time of the accident, but the meterological conditions were good.

The disaster was attributed to a lack of command coordination and decision, as illustrated by the action of the first officer in changing runways; faulty judgement; and insufficient knowledge of the equipment, which created an emergency situation that the crew could not handle.

In addition to the lack of competence in the cockpit, irregularities were identified in the company's operations. These included the finding of rust in the fuel system of *N2737A* and in the truck that had serviced it. And although the contamination was not considered a causative factor in the multiple engine failure, it did reflect a lack of compliance with civil air regulations by Imperial Airlines. As a result, the US Federal Aviation Agency (FAA) revoked the carrier's operating certificate some six weeks after the crash.

Date: 1 March 1962 (10:08)
Location: New York, New York, US
Operator: American Airlines (US)
Aircraft type: Boeing 707-123B (*N7506A*)

Operating as Flight 1, the jetliner took off from Runway 31L at New York International Airport, on a domestic transcontinental service to Los Angeles, California. Following one left turn, the 707 began a second, back towards the south-east, but instead of levelling off it continued rolling to port until it inverted. Then, from an approximate height of 1,500 ft (500 m) and less than 2 minutes after becoming airborne, the aircraft plunged into Jamaica Bay, disintegrating on impact and bursting into flames. All 95 persons aboard (87 passengers and a crew of eight) perished.

Its undercarriage and flaps fully retracted, the jetliner had crashed in the shallow waters of Pumpkin Patch Channel during low tide and at a speed of about 230 mph (370 kmh), leaving a crater some 10 ft (3 m) deep on the bottom of the bay. Much of the debris was buried and had to be excavated from the mud.

The condition of both the wreckage and bodies of the flight crew somewhat hampered the investigation into the tragedy by the US Civil Aeronautics Board (CAB). There was, however, no

The shattered remains of the 707 continue to smoulder on the surface of Jamaica Bay following the accident that took 95 lives. *(AP Images)*

evidence of in-flight fire or explosion, incapacitation of the pilots or malfunction in the aircraft's aileron control system. The weather at the time was excellent, with high, scattered clouds and a visibility of 15 miles (c. 25 km).

Examination did, however, reveal anomalies in the rudder control system of the 707. Wires were found to be frayed or severed in the voltage rate generator of the rudder servo unit, a device designed to convert electrical signals from the automatic flight control system into proportional mechanical forces to adjust the vertical control surface. There were also scratches or gouges on the sleeving enclosing the wires. This apparently did not occur on impact, because similar damage was found in other units still on the production line. It was concluded that the damage resulted from the improper use of tweezers when tying the wire bundles to the motor housing. In its investigative report, the CAB expressed the opinion that the wires were weakened to the point that vibration and other disturbances eventually caused their final separation.

As established by testing, the crossing or otherwise short-circuiting of the wires could cause a 'hard-over' signal by the yaw damper, a mechanism designed to sense the onset of a lateral control abnormality and automatically adjust the rudder, and of which the servo is a component. In the case of N7506A, it apparently resulted in an unexpected rudder deflection to the left, producing yaw, side-slip and roll that in turn led to a loss of control. The reason the crew allowed the aircraft to fall into the stall regime may have been due to a combination of factors, including the initial masking of the control problem by turbulence; difficulty in recognising the situation because of less reliance on instrument references in the visual meteorological conditions; an unintentional nose-high attitude occurring as the crew struggled with the controls; the absence of the stick-shaker warning indication before the initiation of the stall buffet; or the continued operation of the malfunctioning yaw damper. There was also speculation that the pilot's attempt to maintain the specified flight path, which included turns for the purpose of noise abatement and avoiding the traffic pattern of nearby La Guardia Airport, could have been a factor in the accident by preventing a smooth climb-out of the departing aircraft.

There were also indications that, in an attempt to regain control, the crew had throttled back the two port engines, then disengaged the yaw damper and deactivated the rudder boost system.

Differing with the findings of the CAB, the US Federal Aviation Agency (FAA) concluded that the disaster probably resulted from the loss of an improperly installed bolt from the 707's hydraulic boost system. As a consequence, control of the system was lost, causing the rudder to deflect to the full limits of its range, producing a similar yawing action to that which would have been produced by a servo malfunction. The CAB did note in its report that such an occurrence could have been the initiating abnormality that led to the crash.

Despite its own hypothesis as to the cause, the accident prompted the FAA to issue an airworthiness directive requiring the inspection of servo rate generator motors of the type used on N7506A to check for damaged wire bundles.

Date: 4 March 1962 (c. 19:20)
Location: Near Douala, Cameroon
Operator: Caledonian Airways (UK)
Aircraft type: Douglas DC-7C (G-ARUD)

All 111 persons aboard (101 passengers and 10 crew members) perished when the aircraft, which had been leased from the Belgian airline SABENA and was being operated by Caledonian on behalf of Trans-Africa Air Coach Ltd, crashed about a minute after taking off from Runway 12 at Douala Airport, bound for Lisbon, Portugal, its next en route stop during a charter service to Luxembourg from Lourenço-Marques (now Maputo), Mozambique.

Following an unusually long take-off ground run, the DC-7C appeared to gain altitude with difficulty. Flying nearly level longitudinally and banked slightly to the left, the transport first struck trees approximately 1.5 miles (2.5 km) beyond the end of the runway, some 1,500 ft (500 m) to the left of its extended centreline and only about 65 ft (20 m) above its elevation, then slammed into a swamp, disintegrated and burned. At the moment of impact its undercarriage was in the up position, and its flaps were also retracted or nearly so, though there were indications that the crew had tried to re-extend them after observing some abnormality. The accident occurred on a dark, moonless night, and the meteorological conditions at the time consisted of a low, broken overcast, with 3/8 fracto-cumulus clouds at approximately 1,300 ft (400 m), 2/8 stratocumulus at about 2,000 ft (600 m), and a visibility of around 10 miles (15 km). There was also light rain and thunderstorm activity in the area.

The aircraft's starboard elevator spring tab was found to be jammed, and the investigative commission concluded that this could have happened before the crash. A spring tab is designed to reduce the efforts of the pilot, especially when operating at higher air speeds. In this case such a jamming could have increased by up to three times the amount of pull force on the control column required to carry out a successful rotation. This would also account for the long take-off ground run and could have led to a negative rate of climb.

Had it occurred, the mechanical malfunction may have been aggravated by a climb technique adopted by the carrier that emphasised gaining speed and could, in turn, result in flight at a low altitude; by the fact that the flap retraction procedure utilised by the airline did not stipulate a minimum height for such other than that needed for obstacle clearance; and by the presence in the first officer's seat of a check pilot, whose attention might have been directed more towards the captain than the indications of his own instruments. A defect in some flight instrument, such as the pilot's flight director or the emergency artificial horizon, was not completely eliminated by the commission as a possible cause of the accident, though this would not have explained the decision of the crew to re-extend the flaps.

Subsequently, the manufacturer designed a modification of the spring tab mechanism used on this type of aircraft to eliminate the possibility of accidental jamming. Safety improvements were also made at Douala Airport, with the installation of three white lights at an approximate height of 130 ft (40 m) and about 4 miles (6.5 km) from the runway threshold to provide a visual fix along the centreline.

Date: 16 March 1962 (c. 00:30)
Location: Philippine Sea
Operator: The Flying Tiger Line Inc (US)
Aircraft type: Lockheed 1049H Super Constellation (N6921C)

The four-engine transport was en route from Guam to the Philippines, one segment of a transpacific service originating at Travis Air Force Base, California, US, with an ultimate destination of Saigon (Ho Chi Minh City), in (then) South Vietnam, being conducted under contract to the US Military Air Transport Service (MATS). It was carrying 93 US and three South Vietnamese service personnel plus a civilian crew of 11 Americans, a total of 107 persons.

Cruising in darkness and, apparently, good weather conditions, with scattered clouds, the aircraft was last reported at an altitude of 18,000 ft (c. 5,500 m). There was no indication of any difficulty in its final radio transmission, but when the Super Constellation failed to arrive at Clark Air Base, located near Manila, a search was begun that went on for more than a week, involving nearly 50 aircraft and eight vessels and covering 144,000 square miles (c. 230,000 sq km) of open sea. But no trace of it was ever found.

Members of a ship's crew had reported seeing an explosion in the sky from which two flaming objects appeared to fall into the ocean, at the approximate time and location where N6921C was believed to have been, i.e. some 800 miles (1,300 km) east of the Philippines and in an area where the depth of the water ranged from 2 to 3 miles (c. 3–5 km).

In its investigative report, the US Civil Aeronautics Board (CAB) concluded that they had probably witnessed the catastrophic demise of the airliner. But whether it was a victim of mechanical or structural failure, sabotage, or some other adverse factor, could not be determined due to a lack of tangible evidence.

Date: 22 May 1962 (c. 21:15)
Location: Near Unionville, Missouri, US
Operator: Continental Air Lines (US)
Aircraft type: Boeing 707-124 (N70775)

Designated as Flight 11, the jetliner was en route from Chicago, Illinois, to Kansas City, Missouri, the first segment of a domestic service scheduled to terminate at Los Angeles, California, when it crashed along the Iowa/Missouri border, killing all 45 persons aboard (37 passengers and a crew of eight). One passenger was found alive in the wreckage but succumbed to injuries about 1½ hours after his rescue.

Flying in darkness and clear meteorological conditions at an approximate height of 37,000 ft

The main portion of the Continental Air Lines Boeing 707 lies in a field after an in-flight break-up attributed to a bomb blast. *(CORBIS)*

(11,300 m), the aircraft had just circumnavigated some thunderstorm activity when it was rocked by an explosion, and shortly afterward disintegrated. The major part of it fell into a field about 5 miles (10 km) north-north-west of Unionville, though pieces were found over a path 40 miles (c. 65 km) long in a north-easterly direction, and some light debris was found up to 120 miles (c. 190 km) away from the main wreckage area.

Early suspicions of foul play were soon proved correct when the US Federal Bureau of Investigation (FBI) established that dynamite had been detonated within the fuselage of the 707, apparently in the used towel bin underneath the wash basin in its right rear lavatory. Following the blast, the crew must have initiated an emergency descent, donning smoke masks and lowering the undercarriage, but the aircraft broke up at a high altitude. Losing the aft 38 ft (11.5 m) of its fuselage, the jetliner pitched down, causing most of its left wing, the outer portion of its right wing and all four engines to break off.

The bomb was believed to have been carried aboard by a passenger in a suicide-for-insurance plot, with his wife named as the beneficiary. In the process he committed the first successful sabotage of a commercial jet.

Date: 3 June 1962 (*c.* 12:35)
Location: Near Villeneuve-le-Roi, Ile-de-France, France
Operator: Air France
Aircraft type Boeing 707-328 (*F-BHSM*)

The jet airliner was on a charter service to the United States, bound for Atlanta, Georgia, via New York City. Except for one Frenchman, its passengers were all Americans returning home from a tour of Europe sponsored by the Atlanta Art Association.

Using Runway 08, the 707 began its take-off from Orly Airport, located just outside Paris. Accelerating normally, it commenced rotation, and its nose remained slightly raised for about 5 seconds until dropping back to the ground when the brakes were applied, the jet reaching a speed of approximately 200 mph (320 kmh) but never becoming airborne. Thick smoke streamed from its wheels as the crew tried to bring the 707 to a halt, and its path then curved to the right, suggesting a desperate attempt to ground-loop. However, the aircraft ran off the end of the runway while still travelling along its centreline. Rolling on to grass, its main undercarriage was torn off, the left gear first, and after hitting the approach lights the jet began to break apart. Striking a house and garage, it finally came to rest some 1,500 ft (500 m) beyond the end of the runway. Fire, which had erupted during the ground slide, soon engulfed the main part of the wreckage. The accident killed 130 persons aboard the 707, including eight crew members. Two stewardesses seated in the rear of its cabin survived with injuries.

The aircraft's horizontal stabiliser was found to be improperly trimmed, specifically at a setting of 1.5 units nose-up; this was slightly more than 2 units towards the nose-down position. Such a condition would have produced resistance on the control column at the time of rotation and lift-off that may have seemed prohibitive to the pilot-in-command, even to the point that he believed the stabiliser to be jammed.

An investigative board concluded that the incorrect setting resulted from the failure of the trim servo motor, which would also have prevented the crew from rectifying the problem. However, the cause of the malfunction could not be determined. The pilot may have tried to identify the source of the trouble before he abandoned the take-off, but by then it was too late to stop or even slow down on the remaining runway.

Tests revealed that the 707 could have taken off safely despite the out-of-trim condition, although the captain lacked the data required to make a decision on whether to continue in such a short period of time. Soon after the crash, Air France instructed its pilots to adopt new procedures before and during take-off to assure proper operation of an aircraft's flight controls.

The weather conditions at the time on this Sunday, consisting of scattered clouds and good visibility, were not considered a factor in the disaster.

Date: 22 June 1962 (04:01)
Location: Basse-Terre, Guadeloupe, West Indies
Operator: Air France
Aircraft type: Boeing 707-328 (*F-BHST*)

Operating as Flight 117, the jet airliner crashed some 15 miles (25 km) west-north-west of Le Raizet Airport, serving Pointe-à-Pitre, on Grande-Terre, where it was to have landed, one of six en route stops during a service from Paris to Santiago, Chile. All 113 persons aboard (103 passengers and a crew of 10) perished.

Shortly before the accident, the 707 reported passing over the Pointe-à-Pitre non-directional beacon (NDB) at 5,000 ft (*c.* 1,500 m). It then executed a turn back towards the east to begin its final approach. The aircraft was about 10 miles (15 km) off the procedural let-down track when it slammed into a tropical forest on a hill at an approximate elevation of 1,500 ft (500 m) near the town of Sainte-Rose, its undercarriage still retracted at the moment of impact. Some of the wreckage did burn, but there was no major post-crash fire. It was dark at the time and the local meteorological conditions consisted of violent thunderstorm activity, with a visibility of around 5 miles (10 km) and a ceiling of about 1,000 ft (300 m) within the squall and 300–500 ft (100–150 m) higher to the east of that area.

The disaster was attributed to the following sequence of events: 1) breakdown of the very-high frequency omnidirectional range (VOR) station at Pointe-à-Pitre (the pilot of the 707 had expressed concern over the fact that the navigational aid was unserviceable in radio communications with the control tower before the crash); 2) insufficient meteorological information given the flight; and 3) an incorrect automatic direction finder (ADF) indication due to the effects of the poor weather conditions.

A precision approach would not have been possible because the airport had no instrument landing system (ILS). It does today, providing an extra measure of security to arriving aircraft.

Date: 30 June 1962 (time unknown)
Location: Near Krasnoyarsk, Russian Soviet Federative Socialist Republic, USSR
Operator: Aeroflot (USSR)
Aircraft type: Tupolev Tu-104A (*SSSR-42340*)

The jetliner crashed and burned on a scheduled domestic service from Irkutsk to Omsk, and all 84 persons aboard (76 passengers and eight crew members) perished.

Cruising at about 29,000 ft (9,000 m) in daylight and instrument meteorological conditions, the aircraft went into an uncontrolled descent; at an approximate height of 2,600 ft (800 m) above the ground, it began to rotate, and subsequently plunged to earth in a clean configuration with both engines operating.

An investigative commission was unable to determine the cause of the crash, though special research could not identify any mechanical failures prior to impact.

The crash of this Air France Boeing 707 near Paris killed 130 persons after an aborted take-off from Orly Airport. *(CORBIS)*

An Aeroflot Antonov An-10A turboprop, with its high-wing configuration, was the type involved in the disaster in July 1962. *(Philip Jarrett)*

Date: 7 July 1962 (*c.* 00:15)
Location: Near Junnar, Maharashtra, India
Operator: Alitalia (Italy)
Aircraft type: Douglas DC-8 Series 43 (*I-DIWD*)

Originating at Sydney, Australia, Flight 771 was to have made six en route stops during a service scheduled to terminate at Rome, Italy. Following its departure from Bangkok, Thailand, the DC-8 proceeded on towards India, with a planned landing at Santa Cruz Airport, serving Bombay. Cleared for descent to 4,000 ft (*c.* 1,200 m), the pilot was granted permission to make a 360-degree turn over the outer marker. There were no further communications with the flight.

The jet airliner crashed into a hill at an approximate elevation of 3,600 ft (1,100 m), only about 5 ft (1.5 m) from the top, some 50 miles (80 km) east-north-east of the airport and at a position that was about 5 miles (10 km) to the left of the proper track. All 94 persons aboard (85 passengers and a crew of nine) were killed. There were localised fires in the wreckage but no major post-impact blaze. The accident occurred in darkness and instrument weather conditions, with light rain reported by witnesses.

An Indian investigative court attributed the disaster to a navigational error that led to the false impression on the part of the pilot that he was closer to his destination than was actually the case, which in turn resulted in a premature descent below the obstructing terrain. This hypothesis was bolstered by his request to circle over the outer marker, which indicated that he believed the flight to be in close proximity to that navigational aid. There were also indications that, despite his stated intention, the captain had elected to execute a straight-in approach to Runway 27. Considered by the court as contributing factors were the failure of the pilot to make use of the available navigational facilities in order to ascertain his position; infringement of the minimum safe altitude; and his unfamiliarity with the terrain along this particular route.

The airline blamed the crash on 'defective, wrong and incomplete' clearance given by the approach controller. It said that there should have been no such clearance while the DC-8 was still outside the control zone. The company further asserted that air traffic control in the Bombay area was 'poorly organised, constituting a hazard to international aircraft'. Indian authorities disputed the accusations, stating that terrain clearance was the responsibility of pilots, not air traffic controllers, and noted that, in descending below 4,000 ft, the Italian pilot had even disregarded the clearance limit.

Date: 28 July 1962 (time unknown)
Location: Near Adler, Russian Soviet Federative Socialist Republic, USSR
Operator: Aeroflot (USSR)
Aircraft type: Antonov An-10A (*SSSR-11186*)

The four-engine turboprop crashed and burned near the Adler airport, where it was to have landed during a scheduled domestic service from Lvov, Ukraine, killing all 81 persons aboard (74 passengers and seven crew members).

Cleared by the approach controller for descent down to about 5,000 ft (1,500 m), the airliner slammed into a mountainside at an approximate elevation of 2,000 ft (600 m), its undercarriage and flaps still retracted at the moment of impact. The accident occurred in daylight and instrument meteorological conditions, whith a cloud base of about 2,000 ft (600 m), and with the flight not visible on ground radar due to the 'shadow' effect of the mountains.

Combining as causative factors in this crash were the introduction by the air traffic control service of changes in the approach pattern at the Adler airport without approval by state aviation authorities and without informing the flight units about these changes, and inadequacies in the areas of flight control and crew training in operations there and on the part of the authorities over training for flights in mountainous regions in general.

Date: 2 September 1962 (time unknown)
Location: Near Khabarovsk, Russian Soviet Federative Socialist Republic, USSR
Operator: Aeroflot (USSR)
Aircraft type: Tupolev Tu-104A (*SSSR-42366*)

The jetliner crashed and burned about 10 minutes after it had taken off from the Khabarovsk airport, on a scheduled domestic service to Petropavlovsk-Kamchatskiy, located on Kamchatka. All 86 persons aboard (79 passengers and a crew of seven) perished.

As the twin-engine jet was climbing at a height of about 15,000 ft (5,000 m), the crew radioed to the air traffic controller that it had begun shaking, and was experiencing uncontrolled roll and yaw.

They also reported a 'grey-green cloud' near the aircraft. The subsequent crash occurred at night and in instrument meteorological conditions.

With the flight data recorder (FDR) having been destroyed in the crash, the investigative commission had no objective data from which it could reconstruct the development of the abnormal situation. The cause was therefore undetermined. Examination of the wreckage did not disclose any pre-impact failures in the aircraft or its systems.

Date: 27 November 1962 (*c.* 03:40)
Location: Surco District, Department of Lima, Peru
Operator: SA Empress de Viacao Aerea Rio Grandense (VARIG) (Brazil)
Aircraft type: Boeing 707-441 (*PP-VJB*)

Designated as Flight 810, on a service that had originated at Porto Alegre, Rio Grande do Sul, Brazil, with an ultimate destination of Los Angeles, California, US, the jet airliner was preparing for a scheduled landing at the Lima-Callao airport when it crashed some 15 miles (25 km) south of the capital city. All 97 persons aboard (80 passengers and 17 crew members) perished.

The aircraft had initiated an overshoot procedure at the suggestion of approach control because it was too high on its first attempt to land. It then passed over the airport while turning to the left and assumed a southerly heading before initiating a 180-degree turn required for interception of the instrument landing system (ILS) back course to Runway 33.

However, the 707 continued on in a north-north-easterly direction for almost 3 minutes, proceeding through the northbound course, and was on a heading of 333 degrees when it struck La Cruz Peak, which rises to about 2,500 ft (750 m), exploding on impact. At the time of the crash, the aircraft was flying nearly straight and level, with its main undercarriage extended (the position of the nose gear could not be determined).

It was dark at the time of the accident, being before dawn, and the weather conditions in the general vicinity consisted of a low overcast, specifically 8/8 stratus clouds at approximately 2,000 ft (600 m), with a visibility of about 10 miles (15 km) and a slight breeze from a direction of 200 degrees.

Although the cause of the deviation that led to the disaster could not be established, one possible theory centred on the instrument presentation of inaccurate navigational information.

Had the aircraft's automatic direction finder (ADF) equipment been tuned to the wrong non-directional beacon (NDB), and the Collins integral instrument incorrectly adjusted so as to confuse the exactly reversed front and back courses of the ILS, the crew would have been given an indication that the correct approach path was forward and to the right. In reality, an immediate left turn was needed to intercept the west side of the ILS back course.

An ADF indication of 90 degrees to the left, which would have occurred as the 707 continued on a heading of 12 degrees, could have convinced the crew that the ILS at the airport was not functioning properly. The aircraft had turned back just before the accident took place, approximately 8 miles (13 km) east of the proper approach track.

Date: 1 February 1963 (c. 17:15)
Location: Ankara, Turkey
First aircraft
Operator: Middle East Airlines (Lebanon)
Type: Vickers Viscount 754 (*OD-ADE*)
Second aircraft
Operator: Turk Hava Kuvvetleri (Turkish Air Force)
Type: Douglas C-47A (*CBK-28*)

Flight 265 was nearing the end of a service from Nicosia, Cyprus, as it prepared for a scheduled landing at Ankara's Esenboga Airport. It was carrying a relatively light load, with only 11 of its passenger seats filled plus a crew of three. Proceeding under instrument flight rules (IFR), the four-engine turboprop was cleared for a non-directional beacon (NDB) procedure approach, the crew lowering the undercarriage and extending the flaps. Meanwhile, *CBK-28* was returning to Etimesgut Airport under visual flight rules (VFR), its three crew members (and only occupants) having completed a training mission.

The two aircraft collided and crashed, with wreckage from the Viscount falling into the Ulus district of the city, touching off fires and destroying or damaging numerous buildings, houses and vehicles. In the carnage, 87 persons on the ground were killed in addition to the 17 aboard the aircraft, and 50 others suffered injuries. The collision had occurred at a height of under 7,000 ft (c. 2,000 m)

shortly before sunset and in what eyewitnesses described as a 'cloudless' sky. Visibility was reportedly in excess of 10 miles (15 km).

Overtaking the military transport from behind and at an angle of about 40 degrees, the crew of the airliner apparently did not see the C-47 until the last moment, when a pull-up manoeuvre was made, but to no avail. The nose and right wing of the Viscount first struck the C-47, then the former's right inboard propeller sliced off the latter's left horizontal stabiliser. A portion of the fuselage skin on the starboard side of the airliner was torn off, and some of the passengers tumbled out. At the time of impact, the Viscount had been descending on a heading of about 280 degrees and at an estimated air speed of around 150 mph (250 kmh), and the C-47 descending in a clean configuration on a heading of approximately 240 degrees and at an estimated air speed of 140 mph (225 kmh).

Representing the nation of registry of the airliner, the Lebanese Directorate of Civil Aviation expressed reservations about the accident report, which it said did not take into account 'all the important elements' that could have caused or contributed to the collision. One of these was that the Turkish investigative commission did not consider the presence of a military flight training zone extending into the holding and approach pattern allocated to civil aircraft without any coordination or direct contact between the military and civilian air traffic control units.

Also questioned was the meteorological information given in the report, which may not have been accurate. The crew of a US Air Force C-130 transport had in fact reported 6/10 cloud coverage at 5,000 ft (c. 1,500 m) and a visibility of only 5 miles (10 km) over the Ankara NDB, as was noted in the Turkish report.

Date: 3 June 1963 (c. 10:15)
Location: North Pacific Ocean
Operator: Northwest Airlines (US)
Aircraft type: Douglas DC-7C (*N290*)

The aircraft was being flown under contract to the US Military Air Transport Service (MATS) and was en route from McChord Air Force Base, located near Tacoma, Washington state, to Elmendorf Air Force Base, Anchorage, Alaska. Most of its passengers were service personnel and their dependants.

Date: 30 June 1956 (*c*. 11:30)
Location: Northern Arizona, US
First aircraft
Operator: Trans World Airlines (TWA) (US)
Type: Lockheed 1049 Super Constellation
(*N6902C*)
Second aircraft
Operator: United Air Lines (US)
Type: Douglas DC-7 (*N6324C*)

The inadequacies of the US air traffic control (ATC) system were brought to full realisation by this horrifying collision, the first commercial aviation disaster to claim more than 100 lives.

Both four-engine transports had departed on this Saturday morning from Los Angeles International Airport, California, on domestic services. The first to take off was TWA Flight 2, scheduled to stop at Kansas City, Missouri, before continuing on towards its final destination of Washington, DC, with 64 passengers and six crew members aboard. It was followed by United Flight 718, en route to Chicago, Illinois, with an ultimate destination of Newark, New Jersey, and carrying 53 passengers and a crew of five. The two aircraft were operating in accordance with instrument flight rules (IFR), cruising at assigned altitudes along prescribed airways. The proposed true air speed of the Super Constellation was about 310 mph (500 kmh), and that of the DC-7 approximately 330 mph (530 kmh).

At one point, while over the Mojave Desert of Southern California, Flight 2 asked whether it could ascend to 21,000 ft (6,400 m). Since this height had already been allocated to United 718, the request was denied by the Los Angeles ATC Centre. It was, however, cleared to fly 1,000 ft (*c*. 300 m) 'on top of' the general cloud layer. Ironically, this turned out to be 21,000 ft, as later confirmed by the crew. Subsequently, both aircraft would leave the designated airways and proceed north-eastwards (with *N6902C* flying to the north of *N6342C*), taking more direct courses towards their intended destinations. (This was common practice at the time in high-altitude operations, enabling crews to take advantage of the most favourable wind and weather conditions as well as taking the shortest routes possible.) Their paths would cross high over Grand Canyon National Park, some 70 miles (110 km) north of Flagstaff.

In their last regular position reports, both flights estimated they would reach the Painted Desert

An artist's impression of the mid-air crash over the Grand Canyon, based on Civil Aeronautics Board findings, showing how the left wing of the DC-7 sliced into the rear fuselage of the Super Constellation. *(Mel Hunter, Life magazine)*

The ground impact of the Swissair Caravelle left a crater and damaged adjacent houses. *(Swiss Federal Aircraft Accident Investigation Bureau)*

In their last known message, the crew asked whether the aircraft could ascend from its cruising altitude of 14,000 ft (*c.* 4,300 m) to 18,000 ft (*c.* 5,500 m); no reason was given. The Canadian radio operator replied that the requested height was already occupied by a Pacific Northern Airlines flight. Less than 10 minutes later, the DC-7C plunged into the sea some 130 miles (210 km) west-south-west of Annette Island, Alaska, and about 50 miles (80 km) off the north-western tip of the (Canadian) Queen Charlotte Islands, and all 101 persons aboard, including a civilian crew of six, perished.

Subsequently, human remains and approximately 1,500 lb (700 kg) of debris, mostly cabin equipment, were recovered. But the depth of the ocean in the area, around 8,000 ft (2,500 m), precluded any attempt to recover the main wreckage.

The US Civil Aeronautics Board (CAB) concluded that the aircraft was probably intact when it crashed at a high rate of speed, apparently while in a nearly inverted attitude. There was no evidence of an in-flight explosion or fire, although a post-impact blaze apparently burned on the surface of the water.

According to a pilot flying the same route at about the same time, the weather was characterised by scattered clouds at different altitudes and light turbulence; the conditions were also conducive to icing. In fact, the request by the crew of *N290* to ascend could have been motivated by an encounter with either icing or turbulence. Between their last radio transmission and the crash, during which time they did not respond to any calls, the crew may have been preoccupied with an emergency situation or experienced trouble with the communications equipment, possibly due to static (as was reported by the other pilot). However, due to the lack of evidence the cause of the disaster could not be determined.

Date: 4 September 1963 (*c.* 07:20)
Location: Durrenasch, Aargau, Switzerland
Operator: Swissair AG
Aircraft type: Sud-Aviation Caravelle III (*HB-ICV*)

Before its departure from Zürich-Kloten Airport, the pilot of the aircraft was authorised to taxi half-way down Runway 34, probably using the engines to

A water-filled crater marks the scene of the Trans-Canada Air Lines DC-8 disaster that took 118 lives. *(National Archives of Canada)*

disperse the fog that hung low over the area at the time. Returning to the beginning of the runway, the Caravelle, which was designated as Flight 306, took off for Geneva, the domestic segment of an international service scheduled to terminate at Rome, Italy.

Less than 10 minutes later, the jet airliner plunged to earth and exploded about 15 miles (25 km) west-south-west of Zürich and frighteningly close to two farmhouses, leaving a crater approximately 65 ft (20 m) in diameter and some 20 ft (6 m) deep. All 80 persons aboard, including a crew of six, perished in the disaster. Among the passengers were 43 from the Swiss village of Humilkon, who represented about one-quarter of the community's inhabitants.

Fragments of the aircraft's No. 4 left main gear wheel and tyre were found on and beyond the end of the runway. The wheel flange had apparently split as the jet was being positioned for take-off, causing the corresponding tyre to explode, apparently due to overheating in the brake system. Fire then erupted, probably when fuel lines were damaged in the blast and the volatile liquid came in contact with the overheated brake components.

It was considered possible that the similarly stressed No. 3 wheel ruptured after the Caravelle

had become airborne, causing more damage and, in turn, an in-flight blaze. More likely, however, was that the blaze known to have started on the ground in the No. 4 wheel continued to burn following gear retraction, then ignited the No. 3, causing its failure. Whatever the case, the flames must have spread rearward, resulting in serious damage. The aircraft's electrical system apparently malfunctioned, and its flight control and hydraulic systems as well as its structural integrity could also have been adversely affected by the fire. Additionally, there was a loss of power in its left engine, which might have resulted from either deliberate action by the crew or to interruption of its fuel supply.

Reaching a maximum altitude of approximately 9,000 ft (2,700 m), the jet began to descend while on a south-westerly heading, and during this period of time the crew transmitted a 'Mayday' distress message. Before it crashed, the Caravelle shed numerous parts, including a portion of the left wing and rear fuselage, which ultimately must have led to a loss of control.

The overheating was most probably caused by intentional braking on the part of the pilot as the aircraft taxied down the runway. However, the possibility of unintentional braking action resulting from a mechanical defect or irregularity could not be ruled out, even though there was no evidence of such a condition. Safety measures implemented in the wake of the disaster included a discontinuation of the fog dispersal procedure that was an underlying factor in the brake overheating, and the fitting on the Caravelle fleet of temperature gauges and blow-out fuses on the wheel rims. Also, the placement of protective shields over vital hydraulic and fuel lines in the undercarriage bays of aircraft was instituted by Swissair.

Date: 29 November 1963 (*c.* 18:30)
Location: Near Sainte Therese de Blainville, Quebec, Canada
Operator: Trans-Canada Air Lines
Aircraft type: Douglas DC-8 Series 54F (*CF-TJN*)

The jetliner, which was operating as Flight 831 on a domestic service to Toronto, Ontario, plunged to earth about 5 minutes after taking off from Dorval Airport, serving Montreal, disintegrating and erupting into flames on impact. All 118 persons aboard (111 passengers and seven crew members) perished. A water-filled crater marked the scene of the crash, some 10 miles (15 km) north-west of Montreal and approximately 15 miles (25 km) from the airport. The accident occurred in darkness and during a fog and light rain, with a breeze out of the north-east of 12 mph (c. 20 kmh) and a visibility of 4 miles (c. 6.5 km).

The DC-8, which had taken off from Runway 06 and then begun a left turn before disappearing from the airport radar screen, was in a clean configuration and on a north-north-westerly heading when it crashed at a steep angle. At the time of impact, its velocity was calculated to have been between 540 and 560 mph (870–900 kmh).

Examination of the wreckage revealed that the horizontal stabiliser was set to an angle of between 1.65 and 2 degrees nose-down trim and had been moved to that position by hydraulic power, factors that proved very significant. It was concluded that this setting, which would be unusual on an aircraft climbing out from take-off, resulted from action, apparently intentional, by the flight crew.

A number of theories were explored by the investigative commission, but the one considered 'most probable' as causing the disaster was the unprogrammed extension of the aircraft's pitch trim compensator. This would have had the effect of moving the control column back and the elevators up, resulting in a nose-high attitude. The pilot would likely have counteracted this condition by trimming the stabiliser to or near to the limit of the nose-down setting, inadvertently creating an adverse effect on the stability of the jetliner and placing it in a diving descent. As its velocity increased, the force required to pull back on the control column would have become prohibitive. Recovery could, however, still have been made by re-trimming the horizontal stabiliser, but at a high rate of speed the activating motor might not be able to overcome the high aerodynamic forces.

Under the circumstances, the only possibility for recovery would have been to release pressure on the control column, thereby relieving the forces being applied to the empennage and unstalling the hydraulic motor so the stabiliser could be moved. Such action would, of course, have momentarily worsened the situation by actually steepening the descent and increasing the air speed. The upset in this case was believed to have occurred at an approximate height of 6,000 ft (c. 1,800 m), which would not have been sufficient to carry out such a procedure.

Though not severe, existing turbulence could have contributed to the accident by affecting the attitude of the aircraft, minor changes that could have built up into large displacements. An aggravating factor was that the jetliner had been flying at night and in cloud, and its pilots would thus have been without visual reference to either the ground or the horizon.

There were two other possible reasons for the crew to have applied nose-down trim. The first was that icing of the pitot system had caused an erroneously low air speed reading, prompting the pilot to lower the nose of the aircraft to increase velocity. The second possibility was an inaccurate artificial horizon indication due to failure of the associated vertical gyro or a loss of power, leading to the same action. Despite their weaknesses, neither of these two theories could be entirely dismissed.

There was no evidence of structural failure, malfunction of the engines, flight controls or any other major system, collision with another object, in-flight explosion or fire, or incapacitation of the crew.

The recommendation that turbine-powered commercial transports be fitted with flight data recorders, made by the commission in its report on the crash of *CF-TJN*, would later become a requirement for such aircraft registered in Canada.

Data: 8 December 1963 (20:59)
Location: Near Elkton, Maryland, US
Operator: Pan American World Airways (US)
Aircraft type: Boeing 707-121 (*N709PA*)

Originating at San Juan, Puerto Rico, Flight 214 had stopped at Baltimore, Maryland, before proceeding on towards its ultimate destination of Philadelphia, Pennsylvania. The crew were advised that it was to hold for landing, along with five other aircraft, until high winds had subsided at Philadelphia International Airport. During a routine conversation beween the approach controller and a National Airlines DC-8, a distress message was heard from the 707, believed to be 'Mayday . . . Mayday . . . Mayday . . . Clipper two one four out of control. Here we go!'

Trying to contact the Pan American flight, the controller got a reply from the DC-8, its co-pilot stating that 'Clipper two fourteen is going down in flames'.

Spinning uncontrollably, the jet airliner plunged into a cornfield between Elkton and the Delaware border and disintegrated in a fiery explosion. All 81 persons aboard (73 passengers and a crew of eight) perished. The weather in the area of the crash was described as cloudy, with thunderstorm activity and light rain.

Scores of witnesses observed lightning in the night sky, and several reported seeing one bolt hit the 707. Examination of the wreckage revealed an irregularly shaped hole about 1.5 in (5 mm) in diameter and numerous small lustrous craters in its left wing-tip, confirming that the aircraft had indeed been struck.

By eliminating all other conceivable causes, the US Civil Aeronautics Board (CAB) concluded that lightning had precipitated the accident by igniting the fuel–air mixture in the left reserve tank, or possibly in the left surge tank or even at the vent outlet. The resulting explosion blew apart the port outer wing structure as the 707 was in a holding pattern at an altitude of 5,000 ft (c. 1,500 m), causing an immediate loss of control. Before impact with the ground, all four engines broke off due to excessive forces imposed during the fall, and large fires were observed on both wings, attributed to secondary explosions in other fuel tanks.

The exact mechanics of ignition remained a mystery, but, as noted in the investigative report, many strange phenomena have been associated with lightning. Among these are 'streamers' induced by the intense electric field within a storm that extend out from the extremities of an aircraft and toward an approaching lightning stroke, which have sufficient energy to ignite fuel vapours. Other potential sources of ignition are plasma, shock waves and sparking.

Within two weeks of this accident, the US Federal Aviation Agency (FAA) made a recommendation for the installation of lightning discharge wicks on all commercial jet transports registered in the country, and later issued airworthiness directives requiring modification of the fuel tank access door and the thickening of the skin covering the wing-tips on Boeing jets. In 1967 the FAA took further action to reduce the lightning threat by ordering the installation on certain models of the 707 and its close relative, the 720, of either a system designed

to extinguish automatically any flame propagation through the fuel tank outlets, or auxiliary vents that would prevent the accumulation of fuel vapours in the regular ones. (Research conducted subsequently to the CAB inquiry indicated that in the case of N709PA the vapours probably did ignite in a fuel vent.)

Also due to this and other crashes the airline industry began phasing out use of JP-4 jet fuel and switching to the less volatile kerosene.

Date: 25 February 1964 (02:05)
Location: Near New Orleans, Louisiana, US
Operator: Eastern Air Lines (US)
Aircraft type: Douglas DC-8 Series 21 (N8607)

Designated as Flight 304, the jetliner took off from New Orleans International (Moisant) Airport, bound for Atlanta, Georgia, its next scheduled stop during a service from Mexico City to New York City. Approximately 5 minutes later, the DC-8 crashed in Lake Pontchartrain, some 20 miles (30 km) north-east of the airport, and all 58 persons aboard (51 passengers and seven crew members) perished. The disaster occurred in early morning darkness and in instrument meteo-rological conditions. At the airport at around this time there was a ceiling of 1,000 ft (c. 300 m), a visibility of around 5 miles (10 km), turbulence and a 12-knot wind out of the west.

Subsequently, about 60 per cent of the aircraft's wreckage, located in water some 20 ft (6 m) deep, was recovered from the bottom of the lake. The DC-8 had disintegrated on impact, the largest piece found being a 5 ft (1.5 m) section of the rudder, and this, coupled with the fact that the pertinent portion of the flight data recorder (FDR) tape was not recovered, hampered the investigation of the disaster. However, by using the records of N8607, and by studying problems that had afflicted other DC-8s, the US Civil Aeronautics Board (CAB) was able to determine the probable sequence of events leading up to the crash.

Examination of its right and left jack-screws indicated that the aircraft's horizontal stabiliser was set in the nose-down trim. Whether it had been placed that way intentionally or unintentionally by the crew, or resulted from a malfunction, such a setting following take-off was considered unusual. The abnormal longitudinal trim component position coupled with moderate to severe wind shear-type turbulence that the flight was believed to have encountered probably caused a reduction in the aircraft's stability characterstistcs.

A review of its records disclosed a history of trouble with the pitch trim compensator (PTC) installed on N8607 at the time of the accident. It had been removed from various aircraft 15 times over a four-year period, nearly half of these as a result of unprogrammed extensions. The unit was known to have been inoperative since the outbound flight to Mexico City the previous day. Numerous autopilot difficulties had also been reported on this particular DC-8, which could have resulted from such extensions.

Had the PTC actuator been partially or fully extended, it was likely that the pilots trimmed the stabiliser to the full-down position to counteract the nose-up attitude of the aircraft. This could have placed the DC-8 in a steep descent. Failure of the chain sprocket in the stabiliser drive mechanism must then have occurred, probably as the crew tried to apply nose-up trim. This malfunction could have led to either the introduction of a pilot-induced oscillation, or control input, resulting in a loss of control, or contributed to the failure to recover therefrom.

The upset probably took place at a height below 6,000 ft (c. 1,800 m), which would not have allowed the pilots to effect full recovery. Examination of the engines indicated that the crew had employed reverse thrust in an attempt to arrest the descent, and almost succeeded, since the cleanly configured jetliner was believed to have been essentially level at the moment of impact.

Cases of misrigging in the PTC units of other DC-8s were discovered during the investigation into the crash of Flight 304 and it was concluded that maintenance personnel had installed a bushing upside-down in the one used on N8607. This would have caused the actuator to extend even further.

Besides the mechanical failure and the adverse flying conditions, factors that may have played a role in the disaster were the aircraft's attitude indicator, which was difficult to interpret at night, and the unstable characteristics of the DC-8 itself at certain air speeds. In a related matter, it was determined that the functional tests used by Eastern and other carriers were incapable of detecting certain PTC computer malfunctions.

Several modifications in the Douglas transport were made and new maintenance and operating procedures implemented in the wake of this tragedy. These included a reduction in the nose-down travel of the aircraft's horizontal stabiliser and replacement of the PTC actuator bell-crank arm, the latter designed to improve longitudinal stability. There were also changes in the method of dealing with an inoperative PTC or an unwanted extension, and a warning light was installed to alert crews in the event of the latter condition.

Date: 29 February 1964 (c. 15:15)
Location: Near Innsbruck, Austria
Operator: British Eagle International Airlines
Aircraft type: Bristol Britannia 312 (G-AOVO)

Flight 802 had originated at London's Heathrow Airport and was scheduled to land at Kranebitten Airport, serving Innsbruck. Upon arrival over its intended destination, clouds covered the area, and the conditions were in fact below the airline's minima for such a landing. But the pilot-in-command, a veteran who had flown into Innsbruck on nine previous occasions, decided against proceeding to an alternate airport.

The four-engine turboprop was first reported in the holding pattern above the Innsbruck very-high-frequency omnidirectional range (VOR) station, the pilot stating that he could not break through the overcast. It was last reported at a height of 10,000 ft (c. 3,000 m) before the air traffic control centre lost radio contact with the flight. Ground witnesses heard what was believed to have been the Britannia in or above the clouds around this time.

The following day, more than 18 hours later, its wreckage was found on a steep eastern slope of Glungezer Mountain, in the Alps, some 10 miles (15 km) east-south-east of the airport, itself located about 2.5 miles (4 km) west of the city. The aircraft had crashed at an approximate elevation of 8,500 ft (2,600 m), while in a slight nose-up attitude, with its undercarriage retracted and flaps set at 15 degrees, and the impact precipitated an avalanche that carried most of the debris and victims' bodies more than 1,300 ft (400 m) down the mountainside. All 83 persons aboard (75 passengers and a crew of eight) were killed. An evasive pull-up

The tail assembly of the British Eagle International Airlines Britannia lies in snow on Glungezer Mountain following the crash near Innsbruck. *(AP Images)*

manoeuvre may have been initiated an instant before impact; there was no post-crash fire. The mountain at the time was obscured by cloud, with snow flurries in the area.

It was concluded that the pilot had intentionally descended below the minimum safe altitude of 11,000 ft (*c.* 3,300 m) in an apparent attempt to penetrate the overcast. A technical defect in the aircraft, altimeter error or an encounter with severe icing or turbulence were all ruled out. The flight continued to descend while making several turns over the mountains. In the final moments before the crash, the crew were flying without visual contact of the ground, in violation of Austrian regulations pertaining to the Innsbruck airport. At the time of the accident, the Britannia was on a westerly heading but neither in the airport circuit nor on landing approach.

Despite the prevailing conditions, other aircraft were operating in and out of the airport, and this may have been a factor in the erroneous decision by the pilot of Flight 802 to continue the descent.

One of the safety recommendations made in the investigative report was that operations conducted under visual flight rules (VFR) should not be allowed under any circumstances in instrument meteorological conditions.

Date: 1 March 1964 (*c.* 11:30)
Location: Near Zephyr Cove, Nevada, US
Operator: Paradise Airlines (US)
Aircraft type: Lockheed 049 Constellation (*N86504*)

All 85 persons aboard (81 passengers and four crew members) were killed when the aircraft, operating as Flight 901A, crashed approximately 10 miles (15 km) north-east of Tahoe Valley Airport, located across the border in California, where it was to have landed at the end of an intrastate service from Salinas and San José.

It was snowing at the airport shortly before the Constellation arrived over the Lake Tahoe very-high-frequency omnidirectional range (VOR) station, with a visibility of 3 miles (*c.* 5 km) and a ceiling of 2,000 ft (*c.* 600 m), conditions that were not conducive to visual flight rules (VFR) operations. However, the airport had no approved instrument flight rules (IFR) approach procedure. Nevertheless, the pilot attempted to land, and this deviation from the prescribed VFR procedures led to an unsuccessful approach and, subsequently, to 'geographical disorientation'. The aircraft was last seen proceeding out over Lake Tahoe in a northerly direction before it disappeared into a snowstorm.

The wreckage was located the following day on a snow-covered ridge of Genoa Peak, some 5 miles (10 km) east of the lake. Its undercarriage retracted but flaps extended, the Constellation was heading towards the east and in a nearly level attitude when initially it struck trees at an approximate elevation of 8,675 ft (2,650 m).

Under the circumstances, the captain should have either waited for the weather to improve or diverted to an alternate airport. In trying to land either without, or despite, knowledge of the existing meteorological conditions, he violated company policy. The crew may have attempted to fly through Daggett Pass and levelled off at what they believed to be a safe altitude. Or the aircraft might not have been able to climb any higher due to airframe icing, since N86504 was not equipped to fly in such conditions.

Other factors that may have contributed to the accident were a discrepancy in the pilot's altimeter, which could have resulted in an erroneous height display of about 280 ft (85 m) too high; a possible error of 15 degrees or more in the aircraft's compass system, and strong winds over the lake, which could have caused a drift towards the mountains. The procedures used by the general aviation carrier in reporting the weather were also considered unsatisfactory, and in this case the crew had been provided with a falsified meteorological report.

The crash came tragically close to being averted altogether. Had the Constellation been only 300 ft (c. 100 m) higher or 1,000 ft (c. 300 m) further south, it would have cleared the terrain safely and entered VFR conditions.

Date: 2 September 1964 (time unknown)
Location: Island of Sakhalin, USSR
Operator: Aeroflot (USSR)
Aircraft type: Ilyushin Il-18B (*SSSR-75531*)

The four-engine turboprop crashed near the Yuzhno-Sakhalinsk airport, where it was to have landed during a scheduled domestic service from Krasnoyarsk, RSFSR, and all 87 persons aboard (78 passengers and a crew of nine) lost their lives.

After they had insisted upon one, the crew were granted permission by the air traffic controller to make a direct approach without completing the standard traffic pattern. Subsequently, the airliner initiated a premature descent, then slammed into a wooded hillside at an approximate elevation of 2,000 ft (600 m) and caught fire, the accident occurring at night and in adverse weather conditions.

Blamed for the crash were the combined effects of the error by the controller, who lacked the availability of radar with which to monitor the flight, and of the crew, as well as inadequate knowledge of the approach conditions at this particular airport and poor in-flight planning on the part of the latter.

Date: 2 October 1964 (05:45)
Location: Near Trevelez, Granada, Spain
Operator: Union des Transports Aeriens (UTA) (France)
Aircraft type: Douglas DC-6B (*F-BHMS*)

The airliner was on a scheduled international service originating at Paris, with two en route stops

The estimated flight path of the Paradise Airlines Constellation which proceeded out over Lake Tahoe due to suspected crew disorientation and ultimately crashed on a Nevada peak. *(Civil Aeronautics Board)*

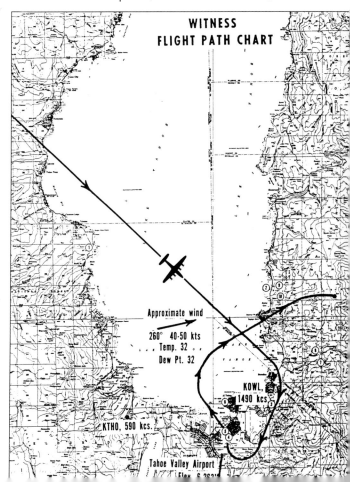

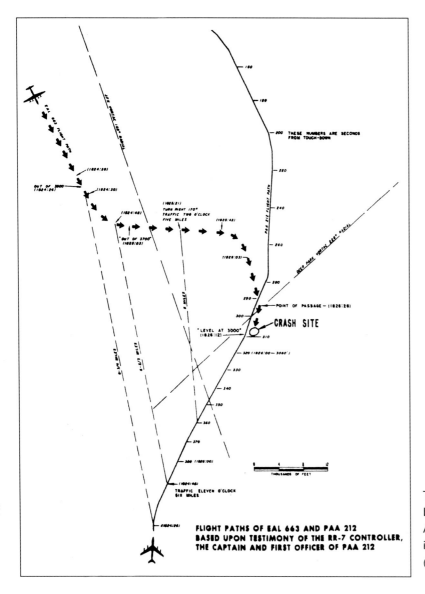

**FLIGHT PATHS OF EAL 663 AND PAA 212
BASED UPON TESTIMONY OF THE RR-7 CONTROLLER,
THE CAPTAIN AND FIRST OFFICER OF PAA 212**

The flight paths of the Eastern Air Lines DC-7B that crashed and the Pan American World Airways Boeing 707 indirectly involved in the accident. *(Civil Aeronautics Board)*

and an ultimate destination of Port-Etienne, Mauritania. About 1½ hours after its departure from Palma de Mallorca, in the (Spanish) Balearic Islands, the transport slammed into a mountain at an approximate elevation of 7,000 ft (2,000 m) in the Sierra Nevada region, some 20 miles (30 km) south-east of the city of Granada. All 80 persons aboard (73 passengers and a crew of seven) perished in the crash, which occurred shortly before sunrise. Around the time of the accident, the weather conditions at Granada were good, with the sky clear and a visibility of between 5 and 10 miles (*c.* 10–15 km).

The aircraft had deviated by about 5 degrees from, but flew at altitudes within the established safety margin for, the planned route. Since the autopilot error could be plus or minus 1 degree, the

remaining 4 degrees may have been caused by the wind or some other undiscovered anomaly.

However, since no instruments or other components were found on which a technical investigation could be conducted, the cause of deviation could not be determined.

Date: 6 February 1965 (08:36)
Location: Near San Jose de Maipo, Santiago, Chile
Operator: Linea Aerea National de Chile (LAN-Chile)
Aircraft type: Douglas DC-6B (*CC-CCG-404*)

Designated as Flight 107, the airliner crashed at an approximate elevation of 11,500 ft (3,500 m) in the Volcan Pass region of the Andes Mountains, some 30 miles (50 km) south-east of the capital city of Santiago, from where it had taken off earlier, bound for Buenos Aires, Argentina, and Montevideo, Uruguay. There was no fire, but the DC-6B disintegrated on impact, and all 87 persons aboard (80 passengers and seven crew members) perished.

An investigative board attributed the accident to a lack of discipline on the part of the pilot-in-command, who followed a route that was neither in accordance with the approved flight plan nor with the carrier's operations manual relating to crossing the mountains. The weather was not considered a factor.

Date: 8 February 1965 (18:26)
Location: Near New York, New York, US
Operator: Eastern Air Lines (US)
Aircraft type: Douglas DC-7B (*N849D*)

Flight 663 had taken off from John F. Kennedy International Airport, bound for Richmond, Virginia, its next scheduled stop during a domestic service originating at Boston, Massachusetts, with an ultimate destination of Atlanta, Georgia. Meanwhile, a Pan American World Airways Boeing 707 jetliner was approaching from the south and preparing to land at the airport at the end of an international service from San Juan, Puerto Rico. The two aircraft were operating under instrument flight rules (IFR) and positive control, with air traffic controllers providing radar vectors to both and maintaining separation in accordance with established guidelines. The shortcomings of the separation criteria then in effect would soon be brought to full realisation by what was about to happen.

The last message from the Eastern crew was a 'Good night'. Less than 2 minutes later the Pan American co-pilot reported a near collision with another aircraft; also the radar target representing Flight 663 was no longer visible. The cleanly configured DC-7B had plunged into the Atlantic Ocean approximately 7.5 miles (12 km) off Jones Beach, and some 15 miles (25 km) south-east of the airport, exploding on impact. All 84 persons aboard (79 passengers and a crew of five) perished. The 707 landed safely without further incident. It was dark at the time of the accident, and the weather consisted of scattered clouds above 10,000 ft (3,000 m) and a visibility of 7 miles (11 km).

Some of the victims' bodies were found, and the aircraft's main wreckage was located on the ocean floor, in about 80 ft (25 m) of water, with more than 60 per cent of it later being recovered. Examination of the debris revealed no evidence of mechanical or structural failure, or pre-impact fire or explosion.

In its inquiry, the US Civil Aeronautics Board (CAB) was able to reconstruct the probable flight paths of both the DC-7B and the 707. Realising a potential conflict with the latter, the departure controller had instructed the eastbound Eastern flight to turn southward, allowing it to continue to climb until it was at least 1,000 ft (300 m) above the descending, northbound jet. In the process, however, he placed the two aircraft on nearly head-on courses. Although the DC-7B was determined to have been indeed higher, the 707 could have appeared to the Eastern pilots as being at the same height and thus a collision threat, when viewed from a distance of 5 miles (*c.* 10 km) against a featureless background, and with the horizon not visible, the single light source not providing sufficient stimulus for depth perception.

It was therefore likely that the crew of *N849D* initiated a descent. Simultaneously, the Pan American crew, fearful of a potential conflict with the piston-engine transport, also began to descend, which probably appeared to negate the action of the Eastern pilot. At that point his only recourse was to make a sharp turn to the right and/or pull up.

The captain and first officer of the 707 confirmed that the DC-7B was in or near a vertical bank when it passed their aircraft left-to-right at about the same altitude, i.e. around 3,000 ft (1,000 m). As a result of the unusual attitude created by the avoidance manoeuvre, the pilots of *N849D* apparently experienced spatial disorientation and were not able to reorient themselves by reference to their instruments in time to effect full recovery. Impact occurred with the aircraft in a nearly level but slight nose-up attitude, with its right wing slightly low.

Subsequently, the US Federal Aviation Agency (FAA) instituted a new procedure at the New York airport in which a minimum of 2,000 ft (*c.* 600 m) would be provided between inbound and outbound air traffic in areas conducive to optical illusions, twice the amount required at the time of the disaster.

An American Airlines Boeing 727–23, identical to the aircraft that crashed during a landing approach to Greater Cincinnati Airport on 8 November 1965. (Boeing)

Date: 20 May 1965 (c. 01:50)
Location: Near Cairo, Egypt
Operator: Pakistan International Airlines
Aircraft type: Boeing 720B (AP-AMH)

Operating as Flight 705 and inaugurating a new route on the carrier's service to London from Karachi, Pakistan, the jetliner was preparing to land when it crashed and burned some 5 miles (10 km) from the Cairo airport, a scheduled stop, killing 121 persons aboard (108 passengers and the entire crew of 13). The six surviving passengers were injured.

Cleared for a non-precision instrument approach to Runway 34, the aircraft was turning left on to the base left of the airport circuit when its rate of descent began to increase, ultimately reaching about 2,400 ft/min (730 m/min), approximately triple the norm. Its indicated air speed also increased slightly until the 720B struck the ground while in a gentle left bank, with its undercarriage retracted and flaps set at 20 degrees. Wreckage was scattered over the hilly, desert terrain on a north-easterly heading for a distance of nearly 1 mile (1.5 km), with the main portion of the aircraft having come to rest upside down. The accident occurred in early morning darkness, although the sky was cloudless, with a visibility of about 5 miles (10 km).

The reason for the abnormal continuation of the descent until impact could not be determined.

Oscillations in the height and speed parameters of the flight data recorder (FDR) read-out indicated the possibility of an attempt to counteract a nose-down condition, although this could not be positively established. It was noted, however, that in the clear weather the bright lights surrounding the airport should have provided the pilot with adequate visual reference in order to detect an abnormal attitude and take immediate corrective action.

This and four other air carrier and military aircraft crashes occurring over a period of less than 10 years prompted the International Federation of Air Line Pilots Associations (IFALPA) to recommend that its members discontinue using Runway 34 at Cairo except in daylight and good meteorological conditions. Among other concerns, IFALPA complained of the absence of an instrument landing system (ILS), poor signal strength and transmission continuity in the locator beacon, inadequate runway lighting and a let-down procedure that did not conform with the practices recommended by the International Civil Aviation Organisation (ICAO), i.e. by allowing an obstacle clearance of less than 1,000 ft (c. 300 m).

Date: 8 July 1965 (c. 17:40)
Location: Near 100 Mile House, British Columbia, Canada
Operator: Canadian Pacific Air Lines
Aircraft type: Douglas DC-6B (CF-CUQ)

Designated as Flight 21, the aircraft was en route from Vancouver to Prince George, its first scheduled stop during a domestic service with an ultimate destination of Whitehorse, Yukon Territory, when it crashed and burned approximately midway between the two cities. All 52 persons aboard (46 passengers and a crew of six) perished.

The DC-6B was last reported cruising at flight level 160 when its crew transmitted three 'Mayday' distress calls. Witnesses who had seen the transport flying in clear conditions reported a mid-air explosion before it plummeted vertically into a wooded area. Its empennage, including the vertical and horizontal stabiliser assemblies, had separated from the rest of the fuselage as a result of the blast, which was determined to have occurred in the left rear lavatory.

It was believed that a saboteur had ignited a mixture of acid and gunpowder, which may have been poured into the toilet bowl, in a possible suicide-for-insurance scheme.

Date: 8 November 1965 (19:01)
Location: Near Constance, Kentucky, US
Operator: American Airlines (US)
Aircraft type: Boeing 727-23 (N1996)

It was dark and the weather was getting worse as Flight 383 prepared for a scheduled landing at Greater Cincinnati Airport, at the end of a domestic service from New York City. Nevertheless, the crew elected to make a visual approach, and were cleared to land on Runway 18.

As the aircraft was turning left on to the final approach course, the first officer radioed 'we'll pick up the ILS here'. Seconds later the jetliner slammed into a wooded hillside approximately 2 miles (3 km) from the threshold of the runway and about a quarter of a mile (400 m) to the left of its extended centreline, and some 225 ft (70 m) below the published airport elevation, bursting into flames on impact. The accident killed 58 persons aboard the 727, including five crew members. A stewardess and three passengers, among them an off-duty American Airlines pilot, survived with injuries.

The aircraft was in a slight nose-up attitude with its undercarriage still retracted and flaps set at 25 degrees at the moment of initial impact. There was thunderstorm activity in the area at the time, with a ceiling of 2,500 ft (*c.* 750 m), a broken overcast at 1,500 ft (*c.* 500 m) and scattered clouds at 1,000 ft (*c.* 300 m), and a visibility of 2 miles (*c.* 3 km). The wind was from the west at a velocity of 8 knots.

The accident was believed to have resulted from the failure of the flight crew to monitor properly the aircraft's height during the approach. Following a level-off, the final descent was continued for 1½ minutes, apparently without sufficient reference to the altimeters. In its investigative report, the US Civil Aeronautics Board (CAB) said that it found the error 'difficult to reconcile' when considering that both pilots were experienced captains, with the one acting as first officer administering a

flight check as part of the other's upgrading to 727 captain status.

Several interrelated factors were thought to have contributed to this failure. Perhaps the most significant was the deteriorating visibility conditions when the flight began to encounter rain and clouds while on the base leg of the airport circuit. The terrain features themselves may have created the illusion of having sufficient altitude. This could have happened had the crew associated the lights of residences located along the Ohio River with the elevation of the airport due to the absence of lighting on the rising terrain in between. Furthermore, since the crew had to look left throughout the final turn in order to keep the airport in sight, the only other ground lights visible under the circumstances would have been those in the river valley.

The configuration of the aircraft at the time of the crash indicated that there had been a delay in the completion of the final checklist by the crew. A rush of cockpit activities could have been an additional element of distraction as the pilots tried to maintain visual contact with the approach lights.

The captain and first officer had flown together several times before, and therefore must have established a pattern of relying on each other's abilities. This could actually have been to the detriment of safety in this case had one pilot concentrated on maintaining visual contact, believing the other was monitoring his instruments.

Another indeterminable factor may have been a reduction in visibility due to the initial effect of the windscreen rain repellent and, possibly, to lightning flashes.

It was not known exactly how the pilots had used the airport's instrument landing system (ILS). Under the existing conditions, it would have been wise to execute a full ILS approach, but because of a 20 minutes delay in the departure of the flight from New York City, they probably decided to carry out a visual procedure in order to expedite the landing.

Date: 24 January 1966 (*c.* 08:00)
Location: French Alps
Operator: Air-India
Aircraft type: Boeing 707-437 (*VT-DMN*)

Operating as Flight 101 and on a service originating at Bombay, India, with an ultimate destination of New York City, the jet airliner was preparing for a scheduled stop at Geneva, Switzerland, when it was instructed to maintain 1,000 ft 'on top' of the clouds. However, the 707 descended below flight level 190 – the minimum safety altitude – then slammed into a ridge of Mont Blanc, approximately 200 ft (60 m) below its summit, and on a probable heading of 330 degrees. The aircraft disintegrated on impact, and all 117 persons aboard (106 passengers and 11 crew members) perished.

The sequence of events began when the pilot-in-command, who knew one of his two very-high-frequency omnidirectional range (VOR) receivers was unserviceable, miscalculated his position relative to the mountain, radioing the message 'I think we are passing abeam Mont Blanc now'. The

Bits of wreckage speckle the snow where the Air-India Boeing 707 hit Mont Blanc in the French Alps. *(CORBIS)*

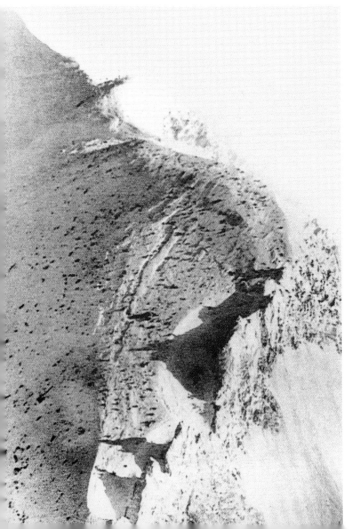

Geneva centre controller noted the error upon checking the radar screen and attempted to correct it by stating that the aircraft had '5 miles to the Mont Blanc'. But due to the controller's imprecise phraseology, the pilot may have misunderstood the comment as merely an acknowledgement of his previous transmission, and not that the 707 had yet to reach this point.

Complicating matters were a number of other factors. It was around dawn, and with the sun being low on the horizon and behind the aircraft, thus producing no obvious shadows, it would have been difficult to distinguish the snow-covered terrain from the clouds.

The crew could also have been faced with a 'white-out'. This phenomenon can cause an absence of shadows combined with diffused illumination (especially when snow or ice crystals are suspended in the air), as well as a reduction in horizontal visibility and an apparent increase in luminance; the physiological characteristics of illumination of the retina, myopia and other minor vision defects; and also have psychological effects, from a disorientation of one's vertical sense to a loss of both a sense of direction and of distance perception.

There was a cloud layer in the area of Mont Blanc that extended up to about 500 ft (150 m) above the elevation of the crash site and shrouded its summit, with light snowfall, severe turbulence and down draughts near the terrain. The speed and direction of the wind was estimated as 35 knots from west-north-west at the level of impact and 60 knots from north-north-west at the peak.

Because of local variations in atmospheric pressure in the vicinity of the mountain, the aircraft's altimeters may have indicated 800 to 1,000 ft (*c*. 250–300 m) higher than its actual altitude.

All of these factors could have led to an inadvertent descent into the cloud bank with insufficient time for the crew to obtain visual reference before hitting the ridge.

Date: 4 February 1966 (*c*. 19:00)
Location: Tokyo Bay, Japan
Operator: All Nippon Airways (Japan)
Aircraft type: 727-81 (*JA8302*)

Designated as Flight 60, the jetliner crashed about 7.5 miles (12 km) east-south-east of Tokyo International (Haneda) Airport, where it was scheduled to land at the end of a domestic service from Chitose Airport, located on Hokkaido, near Sapporo. All 133 persons aboard (126 passengers and a crew of seven) were killed.

It was dark at the time, but the weather conditions in the moonlight were good, with scattered cumulus clouds reported at an approximate height of 2,000–3,000 ft (600–1,000 m) in the area north of Kisarazu. Visibility was some 5–10 miles (10–15 km).

The captain had initiated a descent while operating under visual flight rules (VFR) procedures, and the aircraft was observed at a height of perhaps 2,000 ft (*c*. 600 m) or lower shortly before the accident. It was on its approach to Runway 33R, as cleared, when the co-pilot of a Japan Air Lines jet reported seeing the flash of an explosion, presumably the crash. However, the cleanly configured 727 was not properly aligned with the runway at the moment it slammed into the water.

All of the victim's bodies were later recovered from the bay, as was about 90 per cent of the aircraft's wreckage, and examination of the latter revealed no evidence of any pre-impact fire, explosion or mechanical failure. Nor were there any signs of malfunction or error in the altimeters or other vital instruments. There was no indication of any abnormalities in the last radio message from the flight, which was transmitted only seconds before the accident.

The cause of the disaster and the reason why the aircraft had been at an unusually low altitude for night visual flight before the crash could not be determined.

Date: 4 March 1966 (*c*. 20:15)
Location: Near Tokyo, Japan
Operator: Canadian Pacific Air Lines
Aircraft type: Douglas DC-8 Series 43 (*CF-CPK*)

Flight 402 circled on a holding pattern for nearly half an hour waiting for the fog to lift at Tokyo International (Haneda) Airport, a scheduled stop during a transpacific service from Hong Kong to

The empennage of the All Nippon Airways Boeing 727 is raised from Tokyo Bay after the crash that claimed 133 lives. *(CORBIS)*

Vancouver, British Columbia, Canada, before initiating its descent. When the conditions got worse the landing was abandoned altogether, and the aircraft began to proceed to its alternative airport, at T'ai-pei, Taiwan. Shortly afterwards, however, the flight was advised of an improvement in the visibility at Haneda, with the runway visual range (RVR) increasing to 3,000 ft (c. 1,000 m), and the pilot consequently requested clearance to return and then started descending.

In the darkness the DC-8 would be making a ground-controlled approach (GCA) to Runway 33R, with the crew referring to instrument landing system (ILS) indications. During the final seconds of the flight, the controller warned the aircraft: 'dropping low, ten to fifteen, twenty feet low . . . level off momentarily . . . precision minimum, level off, twenty feet low', but the crewman handling the radio only responded 'Tower, would you turn your . . . runway lights down?'

The jetliner then made a sharp decline, but was in an approximately level attitude with under-carriage and flaps extended when it hit the approach lights, the initial impact occurring with a main gear wheel some 2,800 ft (850 m) from the runway threshold. It then struck a sea-wall with the bottom of its fuselage, was thrown over that structure and finally crashed near the end of the runway, bursting into flames. The accident killed 64 persons aboard the aircraft, including all 10 crew members, and injured the eight surviving passengers, who were seated in the centre part of the cabin and managed to escape through a torn portion of the fuselage or the forward door.

According to the investigative committee, the principal cause of the crash was the decision by the pilot-in-command to attempt a landing under the circumstances. It was believed that he initiated a steep rate of descent with the intention of executing the final approach at a lower altitude. Poor visibility due to the illusive fog condition probably misled the pilot and affected his judgement.

Date: 5 March 1966 (c. 14:15)
Location: Near Gotemba, Shizuoka, Japan
Operator: British Overseas Airways Corporation (BOAC)
Aircraft type: Boeing 707-436 (G-APFE)

It must have been a grisly sight for the occupants of Flight 911 as the 707 taxied by the remains of the Canadian Pacific DC-8 which had crashed on landing the previous night (see above), before taking off from Tokyo International (Haneda) Airport, bound for Hong Kong, one segment of an around-the-world service originating at and destined for London. Little could any of them have known that in less than half an hour they would meet the same fate.

In an apparent attempt to expedite the departure or, perhaps, to give his passengers a scenic view of the majestic Mt Fuji, Capt Bernard Dobson elected to make a visual climb-out, flying off the designated airway. This deviation would be a significant factor in the subsequent accident, because it would take the flight into an area of severe turbulence. It was an exceptionally clear day, but the winds were blowing at the summit of the peak at a velocity of 60 to 70 knots.

The jet airliner was heading towards the west when it began to ascend while shedding parts after flying over Gotemba, located some 50 miles (80 km) south-south-west of Tokyo, at an altitude of approximately 15,000 ft (5,000 m). Its empennage then separated, and, at a height of about 7,000 ft (2,000 m), the forward fuselage section broke away. Other components, including the right outer wing and all four engine/pylon assemblies, were also torn away as the 707 plummeted to earth. Trailing vapour, the main fuselage section and still-attached wings fell into a wooded area at the eastern base of the mountain, and the forward part crashed some 1,000 ft (300 m) away and caught fire. All 124 persons aboard (113 passengers and a crew of 11) were killed. Wreckage was scattered over an area approximately 10 miles (15 km) long and 1 mile (1.5 km) wide.

It was believed that the aircraft broke up in a very short period of time after encountering an abnormally strong gust of wind that generated a load considerably in excess of its design limits. Although it was impossible to forecast, and its existence could not be confirmed, the investigative commission did not deny that turbulence of such severity as to destroy a jet transport could have been produced by a powerful mountain wave present in the lee of Fujiyama. One theory suggested a difference between waves associated with an isolated peak, as was the case here, and those formed in the normal way, i.e. by extended ridges.

Metallurgical tests revealed fatigue cracks in a bolt hole in the vertical stabiliser rear spar starboard attachment fitting of *G-APFE*. However, it could not be determined clearly how this condition contributed to the structural failure. Inspections prompted by the disaster further revealed fatigue cracks in the tail assembly bolts of other aircraft in the BOAC Boeing 707 fleet, necessitating the temporary grounding of some of them for rectification.

Date: 22 April 1966 (20:30)
Location: Near Ardmore, Oklahoma, US
Operator: American Flyers Airline Corporation (US)
Aircraft type: Lockheed 188C Electra (*N183H*)

The aircraft was being operated under contract to the US Military Airlift Command and on a domestic transcontinental service from Monterey, California, to Columbus, Georgia. Except for an off-duty flight engineer riding in the cockpit jump seat, its passengers were recent recruits on their way to Fort Benning for advanced training.

During an approach to land at Ardmore Municipal Airport, and an en route refuelling stop, the four-engine turboprop crashed and burned in the foothills of the Arbuckle Mountains, and 83 persons aboard were killed, including the five members of the regular crew and the sole non-revenue passenger. The 15 survivors suffered various injuries. It was dark at the time of the accident, and the latest given weather consisted of a low ceiling, with broken clouds at 700 ft (*c*. 200 m) and a solid overcast at about 1,000 ft (300 m), and a visibility of 3 miles (*c*. 5 km) in fog and drizzle.

The crew had originally planned a landing on Runway 08, using automatic direction finder (ADF) instrument procedures, but instead deviated to the north of the proper track, possibly to avoid thunderstorm activity. They then started a visual, circling approach to Runway 30. The Electra was in a right turn with its undercarriage down and flaps extended when it slammed into a hill, just below its crest, approximately 1.5 miles (2.5 km) north-east of the airport.

Investigation by the US Civil Aeronautics Board (CAB) revealed no evidence of any mechanical failure or defect in the aircraft. However, an autopsy performed on the body of the 59-year-old captain was considerably more revealing, disclosing severe coronary arteriosclerosis. So dire was his condition that two pathologists concluded that he may have died of heart failure before the crash. Perhaps even more disturbing was that the pilot, who also served as president of the airline, had falsified his application for a first-class medical certificate, required as part of his airline transport rating (ATR). It was learned that he had a history of heart trouble dating back 18 years, and also suffered from diabetes. Both ailments would have been disqualifying factors for issuance of the certificate.

It was believed that the captain was flying the Electra and became incapacitated during the final stages of the approach. He may have slumped across the control wheel or back in his seat, in either case causing the transport to roll to the right. At the time the first officer would probably have been looking outside, trying to keep the airport in sight, and he might not have noticed the pilot's seizure until the change in attitude or, perhaps,

The front fuselage section of the BOAC Boeing 707, with wings still attached, plummets to earth after the in-flight break-up. *(AP Images)*

This Britannia Airways Bristol Britannia 102 was a sister to the aircraft that crashed in Yugoslavia. *(Rod Simpson)*

when alerted by one or both of the other two men on the flight deck. The late recognition of the situation, coupled with the aircraft's response time, precluded a successful recovery at such a low altitude. In addition, a duty time of 16 hours on the day of the accident probably contributed to the captain's susceptibility to such incapacitation.

Following this disaster, the CAB announced that it would work with the US Federal Aviation Agency (FAA) in exploring ways to improve the quality of medical information received from pilots.

Date: 1 September 1966 (00:47)
Location: Near Ljubljana, Slovenia, Yugoslavia
Operator: Britannia Airways (UK)
Aircraft type: Bristol Britannia 102 (*G-ANBB*)

The turboprop airliner was on a charter service from Luton, England, and crashed while attempting to land at Ljubljana's Brniki Airport, killing 98 of the 117 persons aboard (92 passengers and six crew members). All the survivors, who included a stewardess, were injured.

During the approach to Runway 31, the crew reported seeing the airport, then requested radar assistance, implying that visual contact had been lost. Shortly afterwards, the controller observed the target on the radar screen turn to the right, but no correction was made even after he instructed the crew to turn left 3 degrees. Its undercarriage extended and flaps set at 15 degrees, the Britannia slammed into a forest, broke apart and caught fire approximately 1.5 miles (2.5 km) from the threshold of the runway and some 2,300 ft (700 m) north of its extended centreline. The accident occurred in darkness, but despite the presence of shallow fog in the area, the visibility was good, with scattered stratocumulus clouds at about 6,000 ft (1,800 m).

The pilot-in-command probably did not set his altimeter to the given airfield pressure (QFE), but the approach was conducted as though it were, and as a result the aircraft went some 1,250 ft (380 m) below the procedural safety height. Nor was the first officer's altimeter set correctly, though it was not the same as the captain's. The discrepancy was not detected due to the apparent failure of the crew to carry out the required altimeter cross-checks.

The disregard of the proper procedures may be explained by the fact that the approach was conducted in moonlight and good weather conditions, which enabled the crew to sight the runway while still at least 7 miles (11 km) away. But whereas the runway lights may have been visible, the pilots would not have been able to discern their low altitude. The visual effect of the upward-sloping runway made the situation worse, giving them a wrong impression of their approach angle. The controller's failure to provide the crew with altitude information was not considered a contributing factor.

Britannia Airways would later revise its operations manual in view of the opinion of the commission responsible for investigating the crash that the carrier's policy, which allowed the setting of an altimeter to the QFE 'at a convenient time', was imprecise and conducive to pilot error.

Date: 24 November 1966 (c. 16:30)
Location: Near Bratislava, Czechoslovakia
Operator: Transportno Aviatsionno Bulgaro-Soviet Obshchestvo (TABSO) (Bulgaria)
Aircraft type: Ilyushin Il-18B (*LZ-BEN*)

All 82 persons aboard (74 passengers and a crew of eight) were killed when the four-engine turboprop crashed and burned in the 'Little Carpathians' range of mountains about 5 miles (10 km) from the city's international airport, from where it had taken off only 2 minutes earlier.

Operating as Flight 101, a service originating at Sofiya, Bulgaria, and scheduled to terminate at (East) Berlin, the airliner was diverted to Bratislava due to adverse meteorological conditions. Some 5 hours later the captain elected to proceed on to Prague, where he had originally intended to land.

Following its departure, the Il-18 maintained the assigned altitude but did not turn to starboard as instructed. Cleanly configured, the aircraft was in a slight left bank when it hit a wooded hillside at an approximate elevation of 1,380 ft (420 m), the accident occurring in twilight. The airport was completely overcast at the time, with 6/8 stratus clouds at about 1,200 ft (350 m) and 8/8 nimbostratus at around 3,000 ft (1,000 m), a visibility of approximately 4.5 miles (7 km) and a moderate, continuous rain.

Although not determined with certainty, an investigative commission concluded that the most probable cause of the crash was the insufficient evaluation of both the weather and the relief of the terrain by the pilots, and their failure to adapt the flight to these conditions. The situation became dangerous only when the crew did not comply with the accepted flight clearance, which was either intentional or due to an unexpected occurrence that they did not understand or with which they could not cope.

With regard to the former theory, the immediate replies to messages from the ground raised doubts as to whether sufficient and concentrated attention was being given by the entire flight crew in making decisions. One noteworthy item was that the radio operator was not fully proficient in English, which could have complicated matters for the pilot.

With regard to the second theory, the possibility of an incorrect artificial horizon indication due to a defect in the instrument could not be dismissed. Such a faulty reading would have explained the failure of the crew to maintain the required 15-degree bank, which, probably in conjunction with excessive speed, may have caused the deviation. Turbulence was another possible contributing factor.

Date: 20 April 1967 (02:13)
Location: Near Nicosia, Cyprus
Operator: Globe Air AG (Switzerland)
Aircraft type: Bristol Britannia 313 (*HB-ITB*)

The turboprop airliner, on a non-scheduled service from Bangkok, Thailand, to Basel, Switzerland, crashed and burned while trying to land at the Nicosia airport, killing 126 persons aboard (117 passengers and nine crew members). Three passengers and a stewardess, who were found near the wreckage of the tail section, survived with injuries.

The Britannia had diverted from Cairo, one of three planned en route stops, but it could not be determined why the captain did not proceed to the prescribed alternate airport at Beirut, Lebanon, since the weather there was better than at Nicosia.

Following an overshoot, the pilot made a second landing attempt, but during the visual approach to Runway 32 he apparently misjudged the distance while in the airport circuit and descended too low to clear the rising terrain. The aircraft was in a left bank and on a heading of 68 degrees when it struck a hillock about 20 ft (6 m) below its crest.

The accident occurred in darkness and during a thunderstorm, with 5/8 cloud coverage at 250 ft (c. 75 m) and 5/8 estimated at 2,000 ft (c. 600 m), and a visibility of approximately 4.5 miles (7 km). There was also a 7-knot wind from the east.

At the time of the crash, both pilots had exceeded by nearly 3 hours their authorised duty time. It was also noted in the investigative report that the first officer had less than 50 hours flying time in Britannia aircraft.

Date: 3 June 1967 (22:06)
Location: Near Prats-de-Mollo-la-Preste, Roussillon, France
Operator: Air Ferry Ltd (UK)
Aircraft type: Douglas DC-4 (*G-APYK*)

A holiday trip to the Mediterranean ended tragically in this, the first of two major disasters involving British supplemental airlines occurring during a single weekend.

The vintage transport was to have landed at Perpignan, at the end of a charter service from Manston, England. However, while nearing its destination the aircraft started to deviate to the west of the prescribed track, by nearly 10 miles (15 km) at the last reporting point and even further as it began what might have been an approach and landing manoeuvre. In the final moments of the flight, when asked by the approach controller 'Yankee Kilo, you not have my field in sight?', a crewman responded with an 'affirmative', but due to a misunderstanding brought about by the somewhat contradictory question, the controller did not realise that the crew had not in fact made visual contact with the airport.

Just before the accident, the DC-4 initiated a wide left turn, then rolled back into a fast right turn of approximately 90 degrees, which was followed by a steep left turn. During this last turn, and while in a bank of about 60 degrees, the aircraft hit a rock spur at an approximate elevation of 3,800 ft (1,150 m), which sheared off its entire port wing. The transport, which was clearly configured and on a near-northerly heading at the time of the initial impact, finally crashed at the bottom of a ravine some 700 ft (200 m) below that point and burst into flames. All 88 persons aboard (83 passengers and a crew of five) perished.

The accident took place about 25 miles (40 km) south-west of Perpignan, in the Mont Canigou massif of the Pyrenees, at night and in good weather, with scattered cumulus and stratocumulus clouds and a visibility in excess of 5 miles (*c.* 10 km). There was little or no wind.

The accident was believed to have resulted from a series of errors on the part of the flight crew. It appeared that the pilots did not use the Perpignan very-high-frequency omnidirectional range (VOR) station for navigational purposes, erred in dead reckoning, and may have confused two towns, Prades for Rivesealtes. Their estimated time of arrival was also incorrect by 10 minutes behind what normally would be expected, apparently because a fixed amount of time reserved for the landing procedure had been included in the calculations of the company's flight plan. And even though they did not have any runway in sight and were probably not referring to the aircraft's radio-navigational instruments, the crew proceeded to descend below the minimum safety altitude, apparently from a point that had not been properly identified.

It was concluded that the pilot saw the mountain upon turning on the landing lights and endeavoured to turn back on a reciprocal heading by making the tight left bank that preceded the crash.

The irrational conduct of the crew itself had an underlying cause, which was discovered through the medical aspects of the inquiry. Toxicological examinations on the remains of the three flight crewmen (who included a supernumerary pilot) revealed high levels of carbon monoxide. Since the impact was non-survivable, the highly toxic fumes must have been inhaled before the crash and would have been sufficient to cause intoxication to the point of affecting their powers of judgement. Flight at the cruising altitude of 9,000 ft (*c.* 2,700 m), where the air is thinner, would have aggravated the situation, leading to hypoxia. The source of the carbon monoxide could only have been the aircraft's heater; if the joints of its exhaust pipe were cracked or otherwise defective, the fumes could easily seep into the cockpit. (Regulations concerning the inspection and overhaul of Janitrol-type heaters were later tightened.)

Additional factors were the misunderstandings between the crew and the controller, attributed to language difficulties and, in particular, the lack of standard phraseology used, and the failure of the latter to check the bearing of the DC-4 during radio communications and thus detect the deviation in its track.

The crash of this British Midland Airways Argonaut in an open space in the centre of Stockport avoided a potentially higher death toll. *(AP Images)*

Date: 4 June 1967 (*c.* 10:10)
Location: Stockport, Cheshire, England
Operator: British Midland Airways
Aircraft type: Canadair C-4 (*G-ALHG*)

A derivative of the famed Douglas DC-4, the Canadian-built C-4 (dubbed the 'Argonaut' by British operators) had a history of reliability since its introduction into service in the late 1940s. Strangely, it would take this accident two decades later to reveal a potentially serious flaw in the four-engine transport.

This particular aircraft was to have landed at Ringway Airport, serving Manchester, at the end of a non-scheduled service from Palma de Mallorca in the Spanish Balearic Islands. It was carrying a full load of British holidaymakers plus five crew members.

However, during a radar-monitored instrument landing system (ILS) approach to Runway 24, both the aircraft's starboard power plants malfunctioned, and Capt Harry Marlow radioed that he was initiating an overshoot and reported 'a little bit of trouble with rpm'. The C-4 completed a 360-degree right turn, during which it broke through the low overcast, and was approximately on the ILS localiser when it crashed in the centre of town and some 5 miles (10 km) short of the runway

threshold. Its port wing was torn off upon striking a three-storey building, and the airliner hit the ground in a nearly level attitude. At the moment of impact its undercarriage was retracted and flaps were set at 10 degrees.

Initially there were only small, scattered fires, but about 10 minutes after the crash an explosion occurred in the starboard wing, and the blaze rapidly spread to the fuselage. The flames beat back rescuers after only 10 passengers could be saved, all of whom were injured, as was the stewardess, who had been thrown clear through a tear in the cabin. Also found alive was Capt Marlow, who escaped serious physical harm but suffered from retrograde amnesia and could not remember anything about the flight. The other 72 persons aboard lost their lives, including the first officer, a supernumerary engineer and a steward. The meteorological conditions at the airport shortly before the disaster consisted of rain, 3/8 cloud coverage at 300 ft (*c.* 100 m), 7/8 at 400 ft (*c.* 120 m) and 8/8 at 5,000 ft (*c.* 1,500 m), and a horizontal visibility of approximately 1 mile (1.5 km).

The immediate cause of the accident was the loss of power in both starboard engines, resulting in control difficulties, that prevented the crew from maintaining height, especially with one of the propellers windmilling. The source of the problem was not mechanical, however, but rather in the design of the fuel cocks and the location in the cockpit of their actuating levers. So awkward was their placement on the console that a pilot could rather easily put one or more of the levers in the wrong position, and only a slight error in the positioning of a lever could create a situation in which a cross-feed valve would be 'cracked', or improperly closed, allowing for the inadvertent transfer of fuel from one tank to another. This condition could represent a threat to safety after a long flight if fuel had been transferred from a tank that the crew believed was sufficiently filled.

Other C-4 operators had experienced cases of inadvertent fuel transfer, but these were not communicated to the appropriate British government authorities. Nor had users of the type been adequately informed of the potential hazard by the manufacturer. British Midland Airways' engineers in fact did not even realise that such an inadvertent transfer of fuel was possible. But there was no doubt that such a condition had caused fuel starvation and, in turn, the power loss in the No. 4 engine of *G-ALHG*. Its No. 3 power plant may have failed for the same reason or, perhaps, because the pilot misidentified the engine for the one that had initially malfunctioned. It was then possible that the pilot had realised his mistake and correctly feathered the No. 4 propeller, but did not restore power in time to the No. 3 engine to prevent the crash.

Aggravating the woes of the crew were the poor handling characteristics of the C-4 in the event of such a power loss. In its report the investigative board noted that due to that fact, the lack of instruments to indicate engine failure, and the poor design of the fuel system controls, the aircraft would not have been certified under 1967 standards.

Though the outcome proved disastrous, the captain was not faulted for executing a go-around under the circumstances. He did show skill in apparently cutting power and setting the transport down in the only open space available.

Tragically, many of those killed had survived the impact but were trapped and died in the inferno. But it could have been worse. Immediately beyond the crash site were tall blocks of flats, the town hall and police station, and Stockport Infirmary.

Date: 19 July 1967 (12:01)
Location: Near Hendersonville, North Carolina, US
First aircraft
Operator: Piedmont Airlines (US)
Type: Boeing 727-22 (*N68650*)
Second aircraft
Operator: Lanseair Inc (US)
Type: Cessna 310 (*N3121S*)

Designated as Flight 22, the 727 took off 2 minutes before noon from Asheville Municipal Airport, bound for Roanoke, Virginia, one segment of a domestic service originating at Atlanta, Georgia, with an ultimate destination of Washington, DC. Meanwhile, the 1955 model twin-engine Cessna was preparing to land at Asheville at the end of an intrastate flight from Charlotte. Both were operating under instrument flight rules (IFR).

Rather than follow its clearance, i.e. to proceed from the Asheville very-high-frequency omni-directional range (VOR) station to the Asheville radio beacon located north-west of the airport, the corporate aircraft strayed about 10 miles (15 km) to the south-west and into airspace allocated to the jetliner. The two collided at an approximate altitude of 6,000 ft (1,800 m) some 15 miles (25 km) south-east of the city of Asheville. All 79 persons aboard the transport (74 passengers and a crew of five) and the three occupants of the general aviation aeroplane (including an experienced commercial pilot and a qualified private pilot) perished.

The cause of the deviation by *N3121S* could not be determined, but the investigation centred on a possible misidentification of or failure to locate the Asheville beacon.

The first significant event in the accident sequence was a remark by the Atlanta centre controller for the Cessna to 'expect ILS approach at Asheville'. This advisory should not have been accepted as a clearance, but if it were, it could have set the stage for disaster. Asheville has four different approaches, and the instrument landing system procedure uses the Broad River radio beacon, located south-east of the airport, as a fix.

Minutes later, the Asheville approach controller transmitted to *N3121S* a message containing an error, radioing 'Three one two one Sugar cleared over the VOR to the Broad River, correction, make that the Asheville radio beacon'.

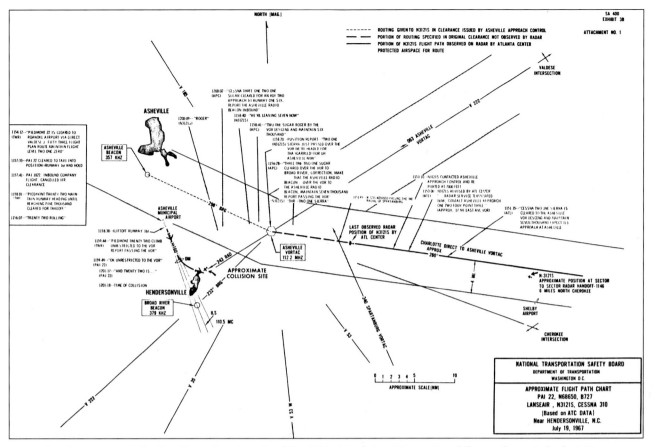

An airways map indicating the assigned route of the light aircraft (east to west) and the south-westerly deviation that led to the collision with the jetliner. *(National Transportation Safety Board)*

Though immediately revised, the initial use of Broad River in the transmission could have continued the chain of misunderstanding. Furthermore, the clearance contained no reference to the type of approach. Later the controller did clear the Cessna for an ADF-2 (automatic direction finder) approach, using the Asheville beacon, but by then the aircraft was already well off course and only 76 seconds away from colliding with the 727.

The crews were unaware of one another, as they were communicating with the ground on different radio frequencies. However, the Cessna pilots could have overheard a message to another Piedmont flight that received clearance for an ILS approach, only adding to their confusion.

A portion of a three-year-old approach chart was found in the wreckage of the corporate aircraft, on which the geographical location of the Asheville beacon was not even depicted. In addition, the Cessna's automatic direction finder (ADF) receiver was determined to have been tuned to the Broad River facility.

The final message from *N3121S* was 'We're headed for the . . . Asheville now'. There was a possibility that the pilots had thought the Asheville and Broad River beacons were one and the same. They must have maintained the same south-westerly heading while trying to locate the navigational aid, or abandoned their efforts altogether and continued visually.

Converging at an estimated speed of 350–400 mph (c. 550–650 kmh), the aircraft approached through a broken overcast, which would have reduced the time available for detection and avoidance. Also, the preoccupation of the Cessna's crew with their navigational difficulties and that of the 727 with normal departure procedures could have reduced their vigilance.

Witnesses reported that the actual collision took place in an area clear of clouds, with the light aeroplane pulling up sharply just before impact. There was no evidence that the airline crew at any point saw the other aircraft.

The initial contact was between the left outer wing and nose of the Cessna and the left forward

A British European Airways Comet 4B of the type destroyed by an explosive device over the Mediterranean Sea. *(BAe Systems)*

Date: 12 October 1967 (*c.* 07:25)
Location: Off south-western Turkey
Operator: British European Airways (BEA)
Aircraft type: de Havilland Comet 4B (G-ARCO)

Originating at London, Flight 284 had stopped at Athens, Greece, before taking off for Nicosia, Cyprus. The last segment of the service was being conducted by BEA on behalf of Cyprus Airways, but retained the same flight number.

At around 07:00, and while cruising at flight level 290, the jetliner passed a westbound BEA Comet, whose captain later stated that the meteorological conditions in the area were clear and smooth. There were no further communications with CY 284 after it contacted Nicosia at 07:18.

Three hours later, wreckage from *G-ARCO* was spotted floating in the Mediterranean Sea some 100 miles (150 km) east-south-east of the island of Rhodes, in the general vicinity where it had fallen. For the 66 persons aboard (59 passengers and a crew of seven), there was no chance for survival. Subsequently, a small amount of debris, mostly cabin furnishings and personal effects, was recovered, as were the bodies of 59 victims. Most of the wreckage sank in water that was more than 6,000 ft (1,800 m) deep and could not be salvaged.

It was apparent from the scattering and state of the flotsam and bodies that a mid-air break-up had occurred. But there was no evidence of structural weakness or prior damage in the aircraft.

A significant lead in the subsequent inquiry was uncovered through the examination of one of the many recovered seat cushions. Its condition, under investigation at the Royal Armament Research and Development Establishment (RARDE), was remarkably similar to cushions used to muffle explosions in cases of safe-breaking. In addition to the numerous superficial characteristics, the cushion was found to contain many small particles of metal and fibres as well as about 20 perforations. Laboratory tests confirmed that it had been subjected to the effects of a high explosive, irrefutable proof that the jetliner had been sabotaged.

The bomb had detonated in the cabin, the specific location believed to have been on the left side of the aircraft's tourist section, and probably between the cabin wall and the support of a seat that was occupied by a passenger (one of the victim's bodies exhibited indications of exposure to

fuselage section of the 727, which at the time was in a gentle left bank and on a heading of 100 degrees. The jetliner then nosed over, plunged into a wooded area in an inverted attitude and a steep angle of descent and exploded. The corporate aeroplane disintegrated in flight and was not observed after the collision.

In summary, the disaster may have resulted from inadequate knowledge of the Asheville area by the Cessna's pilot-in-command and poor flight planning on his part for apparently not reviewing and becoming familiar with the latest charts, and the failure of the air traffic control (ATC) system to provide timely information that could have placed the aircraft on the correct course or at least alerted the pilot to his misunderstanding. It should be noted, however, that at no point did the Cessna pilot request assistance or clarification of any of the ATC instructions.

An underlying factor in this accident was the absence of surveillance radar at the airport, which simply lacked the level of traffic at the time to make it eligible for such an installation. Though not an infallible method of separating aircraft, its use in this case would have given the controller the opportunity to detect and thus correct the deviation of the light aeroplane from is prescribed flight path.

As a safety measure, the US Federal Aviation Administration (FAA) would later require that approach/landing charts display all available navigational aids.

such a blast). The type of explosive used could not be identified.

By analysing the distribution of the debris, it was possible to determine that the Comet did not disintegrate at the cruising altitude of 29,000 ft (c. 9,000 m). The blast apparently caused severe damage and created an out-of-control condition, and the aircraft suffered structural failure at an approximate height of 15,000 ft (5,000 m), its fuselage breaking into at least two major sections.

No suspects were ever apprehended or motive established, though the bombing may have been an attempt to kill the leader of the Greek forces in Cyprus after he was incorrectly identified as being among those who boarded the jetliner at Athens. On the other hand, this may have been some kind of insurance swindle. Two of the passengers were found to have been carrying abnormally high coverage, with one of the policies having been taken out shortly before the flight.

It was recommended in the investigative report that flight data recorders be so equipped as to facilitate their recovery from deep water, a proposal that would see future application.

Date: 16 November 1967 (time unknown)
Location: Near Sverdlovsk, Russian Soviet Federative Socialist Republic, USSR
Operator: Aeroflot (USSR)
Aircraft type: Ilyushin Il-18B (*SSSR-75538*)

All 107 persons aboard (99 passengers and a crew of eight) were killed in the crash of the four-engine turboprop. The accident occurred at night and in instrument meteorological conditions, with a ceiling of around 300 ft (100 m), shortly after the airliner had taken off from the Sverdlovsk airport, on a scheduled domestic service to Krasnoyarsk.

Climbing to an approximate height of 700 ft (200 m) above the ground, and after initiating a left turn while in the clouds, the aircraft suddenly turned right, plunged to earth in a bank of about 90 degrees and caught fire.

Although there had been no distress message and the unprotected flight data recorder (FDR) mounted on the Il-18 was destroyed, investigation revealed that the crash apparently resulted from an incorrect indication of the main artificial horizons and of the compass system due to an electrical power failure, with the pilots then unable to

determine the correct attitude of the aircraft with their back-up instruments and in conditions that precluded flight by visual reference. Action taken to arrest the descent without recovering from the steep bank proved insufficient to save the flight.

Date: 20 November 1967 (c. 21:00)
Location: Near Covington, Kentucky, US
Operator: Trans World Airlines (TWA) (US)
Aircraft type: Convair 880 (*N821TW*)

Flight 128 was scheduled to land at Greater Cincinnati (Ohio) Airport during a domestic transcontinental service from Los Angeles, California, to Boston, Massachusetts, but during the approach to Runway 18 the jetliner crashed and burst into flames, killing 70 persons aboard (65 passengers and five crew members); ten passengers and two cabin attendants survived with various injuries.

The instrument landing system (ILS) localiser was operational at the time, but the glide slope, approach lights and middle marker beacon were inoperative due to runway construction, conditions of which the crew had been informed.

Its undercarriage extended and flaps set at 50 degrees, the aircraft was in a nearly level attitude and on the correct heading of 180 degrees when it began hitting trees at an indicated air speed of about 220 mph (350 kmh). The initial impact took

A Trans World Airlines Convair 880, of the type that crashed during a landing attempt at Greater Cincinnati Airport. *(Trans World Airlines)*

place some 9,350 ft (2,850 m) from the runway threshold and approximately 430 ft (130 m) to the right of its extended centreline, and the jetliner then slammed into a pasture.

The visual approach had been conducted at night and in deteriorating weather conditions without adequate altimeter cross-reference. Additionally, the captain may have been deceived by a sensory illusion with regard to height.

The approach was normal until passage of the outer marker, whereupon there was a breakdown in the application of the prescribed procedures. The first officer did not call out the above-ground altitude of 500 ft, the 100 ft increments below that level or the arrival at the decision height, nor did he announce any deviation from the localiser centreline or in the air speed, altitude or rate of descent of the aircraft. At the time that these call-outs should have been made, as transcribed on the cockpit voice recorder (CVR) tape, the co-pilot and flight engineer were carrying out the final landing checklist, and even though the former may have referred to his instruments, this activity coupled with an atmosphere of complacency due to his confidence in the captain, reinforced perhaps by the fact that the two had flown together before, could have led to the omissions.

Meanwhile, the pilot may have divided his attention between trying to make visual contact with the ground and monitoring his instruments. In the vicinity of the Ohio River the flight encountered a snow shower, which reduced visibility to 1½–2 miles (2.5–3 km). The airport had an indefinite ceiling of 1,000 ft (c. 300 m). Under these circumstances, he may have been faced with trying to reorient himself with the instruments.

It was believed that the captain had used the lights in the river valley as a visual reference to establish his final approach altitude. In darkness and under lowering visibility conditions, it is possible that these lights could be confused as being at the same elevation of the airport, therefore creating the false impression of having sufficient height for terrain clearance. Furthermore, as studies have shown, lights on upsloping terrain in the area could have produced the sensation of being higher than was actually the case.

The cockpit conversation also indicated that the pilot did not have the minimum altitude clearly in his mind and levelled off at 400 ft (c. 120 m) above

the river rather than at the prescribed height of about 1,300 ft (400 m), or 400 ft above the elevation of the airport. He may have realised that something was wrong in the final seconds of the flight, as an instant before initial impact he initiated a pull-up and was heard to say 'Come on you'.

A claim by the airline that the crash may have resulted from erroneous instrument readings due to ice or water blocking the static ports was rejected by the US National Transportation Safety Board (NTSB), which investigated the accident.

Date: 29 February 1968 (time unknown)
Location: Near Bratsk, Russian Soviet Federative Socialist Republic, USSR
Operator: Aeroflot (USSR)
Aircraft type: Ilyushin Il-18D (*SSSR-74252*)

The airliner was en route from Krasnoyarsk to Petropavlovsk-Kamchatskiy, on Kamchatka, one segment of a scheduled domestic service originating at Moscow, and cruising in darkness at flight level 260 when some sort of emergency developed.

Although the crew did not communicate with air traffic control, an abrupt descent was begun and accelerated until aerodynamic forces broke up the four-engine turboprop at an approximate altitude of 10,000 ft (3,000 m) above the ground, and it then crashed and burned. All but one of the 82 persons aboard were killed, including nine crew members; the miraculous survival of a single passenger, who suffered only minor injuries, was attributed to the fact that his seat (to which he remained safety belted) separated together with a large section of airframe skin, gliding slowly to earth like a leaf and landing atop a tree.

The cause of the disaster remained unidentified, although the descent could have been prompted by a fuel leak and the discovery of direct or indirect signs of an in-flight blaze (traces of fire were observed on the port wing).

Date: 5 March 1968 (20:32)
Location: Basse-Terre, Guadeloupe, West Indies
Operator: Air France
Aircraft type: Boeing 707-328C (*F-BLCJ*)

Operating as Flight 212, the jet airliner had been cleared for a visual approach to land at Le Raizet Airport, serving Pointe-à-Pitre, on Grande-Terre,

All 63 persons aboard perished when the Air France Boeing 707 ploughed into the dormant volcano and virtually disintegrated. *(CORBIS)*

which was a scheduled stop. It had also landed at Quito, Ecuador, and Caracas, Venezuela, during a service originating at Santiago, Chile, and ultimately bound for Paris.

The pilot-in-command reported 'airfield in sight' before receiving the clearance; less than 2 minutes later the 707 struck a ridge of La Soufriere, a dormant volcano and the highest point on the island, the accident taking place some 15 miles (25 km) south-south-west of the airport. All 63 persons aboard (49 passengers, a regular crew of 11 and three off-duty crew members) perished.

When it crashed, the aircraft was on a heading of 50 to 60 degrees, and probably in a very shallow descent. Its undercarriage was retracted, and flaps were set at 25 degrees. The jet exploded on impact with the heavily wooded terrain at an approximate elevation of 4,000 ft (1,200 m), and its wreckage was still burning a week later. Found in the debris was an air speed indicator reading about 370 mph (595 kmh), and an altimeter recovered showed a height of between 3,500 and 4,300 ft.

It was dark at the time with a quarter-moon, and witnesses reported the sky as being clear in the vicinity of the accident. However, a few stratiform clouds covering the eastern slopes of the mountains and a cloud cap at the summit of La Soufriere were observed.

It was believed that the crew had initiated a descent from an incorrectly identified point. Difficulties encountered by the flight in establishing radio contact with the airport control tower probably rendered the captain impatient, and as a consequence he may have lost track of the passage of time and the fact that he was not following the normal route. This in turn could have led to the false impression on his part that the aircraft had been closer to its destination than was actually the case.

Despite the pilot's message (which was interpreted to mean that the city lights were visible and not as positive identification of the airport), the French investigative commission doubted that Pointe-à-Pitre could have been seen from his position or height. He must have mistaken for Pointe-à-Pitre the town of Basse-Terre, located on the island of the same name, since witnesses in this area reported seeing an aircraft at an unusually low altitude. The error, resulting in a descent below the minimum safety level, was then not corrected by cross-checking with existing navigational aids.

Despite a lengthy search, the flight data recorder (FDR) belonging to the 707 was not recovered, and this coupled with the location and state of destruction of the wreckage prevented the commission from bringing to light whatever factor, perhaps more than one, that caused the error by the crew. Nor could a reason be found to explain the adoption by the pilot-in-command of a flight profile that would undoubtedly have delayed his arrival at Pointe-à-Pitre by 2 to 3 minutes.

There was no evidence of anything of a technical nature being wrong with the aircraft as directly contributing to the disaster.

Date: 24 March 1968 (*c.* 12:15)
Location: Off Wexford Harbour, Ireland
Operator: Aer Lingus – Irish International Airlines
Aircraft type: Vickers Viscount 803 (*EI-AOM*)

This perplexing crash occurred while the four-engine turboprop, designated as Flight 712, was on a service to London from Cork, Ireland, with 61 persons aboard (57 passengers and a crew of four). Before radio contact was lost, it broadcast a message later determined to be 'Twelve thousand feet, descending . . . spinning rapidly'.

The Viscount was believed to have gone into a spin, spiral dive or similar manoeuvre at the cruising altitude of 17,000 ft (*c.* 5,200 m). It appeared that a recovery had been made at less than 12,000 ft (*c.* 3,700 m), but not without inflicting some structural deformation of the airframe, most probably on the horizontal stabilisers and elevators, causing pitch control difficulties. And it was this condition that sent the airliner plunging into St George's Channel approximately 10 miles (15 km) east of Carnsore Point. Searchers recovered the bodies of 14 victims, but there were no survivors.

Located in water about 230 ft (70 m) deep, some 60 per cent of the wreckage was later salvaged. Additionally, a portion of the spring tab from the inboard end of the port elevator that apparently became detached in flight was found washed up on a beach.

It was concluded that the aircraft had flown in the disabled condition for at least 10 minutes, and before impact its engines were apparently throttled back intentionally. The Viscount then struck the water in a steep angle of descent and with considerable vertical velocity but a relatively low forward speed, i.e. less

than 150 mph (250 kmh). The weather in the general area consisted of 3/8 stratus clouds between 500 and 1,500 ft (*c.* 150–500 m), 6/8 altostratus between 12,000 and 15,000 ft (*c.* 3,700–5,000 m) and high cirrocumulus.

There was insufficient evidence to determine the cause of the initial descent that led to the structural damage. An in-flight fire or explosion, power plant failure, bird strike, crew incapacitation or encounter with severe turbulence were either ruled out or considered highly improbable. Although there was no substantiating evidence of such an occurrence, the known facts did point to the possibility of a collision with another aircraft, possibly a pilotless drone, a near collision that necessitated an evasive manoeuvre, or an upset of the Viscount by its wake turbulence. However, these hypotheses were dispelled more than three decades later by the findings of an independent inquiry, which pointed to excessive spring tab free play leading to a flutter condition as the precipitating factor.

Date: 20 April 1968 (*c.* 20:50)
Location: Near Windhoek, South-West Africa (Namibia)
Operator: South African Airways
Aircraft type: Boeing 707-344C (*ZS-EUW*)

Operating as Flight 228/129, the aircraft had landed at J.G. Strijdom Airport, serving the capital city, before continuing on to Luanda, Angola, its next scheduled stop during a service originating at Johannesburg, South Africa, with an ultimate destination of London. After taking off from Runway 08 the 707 climbed to an approximate altitude of 600 ft (180 m) above airfield elevation, whereupon it levelled off and then began to descend. Only about a minute after becoming airborne, the jetliner crashed some 3 miles (5 km) from the end of the runway, bursting into flames on impact. The accident claimed the lives of 123 persons aboard, including the entire crew of 12 and a passenger who was found alive at the crash site but succumbed days later. Five other passengers, all of whom were seated near the front of the cabin, survived with various injuries.

Since *ZS-EUW* was not equipped with either a flight data recorder (FDR) or cockpit voice recorder (CVR), the exact sequence of events and the actions of the flight crew could not be ascertained. However, through the subsequent investigation it was possible to conclude that the disaster resulted from human error rather than mechanical failure or a defect in the aircraft or any of its systems.

It was evident that the undercarriage had been raised immediately after lift-off, and that soon thereafter the flaps were fully retracted and the engine output reduced from take-off to climb power. Though in accordance with the prescribed procedures, these alterations in flap configuration and thrust would have caused the loss of height unless the pilot checked that tendency and maintained a climbing attitude by appropriate action or until the jetliner attained considerably more speed. Instead, he appeared to have changed the stabiliser trim to maintain the same pitch attitude as though he believed that the aircraft was ascending; at that point, however, the 707 was in fact descending. Additionally, the co-pilot must have monitored the flight instruments

insufficiently to appreciate that the aircraft was losing altitude.

Despite the clear, windless weather conditions, it was a dark, moonless night, and there were few lights on the ground in the area, if any. This absence of external visual references, along with spatial disorientation and the crew's preoccupation with the normal checks that are made after take-off, probably contributed to the accident.

Factors that might have contributed were temporary confusion in the mind of the pilot on the position of the inertial-lead vertical speed indicator, arising from the difference in the instrument panel layout in the 'C' version of the Boeing 707-344 as compared with the 'A' and 'B' models with which the captain and first officer were familiar; the pilot's misreading, by 1,000 ft, of the drum-type altimeter, which is susceptible to ambiguous interpretation on the thousands scale; and distraction on the flight deck caused by a bird or bat strike or some other minor occurrence such as smoke from overheating

Emergency workers and law enforcement personnel search through the wreckage of the Braniff International Airways Electra following the crash in Texas farmland. (CORBIS)

electrical equipment or a startling noise caused by something falling in the galley.

Although crew incapacitation had been ruled out, the investigative report did note that the captain's blood pressure was slightly above normal, and that his vision had deteriorated somewhat.

The impact with the ground took place at a speed in excess of 300 mph (480 kmh), with the 707 banked slightly to the left. Wreckage was strewn over an area nearly 1 mile (1.5 km) long and 700 ft (200 m) wide.

As a result of this accident, it was recommended that the minimum height for flap retraction be raised from 400 to 1,000 ft (c. 120 to 300 m) and the normal altitude for such action be fixed at 2,000 ft (c. 600 m).

Date: 3 May 1968 (c. 16:50)
Location: Near Dawson, Texas, US
Operator: Braniff International Airways (US)
Aircraft type: Lockheed 188A Electra (N9707C)

A SIGMET had been issued concerning a line of thunderstorms stretching across central Texas. Through this area was the planned path of Flight 352, whose pilots were provided with the weather report before their departure from Houston.

Following take-off, the turboprop airliner headed north for Dallas on the initial intrastate segment of a domestic service with an ultimate destination of Memphis, Tennessee. About 20 minutes later, as the Electra approached the cumulonimbus build-up, the crew were faced with finding the fastest, smoothest way of traversing the storm.

Despite a suggestion by the Fort Worth control centre to deviate to the east, where the rest of the air traffic was being re-routed, the crew insisted on proceeding to the west. Minutes later, and after being cleared to descend to and maintain 5,000 ft, the crew reported seeing an opening in the storm, then asked whether there were any reports of hail in the area.

'No, you're the closest one that's ever come to it yet,' the controller replied.

Less than a minute later, the flight asked permission, and was so granted, to make a 180-degree turn. No reason was given for this request, but from their conversation, transcribed by the cockpit voice recorder (CVR), it was obvious that the pilots realised their error in flying into the thunderhead.

'Don't talk to him too much,' the captain advised the first officer regarding the air traffic controller. 'He's trying to get us to admit we made a big mistake coming through here.'

While the pilot's decision to penetrate the storm in the first place had been unsound, and this was considered a major factor in the subsequent accident, his action in reversing direction and attempting to fly out of it would also prove fatally flawed. Such a procedure carried out in turbulent conditions could lead to a loss of control and was in fact against company policy.

The captain initiated a turn to the right, which progressed beyond 90 degrees. This resulted in a loss of lift, causing the nose of the aircraft to pitch down. It was believed that simultaneously the transport encountered turbulence, resulting in a lateral upset, and that it then may have been hit by an upward gust of wind which, coupled with the loss of lift, led to a longitudinal upset or spiral manoeuvre.

As the pilot attempted to bring the aircraft back to level flight from the unusual attitude, the inboard section of the right wing was subjected to bending and twisting forces that ultimately exceeded its designed strength. The wing finally failed, fracturing near the root and just outboard of the No. 4 power plant.

The initial break-up occurred at an estimated air speed of 380 mph (c. 600 kmh), at an approximate altitude of 7,000 ft (c. 2,000 m) and as the transport was on a heading of around 200 degrees. Almost instantly thereafter, the empennage broke off from the fuselage, and this was followed by the separation of the two left engines, left flaps and other components. Fuel from the ruptured wing tanks then ignited, and the Electra fell to earth in flames into farmland some 20 miles (30 km) south-west of Corsicana. All 85 persons aboard (80 passengers and five crew members) perished.

Witnesses in the immediate area of the crash reported rain, hail, high winds and lightning. One bolt seen in close proximity to the aircraft at about the time it broke up was not considered a factor in the accident.

Despite a total lack of evidence, the possibility of prior weakness in the wing structure due to stress corrosion, probably in the form of a small crack, could not be completely discounted.

There was also an indication that the aircraft's weather radar antenna may have been tilted slightly up, which would have resulted in a misleading presentation on the screen, and this, coupled with the effects of hail, which generally has a lesser reflectivity to radar than other forms of moisture, could have induced the crew to press for a deviation to the west.

One of the recommendations made by the US National Transportation Safety Board (NTSB) in its investigative report on this disaster was that greater emphasis be placed on weather radar for avoiding thunderstorms than as an aid in penetrating them. The findings of the NTSB would lead to reviews, amendments and updating in training and procedures used by the airline industry pertaining to the issue of storm avoidance.

Date: 22 May 1968 (*c.* 17:50)
Location: Paramount, California, US
Operator: Los Angeles Airways (US)
Aircraft type: Sikorsky S-61L (*N303Y*)

Probably the most popular and certainly the busiest route in L.A. Airways' commuter helicopter network was the service between the Disneyland amusement park in Anaheim and Los Angeles International Airport. It was on this run that tragedy befell Flight 841.

The turbine-engine rotorcraft departed Anaheim at 17:40 for the 25-mile (40-km) flight, and it was later observed at an altitude of about 2,000 ft (600 m) by the crew of another company aircraft heading in the opposite direction. Not more than a minute afterwards, a distress message was heard from Flight 841, later determined to be 'L.A., we're crashing, help us!'

Witnesses saw the helicopter descend to between 600 and 800 ft (*c.* 180–250 m) above the ground, then yaw to the left from a westerly to a south-westerly heading before it fell almost vertically into a dairy yard in suburban Los Angeles and burst into flames, killing all 23 persons aboard (20 passengers and a crew of three).

Examination of the wreckage indicated that the main rotor blades had undergone extreme lead and lag (fore and aft) over-travel excursions, so severe in fact that in some instances the blade overlapped the adjacent one. These excursions continued as the aircraft descended under partial control until one blade became detached from the rotating swashplate (the mechanism that transmits pitch control inputs) due to the overload failure of its pitch control rod at the lower trunnion end attachment. That blade then became uncontrollable and struck the aircraft, and the resulting imbalance caused the other four blades to do the same. The repeated strikes broke all five blades and caused severe structural damage, including the separation of the aft fuselage and tail rotor pylon assembly.

The main rotor system of the S-61 was designed to allow the blades limited motion both fore and aft and up and down, and each blade had been equipped with a damper to maintain stability. In this case the rotorcraft apparently experienced a loss of effective damper action of one blade or the failure of the damper of another. The reason for the first possibility could not be determined, and although the second could have involved bushing or bearing failure, this could not be substantiated because significant portions of the damper must have fallen off some distance from where the helicopter ultimately crashed and were never found. Studies showed that oscillations of one blade could cause similar anomalies in the two opposing ones.

This accident led to improvements in the S-61 model, including a modification of the helicopter's automatic flight control system. Additionally, the unlimited service life of the horizontal hinge pins used in the main rotor head was reduced to 5,000 hours.

Los Angeles Airways Sikorsky S-61s were involved in the two worst US commercial helicopter disasters, which occurred during a three-month period in 1968. (*Sikorsky*)

This Air France Caravelle is virtually identical to the aircraft that crashed in the Mediterranean Sea owing to in-flight fire. *(Air France)*

Date: 14 August 1968 (*c.* 10:35)
Location: Compton, California, US
Operator: Los Angeles Airways (US)
Aircraft type: Sikorsky S-61L (*N300Y*)

The company's second fatal crash in three months involved an aircraft flying on the same route but in the opposite direction, i.e. from Los Angeles International Airport to the Disneyland/Anaheim heliport.

Designated as Flight 417, the turbine-engine helicopter was seen at an estimated height of 1,500 ft (*c.* 500 m) above the ground when witnesses reported hearing a loud noise and seeing one of its main rotor blades break off. The aircraft fell in uncontrolled gyrations, then crashed and burned in Leuders Park. All 21 persons aboard (18 passengers and three crew members) were killed.

Examination revealed that the separation was caused by a fatigue crack in the spindle, the part of the assembly that attaches each blade to the main rotor head (it also provides pitch control of the blade). The nucleus of the fracture was on the trailing side of the spindle, and the crack, which had propagated through more than two-thirds of the shank cross-section, must have developed slowly over a long period of time. It had apparently been precipitated by substandard hardness of the metal and inadequate shot peening (a shop process designed to increase its strength); to a lesser degree from pitting that may have been present in the structure and possibly by tension on the unpeened metal generated by the nickel plating to which it was connected. Although the crack should have been present during the last overhaul of the spindle, it could not be determined why it was not detected.

An airworthiness directive issued by the US Federal Aviation Administration (FAA) two days after the accident mandated that only new main rotor blade spindles be used on S-61 rotorcraft. Previously, reworked spindles had been allowed, and no service life specified. The new time limit imposed was 2,400 hours.

Date: 11 September 1968 (*c.* 10:30)
Location: Near Cap d'Antibes, Provence-Alpes-Côte-d'Azur, France
Operator: Air France
Aircraft type: Sud-Aviation Caravelle III (*F-BOHB*)

Operating as Flight 1611, the jet airliner plunged into the Mediterranean Sea some 25 miles (40 km) south of Nice airport, where it was scheduled to land at the end of a service from Ajaccio, Corsica. All 95 persons aboard (89 passengers and a crew of six) perished.

The first hint of something amiss came less than 3 minutes before radio and radar contact with the Caravelle was lost, when a member of the crew announced 'Trouble', then shortly afterwards reported 'Fire on board'. Upon receiving this message, the Marseilles control centre cleared the aircraft for an immediate descent without restriction. The final transmission from the flight was 'We are going to crash if this continues'.

Around the time of the disaster, the weather conditions in the area consisted of a broken overcast, with a base of about 1,500 ft (500 m), and a visibility of around 3–5 miles (5–10 km). Since the crew had reported seeing land, the jet must have been under the clouds in the final moments of the flight.

The wreckage was later found on the ocean floor, in water approximately 7,500 ft (2,300 m) deep. Some 8–10 tons (9,000–11,000 kg) of debris were recovered over a period of more than two years, and its fragmented condition indicated a violent impact with the sea at a steep angle of descent. There was also evidence of pre-impact fire in the right rear portion of the aircraft's cabin.

It was believed that the blaze had started in the area of the right lavatory and the galley. Although its cause could not be determined, the fire may have been of an electrical origin, possibly due to a malfunction in the water heater (as had happened to another Caravelle that was destroyed while on the ground). Alternatively, it could have resulted from a passenger carelessly tossing a lighted cigarette into the lavatory waste bin. There was no evidence of sabotage with explosives, but the use of an incendiary device could not be completely ruled out.

It was concluded that the aircraft must have been out of control before the crash. The most probable reasons for this were either interference with the flight crew by passengers who had surged into the cockpit to escape the flames, or incapacitation of the pilots due to smoke inhalation, despite the fact that they must have been wearing masks and goggles.

Date: 12 December 1968 (22:02)
Location: Near Caracas, Venezuela
Operator: Pan American World Airways (US)
Aircraft type: Boeing Advanced 707-321B (*N494PA*)

Designated as Flight 217 and en route from New York City, the jet airliner crashed in the Caribbean

A Boeing 707-321C convertible passenger/freight aircraft, basically the same as the Pan American World Airways jetliner that crashed in the Caribbean Sea. *(Boeing)*

The remains of the Ariana Afghan Airlines Boeing 727 and the house it destroyed while attempting to land at London's Gatwick Airport. *(AP Images)*

Sea and exploded while descending for a landing at Maiquetia Airport, serving Caracas, killing all 51 persons aboard (42 passengers and a crew of nine).

The accident took place some 10 miles (15 km) from shore, during the final approach phase that was being conducted under visual flight rules (VFR) procedures. It was dark at the time, but the meteorological conditions were good, with a ceiling of 2,000 ft (*c.* 600 m) and unlimited visibility under the clouds.

The bodies of more than half of the victims and significant portions of the aircraft, including the tail assembly, two engines and the flight data recorder (FDR), were subsequently recovered from the water, which was about 360 ft (110 m) deep at the crash site. Some of the occupants may have been knocked unconscious on impact and drowned.

Although the cause of the accident could not be determined, it was considered possible that the pilots had been deceived by a sensory illusion produced by town lights on upsloping terrain in the vicinity of the airport, which, as studies have shown, can create the impression of being higher than is actually the case and thus result in an undershoot.

Date: 5 January 1969 (*c.* 02:35)
Location: Horley, Surrey, England
Operator: Ariana Afghan Airlines (Afghanistan)
Aircraft type: Boeing 727-113C (*YA-FAR*)

The jetliner, which was operating as Flight 701, had been scheduled to land at London's Gatwick Airport at the end of a service from Kabul, Afghanistan, with four en route stops. In the early morning darkness, the 727 began its approach to Runway 27; the aircraft's autopilot was coupled to the instrument landing system (ILS), but the crew would still be responsible for flap and power settings.

As the approach continued, the flaps were lowered to 15 degrees, which was contrary to the recommended setting of 25 degrees; this seemingly innocuous error would be the first in a chain of events that would ultimately lead to the crash of the 727. The incorrect flap setting meant that the aircraft had less drag than anticipated, so the autopilot had to demand a greater than normal nose-down pitch in order to position the aircraft on the glide slope. This attitude caused its air speed to increase, producing more lift and requiring even further nose-down trim to keep the jetliner on the correct glide path. The increasing application of nose-down elevator pressure eventually outstripped the ability of the system to trim out the load on the horizontal stabiliser, resulting in the illumination of the 'stabiliser out of trim' warning light in the cockpit. Unaware of the incorrect flap setting, the captain interpreted the warning light as indicating a possible malfunction and he disconnected the autopilot.

Following extension of the undercarriage and passage of the outer marker, and as the aircraft was being flown manually, the flaps were repositioned from 15 to 30 degrees without the intermediate setting of 25 degrees being selected first. This uninterrupted 15 degree change in flap position resulted in a marked nose-down pitch, an increase in the rate of descent and a reduction in air speed that was not offset by an increase in power. The aircraft, which was then at an approximate height of 1,200 ft (c. 350 m), immediately dropped below the glide slope, and its rate of descent reached approximately double the norm. The pilots did not appear to notice this deviation, and no corrective action was taken for about 45 seconds. Six seconds after the first officer called out 'We have four hundred feet', the captain pulled back on his control column and applied full power, but by then it was too late.

Just after its nose began to rise, the jetliner brushed treetops approximately 1.5 miles (2.5 km) from the runway threshold, knocked chimney-pots off a house, then struck more trees, the impact with which tore off its starboard wing tip, aileron and outer flap. Touching the ground with its right main gear, the aircraft became airborne again and, after demolishing a second residence, broke apart and burst into flames.

Killed in the accident were 48 of the 62 persons aboard the 727, including five of its eight crew members, and two occupants of the dwelling. The effects of the fire, rather than impact forces, were responsible for nearly all of the fatalities. The three members of the flight crew, the 11 surviving passengers and an infant on the ground, the daughter of the couple who lost their lives, suffered injuries.

The airport weather around this time consisted of freezing fog and a runway visual range (RVR) of only about 300 ft (100 m), which was less than the prescribed minimum. The airline did allow its pilots some discretion on this matter, but regardless of

that, the captain's decision to continue the approach under the circumstances was not itself a causative factor in the crash.

There was no evidence to suggest that the aircraft's flight director had not been working properly. However, had it been inadvertently selected to the wrong mode, it would not have provided tracking information until YA-FAR had intercepted the glide slope again after the deviation, or perhaps not at all.

The pilot's attention was probably directed outside the aircraft at a critical time, in an attempt to obtain visual reference, rather than on the instruments, and for that reason he may not have detected the descent below the correct glide path. The crew did report seeing one light during the approach, but this was established to have been the hazard beacon on Russ Hill. Under the conditions, the light could have appeared higher than was actually the case, creating the false impression of being too high.

Date: 16 March 1969 (c. 12:00)
Location: Maracaibo, Zulia, Venezuela
Operator: Venezolana Internacional de Aviación SA (VIASA) (Venezuela)
Aircraft type: McDonnell Douglas DC-9 Series 32 (YV-C-AVD)

Originating at Caracas, Flight 742 had landed at Grano de Oro Airport, as scheduled, before taking off on the second leg of an international service that was to have terminated at Miami, Florida, US. Seconds after becoming airborne, the jet airliner struck an electric power line at an approximate height of 150 ft (50 m) above the ground, then plunged into the La Trinidad section of the city. All 84 persons aboard the DC-9 (74 passengers and a crew of 10) and 70 others on the ground lost their lives in the disaster, while more than 100 persons were injured, 20 seriously. Numerous vehicles, including a bus, and at least 20 houses were destroyed in the impact and ensuing fires.

The accident was attributed to faulty temperature sensors along the runway and the take-off calculations made from the erroneous information they had provided, which resulted in an overloaded aircraft for the prevailing conditions. This in turn necessitated a longer-than-planned ground run that led to a climb gradient too low to clear the power line (which, interestingly, had been installed over the objections of aeronautical authorities). Although the local weather was good at the time, the ambient air temperature of more than 100 degrees Fahrenheit (37 degrees Celsius) would have affected the performance of the jet. Only two days after the crash, Venezuela's Public Works Minister announced that in order to enhance safety at the airport, the runway would be extended by approximately half a mile (0.8 km).

The DC-9 involved in the accident was on lease to VIASA from another Venezuelan carrier, AVENSA, which also provided the crew for this particular flight.

Date: 20 March 1969 (c. 02:00)
Location: Near Aswan, Egypt
Operator: United Arab Airlines (Egypt)
Aircraft type: Ilyushin Il-18D (*SU-APC*)

The four-engine turboprop, which was on a non-scheduled service from Jiddah, Saudi Arabia, its passengers Muslim pilgrims, crashed and burned while attempting to land at Aswan Airport, killing 100 persons aboard, including the seven members of the crew. All five survivors were seriously injured.

It was dark and the horizontal visibility had been reduced to around 1.2–2 miles (2–3 km) by blowing sand as the aircraft, following two unsuccessful approaches, began its third, using non-directional beacon (NDB) guidance. Banked to the right, the Il-18 hit the left side of the runway approximately 3,675 ft (1,120 m) beyond its threshold. The impact sheared off its starboard wing, and the resulting spillage of some 6,000 lb (2,700 kg) of fuel caused the fire.

The pilot had apparently descended below the minimum safe altitude without having the runway lights clearly in sight. Fatigue due to continuous work without sufficient rest was a contributing factor.

Date: 4 June 1969 (08:42)
Location: Near Salinas Victoria, Nuevo Leon, Mexico
Operator: Compania Mexicana de Aviación SA (Mexico)
Aircraft type: Boeing 727-64 (*XA-SEL*)

Operating as Flight 704, the jet airliner crashed and burned some 20 miles (30 km) north of Monterrey while preparing to land at the city's airport, at the end of a domestic service from Mexico City. All 79 persons aboard (72 passengers and a crew of seven) perished.

According to its flight data recorder (FDR) read-out, the 727 had made a continuous descent in the last 5 minutes before impact at a rate of approximately 1,500 ft (500 m) per minute and an indicated air speed of about 290 mph (465 kmh). During this time, and on passing over the

The wreckage of the Allegheny Airlines DC-9 is spread across an Indiana field and nearby trailer park after the collision with a light aircraft. *(AP Images)*

Monterrey very-high-frequency omnidirectional range (VOR) station, the pilot turned left instead of right, which was required in order to enter the holding pattern, apparently doing so without having established his exact position. Its excessive speed and the wide radius of the turn took the aircraft out of the designated descent area and over rising terrain.

Its undercarriage still retracted, the jet struck a mountain at an approximate elevation of 5,000 ft (1,500 m), or less than 1,000 ft (300 m) below its peak. The airport weather at the time was overcast, with one layer of clouds at roughly 500–1,500 ft (c. 150–500 m) and another between 2,000 and 7,500 ft (c. 600–2,300 m). There was also fog and drizzle in the area.

Date: 9 September 1969 (15:29)
Location: Near London, Indiana, US
First aircraft
Operator: Allegheny Airlines (US)
Type: McDonnell Doulgas DC-9 Series 31 (*N988VJ*)
Second aircraft
Operator: Private
Type: Piper PA-28-140 Cherokee (*N7374J*)

Designated as Flight 853, the DC-9 had begun its descent in preparation for landing at Weir Cook Municipal Airport, serving Indianapolis, a scheduled stop during a domestic service originating at Boston, Massachusetts, with an ultimate destination of St Louis, Missouri. It was operating under instrument flight rules (IFR) and positive control and on a heading of 282 degrees.

Meanwhile, the single-engine Cherokee, which had been leased from the Forth Corporation, was heading towards the south-east, a student pilot at the controls. It was operating under visual flight rules (VFR). Neither crew was aware of the other's presence.

The aircraft collided at an approximate altitude of 3,550 ft (1,080 m) and some 10 miles (15 km) south-east of the state capital. Impact was at an obtuse angle, with the initial contact taking place between the vertical stabiliser of the commercial transport and the left side of the general aviation aeroplane, just forward of its wing. The former's horizontal stabiliser was sheared off, and the jetliner then plunged into a field, hitting the ground in an inverted, nose-down attitude, almost

level laterally, with its undercarriage and flaps retracted. The light aircraft fell in pieces about 1 mile (1.5 km) away. All 82 persons aboard the DC-9 (78 passengers and four crew members) and the sole occupant of the Cherokee perished. Some of the wreckage was scattered over a nearby trailer park, although there were no injuries on the ground. There was also no fire.

The local meteorological conditions at the time consisted of a broken overcast, with a cloud base of approximately 4,000 ft (1,200 m). Even though the collision occurred about 500 ft (150 m) below the overcast, where the visibility was in excess of 15 miles (c. 25 km), the jetliner had been in the clouds until 14 seconds before impact, giving both crews only that amount of time to make visual contact and initiate evasive action. Witnesses observed no such manoeuvres by either aircraft before they hit. It was noted in the investigative report of the US National Transportation Safety Board (NTSB) that the first officer of *N988VJ* was in the best position to see *N7374J*, but would then have been monitoring the altimeter and not watching for conflicting traffic. In addition, the speed of the transport, nearly 300 mph (c. 480 kmh), was slightly high when considering the weather and operational regulations in effect at the time, though still within the prescribed limits.

The NTSB attributed the disaster to deficiencies in the capability of the air traffic control system maintained by the US Federal Aviation Administration (FAA) in a terminal area wherein there was a mix of IFR and VFR traffic flying at different speeds. These deficiencies included the inadequacy of the 'see-and-avoid' concept under the circumstances of the accident; the technical limitations of radar in detecting all aircraft; and the absence of regulations providing a system of separating such mixed traffic in terminal areas.

Neither the Indianapolis control centre nor Indianapolis approach control, which were handling the DC-9, reported observing the Cherokee on their radar equipment before the collision. In the case of the former, this resulted from the inadequate cross-section of the aircraft and the fact that the radar was being operated on lower power at the time to counteract the effects of 'anomalous propagation' associated with a temperature inversion. (This phenomenon consists of the return from objects beyond the normal range of the radar appearing as close-in targets and cluttering the screen.) In the case of the latter, the Cherokee was initially not detected because of the tangential blind speed effect. (This occurs when the relative speed of the target falls below that of the revolving antenna.) Later, the light aeroplane was not seen on approach control radar either due to the effects of the same inversion or simply because the controller's attention had been diverted by other duties, which precluded his monitoring of the radarscope.

The following year the FAA implemented a terminal control system around major US airports, requiring positive control of all aircraft flying within. Climb and descent corridors for higher-speed IFR traffic were established at numerous other less-congested airports.

Date: 20 September 1969 (*c.* 16:00)
Location: Near Hoi An, (South) Vietnam
First aircraft
Operator: Air Vietnam (South Vietnam)
Type: Douglas DC-4 (*XV-NUG*)
Second aircraft
Operator: US Air Force
Type: McDonnell F-4E Phantom II (*67-393*)

Both aircraft were approaching to land at Da Nang Air Base, the commercial transport at the end of a scheduled domestic service that had originated at Saigon (now Ho Chi Minh City), and the jet fighter returning from a combat mission, when they collided at a height of about 300 ft (100 m). The DC-4 then crashed, killing all but two of the 77 persons aboard, including the entire crew of six, plus two others on the ground. Both surviving passengers were injured. The Phantom's navigator also suffered minor injuries when he ejected and parachuted to earth, while the pilot managed to land the damaged aircraft safely.

Although it was supposed to use Runway 17-Left, *XV-NUG* had strayed into the path of *67-393* as the latter approached for a landing on the adjacent 17-Right. In the resulting collision, the starboard horizontal stabiliser of the DC-4 was torn off. The crew retracted the undercarriage and attempted a go-around, but the aircraft plummeted into a field and exploded.

A transcript of air/ground radio transmissions revealed that the pilot of the DC-4 must have either misconstrued or, on account of overlapping communications, did not completely hear the instructions sent from the control tower to the F-4, 'You are cleared to land on 17-Right', The fact that he believed the message to be intended for him was indicated by his immediate response, 'Roger, 17-Right.' The local weather at the time, which consisted of a high overcast, scattered clouds at lower altitudes and a visibility of approximately 10 miles (15 km), was apparently not a factor in the accident.

Date: 20 November 1969 (*c.* 08:30)
Location: Near Lagos, Nigeria
Operator: Nigeria Airways
Aircraft type: BAC VC-10 (*5N-ABD*)

Operating as Flight 925, the jet airliner crashed and burned some 8 miles (13 km) north of Ikeja Airport, itself located some 10 miles (15 km) north-north-west of and serving Lagos, where it was to have landed at the end of a service from London, with en route stops at Rome, Italy, and Kano, Nigeria. All 87 persons aboard (76 passengers and 11 crew members) were killed.

The disaster occurred during a straight-in very-high-frequency omnidirectional range (VOR) instrument procedure approach to Runway 19. Its undercarriage down and flaps set at 35 degrees, the VC-10 initially hit trees, and after rolling to the left slammed to earth in a pronounced nose-up, port wing-down attitude. Some of the victims apparently survived the crash but succumbed to the effects of the post-impact fire. Though clear at the airport, the weather in the area of the accident was characterised by a layer of fog that extended from treetop level to at least 1,000 ft (300 m), possibly above 2,000 ft (600 m).

There was no evidence of any pre-impact mechanical failure or defect in the aircraft. Although the cause could not be determined with certainty, the crash was believed to have resulted from a lack of altitude awareness on the part of the pilot while in the final approach phase, which led to a descent below a safe height. During this time, the other three members of the flight crew were probably involved in their normal pre-landing checks. Meanwhile, the captain may not have been properly monitoring his instruments while trying to make visual contact with the ground.

G-ARVA, later re-registered as 5N-ABD, was the Nigeria Airways VC-10 that crashed during an attempted landing at Lagos airport. *(Rod Simpson)*

Fatigue may have contributed to the suspected human error.

Date: 3 December 1969 (*c.* 19:10)
Location: Near Caracas, Venezuela
Operator: Air France
Aircraft type: Boeing Advanced 707-328B (*F-BHSZ*)

Designated as Flight 212, the jet airliner crashed in the Caribbean Sea approximately 5 miles (10 km) from shore, and all 62 persons aboard (51 passengers, including a relief crew of 10, and 11 regular crew members) perished.

The disaster occurred in darkness about 3 minutes after *F-BHSZ* had taken off from Maiquetia Airport, serving Caracas, bound for Guadeloupe, one segment of an international service originating at Santiago, Chile, with an ultimate destination of Paris. Climbing to an approximate height of 3,000 ft (1,000 m), its nose suddenly dropped, and the 707 then plummeted into water some 150 ft (50 m) deep. An examination of recovered debris disclosed no evidence of pre-impact fire or explosion.

As an indication of a major technical failure, the pilot had radioed that he was losing altitude and could not control the aircraft before impact. However, the cause of the crash remains a mystery.

Date: 8 December 1969 (20:46)
Location: Near Keratea, Attiki, Greece
Operator: Olympic Airways (Greece)
Aircraft type: Douglas DC-6B (*SX-DAE*)

All 90 persons aboard (85 passengers and a crew of five) perished when the aircraft crashed some 25 miles (40 km) south-east of Athens while preparing to land at the airport serving the capital city, at the end of a scheduled service from Canea, on the Greek island of Crete.

Its undercarriage still retracted, the DC-6B had struck Mt Pan at an approximate elevation of 2,000 ft (600 m), bursting into flames on impact. The accident occurred in darkness, and thunderstorm activity had been reported in the area, accompanied by rain and high winds. Though adverse, the meteorological conditions were not considered dangerous.

According to the Accidents Investigation Bureau of Greece, the flight crew of *SX-DAE* had deviated from the proper track and had also descended below the minimum safety altitude during the initial phase of the instrument landing system (ILS) approach.

THE 1970S

The Boeing 747 introduced air travellers to the 'jumbo jet' era in 1970. This massive transport was joined in succession by the McDonnell Douglas DC-10, the Lockheed L-1011 TriStar and, a while later, the Airbus family of jetliners. The size of the aircraft actually created the problem of over-capacity in the airline industry, literally offering more seats than there were passengers to fill them.

Wide-bodied jets brought about unparalleled standards of safety and performance. The first fatal 747 crash would not occur until nearly five years and more than 2 million flying hours into its service life. The L-1011 had the unfortunate distinction of being the first of the new generation of airliners to be involved in a fatal accident. Subsequently, however, it would amass an equally impressive record of safety.

The consequences of what everyone had feared the most – the non-survivable crash of a fully loaded wide-bodied transport – were fully realised in March 1974, when a Turkish Airlines DC-10 crashed near Paris with a loss of 346 lives, a death toll that was nearly double that of the worst previous aviation disaster. The tragedy also brought to light a serious design flaw in the aircraft's cargo door, proving that even the most sophisticated and up-to-date technology is fallible. Five years later in 1979 another catastrophic DC-10 accident in the United States led to the temporary grounding of the giant jet. Again a weakness in design proved to be an underlying factor.

The worst possible scenario took place in the spring of 1977, when two 747s collided inexplicably on a fog-cloaked airport runway in the Canary Islands. Nearly 600 persons were killed in the disaster.

Date: 6 February 1970 (time unknown)
Location: Near Samarkand, Uzbek SSR, USSR
Operator: Aeroflot (USSR)
Aircraft type: Ilyushin Il-18 (*SSSR-75798*)

Operating on a scheduled domestic service from Tashkent, the four-engine turboprop airliner crashed and burned on a cloud-obscured mountain, in daylight hours and at an approximate elevation of 5,000 ft (1,500 m), as it was approaching to land at the Samarkand airport. Bad weather prevented searchers from locating the wreckage until three days later, after which the few who survived the impact had frozen to death, leaving no survivors among the 92 persons aboard (85 passengers and a crew of seven).

The air traffic controller had misidentified the aircraft's location, which placed the flight some 20 miles (30 km) from the airport, or about 5 miles (10 km) closer than its actual position. The resulting incorrect information provided to the crew, combined with their own violation of the approved approach pattern, led to a premature descent below the obstructing terrain.

Date: 15 February 1970 (*c.* 18:30)
Location: Near Santo Domingo, Dominican Republic
Operator: Compania Dominicana de Aviación C por A (Dominican Republic)
Aircraft type: McDonnell Douglas DC-9 Series 32 (*HI-177*)

The jet airliner plunged into the Caribbean Sea approximately 2 miles (3 km) offshore, and all 102 persons aboard (97 passengers and five crew members) perished.

Only about 2 minutes after the DC-9 had taken off from the city's international airport, on a scheduled service to San Juan, Puerto Rico, a crewman reported a loss of power in one of its two engines and that the flight was turning back. The aircraft descended rapidly after initiating a right turn and finally crashed some 3 miles (5 km) from the airport. The disaster occurred in twilight conditions, but the weather was excellent.

Some debris and the remains of two dozen victims were found, but most of the wreckage, including the power plants, instruments and the flight data recorder (FDR), was lost in about 1,000 ft (300 m) of water and could not be recovered for examination. There was no trace of fire on any of the recovered parts.

Date: 3 July 1970 (19:05)
Location: Near Arbucies, Girona, Spain
Operator: Dan-Air Services Ltd (UK)
Aircraft type: de Havilland Comet 4 (*G-APDN*)

All 112 persons aboard (105 passengers and a crew of seven) perished when the jet airliner crashed in the Sierra de Montseny region some 30 miles (50 km) north-east of Barcelona and approximately 40 miles (65 km) from the city's airport, where it was to have landed at the end of a charter service from Manchester, England.

Cleanly configured, the Comet was on an approximate heading of 140 degrees and in a slight descent when it struck the wooded slope of Les Agudes Peak, at an elevation of about 4,000 ft (1,200 m), exploding in flames on impact. At the time of the crash its true air speed was in excess of 250 mph (400 kmh). The accident occurred in daylight, but the mountains were obscured by a mass of stratus and stratocumulus clouds, with a base of roughly 2,500–3,000 ft (750–1,000 m), which reduced visibility to nil.

Due to heavy traffic in the vicinity of Paris, the jet was intentionally diverted from the route laid down in its flight plan, but it subsequently began to deviate to the left of the assigned airway. The displacement of the flight track could have resulted from a defect in the aircraft's equipment. Significantly, its position could only have been determined by the intersection of radials following passage of the Toulouse very-high-frequency omnidirectional range (VOR) station, in France. There was no evidence of any aberrations in the Barcelona VOR.

The Spanish approach controller did not realise that the Comet was flying some 15 miles (25 km) to the east and not above the Berga reporting point. This, coupled with an incorrect estimated time of arrival at the Sabadell non-directional beacon (NDB), made it difficult for him to identify the radar target of the airliner. In an attempt to facilitate identification, he instructed it to turn on to the south-easterly heading that was continued until impact.

About 3 minutes before it crashed, the jet reported passing the Sabadell NDB, when in fact it was still 32 miles (52 km) from that position. By

The flight track and times (given in GMT) of the Dan-Air Comet 4, including the turn on to the course that ended in the crash on a Spanish mountainside.
(Spanish Air Ministry)

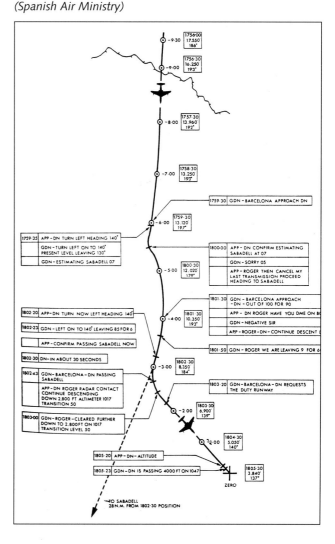

An Air Canada DC-8 Super 63, identical to the aircraft that crashed after a baulked landing at Toronto International Airport. *(Programmed Communications Ltd)*

coincidence, the controller had observed on his radar screen the echo of another aircraft (whose speed was similar to that expected from a Comet) over the beacon at the same time, which he misidentified as *G-APDN*. He then cleared the transport for descent to 2,800 ft (*c.* 850 m), the minimum altitude where it was believed to have been, but not at its actual location.

The installation of a secondary radar system at Barcelona after this disaster would assure proper identification of an aircraft equipped with a transponder, as was the Comet. The investigative report on the accident also noted the importance of using all navigational aids, and recommended that radio-navigational charts illustrate the heights of significant points along designated routes.

Date: 5 July 1970 (08:09)
Location: Near Malton, Ontario, Canada
Operator: Air Canada
Aircraft type: McDonnell Douglas DC-8 Super 63 (*CF-TIW*)

Flight 621, which had taken off earlier on this Sunday morning from Montreal, Quebec, was cleared to land on Runway 32 at Toronto International Airport, a scheduled stop during a service with an ultimate destination of Los Angeles,

California, US. The airport weather at the time was ideal, with scattered clouds at 3,500 ft (*c.* 1,050 m) and a visibility of 20 miles (*c.* 30 km).

As transcribed on the cockpit voice recorder (CVR) tape, Captain Peter Hamilton and First Officer Donald Rowland omitted the 'spoilers armed' item in their pre-landing checks. They agreed that the lift-reduction devices would be armed during the flare, allowing for their automatic extension when the wheels of the aircraft made contact with the pavement. However, as the DC-8 passed over the runway threshold at an approximate height of 60 ft (20 m), the co-pilot committed an error that would prove fatal. When authorised by the pilot to arm the ground spoilers, which would involve lifting the appropriate lever on the control console, he instead pulled it to the rear, resulting in their immediate deployment. The captain commanded 'No, no, no!' and the first officer, realising his mistake, responded with 'Sorry. Oh, sorry, Pete'.

Action by the pilot, who applied full power to all four engines and rotated the aircraft's nose upward to counter the high rate of descent that had developed, was unsuccessful in preventing the exceptionally hard landing that resulted from the spoiler extension. The impact on the main undercarriage, after which the tail skid hit the ground, generated forces that caused the separation of the No. 4 engine pod and pylon assembly and also punctured the bottom of the No. 4 alternate fuel tank. Escaping fuel then ignited, possibly after coming in contact with wiring severed when the power plant broke off.

On the ground for only a fraction of a second, the DC-8 then climbed away, the captain radioing his intention to circle the airport and land again on the same runway. The aircraft's undercarriage, which had apparently not been badly damaged, was raised for the go-around, and its flaps brought up to 20 degrees; the spoilers were by then fully retracted.

Only about 3 minutes after the hard landing *CF-TIW* was rocked by three explosions, the second of which ripped free the No. 3 engine pod and pylon, the last one blasting away a large segment of the right outer wing. Unable to sustain flight, the jet airliner plunged from an approximate height of 3,000 ft (1,000 m) into a field some 5 miles (10 km) north of the airport and at an indicated air speed in excess of 250 mph (400 kmh), disintegrating in a ball of fire on impact. All 109 persons aboard (100 passengers and nine crew members) perished.

It might be difficult to understand how such an innocuous mistake as the one made by the first officer could have such catastrophic consequences, but in its investigative report a board of inquiry blamed the disaster as much on faulty design as human error. It argued that while a mechanism using one handle to perform completely different tasks might be acceptable for a secondary system, such as heating or ventilation, it was not appropriate for one that operated something as vital as the spoilers. At the very least, it ruled, the activating lever should have been fitted with some kind of guard or gate. Preferably the system would have been made so as to prevent deployment while the aircraft was in the air.

Furthermore, the inquiry found that the instruction manuals provided by the manufacturer contained information that was misleading, incomplete and even inaccurate, stating in fact that a mechanism built into the system would prevent

The shattered remains of the Air Canada Super DC-8 are strewn across the Canadian countryside following the disaster that claimed 109 lives. *(CORBIS)*

such an air-flight spoiler extension. As a result, even the Air Canada training staff did not realise that such inadvertent deployment as that which happened to *CF-TIW* was possible, which meant that the airline's pilots were not being made aware of this potential threat to safety.

These factors, coupled with the failure of the Canadian Ministry of Transport to note differences between the DC-8 operating manuals used by Air Canada and the nation's other carriers, and the acceptance by both the government agency and the company of an aircraft employing a spoiler system that the board had labelled as defective, were considered as contributory to the crash. The board also criticised the design of the pod/pylon structure and what it described as the failure of the manufacturer to ensure the integrity of the fuel and electrical systems built into the DC-8.

In using their own method of activating the spoilers, the crew of Flight 621 were not adhering to the prescribed Air Canada procedures, which dictated that the system be armed for automatic deployment at an altitude of 1,000 ft (*c.* 300 m). Interestingly, on the day of the accident the pilots did not even use the technique they had adopted when flying together previously, i.e. to extend manually the spoilers after touchdown.

Had the aircraft continued the landing after the error by the first officer, this would probably have been only a minor incident, with no casualties; but the captain was not faulted for his decision to execute the overshoot procedure. The board noted that in trying to prevent or lessen the impact with the runway, he had placed the jet in a position normally used for such a manoeuvre, and under the circumstances continuing the take-off was the logical thing to do. Furthermore, there was no evidence that the crew had realised the extent of the damage sustained by the DC-8 until it was too late.

As a result of this disaster, the US Federal Aviation Administration (FAA) issued an air-worthiness directive (AD) requiring placard warnings against in-flight deployment of ground spoilers by DC-8 operators. Following a non-fatal accident some three years after the Air Canada crash, the FAA issued another AD requiring that all aircraft of the type be fitted with spoiler locking mechanisms to prevent such an occurrence.

Date: 9 August 1970 (*c.* 15:00)
Location: Near Cuzco, Peru
Operator: Lineas Aereas Nacionales SA (LANSA) (Peru)
Aircraft type: Lockheed 188A Electra (*OB-R-939*)

The four-engine turboprop crashed shortly after its departure from the city's airport, on a scheduled domestic service to Lima, killing 99 persons aboard, including eight members of the crew, plus two others on the ground. Only the first officer, who was seriously injured, survived the disaster.

Its No. 3 power plant having failed during take-off, the Electra continued climbing straight ahead following a ground run that was nearly half a mile (0.8 km) longer than normal. The flaps were then retracted and a left turn commenced at an approximate height of 300 ft (100 m) above the ground, which was probably an attempt to return to its departure point. Due to the limited space available, a steep bank was required, but during the turn the airliner slammed into a hill about 5 miles (10 km) south of the airport and exploded. Reportedly, it was foggy in the area of the crash at the time.

Besides the mechanical malfunction, the accident was attributed to a procedural error on the part of the captain. In view of an apparent maintenance deficiency that may have been a factor in the power plant failure, the Peruvian government fined LANSA, and about a month after the accident suspended its operations pending a review of the carrier's safety practices.

Date: 14 November 1970 (19:35)
Location: Near Huntington, West Virginia, US
Operator: Southern Airways (US)
Aircraft type: McDonnell Douglas DC-9 Series 31 (*N97S*)

Tragedy struck the Marshall University football team as it was returning home from an interstate game at Greenville, North Carolina, when the chartered jetliner, carrying 36 players, five coaches, the team trainer, boosters and a crew of five, crashed west of Tri-State Airport, where it was to have landed. All 75 persons aboard were killed.

The aircraft had been cleared for a non-precision approach to Runway 11, using localiser guidance, before the accident occurred in evening darkness and during a light rain, with fog, smoke, scattered clouds at 300 ft (100 m), a broken overcast at 500 ft (c. 150 m), solid coverage at 1,000 ft (c. 300 m), and a visibility of 5 miles (10 km). Its undercarriage down and flaps fully extended, the DC-9 hit trees, then slammed into a hill about 1 mile (1.5 km) from the threshold of the runway and some 280 ft (85 m) to the right of its extended centreline, exploded and burned.

The jetliner had continued more than 300 ft (100 m) below the minimum descent altitude (MDA) before the flight crew initiated a missed approach procedure. The reason for this could not be determined, although the two most likely explanations were an error in the aircraft's static system that caused the barometric altimeters to indicate a reading higher than its actual altitude and the vertical speed indicators to show a decrease in the rate of descent, or reliance by the crew on the radio altimeters as a primary reference for determining height.

The first hypothesis was supported by the read-out from the flight data recorder (FDR), which uses a separate static system, showing a higher-than-normal rate of descent, and by analysing the cockpit voice recorder (CVR) tape, showing that all but one of the first officer's altitude call-outs were approximately 200 ft (60 m) above the actual height of the aircraft. One weakness to this theory was that an error in the static system should have caused a similar discrepancy in the air speed indicators, which probably would have been noticed by the crew, but there was no evidence of such an erroneous indication.

Regarding the second hypothesis, the call-outs by the co-pilot, when correlated with the FDR data, were similar to those that would be expected if the radio altimeter were being used. But the US National Transportation Safety Board (NTSB) expressed doubt that an experienced crew would rely only upon the radio altimeter when the instrument is not intended for use, and is not reliable, over the kind of uneven terrain found under the approach path to Tri-State Airport. Sound operating procedures dictate that the captain also refer to his barometric altimeter, and the disparity between that and the reading of either his radio altimeter or that of the first officer, reflected in the call-outs, would have been detected.

It was determined that the co-pilot did not make all of the required call-outs, including 500 ft above airport elevation, 100 ft above minimum altitude and the decision height, and the captain, who had been using the autopilot throughout the approach, did not start levelling off until after the DC-9 had descended through what he thought was the MDA. The effects of these deviations on the subsequent accident were difficult to assess.

The crew apparently observed the glow from the lights of a refinery, and this, coupled with the fact that the pilot knew he was approaching the bottom layer of the overcast, could have induced him to continue below the decision height. The NTSB concluded, however, that the crew never made visual contact with any part of the airport and were not aware that the aircraft had descended below the MDA.

Although the airport did have an instrument landing system (ILS) localiser, no glide slope had been included because the terrain was not suitable to provide an adequate reflecting surface for the antenna. A non-standard glide slope that might have prevented this accident was later installed.

One of the recommendations made by the NTSB in its report on the crash was for the development of specific crew procedures for non-precision approaches as in the case of those that utilise the ILS.

Date: 23 May 1971 (c. 20:00)
Location: Near Rijeka, Yugoslavia
Operator: Aviogenex (Yugoslavia)
Aircraft type: Tupolev Tu-134A (YU-AHZ)

The jet airliner was on a charter service from London and carrying mostly British tourists when it crashed on landing at Rijeka Airport. Among the 83 persons aboard, only one passenger and the four members of the flight crew survived, all of whom escaped serious injury. The 78 persons killed included the aircraft's three stewardesses.

Dusk had set in and it was heavily overcast, with thunderstorm activity in the area and the cloud level down to about 2,000 ft (600 m), as the twin-engine jet made its approach to Runway 14, using instrument landing system (ILS) guidance. At a point some 2.5 miles (4 km) from the runway threshold and at an approximate height of 1,000 ft (300 m) above the ground, the aircraft entered an area of heavy rain. It also encountered turbulence and, less than a minute before touchdown, was carried upward and rolled to the right. This disturbance, which could be explained by a moderate gust, a change of wind velocity and by the aircraft coming out of the zone of heavy rain, caused a deviation from the correct flight path.

Unable to return to the ILS, the crew attempted to regain alignment with the runway visually, and succeeded in doing so. Still above the glide slope, though, the pilots lowered the nose of the Tu-134 and reduced power. Subsequently there was a decrease in air speed and a steepening in the angle of descent. In the resulting hard landing, which was at a speed of around 150 mph (250 kmh), the extended main gear bore the brunt of the initial impact, and the port wing broke just inside the undercarriage leg. The aircraft then turned over and slid, inverted, some 2,300 ft (700 m) down the runway, bursting into flames before coming to a stop. Its fuselage rapidly filled with carbon monoxide, preventing rescuers from saving any more of the occupants, even though all must have survived the actual crash.

The improper handling of the flight and power plant controls that preceded the accident could be attributed to the false perceptions of the crew due to the intense rain, which caused a refraction of light. This optical illusion gave the pilots the impression of being closer to the runway and higher above the ground than was actually the case.

Date: 6 June 1971 (*c.* 18:10)
Location: Near Duarte, California, US
First aircraft
Operator: Hughes Air West (US)
Type: McDonnell Douglas DC-9 Series 31 (*N9345*)
Second aircraft
Operator: US Marine Corps
Type: McDonnell F-4B Phantom II (*151458*)

Designated as Flight 706, the DC-9 departed from Los Angeles International Airport bound for Salt Lake City, Utah, its first stop during a domestic service with an ultimate destination of Seattle, Washington. The jet airliner was operating under instrument flight rules (IFR) and positive control.

Less than 10 minutes after take-off, and while climbing on a north-easterly heading to its assigned altitude, the transport collided with the southbound jet fighter, which was en route to the El Toro Marine Air Station, in Southern California. Colliding almost at right-angles, the vertical stabiliser of the F-4B passed through the lower left cockpit area of the DC-9, and its right wing passed through the passenger cabin.

The collision occurred at an approximate height of 15,000 ft (5,000 m) and some 20 miles (30 km) north-east of downtown Los Angeles, and both aircraft then plummeted into the San Gabriel Mountains. The transport erupted into flames when it crashed in Fish Canyon, and the fighter, which had caught fire in flight, fell less than 1 mile (1.5 km) away. All 49 persons aboard the airliner (44 passengers and a crew of five) and the pilot of the military jet, who was apparently unable to eject because the front canopy would not jettison, perished.

The fighter's radar intercept officer (RIO) parachuted to safety and was the sole survivor of the disaster.

The US National Transportation Safety Board (NTSB) blamed the collision on the failure of both crews to see and avoid each other's aircraft, but recognised that their ability to detect one another, assess the situation and initiate evasive action was

The charred remains of the Hughes Air West DC-9 lie in a canyon after the collision with a US Marine Corps jet fighter. *(AP Images)*

A Toa Domestic Airlines YS-11A-200, in the same livery as the aircraft that crashed in northern Japan. *(K. Hoashi/Ikaros/Uniphoto Press International)*

only marginal. Contributing to the accident were a high closure rate, calculated to have been almost 750 mph (*c.* 1,200 kmh), and the fact that the Marine jet had entered a busy air corridor under visual flight rules (VFR) while not in contact with the regional air traffic control centre.

Because of an oxygen system leak, the Phantom was being flown below its normal cruising altitude, and as a result of an inoperative transponder, reduced detectability due to design and configuration, and a low-level temperature inversion in the area, the fighter's target did not show up well enough on the radarscope to be noticed by a controller otherwise unaware of its presence. Furthermore, its pilot did not request air traffic control assistance, which could have prevented the disaster.

The F-4 did have its own air-to-air radar system, but, besides being in a degraded state, it was in a mapping rather than a search mode, at the request of the pilot. As a result no airborne targets were observed, including the DC-9. Under the circumstances, the pilot should have used the RIO to help maintain a lookout for other air traffic. Actually, the latter did see the airliner after turning away from his radarscope, and he shouted to the pilot, who had already initiated a left roll. The air carrier crew may not have even seen the fighter, or

saw it when it was too late to take evasive action. (The latter's failure was probably partly attributable to a lack of recurrent training in lookout and scanning techniques and reliance on ground controllers to provide traffic separation.)

Visibility was generally good in the vicinity at the time, although a layer of haze in the background would have made the DC-9 less conspicuous to the Phantom crew. Cockpit visibility and limitations of human eyesight would further have hampered the 'see-and-avoid' principle. Additionally, both aircraft were on an essentially constant bearing with respect to one another, and would thus have remained almost stationary from each other's perspective.

Following this accident, most military flights began to switch to IFR procedures, and the NTSB recommended to the US Department of Defense that air intercept radar on such aircraft as the F-4 also be used for collision avoidance.

Date: 3 July 1971 (*c.* 18:10)
Location: Hokkaido, Japan
Operator: Toa Domestic Airlines (Japan)
Aircraft type: NAMC YS-11A-227 (*JA8764*)

All 68 persons aboard (64 passengers and four crew members) were killed when the twin-engine turboprop, on a domestic intra-island service from Sapporo to Hakodate, crashed near its destination.

In the last radio transmission from Flight 63, the pilot reported approaching the Hakodate non-directional beacon (NDB). Its undercarriage retracted and flaps partially extended, the aircraft was flying on an east-north-easterly heading with its right wing slightly low when it struck a mountain ridge at an approximate elevation of 3,000 ft (1,000 m), some 10 miles (15 km) north-north-west of the city's airport. Hampered by bad weather, searchers were not able to locate the wreckage until the following day. Although a small fire did erupt in the area of the left power plant, there was no major post-impact blaze.

The meteorological conditions at the airport around the time of the accident were near the minima for an automatic direction finder (ADF) instrument procedure landing. Just before the crash, the YS-11 was believed to have been in the midst of an overcast, with possible rain and turbulence within the clouds. The velocity of the wind in the area could have been high and the direction changeable because of the terrain.

Presumably the pilot had mistaken his position as being over the NDB, when in fact the aircraft was about 5 miles (10 km) north of the navigational aid, which he attempted to circle. A strong south-westerly wind also caused it to drift northward. The expected passage of the beacon was about 2 minutes early, but the crew must not have detected the error, apparently due to an incorrect ADF indication, with the instrument having been affected by the atmospheric conditions. Though revised by 1 minute, the flight plan that had been prepared by the airline was not modified to compensate for wind, temperature and altitude factors.

A number of safety recommendations were made in the investigative report on this accident, including the installation of distance-measuring equipment (DME), an instrument landing system (ILS) and a very-high-frequency omnidirectional range (VOR) station at Hakodate, and the establishment of a long-range radar facility that in this case would have covered the entire route of the flight. Some of these proposals were incorporated into an extensive programme designed to improve Japan's airport/airway system, which was initiated even before the crash of Flight 63.

Date: 25 July 1971 (time unknown)
Location: Near Irkutsk, Russian Soviet Federative Socialist Republic, USSR
Operator: Aeroflot (USSR)
Aircraft type: Tupolev Tu-104B (*SSSR-42405*)

The jet airliner crashed as it was attempting to land at the Irkutsk airport, an en route stop during a scheduled domestic service from Novosibirsk to Vladivostok, killing 97 persons aboard. Four of its eight crew members and 25 passengers survived. The accident occurred at night and in instrument meteorological conditions.

During the approach and when over the outer marker beacon, the ground controller advised that the aircraft was to the left of the runway axis. The subsequent corrective action was excessive, however, necessitating another turn in the opposite direction. As a result of the second manoeuvre, the Tu-104 was banked slightly to the left when it touched down on its main undercarriage, the port gear first followed by the starboard, some 500 ft (150 m) short of the runway threshold. The final approach had been conducted some 15–20 mph (25–35 kmh) below the required speed, but with a high descent rate, and in the hard undershot landing the aircraft's left wing separated from the fuselage. The twin-engine jet then rolled to the left, turned over and burst into flames.

Although no flight data recorder (FDR) information was available to the investigative commission, and the exact cause remained unidentified, the accident probably resulted from a combination of faulty piloting technique and an incorrect altimeter indication that was too high.

Date: 30 July 1971 (*c.* 14:00)
Location: Near Morioka, Iwate, Japan
First aircraft
Operator: All Nippon Airways (Japan)
Type: Boeing 727-281 (*JA8329*)
Second aircraft
Operator: Japan Air Self-Defence Force (JASDF)
Type: North American F-86F Sabre (*92-7932*)

Operating as Flight 58, the jetliner had taken off earlier from Chitose Airport, located on Hokkaido and serving Sapporo, on a domestic service to Tokyo. Cruising along a prescribed airway at a height of 28,000 ft (*c.* 8,500 m) and on an approximate heading of 190 degrees, the transport collided with the jet fighter over the village of Shizukuishi, some 275 miles (440 km) north of the capital city. Both aircraft then crashed, and all 162 persons aboard the 727 (155 passengers and a crew of seven) perished. Additionally, an elderly woman on the ground was reportedly injured when a piece of wreckage fell through the roof of a house.

A 22-year-old student pilot was at the controls of the fighter, accompanied by his instructor in another F-86. The former had not been briefed on either the altitude at which they would be flying or the route they would take.

Shortly before the accident, the instructor began a left turn, with the trainee following about 3,000 ft (1,000 m) below his aircraft; the student was concentrating on maintaining his position with the flight leader, rather than watching out for air traffic. Seeing the 727, the instructor immediately ordered him to take evasive action, and the trainee, who saw the jetliner approximately 2 seconds before impact, did so, but too late to prevent the disaster. Though the airline crew may have observed the fighter a few seconds before the collision, there was no evidence of an avoidance manoeuvre.

When they hit, the indicated air speed of the transport was approximately 560 mph (900 kmh), and that of the military jet around 520 mph (840 kmh), with the former in level flight and the latter still banked to the left. Initial contact was at the leading edge of the 727's left horizontal stabiliser and the trailing edge of the Sabre's right wing. The fighter then nosed over and struck, with the bottom of its front fuselage section, the upper left-hand side of the jetliner's vertical stabiliser. The fighter's right wing was torn off and the horizontal tail assembly of the 727 damaged. Both aircraft became uncontrollable and plummeted to earth in pieces, scattering wreckage over a wide area.

The canopy of the Sabre had come off, and although he was unable to reach the ejection lever, the pilot managed to climb out of the cockpit and abandon the aircraft as it spiralled down. He landed safely by parachute in a rice paddy.

Despite the fact that the formation and turn training required substantial airspace, the military exercise was being conducted in a rather small area, at a considerable height and under visual flight rules (VFR) procedures, making it impossible

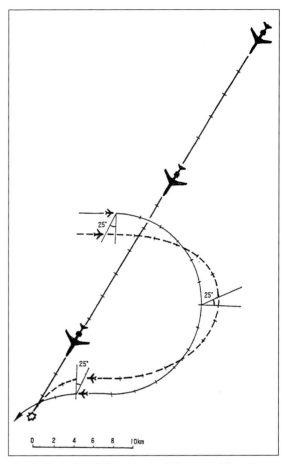

The flight paths of the F-86 jet fighters and the All Nippon Airways Boeing 727 in the final moments before the mid-air crash. (Japanese Ministry of Transport/Ikaros/Uniphoto Press International)

to determine an exact position. As a result, the instructor did not realise that he and his student had strayed out of the designated training area and into the airway. The weather was apparently not a factor in the accident, with good visibility and scattered clouds at lower altitudes.

The two airmen were later convicted of involuntary manslaughter and sentenced to prison, and the disaster also led to a shake-up within the JASDF, with its Director General accepting responsibility and submitting his resignation.

Among the safety recommendations made in the investigative report on the collision were the expansion of radar control zones, the prohibition of aircraft that constantly change their heading and/or height from entering these areas, and the establishment of specific regions for military training flights. A five-year plan launched by the government of Japan to modernise the nation's air traffic control system, which had begun even before this accident, was consequently accelerated. Additionally, most JASDF training was moved out over the sea, away from commercial airways.

Date: 4 September 1971 (*c.* 12:15)
Location: Near Juneau, Alaska, US
Operator: Alaska Airlines (US)
Aircraft type: Boeing 727-193 (*N2969G*)

Alaska is without a doubt the most air-minded of all the American states. It also has some of the most treacherous flying conditions anywhere, with terrain and weather that can place a heavy demand on both pilots and equipment – during the year 1971, the state actually experienced more fatalities in air crashes than in road traffic accidents, the primary reason for this being the disaster that befell Flight 1866.

Although a portion of the trip would take place over foreign territory, this was still classified as a domestic service, originating at Anchorage, Alaska, with an ultimate destination of Seattle, Washington. One of the four scheduled stops along the way was at the Alaskan state capital.

Shortly before noon, the 727 was reported in a holding pattern, and it completed the circuit once before receiving clearance for a straight-in approach to land on Runway 08 at Juneau Municipal Airport, using localiser directional aid procedures. The airport control tower relayed the latest meteorological information, but there was no further communication with the flight.

The jetliner crashed in the Chilkat Mountain Range some 20 miles (30 km) west of the airport, and all 111 persons aboard (104 passengers and seven crew members) perished. Configured with its undercarriage extended and flaps retracted, the aircraft struck the eastern side of a canyon at an approximate elevation of 2,500 ft (750 m) and disintegrated. At the moment of impact, its indicated air speed was about 230 mph (370 kmh) and its heading approximately 70 degrees. There was evidence of scattered, independent fires throughout the wreckage area.

The accident apparently resulted from the display of misleading navigational information that made the crew believe that the flight had progressed further along the localiser course than was actually the case, which resulted in a premature descent below the obstructing terrain. This theory was borne out through the correlation of comments transcribed on the cockpit voice recorder (CVR) tape with the flight data recorder (FDR) read-out – at one point the 727 was about 10 miles (15 km) west of its reported position. Similar erroneous indi-

Little remains of the Alaska Airlines Boeing 727 that slammed into the mountain, with a loss of 111 lives.
(*AP Images*)

cations were evident in subsequent intracockpit conversation. The origin or nature of the information could not be determined.

There was no evidence of a malfunction in the Doppler very-high-frequency omnidirectional range (VOR) system, but this could not be ruled out completely. Nor were there indications of any problems with the 727's navigational equipment, although the degree of destruction could have masked such a technical failure. Spurious signals affecting the VOR reception were discounted, and incompatibility between the aircraft's navigational receivers and the system could not be substantiated.

A possible operational factor leading to the crash was the presence of a twin-engine Piper Apache that had accepted an improper clearance and was lost in the area. Compounding its plight were communications difficulties, and as a result the regional air traffic control centre asked the jetliner to relay messages between it and the general aviation aircraft. Besides adding to the workload of the airline crew and maybe even affecting their coordination, the light aeroplane represented a potential conflict with the 727. From his comments recorded by the CVR, the captain of Flight 1866 seemed rather irritated about the situation. This distraction could have been significant had he tuned in the Juneau localiser in preparation for holding before the three-way conversation, then in oversight selected one of the radials emanating from the Sisters Island VOR, which was being used as a fix to determine the progress of the aircraft along the course, without changing the frequency to that of the navigational station. The resulting inconsistent instrument indications would have been transient in nature and perhaps gone unnoticed by the crew.

The only apparent deviation in the crew's routine was the absence of aural identification procedures when tuning in the different navigational facilities (this consists of increasing the volume again until the 'navaid' code can be heard). The crew did not use either of the two available non-directional beacon (NDB) navigational aids that could have helped determine the progress of the flight, although this was not part of the prescribed procedure.

The weather in the vicinity of the accident site at the time was characterised by multiple layers of cloud with bases between 1,000 and 1,500 ft (c. 300–500 m), which would have obscured the terrain and prevented the crew from noticing and correcting the navigational error.

Not long after the disaster, distance-measuring equipment (DME) was installed at the Juneau airport to provide pilots with an additional means of establishing their position.

Date: 2 October 1971 (11:10)
Location: Near Aarsele, West Vlaanderen, Belgium
Operator: British European Airways (BEA)
Aircraft type: Vickers Vanguard 951 (*G-APEC*)

Everything was normal as Flight 706 cruised over the Belgian countryside at 19,000 ft (c. 5,800 m) while en route from London to Salzburg, Austria. Then a sudden message of distress: 'Mayday, Mayday, Mayday . . . We're going down vertically', transmitted from the Vanguard, was heard at the Brussels air traffic control centre, followed by 'Out of control!'.

Slowly rotating in a clockwise direction, the turboprop airliner plunged into a field at a steep angle, beyond the vertical, some 10 miles (15 km) west-south-west of Ghent, bursting into flames on impact. All 63 persons aboard (55 passengers and a crew of eight) perished. Additionally, an occupant of a passing automobile was injured by flying debris.

The nature of the crash seemed to indicate the possibility of structural failure, and this was soon confirmed when both horizontal stabilisers and the corresponding elevators were found in pieces some distance from the main wreckage area, having obviously separated in flight. But the root cause of the failure was internal, not external. Examination revealed corrosion in the lower part of the rear pressure bulkhead, over an area of 18 in (48 cm), under plating that was bonded to the structure. The bond was completely delaminated in this area and the bulkhead material literally eaten away. Tears ran upward and outward from the corroded area.

The corrosion had probably required a relatively long period of time to develop, but on this particular flight the crack-weakened structure finally gave way to the stress created by pressurisation. When the bulkhead ruptured, air from the cabin rushed into the empennage, which was not designed to withstand such internal pressure. Interior damage and severe distortion of the outer skin led to the failure of both tailplanes

A British European Airways Vanguard 951, the type that crashed during a London-to-Salzburg service. *(BAe Systems)*

under existing loads. The loss of aerodynamic support provided by the tail surfaces caused the Vanguard to enter the steep dive, from which recovery was not possible.

The corrosion was attributed to fluid contamination that may have been initiated by spillage from the lavatory, although this could not be substantiated. It was not detectable through the normal maintenance procedures used at the time, which consisted of both visual and radiographic inspection.

Subsequent to the accident, similar corrosion was found in eight other aircraft of the same type flown by BEA, nearly half of the airline's Vanguard fleet. Revised inspection techniques and a modification of the transport to improve access were later introduced with the objective of detecting corrosion before the structural integrity of the rear bulkhead could be affected. Additionally, the number of inspections was increased considerably.

Date: 24 December 1971 (*c.* 12:40)
Location: Near Puerto Inca, Huánuco, Peru
Operator: Lineas Aereas Nacionales SA (LANSA) (Peru)
Aircraft type: Lockheed 188A Electra (*OB-R-941*)

Designated as Flight 508, the turboprop airliner was on a domestic service from Lima to Iquitos, with an en route stop at Pucallpa, when it entered a thunderstorm, the cumulonimbus build-up containing severe lightning and heavy turbulence, with wind gusts of up to 190 knots.

Suddenly, while flying at an altitude of 21,000 ft (6,400 m), or about 10,000 ft (3,000 m) above the ground, the Electra suffered catastrophic structural failure. Both its wings snapped, the right one separating completely, and its fuselage broke in several places. Burning wreckage was scattered some 10 miles (15 km) over the mountainous terrain.

The aircraft was still missing when three hunters found one of the passengers, a 17-year-old-girl, alive. Injured in the crash, she was also treated for exposure to the elements after trekking through the forest for 10 days. The wreckage of *OB-R-941* was located two weeks after its disappearance, with no survivors among the other 91 persons aboard, including six crew members. However, there were indications that at least a dozen others had lived through the break-up and ground impact; it was theorised that the fall may have been cushioned by an enormous updraught.

The initial loss of the starboard wing apparently resulted from the effects of a lightning-induced explosion coupled with both the aerodynamic load imposed by the turbulence and the stresses generated as the crew tried to regain level flight.

Date: 7 January 1972 (*c.* 12:15)
Location: (Spanish) Balearic Islands
Operator: Lineas Aereas de Espana SA (Iberia) (Spain)
Aircraft type: Sud-Aviation Caravelle VI-R (*EC-ATV*)

The jet airliner, which was operating as Flight 602 and had stopped at Valencia, on the Spanish mainland, during a domestic service originating at Madrid, crashed on the island of Ibiza. All 104 persons aboard (98 passengers and a crew of six) perished.

Its undercarriage still retracted, the Caravelle struck Rocas Altas Peak at an approximate elevation of 1,000 ft (300 m), or only about 100 ft (30 m) from the top of the mountain, while attempting to land at Ibiza Airport, located near San José. The aircraft exploded and disintegrated on impact, which took place at an indicated air speed of around 320 mph (515 kmh). At the time of the accident the weather consisted of a high overcast and patches of broken clouds between about 800 and 1,500 ft (250–500 m), with a visibility of approximately 5–10 miles (10 15 km). The wind was from the north at 10 knots.

It was ruled that the pilot had failed to maintain the minimum flight altitude during the final phase of a visual approach to Runway 07.

Date: 14 March 1972 (*c.* 22:00)
Location: Near Al Fujayrah, United Arab Emirates
Operator: Sterling Airways (Denmark)
Aircraft type: Aerospatiale Caravelle Super 10B (*OY-STL*)

All 112 persons aboard (106 passengers and six crew members) perished when the jetliner crashed while preparing to land at the Dubai international airport, a refuelling stop during a charter service from Colombo, Ceylon (Sri Lanka), to Copenhagen, Denmark.

Flight outside of the airport traffic circuit resulted in the crash of an Alitalia DC-8 in which 115 persons were killed. *(CORBIS)*

Cleared for a straight-in approach to Runway 30 using very-high-frequency omnidirectional range (VOR) instrument procedures, the crew had also been asked to report when at 2,000 ft (c. 600 m) or when the airport was in sight. Subsequently, the Caravelle struck a mountain ridge at an approximate elevation of 1,500 ft (500 m), some 50 miles (80 km) from the airport and about 20 miles (30 km) to the north of the extended centreline of the runway, bursting into flames on impact. It was dark at the time, and the meteorological conditions at the airport consisted of scattered cumulus and stratocumulus clouds at 2,000 ft (c. 600 m), a broken overcast at 8,000 ft (c. 2,500 m) and a visibility of around 5 miles (10 km).

The aircraft had descended below the prescribed minimum altitude because the pilots probably believed they were closer to the airport than was actually the case. This mistake apparently resulted from incorrect information on the outdated flight plan being used, misreading of the weather radar, or from a combination of these factors. The position error must have been reinforced when the crew saw Al Fujayrah or some other town and mistook it for Dubai.

Date: 5 May 1972 (22:24)
Location: Near Carini, Sicily, Italy
Operator: Alitalia (Italy)
Aircraft type: Douglas DC-8 Series 43 (*I-DIWB*)

Designated as Flight 112, the jet airliner crashed some 3 miles (5 km) south-east of Punta Raisi Airport, serving Palermo, where it was scheduled to land at the end of a domestic service from Rome. All 115 persons aboard (108 passengers and a crew of seven) were killed.

Its undercarriage still retracted, the DC-8 struck Montagna Lunga ('Long Mountain') at an approximate elevation of 2,000 ft (600 m), or less than 300 ft (100 m) from its crest, bursting into flames on impact, the accident occurring in darkness during the intermediate phase of an approach begun from the north. The weather at the time consisted of a broken overcast, with 3/8 cumulus clouds at 1,700 ft (c. 520 m) and high cirrus, and a visibility of around 3 miles (5 km). The wind was calm.

The disaster was attributed to the crew's non-adherence to the airport traffic circuit regulation, which resulted in flight at an insufficient altitude to

clear the terrain. At the time of the crash, the aircraft was apparently being flown by the first officer, who had been described as 'a good collaborator if constantly watched' and one who at times made 'unorthodox' decisions, 'perhaps as a result of conceit or levity'.

Not quite six months later an additional tragedy took place at the scene of the accident when a man who had come to pray for his daughter, who had been a passenger on the flight, was himself killed by a piece of falling wreckage.

Date: 18 May 1972 (time unknown)
Location: Near Kharkov, Ukraine, USSR
Operator: Aeroflot (USSR)
Aircraft type: Antonov An-10A (*SSSR-11215*)

The four-engine turboprop crashed some 15 miles (25 km) from the Kharkov airport, where it was to have landed during a scheduled domestic service from Moscow, and all 122 persons aboard (114 passengers and a crew of eight) perished.

While descending from its cruising level to about 5,000 ft (1,500 m), with its undercarriage and flaps still retracted, the airliner suffered structural failure, resulting in the separation of both wings, and the fuselage then fell in a ballistic trajectory, plunging into a wooded area. There was no fire. The crash occurred in daylight, visual meteorological conditions, with a cloud base of around 5,000–7,000 ft (1,500–2,000 m) and a visibility of approximately 5 miles (10 km). The wind was calm.

The in-flight failure of the centre wing section was attributed to a fatigue crack in the lower central wing panel. Eleven years old, the aircraft had recorded 15,483 flight hours and 11,105 landings, and was overhauled three times, each of which should have extended its service life by 5,000 hours and 3,200 landings.

As a consequence of this accident, Aeroflot ceased operations with the An-10 model transport.

Date: 14 June 1972 (c. 20:20)
Location: Near New Delhi, India
Operator: Japan Air Lines (JAL)
Aircraft type: Douglas DC-8 Series 53 (*JA8012*)

Flight 471 had been cleared to land at Palam International Airport, serving the Indian capital and a scheduled stop during a service originating at Tokyo, with an ultimate destination of London, but during a straight-in instrument landing system (ILS) approach to Runway 28, the jetliner went below the minimum altitude, then crashed and burned on a bank of the River Yamuna, some 10 miles (15 km) from its threshold. All but three of the 89 persons aboard the aircraft, including its 11 crew members, were killed, along with four others on the ground. The surviving passengers suffered various injuries.

It was dark at the time of the accident, and the visibility had been reduced to approximately 1 mile (1.5 km) in dust haze, with the sky obscured. The wind was from the west at around 15 knots.

The crash was attributed to the disregard of the prescribed procedures by the crew, specifically the abandonment of all instrument references before visual contact with the runway had been established. A number of factors were identified in the investigation, some or all of which may have contributed to the disaster. Cited were the relative lack of experience of both the captain and first officer; the decision by the former to allow the latter to make the approach despite his insufficient instrument flight time, and while not performing the duties of the co-pilot himself; the lack of familiarity of both pilots with the route and misconceptions on their part regarding the facilities available at the New Delhi airport; and their failure to carry out the required landing checks, which indicated laxity and poor discipline. Rather than levelling off, the DC-8 descended through the minimum altitude of 2,100 ft (640 m), apparently after the crew saw what they incorrectly identified as the runway lights, and from that point on the altimeters were ignored. Poor orientation led the pilots to believe that they had reached the outskirts of the airport.

Configured with its undercarriage down and flaps set at 35 degrees, the aircraft had descended almost to the height at which it should have been upon passing over the runway threshold before the error was realised and full power applied. However, the initial impact occurred 6 seconds after the 'overshoot' command, before the engines could develop maximum thrust.

The Indian investigative report noted that had the flight director transfer switch been in the very-high-frequency omnidirectional range/glide slope (VOR/GS) position, a warning flag would have appeared and the descent perhaps arrested by the crew, providing the instrument was being monitored. However, the report rejected the contention of the airline and Japanese government authorities that the premature descent resulted from a false glide path signal transmitted by the ILS. A factor that apparently contributed to the severity of the crash was a rise in the embankment on the west side of the river.

Subsequent to this and a second fatal DC-8 accident about six months later (see separate entry, 28 November 1972), JAL equipped its entire fleet of aircraft with altitude alert systems, and also implemented changes in the training and evaluation of its pilots.

Date: 15 June 1972 (c. 14:00)
Location: Near Pleiku, (South) Vietnam
Operator: Cathay Pacific Airways (Hong Kong)
Aircraft type: Convair 880M (*VR-HFZ*)

Operating as Flight 700Z, which had stopped at Bangkok, Thailand, during a service from Singapore to Hong Kong, the jetliner was reported to have been cruising at 29,000 ft (c. 9,000 m) before radio contact was lost. Its burning wreckage was located shortly afterwards scattered in an east-south-easterly direction over an approximate area of 1 by 1.5 miles (1.5 by 2.5 km) in a Central Highlands jungle. All 81 persons aboard (71 passengers and a crew of 10) perished.

It was obvious that the disaster was sudden and catastrophic. When considering the decade-old war raging below, early suspicion that the aircraft had been shot down, either accidentally or intentionally, was understandable. But as investigators began to examine the debris, the tell-tale signs of such a hit were simply not present. Metallic fragments associated with military missiles or projectiles should have been much larger, heavier and thicker than those found in parts of the aircraft and some of the victims' bodies. Furthermore, the fragments had travelled from inside out, pointing to an internal explosion. The known facts led to the undeniable conclusion that *VR-HFZ* had been destroyed by a bomb.

With the assistance of the flight data recorder (FDR) read-out, the sequence of events was reconstructed. Flying in good weather conditions at

A British European Airways Trident 1C, shown in the same colour scheme as the aircraft that crashed after taking off from Heathrow Airport. *(Rod Simpson)*

the last reported cruising altitude and an indicated air speed of about 350 mph (560 kmh), the jetliner was on a heading of approximately 70 degrees when the high-explosive device detonated within its passenger cabin, in or near the centre section. At least one victim and possibly some seats were ejected from the fuselage, striking the vertical stabiliser, which subsequently broke off. The blast also ruptured the No. 3 wing tank, and escaping fuel ignited in the air.

It was considered 'highly probable' that the flying controls routed beneath the cabin floor were damaged, and this, together with the loss of the stabiliser, resulted in erratic, high-speed man-oeuvres that led to the progressive break-up of the aircraft. All the components struck the ground in a flat attitude after a vertical descent. The occupants not killed by the initial blast were probably rendered unconscious in the consequent explosive de-compression.

A Thai police lieutenant accused of planting the bomb in a suitcase at Bangkok in order to kill his fiancée and daughter by another marriage, both passengers on the flight and whom he had insured prior to its departure, was acquitted two years later due to insufficient evidence.

It was recommended in the investigative report that the sale of flight insurance at airports be discouraged, and that insurance companies advise the proper authorities and the airlines about passengers who are heavily covered on a short-term basis.

Date: 18 June 1972 (17:11)
Location: Staines, Surrey, England
Operator: British European Airways (BEA)
Aircraft type: Hawker Siddeley Trident 1C (*G-ARPI*)

Designated as Flight 548, the jetliner was fully loaded when it departed from London's Heathrow Airport, bound for Brussels, Belgium. Following take-off from Runway 28R, the Trident initiated a turn to the left. A terse 'Up to 60', acknowledging its clearance to 6,000 ft (*c.* 1,800 m), was the last message received from the flight. About 40 seconds later, or 1 minute 46 seconds after becoming airborne, it plummeted in a relatively flat attitude into a field adjacent to the A30, a major thoroughfare, and some 3 miles (5 km) south-west of the airport.

A fire that erupted was quickly extinguished before it could spread, and rescuers actually removed one man alive from the wreckage, but he died soon afterwards, leaving no survivors among the 118 persons aboard (112 passengers and six regular crew members). This was the first time more than 100 lives had been lost in an aviation disaster occurring in the British Isles.

It was apparent that the accident did not result from any failure or defect in the aircraft, but rather from the actions of the crew. The absence of a cockpit voice recorder (CVR) on *G-ARPI* prevented the investigative board from determining with certainty the events that took place on the flight deck. But using information from the flight data recorder (FDR) and other facts gathered through the inquiry, the probable sequence of events could be established. Particularly revealing was an autopsy performed on the body of the captain, 51-year-old Stanley Key, which revealed a severe case of arteriosclerosis, or a narrowing of the arteries through a build-up of fatty deposits, in his heart. There was also a tear in the wall of one artery, indicating that he had suffered a haemorrhage not more than 2 hours before his accidental death.

At the least, Capt Key may have experienced considerable pain; at worst, he could have collapsed at the controls. He had been declared as fit to fly and had in fact passed an electrocardiographic examination the previous November. Yet his condition was bad enough to have sharply reduced his life expectancy. Before the flight he had had what was described as a 'violent' verbal outburst with another pilot in the crew room regarding a labour issue, which could have raised his blood pressure sufficiently to cause the haemorrhage.

The airline did have specific instructions in the event of pilot incapacitation, but Capt Key's ailment had adverse effects on the other members of the flight crew, acting First Officer Jeremy Keighley, 22, and Second Officer Simon Ticehurst, 24. Also travelling in the cockpit, as a passenger, was an off-duty BEA captain, John Collins. Capt Key's attention was obviously diverted from the operation of the aircraft by his illness, leading to a steady deterioration of air speed. The primary factor in the accident was the retraction of the 'droops', high-lift devices on the leading edges of the wings, at an indicated air speed of only 186 mph (299 kmh), or some 70 mph (110 kmh) below that prescribed. The 'droops' were selected up at an altitude of 1,772 ft (540 m) following flap retraction and after thrust had been reduced as part of the regular noise-abatement procedure, placing the jetliner precariously close to a stall condition.

The Trident's then-unique stall-warning/ prevention system had been designed to both shake the control yoke to alert the crew of an impending stall and move it forward to lower automatically the nose of the aircraft in the event of such a condition

Wreckage of G-ARPI lies in a field in Staines, England, after the disaster that took 118 lives. *(AP Images)*

developing, as was the case here. However, the system on *G-ARPI* was manually overridden after it activated a third time. Subsequently, the jetliner pitched up rapidly, losing height and further speed, entering first an aerodynamic stall, then a deep stall from which recovery was not possible. It was raining on this late Sunday afternoon, with a solid overcast at 1,000 ft (*c.* 300 m) and scattered clouds below that. At the most crucial time, therefore, the aircraft was operating in cloud, and the crew had no outside visual reference.

Either the pilot or the co-pilot must have moved the 'droop' lever. In the case of Capt Key, and especially considering his ailment, he may himself have mistaken it for the flap lever. On the other hand, First Officer Keighley may have moved it intentionally after misidentifying the stall-recovery low pressure light for the 'droop' out-of-position indicator; after misinterpreting an order from the pilot (in the vein of 'Put that up', actually meaning a new number in the height acquire window), for the 'droops' to be retracted; or, in following a similar command, by mistaking the 'droop' for the flap lever.

For whatever reason, the crew had failed to diagnose the premature 'droop' retraction as the reason for the activation of the stall-recovery system. Besides Capt Key's condition, the underlying causes of the accident were the lack of training of pilots in the dangers of subtle incapacitation; a lack of experience by First Officer Keighley; and a lack of knowledge by the crew of the implications of a change in configuration as well as the fact that the stall-warning/prevention system could be experienced almost simultaneously and what could prompt such an event. There may have been some additional distraction, possibly the presence of Capt Collins, that diverted the attention of Second Officer Ticehurst.

Despite the predicament, the aircraft could still have been saved by reselecting the 'droops' to the extended position, moving the control column forward either manually or through continued automatic activation of the stall-recovery system, and increasing thrust.

Another factor in the crash was the lack of a mechanism to prevent retraction of the 'droops' at too low an air speed. A speed-operated baulk was one of the suggestions made by the British Air Accidents Investigation Branch in its report on the

crash of *G-ARPI*. Among the other recommendations were that trainee pilots be given more experience before being placed in the position of first officer and that a 'stress test' rather than a 'resting' electrocardiogram be used on flight crews. Many of these proposals were subsequently implemented, including a requirement that all large commercial aircraft registered in Great Britain be fitted with cockpit voice recorders to aid in accident investigation.

Date: 14 August 1972 (*c.* 17:00)
Location: Near Königswusterhausen, (East) Germany
Operator: Interflug Gesellschaft (East Germany)
Aircraft type: Ilyushin Il-62 (*DM-SEA*)

The jet airliner took off from Schonefeld Airport, serving (East) Berlin, on a charter service to Burgas, Bulgaria. About 30 minutes later it crashed and exploded in a field some 10 miles (15 km) south-east of the capital city, and all 156 persons aboard (148 passengers and a crew of eight) perished.

While at an altitude of about 30,000 ft (10,000 m), the captain reported difficulties in controlling the aircraft's elevator, and decided to turn back. Subsequently, radio contact was lost.

Investigation revealed that a fire, of which the crew were apparently not aware, had weakened the rear structure of the Il-62 to the extent that the tail assembly broke off in flight. Due to the extreme disintegration of the aircraft, it was not possible to determine the cause of the blaze.

Date: 31 August 1972 (time unknown)
Location: Near Magnitogorsk, Russian Soviet Federative Socialist Republic, USSR
Operator: Aeroflot (USSR)
Aircraft type: Ilyushin Il-18 (*SSSR-74298*)

The airliner crashed as it attempted a forced landing at the Magnitogorsk airport, killing all 101 persons aboard (92 passengers and nine crew members).

Cruising at an altitude of about 23,000 ft (7,000 m), the four-engine turboprop had been on a scheduled domestic service to Moscow from Karaganda, Kazakh SSR, when the crew requested clearance for an emergency descent due to heavy smoke in the cabin. After the crew had disengaged

An Aeroflot Ilyushin Il-18, two of which were involved in catastrophic crashes only 32 days apart during the latter half of 1972. *(Aviation Photo News)*

the autopilot in order to perform a straight-in approach, the air traffic controller radioed that the aircraft was flying towards mountainous terrain and instructed it to turn left. Descending in daylight conditions to an approximate height of 2,000 ft (600 m), the Il-18 was by this time heading away from the airport, and when advised of this fact by the controller a crew member responded that the smoke was 'very very thick'. About 20 minutes elapsed from the time that the emergency situation was first reported until the moment the aircraft struck the ground some 25 miles (40 km) from the airport.

The dense smoke and related carbon monoxide in the cockpit had resulted in the partial or complete incapacitation of the flight crew, with the impossibility of continuing visual flight and of monitoring the instruments. The underlying cause was a fire in the cargo compartment, which stemmed from the spontaneous ignition of passenger baggage. The weather was not a factor.

Date: 1 October 1972 (*c.* 18:00)
Location: Near Adler, Russian Soviet Federative Socialist Republic, USSR
Operator: Aeroflot (USSR)
Aircraft type: Ilyushin Il-18B (*SSSR-75507*)

All 109 persons aboard (101 passengers and a crew of eight) were killed when the four-engine turboprop crashed in the Black Sea shortly after taking off from the Adler airport, serving Sochi, on a scheduled domestic flight to Moscow.

Climbing through an altitude of about 500 ft (150 m), the airliner started to descend until it plunged into the water and sank approximately 3.5 miles (6 km)) offshore, the accident occurring at dusk and in visual meteorological conditions. There was no distress message before the crash, and an investigation failed to reveal the nature of the difficulty. Nor was the aircraft's flight data recorder (FDR) recovered.

The cause of the disaster was therefore undetermined.

Date: 13 October 1972 (21:50)
Location: Near Krasnaya Polyana, Russian Soviet Federative Socialist Republic, USSR
Operator: Aeroflot (USSR)
Aircraft type: Ilyushin Il-62 (*SSSR-86671*)

The jet airliner, which had stopped at Leningrad during a scheduled international service from Paris, France, crashed and burned while attempting to land at Sheremet'yevo Airport, serving Moscow. All 174 persons aboard (164 passengers and 10 crew members) perished.

It was dark at the time of the accident, and the local weather consisted of a low overcast, with a cloud base of about 300 ft (100 m) and a visibility of around 1 mile (1.5 km) in haze and drizzle. The wind was light, with no reported turbulence.

During the approach, the crew reported reaching an approximate height of 4,000 ft (1,200 m), after which the aircraft's descent rate decreased, then increased again. After beginning a turn on to the base leg of the circuit, the jet continued down through an altitude of about 1,300 ft (400 m), still banked at 25 degrees, with no decrease in the descent rate and with forward speed increasing to more than 370 mph (600 kmh). Cleanly configured, the aircraft ultimately struck the ground some 7.5 miles (12 km) north of the airport.

The exact cause of the accident could not be determined; the most probable cause was the sudden 'psycho-physiological' incapacitation of the pilots for some unknown reason. It was noted in the investigative report that this particular crew were highly experienced, with considerable flight time in the type.

Date: 27 October 1972 (*c.* 19:20)
Location: Near Noirétable, Rhône-Alpes, France
Operator: Air Inter (France)
Aircraft type: Vickers Viscount 724 (*F-BMCH*)

Operating as Flight 696, the four-engine turboprop was on a domestic service from Lyon to Clermont-Ferrand. Following one orbit in a holding pattern, the Viscount was cleared for descent to 3,600 ft (*c.* 1,100 m), and a crewman reported making a procedural turn in preparation for landing at Aulnat Airport. There was no further radio contact with the flight.

Early the next morning its wreckage was located 27 miles (44 km) east of the airport, along the axis of the runway and generally on the correct heading of the approach track. Its undercarriage retracted and flaps partially extended, the airliner had crashed near the top of a hill at an approximate elevation of 3,000 ft (1,000 m). The accident killed 60 persons aboard, including the entire crew of five, and injured the eight surviving passengers. It was dark at the time, and the airport weather consisted of rain, a visibility of around 5 miles (10 km) and a low ceiling, with 4/8 cloud coverage at about 2,300 ft (700 m) and a solid overcast at approximately 8,000 ft (2,500 m).

The disaster was primarily attributed to a 180-degree shift of the Viscount's radio compass needle.

This erroneous indication could have resulted from a defect in *F-BMCH*, caused by the faulty installation of its antenna system in combination with certain atmospheric conditions. More likely, however, it was associated with the effect of localised rainfalls over the mountainous terrain, which emitted electrical discharges powerful enough to block out the signals from the Clermont-Ferrand non-directional beacon (NDB). The passage of the aircraft through nimbostratus clouds, which subjected it to an intense electric field, and the presence of thunderstorm activity in the area, could have contributed to the bearing error. Meanwhile, the interception of signals from the instrument landing system (ILS) may have further reinforced the crew's misconception, as might have the lights from the town of Thiers, which were probably visible. The combined effects of these events led to a premature descent below the obstructing terrain.

Though the pilots could have cross-checked their position, this apparently was not done. Over-confidence in the radio compass, coupled with either the failure to check or an error in the reading of the flight time, could have been a factor in the crew's incorrect estimate of when the aircraft was to have passed the NDB. Compounding the mistake was the possible distraction of the captain and first officer, either by the turbulence encountered by the flight or by the presence of an instructor pilot in the cockpit.

Date: 28 November 1972 (19:51)
Location: Near Moscow, Russian Soviet Federative Socialist Republic, USSR
Operator: Japan Air Lines (JAL)
Aircraft type: McDonnell Douglas DC-8 Super 62 (*JA8040*)

The accident occurred in evening darkness immediately after the jetliner, which was designated as Flight 446, had taken off from Sheremet'yevo Airport, a scheduled stop during a service to Tokyo from Copenhagen, Denmark.

Climbing to approximately 300 ft (100 m) while on a heading of 248 degrees, the aircraft abruptly lost height and crashed some 500 ft (150 m) from the end of the runway and about 150 ft (50 m) to the left of its extended centreline. Hitting the ground tail first with its undercarriage extended, the DC-8 broke up and burst into flames, killing 62

A Convair 990A Coronado of the Spanish non-scheduled carrier Spantax, identical to the aircraft that crashed on Tenerife. *(Rod Simpson)*

of the 76 persons aboard (53 passengers and nine of its 15 crew members). All of the survivors suffered injuries.

Following the attainment of the safety speeed, the crew put the aircraft into a supercritical angle of attack, which resulted in a loss of air speed and altitude. A Soviet investigative commission attributed this condition to either an inadvertent extension of the spoilers, leading to a reduction in lift and an increase in drag, or a loss of control by the pilots associated with the malfunctioning of one of the two left power plants after ice formation on the engine intake at a time when the de-icing system was switched off.

With regard to the second theory, there were indications of engine trouble before the crash. A comment by a member of the flight crew, who reported irregularities in the functioning of the No. 2 power plant, was heard on the cockpit voice recorder (CVR) tape, as was a sound typical of an engine surge. Additionally, a surviving hostess reported seeing a flame in the vicinity of the port engines, and some of the passengers said they felt the aircraft decelerate several times after becoming airborne. Examination also revealed that three first-stage fan blades in the No. 2 power plant were bent, characteristic of damage produced by the impact of ice particles.

Had a loss of thrust occurred, the pilots could have tried to continue the climb-out by pulling back

on their control columns, leading to the nose-high attitude and, consequently, an increase in drag followed by a loss of vertical speed. Complicating matters were the night-time conditions, which would have reduced visual reference and possibly contributed to the high angle of attack ending in a stall.

On the other hand, the anomalies in the engines may have arisen after the DC-8 assumed the extreme attitude with its spoilers extended.

Date: 3 December 1972 (*c.* 06:45)
Location: Tenerife, (Spanish) Canary Islands
Operator: Spantax SA Transportes Aereos (Spain)
Aircraft type: Convair 990A Coronado (*EC-BZR*)

Taking off around sunrise and during a low overcast from Los Rodeos Airport, located near Santa Cruz de Tenerife, the jet airliner, on a charter service and bound for Munich, (West) Germany, climbed to an approximate height of 300 ft (100 m) above the ground. Its undercarriage and flaps still extended, the Coronado then plunged to earth and burst into flames, coming to rest inverted about 50 ft (15 m) to the left and some 1,000 ft (300 m) beyond the end of the runway. All 155 persons aboard (148 passengers and a crew of seven) were killed.

A loss of control at or about the time of rotation, believed to have been precipitated by abnormal manoeuvres made by the pilot that were attributed to the conditions of zero visibility, was blamed for the crash.

Date: 29 December 1972 (23:42)
Location: Near Miami, Florida, US
Operator: Eastern Airlines (US)
Aircraft type: Lockheed L-1011-1 TriStar (*N310EA*)

The first fatal crash of a wide-bodied jet airliner involved Flight 401, on a non-stop domestic service from New York City, and scheduled to land at Miami International Airport.

During the approach, and when the undercarriage was lowered, trouble arose when, in what had been up until then an uneventful trip, the green light indicating that the nose gear was down and locked failed to illuminate. Incredibly, this seemingly minor annoyance would play a key role in the ultimate destruction of the aircraft and the loss of more than 100 lives.

Recycling the gear to no avail, the crew reported the problem to the control tower and the TriStar was cleared to circle at 2,000 ft (*c.* 600 m). The captain then instructed the first officer to engage the autopilot and the second officer to enter the electronics compartment, located underneath the flight deck, to check the position of the gear visually by means of an optical sight. The flight engineer was then joined by a maintenance specialist, who had been riding as a passenger in the forward observer's seat. Meanwhile, the pilot and co-pilot continued to concentrate on the nose light unit itself, trying unsuccessfully to remove the lens from its retainer. During this time the cockpit voice recorder (CVR) transcribed a C-chord, an aural alert indicating a deviation from the selected altitude, but there was no indication that either of the pilots heard the warning.

About a minute later the Miami approach controller, who had been monitoring the flight, noted a height of only 900 ft (274 m) on the aircraft's alphanumeric data block on his radarscope. He then asked, 'Eastern 401, how are things coming along out there?' Unfortunately, his query made no reference to the altitude of the aircraft, which continued to deteriorate. Acknowledging the

The first wide-bodied commercial jet to be involved in a fatal accident was an Eastern Airlines Lockheed L-1011 TriStar. *(Eastern Airlines)*

INITIAL IMPACT AREA

Wreckage of the Eastern Airlines L-1011 is strewn across the Florida Everglades after the crash that claimed more than 100 lives. *(National Transportation Safety Board)*

controller, the captain requested and was granted clearance to turn back towards the airport.

In the final few seconds of the flight, the crew finally realised that something was amiss. The first officer remarked 'We did something to the altitude', and the captain responded 'What?'.

The co-pilot then asked 'We're still at two thousand feet, right?', and the pilot immediately exclaimed 'Hey, what's happening here?'.

The radio altimeter then began to beep, but there was no time for corrective action.

The TriStar crashed in the Everglades some 20 miles (30 km) west-north-west of the airport, scattering wreckage across the marshland over an area approximately 1,500 ft (500 m) long and some 300 ft (100 m) wide. Including those who succumbed later, a total of 103 persons aboard (98 passengers, the entire flight crew of three and two cabin attendants) were killed. Almost miraculously, 73 others, including the eight other crew members assigned to *N310EA* and the maintenance specialist, escaped with their lives. Most of the fatalities resulted from impact trauma, although a few drownings were reported in water that was about 6 to 12 in (15–30 cm) deep. Injuries among the survivors ranged from minor to critical. An autopsy revealed a tumour in the brain of the captain, 55-year-old Robert Loft, and although this received media attention, it was not considered significant to the accident.

A technical anomaly, however, was found. The autopilot/flight director system on the L-1011 has two roll and pitch computers, one for each pilot, which control up or down attitude. As designed, a force applied to either control column will cause disengagement of the altitude hold function, and such disengagement would normally extinguish the altitude mode select light on the glare shield and the disappearance of the ALT annunciation on both panels, alerting both pilots that the height was no longer being automatically maintained. However, on this particular aircraft the computers were mis-matched so that the first officer's autopilot could be disengaged by 20 lb (9 kg) of pressure and the captain's by only 15 lb (6 kg) of pressure. The pilot could thus disengage the autopilot without the co-pilot's altitude indicator going out, giving the latter the false impression that the autopilot was still engaged in the altitude hold. But since the first officer's autopilot was believed to have been the one engaged, this mismatch should not have been a critical factor.

Nevertheless, correlation of the read-out from the digital flight data recorder (DFDR), which transcribed 62 parameters, with the CVR tape pointed to the possibility of an inadvertent disengagement. A slight change in pitch was recorded at the same time the captain asked the second officer, seated behind and to his right, to check the nose gear position visually, an indication that the pilot could have bumped the control column when he turned to speak to the flight engineer. A pitch change was also noted concurrent with a change in heading. In addition, there were several power reductions, which could have been intentional or, if unintentional, may have resulted from either pilot bumping the thrust levers. These power reductions coupled with the slight pitch control movements were responsible for the unrecognised descent that followed. (The investigation revealed a surprising lack of knowledge among flight crews about the capabilities and operation of the autopilot system on the L-1011.)

Just before the crash, it could be said that neither pilot actually had taken responsibility for flying the aircraft. The two had become so preoccupied with the nose gear indicating system that there was no monitoring of the flight instruments during the final 4 minutes of the flight. In addition, it was dark at the time, with no moon, and despite unrestricted visibility there were no visual references by which the crew could have detected the loss of height.

It could be argued that the approach controller might have prevented the accident by notifying N310EA of its apparent low altitude. He later testified that he had contacted the aircraft only because it was nearing the airspace boundary within his jurisdiction, and added that momentary deviations in height on radar displays are not uncommon. Furthermore, air traffic controllers were not, at least at the time, required to offer such guidance. (This issue would surface again two years later after another major airline disaster in the US, and would result in a change of policy regarding the responsibility of controllers in providing altitude information to crews.)

The crash occurred as the transport was in a left bank of 28 degrees and on a heading of 240 degrees. Its indicated air speed at the moment of impact was about 230 mph (370 kmh). There was a flash fire, but no sustained blaze. Disintegration of the aircraft was such that the US National Transportation Safety Board (NTSB) actually classified the accident as 'non-survivable', and the survival of more than a third of the occupants can probably be ascribed to the fact that either their seats remained attached to large floor sections or they were thrown clear of the wreckage at considerably reduced velocities. The energy-absorbing design of the passenger seats was an additional significant factor.

Examination of the wreckage showed that the flap handle was set at 18 degrees and the undercarriage lever was down. As it turned out, the crew's concern over the position of the nose gear was unfounded. It, as well as the two main gears, were found extended and locked – the two bulbs in the nose gear unit had merely burned out.

As recommended by the NTSB, a switch for the nose wheel well light located near the gear indicator optical sight was later installed in the TriStar, the presence of which would probably have sped up the actions of the men in the lower compartment of N310EA and perhaps prevented its crash. In addition, Eastern Airlines was required by the US Federal Aviation Administration (FAA) to modify the altitude select alert system in its L-1011 fleet, which had been configured so that the amber warning lights would be inhibited from operating below 2,500 ft (c. 750 m). The only warning of a height deviation under this altitude was the single C-chord.

Date: 22 January 1973 (c. 09:30)
Location: Near Kano, Nigeria
Operator: Alia Royal Jordanian Airlines
Aircraft type: Boeing 707-3D3C (JY-ADO)

Chartered by Nigeria Airways, the jetliner was on a non-scheduled service from Jiddah, Saudi Arabia, its passengers Muslim pilgrims. Diverted by bad weather from Lagos, its original destination, to Kano, the 707 crashed while landing at the city's airport, killing 176 persons aboard, including six of its nine crew members. Most of the 33 survivors were injured.

Based on unconfirmed reports, JY-ADO touched down hard in a nose-high, right wing-low attitude, upon which its two starboard engines and rear fuselage area struck the ground. After rocking to the left, its No. 1 and No. 2 power plants hit the ground, and its port wing separated from the fuselage. The transport then swung completely round, skidded off the runway and was subsequently destroyed by flames. At the time of the accident, visibility had been reduced by haze and there were gusting crosswinds.

There were other accounts that the aircraft's right main gear was torn off when it either hit the edge of the runway following an undershoot or struck some obstruction or depression in or to the side of the pavement. However, the American captain in command of the 707, who survived, would later be blamed for the disaster, reportedly displaying a piloting technique that was, according to the investigative tribunal, 'tantamount to recklessness'.

Date: 21 February 1973 (c. 14:10)
Location: Near Ismâ'ilîya, Egypt
Operator: Libyan Arab Airlines
Aircraft type: Boeing 727-224 (5A-DAH)

Originating at Tripoli, Flight 114 had stopped at Banghāzī, also in Libya, before proceeding on towards its ultimate destination of Cairo, Egypt.

However, following its passage of Sîdi Barrâni, Egypt, the jetliner began to stray from the intended route. Flying to the south of Cairo, the aircraft passed the capital city, and while approaching the Gulf of Suez it was first spotted on radar by Israeli defence forces, which promptly dispatched two F-4 Phantom II jet fighters. The military pilots, who identified the intruder as a Libyan commercial transport, tried to get it to land, using hand gestures, rocking the wings of their aircraft and, finally, by firing their cannons across its nose.

Over the Sinai Peninsula, the 727 turned back towards the west, but shortly afterwards, and while it was at a height of 5,000 ft (c. 1,500 m), the fighters attacked the jetliner, hitting its starboard wing-tip with tracers and starting a fire. As the aircraft descended, apparently still under control, the blaze spread to its cabin.

The 727 crashed approximately 10 miles (15 km) east of the Suez Canal while attempting a belly-landing in the desert, with an explosion occurring in the area of its right main gear almost simultaneously with ground impact. All but five of the 113 persons aboard were killed, including eight crew members; four passengers and the aircraft's co-pilot survived with various injuries. An examination of the wreckage revealed that only one of the transport's three engines had been operating at the time of the crash.

Although the flight had generally assumed the correct heading, its track was displaced to the east, and when the first officer reported it as over Qarum, the jetliner was actually some 100 miles (150 km) east-south-east of that location. Furthermore, all air traffic control instructions to the aircraft were based on its own erroneous position reports, and when the crew radioed that they were not receiving navigational signals, the controller advised them to 'Stick to the Cairo non-directional beacon'. The drift was apparently related to an encounter with a strong tail wind.

During much of the flight, the 727 was over clouds, with low stratocumulus and 6/8 to 8/8 altocumulus up to about 18,000 ft (5,500 m). Once over the Sinai, the ground was visible, and at around this time the crew appeared to realise their error. By then, however, the aircraft was out of the range of the navigational facilities.

Although records did not indicate any such faults in the Cairo beacon, the International Civil Aviation Organisation (ICAO) investigative report on the disaster considered it probable that it was not functioning properly at the time. Additionally, the Cairo approach control radar was out of order.

The crew of 5A-DAH apparently did not understand the orders of the fighter pilots, and when they turned back towards Cairo and raised the aircraft's gear, which had been lowered, it was construed by the Israelis as an attempt to escape. Defence Minister Moshe Dayan admitted an 'error of judgement' in shooting down the transport, and the Israeli government agreed to compensate the families of the victims.

Date: 5 March 1973 (c. 13:50)
Location: Near Nantes, Payes de la Loire, France
First aircraft
Operator: Lineas Aereas de Espana SA (Iberia) (Spain)
Type: McDonnell Douglas DC-9 Series 32 (EC-BII)
Second aircraft
Operator: Spantax SA Transportes Aereos (Spain)
Type: Convair 990A Coronado (EC-BJC)

This mid-air crash between two jet transports occurred during a strike by civilian controllers, wherein the French air traffic control (ATC) system had been taken over by military personnel.

Both aircraft were bound for London, the DC-9, operating as Flight 504, en route from Palma de Mallorca, in the (Spanish) Balearic Islands, and the Coronado on a charter service from Madrid. Only minutes earlier they had been transferred to the same ATC centre from another facility, which had assigned them to the same flight level despite the fact that both crews had estimated that they would reach the Nantes very-high-frequency omni-directional range (VOR) station at the same time.

To avoid a potential conflict, the Spantax aircraft was instructed to delay by 8 minutes its arrival at the navigational aid, but the fact that the jet at that point was only about 10 minutes flying time from VOR made this an unrealistic request. Asking for confirmation of these instructions, the controller only responded with a 'Stand by'. In international phraseology, this expression normally means that a message will be immediately forthcoming; however, the crew were left in uncertainty for nearly 2 minutes before communications were re-established. Shortly afterwards the pilot asked if he could carry out a 360-degree turn, because a speed reduction would be insufficient to delay passage of the station.

This manoeuvre was subsequently initiated without clearance and in proximity to the VOR, and led to the interception by *EC-BJC* of the adjacent airway, along which *EC-BII* had been flying. The resulting collision occurred at a height of 29,000 ft (*c.* 9,000 m) over La Planche, a village located south-east of Nantes, and in the midst of an overcast, which had reduced visibility to zero.

All 68 persons aboard the DC-9 (61 passengers and a crew of seven) perished when the aircraft broke up in flight, scattering wreckage over an agricultural area. There were no injuries among the 106 persons aboard the Coronado, which was still in the right-hand turn at the time of impact and lost a portion of its left wing, outboard of the No. 1 engine, but nevertheless managed a safe landing at a military air base.

Whereas the solution to the conflict was based on separation by time, a simple change of altitude would have been possible. Complicating matters was the poor quality of radio transmissions between the Spantax jet and control. The Coronado had not yet made radio contact with nor been positively identified on radar at the facility responsible for its control, and was no longer in radar contact with the one from which it had been transferred. Thus, in the final moments before the collision it was virtually cut off from ATC services. The crew themselves had erred in not properly assessing the situation and establishing radio contact with the appropriate controlling facility.

The method used to provide for separation of the aircraft required either precise navigation by the Spantax crew or complete radar coverage and, in whichever case, trouble-free communications, conditions that were not realised.

Date: 10 April 1973 (10:13)
Location: Near Hochwald, Solothurn, Switzerland
Operator: Invicta International Airlines (UK)
Aircraft type: Vickers Vanguard 952 (*G-AXOP*)

The turboprop transport, on a charter service from Luton and Bristol, England, was to have landed at Basel-Mulhouse Airport, located just across the border in France. Its first instrument landing system (ILS) approach, which was to Runway 16, ended in an overshoot. Minutes later, a meteorologist

and retired aviator telephoned the control tower, stating that he had just seen a four-engine aircraft, later identified as *G-AXOP*, fly over the Binningen Observatory at a dangerously low altitude. He urged that it be instructed to climb. However, the gallant effort by the ground observer to perhaps prevent a crash was to no avail. Shortly afterwards the Vanguard, its undercarriage apparently retracted and flaps set at 20 degrees, brushed against a wooded ridge, then slammed into a snow-covered forest area.

The accident, which took place some 10 miles (15 km) south of the airport, claimed the lives of 108 persons aboard the aircraft, including four crew members. Among the 37 survivors, 35 passengers and a cabin attendant suffered injuries, and a second stewardess escaped unscathed. Fire erupted in the right wing after impact but was extinguished before it could spread over the rest of the wreckage, and this absence of a major blaze, coupled with the fact that the rear section of the fuselage remained intact, probably accounted for the relatively high rate of survival. Most of the victims were women from five towns in the English county of Somerset on a one-day 'shopping tour' of Switzerland.

The weather in the area of the crash at the time was characterised by a driving snow, which reduced visibility to approximately 150 ft (50 m). The clouds were down to the level of the terrain and the wind was blowing from the north at about 15 knots. At the airport, the runway visual range (RVR) was in fact below the minimum allowed in Vanguard operations, but the control tower relayed the incorrect measurement to the aircraft, one slightly above the minimum. The crew made no further enquiries regarding the meteorological conditions.

Although the actions of the two pilots could not be determined with certainty due to the absence of a cockpit voice recorder (CVR) on *G-AXOP*, the accident apparently resulted from a loss of orientation on their part. Contributing factors were unsatisfactory navigational procedures, most significantly the initiation of the final approach despite the incorrect assessment of height and position, and the confusion of navigational aids. An additional factor was the poor reception of radio-navigational signals due to defects in the aircraft's equipment, which made the task of the crew more difficult.

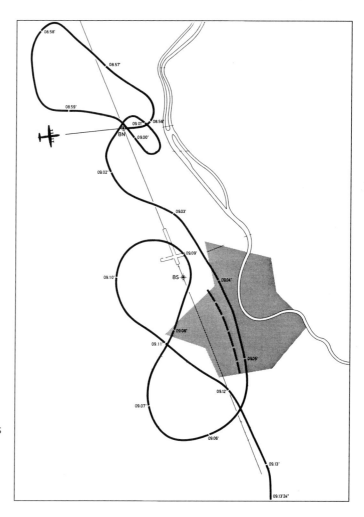

The meandering flight path of the Invicta International Airlines Vanguard (with times given in GMT) indicates the disorientation of the crew that led to the disaster. (*Swiss Federal Aircraft Accident Investigation Bureau*)

With regard to the technical aspect, the No. 1 automatic direction finder (ADF) receiver may not have been functioning properly due to faulty repair work, specifically poor soldering of joints in its loop servo amplifier. And both the No. 1 very-high-frequency omnidirectional range (VOR) and No. 2 glide slope receivers were improperly set, so that in neither case would a warning flag, indicating an anomaly, have appeared at the correct time. Unsatisfactory readings could also have given the crew the false impression of being properly on the glide path. There could also have been 'jittery' indications making it difficult to intercept the localiser signal.

The pilots, who apparently believed that their navigational difficulties were due to the atmospheric conditions (as evidenced by the statement that the ADF indicators were 'all over the place in this weather'), were probably remiss in cross- and double-checking of the instruments, through which the discrepancies could have been detected and perhaps corrected. Nor did they ask for any navigational assistance from the air traffic control service.

The flight path of the Vanguard became erratic following passage of the non-directional beacon (NDB) designated 'BN'. This may have resulted from the fact that its ADF receivers were not tuned to two navigational aids being used in the normal sequence.

Actually, the first approach, during which the transport deviated considerably to the right and then the left of the runway centreline, almost ended in a crash after the crew had apparently established visual contact with the ground. During the second approach a descent was begun, indicating that the pilots had a glide slope indication. By then, however, the disorientation was such that a successful landing would probably not have been possible. In the final moments of the flight, the aircraft was headed towards the south, i.e. away from the airport, and the accident occurred during a climb-out manoeuvre.

Both flight crewmen were qualified captains, though this could actually have been a hindrance had the one serving as co-pilot behaved more as a

The aftermath of the Vanguard crash in Switzerland that killed 108 persons. *(Swiss Federal Aircraft Accident Investigation Bureau)*

pilot-in-command than as a first officer. A change in the operator of the radio indicated that there was a switch in the pilot flying the Vanguard after the first overshoot.

Among the recommendations made by the Swiss investigative commission were that all medium wavelength radio beacons be readjusted to a modulation in conformity with International Civil Aviation Organisation (ICAO) standards; that international regulations require the suppression of unpublicised ILS back beams; and that every large commecial aircraft carry both a flight data recorder (FDR) and a voice recorder. An FDR had been fitted to *G-AXOP*, and the installation of a CVR on similar types would later become a British civil aviation requirement.

Date: 18 May 1973 (time unknown)
Location: Southern Siberia, USSR
Operator: Aeroflot (USSR)
Aircraft type: Tupolev Tu-104B (*SSSR-42411*)

All 81 persons aboard perished, including an estimated crew of five to 10, when the jet airliner crashed east of Lake Baikal during an attempted hijacking.

The aircraft had been on a scheduled domestic service from Moscow to Chita, RSFSR, when a passenger demanded to be taken to China; subsequently the explosive device he was carrying apparently detonated at an altitude of approximately 30,000 ft (10,000 m).

Date: 11 July 1973 (*c.* 15:00)
Location: Near Saulx-les-Chartreux, Ile-de-France, France
Operator: SA Empresa de Viacao Aerea Rio Grandense (VARIG) (Brazil)
Aircraft type: Boeing 707-345C (*PP-VJZ*)

Everything was routine for Flight 820 during most of its 11-hour transatlantic journey from the time of departure at Rio de Janeiro, Brazil, until shortly before it was scheduled to land at Orly Airport, serving Paris. Then came the first hint of trouble, at 14:58, when the message 'Problem with fire on board' was received from the aircraft, and an 'emergency descent' was requested.

Cleared for a direct approach to Runway 07, the jet airliner flight was about 10 miles (15 km) from the airport when the pilot reported 'total fire'. This message was prompted by the alarming announcement from the chief steward that smoke had entered the cabin and passengers were being asphyxiated. The flight crew donned oxygen masks and goggles, but the smoke became so dense in the cockpit that not even the instruments could be seen. In view of the desperate situation, the captain decided that a forced landing was necessary.

Looking through the side cockpit windows, which had been opened, the pilots managed to set the aircraft down in a field some 3 miles (5 km) from the threshold and in near alignment with the axis of the runway. Its extended main undercarriage collapsed almost immediately, and the left outer wing and all four engines were then torn off as the 707 slid on its belly for approximately 1,500 ft (500 m).

Despite the exceptional skill displayed by the crew in landing the aircraft and the quick action by emergency personnel, who were on the scene in minutes, the fuselage was gutted by flames. Except for the flight engineer, who was not wearing his safety belt and died of impact trauma, the 123 persons killed in the disaster succumbed to the effects of the fire (about three-quarters of them from carbon monoxide poisoning and the rest from inhaling other toxic gases). Only one passenger,

who was rescued by firefighters, and 10 of the 17 crew members assigned to the flight, who managed to escape on their own, survived. It was considered probable that the fire developed in the washbasin unit of the aft right lavatory. The blaze may have been due to an electrical fault, or may have resulted from human carelessness, such as the discarding of a lighted cigarette; the exact cause was never determined.

There was no evidence of foul play, and no defect could be found in the aircraft. However, there was a material factor with respect to the seriousness of the fire. Samples of cabin furnishings examined were found to be readily combustible, and the waste towel disposal containers did not satisfy the requirements of being flame-resistant.

Members of the cabin crew took action with fire extinguishers as soon as smoke was discovered, but their efforts were ineffective because the origin of the blaze could not be located. The actions of the flight crew were considered somewhat incoherent but still sound, including the decision not to release the cabin oxygen masks (the output of oxygen from unused masks would have worsened the situation, and since the masks supply a mixture of pure oxygen and ambient air, they would not have provided any protection from the noxious fumes).

Most of the safety measures recommended by the French investigative commission in its report on the

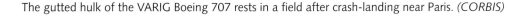

The gutted hulk of the VARIG Boeing 707 rests in a field after crash-landing near Paris. *(CORBIS)*

crash of Flight 820, which included the use of non-flammable waste bins, the elimination of inflammable objects and the enforced prohibition of smoking in aircraft lavatories, were subsequently put into effect by many national aviation regulatory bodies.

Date: 22 July 1973 (22:06)
Location: Off Papeete, Tahiti
Operator: Pan American World Airways (US)
Aircraft type: Boeing Advanced 707-321B (N417PA)

This inexplicable crash involved Flight 816, which had originated at Auckland, New Zealand, and landed at Faaa Airport, serving Papeete, before continuing on towards the US, with a planned stop at Honolulu, Hawaii, and an ultimate destination of Los Angeles, California.

Using Runway 04, the 707 took off into the darkness, then initiated a left turn, as cleared. About 30 seconds after becoming airborne, however, the jet airliner plunged into the Pacific Ocean approximately 2 miles (3 km) from the end of the runway and to the left of its extended centreline, killing 78 persons aboard, including the entire crew of 10; though he was seriously injured, one passenger survived. Among the victims was a stewardess who succumbed in a hospital after also being rescued alive. There were reports of an additional fatality, a man whose wife was on the flight who himself jumped into the water and vanished.

Ten bodies and a small amount of debris, including the aircraft's nose gear and pieces of its cabin furnishings, were recovered. Most of the wreckage, however, was lost in water some 2,300 ft (700 m) deep and could not be located, despite a three-day search using sonar equipment. This lack of evidence and, especially, the failure to find either the flight data (FDR) or cockpit voice (CVR) recorders, prevented the French investigative commission from determining the cause of the disaster.

The jet reportedly ascended at a lower than normal climb gradient after taking off. During the low-altitude left turn, the 707 lost height, descending at a shallow angle, and at the moment of impact its undercarriage was apparently up and its flaps were either at the take-off position or in the process of being retracted.

As noted in the accident report, a malfunction in one power plant should not have jeopardised the flight, and obtained evidence cast doubt on the theory that the aircraft had experienced multiple engine failure. Nor were there any indications, including the absence of a distress message, of a control system malfunction or other serious emergency.

Considered more likely was that the failure of an instrument or system had diverted the crew's attention while in the turn, with a resultant excessive bank leading to the loss of altitude. Also, since the turn was made out towards the sea, no visual references would have been available to counter the change in the angle of the town lights visible on the right-hand side of the aircraft. This could have created the illusion of ascent. Whether involuntary or intentional, the steep bank in itself could have created a hazardous situation.

Both the captain and first officer, who were but a year from retirement, had been undergoing regular treatment for hypertension, and an autopsy performed on the latter revealed a serious arteriosclerotic condition. However, there was no evidence that the health of either pilot played a role in the crash.

The weather, which only minutes before the disaster consisted of rain, a solid overcast at about 8,000 ft (2,500 m) and scattered clouds down to around 2,300 ft (700 m), and a visibility of approximately 5 miles (10 km), was not considered a factor.

Date: 31 July 1973 (11:08)
Location: Boston, Massachusetts, US
Operator: Delta Air Lines (US)
Aircraft type: McDonnell Douglas DC-9 Series 31 (N975NE)

Designated as Flight 723, which had stopped at Manchester, New Hampshire, during a domestic service originating at Burlington, Vermont, the jetliner crashed and burned while attempting to land at Logan International Airport. All 89 persons aboard (83 passengers and six crew members) were killed. One of the victims lived for nearly five months before succumbing to his injuries.

The accident apparently resulted from the failure of the pilots to monitor their altitude and recognise the passage of the aircraft through the decision height during an unstabilised instrument landing system (ILS) approach to Runway 04R, conducted in rapidly changing meteorological conditions.

Descent into a fog ended in a crash at Boston's Logan International Airport of a Delta Air Lines DC-9 Series 30, similar to this one. *(McDonnell Douglas)*

The sequence of events began with vectors of *N975NE* by approach control that were not in accordance with standard operating procedures. At the time that the controller should have issued the clearance, as required, he was preoccupied with a potential conflict between two other flights. As a result, the crew of the DC-9 had to request approach clearance and other instructions. Communication difficulties with one of the other aircraft further delayed the descent of Flight 723 to the correct approach altitude and its release to the control of the airport tower. Despite the non-standard air traffic control services that were partly to blame for the poor positioning of the aircraft, its progress could still have been ascertained through proper monitoring by the crew.

The jetliner passed over the outer marker at a velocity of about 240 mph (385 kmh), or some 50 mph (80 kmh) above that recommended by the carrier. It was also more than 200 ft (60 m) above the normal height at the same point, and, at such an air speed, a high rate of descent would have been required to intercept the glide slope. A high rate of descent would, in turn, have made it difficult for the crew to reduce air speed to that considered acceptable and would have forced the pilots to act more quickly than usual.

An additional factor was the crew's use of the aircraft's flight director system, which they had employed as an approach aid. If it were in its normal mode and the aircraft too high to intercept the glide slope, no pitch guidance would be provided. It was believed, however, that the flight director had been inadvertently placed in the go-around position, which corresponded to the approach mode on the system to which this crew were accustomed. The resulting abnormal display must have led to the lateral corrections that caused the deviation from the localiser centreline. The first officer, who was actually doing the flying, seemed preoccupied by the display to the detriment of his attention to altitude, heading and air speed. Meanwhile, the captain divided his attention among the problems with the flight director, com-munications with the ground and the weather information given by the approach controller.

It was foggy at the time, with an overcast estimated at 200 ft (60 m) and a light wind. The runway visual range (RVR) was reported to the flight to have been in excess of 6,000 ft (1,800 m), but due to the rapid change in weather and a delay of nearly a minute in the cycling of the RVR digital display, the information was not indicative of the actual conditions. In fact, the RVR had dropped to only about 1,500 ft (500 m) just before the aircraft was to have landed.

The presence of an off-duty pilot riding in the cockpit jump seat and, especially, his participation in the reading of the checklist, which was contrary to normal procedures, could also have distracted the regular two-man flight crew.

The descent continued until the jetliner, its undercarriage down and flaps fully extended, struck a sea wall. The initial impact took place some 3,000 ft (1,000 m) from the threshold of the runway and about 150 ft (50 m) to the right of its extended centreline, and the DC-9 then disintegrated. Due to the poor visibility, the accident was not seen from the control tower; moreover, tower personnel silenced an alarm, which they believed to be false, set off when the crash damaged the airport's approach light system (ALS), without notifying inbound flights, as required. Fortunately, two aircraft cleared to land on the same runway over which wreckage was scattered abandoned their approaches because of the weather.

A programme for controllers in the use of the ALS was later initiated at Boston, and the US Federal Aviation Administration (FAA) also modified its terminal air traffic control procedures so that pertinent information would be forwarded to the ground controller when the active runway was not visible from the tower cab.

Date: 13 August 1973 (*c.* 11:40)
Location: Near La Coruña, Spain
Operator: Aviacion y Comercio SA (AVIACO) (Spain)
Aircraft type: Sud-Aviation Caravelle 10-R (*EC-BIC*)

Having completed a domestic service from Madrid as Flight 116, the jet airliner had already made three unsuccessful attempts to land at La Coruña Airport. On the third try, the tower controller reported seeing the Caravelle in the low, ragged fog, relaying this information to the crew. This must have led the captain to believe that by going slightly below the minimum altitude he would be able to carry out a safe landing, so he began his fourth attempt.

During the approach the pilots probably tried to make visual contact with the ground and did not properly refer to their altimeters. A pull-up was initiated and full power applied just before the aircraft clipped with its right flap and part of the

fuselage some eucalyptus trees atop a hill, and the twin-engine jet then crashed inverted about 2 miles (3 km) from the threshold of Runway 22, bursting into flames on impact. All 85 persons aboard (79 passengers and a crew of six) and a worker on the ground were killed.

Shortly before the accident, the vertical visibility was between 800 and 1,000 ft (*c.* 250–300 m) and the horizontal visibility approximately 1 mile (1.5 km).

By attempting to land in meteorological conditions that were below minima, the pilot violated both the nation's regulations and instructions and the international standards in force in Spain. Under the circumstances he should have diverted to an alternative airport.

A possible extenuating factor was that the approach chart used by the crew depicted the 345 ft (105 m) hill as the highest obstacle, whereas the trees rose 40 to 50 ft (12–15 m) above the terrain.

One of the recommendations made in the investigative report was for air traffic control services to inform pilots before reaching their destination when the weather falls below the minimum criteria.

Date: 30 September 1973 (20:40)
Location: Near Sverdlovsk, Russian Soviet Federative Socialist Republic, USSR
Operator: Aeroflot (USSR)
Aircraft type: Tupolev Tu-104B (*SSSR-42506*)

The jetliner, which was on a scheduled domestic service, crashed shortly after taking off from the city's airport, and all 108 persons aboard (100 passengers and eight crew members) perished. It was dark at the time, and the weather was overcast, with a cloud base of about 800 ft (250 m) and a visibility of around 3.5 miles (6 km). The wind was blowing from a north-north-westerly direction at approximately 15 mph (25 km).

In the final radio transmission from the flight, the crew acknowledged departure instructions and advised that they would report upon reaching about 5,000 ft (1,500 m). At an approximate height of 1,200 ft (350 m) above the ground, the aircraft commenced a left turn, with the bank angle then decreasing simultaneously with the start of a steep climb. The bank angle steepened again and engine thrust was reduced, whereupon the twin-jet transport went into a descent. The crew's energetic effort in pulling back on the control wheel without recovering from the bank was unsuccessful, and the Tu-104 struck the ground some 5 miles (10 km) south-west of the airport and caught fire. Impact occurred at a speed of about 500 mph (800 kmh), with the aircraft in a near vertical left bank, descending at an angle of 20 degrees and on a west-south-westerly heading.

The accident was attributed to incorrect indications by the main artificial horizons and the compass system due to an electrical supply failure, coupled with the inability of the pilots to determine their attitude using their back-up instruments at night and in clouds, conditions that precluded flight by visual reference.

The electrical system malfunction could have resulted from a temporary failure of the transducer or its inadvertent switching off by the crew after engine start during their pre-flight preparations. They apparently switched on the transducer about a minute before the crash, but it was too late to ensure normal operation of the attitude instruments.

Date: 13 October 1973 (*c.* 20:15)
Location: Near Domodedovo, Russian Soviet Federative Socialist Republic, USSR
Operator: Aeroflot (USSR)
Aircraft type: Tupolev Tu-104B (*SSSR-42486*)

The jet airliner, which was designated as Flight 964 and on a domestic service from Kutaisi, Georgian SSR, crashed and burned about 5 miles (10 km) from Domodedovo Airport, serving Moscow, where it was scheduled to land. All 119 persons aboard (114 passengers and a crew of five) perished.

Its undercarriage having been lowered but its flaps still retracted, the aircraft was on a south-south-easterly heading when it plunged to earth from an approximate height of 1,300 ft (400 m) following a right turn and then a steep left spiral manoeuvre, the latter with a banking attitude of up to 75 degrees. It was determined that an electrical power failure had rendered inoperable the aircraft's compass system and main gyros. As a result, the magnetic heading indication froze and the pilots could not ascertain their attitude using their standby instruments.

The accident occurred in darkness, but the weather was not considered a factor.

Date: 22 December 1973 (22:10)
Location: Near Tetouan, Morocco
Operator: Sobelair SA (Belgium)
Aircraft type: Sud-Aviation Caravelle VI-N (*OO-SRD*)

All 106 persons aboard perished when the jet airliner, which was owned by the Belgian carrier SABENA and sub-leased to Royal Air Maroc, crashed while preparing to land at Boukhalf Airport, serving Tangier, an en route stop during a non-scheduled service from Paris, France, to Casablanca, Morocco. Many of the passengers were Moroccans on their way home for the holidays; except for one, the crew of seven were Belgian.

Apparently failing to capture the outer marker signal for an instrument landing system (ILS) approach to Runway 28, the Caravelle proceeded too far east on the outbound leg of a procedural turn, outside the protected area and over hazardous terrain, before turning back on to the final approach course. Its undercarriage retracted, the aircraft struck a mountain at an approximate elevation of 2,300 ft (700 m) and some 25 miles (40 km) from the airport, bursting into flames on impact.

The accident occurred in darkness and meteorological conditions consisting of rain and a low ceiling, with a broken overcast at around 2,000 ft (600 m) and scattered clouds down to about 1,000 ft (300 m). The winds were blowing from a south-south-westerly direction at 20 to 40 knots.

Date: 26 January 1974 (*c.* 07:30)
Location: Near Izmir, Turkey
Operator: Turk Hava Yollari AO (Turkish Airlines)
Aircraft type: Fokker-VFW F.28 Fellowship Mark 1000 (*TC-JAO*)

The jetliner was on a scheduled domestic service to Istanbul and crashed while taking off from Cumaovasi Airport, killing 66 persons aboard (62 passengers and four crew members). Six passengers, including an infant, and one crew member survived with injuries.

Using Runway 35, the aircraft became airborne before yawing to the left at a height of about 30 ft (10 m). It struck the ground in a nearly level attitude, first with the outboard fairing doors of its left wing flap, then with the left side of its belly, and finally ran into the bank of a drainage ditch that

TC-JAO, the Turkish Airlines Fokker F.28 Fellowship that crashed on take-off from Izmir airport. *(Fokker-VFW)*

parallels the west side of the runway. The twin-engine jet disintegrated and burst into flames, and the main part of its fuselage came to rest inverted.

The weather around the time of the accident consisted of a slight mist, with a broken overcast and a visibility of approximately 3 miles (5 km).

Frost on the wings of the F.28, which had accumulated during the night, combined with over-rotation during the take-off had resulted in a stall, and the low altitude of the aircraft precluded recovery by the pilot.

Date: 30 January 1974 (c. 23:40)
Location: Near Pago Pago, Tutuila Island, American Samoa
Operator: Pan American World Airways (US)
Aircraft type: Boeing Advanced 707-321B (N454PA)

Operating as Flight 806, the jet airliner was scheduled to land at Pago Pago International Airport, the first of two en route stops during a service from Auckland, New Zealand, to Los Angeles, California, US. The 707 crashed and burned while conducting an instrument landing system (ILS) approach to Runway 05, killing 97 persons aboard, including the entire crew of 10. Four passengers survived with injuries.

The accident occurred in darkness, and the airport weather around this time consisted of heavy rain showers, a broken overcast down to approximately 1,500 ft (500 m), a visibility of 1 mile (c. 1.5 km) and north-easterly winds of about 20 knots, with gusts to 35.

In its official report, released nearly a year later, the US National Transportation Safety Board (NTSB) attributed the crash to the apparent failure of the flight crew to correct an excessive rate of descent after the aircraft had passed through the decision height. More than two years after the accident, the US Air Line Pilots Association petitioned to have the probable cause reconsidered, and knowledge gained from other wind-related airline disasters prompted the NTSB to re-open its investigation, examining anew the flight data recorder (FDR) read-out, the cockpit voice recorder (CVR) transcript and the aircraft's engineering performance data.

The revised report, released in 1977, again ascribed crew error as the primary cause, but also injected an environmental factor, namely the destabilising winds that were encountered during the final approach. One Board member who dissented from the majority believed that the winds were in fact the primary cause of the crash.

The jet flew into a predominantly increasing headwind and/or an updraught about 50 seconds before impact, causing it to deviate above the proper glide path. Recognising the situation, which was believed to be related to the winds flowing out of the rainstorm which were affected by the upsloping terrain on the island, the captain reduced thrust in order to correct the aircraft's flight profile. However, he apparently did not, realise what was happening when the 707 came out of this condition and probably encountered a decreasing headwind and/or downdraught; the resulting increase in the descent rate may have gone unnoticed because he was looking outside and not observing his instruments. Moreover, since the aircraft was over an area devoid of lights (the so-called 'black hole' effect) and flying in heavy rain at the time, there would have been no visual clues by which the high sink rate could have been detected. The rain may also have reduced the pilot's visual segment (the ground observable looking forward from the cockpit) and created the illusion of a nose-up attitude, and, under the circumstances, the natural response would be to ease forward on the control column and reduce thrust.

It was determined that the first officer had not set his navigational receiver to the ILS frequency, and would thus have had to look across the cockpit at the captain's instruments for glide slope information and flight director commands. In the process he may not have noticed the visual approach slope indicator (VASI) lights showing that the aircraft had gone below the glide slope. Nor did the co-pilot call out the descent rate, which, combined with the restricted visibility, absence of lighting and failure to monitor the instruments, contributed to the disaster. As transcribed on the CVR tape, he stated that the jet was 'a little high', and after the radio altimeter warning sounded, reported to the pilot, 'You're at minimums', followed by 'Field in sight'.

Its undercarriage down and flaps set at 50 degrees, the 707 hit trees some 3,865 ft (1,180 m) from the runway threshold, then ploughed into a tropical forest. In the impact its nose and main gears, all four engines, outer wings and numerous other components separated.

This accident should have been nearly 100 per cent survivable, since only the first officer died of traumatic injury, but all the other fatalities resulted from burns and/or smoke inhalation.

Date: 3 March 1974 (*c.* 12:40)
Location: Near Ermenonville, Ile-de-France, France
Operator: Turk Hava Yollari AO (Turkish Airlines)
Aircraft type: McDonnell Douglas DC-10 Series 10 (*TC-JAV*)

The disaster that had been feared since the start of the jumbo jet era – a non-survivable crash involving a heavily-loaded wide-bodied transport –

A post-impact fire resulted in much of the damage and all but one of the fatalities in this crash of a Pan American World Airways Boeing 707 on Samoa. *(AP Images)*

The McDonnell Douglas DC-10 became the centre of controversy following the disaster involving the Turkish Airlines aircraft that was identical to this one. *(Ikaros/Uniphoto Press International)*

left commercial aviation reeling for more than a year. This accident has been used by industry critics as an example of corporate ineptitude, design short-sightedness and government laxity.

At the centre of the controversy was a serious defect in the McDonnell Douglas aircraft. The fault lay not in its performance or handling, but something far more mundane, namely the locking mechanism of its rear cargo door. Previously, most jetliner doors had been of the 'plug' type, opening inwards and held firmly in place by cabin pressure when the aircraft is in flight. But the door on the DC-10, which was built by the Convair division of General Dynamics, opened outwards. Due to the constant force being exerted against the door while operating at high altitudes, a durable and foolproof locking system was an absolute necessity.

The door was designed to be closed with a switch. An electrically powered actuator was used to turn a torque tube to which four latches were attached. As the tube revolved during the locking process, the talon of each latch snapped over a corresponding spool. An external lever was then pulled down, driving a locking pin into place on the outside of each latch. Any jamming of the lever should have been an immediate indication that the latches were not in the correct 'over-centre' position, i.e. properly secured. In addition, at the

end of its travel the locking pin bar was supposed to activate a mechanical switch in order to extinguish an open-door warning light in the cockpit. As a final back-up, a small vent located on the outside of the door was designed to close when the locking pins were in place.

If, however, the actuator did not extend sufficiently because the external switch was not held long enough, or for some other reason, the latches would be incorrectly secured. Significantly, the linkages between the lever and the locking pin bar were found to be too weak.

The shortcomings of the locking mechanism were fully realised in June 1972 when an American Airlines DC-10 on a domestic US service nearly met with disaster soon after taking off from Detroit, Michigan. As the jet was at an approximate height of 12,000 ft (3,700 m) and climbing to its cruising altitude, the door, located on the port side and towards the aft of the fuselage, blew open. Due to the absence of relief valves, the resulting explosive decompression was more intense in the cargo hold than in the passenger cabin above it, and the pressure differential imposed a downward load on the cabin floor that exceeded its designed strength, causing it to partially collapse. This in turn damaged the elevator and rudder control cables that ran from the flight deck to the empennage.

Using skill and resourcefulness, the captain and his crew managed a safe landing, relying primarily on the engines to maintain control, and there were no serious injuries among the 67 persons aboard.

Investigation revealed that the door had indeed been improperly closed by the baggage handler – the latches were but one-third of an inch from the 'over-centre' point. In accordance with the prescribed procedures, the handler had attempted to secure the mechanism with the external locking lever, but instead of fitting neatly around the latches, the locking pins had jammed against the lugs. Using his knee for support, he was able to force the lever down, but in doing so merely bent the internal rods and tubes without properly locking the door. The same deflection may have permitted the indicator switch to make contact, preventing the illumination of the cockpit warning light. In addition, the tiny vent door proved to be useless as a safety feature; as designed, it would close whenever the handle was pulled down, regardless of whether the pins were correctly in place.

Almost immediately after the American Airlines incident, the locking mechanism became suspect, prompting action by the Western Division of the US Federal Aviation Administration (FAA). Officials began to produce an airworthiness directive (AD), which would have required, as an interim measure, the placement of a small viewing port over one of the locking pins in the rear cargo door of every DC-10 – a simple peek would thus accurately determine the position of the latches. Also suggested was a placard warning against excessive force in using the external handle. But in the now infamous 'gentleman's agreement', between then FAA Administrator John Shaffer and Jackson McGowen, at the time president of the Douglas divison of McDonnell Douglas, the AD was downgraded to three service bulletins. These not only requested the modification of the directives but also the re-wiring of the electric actuators, alteration of the torque tube and the installation of a support plate to help prevent it from bending, and adjustment of the locking pins to allow for greater travel. While the changes could be practically guaranteed, they would not be carried out with the same urgency as they would have had they been stipulated in an AD.

Perhaps as a result, nearly two years after the issuance of the service bulletins, *TC-JAV* was flying

with only two of the requested modifications, and that set the stage for disaster on the Sunday that Turkish Airlines Flight 981 took off from Orly Airport, serving Paris, bound for London, the second leg of a service originating at Istanbul, Turkey. A British Airways strike had forced many travellers to switch to the Turkish carrier. Consequently, the aircraft was almost loaded to capacity upon its departure, and more than half of the passengers were British.

The weather at the time was ideal, with only scattered cumulus clouds at about 3,000 ft (1,000 m). Cleared for ascent to flight level 230, the wide-bodied jet airliner was observed on radar as it assumed a north-north-westerly direction. Shortly afterwards the primary echo was seen to split in two, with one part remaining stationary before disappearing from the radarscope. The second part turned left to a heading of 280 degrees before it too vanished. What the air traffic controller had observed was the separation of the cargo door, which occurred at an approximate height of 11,000 ft (3,400 m) over the village of Saint-Pathus, at a point

A scar in the forest marks the scene of the first non-survivable crash of a heavily loaded wide-bodied commercial jet transport. *(AP Images)*

when the cabin pressure should have still roughly equalled that at sea level.

As with the American Airlines DC-10, the loss of the door caused a sudden depressurisation, which was followed by the failure of the cabin floor. However, with the extra weight imposed on the structure, the collapse was even more extensive, and six occupants in two triple-seat units were ejected through the opening. There must also have been serious impairment not only to the elevator and rudder cables, but to the No. 2 (centre) power plant controls.

The noise of the decompression was heard on the cockpit voice recorder (CVR) tape, and the first officer, responding to the captain's query of what had happened, said 'The fuselage has burst'. Both the No. 1 and No. 3 engines were also throttled back, apparently automatically, and the aircraft pitched down into a steep descent, the crew unable to regain control. The angle had flattened to about 4 degrees nose-down before the DC-10 ploughed into a forest at an indicated air speed of nearly 500 mph (800 kmh) and while banked slightly to the left, disintegrating in a huge fireball. All 346 persons aboard, including 12 crew members, perished. The main wreckage was strewn over an area approximately 2,300 ft (700 m) long and 300 ft (100 m) wide, some 25 miles (40 km) north-north-east of the French capital. There were only a few small post-crash fires. The duration of the flight was about 10 minutes, and 77 seconds expired between the time of the door failure and the final impact.

The remains of the cargo door revealed various deficiencies. It was obvious that the latches had not achieved the 'over-centre' position. The forces against the door generated by the increasing pressure in flight had been transmitted back to the actuator, which withstood the compression, and in turn to the two bolts that attached it to the door structure, which did not. When the bolts gave way, the latches lost their support, causing the door to open and the top shaft of the actuator to break. The door then shattered into several pieces and became detached from the aircraft.

Studies indicated that, once again, the improper securing of the latches was attributed to the incomplete extension of the actuator shaft. This was believed to have resulted from the intentional cut-off of power when the operator did not hold the switch long enough, or unintentionally, due to slippage of the torque limiter, the normal action of

the thermal protection trip device, or the accidental stoppage of the electrical power supply.

Company records indicating that all of the suggested modifications had been completed on *TC-JAV* prior to its delivery to the airline in December 1972 proved to be erroneous. Although adjustments to the locking pins and lock limit warning switch were made, the work was not in accordance with aeronautical standards. Of course the installation of the viewing port, one modification that had been carried out, could alone have prevented the tragedy, had someone used it to make a visual inspection prior to the take-off. The warning placard was also in place, but of no use for two reasons. First, it had been printed in English, which the Algerian-born baggage handler could not read; and perhaps more importantly, the design of the mechanism and the shoddiness of the modifications made it impossible to pull down the locking lever, bending the internal components, without the use of any abnormal force. The misrigging must also have accounted for the fact that the warning light on the flight engineer's panel had failed to illuminate.

Following the disaster, the FAA issued an AD mandating a 'closed-door' system on all DC-10 cargo doors. Similar to that used on the Boeing 747, the mechanism is designed so as to prevent closure of the vent door unless the locking pins are correctly in place. Subsequently, the government agency took action to further enhance safety in the DC-10, 747 and Lockheed's L-1011 TriStar. Cabin floors were to be reinforced and venting improved so as to increase survivability of the aircraft in the event of a major decompression or structural failure.

The McDonnell Douglas transport recovered from the black eye it suffered in the wake of this accident. But five years later, it would again come under close scrutiny after another catastrophic crash in the US (see separate entry, 25 May 1979).

Date: 22 April 1974 (22:26)
Location: Near Grogak, Bali, Indonesia
Operator: Pan American World Airways (US)
Aircraft type: Boeing 707-321C (*N446PA*)

Designated as Flight 812, the jet airliner was on a transpacific service from Hong Kong to Los Angeles, California, US, and scheduled to land at Ngurah Rai Airport, located near Denpasar, the first of four en route stops. During the intermediate phase of an approach using automatic direction finder (ADF) instrument procedures, and after being cleared to descend to 2,500 ft (c. 750 m), the 707 struck Mt Mesehe, disintegrated and burned. All 107 persons aboard (96 passengers and a crew of 11) perished.

The accident occurred in evening darkness with no moon, and in an area of clear weather conditions. Its undercarriage extended, the aircraft was banking to the right and on a heading of between 155 and 160 degrees when it crashed in a wooded area at an approximate elevation of 3,000 ft (1,000 m).

It was believed that, in an attempt to expedite the landing, the crew executed a right-hand procedural turn prematurely to join the 263-degree outbound track of the traffic pattern. This manoeuvre was apparently based on the indication of only one of the aircraft's ADF receivers, while the other one remained in a steady condition. However, the indication of being over the non-directional beacon (NDB) had been false; the jet was in fact some 35 miles (55 km) north of that point, and the use of a non-standard procedure had prevented the pilots from knowing their exact position.

Although attempts to obtain a proper ADF indication were subsequently made by the crew, this would probably not have been possible because at the time the beacon was shielded by a mountain range. The approach was then continued until impact.

The investigative board was unable to determine what caused one ADF needle to swing as if to give an over-station indication, though it may have resulted from either external or internal interference. There was no evidence of interference by a radio broadcasting station. It was also believed that the pilot-in-command of the flight lacked familiarity with the procedures at this particular airport.

A recommendation made by the board for the installation at Denpasar of distance-measuring equipment (DME) to supplement the existing very-high-frequency omnidirectional range (VOR) facility would later be implemented.

Date: 27 April 1974 (time unknown)
Location: Near Leningrad (St Petersburg), Russian Soviet Federative Socialist Republic, USSR
Operator: Aeroflot (USSR)
Aircraft type: Ilyushin Il-18B (SSSR-75559)

All 109 persons aboard (102 passengers and seven crew members) were killed when the four-engine turboprop airliner crashed and exploded in a field shortly after leaving the city's airport, bound for Zaporozhye, Ukraine, the first segment of a scheduled domestic service with an ultimate destination of Krasnodar, RSFSR.

While climbing after the take-off, the crew reported that the aircraft's No. 4 power plant had caught fire and was vibrating dangerously. The flight crew were cleared to land on the same runway in the opposite direction of the departure path, but after it had turned on to a heading of about 280 degrees and following passage of the outer marker beacon, the Il-18 rolled abruptly to the right into an inverted attitude and slammed to earth approximately 1 mile (1.5 km) short of the runway. The accident occurred in daylight conditions; the weather was not a factor.

The blaze in the nacelle of the No. 4 engine was attributed to the structural failure of the third stage turbine disc, which itself resulted from the gradual growth of a fatigue crack. Burning out a part of the right flap in the area of its jack caused the spontaneous retraction of the unit, which had been extended to 35 degrees. This in turn led to the uncontrolled rolling of the aircraft despite action by the flight crew.

Date: 8 September 1974 (c. 09:40)
Location: Off Kefallinía, Greece
Operator: Trans World Airlines (TWA) (US)
Aircraft type: Boeing Advanced 707-331B (N8734)

Operating as Flight 841, the jetliner had taken off earlier from Athens bound for Rome, Italy, one segment of a service originating at Tel Aviv, Israel, with an ultimate destination of New York City. There was no distress message, but the occupants of another aircraft saw the 707 pitch up, roll to the left and spiral down before it plunged into the Ionian Sea approximately 50 miles (80 km) west of the island and some 200 miles (320 km) west-north-west of the Greek capital. All 88 persons aboard (79 passengers and a crew of nine) were killed.

The water in the crash area was around 10,000 ft (3,000 m) deep, and searchers were able to recover only about 2,500 lb (1,140 kg) of floating wreckage, most of it non-structural interior material and personal effects, and the bodies of 24 victims.

Neither the flight data recorder (FDR) nor the cockpit voice recorder (CVR) were located.

On some of the debris that was picked up there were indications of an explosion having occurred before impact. Metallic and non-metallic particles were found in the foam lining of a suitcase lid and in a seat cushion. There were also penetration markings in a recovered floor panel section. These findings were similar to those uncovered in the investigation of the 1967 crash of a British European Airways Comet jet in the Mediterranean Sea (see separate entry, 12 October 1967), a disaster that was ascribed to sabotage. The 707 had apparently been a victim of the same fate.

It was concluded that a high-explosive device had detonated in the aft cargo compartment of the aircraft while it was cruising at an altitude of 28,000 ft (c. 8,500 m). The blast probably buckled and damaged the cabin floor in such a manner that one or more of the elevator and rudder system cables were stretched and perhaps broken, which would have caused the violent pitch-up and yaw and resulted in a loss of control. The No. 2 engine apparently separated during the manoeuvre due to over-stressing.

There were no suspects in the bombing, but a Palestinian organisation claimed responsibility. The device must have been put aboard at Athens airport, which was notorious for its lax security. (Just two weeks earlier, in fact, a sabotage attempt had been made against the same airline and flight number, but the bomb malfunctioned in the cargo hold of the jetliner.) Only carry-on luggage was being inspected at the time, but, in accordance with TWA procedures, no unaccompanied checked-in baggage would be allowed on to an aircraft. The carrier later instituted a policy to ensure that all luggage would be examined at the boarding point.

Date: 11 September 1974 (c. 07:35)
Location: Near Charlotte, North Carolina, US
Operator: Eastern Airlines (US)
Aircraft type: McDonnell Douglas DC-9 Series 31 (*N8984E*)

Although it was not the worst US air carrier disaster of the year, the circumstances surrounding the crash of Flight 212 made it particularly notorious. Investigation revealed a serious departure from the prescribed procedures on the part of the flight crew, which resulted in a lack of altitude awareness during a landing attempt, with fatal results.

The accident occurred as the crew were conducting a very-high-frequency omnidirectional range/distance-measuring equipment (VOR/DME) instrument procedure approach to Runway 36 at Douglas Municipal Airport, a scheduled stop during a domestic service from Charleston, South Carolina, to Chicago, Illinois. Its undercarriage down and flaps set at 50 degrees, the jetliner hit trees, then crashed into a field in approximate alignment with, but some 3 miles (5 km) short of, the runway. Upon impact, the aircraft broke up and burst into flames, killing 72 of the 82 persons aboard, including the captain and one cabin attendant. One of the victims succumbed a month later. Among the survivors, eight passengers and the first officer were injured; the other hostess escaped unscathed.

The weather in the area at the time was characterised by shallow, patchy ground fog. Though visual meteorological conditions existed above it, visibility was drastically reduced within the fog.

Up until about 2½ minutes before impact, the pilots were engaged in a conversation that was not pertinent to the operation of the aircraft. The discussion was considered distractive and reflected a lax cockpit atmosphere that continued throughout the rest of the flight and ultimately contributed to the accident. As transcribed by the cockpit voice recorder (CVR), the two men covered a variety of topics, from politics to used motor cars, with both expressing strong views and mild aggravation regarding these subjects. In the process they may have relaxed their instrument scan and relied more heavily on visual cues to carry out the approach. And when the DC-9 entered the fog, there would not have been enough time for them to switch back to instrument procedures.

The aircraft passed over the final approach fix (FAF) some 450 ft (135 m) below the minimum crossing altitude and about 50 mph (80 kmh) above the recommended air speed. Its terrain warning system sounded at a height of 1,000 ft (c. 300 m) above the ground, but the alert was not heeded by the crew. Nor did the captain call out when 500 ft above airport elevation, or 100 ft above the minimum descent altitude (MDA), as required.

The first fatal crash of a Boeing 747 involved an aircraft operated by the German carrier Deutsche Lufthansa, in the same livery as the one shown here. *(Philip Jarrett)*

An analysis of the CVR tape indicated that the captain had been referring to his No. 2 altimeter, which was set to the above sea level height (QNH) of 1,800 ft, rather than the given airfield elevation (QFE) of 1,074 ft. The first officer, who had been flying the DC-9 during the approach, later testified that he thought the aircraft was only about 130 ft (40 m) below the minimum altitude upon reaching the FAF. This would have been possible had he accepted 1,800 as the QFE, then misread by 1,000 ft his own altimeter, which was set to airport elevation. Such a reading error could have happened if the co-pilot saw one of the altimeter pointers between the 6 and 7 while failing to observe the window of the instrument, which indicates height in 1,000-ft increments. Considering the incorrect QFE, his assumed altitude would have been 1,670 ft (*c.* 510 m), giving him about 1,300 ft (400 m) to go before reaching the MDA of some 400 ft (120 m) above the ground. The descent was thus continued and in fact steepened seconds before impact. This would also account for the absence of call-outs. In its investigative report, the US National Transportation Safety Board (NTSB) described this theory as 'speculative in nature'.

Whatever the reason for the failure to assess properly and maintain a safe height, it was merely a manifestation of the poor discipline displayed by the crew.

Date: 20 November 1974 (*c.* 07:50)
Location: Near Nairobi, Kenya
Operator: Deutsche Lufthansa AG (West Germany)
Aircraft type: Boeing 747-130 (*D-ABYB*)

The first fatal crash of a Boeing 747 was not the catastrophe many had feared, the death toll being within that recorded in accidents involving conventional jets, and even propeller-driven transports. However, commercial aviation had, of course, already experienced its first 'titanic' disaster earlier in the year with the DC-10 crash in France.

Operating as Flight 540, and on a service from Frankfurt, (West) Germany, to Johannesburg, South Africa, the wide-bodied jet airliner was cleared for take-off on Runway 24 at the Nairobi airport, a scheduled stop.

Accelerating to about 150 mph (250 kmh), the aircraft commenced rotation and became airborne at an approximate speed of 165 mph (265 kmh) some 8,000 ft (2,500 m) from the beginning of the runway. Seconds later a buffeting or strong vibration was felt, prompting the captain first to suspect engine trouble, then unbalanced wheels. Continuing the take-off, gear retraction was begun, but the co-pilot lost all feeling of acceleration.

The jet reached a height of around 100 ft (30 m) before starting to descend, and the control wheel stick-shaker then activated, warning of an impending stall. Realising that a crash was imminent, the first officer fully retarded all four thrust levers.

Its undercarriage was still in the retraction cycle when the 747 grazed bushes and grass approximately 3,700 ft (1,130 m) beyond the end and some 100 ft (30 m) to the left of the extended centreline of the runway, then struck a slightly elevated access road and began to break up. In the impact and subsequent fire, which was started by an explosion in the left wing, then spread to the fuselage, 59 persons aboard (55 passengers and four crew members) were killed. Among the 98 survivors, who included all three flight crewmen and 10 of the 14 cabin attendants, 54 persons suffered injuries and 44 escaped unscathed.

The cause of the accident became known soon afterwards when it was discovered that the flight crew had failed to extend the leading-edge flaps. Further investigation suggested a high probability that the pneumatic system used to power the flap unit was not functioning at the time they were selected to the take-off position, this because the flight engineer had inadvertently failed to open the system's bleed valves. He must have also failed to notice that the four 'valve closed' amber lights were continuously illuminated and the pneumatic gauge was indicating zero duct pressure.

The crew had in fact failed to satisfactorily complete the pre-flight checklist. Whether or not the flight engineer had verbally responded to the question concerning the bleed valves could not be determined, since the three men were not using the intercom system and their voices were not clearly transcribed on the cockpit voice recorder (CVR) tape.

As a result of the flap setting, the aircraft, after becoming airborne, entered into a 'partially stalled' condition due to abnormally high drag and substantial air-flow separation. This condition resulted directly in the loss of acceleration noted by the first officer and the low rate of climb following take-off. The situation may have been aggravated by the fact that rotation was initiated slightly below the prescribed speed.

The pilots attempted to maintain or increase air speed by lowering the nose, but this action could only be done to a limited extent because of their proximity to the ground, and was largely ineffective anyway. This may have been partly due to the presence of wind shear in the area, but was primarily blamed on the increase in drag occurring at this time, probably because of further separation in the air-flow and as the aircraft lost the benefit of ground effect. An additional but less significant factor may have been an increase in drag resulting from the opening of the undercarriage doors during gear retraction, which could have been greater than predicted.

The crash probably could have been prevented by reducing the pitch angle and increasing power earlier, but the crew suspected engine trouble due to a bird strike and did not take the appropriate action. Furthermore, the stall-warning system was not programmed to take account of the leading-edge flap position.

In terms of detecting an incorrect setting, a green light on the pilot's centre panel and eight additional green lights on the flight engineer's annunciator panel were still regarded as inadequate.

A number of previous incidents in which 747s took off with the leading-edge flaps not properly set had taken place, though none proved disastrous because the additional factors that came into play in this accident were not present. As a result of the first case, occurring in August 1972 and involving a British Airways jet, the manufacturer agreed to a modification by the carrier that wired the leading-edge flap system to the undercarriage/trailing-edge flap warning horn.

Boeing did send advisories to all 747 operators about the importance of checking the leading-edge flap position, but made no mention of the British modification. Inadequacies in the international incident reporting network thus contributed to the Lufthansa crash. Even a revised cockpit checklist procedure that came out of the Boeing advisory did not specifically require a verification of the pneumatic system before take-off.

The following year, the US Federal Aviation Administration (FAA) issued an airworthiness directive for additional safety features on the jet, as proposed by the manufacturer, designed so that when the aircraft's trailing-edge flaps were set in the take-off configuration, an amber light would illuminate on the pilot's panel if the leading-edge flaps were not fully extended and an aural warning sound if any flap unit was not properly positioned.

Deemed culpable for the errors leading to the accident, both the captain and the flight engineer of Flight 540 were later dismissed by the airline.

A Trans World Airlines Boeing 727-231, the type that hit Mt Weather near the US capital. *(Trans World Airlines)*

Date: 1 December 1974 (11:09)
Location: Near Berryville, Virginia, US
Operator: Trans World Airlines (TWA) (US)
Aircraft type: Boeing 727-231 (N54328)

This could be classified as a 'milestone' accident because of the repercussions it generated and the changes that ensued. It also brought to an end a frustrating year, in terms of safety, for the US air carrier industry.

Flight 514 had originated at Indianapolis, Indiana, on a domestic service to Washington, DC, with an en route stop at Columbus, Ohio. Washington National Airport, where it was to have landed, had been closed due to high crosswinds, diverting the aircraft to Dulles International Airport.

Three minutes after its transferral from the regional air traffic control centre, approach control radioed the flight: 'TWA 514, you're cleared for a VOR/DME approach to Runway 12' (using very-high-frequency omnidirectional range/distance-measuring equipment instrument procedures). This was only intended as a traffic advisory, meaning that the 727 could descend without conflicting with another aircraft; since it was proceeding under its own navigation, the crew would be responsible for obstacle clearance. However, as an analysis of the cockpit voice recorder (CVR) tape would later confirm, the message was construed by the pilot to

mean that the flight could safely initiate an immediate descent.

The captain was heard to say 'Eighteen hundred is the bottom', in reference to the minimum descent altitude inside the Round Hill airway intersection, as depicted on the approach chart.

The profile view of the map did not indicate the minimum height of 3,400 ft (*c.* 1,040 m) outside that point, which the aircraft had yet to reach, although the minimum did appear on the plan (overhead) view of the chart, but the pilot must have felt he could go below it because the 727 was not on any of the published airways. His comment 'When he clears you, that means you can go to your . . . initial approach altitude' showed his confidence in the controller, and the final approach was thus begun by the co-pilot.

The local weather at the time consisted of low clouds, rain mixed with snow and a visibility of only 50–100 ft (*c.* 15–30 m); the wind was from the east at about 40 mph (65 kmh). There were indications that both the captain and first officer had fleeting glimpses of the ground, but neither must have been able to derive any height reference from what they had seen.

Though it would have been precariously low, the aircraft could have cleared the terrain had it maintained an altitude of 1,800 ft (*c.* 550 m), but apparently due to a combination of the co-pilot's flying technique and the turbulence encountered, the descent could not be arrested. The altitude alert system sounded upon reaching the minimum height, and the radio altimeter warning went off twice, at 500 ft (*c.* 150 m) and 100 ft (*c.* 30 m) above the ground, the last time an instant before impact and just after the pilot was heard to say 'Get some power on'. But by then it was too late.

The cleanly configured jetliner was generally aligned with the runway and in a slight descent when it struck Mt Weather at an approximate elevation of 1,670 ft (*c.* 510 m), about 30 miles (50 km) north-west of the airport and some 50 miles (80 km) from the capital city. Initial impact was with trees about 70 ft (20 m) above the ground, and at an indicated air speed of around 250 mph (400 kmh), and the aircraft then slammed into a rocky outcrop, disintegrated and burned. All 92 persons aboard (85 passengers and seven crew members) perished.

During the inquiry into the disaster, witnesses from the US Federal Aviation Administration (FAA) testified that since it had not been vectored to the final approach course, the flight was not considered a 'radar arrival'. As a result it was not given any altitude restrictions. But the US National Transportation Safety Board (NTSB) ruled that since it had just before received vectoring from the control centre, the aircraft was in a 'radar environment' and that such restrictions should have been included in the clearance. This particular issue led the investigative board to conclude that the clearance was inadequate and therefore a contributing factor in the accident. Two of the five members of the NTSB went even further, disagreeing with the findings of the majority and placing more importance on the actions of the controller as a causative factor coupled with the pilot's failure to follow the approach chart.

The three other members ascribed the crew's decision to descend below a safe height to inadequacies and a lack of clarity in the air traffic control procedures then in use, leading to confusion by both pilots and controllers regarding each other's responsibilities during operations in instrument meteorological conditions. They noted, however, that the plan view of the chart indicating the minimum altitude in the general area should have been apparent to the crew.

The investigation revealed that pilots were not always aware of the type of radar services they were receiving, i.e. only traffic separation, navigational assistance with course guidance only, or monitoring to observe deviations in both flight path and altitude. It was also noted in the investigative report that with the then new automated radar terminal system (ARTS III) equipment, which provides a three-dimensional view, pilots had become increasingly dependent on controllers, which lessened their need to know the terrain over which they were flying and, in some cases, even their position relative to the obstacles or the airport itself.

The NTSB made 14 recommendations to the FAA as a result of this crash, and three of those adopted were particularly important. One was procedural, in that controllers would issue altitude restrictions to pilots making non-precision instrument approaches. The other two were technical innovations. First, ARTS III units would be modified so as to alert controllers when aircraft operating in terminal areas deviated from predetermined altitudes. Second, and perhaps even more significant, was the requirement that all American-registered air carrier aircraft be equipped with a so-called ground proximity warning system (GPWS). This device, which works similarly to a radio altimeter but is more sophisticated, provides the crew with warnings pertaining to height over terrain, descent rate, glide slope deviation, and even flap positions. GPWS units have since become standard on airliners throughout the world.

During the first five years of the 1970s, major US airlines suffered nine fatal 'controlled-flight-into-terrain' crashes during passenger operations, taking nearly 700 lives. In the last half of the decade they had only two such accidents, resulting in 13 deaths. The tragedy of Flight 514 left a legacy of safety for all future air travellers.

Date: 4 December 1974 (*c.* 22:15)
Location: Near Maskeliya, Sri Lanka
Operator: Martinair Holland NV (The Netherlands)
Aircraft type: Douglas DC-8 Series 55F (*PH-MBH*)

The jet airliner was being operated on behalf of Garuda Indonesian Airways on a non-scheduled service from Surabaya, on Java, to Jiddah, Saudi Arabia, with a planned 'technical' stop at Bandaranaike International Airport, located about

10 miles (15 km) north and serving the Sri Lankan capital of Colombo. Except for two Indonesian stewardesses, its crew of nine were Dutch; the 182 passengers were Indonesian Muslims on a pilgrimage to Mecca.

During its descent to land, the aircraft struck a mountain in the Anjimalai Range at an approximate elevation of 4,500 ft (1,400 m) and some 45 miles (70 km) east-south-east of the airport, exploded and burned. All 191 persons aboard perished.

Having lost approximately one-third of its port wing in the initial impact with an adjacent ridge, the DC-8 had crashed while banked at about 30 degrees to the left and with its nose slightly raised and undercarriage retracted. The disaster occurred in darkness, but the weather at the time was fair and not considered a factor.

The foil from the aircraft's flight data recorder (FDR) was torn to pieces and yielded no useful information, but by analysing the known facts Sri Lankan aviation authorities were able to reconstruct what probably happened.

It was apparent that the crew had descended below a safe altitude due to a position error. As noted in the investigative report, both the Doppler navigational system and the weather radar installed in this aircraft were different from others in the company's fleet, and although this had been brought to the attention of the flight crew, it still left room for misinterpretation. Specifically, the 'distance to go' counter in the Doppler system was of a different make so that only the 100-mile indications would be accurate; the positions of the 10-mile and 1-mile discs in the unit were considered arbitrary. In addition, the range in this particular radar screen was 180 nautical miles, 30 more than those in other Martinair aircraft.

Since the navigational aids in this area were sparse and unreliable, the crew probably used the weather radar to re-establish their position while over the Indian Ocean and approaching the Sri Lankan coast. But if the radar had been misread, it could have resulted in a navigational error. Also, the possibility of an overlapping cloud giving a false impression of the coastline could not be ruled out.

Another point mentioned was that the pilot-in-command had no recent experience on the route and did not receive a proper route check, which was not in strict compliance with international aviation regulations. Also the co-pilot had little experience in the type of aircraft and none in either this particular DC-8 or on the course being taken.

Besides the matter of route qualification for crew, the report also noted the shortcomings on the part of the airline in the maintenance of technical records pertaining to aircraft. The officers responsible for the operation at Surabaya also displayed 'a certain degree of negligence' for failing to retain copies of maintenance records and navigational documentation relevant to this flight. Finally, both the captain and first officer were unaware of the correct reporting points in the Colombo Flight Information Region.

Generally, The Netherlands Aircraft Accident Investigation Board agreed with the Sri Lankan findings, especially regarding the weather radar discrepancy. It remarked that this could have led to a continuous error of 30 nautical miles from the time the pilots attempted to re-establish their position.

The Dutch board concluded that as a result of the mistake in navigation, the crew believed the aircraft to be that distance closer to the airport than was actually the case. Therefore when they reported being 14 miles out, it was closer to 50; the pilots presumably adjusted their 'distance to go' counters to agree with the radar information when the two readings were different.

One of the recommendations made in the Sri Lankan report was that instruments that did not give accurate indications be masked. The Dutch board also noted that a requirement for ground-proximity warning system (GPWS) devices on transport aircraft registered in the Netherlands, which went into effect in 1976, would help to prevent this type of accident in the future.

Date: 24 June 1975 (16:05)
Location: New York, New York, US
Operator: Eastern Airlines (US)
Aircraft type: Boeing 727-225 (N8845E)

The first of three major US air carrier accidents attributable to wind shear that occurred during the 1975–85 period (see also separate entries, 9 July 1982 and 2 August 1985) involved Flight 66, which was scheduled to land at John F. Kennedy International Airport at the end of a domestic service from New Orleans, Louisiana.

The wreckage of the Eastern Airlines Boeing 727 litters Rockway Boulevard near the threshold of Runway 22L at John F. Kennedy International Airport. *(AP Images)*

A severe thunderstorm was raging as the aircraft made its approach to Runway 22L under instrument landing system (ILS) guidance. According to witnesses in the immediate area, the storm was accompanied by heavy rain and strong, divergent winds. Less than 10 minutes before the crash, the captain of a DC-8 cargo jet that had landed on the same runway reported a 'tremendous' wind shear near the ground. Told by the controller that the indicated wind was only 15 knots, the pilot responded tartly, 'I don't care what you're indicating – I'm just telling you that there's such a wind shear on the final on that runway you should change it to the north-west.'

Moments later an Eastern Airlines L-1011 TriStar wide-bodied jet nearly crashed while attempting to land after encountering adverse winds before successfully initiating an overshoot procedure. Its pilot also reported 'a pretty good

shear'. Two other aircraft landed safely before Flight 66 began its final approach.

The US National Transportation Safety Board (NTSB) concluded that *N8845E* probably encountered an increasing headwind and possibly an updraught while descending at a height of about 500 ft (150 m) above the ground, causing it to deviate slightly above the ILS glide slope. Suddenly the wind changed to a downdraught, and the headwind diminished. The downward velocity of the wind increased almost simultaneously with the change in direction of the horizontal outflow from the storm cell, resulting in a decrease in the indicated air speed of the 727 and an increase in its rate of descent. This in turn caused the aircraft to deviate below the proper glide path, and as it descended towards the ground both the downdraught and the longitudinal (head and tail) wind component continued to increase.

Its undercarriage extended and flaps set at 30 degrees, the jetliner began striking approach light towers some 2,400 ft (730 m) from the runway threshold, then rolled into a steep left bank after the outboard section of its port wing was severed. The 727 continued through more light stanchions, burst into flames and virtually disintegrated, with the main wreckage coming to rest on Rockaway Boulevard. Including those who succumbed later, a total of 115 persons aboard (109 passengers and six crew members, among them an additional second officer who was giving the regular flight engineer his annual line check) were killed. Seven passengers and two cabin attendants, all of whom were seated in the rear portion of the cabin, survived with various injuries. The non-frangible light towers were largely responsible for the extensive break-up of the aircraft.

Through a correlation of the flight data recorder (FDR) read-out and cockpit voice recorder (CVR) transcript, it was determined that the captain had made visual contact with the approach lights while passing through 400 ft (*c.* 120 m). Seconds later he was heard to say 'Runway in sight', and the first officer responded 'I got it'. This comment seemed to indicate that despite the pilot's instructions to the co-pilot that he continue to monitor the instruments, the latter, who was actually flying the jetliner, began transitioning to the visual references he would need to complete the landing. Since the two men were relying on visual cues rather than their instruments, and with visibility obscured by the heavy rain, neither apparently recognised the deviation below the normal approach path until it was too late. The first officer commanded 'Take-off thrust' a second before the initial impact, but by then the crash was inevitable. The NTSB admitted that the winds may have been too severe for a successful landing even had the crew relied upon and responded rapidly to the instrument indications.

During the inquiry, investigators sought to determine why the runway was left open in such obviously bad meteorological conditions, especially considering the reports from other aircraft. The tower controller said he did not consider changing runways because the surface winds were most nearly aligned with 22L. He added that he was too busy to forward the recommendations of the DC-8 pilot to his superiors. In its investigative report, the Board expressed belief that a runway change was not made out of concern that it would have disrupted and delayed the flow of air traffic.

In the end, of course, it is the pilot-in-command who determines what course of action will be taken. In this case the captain of Flight 66 may have been influenced by the successful landings of two preceding aircraft. Furthermore, abandoning the approach and switching runways could have caused a delay of up to 30 minutes.

The NTSB made 14 recommendations as a result of this accident, mostly dealing with detection and avoidance of wind shear, but despite procedural changes and technological advances over the next few years, this weather phenomenon would continue to plague commercial aviation and, tragically, claim more lives.

Date: 3 August 1975 (*c.* 04:30)
Location: Near Immouzer, Morocco
Operator: Alia Royal Jordanian Airlines
Aircraft type: Boeing 707-321C (*JY-AEE*)

Chartered by Royal Air Maroc, the jetliner crashed and exploded in mountainous terrain some 25 miles (40 km) north-west of Agadir while preparing to land at the city's Inezgane Airport, at the end of a non-scheduled service from Paris, France. All 188 persons aboard (181 passengers and a crew of seven) perished.

Cleared to descend, the crew were asked by the control tower to report when properly aligned with

the instrument landing system (ILS) of Runway 29. Shortly afterwards the aircraft's right wing-tip and No. 4 engine struck a peak at an approximate elevation of 5,000 ft (1,500 m) and were torn off. The main wreckage came to rest about 5 miles (10 km) to the south-west and some 2,500 ft (750 m) below the point of initial impact. The accident occurred in pre-dawn darkness, and it was reportedly foggy in the area at the time.

Other than the pilot's acceptance of the descent clearance, the reason why the 707 had gone below the minimum safe altitude could not be determined.

Date: 20 August 1975 (*c.* 03:00)
Location: Near Damascus, Syria
Operator: Ceskoslovenske Aerolinie (CSA)
Aircraft type: Ilyushin Il-62 (*OK-DBF*)

Designated as Flight 542 and on a service from Prague, Czechoslovakia, to Tehran, Iran, the jet airliner crashed some 10 miles (15 km) north-east of the Damascus international airport, where it was scheduled to land, killing 126 persons aboard, including the 11 crew members. Both surviving passengers were seriously injured.

Though dark, the weather at the time was good, in moonlight, when the Il-62 struck a sandy hill and burst into flames during the approach, its undercarriage down at the time of impact. Significant to the investigation was that the aircraft's flight data recorder (FDR) had been destroyed by fire. Examination of the wreckage did not, however, reveal any indication of mechanical or structural failure, and evidence excluded the possibility of a loss of control or explosion occurring prior to the crash.

The accident was attributed to the failure of the crew to maintain the minimum flight altitude.

Date: 30 October 1975 (*c.* 09:20)
Location: Near Prague, Czechoslovakia
Operator: Inex Adria Aviopromet (Yugoslavia)
Aircraft type: McDonnell Douglas DC-9 Series 32 (*YU-AJO*)

The jet airliner, which was on a non-scheduled service from Tivat, Yugoslavia, crashed and burned on a hillside to the east of Ruzyne Airport, serving the Czech capital city, where it was to have landed. Of the 120 persons aboard, 77 were killed in the accident; 42 passengers and one of the aircraft's five crew members survived with various injuries.

During the instrument approach to Runway 24 in meteorological conditions consisting of scattered clouds, with 1/8 coverage at approximately 10,000 ft (3,000 m) and fog reducing the horizontal visibility to about 1 mile (1.5 km), the aircraft descended below the altitude to which it had been cleared. Following a procedural turn to the right, the pilots realised they were in a gorge over the River Vltava, with high ground ahead and to the sides. A full-power climb was initiated before the DC-9, configured with its undercarriage extended, struck trees and a building, then slammed to earth about 5 miles (10 km) short of and some 300 ft (100 m) below the runway threshold, and to the right of its axis.

Some of the airport's navaids were reportedly unserviceable at the time of the crash.

Date: 1 January 1976 (*c.* 05:30)
Location: North-eastern Saudi Arabia
Operator: Middle East Airlines (Lebanon)
Aircraft type: Boeing 720B (*OD-AFT*)

Operating as Flight 438, the jetliner crashed in the desert some 25 miles (40 km) north-west of Al Qaysumah, and all 81 persons aboard (66 passengers and a crew of 15) perished.

The aircraft was on a service from Beirut, Lebanon, to Muscat, Oman, with an en route stop at Dubai, United Arab Emirates, and was cruising in pre-dawn darkness when it disintegrated at an altitude of 37,000 ft (*c.* 11,300 m).

It was concluded that the 720B had been sabotaged with a high-explosive device, which must have detonated in its forward cargo compartment.

Date: 6 March 1976 (*c.* 01:00)
Location: Near Voronezh, Russian Soviet Federative Socialist Republic, USSR
Operator: Aeroflot (USSR)
Aircraft type: Ilyushin Il-18D (*SSSR-75408*)

All 111 persons aboard (100 passengers and 11 crew members) perished when the four-engine turboprop airliner, which was designated as Flight 909, crashed and burned during a domestic service from Moscow, RSFSR, to Yerevan, Armenia.

Cruising at an approximate height of 26,000 ft (8,000 m) in darkness and above a thick layer of clouds, with tops of about 13,000 ft (4,000 m) and the natural horizon invisible, the Il-18 had experienced an electrical power failure, which rendered its compass system, two main gyros and autopilot inoperable. The crew were unable to determine whether the right or left gyros or the standby gyro were giving a correct indication, and the aircraft performed some complicated banking manoeuvres before it plunged to earth.

Date: 10 September 1976 (*c.* 11:15)
Location: Near Gaj, Hrvatska, Yugoslavia
First aircraft
Operator: British Airways
Type: Hawker Siddeley Trident 3B (*G-AWZT*)
Second Aircraft
Operator: Inex Adria Aviopromet (Yugoslavia)
Type: McDonnell Douglas DC-9 Series 32 (*YU-AJR*)

Largely due to the location of the nation, the skies over Yugoslavia are among the busiest in Europe, which places a very heavy burden on its air traffic control (ATC) system and requires strict adherence to proper procedures. The consequences of even a slight departure from those procedures were realised with this catastrophic mid-air collision.

Designated as Flight 476, the Trident left London's Heathrow Airport earlier on this Friday morning bound for Istanbul, Turkey, and carrying 54 passengers and a crew of nine. Cruising at flight level (FL) 330, its course would take it directly over Yugoslavia, and shortly after passage of the Austrian/Yugoslav border it came under the jurisdiction of the Zagreb Area Control Centre.

In the meantime the DC-9, carrying 108 passengers and five crew members, had taken off from Split, Hrvatska, on a charter service to Cologne, (West) Germany. Before departure, its pilot had requested a cruising height of FL 310, but he was subsequently denied ascent above 26,000 ft (*c.* 8,000 m) due to other aircraft in the area. However, the crew were asked if they could climb to FL 350, giving the response 'Affirmative . . . with pleasure'.

The Zagreb ATC centre consisted of three sectors, each one of which was responsible for controlling air traffic at certain altitudes. A display on the radarscope identifying each target and showing its height would only be visible in the sector that had it directly under control. In the other sectors, i.e.

above or below, the aircraft would only appear as a plain blip.

The change in altitude of the DC-9 would thus require a transfer from the middle sector, responsible for control between the flight levels of 250 and 310, to the upper sector, but this time the transfer was not carried out with proper coordination. A new flight progress strip, used to mark the radar target, was not prepared. Instead, the same one used in the transfer from the lower sector was merely modified, but without an arrow to indicate that the aircraft had received clearance by the middle sector to climb. The actual identification of the blip was accomplished by the middle sector controller physically pointing it out to the one handling the upper sector.

Another significant factor was the instruction by the middle sector controller for the Yugoslav transport to squawk 'stand by' temporarily, in preparation for the transfer. As a result of this action, which also went against good operating procedures, the identification display and height information would not appear beside the echo marking the DC-9, giving the upper sector controller only a two-dimensional presentation of the target. Means were available to bring in the display, but for lack of time none was implemented. In fact, the controller had less than 30 seconds to take action upon realising that a potential conflict existed between YU-AJR and G-AWZT. Hampering his plight was the fact that the crew of the DC-9 delayed for nearly 2 minutes in establishing radio contact with the upper sector.

The Trident was also under the jurisdiction of the upper sector, but the controller later stated that he could not recall whether its displayed flight level had been 332 or 335. However, the British crew had minutes earlier reported as being at 33,000 ft (c. 10,050 m), and the controller's actions indicated that he believed this to be the correct height.

In the final moments before the disaster, the controller attempted to hold the DC-9 at its last reported altitude, FL 327. This would have allowed a narrow clearance of around 300 ft (100 m), but due to faulty instructions this chance was also thwarted. The controller gave the order to 'Hold yourself at that height and report passing Zagreb'. In response to the crewman's query for the altitude at which the aircraft should be levelled off, the controller said 'The height you are climbing through'. He also

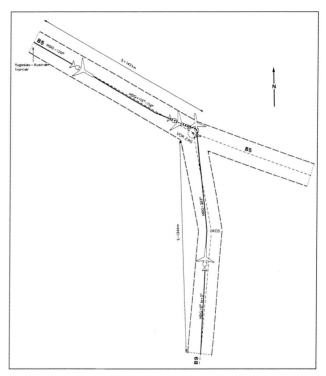

Chart showing the courses of the Trident (flying airport along Airway B5) and the DC-9 (using Airway B9) that collided over Yugoslavia. (Yugoslavia Federal Committee for Transportation and Communications)

warned it of the presence of the Trident. This conversation was carried out in Serbo-Croatian, which went against the rule that English shall always be used in air/ground communications.

Agonisingly, had it been allowed to continue its ascent, YU-AJR would probably have safely cleared G-AWZT, but its altitude at the time that the crew received the level-off order was, tragically, 33,000 ft. The two jet transports thus collided over or in close horizontal proximity to the Zagreb very-high-frequency omnidirectional range (VOR) station, within 100 ft (c. 30 m) of that height and at an angle slightly in excess of 90 degrees.

At the moment of impact the Trident was flying along Airway B5 on a heading of 116 degrees and at a ground speed of approximately 560 mph (900 kmh), and the DC-9 flying along Airway B9 on a heading of 353 degrees and at a ground speed of around 535 mph (860 kmh). Only seconds before the collision the Yugoslav aircraft was actually slightly above the British jet, carried upward by inertia even after the crew had levelled off.

Therefore the DC-9 was in a slight descent and the Trident in level flight when the former's left wing slashed into the latter's flight deck, instantly killing the British crew.

Both aircraft fell to earth vertically with little or no forward motion, *G-AWZT* plummeting into a field and *YU-AJR*, which lost a portion of its port wing and its tail surfaces, crashing into a forest. The latter then caught fire. All 176 persons aboard the two transports perished. According to press reports, a woman on the ground was struck by falling wreckage and also killed. The collision occurred some 15 miles (25 km) north-east of the city of Zagreb, and the aircraft crashed about 4.5 miles (7 km) apart, although debris was scattered over an area of approximately 5 by 20 miles (10 by 30 km).

Besides improper ATC procedures, the investigative committee blamed the accident on the failure of both crews to maintain a lookout for other traffic. The collision occurred in conditions of good visibility, with no clouds in the area at that altitude, and it was determined that the pilots had some 30 seconds to make visual contact with the opposing aircraft and initiate evasive manoeuvres, but no such action was taken.

The committee was particularly critical of the British crew for not being more vigilant when crossing the intersection of two airways. It noted that the radio transmissions between the DC-9 and the controller were heard on the Trident's cockpit voice recorder (CVR) tape and stated that this should have alerted the pilots as to the potential conflict. Instead they discussed items that were not pertinent to the operation of the aircraft, and the first officer was apparently working on a crossword puzzle.

England's representative in the investigation, however, challenged this aspect of the final report. He noted that the closing speed of about 850 mph (1,370 kmh) would have negated an attempt by the crew to observe the DC-9. He further wrote that the Yugoslav pilots, looking down from the sun at an aircraft that was producing a condensation trail, had a better opportunity to see than the British crew, who were looking into the sun. Instead he attributed the collision to the failure of the ATC system to provide adequate separation.

An additional contributing factor was the heavy workload imposed on the upper sector controller, due to the absence of his assistant. This was not known to the supervisor.

Under the harsh Yugoslav law, eight ATC personnel were subsequently charged with criminal negligence, and the upper sector controller, the only one convicted, served two years in prison.

Date: 19 September 1976 (*c.* 23:15)
Location: Near Isparta, Turkey
Operator: Turk Hava Yollari AO (Turkish Airlines)
Aircraft type: Boeing Advanced 727-2F2 (*TC-JBH*)

The jetliner was en route from Istanbul to Antalya, the domestic sector of a scheduled international service originating at Milan, Italy, when it struck a mountain at an approximate elevation of 3,700 ft (1,130 m), some 65 miles (105 km) north of its intended destination, bursting into flames on impact. All 155 persons aboard (147 passengers and a crew of eight) perished.

After passing the Afyon very-high-frequency omnidirectional range (VOR) station, *TC-JBH* requested descent from flight level 250 to 130. The aircraft then made contact with the Antalya airport control tower and descended to 12,000 ft (*c.* 3,700 m). Radio contact with the 727 was lost after the pilot had reported the lights of Antalya in sight and been granted permission to circle over the city and make a direct landing approach to Runway 36.

Soon after the investigation of the crash began, it became apparent that in the darkness and clear weather conditions the crew had mistaken Isparta for Antalya, resulting in a descent below the obstructing terrain.

Date: 12 October 1976 (01:37)
Location: Near Bombay, India
Operator: Indian Airlines
Aircraft type: Sud-Aviation Caravelle VI-N (*VT-DWN*)

The jetliner crashed in flames while attempting an emergency landing in early morning darkness at Santa Cruz Airport, from where it had taken off only about 3 minutes earlier, on a scheduled domestic service to Madras, Tamil Nadu, and all 95 persons aboard (89 passengers and a crew of six) were killed.

Its right power plant had failed during the initial climb, prompting the pilot to turn back. Fire then erupted in the same engine and, during its approach to Runway 09, pitch control of the

Survivors congregate on the grass beside the runway after escaping from the flaming Pan Am 747, which was struck by a KLM aircraft of the same type while still on the ground at Los Rodeos Airport. *(Getty Images)*

aircraft was apparently lost. Its undercarriage down, the Caravelle plunged to earth in a 45-degree nose-down attitude from an approximate height of 300 ft (100 m) and some 1,000 ft (300 m) short of the runway.

A fatigue crack in the tenth stage compressor disc was blamed for the power plant failure. This malfunction was followed by the bursting of the compressor casing and the cutting of fuel lines that spanned the structure, which in turn led to the extensive in-flight blaze in the engine bay. The fire, which was allowed to spread partly because of the crew's failure to shut off the fuel supply to the No. 2 power plant, must have consumed the supply of hydraulic fluid before the aircraft could land.

Date: 13 January 1977 (*c.* 18:15)
Location: Near Alma-Ata, Kazakh SSR, USSR
Operator: Aeroflot (USSR)
Aircraft type: Tupolev Tu-104A (*SSSR-42369*)

All 90 persons aboard (82 passengers and eight crew members) were killed when the jet airliner crashed and burned while attempting an emergency landing at the Alma-Ata airport.

Operating as Flight 3843 and nearing the end of a domestic service originating at Khabarovsk, RSFSR, the aircraft had begun its approach and been flying about 7.5 miles (12 km) from the

airport, with undercarriage down and flaps partially extended, when the crew were notified of a fire in its left engine. Emergency procedures, which included altering the flap setting and shutting down the malfunctioning power plant, were immediately implemented. Shortly afterwards, however, the Tu-104 slammed to earth approximately 2 miles (3 km) from the threshold of the runway and some 1,300 ft (400 m) to the left of its axis.

The engine fire could have led to any or all of the following situations: failure of the flight control system or the elevator trimmer; incapacitation of the pilots by carbon monoxide poisoning; and displacement of the aircraft's centre of gravity due to panic among the passengers. The accident occurred at dusk; the weather was not considered a factor.

Date: 27 March 1977 (*c.* 17:00)
Location: Tenerife, (Spanish) Canary Islands
First aircraft
Operator: KLM Royal Dutch Airlines
Type: Boeing 747-206B (*PH-BUF*)
Second aircraft
Operator: Pan American World Airways (US)
Type: Boeing 747-121 (*N736PA*)

In history's worst commercial aviation accident, the two wide-bodied jet airliners collided at Los Rodeos Airport, located near Santa Cruz de Tenerife, and

The empennage and a portion of the fuselage are still recognisable but little else remains of the KLM transport. *(CORBIS)*

583 persons were killed. In examining the circumstances of this tragedy it is noteworthy how the combined efforts of several seemingly innocuous factors led to catastrophic consequences.

Both transports were engaged in charter operations originating within the respective nations of registry, KLM's *Rhine River* en route from Amsterdam and Pan American's *Clipper Victor* having stopped at New York City during a service from Los Angeles, California.

The first event in the sequence leading up to the accident was a terrorist bombing in the terminal building at Las Palmas Airport, on the nearby island of Gran Canaria, the intended destination of both aircraft. As a result of the blast, which injured eight persons, and the threat of a second bomb, the airport was closed, diverting the two 747s and several other aircraft to Tenerife.

Once Las Palmas had reopened, the crews prepared for the short inter-island flight. Though ready to leave immediately, Pan Am's *N736PA* could not. Its path had been blocked by *PH-BUF*, whose own departure was being delayed by the boarding of its passengers, who had been allowed to

wait in the terminal, and by the decision of its crew to refuel for the trip from Gran Canaria back to Amsterdam. Finally, the KLM crew were authorised to begin taxiing to the start of Runway 30 in order to await clearance to take off.

Due to the heavy concentration of aircraft on the ground at the airport, with some even parked on the taxiway, the Dutch and American jets were forced to backtrack on the runway itself, with the latter following a distance behind the former. Meanwhile, the meteorological conditions continued to deteriorate on this late Sunday afternoon, with the visibility decreasing to approximately 1,500 ft (500 m) in light rain and fog.

Having reached the end of the runway and turned completely about, the KLM crew reported by radio that they were 'ready for take-off'. The control tower operator then proceeded to provide air traffic control (ATC) clearance and navigational information, which did not include specific clearance to take off.

Meanwhile, as the Pan Am 747 continued to taxi, the American pilots observed a horrifying sight: looming out of the mist was the Dutch transport accelerating to its rotation speed, on a head-on course with their aircraft. Applying full thrust and turning to the left, the Pan American crew attempted to clear the runway, but could not prevent the collision, which occurred at 17.06.50.

Its tail skid dragging along the ground for a distance of about 65 ft (20 m) due to over-rotation, *PH-BUF* had just become airborne when its main gear slashed into the side of *N736PA* in the area of the latter's No. 3 engine. The KLM aircraft then slammed back on to the pavement some 500 ft (150 m) beyond the point of the collision and slid approximately 1,000 ft (300 m) further, turning in a clockwise direction and coming to rest almost sideways to the runway axis. Although neither the collision nor the impact with the ground could have been excessively violent, the *Rhine River* was swept by flames before anyone could escape, and all 248 persons aboard, including the crew of 14, perished.

The top of its fuselage having been ripped open and vertical stabiliser sheared off, the *Clipper Victor*, which had been at an angle of about 45 degrees relative to the runway at the time of the crash and may have continued to roll for a slight distance afterward, was itself gutted by explosions and fire. Among the 396 persons aboard, 326 passengers and nine of its 16 crew members lost their lives, some of whom succumbed days or weeks after the accident. All but two of the survivors, who included the pilot, co-pilot and flight engineer, were injured.

Obviously the primary responsibility for the tragedy rested with KLM Capt Jacob van Zanten, a senior training pilot for the carrier with some 21,000 hours in the air, whose action in taking off without clearance seemed difficult to understand. However, there were a number of extenuating circumstances that could at least help to mitigate his basic error.

Before the collision, the Dutch crew were facing an increasingly urgent time factor. They would have to take off soon in order to pick up the passengers waiting at Las Palmas Airport and complete the flight back to Amsterdam within the maximum duty time allowed by the airline. The situation was aggravated by the time it took to refuel the aircraft, and other possible delays including ATC tie-ups and the worsening weather. They also faced adversities in preparation for the departure, such as taxiing in heavy fog and having to complete a 180-degree turn in a comparatively small area at the end of the

runway in the huge 747. So, when there appeared to be a momentary improvement in the visibility, the pilots must have felt somewhat relieved, which increased their desire to take off.

Communications played a major role in the disaster. After reporting that they were ready to go, the instructions to the Dutch crew from the tower controller included the remark 'You are cleared to the Papa Beacon'. This definitely was not intended as clearance to take-off, but must have been construed as such by the KLM captain. Reading back the ATC information, the first officer ended the transmission with the ominous message 'We are now at take off' or 'now taking off'. The controller, apparently not realising the implications of the statement, merely responded 'Stand by for take-off. I will call you.'

Meanwhile, this conversation was being monitored, with some apprehension, by the Pan American crew, prompting radioed remarks from both the pilot and co-pilot, the latter saying 'We're still taxiing down the runway'. Unfortunately, this was sent simultaneously with the tower transmission, causing a shrill noise in the cockpit of the Dutch transport that blocked out both messages.

A subsequent request by the tower to the American crew asking them to 'report runway clear', and the response 'Okay, will report when we're clear', were both clearly heard on the cockpit voice recorder (CVR) tape of *PH-BUF*. The messages concerned the KLM second officer enough for him to ask 'Is he not clear, that Pan American?' His captain responded emphatically 'Oh yes'.

By that time the *Rhine River* was already on its take-off run, and only about 15 seconds later it struck the *Clipper Victor*.

Though speaking in English, the failure of both the Dutch co-pilot and the Spanish tower controller to use proper aviation terminology contributed to the accident, as did a comparatively minor error by the American pilots. Their confusion pertained to the intersection at which their aircraft was to have turned off the runway in order to get back to the taxiway. Clarifying the instructions, the tower controller radioed 'The third one, sir. One, two, three . . . third, third one'. Nevertheless, the 747 taxied past ramp C-3 and headed towards C-4, which the crew apparently mistook for the third one. This slight miscue accounted for *N736PA* still being on the runway when *PH-BUF* began its unauthorised take-off. As noted in the Spanish investigative report, the fact that the aircraft were taxiing on the runway was in itself potentially hazardous. The use of reduced power by the KLM crew when taking off also contributed to the collision, though indirectly, by affecting the performance of the aircraft.

There was another seemingly paradoxical factor that could have contributed to the disaster. Though Capt van Zanten was highly experienced, his work as an instructor for more than 10 years may have diminished his familiarity with route flying, including such items as take-off clearances. In simulated flights, the instructor normally assumes the role of the controller, and practice take-offs often take place without any clearance whatsoever. Conversely, the first officer was faced with serving with one of the carrier's most prestigious pilots, and had little experience in Boeing jets, which could have reduced the likelihood of his questioning or challenging the latter's actions.

Commenting on the report, authorities from the Netherlands, adding that the KLM crew appeared to have taken off with the 'absolute conviction' that they had the proper clearance. In an additional finding, they noted that sounds suggesting a broadcast football match in the control tower were heard in the recorded radio transmissions, which if true could have been an element of distraction. The Dutch observers also noted that the tower controller should have asked for confirmation of his instruction to 'Stand by for take-off'.

In a difference of opinion, officials from the nation of registry doubted that the 'prestige' factor influenced the KLM first officer, and said there was no evidence of haste on the part of the captain. They dismissed his slight advancement of the thrust levers before his co-pilot had asked for clearance, which was noted in the Spanish report, as a normal check of the engines.

Recommendations from both countries included an emphasis on the importance of strict adherence to instructions and clearances, the use of standard, concise and unequivocal aeronautical terminology in all radio communications, and the greater application of ground radar and special light mechanisms to improve safety. Some of the latter proposals would later be adopted for use in Spain, but not until after another disastrous collision between two commercial jets, this one at Madrid's airport, in 1983 (see separate entry, 7 December 1983).

Date: 4 April 1977 (*c.* 16:15)
Location: Near Atlanta, Georgia, US
Operator: Southern Airways (US)
Aircraft type: McDonnell Douglas DC-9 Series 31 (*N1335U*)

Neither Capt William McKenzie nor First Officer Lyman Keele, the two pilots of Flight 242, had any idea of the meteorological conditions facing them along the domestic route to Atlanta before their departure from Muscle Shoals, Alabama. Nor could they have known that this would be the last flight for both of them.

Following a scheduled stop at Huntsville, Alabama, the twin-jet airliner headed east towards its destination – and an encounter with what would later be classified as one of the worst storm systems recorded in the United States in years.

Earlier, the US National Weather Service (NWS) had issued two SIGMET reports and two tornado watches for the general area where the DC-9 was to fly. One watch also called for a few severe thunderstorms, with hail up to 3 in (10 cm) in diameter, extreme turbulence, surface winds of almost hurricane velocity and cumulonimbus clouds topping off above 50,000 ft (15,000 m). Though received by the crew, this information was only a forecast. The pilots, who had flown the route in the opposite direction only 2 hours earlier, would probably rely more on their personal knowledge of the weather than on a prediction of the conditions that might develop.

As it continued on a south-westerly heading, the flight enountered a thunderstorm in the vicinity of Rome, Georgia, some 50 miles (80 km) north-west of Atlanta. From the cockpit voice recorder (CVR) tape, it was apparent that the crew had spotted the build-up on the aircraft's radar. Capt McKenzie was heard to say 'Looks heavy . . . nothing going through that', and he and First Officer Keele then discussed a possible hole within the area of intense precipitation.

The jet penetrated the storm at an altitude of between 17,000 and 14,000 ft (*c.* 5,200–4,300 m). Minutes later came the first hint of trouble, when the pilot reported the aircraft's windscreen as having been cracked, apparently by hail, and that its left power plant had failed. In less than 30 seconds there came an even more ominous message: 'Got the other engine going too'.

The Atlanta control centre asked for a repeat, and the situation was made frighteningly clear by the captain: 'Stand by. We lost both engines.' Without power, the DC-9 was literally a huge glider with no place to land.

The crew first requested a vector to Dobbins Air Force Base, which could have accommodated an aircraft of that size, but instead of continuing on towards the military installation, the jet turned about 180 degrees back in the other direction. It was believed that the crew did not select emergency (battery) power, and instead attempted an engine restart while trying to remain in visual meteorological conditions. Finally, the auxiliary power unit was activated, and radio communications with the ground resumed after a lapse of 2 minutes.

Before turning back towards the east, the flight came within 10 miles (c. 15 km) of Cornelius Moore Airport, which, despite a relatively short runway and a lack of emergency equipment, could have been used as a last-resort landing strip. However, the pilots were apparently not aware of their proximity to it, and since it was outside their airspace, the airport was not depicted on the controllers' displays.

More than 7 minutes had now elapsed since the engine failure and the situation was reaching critical proportions. The crew had to find a place – any open space – on which to set down. It was then that Capt McKenzie pointed out a highway. 'We'll have to take it,' First Officer Keele responded. The aircraft's undercarriage was lowered and flaps extended to 50 degrees in preparation for the desperation landing on the road, actually State Spur 92.

The left outer wing of N1335U first hit two trees, and both wings then struck more trees and utility poles, as the aircraft was still airborne. Simultaneous with its left main gear touching the pavement, its port wing struck an embankment, and the DC-9 veered to the left, ploughing into more trees, fences and other obstacles and breaking apart. Fire erupted on impact and swept over much of the wreckage. The disaster, which took place in the small community of New Hope, located some 20 miles (30 km) north-west of Atlanta, killed 63 of the 85 persons aboard the aircraft, including the

pilots, and nine others on the ground, some of whom were in an automobile that was crushed by the jet. Two of the victims, one of whom had been on the ground, succumbed about a month after the crash. The 22 survivors, including both cabin attendants, suffered various injuries. Seven vehicles and a combination grocery store/gasoline station were destroyed.

The exact conditions encountered by the aircraft could not be determined. It was concluded, however, that the ingestion of large amounts of rain and hail had caused a decrease in the rotational speeds of both power plants, below that required for operation of the engine-driven generators. This accounted for the 36-second loss of electrical power before the engines failed completely. The intentional thrust reduction of the crew in preparation for the descent had apparently contributed to the loss of rotational speed.

Calculations illustrated how massive water ingestion, leading to surging in the aft stages of the high-pressure compressors, could cause upstream over-pressures and correspondingly high aerodynamic forces in excess of any experienced during the development and service history of the power plant. An examination of both low-pressure compressors revealed that the sixth-stage blades were deflected forward and had clashed with the fifth-stage stator vanes. Pieces from the broken blades and vanes were then ingested into the high-pressure compressors, causing severe damage. Furthermore, advancement of the thrust levers – a normal pilot reaction to a loss of engine rpm – only aggravated the situation. Evidence of over-temperatures before the engines failed indicated that high thrust settings were maintained even after the compressors were damaged. Neither power plant could have been restarted in such a condition, making the crash inevitable.

The US National Transportation Safety Board (NTSB) tried to determine why the pilots had flown into such a severe storm. There was circumstantial evidence to indicate that their rest time, just under the prescribed minimum, combined with inadequate food intake and long duty hours on the day of the accident could have produced fatigue leading to a deterioration in the captain's judgement. Neither the crew nor flight dispatch personnel had apparently made any significant attempt to seek information on the current weather between

The burned-out hulk of
the TAP Boeing 727
following the runway
overrun accident on
Madeira. *(AP Images)*

Huntsville and Atlanta. It was concluded that both parties had not only over-relied on the pilots' personal knowledge of the conditions coming from their earlier flight, but also on the aircraft's weather radar.

As had happened in previous air disasters, the crew in this case tried to navigate through a thunderstorm using airborne radar. However, since the jet was at the time flying in rain, its radar may have been affected by attenuation. Thus the contour hole noted by the pilots would have been distorted so as to appear as being free of pre-cipitation, and when its course was altered to the left the DC-9 in fact entered the most intense part of the storm.

Also identified was the failure of the company's dispatching system to provide up-to-date reports on the meteorological conditions along the intended route of the flight. Limitations in the air traffic control (ATC) sytsem of the US Federal Aviation Administration (FAA), which that precluded timely dissemination of hazardous weather information, were another contributing factor. As a result of these shortcomings, the crew were not made aware of several tornado sightings in eastern Alabama and the radar identification of thunderstorm activity in the vicinity of Rome. One dissenting board member believed that the probable cause of the accident was the captain's decision to penetrate a known area of severe weather.

Subsequently, the US ATC system implemented one of the recommendations made by the NTSB in its investigative report on the crash of Flight 242 by establishing a standard scale of thunderstorm activity intensity, based on the one in use by the NWS. This information was also published in the Airman's Information Manual. The FAA also took action to enhance the dissemination of significant weather information and issued an advisory circular emphasising the need for pilots to avoid hazardous meteorological conditions. In response to another NTSB recommendation, the FAA noted that a research and development programme exploring ways of improving radar detection of such phe-nomena had been initiated back in August 1975.

Date: 19 November 1977 (21:48)
Location: Near Funchal, Island of Madeira, Portugal
Operator: Transportes Aereos Portugueses EP (TAP) (Portugal)
Aircraft type: Boeing Advanced 727-282 (*CS-TBR*)

After two unsuccessful attempts, Flight 425 tried a third time to land at Santa Catarina Airport at the end of a service from Brussels, Belgium, via Lisbon,

Portugal. Following a non-directional beacon instrument procedure approach in darkness and meteorological conditions consisting of rain, a low, broken overcast, with 6/8 cumulus clouds at about 1,500 ft (500 m), and an approximate visibility of 2 miles (3 km), the jet airliner landed on Runway 24 some 2,000 ft (600 m) beyond its threshold.

Despite the use of full reverse thrust and extension of the spoilers, it could not be stopped. Overrunning the runway, the 727 plunged off a cliff and struck a stone bridge, at which location its right wing and empennage, including all three engines, were found. The rest of the fuselage, with the left wing still attached, crashed almost vertically on to a beach about 130 ft (40 m) below the level of the airport, exploding in flames on impact. The accident killed 131 persons aboard the aircraft, including six crew members; nine of the victims' bodies were apparently swept out to sea and not recovered. Two cabin attendants and 31 passengers survived with various injuries.

According to the digital flight data recorder (DFDR) read-out, its indicated air speed was approximately 20 mph (30 kmh) above the prescribed velocity when the transport touched down some 1,000 ft (300 m) past the aiming point, despite the fact that it had passed over the threshold at the correct height and properly configured. Just before the landing, and in a possible attempt by the crew to get the aircraft on the ground, the flaps were retracted from 40 to 25 degrees. This, coupled with the speed of the 727 and a slight incline in the runway, could have contributed to an abnormal extension of the flare, which itself factored in the overrun.

Almost simultaneous with the touchdown, there was a significant deflection of the aircraft's rudder to the left, which made the jet skid to the right. There were also indications of hydroplaning, possibly due to poor runway drainage resulting from deformations in the surface of the pavement. One lesser item that could have contributed to the disaster along with the aforementioned factors and the weather itself was that the indicator lights at the 1,000-ft mark along the runway were inoperative.

It was noted in the investigative report that due to the possibility of wind shear in the approach area, the carrier had recommended a speed of about 10 mph (15 km) above the norm when using Runway 24 at the Funchal airport, which could partially account for the 'hot' landing.

Subsequent to the crash, TAP restricted landings and take-offs on this particular runway to dry conditions.

Date: 4 December 1977 (*c.* 20:15)
Location: Near Kampung Ladang, Malaysia
Operator: Malaysian Airline System
Aircraft type: Boeing Advanced 737-2H6 (*9M-MBD*)

During the approach to land at the Kuala Lumpur international airport at the end of a domestic service from Penang, the captain of Flight 653

A Boeing 737-200 in the Malaysian Airline System livery at the time of the hijacking disaster. *(Ikaros/Uniphoto Press International)*

reported that a hijacker had commandeered the aircraft, and that it was proceeding on to Singapore. Subsequently, the 737 descended from 21,000 to 7,000 ft (6,400 to c. 2,000 m) before radio and radar contact was lost.

According to eyewitnesses, the jetliner, observed in darkness, pitched up from level flight, then plunged to earth in a steep nose-down attitude, with some bank. The impact was at a high rate of speed in a swamp some 30 miles (50 km) south-west of Johor Baharu, and the aircraft then exploded and disintegrated. All 100 persons aboard (93 passengers and a crew of seven) perished.

Although there were reports of a fire or explosion in the air before the crash, it was later concluded that both pilots had been shot. Security measures were implemented in the wake of this disaster.

Date: 1 January 1978 (c. 20:15)
Location: Near Bandra, Maharashtra, India
Operator: Air-India
Aircraft type: Boeing 747-237B (*VT-EBD*)

Designated as Flight 855, the aircraft took off from Santa Cruz Airport, serving Bombay, bound for Dubai, United Arab Emirates. Proceeding in darkness and weather conditions described as 'calm and clear', it was instructed to climb to flight level 310, and report upon leaving 8,000 ft (c. 2,500 m). The last message from the 747, received about a minute after its departure, was 'Happy New Year to you, sir. Will report leaving 80.'

Only 20 seconds later, the wide-bodied jet airliner plunged into the Arabian Sea approximately 2 miles (3 km) from the shore, exploding on impact. All 213 persons aboard (190 passengers and 23 crew members) perished. Most of its wreckage, including both the digital flight data (DFDR) and cockpit voice (CVR) recorders, was subsequently recovered, as were the remains of 90 victims. The depth of the ocean at the site of the crash was less than 30 ft (10 m), sufficiently shallow for parts of the aircraft to protrude above the surface.

An Indian court of inquiry ruled that the disaster apparently resulted from 'irrational' control wheel inputs on the part of the captain related to a complete unawareness of his attitude after his attitude director indicator (ADI) had malfunctioned, with the instrument probably remaining in a right-bank indication even after the jet had returned to level flight following a gentle right turn. This led to the continuation of a roll to the left beyond a 90-degree position, from which a successful recovery could not be made. He had also failed to use other instruments, including the standby horizon indicator, to correct the situation. Additionally, the first officer had failed to monitor the flight instruments, including his ADI which functioned independently of the pilot's, and rendered no assistance to the captain in ascertaining the attitude of the transport.

According to the CVR tape, the pilot-in-command realised there was something wrong with his ADI, and the flight engineer also noted the difference in the indication between that one and the standby instrument. However, the co-pilot did not respond to the concern of the captain. And apparently, no failure flag had appeared on the ADI after the instrument malfunctioned. The aircraft reached a maximum height of just under 1,500 ft (500 m) before it began to descend, hitting the water beyond a wings-vertical attitude and at a nose-down angle of 35 to 40 degrees.

Boeing and the manufacturers of the avionics used on the 747, who were named as defendants in a subsequent legal action, claimed that the pilot had a history of diabetes and drinking, and may have been under the influence of both alcohol and medication on the day of the accident, and merely experienced spatial disorientation. All three companies were exonerated from charges of negligence in a 1985 US federal court decision.

Among the recommendations made in the Indian investigative report were those intending to rectify identified deficiencies in specific crew training and procedures, including those pertaining to ADI failure and recovery from unusual attitudes.

Date: 25 September 1978 (c. 09:00)
Location: San Diego, California, US
First aircraft
Operator: Pacific Southwest Airlines (PSA) (US)
Type: Boeing 727-214 (*N533PS*)
Second aircraft
Operator: Gibbs Flite Center Inc (US)
Type: Cessna 172M (*N7711G*)

Southern California, with its relative opulence and ideal flying weather, is known for having the highest concentration of general aviation aircraft in

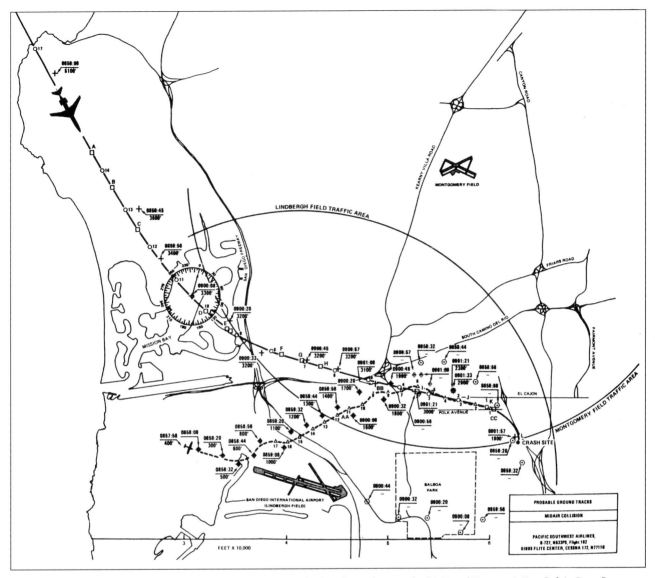

The respective flight paths of the 727 and Cessna involved in the mid-air crash. *(National Transportation Safety Board)*

the world. Though the often-used term 'crowded' is a misnomer, the skies over this region could perhaps best be described as 'busy'. This is certainly the case around Los Angeles, but also true to a lesser degree in San Diego, located some 100 miles (150 km) to the south. Yet until this date, despite the potential for one, both areas had been spared a major collision between a light aircraft and a large commercial transport; but any over-confidence on the part of private and air carrier pilots that may have developed as a result of their good record was quickly eradicated by this horrifying accident.

PSA Flight 182 had stopped at Los Angeles during an intrastate service from Sacramento to San Diego, and was scheduled to land at Lindbergh Field; it was operating under instrument flight rules

(IFR). The meteorological conditions on this Monday morning were excellent, with not a cloud in the sky and a visibility of 10 miles (*c.* 15 km), so the 727 was cleared for a visual approach to Runway 27. Coming in from the north-west, the aircraft assumed a south-easterly course while on the downwind leg of the circuit before it was to have turned back towards the west to begin its final approach.

Meanwhile, the single-engine Cessna had just completed a practice instrument landing system (ILS) approach to the airport, using Runway 09, the reverse of 27, because it was equipped with ILS facilities. At the controls of the light aeroplane was 35-year-old David Boswell, a qualified private pilot working on his instrument rating; his instructor was Martin Kazy, who had logged more than 5,000 hours in the air. Though operating under visual flight rules (VFR), the Cessna was in radio and radar contact with both the Lindbergh control tower and approach control. It was also fitted with an altitude encoding transponder as are airliners, enabling the controllers to track its height and computed ground speed as well as position.

At 08.59.30, the 727 received the first of four significant traffic advisories when the approach controller reported 'PSA one eighty-two, traffic twelve o'clock, one mile, northbound'.

Capt James McFeron responded, 'We're looking'.

Seconds later, the controller advised, 'Additional traffic's twelve o'clock three miles, just north of the field, north-eastbound, a Cessna one seventy-two climbing VFR out of one thousand four hundred.'

First Officer Robert Fox radioed, 'Okay, we've got that other twelve'.

Following a third advisory, in which the approach controller reported 'traffic's at twelve o'clock, three miles, out of one thousand seven hundred', the PSA pilot confirmed 'Traffic in sight'.

The controller then cleared the flight to 'maintain visual separation'.

During this period of time the Cessna was instructed to maintain VFR at or below 3,500 ft (c. 1,050 m) and to proceed on a heading of 70 degrees. It was also given a traffic advisory by the approach controller who reported the 727 at its 6 o'clock position and that the PSA crew had the light aeroplane in sight. The final advisory to the 727 came from the tower controller, who reported 'traffic twelve o'clock, one mile, a Cessna' at 09.00.38.

The captain this time replied with the statement, 'Okay, we had it there a minute ago', followed by a tentative 'I think he's pass(ed) off to our right'.

The tower controller would later testify that he heard the pilot say 'He's passing off to our right', and for that reason took no further action, responding only with a 'Yeah'.

At 09.01.28 a conflict alert warning sounded at the approach control facility. This collision avoidance mechanism, which was built into the radar system, uses a computer to predict that two targets will cross paths at the same point. The only subsequent action taken, however, was a second traffic advisory to the Cessna by the approach

controller regarding the 727. The time was 09.01.47.

At that moment, and almost inexplicably considering the equipment in use and the warnings issued, the aircraft collided at an approximate altitude of 2,500 ft (750 m) and about 3.5 miles (6 km) north-east of the airport. Just before impact the commercial transport was descending and banked slightly to the right, and the general aviation aeroplane climbing with its wings level. The 727 overtook and struck the Cessna with the underside of its starboard wing, and the latter then broke apart, exploded and fell immediately to the ground, crashing on a street below. The collision inflicted serious damage to the 727's wing, with large sections of both the leading and trailing edges having been torn away. Fire also erupted in this area, probably from ruptured fuel lines.

Apparently rendered uncontrollable, the jetliner began a shallow descending right turn and, only 20 seconds after the collision, slammed into the North Park section of the city just west of Highway 805 and less than 1 mile (1.5 km) from Balboa Park, home of the famous San Diego Zoo. It crashed in a street on an approximate heading of 200 degrees and an indicated air speed of about 270 mph (435 kmh), with its right wing slightly low, under-carriage down and flaps partially extended, and exploded in flames, devastating a residential neighbourhood. All 135 persons aboard the transport (128 passengers and a crew of seven), the two occupants of the light aeroplane and seven on the ground perished. Nine others suffered injuries, including a woman and her infant son who were driving through the area when a body smashed through the windscreen of their automobile. The impact and subsequent fires destroyed or damaged 22 dwellings.

As has been the case in other accidents of this type, immediate press reports put most of the blame on the small aircraft, and inevitaby there were calls for limiting general aviation operations at major airports. However, this charge was an unfair one, since this could hardly be considered a classic IFR/VFR conflict. Despite a VFR clearance, the Cessna was being flown under positive control in an area where terminal radar services were available. Traffic advisories to both aircraft were seemingly adequate.

In its investigative report, the US National Transportation Safety Board (NTSB) blamed the

One engine of the PSA jetliner rests amid the ruins of the San Diego neighbourhood. *(National Transportation Safety Board)*

collision on the failure of the airline crew to maintain visual separation with the light aircraft as instructed and to inform the controller that they no longer had the Cessna in sight. It named as contributing factors the air traffic control (ATC) procedures in effect at the time, which authorised controllers to separate two aircraft using visual advisory procedures, when the technological capability existed to provide lateral and vertical separation.

But the findings of the inquiry were not unanimously accepted. In a dissenting opinion, NTSB member Francis McAdams cited inadequacies in the ATC system as the probable cause and not just a contributing factor. He cited a number of other factors as contributing to the accident, all of which were mentioned in the report. The absence of any one of these occurrences may well have prevented the disaster.

Had the Cessna maintained the 70-degree heading as assigned by the approach controller, it would have crossed the path of the 727 earlier and the collision would have been avoided; its slight turn to the right, which was not reported to the controller, placed the light aeroplane on a track coinciding with that of the jetliner. The turn also took the 727 out of the visual range of the Cessna's pilots by putting it directly behind them, and since they had been informed that the airline crew had them in sight, there would have been no reason to turn their aircraft in order to look for the transport. The approach controller also erred in not instructing Flight 182 to maintain an altitude of 4,000 ft

(c. 1,200 m) until clear of the traffic area of nearby Montgomery Field, as required, to prevent conflict with operations at that general aviation airport. Even though the Cessna was operating out of Lindbergh Field, the 727 would have safely cleared the light aeroplane had it been at that height.

Neither the approach controller's third advisory given to the PSA crew nor the tower's warning were in accordance with prescribed regulations because they did not contain the direction of the said traffic nor the aircraft type. The investigative board also tried to determine why the conflict alert was not resolved. The approach controller stated that when the alert sounded, the data blocks representing the two aircraft were beginning to merge on the radarscope, but he took no action because the airline crew had already said that they had the reported traffic in sight. He and his coordinator both noted that such alerts were common.

Of course, the 727 was the overtaking aircraft and its crew would have been responsible for seeing and avoiding the Cessna. The cockpit voice recorder (CVR) tape indicated some confusion on the part of the pilots over the location of the light aeroplane after the initial 'Traffic in sight' message.

Following the tower's advisory, the pilot asked 'Is that the one we're looking at?', and the co-pilot replied 'Yeah, but I don't see him now'.

Moments later First Officer Fox questioned 'Are we clear of the Cessna?', and Capt McFeron answered 'I guess'.

Then, expressing a note of misdirected optimism, he was heard to say 'I saw him about one o'clock; probably behind us now'.

Nine seconds before the collision, the co-pilot remarked that 'There's one underneath', followed immediately by 'I was looking at that inbound there'.

Despite the good visibility and the fact that the Cessna was below the horizon, so the PSA pilots would not have had to look directly into the morning sun to see it, there would have been other factors making N7711G less observable as they closed in on the light aeroplane. In the final seconds before the collision the Cessna would have been masked to the crew by the cockpit structure of the jetliner, and the fact that both aircraft were virtually on the same heading would have reduced the apparent motion of the 172. Furthermore, the angle would have caused a foreshortening of the Cessna, making it appear smaller, and the aircraft would also have blended into the multiple colours of the residential area against which it was seen.

Not long after the accident the possible presence of a third or 'mystery' aircraft in the area at around the time of the collision came to light. It was first thought that the PSA crew may have mistaken another aircraft for the one that had been the object of the traffic advisories, and this theory was bolstered by witness accounts and, particularly, by the initial traffic report given to Flight 182. Board member McAdams in fact mentioned a possible misidentification in his dissenting opinion.

Two years later it was confirmed that a small single-engine Cessna 150 had indeed been in the general area at around 09:00 on the day of the disaster, and this revelation prompted the US Air Line Pilots Association (ALPA) to petition the NTSB for a reconsideration of the probable cause. The request was rejected on the basis that the 150 had crossed the flight path of the 727 too early to have been confused with the subsequent traffic advisories. Nor did the NTSB accept the premise that the co-pilot of Flight 182 mistook another PSA jetliner that was in front of his aircraft as the mentioned traffic. Never resolved, however, was the identity of the traffic referred to by First Officer Fox in his message 'We've got that other twelve', whether the aircraft in the first advisory or N7711G.

The NTSB was, however, sufficiently moved by the ALPA petition to modify its original findings. In the new probable cause, the ATC procedures joined the error by the PSA crew as a primary factor.

Considered as contributing factors were the failure of the controller to advise Flight 182 of the Cessna's direction, the failure of the light aeroplane to maintain the assigned heading, and improper resolution of the conflict alert.

NTSB recommendations included the implementation of a full-scale terminal radar service area at Lindbergh Field, which would later be acted upon by the US Federal Aviation Administration (FAA), and procedural changes for the separation of aircraft in all terminal areas. That did not mean that the San Diego disaster was the result of a failure in the ATC system. The equipment was more than adequate and functioned perfectly on the day of the collision. Nor was there any gross negligence by any of those involved, but rather a series of seemingly small but nevertheless critical errors. The underlying reason for the tragedy could perhaps best be summed up in one word: complacency.

Date: 15 November 1978 (23:30)
Location: Near Katunayake, Sri Lanka
Operator: Loftleidir HF (Icelandic Airlines)
Aircraft type: McDonnell Douglas DC-8 Super 63CF (*TF-FLA*)

The jetliner was being flown on behalf of Garuda Indonesian Airways on a non-scheduled service from Saudi Arabia to Indonesia, its passengers Muslim pilgrims returning home from Mecca, and it crashed in the vicinity of Bandaranaike International Airport, located some 20 miles (30 km) north of Colombo, and an intermediate stop. The disaster killed 184 persons aboard the aircraft, including eight of its 13 crew members. Many of the 78 survivors suffered serious injuries.

After beginning an instrument landing system (ILS) approach, the DC-8 ploughed into a coconut plantation approximately 1 mile (1.5 km) from the threshold of the assigned runway, No. 22, broke apart and burst into flames, its undercarriage down at the moment of impact. The accident took place in darkness and during a light to moderate rain, a low overcast consisting of 5/8 cloud coverage at about 1,000 ft (300 m), and a visibility of around 3.5 miles (6 km). There was also thunderstorm activity in the area.

Sri Lankan aviation authorities attributed the disaster to the flight crew's nonconformance with the established approach procedures. Specifically, they ruled that the pilots failed to check and utilise all the instruments available for altitude and rate-of-descent awareness; that the first officer did not make the required altitude and descent rate callouts at various levels; and that the captain failed to initiate a missed approach procedure at the appropriate height when the runway was not visible. (Subsequently, he did commence an over-shoot, asking for full power, but at too low an altitude to prevent the crash.)

Additionally it was considered probable that the captain's radio altimeter had been erroneously set at 150 ft (c. 50 m), which would have deprived him of the ground-proximity warning system (GPWS) alert at the intended break-off height of 250 ft (c. 75 m).

In a dissenting opinion, the Icelandic Directorate of Civil Aviation blamed the accident on inadequate maintenance of the ILS facilities, which it said caused a downward bending of the glide slope into the ground and, in turn, of the jetliner arriving at its decision height too far from the runway and over terrain where a successful recovery could not be made. The Directorate also considered erroneous information supplied by the radar controller and the lack of an operational approach lighting system at the airport as contributing factors.

Icelandic and Sri Lankan investigators did agree that an encounter with heavy rain and/or a downdraught during a critical portion of the flight hampered the crew's attempt to regain altitude.

Date: 23 December 1978 (00:39)
Location: Near Cinisi, Sicily, Italy
Operator: Alitalia (Italy)
Aircraft type: McDonnell Douglas DC-9 Series 32 (*I-DIKQ*)

Operating as Flight 4128 and on a supplemental domestic service from Rome, the jet airliner crashed in the Tyrrhenian Sea while attempting to land at Punta Raisi Airport, serving Palermo, killing 108 persons aboard, including the entire crew of five. Fishing boats rescued the 21 surviving passengers.

The accident occurred during the final approach to Runway 21, using very-high-frequency omni-directional range and distance-measuring equipment (VOR/DME) procedures and while under radar contact. It was dark at the time, and the meteorological conditions consisted of light rain and low clouds, with 4/8 cumulus at about 2,500 ft (750 m) and 8/8 altostratus at 8,000 ft (c. 2,500 m), a visibility of approximately 5 miles (10 km), and a 17-knot wind from a direction of 190 degrees.

Having levelled off at a height of about 150 ft (50 m) with its undercarriage extended, the DC-9 hit the surface of the water with its right wing some 3.5 miles (6 km) from the runway threshold after a final loss of height attributed to the wind, the second impact breaking its fuselage into three main sections and tearing off both wings and one engine. The main wreckage, containing many of the victims' bodies, was subsequently recovered.

The crash apparently resulted from the poor monitoring of altitudes and too early a transition from instrument to visual flight procedures by the pilots while descending over an area devoid of lights and conducive to optical illusions. Significantly, the airport surveillance radar had no altitude reporting capability and a 'blind spot' in the area where the accident took place.

Date: 25 May 1979 (15:04)
Location: Near Chicago, Illinois, US
Operator: American Airlines (US)
Aircraft type: McDonnell Douglas DC-10 Series 10 (*N110AA*)

Five years after the crash near Paris (see separate entry, 3 March 1974), the DC-10 once again became the centre of controversy as a result of this, the worst US domestic airline accident to date.

Flight 191 began its take-off, as cleared, from Runway 32R at O'Hare International Airport, on a non-stop domestic service to Los Angeles, California. The weather on this Friday afternoon was perfect, with the sky clear and a visibility of 15 miles (c. 25 km). Accelerating normally, the aircraft commenced to lift off, whereupon a serious structural failure occurred. At or just before rotation, its No. 1 engine, with the pylon attached, broke off. Tossed completely over the left wing, the power plant came to rest along the right-hand side of the runway.

The DC-10 then climbed to a height of about 300 ft (100 m) above the ground before it rolled to the left and started to descend, despite the

The American Airlines DC-10, minus its left engine/pylon assembly, is photographed an instant before impact. *(CORBIS)*

application of aileron and rudder deflections in the opposite direction. Only 31 seconds after becoming airborne, the wide-bodied jetliner plunged into an open field in a nose-down attitude of approximately 20 degrees, with its undercarriage still extended and flaps at the take-off setting. The transport disintegrated in a massive explosion on impact, which took place about 1 mile (1.5 km) from the end of the runway and some 1,000 ft (300 m) to the left of its extended centreline, and at a speed of around 180 mph (290 kmh). All 271 persons aboard (258 passengers and 13 crew members) and two men on the ground perished. Two others were seriously injured and several vehicles, a mobile home and an old aircraft hangar were destroyed.

As with the Turkish crash in 1974, design shortcomings played an important role in this accident, but the primary factor in the tragedy that befell Flight 191 was not design-based, but operational – specifically, improper maintenance procedures.

Examination of the wreckage revealed a fracture in the forward flange of the left pylon's aft bulkhead. Resulting from overstressing, the total length of the main break and associated fatigue cracking was about 13 in (33 cm). At one end of the fracture, the cracking progressed to the upper inboard fastener that attached the forward section of the bulkhead to the aft part. At the other end, the fatigue propagated forward and slightly outboard towards the farthest-out hole in the upper flange. Weakened by the crack, the structure failed

from stresses generated as the DC-10 took off. The sequence and direction of the separation were consistent with forces imposed during the upward rotation of the aircraft, combined with aerodynamic loads and the thrust from the engine itself.

The loss of the power plant should not have doomed the flight, but what proved fatal was the damage it inflicted. When the pod/pylon assembly tore away, it took with it a chunk of the wing's leading edge 3 ft (*c.* 1 m) long. Both the No. 1 and No. 3 extension and retraction lines of the corresponding hydraulic systems and the follow-up cables for the drive actuators of the outboard slats were severed. Due to the loss of hydraulic fluid, the force of the rushing air caused the outboard slats on the left wing to retract, while the inboard slats on the same wing and both the inboard and outboard ones on the right wing remained extended. This asymmetrical slat configuration would have created handling difficulties for the pilots, and had the effect of increasing the stalling speed of the port wing. There were other problems as well. The No. 1 engine powered a number of systems and instruments, all of which failed when it separated. Particularly significant was the loss of the stick-shaker stall-warning device and the slat disagreement warning system.

Whatever action was taken by the crew could not be ascertained; the cockpit voice recorder (CVR) also received its electrical supply from the missing engine, as did certain parameters of the digital flight data recorder (DFDR). It was concluded, however, that the power had not been restored, possibly due to the distraction associated with the

A fiery explosion marks the end of Flight 191 seconds after its departure from Chicago's O'Hare International Airport. *(CORBIS)*

multiple failures, or due to the insufficient time available.

Especially considering the absence of the stick-shaker activation, the roll of the DC-10 must have confused the pilots, who could not have recognised the manoeuvre as the beginning of a stall. The buffeting associated with a stall could have been masked by air turbulence, the presence of which was confirmed. Also, neither the missing engine nor the slats would have been visible from the flight deck. It was therefore considered unreasonable for the crew to have recovered from such a situation.

The fracture that led to the pylon failure was attributed to a questionable maintenance practice used by American and another US carrier, Continental Air Lines. This procedure involved the removal and reinstallation of wing engine and pylon assemblies in one piece. A stand and cradle were affixed to the engine, and the entire unit was supported by a forklift. Though certainly a time-saving measure, safety was also a consideration in the adoption of the procedure. The one-step technique would reduce the number of disconnects of hydraulic and fuel lines, electrical cables and wiring. McDonnell Douglas, however, had prescribed removal and replacement of the pod and pylon separately, and, learning of the new method, the manufacturer stated that it 'did not encourage' it.

The procedure was delicate, and presented numerous possibilities for the application of a fracture-producing load either during disassembly or reassembly. Damage could result from contact between the bolts attaching the spar web to the upper flange of the aft bulkhead with the wing-mounted clevis, or, if the entire assembly were to be lowered too far, from the transferral of its total weight to the bulkhead. It was learned that the forklift drivers did not receive adequate instruction in the need for precision when carrying out the work.

The fracture found on *N110AA* was believed to have been inflicted about two months before the crash, at the airline's maintenance facility in Tulsa, Oklahoma, when the power plant had been removed in order to replace the spherical bearings that are used in the joints that attach the pylon to the wing. As the aircraft was being serviced, the forklift had to be re-positioned, and there were also indications that the vehicle ran out of fuel during the same time span.

Examination also revealed that three shims had been installed on the upper surface of the forward upper flange on this particular DC-10 in order to reduce clearance. In its investigative report, the US National Transportation Safety Board (NTSB) concluded that the shims could have spread out the load and increased the size of the crack, or could have actually added strength to the structure; no conclusion could be made as to their effects. Whatever the case, the fracture was believed to have increased in size during the period of service until the final failure due to normal operational stresses.

Damage resulting from the one-step maintenance procedure had been reported by Continental Air Lines to McDonnell Douglas some months before the Chicago disaster, but in a lapse in safety communications this information was not relayed to the US Federal Aviation Administration (FAA).

The NTSB considered the design of the pylon structure as contributing to the loss of the engine from *N110AA*. It noted that in some places clearances were unnecessarily small, making maintenance difficult to perform. The inter-relationship and lack of redundancy of essential aircraft systems were also a factor in the accident. The stick-shaker had only one motor and, deriving its electrical energy from the port engine, there was no way by which it could operate by battery power; and even had it continued to function after the engine separation, there would have been no warning based on the slats-retracted stall speed schedule, because the computer designed to receive information concerning the position of the outboard slats was itself knocked out by the power loss.

Though the DC-10 had been certified by the FAA in accordance with the rules in effect at the time, the NTSB concluded that those regulations were inadequate. Safe flight characteristics despite an asymmetrical slat configuration had been demonstrated, although not under take-off conditions. And although an analysis did show that the capability of the aircraft to accelerate to and maintain a safe margin above the stall regime was compromised in the event of both a loss of engine thrust and unwanted slat retraction, this combination was considered 'extremely improbable'. The NTSB also identified deficiencies in the surveillance and reporting procedures of the FAA, and shortcomings in the production and quality control standards of the manufacturer. Some three years after the crash, the FAA did take action to rectify one of the identified flaws in the transport when it ordered changes in its slat mechanism. Added to every DC-10 would be a spring assembly providing tension in order to hold the slats in place, even if one of the cables attached to them were to break, and a valve, designed to maintain hydraulic pressure in the system should a line experience a loss of fluid.

The crew of Flight 191 were not faulted for continuing the take-off after the structural failure, since they could not have known the nature of the emergency. In trying to maintain the same air speed, the first officer complied with the procedures specified by the airline in the event of a power plant failure. Unfortunately, his action had the effect of decelerating the jetliner, which led to the initiation of the stall. (As a result of this accident, higher climb-out speeds in the event of a power plant failure occurring during this phase of flight were recommended and later implemented.)

Inspections carried out in the wake of the crash revealed numerous discrepancies in the DC-10 fleet, including fractures that were found in the upper flanges of the aft bulkheads on the pylons of six different aircraft. Concern over these matters prompted the FAA to suspend the transport's type

certificate, which remained in effect in the US for 37 days.

This temporary grounding order was the first involving an American-built commercial airliner in more than 30 years, and proved to be a tremendous blow not just to the DC-10 but also to the supremacy of the nation's aviation industry. As for American Airlines, which abandoned the one-step technique, this served as a bitter lesson in performing maintenance 'by the book'.

Six months after the crash, the carrier was fined US $500,000 for the faulty maintenance procedures it had employed.

Date: 11 August 1979 (*c.* 13:35)
Location: Near Dneprodzerzhinsk, Ukraine, USSR
First aircraft
Operator: Aeroflot (USSR)
Type: Tupolev Tu-134A (*SSSR-65735*)
Second aircraft
Operator: Aeroflot (USSR)
Type: Tupolev Tu-134A (*SSSR-65816*)

The two jet transports collided at an approximate height of 27,500 ft (8,400 m), and both then crashed. A total of 178 persons perished in the disaster and there were no survivors.

An Aeroflot Tupolev Tu-134A, two of which were involved in the disastrous collision over the Ukraine. *(Aeroflot)*

Carnage at Mexico City's international airport following the crash of a Western Air Lines DC-10. *(AP Images)*

Both aircraft were on domestic operations, *SSSR-65735*, designated as Flight 7880, en route from Donetsk, Ukraine, to Minsk, Belorussia, the last segment of a service originating at Tashkent, Uzbek SSR, and carrying 77 passengers and a crew of seven, and *SSSR-65816*, operating as Flight 7628, from Chelyabinsk and Voronezh, RSFSR, to Kishinev, Moldavian SSR, with 88 passengers and a crew of six aboard. As they were flying on crossing tracks, air traffic controllers sought to provide separation through altitude assignment, but after clearing Flight 7880 for ascent to about 30,000 ft (10,000 m), they failed to monitor its position on radar. The resulting collision took place in the clouds, with the nose of *SSSR-65816* probably striking the rear of *SSSR-65735*. Wreckage was scattered over an area of some 2 by 10 miles (3 by 15 km).

Date: 31 October 1979 (05:42)
Location: Mexico City, Mexico
Operator: Western Air Lines (US)
Aircraft type: McDonnell Douglas DC-10 Series 10 (*N903WA*)

Designated as a supplemental service, Flight 2605 was the second of two aircraft that departed from Los Angeles, California, US, bound for Mexico City.

As the wide-bodied jetliner prepared to land at Benito Juarez International Airport, the control tower operator informed its crew that the runway in use was 23-Right. However, the adjacent 23-Left, which had been closed for resurfacing, was the runway equipped with both instrument landing system (ILS) facilities and approach lights. For that reason the captain apparently elected to execute a 'side-step' manoeuvre, using the ILS of 23L before transitioning over to 23R. In accordance with this procedure, the crew would be required to abandon the approach if no visual contact was established at an above-ground height of 600 ft (*c.* 180 m).

During the final approach, the tower controller drew the crew's attention to the fact that the aircraft had deviated to the left of the correct flight path, and again advised that Runway 23L was closed. The DC-10 then entered a fog bank at an approximate altitude of 800 ft (250 m), and a crewman reported that the approach lights could not be seen.

Inexplicably, the jetliner did not land on 23R. Instead, its left main undercarriage wheels touched down on the grass to the left of the pavement of 23L, and the right ones on that runway's shoulder. The aircraft then entered the runway, after which full power was applied and a go-around initiated.

However, just after becoming airborne the DC-10 collided with an earth-laden dump truck that was being driven on the shoulder of the closed runway. The impact sheared off the right main gear, and the undercarriage leg itself then hit and severed the aircraft's starboard horizontal tailplane. Portions of the right wing flaps were also torn away. Due to this damage, the jetliner banked steeply to the right, and its starboard wing was fractured when it scraped along the taxiway.

The DC-10's right wing then struck a repair hangar, rupturing the fuel tanks, and the aircraft finally slammed into another building, broke apart and was swept by flames. The accident killed 72 of the 89 persons aboard the aircraft (61 passengers and 11 crew members), along with the driver of the dump truck. Except for two passengers, the 17 survivors, who also included two cabin attendants, suffered various injuries. The crash occurred around dawn, and in addition to the fog there was mist and haze in the area. Visibility had been reduced to zero. The flight crew had not complied with the approach procedure being used and had descended below the minimum height without reporting the runway in sight. Analysis of the cockpit voice recorder (CVR) tape also indicated that the required altitude call-outs had not been made during the descent.

Date: 26 November 1979 (c. 02:00)
Location: Near At Tā'if, Saudi Arabia
Operator: Pakistan International Airlines
Aircraft type: Boeing 707-340C (AP-AWZ)

Flight 740 had been airborne less than half an hour when a cabin attendant reported a fire in the aft cabin area. Seventeen horrifying minutes later, and while on a south-south-easterly heading, the jetliner plunged into a rocky desert and disintegrated in a fiery explosion that was witnessed by the pilots of another aircraft some 30 miles (50 km) away. All 156 persons aboard the aircraft (145 passengers and a crew of 11) perished.

The accident took place in darkness and clear weather conditions approximately 90 miles (145 km) east of Jiddah, where the 707 had stopped, as scheduled, during a service originating at Kano, Nigeria, with an ultimate destination of Karachi, Pakistan. Due to the condition of the wreckage, the cause of the in-flight blaze that had led to the crash could not be determined.

The aircraft's flight data recorder (FDR) yielded nothing of any significance, but its cockpit voice recorder (CVR) tape was recovered intact and provided much valuable information relative to the investigation. According to facts obtained from the CVR transcript, the fire had started near the cabin door and/or in the lavatory. Someone was heard to say 'Fire, fire, it is totally on fire', and the sound of numerous other voices indicated that panic-stricken passengers had crowded forward towards or into the cockpit to escape the flames.

There was evidence that valuable time had been lost in notifying the flight crew about the fire, and that the captain delayed in turning back towards Jiddah. In fact, the pilot presumably continued climbing towards the assigned altitude even after learning of the blaze, then executed an emergency descent at a rate too slow under the circumstances. He also seemed preoccupied with trying to depressurise the cabin.

It was not known whether the passenger oxygen masks were deployed; had they been, the release of pure oxygen into the cabin would have intensified and extended the fire.

The aircraft had been given an incorrect descent clearance by an air traffic controller, who failed to note the minimum height for the area. This was not a factor, however, as the crew realised the error and levelled off at 11,000 ft (c. 3,400 m). With the elevation of the terrain being about 3,000 ft (1,000 m) at the crash site, it was concluded that the 707 was out of control during the last 8,000 ft (c. 2,500 m) of the descent.

Because it could find no evidence of a pre-impact explosion, and since the use of incendiary devices was not consistent with previous terrorist activity in the Middle East, the investigative board considered sabotage unlikely. There were indications, without confirmation, that the fire was electrical in origin.

Considered most probable, however, was that the blaze had been started unintentionally by a passenger. Most of those aboard were Muslim pilgrims, returning from Mecca, and many had been carrying small gasoline or kerosene stoves used to make tea. If one or more of these stoves were fuelled and pressurised, the pressure differential would increase as the aircraft continued

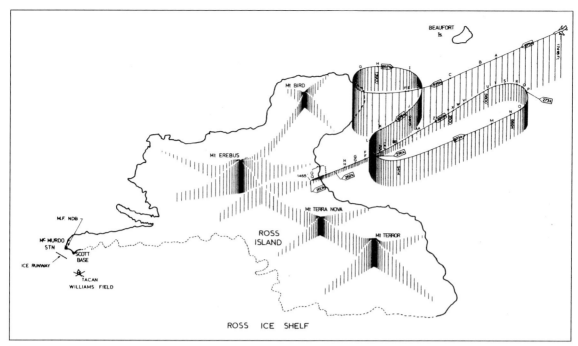

A three-dimensional diagram showing the flight path in the final minutes before the Air New Zealand DC-10 crashed in Antarctica. *(International Civil Aviation Organisation)*

to ascend. A poorly sealed gasket could allow leakage into the cabin or cargo areas, and only a spark or cigarette ember would be needed to set the stage for disaster. Smoke from the rapidly spreading fire must have eventually incapacitated the pilots despite their use of emergency oxygen.

In its accident report, the board recommended that Pakistan International Airlines review its training policies so as to impress cabin crews with the importance of reporting any unusual occurrence, especially a fire, by the most expeditious means available, and flight crews with the importance of implementing emergency procedures without hesitation when facing such a situation. It also suggested that the Saudi Arabian air traffic control system review its procedures to ensure that controllers be aware of minimum safe altitudes in all sectors, and that separate communication frequencies be assigned immediately in the event of an emergency such as the one encountered by Flight 740.

Date: 28 November 1979 (12:49)
Location: Ross Island, Antarctica
Operator: Air New Zealand Ltd
Aircraft type: McDonnell Douglas DC-10 Series 30 (ZK-NZP)

What began as the last of four sightseeing flights conducted by the carrier during the Antarctic

Summer of 1979 would end in the first commercial aviation disaster ever to occur on the frozen continent, involving an airline that had never lost a paying passenger in nearly 40 years of operations and a nation that until this date had not experienced a civilian air crash resulting in more than a couple of dozen fatalities.

Following its departure from Auckland, on New Zealand's North Island, the aircraft proceeded south on what was designated as a non-scheduled service with an ultimate destination of Christchurch, on the country's South Island, and no planned stops in between. The DC-10 was dispatched in accordance with a computerised flight plan, which had been fed into its inertial navigation system (AINS).

The cockpit crew consisted of a captain, two first officers and two flight engineers. The extra co-pilot was in lieu of a second captain, which had been a requirement of Air New Zealand in its Antarctic operations. Interestingly, of these five men only one of the flight engineers had ever been on a polar trip. However, two of the three pilots had been subjected to a specially devised audio-visual, written and simulator route qualification briefing. There were also 15 cabin attendants to serve the 237 passengers on this particular flight.

Inasmuch as compasses are useless so close to the magnetic pole, and for the purpose of maintaining some consistency in an area where determining one's position and direction can be confusing, a method of grid navigation would be employed. This technique involved the placement of a grid over the navigational chart, which in effect reversed directions for a crew flying towards Antarctica from New Zealand. Due north would thus become 180 degrees Grid, and vice versa. This was just one of several factors that added to the complexity of the polar flights.

At the time, Ross Island was under a low overcast, with a reported ceiling of 2,000 ft (c. 600 m) and light snow. However, the weather office at McMurdo Station advised the crew that the visibility under the clouds was 40 miles (c. 65 km). The US Navy air traffic control centre, also located at McMurdo, then suggested that the aircraft take advantage of the facility's surveillance radar to initiate a descent.

While over the Ross Sea, the captain decided to let down through a break in the overcast, doing so in two descending orbits, first to the right, then the left. Following the second loop, the DC-10 continued down to 2,000 ft (c. 600 m), then another 500 ft (c. 150 m) in an attempt to obtain a better view under the cloud base. This action by the pilot represented a violation of the specified minimum altitude of 16,000 ft in instrument meteorological conditions until the passage of McMurdo, and even the absolute minimum of 6,000 ft in any weather.

The crew had just begun ascent procedures, applying full power to the three engines, when the wide-bodied jet airliner slammed into the upward-sloping ice at an approximate elevation of 1,500 ft (500 m) and disintegrated in a mass of flames. All 257 persons aboard perished.

In its report, New Zealand's Office of Air Accidents Investigation ascribed as the primary cause of the disaster the captain's decision to descend visually below the minimum safety height before reaching McMurdo. However, the inquiry also identified numerous shortcomings in the practices of the airline with regard to its Antarctic operations that contributed to, and some even feel caused, the crash.

Particularly noteworthy was a single-digit error in the computer-stored flight plan that resulted in the incorrect coordinates of Williams Field located near McMurdo and the site of a non-directional beacon (NDB) and a tactical air navigation (TACAN) aid,

which was used by Air New Zealand crews. As a consequence the facility was depicted as being 2 degrees 10 minutes further true west than its actual position. Though seemingly insignificant, this lapse actually displaced the direct track to McMurdo by nearly 30 miles (50 km) to the right, relative to the grid. Since past flights had been conducted in visual meteorological conditions (VMC) and did not strictly adhere to the prescribed route, the error was not detected during the operations taking place over the previous 14 months until exactly two weeks before the crash of ZK-NZP, and was not corrected until the night before.

The alteration moved the course back due east almost directly over Mt Erebus, an active volcano rising to about 12,500 ft (3,800 m) and the highest point on Ross Island. Although two of the pilots from the doomed DC-10 had seen a print-out containing the erroneous information, i.e. with the track over the sea-level ice, they were not shown a chart indicating that the intended route passed over the high ground. One track and distance diagram issued at the route qualification briefing, some three weeks earlier, did not show the location of any topographical feature, and the relief maps carried aboard the aircraft were of a very small scale. The audio-visual presentation was also found to be potentially misleading, with one slide showing a view of Mt Erebus, taken from behind the co-pilot's seat, giving no indication of the flight path in relationship to the volcano. The stage was thus set for disaster on the Wednesday morning that the jet took off from Auckland, its AINS programmed with the proper navigational information but the crew unaware of either the original error or the correction.

An important omission in the briefing was a comprehensive discussion of the 'white-out' phenomenon, which is commonplace in areas where large, unbroken expanses of snow are illuminated by a sky overcast with dense, low clouds, blotting out all trace of surface texture or shadow and merging the terrain and horizon into a flattened, white background. The conditions on the day of the accident were highly conducive to such a 'white-out'.

From the comments transcribed from the aircraft's cockpit voice recorder (CVR) tape, it was obvious that the crew had misconceptions about the flight level to be used for the resetting of the altimeters to the local atmospheric pressure, the minimum descent height allowed in VMC and the terrain beneath the track from Cape Hallett to McMurdo. With regard to the first issue, the main altimeters were not reset until the DC-10 had descended to 3,500 ft (c. 1,050 m), instead of the required flight level 180. This resulted in a reading 570 ft (c. 175 m) higher than its actual altitude.

Despite the suggestion of the control centre, ZK-NZP was not observed on radar during the let-down, which went against company policy. When clearance for descent to 2,000 ft was requested while on a heading of 180 degrees Grid, the controller had no reason for concern, but without further comment to the centre, the pilot reversed his course during the descent to 357 degrees Grid, which was back towards the cloud-covered high ground.

Although the navigational aids were functioning properly, the crew could not lock the aircraft's distance-measuring equipment (DME) on to the TACAN, and also experienced a loss in radio communications with McMurdo. These difficulties were probably attributable to the low height of the jet, which placed the mountain in its 'line of sight' with the facilities.

No evidence could be found of any abnormal functioning of the aircraft's navigational and flight guidance system, and the indicated position was within its accuracy limitations. Also, the captain was qualified as a navigator, and could be expected to keep a realistic mental plot of the terrain, particularly Mt Erebus. Nevertheless, both he and the first officer were apparently unaware of their position in the final minutes of the flight. The weather and terrain had even fooled famed polar explorer Peter Mulgrew, who was serving as a tour guide for his fellow passengers and riding in the cockpit. The two flight engineers were not so confident, however, and seconds before impact, one was heard to say 'I don't like this'.

The pilot finally elected to initiate a climb-out of the area, which he must have believed to be due west of the island, and was discussing with the co-pilot the most suitable path to take when the ground-proximity warning system (GPWS) sounded,

announcing 'Pull up'. The crew reacted to the alarm without undue hesitation, with the captain asking for 'go-round power', but the 6½ seconds between the activation of the warning and impact were insufficient for the DC-10 to respond to their commands. At the time of the crash, the aircraft's nose was slightly raised and its wings were approximately level. The GPWS did not go off sooner because the approach was made over a cliff some 300 ft (100 m) high rather than a steadily increasing slope, and because of the transport's high speed, nearly 300 mph (c. 480 kmh) when it slammed into the ice. A slower cruising speed could have been accomplished through the extension of its flaps and slats, but this was prohibited on the Antarctic flights, ironically for safety reasons. The concern was that the high drag resulting from a configuration would increase fuel consumption and perhaps not allow for a safe return should a malfunction prevent their retraction.

While the pilot had initiated the descent, the co-pilot was blamed for not monitoring him nor offering any criticism of his actions. Instead the first officer had devoted an inordinate amount of time in trying to establish radio contact with McMurdo. Also noted in the investigative report was the apparent failure of the crew to use the 'mapping' mode of the aircraft's weather radar for terrain avoidance.

A separate, one-member Royal Commission of Inquiry differed from the conclusions of the Air Accidents office. It ascribed as the 'single, dominant and effective cause' of the disaster the decision by airline officials to change the flight plan without notifying the crew. The commission said that the carrier was guilty of 'incompetent administrative procedures' and charged that company personnel had orchestrated a 'litany of lies' in attempting to cover up their mistake. Nearly 20 years after the tragedy, the government of New Zealand officially accepted the findings of the independent commission regarding the cause of the crash. Discontinued after the accident, the Antarctic scenic flights were resumed in 1994 by the Australian airline Qantas, under a new set of safety guidelines.

THE 1980S

The 1980s could be described as both the best and the worst of times for air safety. In 1984 the industry had its safest year to date, with but two major crashes (both occurring in the Soviet Union); the death toll during the 12-month period was lower than it had been back in the years when airline passengers numbered only thousands and not hundreds of millions.

But the very next year there was a dramatic turn for the worse, as air carrier fatalities burgeoned to more than 2,000. Six major disasters accounted for a majority of those deaths, and for the first time in history more than 500 lives were lost in an accident involving a single aircraft.

It also became apparent that the threat of terrorism, which had plagued commercial aviation throughout the 1970s, had yet to be defeated. The two worst cases of recorded aerial sabotage were the bombing of an Air-India Boeing 747 over the North Atlantic in June 1985, and the destruction of Pan American World Airways Flight 103 over Lockerbie, Scotland, four days before Christmas 1988. Besides terrorism, there were other cases of hostilities against civil aircraft, the most noteworthy of which (due to involvement of 'Super Power' forces) occurred in September 1983 when a Korean Air Lines Boeing 747 was shot down by the USSR after straying off course, and nearly five years later when a US Navy warship on patrol in the Persian Gulf downed an Iranian Airbus. Both appeared to be tragic cases of misidentification.

Hostile action had, in fact, become the greatest single threat to commercial aviation, with four major cases during the last two years of the decade costing more than 800 lives. Three of these incidents and most of the fatalities were related in some manner to the volatile Middle East.

Date: 21 January 1980 (*c.* 19:10)
Location: Near Laskarak, Markazi, Iran
OperatorIran National Airlines Corporation (Iran Air)
Aircraft type: Boeing 727-86 (*EP-IRD*)

All 128 persons aboard (120 passengers and eight crew members) were killed when the jetliner crashed and burned in the Elburz Mountains, some 20 miles (30 km) north of Tehran, while attempting to land at the city's Mehrabad International Airport. The accident occurred in darkness, fog and snow after the aircraft had been cleared for an instrument landing system (ILS) approach to Runway 29L, at the end of a scheduled domestic flight from Bābol Sar (Meshed-i-Sar).

The 727 had flown through the west-north-westerly localiser course, proceeding almost due north until the impact at an approximate elevation of 8,400 ft (2,560 m). According to a government announcement, the disaster was related to the fact that the ground radar and ILS were inoperative, and other airport equipment had not been functioning properly at the time. The head of the nation's Civil Aviation Organisation and five other officials were later charged with manslaughter.

Date: 14 March 1980 (*c.* 11:00)
Location: Near Warsaw, Poland
Operator: Polskie Linie Lotnicze (LOT) (Poland)
Aircraft type: Ilyushin Il-62 (*SP-LAA*)

The passengers who boarded Flight 007 at John F. Kennedy International Airport, serving New York City, included 14 members and eight officials of the US amateur boxing team on their way to matches in Poland.

As the jetliner made its approach to land at Okecie Airport following the transatlantic service, there was an indication that its undercarriage may not have been fully down and locked, prompting the pilots to initiate an overshoot procedure. However, when thrust was increased only slightly, the No. 2 (left inboard) power plant suddenly disintegrated. Flying debris then damaged two other engines and severed vital rudder and elevator control lines.

Rendered uncontrollable, the Il-62 plunged into a moat adjacent to a nineteenth-century fortress in a nose-down angle of about 20 degrees and approximately half a mile (0.8 km) from the runway threshold, exploding on impact. All 87 persons aboard, including a crew of 10, perished in the crash.

Metal fatigue had apparently caused a turbine disc in the power plant to break.

Date: 25 April 1980 (13:21)
Location: Tenerife, (Spanish) Canary Islands
Operator: Dan-Air Services Ltd (UK)
Aircraft type: Boeing 727-46 (*G-BDAN*)

The jet airliner, on a charter service from Manchetser, England, was to have landed at Los Rodeos Airport, located near Santa Cruz de Tenerife. Following their transfer to Tenerife Approach Control, the crew were given the latest weather, and were then authorised for descent to flight level 60. They then reported passing the Tenerife (TFN) very-high-frequency omnidirectional range (VOR) station and heading for the locator beacon 'FP' before being notified of an unpublished holding pattern. Radioing that it was 'taking up the hold', the aircraft received clearance down to 5,000 ft (*c*. 1,500 m). Less than a minute later, the crew reported 'we've had a ground-proximity warning'.

Seconds after that final transmission, the 727 slammed into a mountain some 5 miles (10 km) south-west of the airport and at an approximate elevation of 5,450 ft (1,660 m). The aircraft disintegrated on impact, and all 146 persons aboard (138 passengers and eight crew members) perished. Only small fires erupted in the wreckage after the crash and extinguished themselves. The meteorological conditions in the area around the time consisted of a broken overcast, with the cloud base down to about 3,000 ft (1,000 m), a light wind and no significant turbulence.

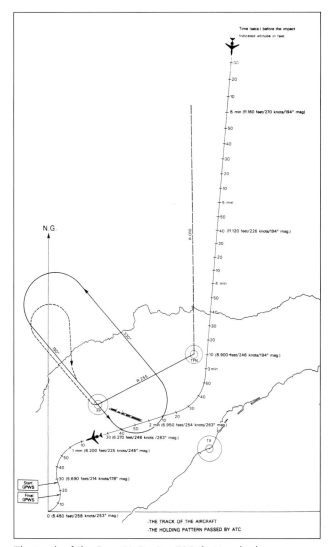

The track of the Dan-Air Boeing 727 that crashed on Tenerife after flying past the holding pattern. (*Spanish Civil Aviation Accident Commission*)

The initial approach of the jet was indicative of the imprecise navigation that continued until the moment of impact. Specifically, its flight path was displaced by nearly 1 mile (1.5 km) to the east of the correct radial upon arrival at TFN. Also, the flight crew did not report passing the VOR until 33 seconds after the fact. There was no interception of Radial 255, as required in order to enter the holding pattern. Moreover, contrary to their radio message, they did not assume a heading towards FP, but instead passed approximately 2 miles (3 km) south of the navigational aid. Rather than entering the holding pattern, the 727 continued on a south-westerly heading, which took it into a mountainous area where the minimum safe altitude was 14,500 ft (*c.* 4,400 m).

As transcribed on the cockpit voice recorder (CVR) tape, the ground-proximity warning system (GPWS) first sounded 27 seconds before the crash, but it deactivated when the aircraft flew over a valley. The alert prompted the pilot to initiate a turn to the right and order an overshoot. At that point he apparently did not know his position.

The CVR transcript also revealed confusion on the part of the crew regarding the radio transmission from the approach controller regarding a 'standard holding', which included instructions to 'turn to the left'. The lack of clarity came from the fact that a standard holding involves a right turn. This led the first officer to remark 'Bloody strange hold, isn't it?'. There was, however, no request for clarification from the approach controller.

Subsequently, the crew expressed concern over their location, with the captain, in reference to the controller, stating 'He's taking us round to the high ground'. There was also evidence of a lack of teamwork between the pilot and the co-pilot, with the latter suggesting a heading more towards the south-east while the former continued with the turn to the right because of his conviction that the jet was flying in the direction of the mountains.

The impact took place some 130 ft (40 m) below the summit of the mountain as the cleanly configured 727 was flying in cloud at an approximate speed of 300 mph (480 kmh), on a heading of about 250 degrees, banked an estimated 30 to 40 degrees to the right and in a slight descent. In not levelling the wings the pilot did not take advantage of the aircraft's optimum climb performance, and as a result he merely reduced its descent rate. Also the speed of the jet was higher than that advisable and this was probably a factor in the short time span between its receipt of the holding information and its passage of FP, which contributed to the accident.

The British representative in the investigation generally agreed with the findings of the Spanish commission, though he labelled the information provided by the approach controller as 'ambiguous' and said it contributed to the disorientation of the crew. He further claimed that it was not practicable for an aircraft to follow the prescribed track because of its sharp angles, and noted that no minimum

safe altitude calculations had been carried out by proper authorities for the approach and holding patterns. He claimed that the crash would not have occurred had the 727 not been cleared by the controller to below 7,000 ft (*c.* 2,000 m).

Of course, the approach controller was operating without the assistance of radar, and could not have known the exact position of *G-BDAN* – he thought it had already entered the holding pattern when he authorised the descent to 5,000 ft. Had the aircraft been where he believed it to be, a left turn would have been required to remain in the circuit.

Three months after the accident, and even before the issuance of the final report, the UK Civil Aviation Authority (CAA) advised all British carriers operating into Los Rodeos Airport to use greater safety altitudes than those published during certain types of approach procedures.

Date: 27 June 1980 (*c.* 20:00)
Location: Off Western Italy
Operator: Aerolinee Itavia SpA (Italy)
Aircraft type: Douglas DC-9 Series 15 (*I-TIGI*)

Operating as Flight 870, the jet airliner had departed earlier from Bologna, on a domestic service to Palermo, Sicily, and it was last known to have been cruising on an almost due southerly heading in darkness and at an altitude of approximately 25,000 ft (7,500 m) before it plunged into the Tyrrhenian Sea some 15 miles (25 km) north-east of the Italian island of Ustica, in water nearly 12,000 ft (3,700 m) deep. Searchers later found the bodies of 38 victims, but there were no survivors among the 81 persons aboard (77 passengers and a crew of four).

Tests performed on recovered debris and pathological examinations of the deceased seemed to indicate that the DC-9 had been struck by, or suffered damage from, the nearby explosion of a missile, in either case resulting in an in-flight break-up. Speculation ranged from the intentional destruction of the airliner by a Libyan jet fighter, to an accidental hit during NATO manoeuvres. After one investigative commission was unable to come to a conclusion as to the probable cause of the tragedy, a second one was established, composed of international members.

The recovery of additional wreckage enabled the second commission to form another determination as to the fate of Flight 870. Particularly revealing was the damage and distortion in and around the right rear lavatory, which must have preceded the more general disintegration of the aircraft. It was ruled that such damage could only have been caused by the detonation of an explosive device. The bomb, which must have been composed of a relatively small amount of explosive probably wrapped only in plastic, was believed to have been placed between the outer wall of the lavatory and the skin of the aircraft. (Access to this area would have been possible in several ways, but the placement of something there would have been difficult to detect.)

Reconstruction of the destruction sequence indicated that the blast produced a shock wave that initially tore off skin from the top rear fuselage section and subsequently led to the separation of both engines and the empennage. The DC-9 then pitched down, creating a down-load force that snapped off its left outer wing. The break-up occurred in a matter of a few seconds, after which the airliner plummeted almost vertically into the water.

No claim for responsibility was ever made in connection with the destruction of *I-TIGI*, but it may have been related to a wave of terrorism that plagued Italy from the late 1960s into the 1980s. It was noted in the commission's report, however, that the findings that a bomb brought down Flight 870 had 'still not been accepted by all parties'.

Date: 8 July 1980 (00:39)
Location: Near Alma-Ata, Kazakh SSR, USSR
Operator: Aeroflot (USSR)
Aircraft type: Tupolev Tu-154B (*SSSR-85355*)

Designated as Flight 4225 and on a domestic service to Simferopol, Ukraine, the jet airliner crashed and burned less than 2 minutes after take-off from the Alma-Ata airport. All 166 persons aboard (156 passengers and a crew of 10) perished, and nine others on the ground were injured. The accident occurred in early morning darkness and cloudy weather conditions, with a visibility of around 5 miles (10 km).

The crash was attributed to an encounter with wind shear, consisting of a down-flow of up to about 30 mph (50 kmh) and a tail wind of approximately 45 mph (70 kmh), which occurred at the end of the process of retracting the high-lift devices, when the aircraft's take-off weight was close to the maximum and in mountain conditions, with high ambient temperatures. Climbing to an approximate height of 500 ft (150 m), the Tu-154 began an abrupt descent, then, despite all attempts by the crew to effect recovery, slammed to earth at a speed of around 250 mph (400 kmh), with its undercarriage in the up position.

Date: 19 August 1980 (*c. 22:00*)
Location: Near Riyadh, Saudi Arabia
Operator: Saudi Arabian Airlines (Saudia)
Aircraft type: Lockheed L-1011-200 TriStar (*HZ-AHK*)

One of the worst disasters in the history of commercial aviation, this bizarre accident cannot even be classified as a crash. Despite a successful emergency landing, the wide-bodied jetliner was gutted by flames, and all 301 persons aboard (287 passengers, including 15 infants, and 14 crew members) were killed.

Flight 163 had made a scheduled stop at Riyadh before continuing on the second leg of a service to Jiddah from Karachi, Pakistan. Only 7 minutes after take-off from the city's international airport, as transcribed on the cockpit voice recorder (CVR) tape, the flight crew were alerted by both visual and aural warnings to the presence of smoke in the aft cargo compartment, designated as 'C-3'.

The initial alert occurred as the TriStar was climbing through 15,000 ft (*c.* 5,000 m), and the

Despite a safe landing, none of the 301 persons aboard the Saudia L-1011 survived the fire that ultimately gutted the aircraft's fuselage. (*CORBIS*)

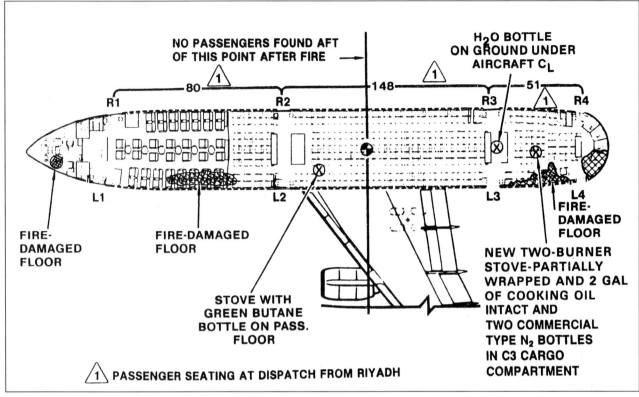

NO PASSENGERS FOUND AFT
OF THIS POINT AFTER FIRE

H₂O BOTTLE
ON GROUND UNDER
AIRCRAFT C_L

FIRE-DAMAGED FLOOR

FIRE-DAMAGED FLOOR

STOVE WITH
GREEN BUTANE
BOTTLE ON PASS.
FLOOR

L4
FIRE-
DAMAGED
FLOOR

NEW TWO-BURNER
STOVE-PARTIALLY
WRAPPED AND 2 GAL
OF COOKING OIL
INTACT AND
TWO COMMERCIAL
TYPE N₂ BOTTLES
IN C3 CARGO
COMPARTMENT

1 PASSENGER SEATING AT DISPATCH FROM RIYADH

Diagram showing the passenger placement and damage in the TriStar disaster. *(International Civil Aviation Organisation)*

crew spent more than 4 minutes trying to confirm the warning and looking for the smoke warning procedure. The captain then decided to return to the airport. Confirmation of the fire came as the aircraft was on its way back.

The actions of the flight crew could be considered normal until the turnaround, when things began to deteriorate, as illustrated by the CVR. The pilot-in-command failed to utilise properly his first and second officers, especially the former, to whom he should have delegated the function of flying the jetliner as he concentrated his attention on the emergency at hand. In fact, the captain appeared to reject the seriousness of the situation throughout the accident sequence. This may have been largely due to the flight engineer, who failed to give him an accurate picture of what was happening and kept saying 'No problem' when a serious one existed. The second officer himself may have been afflicted with dyslexia, which can cause confusion of both instruments and procedures. And the first officer, who had only limited experience in

the type of aircraft, did not assist the pilot in monitoring the safety of the flight. None of the three was apparently affected by the smoke that was filling the passenger compartment until after the landing.

In contrast, evidence pointed to a commendable performance on the part of the cabin crew in both battling the blaze and trying to calm the panic-stricken passengers. However, circumstances would prevent the attendants from carrying out their most important function in the event of an emergency – aiding in the evacuation of the aircraft – even had the captain made preparations for such action.

Despite a stuck thrust lever, which necessitated the shutting down of the No. 2 (centre) engine, the L-1011 landed safely, but it was then that the pilot committed another critical error, one that probably led to the catastrophic results in what should have been a survivable accident. Rather than using the maximum available braking power to stop the aircraft as soon as possible, he continued off the runway and finally came to a stop on a taxiway 2 minutes

40 seconds after touch-down. Moreover, by keeping the two wing engines running for another 3 minutes 15 seconds, he prevented the emergency personnel who had arrived on the scene from taking immediate action and also thwarted any attempt by the cabin crew members to initiate an emergency evacuation on their own.

There was no evidence that an evacuation had been started, nor that anyone had tried to open the cabin doors from inside. This may have been at the request of the captain (since he was heard to instruct his fellow cockpit crewmen before the landing not to evacuate) or because passengers were blocking the doors, which have to move a few inches inward to be opened. More likely, however, the flight and cabin crew were incapacitated by a flash fire, which depleted any oxygen left in the aircraft. This second blaze was caused by a reduction of oxygen and an accompanying increase in toxic gases, and must have taken place shortly after the last message from the TriStar, 'We are trying to evacuate now', transmitted at 21:40.

Aggravating the situation was the fact that the environmental control system (ECS) packs had been turned off, in accordance with normal procedures, which prevented any fresh air being introduced into the fuselage.

The crash/fire/rescue services were also proved to be woefully inadequate; they lacked the correct tools, protective clothing and proper training in forced-entry procedures as well as knowledge of the number and operation of doors in the L-1011 and other aircraft that served the airport. It took the personnel 23 minutes after engine shutdown to get into the fuselage, and by the time the No. 1 door on the left side could be opened, any rescue attempt was futile. Burns, oxygen starvation and the inhalation of such toxic gases as carbon monoxide, nitrous oxide, hydrogen cyanide, formic acid and ammonia had resulted in all the fatalities. The fire ultimately consumed almost the entire upper fuselage structure, leaving the wings, empennage, power plants and extended under-carriage intact. The entire drama was played out in moonlit darkness.

There was no doubt that the blaze had erupted in compartment C-3; the sticking of the No. 2 thrust lever was further proof of this (the throttle controls are routed through the area between the ceiling of the cargo hold and the cabin floor, and

the fairlead rollers that suspend them can, when heated, soften, melt and adhere to these cables, with only a small amount of cooling needed to cause an increase in friction).

The smoke and then the flames must have followed the same path, travelling through the transversals between the cargo compartment and the floor to the sidewall of the aircraft and up into the passenger cabin. The victims' bodies were all found in the forward half of the aircraft. As in previous accidents, the deadly fumes were produced by the burning of furnishings and other cabin materials.

The origin of the fire could not be determined, since the source of ignition had been obliterated in the blaze, but, of course, there are many potential sources of fire in the baggage compartment of an airliner. As noted in the investigative report, three such previous fires were started by the accidental lighting of matches in a suitcase. There was no evidence of an incendiary device.

Several modifications in the L-1011 were made by Lockheed as a result of this tragedy. These included the removal of insulation under the aft lavatories, a replacement in the type of insulation used for heat exchange in the C-2 and C-3 cargo holds, and the replacement of the cargo com-partment ceiling panels with those made of a high-strength glass laminate.

In addition to these changes, the US National Transportation Safety Board (NTSB), which par-ticipated in the investigation, recommended that the certification of the cargo holds be re-evaluated. The principle behind previous requirements was that a fire occurring within the compartment would be extinguished by oxygen deprivation. This concept was considered successfully applied in narrow-bodied aircraft with compartments of limited volume, but tests showed that a fire in the larger cargo holds on such aircraft as the TriStar could be sustained for more than 10 minutes, sufficient time to burn through the ceiling liner.

The US Federal Aviation Administration (FAA), however, responsible for enforcing safety standards on American-built aircraft, said the situation did not warrant the action proposed by the NTSB.

Saudia took its own remedial action in the wake of the disaster, which included a revision of emergency checklists and improvements in emer-gency evacuation training. Additionally, the carrier sealed off the C-3 compartments in its L-1011 fleet, with the intention of confining fires that could occur in them.

Date: 22 August 1981 (*c.* 10:00)
Location: Near Miao-li, Taiwan
Operator: Far Eastern Air Transport Corporation (Taiwan)
Aircraft type: Boeing Advanced 737-222 (*B-2603*)

Designated as Flight 103, the jet airliner plummeted into a mountainous region and burned some 100 miles (150 km) south-south-west of T'ai-pei, from where it had taken off earlier on a domestic service to Kao-hsiung. All 110 persons aboard (104 passengers and a crew of six) perished.

Severe corrosion in the belly area, possibly combined with undetected cracks, had led to the structural failure of its forward fuselage at a high altitude. The same aircraft had lost pressurisation during a flight some two weeks before the crash, and earlier on during the day of the accident.

Date: 16 November 1981 (*c.* 19:40)
Location: Near Noril'sk, Russian Soviet Federative Socialist Republic, USSR
Operator: Aeroflot (USSR)
Aircraft type: Tupolev Tu-154B-2 (*SSSR-85480*)

Operating as Flight 3603 and on a domestic service from Krasnoyarsk, the jetliner crashed and burned near the Noril'sk airport, where it was scheduled to land, killing 99 persons aboard. Three of the aircraft's seven crew members and 65 passengers survived the accident, all of whom suffered injuries. The crash occurred in darkness and during a low overcast, with a cloud base of around 400 ft (120 m) and a visibility of approximately half a mile (0.8 km).

Due to a lower-than-expected consumption of fuel, the Tu-154 was about 5,070 lb (2,300 kg) above its calculated weight, and its centre of gravity beyond the forward limit. This nose-heavy condition caused it to descend below the guide path during the final approach, which could not be countered by the captain's manipulation of the elevator controls. Seconds before impact, he increased thrust and initiated a go-around manoeuvre, but the jetliner slammed into an earthen mound some 1,500 ft (500 m) short of the runway and at an indicated air speed of around 170 mph (270 kmh), with its undercarriage still extended.

Besides failing to calculate adequately the landing weight of the aircraft and its centre of gravity, the crew had not increased its approach speed by about 3 mph (5 kmh), which was required in order to compensate for the former condition.

Date: 1 December 1981 (08:53)
Location: Near Petreto-Bicchisano, Corsica, France
Operator: Inex Adria Aviopromet (Yugoslavia)
Aircraft type: McDonnell Douglas DC-9 Super 82 (*YU-ANA*)

The jet airliner had taken off from Ljubljana, Yugoslavia, on a non-scheduled service to the Mediterranean island, and was to have landed at Campo dell'Oro Airport, serving Ajaccio. It carried 173 passengers, a mechanic and a regular crew of six.

Following its descent from flight level (FL) 330, the DC-9 was instructed to maintain an altitude of 11,000 ft (*c.* 3,400 m) until reaching the Ajaccio very-high-frequency omnidirectional range (VOR) station, and the pilot then reported being in the holding pattern at that height. Subsequently, the approach controller cleared the aircraft down to 3,300 ft (1,005 m).

In the final message from the jet, the captain reported turning inbound to Ajaccio while being in clouds. Less than a minute later, as transcribed on the aircraft's cockpit voice recorder (CVR) tape, the ground-proximity warning system (GPWS) began to sound, announcing both 'Terrain' and 'Pull up'. The captain was heard to ask for 'Power' 9 seconds later. His request was not made in a commanding tone, however, perhaps accounting for the relatively slow application of thrust. Three seconds after the pilot's remark, while turning left in a bank of 25 to 30 degrees and flying in a north-westerly direction at an indicated air speed of about 250 mph (400 kmh), the DC-9 struck Mont San Pietro with its port wing, the initial impact occurring at an elevation of 4,478 ft (1,365 m), or approximately 100 ft (30 m) from the top of the peak.

About half of the wing having been torn off, the aircraft rolled uncontrollably to the left, then crashed in a rocky ravine some 2,300 ft (700 m) below the summit of the mountain, disintegrating in the second or main impact. All 180 persons aboard perished. Wreckage was scattered over the rugged terrain on a heading of about 300 degrees, around 20 miles (30 km) south-west of Ajaccio. There was practically no post-crash fire.

The weather in the area at around the time of the accident consisted of strong winds from the west, heavy turbulence and a solid overcast of altocumulus and cumulus clouds that obscured the mountain tops.

A French investigative commission attributed the disaster to the descent by the crew which placed *YU-ANA* below the safe instrument flight altitude during that portion of its trajectory within the holding pattern, the published minimum height of the circuit being 6,800 ft (*c.* 2,070 m). The commission further observed that when the pilots, alerted by the GPWS alarm, tried to regain altitude, the manoeuvre proved insufficient to overcome the effects of severe down draughts caused by the relief of the terrain and the high winds that were present in the area.

Five contributing factors were outlined in the accident report. First, it was ruled that the crew had apparently not adequately prepared for the approach. The minimum altitude and maximum

A DC-9 Super 80 series, the type operated by the Yugoslav carrier Inex Adria Aviopromet that crashed on French Corsica. *(McDonnell Douglas)*

speed limits of the holding pattern were probably not retained. Additionally, the two pilots may have been distracted by the presence of a third person on the flight deck, a child identified as the son of the first officer, who was heard on the CVR tape. There

A section of the fuselage from YU-ANA rests between the rocks below Mont San Pietro after the disaster that claimed the lives of 180 persons. *(SIPA)*

were also misunderstandings between the captain and the approach controller, attributed to imprecise terminology. Specifically, the latter believed that the aircraft was going to make a direct descent in order to begin the final approach to the airport, while the former elected to enter the 'racetrack' holding pattern, and then initiated the descent. As a result of these misunderstandings, the controller was not fully aware of the progression of the flight. Had he better interpreted the messages 'Call you inbound on radial two forty seven' and 'Rolling inbound out of six thousand' sent by the pilot, an ambiguous situation in the case of the first transmission and an abnormal and dangerous one in the case of the second could have been avoided. Also the receipt of a message from the controller occurring simultaneously with the activation of the GPWS warning may have affected the crew's ability to react to the alarm.

Examination of the digital flight data recorder (DFDR) read-out revealed that the velocity of the DC-9 was greater than the maximum air speed prescribed in the holding pattern, and the crew made no correction for the winds, later calculated to have been approximately 70 knots at FL 110 and averaging 65 knots from that height down to 5,000 ft (c. 1,500 m), which were blowing in the path of the jet. However, the symbolic representation of the holding pattern on the approach chart corresponded to the trajectory of an aircraft flying at about 170 mph (270 kmh) with no wind.

A US Park Police helicopter rescued the survivors from the downed Air Florida Boeing 737, the tail section of which can be seen barely protruding from the Potomac River. *(CORBIS)*

Furthermore, the chart neither indicated the real dimensions of the circuit nor the elevation of the terrain below.

The commission in its inquiry found that habits formed during radar-guided operations could lead to overconfidence on the part of some pilots with regard to minimum safe altitudes. Differing with the French findings, a Yugoslav commission concluded that the crash resulted directly from the misunderstanding between the crew and the controller, and maintained that it should have been obvious to the latter that the former was entering the holding pattern and not making a direct approach.

The accident report emphasised the need for the use of a standard vocabulary in radio communications by pilots and air traffic controllers, and also recommended revisions in approach charts to improve clarity, a change in the location of the Campo dell'Oro Airport holding pattern, and the installation of radar at Ajaccio, or at the very least radar surveillance of the area by another facility.

Date: 13 January 1982 (*c.* 16:00)
Location: Washington, DC, US
Operator: Air Florida Inc (US)
Aircraft type: Boeing 737-222 (*N62AF*)

Snow continued to fall throughout the day on the nation's capital, which, as with the rest of the American North East, had been battered by the weather during an exceptionally harsh January. At Washington National Airport operations had resumed shortly before 15:00, after a closure of more than an hour for the purpose of snow removal.

Through technological advances and improved operating procedures, aviation has managed to overcome many meteorological hazards that would have grounded aircraft in the earlier years of flying. In addition, passengers travelling in and out of the airport, located in Virginia along the bank of the Potomac River, had another reason to feel secure: it had been more than two years since the last fatal crash of a US commercial jet. But as Flight 90 prepared to take off on a domestic service to Fort Lauderdale and Tampa, Florida, that record was about to come to a shattering halt.

Following the de-icing of *N62AF*, and some difficulty in moving it back from the terminal on the slippery ramp, the 737 got in line with numerous other aircraft, awaiting its turn for departure. Flight 90 finally received clearance to take off on Runway 36 nearly an hour after the de-icing had been completed and during a period of continuous light to moderate snowfall, with the temperature remaining below freezing. By the time it received the clearance, considerable snow or ice had once more accumulated on the jetliner, about ¼–½ in (c. 0.5–1 cm) on its wings, of which Capt Larry Wheaton and First Officer Roger Pettit were aware, as confirmed by their comments transcribed on the cockpit voice recorder (CVR) tape.

The most significant effect of even a small amount of snow on an aircraft wing is its influence on the smooth flow of air over the surface contour. This will cause airflow separation at a lower angle of attack than normal, which in turn increases the stalling speed while reducing lift. Even more critical, at least in this case, was the suspected build-up of ice in the compressor inlets of the two engines which, in conjunction with the power plant discharge probes, are used to determine the correct thrust setting. Tests confirmed that the blockage on an inlet tube will result in a false indication of thrust, higher than the amount actually being developed. This blockage could be explained by the simple failure of the crew to turn on the engine anti-ice system. (This was confirmed by the CVR when, during the checklist routine, the captain responded to the first officer as to the status of the anti-ice equipment with the word 'Off'.)

From his recorded remarks, the co-pilot seemed to recognise an anomalous engine pressure ratio (EPR) reading, the take-off 'target' value apparently having been obtained despite an abnormal position of the thrust levers and with inconsistencies in other instrument indications, noting after the ground run had commenced that something did not 'seem right'. First replying 'Yes it is, there's eighty' with regard to the air speed indication, the pilot did not respond to further comments by his first officer and continued the take-off. Due to the blockage of the pressure probes, the actual EPR was believed to have been only 1.70, rather than the required 2.04, which must have been indicated.

Besides degrading its performance, the accumulation of snow and/or ice apparently caused the 737 to pitch up immediately after it had become airborne, resulting in the activation of the stick-shaker stall-warning device; with the reduced power setting, it entered the stall regime and was unable to sustain flight. The aircraft probably reached a peak altitude of between 200 and 300 ft (c. 60–100 m) before it started to descend, turning slightly to the left but maintaining a generally northerly course. It was believed that the crew first lowered the nose, then raised it to maintain height, and in the final moments of the flight applied power, but too late for it to have any effect. Seconds before impact the co-pilot was heard to say 'Larry, we're going down, Larry!'. The pilot replied with 'I know it'.

Its undercarriage still down and flaps partially extended, the jetliner was flying in a nose-high attitude estimated at 30 to 40 degrees, its wings approximately level, when it struck the northbound span of the 14th Street bridge, which connects Virginia with the District of Columbia, about 1 mile (1.5 km) from the end of the runway. Actually skimming over the roadway, which was heavily congested with vehicles moving at a snail's pace because of the weather, it destroyed six occupied cars and a truck and tore away a section of the bridge and some 100 ft (30 m) of railing, then pitched down and plunged into the ice-covered Potomac River.

All but five of the 79 persons aboard the aircraft, including four crew members, were killed in the accident, along with four others in the vehicles. The four passengers and one stewardess who survived (all of whom had been seated at the rear of the cabin near the empennage, which broke off on impact and remained partially above the water) suffered injuries, as did four persons on the bridge. Autopsies performed on the victims' bodies, all of which were recovered along with most of the wreckage, revealed that a majority of the deaths resulted from trauma.

In its investigative report, the US National Transportation Safety Board (NTSB) ascribed the crew's failure to use the engine anti-ice system as the direct cause of the disaster. Had the power plant probes not been blocked, the correct EPR values would have been indicated and the thrust correctly set. On the other hand, had the icing been so severe as to remain in the tubes despite the use of anti-icing, the pilots would have been unable to set the power at the correct EPR, undoubtedly prompting them to discontinue the take-off.

Also regarded as a primary factor in the crash was the decision by the crew to take off despite knowledge of the snow on the aircraft's wings. The pilots may have been influenced by the prolonged departure delay and the inevitability of another long wait in the freezing precipitation had they returned to the ramp for another de-icing. But there were two areas where faulty action by the captain may actually have intensified the contamination of the jetliner. One was the use of reverse thrust in an attempt to back the aircraft away from the terminal. Heat from the engines and reversers and the blowing snow and slush could have deposited a wet mixture on the airframe, particularly on the leading edge of the wings, which subsequently froze. There were also indications that he intentionally positioned the 737 close behind another aircraft, trying to use the heat from the latter's engines to remove the snow on his own aircraft's wings. However, the heat may actually have turned the snow, which otherwise might have blown off during the take-off, into a slushy mixture that then froze on the leading edges or the inlet nose cones of the power plants.

Another factor that directly contributed to the disaster was the continuation of the take-off despite the abnormalities in the engine instrument readings. Since the co-pilot was actually flying the 737, the pilot could be expected to have been the most attentive to the indications; in this case, however, the former seemed the most observant. The crew may have been somewhat hurried when the controller asked for 'No delay on departure' due to landing traffic. Indeed, the NTSB determined that an Eastern Airlines Boeing 727 touched down on the same runway even before the 737 had lifted off, which was a violation of the established separation criteria.

The actions of the flight crew, particularly the captain, reflected a general lack of experience in cold weather operations. It was believed that he missed this exposure to the harsh winter climate of the Eastern American states because of the rapid expansion of the airline in the late 1970s and early 1980s, wherein pilots were being upgraded faster than the industry norm to meet the increasing demands of its growing schedules.

Other contributing factors were the long delay between de-icing and take-off clearance and the tendency of the Boeing 737 to pitch up when the leading edges of its wings become coated with snow

or ice, something that had been suspected for some years before this crash.

Though the Board could not determine whether it also contributed to the accident, the de-icing of N62AF was found to be deficient. It was concluded that the American Airlines personnel who carried out the operation had used an incorrect mixture of de-icing fluid, composed of glycol and water, this due to the non-availability of a monitoring device.

Amid the human errors that led to the disaster, the crash itself brought forth some individual cases of heroism and self-sacrifice. The survivors, who were able to cling to wreckage, owe their lives primarily to the crew of a US Park Police LongRanger helicopter, which arrived on the scene in about 20 minutes and hoisted or towed them to safety. To accomplish one rescue the pilot hovered the aircraft just above the water, and the passenger was lifted on to its skid. Two bystanders actually jumped into the frigid river, and one of them, a US Congressional Budget Officer clerk named Lenny Skutnik, gained national fame for saving a woman who had lost her grip on the rescue line. Another passenger who lived through the crash unselfishly passed the line to the other survivors; by the time the helicopter returned for him, he had slipped beneath the surface of the water and drowned.

Only about two weeks after the accident, the NTSB recommended that the US Federal Aviation Administration (FAA) immediately review de-icing procedures used before take-off in air carrier operations and the information being provided to flight crews, emphasising the inability of de-icing fluid to protect against the subsequent formation of ice. In response, the FAA transmitted the recommendation to every operator, and the agency subsequently requested that carriers review their manuals and the information they provide for cold weather operations. Extensive guidance on the issue of wing contamination was also contained in a 37-page advisory circular issued by the FAA about a year after the crash. The Air Florida disaster also revealed inadequacies in the emergency services provided at Washington National Airport, and led to such improvements as the acquisition of two rescue boats, one with limited ice-breaking capabilities. Additionally, the runway overrun area was extended, which could prove useful in the event of an aborted take-off.

Date: 26 April 1982 (*c.* 16:45)
Location: Near Yangshuo, Guangxi, China
Operator: Civil Aviation Administration of China (CAAC)
Aircraft type: Hawker Siddeley Trident 2E (*B-266*)

Operating as Flight 3303 and on a domestic service originating at Canton, Kwangtung, the jetliner struck a mountain some 30 miles (50 km) south-east of Kweilin as it was approaching to land at the city's airport. All 112 persons aboard (104 passengers and a crew of eight) perished.

The crash reportedly occurred during a light rain and apparently resulted from operational factors.

Date: 8 June 1982 (02:25)
Location: Near Pacatuba, Ceara, Brazil
Operator: Viacao Aerea São Paulo SA (VASP) (Brazil)
Aircraft type: Boeing Advanced 727-212 (*PP-SRK*)

Designated as Flight 168, the jet airliner crashed some 15 miles (25 km) south-west of Fortaleza while preparing to land at the city's Pinto Martins Airport, at the end of a domestic service originating at São Paulo, via Rio de Janeiro. All 137 persons aboard (128 passengers and nine crew members) perished.

Initiating a descent from flight level (FL) 330, the 727 had been cleared only down to 5,000 ft (*c.* 1,500 m). Nevertheless, it continued well below that height until finally slamming into a hill in the Serra de Aratanha region at an approximate elevation of 2,000 ft (600 m) and exploding on impact. The accident occurred in early morning darkness, but the weather was good, without indications of heavy cloud formations or significant obstructions to visibility in the area.

According to the cockpit voice recorder (CVR) tape, the aircraft's altitude alert system had sounded twice before the crash. Also, upon passing through a height of 3,800 ft (*c.* 1,150 m), the first officer warned the captain of the terrain ahead, without the latter interrupting the descent. Besides the crew's failure to maintain the minimum authorised altitude, an analysis of the flight data recorder (FDR) read-out established the maximum speed limit of 250 knots (*c.* 465 kmh) below FL 110 had been exceeded.

The disaster was attributed to a deficient descent plan, non-observance of both air traffic regulations and the carrier's operational procedures, and a lack of cockpit discipline. A contributing factor was that the pilot-in-command had apparently concentrated his attention on the lighted city and ignored other aspects of the flight, such as the observation of distance and height.

As was noted in the recommendations portion of the investigative report, in-flight decisions must result from teamwork, and the captain, who is ultimately responsible for the safe operation of an aircraft, should never disregard the advice of an inferior. It was further emphasised that the non-flying pilot has a 'right and obligation' to intervene when safety is being compromised, and also suggested that Brazil's airlines develop a better system of evaluating the performance of their flight crews.

Date: 28 June 1982 (*c.* 10:50)
Location: Southern Belorussia, USSR
Operator: Aeroflot (USSR)
Aircraft type: Yakovlev Yak-42 (*SSSR-45229*)

The jet airliner, which was operating as Flight 8641 and on a domestic service from Leningrad, RSFSR, to Kiev, Ukraine, crashed some 20 miles (30 km) south-east of Mozyr and about 125 miles (200 km) north-west of its destination. All 132 persons aboard (124 passengers and a crew of eight) perished.

Shortly after it had initiated a descent from an altitude of about 30,000 ft (10,000 m), a serious malfunction occurred, with the aircraft's stabiliser almost instantaneously moving to a position of +2 degrees, or beyond the mechanical stop. The abrupt change in the stabiliser setting caused an increase in vertical acceleration, which decreased when the autopilot deflected the elevator. Three seconds later the autopilot disengaged and the elevator deflected to a position of –5 degrees, which caused an increase in the vertical acceleration.

Simultaneous with an attempted pull-out, the Yak-42 entered a left bank, which ultimately surpassed 90 degrees. Meanwhile, its nose-down angle exceeded 50 degrees as the aircraft plunged to earth at a vertical rate of descent of around 1,000 ft/sec (300 m/sec). At a height of about 19,000 ft (5,800 m) and an indicated air speed of more than 500 mph (800 kmh), the aircraft suffered structural failure due to aerodynamic stresses that were beyond the permitted limits and the excessive pressure in the cabin associated with the rapid descent. Complete disintegration of *SSSR-45229* occurred on impact with the ground; there was no post-crash fire.

The disaster resulted from the in-flight failure of the aircraft's stabiliser screw-jack mechanism due to excessive wear and jamming of the nut. It was later discovered that because of a manufacturing error, the thread of the screw-jack had been cut at the wrong pitch. Also factoring in the failure was the use of a non-standard lubricating substance. The entire Yak-42 fleet was grounded while this fault could be rectified.

Date: 6 July 1982 (*c*. 00:05)
Location: Near Moscow, Russian Soviet Federative Socialist Republic, USSR
Operator: Aeroflot (USSR)
Aircraft type: Ilyushin Il-62M (*SSSR-86513*)

All 90 persons aboard (80 passengers and a crew of 10) were killed when the jet airliner, designated as Flight 411, crashed and burned in farmland about 5 miles (10 km) west of the city's Sheremet'yevo Airport, from where it had taken off shortly before, en route to Africa, with a planned stop at Dakar, Senegal, and an ultimate destination of Freetown, Sierra Leone. The accident occurred in darkness, but the weather was not considered a factor.

An Aeroflot Ilyushin Il-62M, identical to the aircraft that crashed after taking off from Moscow's Sheremet'yevo Airport. *(Aeroflot)*

The crash was attributed to the failure of the aircraft's power plant fire warning system, due to design deficiencies. This resulted in false fire indications in the two port engines, the No. 1 only seconds after rotation and the No. 2 moments later, both of which were shut down by the crew. The Il-62 was incapable of sustaining flight on only two engines, with its flaps set at 30 degrees and its take-off weight near the maximum. Additional difficulties were associated with the night-time conditions and the populated area below its flight path.

Turning back in an attempted off-airport forced landing in the opposite direction of the take-off and with its undercarriage retracted, the jet lost speed during a right and then a left turn, leading to a loss of lateral control while in a left bank that exceeded 70 degrees, finally stalling at an approximate height of 250 ft (75 m).

Date: 9 July 1982 (16:09)
Location: Kenner, Louisiana, US
Operator: Pan American World Airways (US)
Aircraft type: Boeing 727-235 (*N4737*)

The second of three major wind shear-related US air carrier disasters occurring in the 1975–85 period (see also separate entries, 24 June 1975 and 2 August 1985) involved Flight 759, which took off from Runway 10 at New Orleans International (Moisant) Airport, bound for Las Vegas, Nevada, its next scheduled stop during a domestic transcontinental service from Miami, Florida, to San Diego, California. Less than 30 seconds after becoming airborne, the jetliner crashed and exploded approximately 1 mile (1.5 km) beyond the end of the runway, devastating a residential neighbourhood. A total of 153 persons perished, the victims including eight on the ground in addition to all 145 aboard the aircraft; among the latter were the eight regular members of its crew, a cockpit jump-seat occupant and one passenger who was pregnant, which accounted for the additional fatality mentioned in some press reports. Another 16 persons suffered injuries, and about a dozen houses were destroyed or substantially damaged.

A thunderstorm was sweeping over the area at the time, accompanied by heavy rain, an east-north-easterly wind of some 15 knots, a broken overcast at around 4,000 ft (1,200 m) and a

Houses were reduced to rubble in this disaster near New Orleans International Airport which killed 153 persons. *(CORBIS)*

visibility of 2 miles (*c.* 3 km). Though not outwardly hazardous, the weather contained at least one insidious element that was believed to have been responsible for the tragedy.

In its investigative report, the US National Transportation Safety Board (NTSB) concluded that *N4737* had apparently encountered a 'microburst' following rotation. This wind shear phenomenon is fundamentally a downward gust that flows outward in all directions upon reaching the ground.

At the moment of take-off, the aircraft would have been operating in a headwind, after which it experienced a downdraught while in the centre of the microburst, then an increasing tail wind. These divergent winds led, in rapid succession, to an increase then a decrease in indicated air speed, lift, drag and pitch. Reaching a height of 100 to 150 ft (*c.* 30–50 m) above the ground, the 727 began to descend. It initially struck three tall trees some

2,400 ft (730 m) from the end of the runway, then a second group of trees, the impact shearing off segments of its leading-edge wing devices, which were extended, and trailing-edge flaps, which were set at 15 degrees. Its undercarriage retracted, the jetliner slammed to earth after turning on to a northerly heading and rolling to the left beyond 90 degrees.

Since the aircraft was in the midst of heavy rain, the crew had to fly exclusively by instrument reference, and in this case the time required for response by the pertinent instruments and recognition and corrective action by the pilots was insufficient to prevent the crash. Other factors that would have complicated the crew's recognition of the wind shear were the precipitation itself, the turbulence associated with the storm and the need to apply an abnormal force to the control column and adopt an unusually nose-high attitude. It was determined that the co-pilot, who was flying the 727, did indeed take corrective action and had actually managed to arrest the descent at around the time of the initial tree impact. An analysis of the cockpit voice recorder (CVR) tape indicated that the safety-conscious captain had prepared for the possibility of wind shear before departure, instructing his first officer to 'Let your air speed build up on take-off'.

Contributing to the accident was the inability of the ground-based low-level wind shear detection technology then available to provide definite guidance for air traffic controllers and pilots for use in avoiding this potential hazard. The system such as the one employed at New Orleans, though described as 'state of the art', had several limitations. The sensors, or anemometers, could not detect winds directly above or beyond their periphery; nor could they discern updraughts or down draughts. Also, the simultaneous passage of a peripheral and the centrefield sensor by a gust would not set off a wind shear alarm. Most significantly, perhaps, was that a microburst would not be detected if sufficiently small as to occur between sensors. In addition, the reading of a particular unit could have been lower than was actually the case due to the slowing effect of the winds flowing over nearby trees.

Despite its shortcomings, the system did detect the presence of wind shear before the crash, which prompted the control tower to issue an advisory for wind shear 'in all quadrants' some 5 minutes before the departure of Flight 759. Though this was a relatively long period of time for such a fleeting event, the NTSB expressed satisfaction that the Pan American crew had received adequate meteorological information. It further concluded that the decision by the captain to take off was reasonable under the circumstances. When it began its ground run, only light rain was falling on the aircraft, which became progressively heavier; no lightning or thunder had been observed in the immediate area, and the microburst that proved so deadly was not detected until after N4737 had started to take off.

Though the effects of the heavy precipitation on the 727 could not be determined, the NTSB expressed concern that it could have produced a film of water on its wings, roughening their surface and lowering aerodynamic efficiency. The rain was also suspected of reducing the effectiveness of the aircraft's weather radar, which the crew had used while still on the ground in an attempt to determine the conditions existing in the flight path of the jetliner. This attenuation apparently prevented the observance on the radarscope of the storm cells located east of the airport, including the one that spawned the microburst.

Investigators were hampered somewhat in trying to establish the exact effects of the microburst by the early model flight data recorder (FDR) installed on the 727. For this reason the NTSB suggested that all US commercial jet transports be fitted with digital systems capable of transcribing many more parameters, including pitch and roll attitude, stabiliser trim position and engine thrust. The Board also recommended to the US Federal Aviation Administration (FAA) several improvements in the way wind shear information is disseminated to pilots, including the need for the constant updating of advisories.

Date: 11 July 1983 (07:28)
Location: Near Cuenca, Azway, Ecuador
Operator: Transportes Aereos Militares Ecuatorianos (TAME) (Ecuador)
Aircraft type: Boeing Advanced 737-2V2 (*HC-BIG*)

Operating as Flight 173 and on a domestic service from Quito, the jet airliner crashed during an attempted landing at Mariscal Lamar Airport, serving Cuenca. All 118 persons aboard (112 passengers and a crew of six) were killed.

The accident occurred as the aircraft was on its final approach to Runway 23, and in conditions of reduced visibility due to haze, with a few clouds at 1,000 ft (*c.* 300 m) and no wind. Its undercarriage apparently down, the 737 slammed into a hill approximately 2 miles (3 km) short of the runway, exploding in flames on impact.

The crash was blamed on the failure of the flight crew to observe the proper instrument approach procedure and the minimum safety altitude. With regard to the former factor, the aircraft's cockpit voice recorder (CVR) tape revealed that the pilots had not been adequately monitoring their instruments during the landing attempt. Additionally, the runway was not equipped with visual approach slope indicator (VASI) lights to help in determining the proper glide path.

Date: 30 August 1983 (23:17)
Location: Near Alma-Ata, Kazakh SSR, USSR
Operator: Aeroflot (USSR)
Aircraft type: Tupolev Tu-134A (*SSSR-65129*)

The jet airliner crashed and burned while attempting to land at the Alma-Ata airport, at the end of a scheduled domestic service from Kazan, RSFSR. All 90 persons aboard (84 passengers and six crew members) were killed.

After the aircraft had erroneously assumed a heading of 145 degrees, the approach controller instructed the crew to change its course to 140 degrees so it could land behind an Aeroflot Il-62. During a subsequent vector on to a course of 40 degrees, however, the final controller cleared the Tu-134 down to about 2,000 feet (600 m) at a location where the minimum safety altitude was nearly 15,000 ft (*c*. 5,000 m). Around a minute later the aircraft slammed into a hillside at an approximate level of 2,300 feet (700 m), some 20 miles (30 km) from the airport. The disaster occurred in darkness and fair weather conditions.

The crash was attributed to the following factors: 1) violation of the approved approach scheme to the Alma-Ata airport; 2) failure of the executive flight manager to monitor the situation and thus prevent the accident; and 3) violation of the flight operations manual by the crew for following the final controller's instructions to descend below a safe height and for failing to respond appropriately to the ground-proximity warning system (GPWS), which first sounded nearly half a minute before impact.

Date: 1 September 1983 (*c*. 03:30)
Location: North-west of Hokkaido, Japan
Operator: Korean Air Lines (South Korea)
Aircraft type: Boeing 747-230B (*HL7442*)

Different theories have circulated as to the reasons behind the infamous downing of Flight 007 by Soviet defence forces. Some are extreme, from the belief that the aircraft had been sent on a provocative mission by the US, to, the suggestion that it was lured to destruction by the USSR in order to disgrace its long-time arch-rival Super Power. Such hypotheses lie at the borders of logic and can be disputed on both political and technical grounds.

Most reasonable observers feel that the incursion of the wide-bodied jetliner into Soviet airspace was

An illustration of the correct route and the course believed to have been taken by Flight 007 that led to its destruction. (*International Civil Aviation Organisation/Ikaros/Uniphoto Press International*)

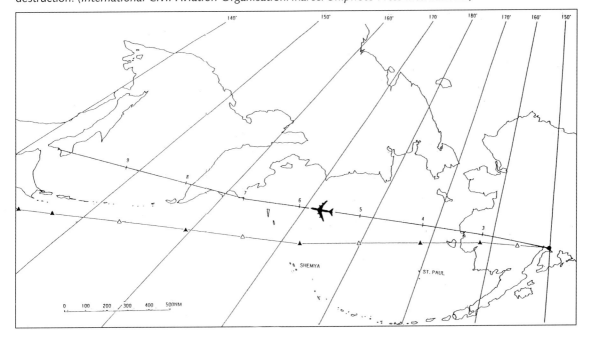

totally inadvertent, and that the subsequent attack resulted from its misidentification as an intelligence aircraft. This was also the conclusion of the International Civil Aviation Organisation (ICAO), which conducted its own investigation into the tragedy.

Flight 007 had originated at New York City, with an ultimate destination of Seoul, South Korea, and a scheduled intermediate stop at Anchorage, Alaska, US, for refuelling and a change of crew. While on the ground at Anchorage International Airport, the aircraft's three independent inertial navigation system (INS) units ·vould also have to be reprogrammed for the second leg of the trip; this would involve keying into the system the exact position of the 747 as it sat on the airport tarmac. The proper routeing of the flight would then be pre-arranged by punching in the coordinates of certain positions, or way-points, along the prescribed track, which might be navigational facilities or even certain geographical points. Once interfaced with the autopilot, the INS would automatically steer the aircraft to its intended destination, even compensating for any wind conditions that might be encountered.

Following a 50-minute layover, the jetliner took off on the final leg of the transcontinental service, carrying six off-duty company personnel in addition to the three regular flight crewmen, and 20 cabin attendants to serve its 240 passengers. The latter included American Congressman Lawrence McDonald. They had but 5 1/2 hours left to live.

Subsequent analysis of radar data indicated that the aircraft began to stray to the right of the prescribed route about 10 minutes after its departure from Anchorage, and it was approximately 7.5 miles (12 km) north of the track at the time of radar service termination. This discrepancy was not considered abnormal, and the Anchorage control centre made no attempt to advise the crew of such. A military radar recording showed the flight to be nearly 15 miles (25 km) too far north upon its passage of the Bethel (Alaska) very-high-frequency omnidirectional range/tactical air navigation (VORTAC) facility. At the time, however, there was no interaction between military and civilian controllers, and the deviation went unchecked, and resulted in a progressively greater lateral displacement. Ultimately, and when some 250 miles (400 km) west of the normal route, the 747 entered Soviet airspace.

In a major foul-up of Soviet defence forces, jet fighters that were scrambled into action failed to locate the commercial transport as it flew over the southern tip of the Kamchatka Peninsula, the location of both a missile and a submarine base. Military authorities could only watch helplessly as the radar target representing Flight 007 proceeded out over the Sea of Okhotsk on its south-westerly heading.

About an hour later, HL7442 had again penetrated the border of the USSR, this time passing over southern Sakhalin Island, another militarily sensitive area. The aircraft would still have been flying in darkness at the time, with a half-moon providing partial illumination. The weather in the area was reportedly good, with 5/8 cirrus clouds at around 30,000 ft (10,000 m).

At 03:05 the pilot of a Soviet Air Force Sukhoi Su-15 jet fighter radioed that he had made visual contact with the intruder. The communications between him and his ground command were recorded by US monitoring stations, and a transcript was released at a special meeting of the United Nations Security Council. There were no indications in any of the air-to-ground messages that the 747 had been identified as an airliner; the pilot's only reference to it was as a 'target'. Nor was there any evidence, in its transmissions to the Japanese control centre, that the 747's Korean crew knew of, nor made any contact with, the fighters that were in pursuit. During the chase, which lasted about 20 minutes, the Su-15 pilot was believed to have implemented the IFF (identification friend or foe) code procedure, then fired his cannon, presumably in an attempt to get the attention of the airline crew, neither of which actions were successful.

In the final moments of the flight, HL7442 initiated a climb from 33,000 to 35,000 ft (c. 10,050–10,700 m). This is a common procedure for aircraft that have consumed most of their fuel, but it was apparently construed as an evasive manoeuvre. The ascent actually slowed the 747 and caused the Su-15 to fly past it. The Soviet pilot then repositioned himself for the attack. Once locked on, he launched two air-to-air missiles, at least one of which struck the jetliner, possibly in the area of the left wing. It was then that he broadcast the now immortal words 'The target is destroyed'.

At that point, however, the transport was only damaged, badly no doubt, but still able to fly. During its agonising descent, most or all of its occupants probably still alive, the first officer was able to transmit a distress message later interpreted to be 'Korean Air zero zero seven . . . all engines . . . rapid (de)compression. Descending to one zero delta.'

The 747 finally plunged into the Sea of Japan, possibly after a mid-air explosion, an estimated 50 miles (80 km) south-west of Sakhalin and near the island of Moneron, in international waters. All 269 persons aboard perished. Subsequently, a small amount of debris, including personal effects, was recovered, as were the remains of several victims.

Some of the wreckage was found in salvage operations conducted by the USSR and later turned over to American or Japanese authorities. Otherwise the Soviets failed to cooperate in the post-crash search-and-rescue operation, and refused to accept a visit of the investigative team, for which they were strongly rebuked. Neither the aircraft's flight data recorder (FDR) nor its cockpit voice recorder (CVR) was available for analysis. The ICAO thus had to conduct its investigation on the basis of limited hard evidence and facts, assumptions and calculations.

A premeditated detour for intelligence-gathering purposes, a major mechanical or navigational system failure or incapacitation of the crew were all considered too unlikely to warrant further examination. Also ruled out was that the captain had deliberately taken a short-cut with the intention of either conserving fuel or saving time. In fact, no evidence could be found to indicate that the crew were aware of the deviation. The number of plausible explanations was eventually reduced to two, which simulated flights proved would have resulted in roughly the same track as that believed to have been taken.

The first theory was that the crew had inadvertently left the autopilot in the heading mode. Following the departure from Anchorage, a heading of 246 degrees would presumably have been selected to take the flight towards Bethel, after which the autopilot switch should have been turned one notch in an anti-clockwise direction, allowing the INS to take over the function of navigation. Significantly, the fighter pilot had reported that the jetliner was on a heading of 240 degrees before he shot it down, which would lend credence to this hypothesis.

The second postulation was that while the aircraft sat on the ground at Anchorage, an erroneous ramp position was inserted into the INS unit that would be responsible for controlling the autopilot. An error of 10 degrees (139 instead of 149 W) would also explain the track taken by the flight.

As noted in the ICAO report, each of these scenarios 'assumes a considerable degree of lack of alertness and attentiveness on the part of the flight crew, but not to the degree that is unknown in international civil aviation'.

Flying with the autopilot in the heading mode should have caused the illumination of lights on the instrument panel indicating that the INS was not engaged. On the other hand, had an erroneous ramp position been inserted into one of the INS units, the system would automatically detect the discrepancy and flash. This warning indication could be overridden with the 'clear' button, but the incorrectly set unit would continue to display in rather obvious disagreement with the other two. Also the inaccurate original setting would have resulted in the indication of way-point passages that differed from those estimated, which should have alerted the crew that something was amiss. (In fact, the Anchorage control centre, which had to rely exclusively on pilot reports to determine the progress of the flight, did note differences between the estimated and the actual times, but did not attach any importance to them.)

Furthermore, there would have been other ways of determining the position of the aircraft. Since it was out of their range due to the incorrect heading, the navigational aids on St Paul's Island and at Shemya would not have been received, and this discordancy should have prompted the pilots to recheck their navigational progress. Also the weather radar with which HL7442 was fitted had a ground-mapping mode capable of detecting the outline of the Kamchatka Peninsula and Sakhalin Island, serving as an additional reminder of the track error.

Conducting its own inquiry, the State Commission for Civil Aviation Flight Safety in the USSR (GOSAVIANADZOR) rejected the findings of the ICAO. Its conclusion generally followed statements made by the Kremlin in the days and weeks immediately following the tragedy, i.e. that the 747 was on a reconnaissance mission. It also criticised the air traffic control services of the US and Japan for not detecting the error and returning the aircraft to the proper route (though this would imply that the deviation was accidental).

There were some other inconsistencies in the Soviet report, most notably that the fighter had followed established guidelines in trying to warn the Korean crew, and that the jetliner had been flying with its navigational lights out. With regard to the former statement, the ICAO found no evidence that the fighter had flown close beside or in front of the transport, as dictated in normal intercept procedures. The second statement was contradicted by the recorded radio message from the Soviet pilot, who reported that 'The light is flashing'. In its report the ICAO concluded that extensive measures had not been taken to identify *HL7442* before its destruction.

The Soviets maintained that the 747 was just one element in a concerted espionage operation, which they claimed also involved a US Air Force RC-135 reconnaissance jet, and stated that at one point the two aircraft, flying in opposite directions, came so close together 'that their blips merged on the radarscope'. The US later confirmed the presence of an RC-135 in the area on the night that Flight 007 was shot down, though the former had returned to its base in Alaska more than an hour before the attack on the latter.

The thawing of the Cold War that began in the mid-1980s brought forth little additional information to help explain exactly what happened to the 747. More than seven years after the disaster it was reported that Soviet authorities had indeed recovered the aircraft's two 'black box' recorders, which directly contradicted earlier statements. This new information seemed to confirm one of the two ICAO theories, i.e. that the crew had failed to engage the aircraft's INS.

In December 1984 a civilian radar system set up on St Paul's Island went into operation, one capable of monitoring commercial flights using the North Pacific route. Had it been available 16 months earlier, the tragedy of Flight 007 might have been averted.

Date: 23 September 1983 (*c.* 15:30)
Location: Near Mina Jebel Ali, United Arab Emirates
Operator: Gulf Air Ltd (Bahrain, Oman, Qatar, United Arab Emirates)
Aircraft type: Boeing Advanced 737-2P6 (*A40-BK*)

Designated as Flight 771, the jet airliner crashed and burned in the desert some 30 miles (50 km) north-east of Abu Dhabi while preparing to land at the capital city's airport, which was a scheduled stop during a service from Karachi, Pakistan, to Manama, Bahrain. All 112 persons aboard (107 passengers and five crew members) perished.

A distress message had been transmitted from the aircraft as it was descending to 6,000 ft (*c.* 1,800 m) from flight level 310. Additionally, there were indications of a pre-impact explosion having occurred in the forward cargo hold, with resultant structural damage and an uncontrollable fire producing toxic fumes that rapidly overcame the flight crew, leading to a loss of control.

The evidence pointed away from a blaze of either electrical or fuel origin, and it was later concluded that the 737 had been sabotaged with an explosive or incendiary device. Some articles of luggage assigned to the flight had been checked in by a ticket-holder who did not board the aircraft.

Date: 8 November 1983 (*c.* 15:20)
Location: Near Lubango, Huila, Angola
Operator: Linhas Aereas de Angola (TAAG-Angola Airlines)
Aircraft type: Boeing Advanced 737-2M2 (*D2-TBN*)

The jetliner crashed immediately after taking off, on a scheduled domestic service to the capital city of Luanda, and all 130 persons aboard (126 passengers and a crew of four) were killed.

Climbing to an approximate height of 200 ft (60 m), the aircraft commenced a steep turn to the left, then plunged to earth about half a mile (0.8 km) beyond the end of the airport runway, exploding on impact.

Occurring in weather conditions described as 'very bad', the disaster was attributed by Angolan authorities to 'technical failure'; however, guerrillas who had been fighting the government for some time claimed to have shot down the 737 with a surface-to-air missile.

Date: 27 November 1983 (01:06)
Location: Near Majorada del Campo, Madrid, Spain
Operator: Aerovias Nacionales de Colombia SA (AVIANCA)
Aircraft type: Boeing 747-283B Combi (*HK-2910*)

Operating as Flight 11, the wide-bodied jet airliner had been cleared to land at Barajas Airport, serving the city of Madrid, the first of two en route scheduled stops during a service originating at Paris, France, with an ultimate destination of Bogota, Colombia. During the instrument landing system (ILS) approach to Runway 33, the 747 crashed on a hill approximately 7.5 miles (12 km) south-east of the airport, killing 181 persons aboard, including 19 on-duty and four off-duty crew members. The 11 surviving passengers were seriously injured.

It was dark at the time of the accident, and the airport meteorological conditions just beforehand consisted of 3/8 stratus clouds and mist at 1,000 ft (c. 300 m), 5/8 stratocumulus at 1,800 ft (c. 550 m) and a visibility of about 5 miles (10 km). The wind was calm.

The disaster was attributed to error by the pilot-in-command, who, while apparently unaware of his precise position, set out to intercept the ILS on an incorrect track without executing the published instrument approach manoeuvre, and in doing so continued his descent through the minimum safe altitude until impact.

Between Barahona and the initiation of a turn to the right, the flight crew did not adhere to the proper procedures, and as a consequence committed a navigation error. It was also at around this time that the co-pilot experienced difficulties in inserting the coordinates for the Madrid very-high-frequency omnidirectional range (VOR) station into the aircraft's inertial navigational system (INS).

The crew in fact flew below the minimum height for more than a minute before entering the designated protection area, and the captain, in an apparent attempt to reduce speed, lowered the undercarriage out of sequence, i.e. before extending the flaps to a 20-degree setting (the 747 was in this configuration when it hit the ground).

The captain then began the turn before reaching the VOR, the prescribed point for initiation of the manoeuvre, probably because he no longer had a distance-measuring equipment (DME) reading to the station, or perhaps due to a cumulative error in the INS that gave him the impression of being closer to the navigational aid than was actually the case. Following the turn, the crew continued to fly without checking the distance to the VOR or capturing any signal from the ILS, apparently relying only on their automatic direction finder (ADF) indications.

Before this the captain had accepted uncritically an erroneous outer marker crossing altitude given by the first officer, who inverted two digits, resulting in the figure of 2,382 ft instead of the correct one, which was 3,282.

Only 37 seconds before impact, the co-pilot made a remark that indicated the crew's false belief as to the nearness of the aircraft to the marker. The cockpit voice recorder (CVR) tape also revealed deficient teamwork on the flight deck and the fact that the pilots failed to take corrective action in response to the activation of the ground-proximity warning system (GPWS). The altitude alert first sounded 23 seconds before impact, and the captain initially took no action, then disconnected the autopilot, which had been coupled to the ILS, and slightly reduced the rate of descent. Just before the crash the first officer was heard to ask, in a calm tone, 'What does the ground say, captain?', in an apparent reminder to take positive action.

The communications phraseology and procedures used by both the crew and air traffic controllers did not conform to those recommended by the International Civil Aviation Organisation (ICAO). These actions included that of the centre controller, who transferred the flight to the approach controller at a time and place different from that which had been agreed upon, and that of the approach controller, who handed off the aircraft without giving any precise positional reference to either the crew or the tower, or receiving confirmation from the crew that they had intercepted any approach aid or had any visual cue of their position.

Perhaps more significant, however, was the incomplete information provided to the crew by the approach controller, who stated that the aircraft had been 'approaching' the VOR without giving the exact distance. This, or the possibility of a glimpse through the two layers of cloud, may have reinforced the pilot's belief regarding his position.

An additional factor in the accident was that the approach controller failed to inform the flight that radar service had been terminated. He either did not pay sufficient attention to the radarscope, or the echo representing HK-2910 was not conspicuous enough for him to detect the aircraft's deviation in both direction and altitude, preventing the crew from learning of their navigational error.

The resulting crash occurred at an approximate elevation of 2,250 ft (685 m), and while the jet was on a heading of 284 degrees and in a slight nose-up attitude; its indicated air speed at the time was around 160 mph (260 kmh). There were actually three successive impacts, and on the third the 747 began to disintegrate and also burst into flames. The fuselage broke into five sections and came to rest inverted.

In its report on the disaster, the Spanish investigative board emphasised the need for standard phraseology in air/ground radio communications, and for strict adherence to prescribed procedures, proper utilisation of navi-gational aids in terminal control areas and thorough familiarisation in the use of the GPWS by flight crews.

Date: 7 December 1983 (*c.* 09:40)
Location: Near Madrid, Spain
First aircraft
Operator: Aviacion y Comercio SA (AVIACO) (Spain)
Type: McDonnell Douglas DC-9 Series 32 (*EC-CGS*)
Second aircraft
Operator: Lineas Aereas de Espana SA (Iberia) (Spain)
Type: Boeing Advanced 727-256 (*EC-CFJ*)

In the midst of a heavy fog, the two jet transports collided at Barajas Airport. A total of 93 persons were killed in the crash – all 37 passengers and the crew of five from the DC-9 and 51 of the 93 aboard the 727, including one of its nine crew members. All but 12 of the survivors suffered injuries.

Designated as Flight 134 and on a domestic service to Santander, Ca Tabria, *EC-CGS* was preparing for its departure when it inadvertently taxied on to Runway 01, crossing left-to-right at an obtuse angle in the path of *EC-CFJ*, which, operating as Flight 350, was taking off for Rome, Italy. The latter had reached the decision speed, and its captain initiated an evasive manoeuvre in an unsuccessful attempt to avoid the collision. Fire erupted in both aircraft, and the 727, which lost practically all of its port wing and its left main undercarriage in the impact, skidded to a stop on the pavement but facing in the opposite direction from the correct runway heading.

The poor visibility, officially reported as about 1,000 ft (300 m) but probably much less at the scene of the accident, had prevented the AVIACO crew from obtaining sufficient visual references in order to determine that they were not taking the correct route to the beginning of Runway 01. The weather was still above the minimum take-off requirements, however.

Pilot complaints of poor ground control and the absence of both marker lights and painted stop signs at taxiway/runway intersections had previously been lodged against Barajas Airport. Plans had actually been made for improvements that should have satisfied most of these concerns but, tragically, the renovation programme was not to be budgeted until the year after the AVIACO/ Iberia disaster.

The charred remains of the Iberia Boeing 727 that collided with an AVIACO DC-9 on the ground at Madrid airport. (*Getty Images*)

An Aeroflot Tu-154B, two of which crashed fatally during the last three months of 1984. *(Aircraft Photographic)*

Date: 11 October 1984 (*c*. 05:40)
Location: Near Omsk, Russian Soviet Federative Socialist Republic, USSR
Operator: Aeroflot (USSR)
Aircraft type: Tupolev Tu-154B-1 (*SSSR-85243*)

Operating as Flight 3352, the jet airliner collided with vehicles while landing at the Omsk airport, a scheduled stop during a domestic service from Krasnodar, Kazakh SSR, to Novosibirsk, RSFSR. The death toll of 178 included two dozen children and young adults, five crew members and four persons on the ground. One passenger and four other crew members survived the disaster, with three of the latter escaping virtually unscathed.

The crash occurred shortly before dawn and in weather conditions consisting of light rain, a visibility of about 2 miles (3 km) and a ceiling of around 300 feet (100 m). The drizzle caused a reflection when the aircraft's landing light was turned on just before landing, prompting the crew to switch it off. Following an automatic-coupled approach, the Tu-154 touched down at a speed of approximately 160 mph (260 kmh).

Just after the crew had noticed something on the runway and started an evasive turn to the right, the aircraft crashed into two cleaning vehicles with heaters and an escort car, then broke apart and caught fire. The vehicles had been on the active runway due to a lack of coordination between the flying control officer, who had fallen asleep and failed to inform the approach controller of the presence of the vehicles, and the final controller and airport service personnel. Additionally, the vehicles had no warning lights.

Date: 23 December 1984 (*c*. 18:10)
Location: Near Krasnoyarsk, Russian Soviet Federative Socialist Republic, USSR
Operator: Aeroflot (USSR)
Aircraft type: Tupolev Tu-154B-2 (*SSSR-85338*)

All but a single passenger among the 111 persons aboard, including the crew of seven, lost their lives when the jet airliner crashed while attempting an emergency landing at the Krasnoyarsk airport, from where it had taken off minutes earlier. The sole survivor of the early evening accident was injured.

Designated as Flight 3519 and on a domestic intrastate service to Irkutsk, the aircraft had been climbing at a height of about 6,000 ft (1,800 m) and on a west-north-westerly heading when its No. 3 (right) power plant disintegrated and caught fire. The failure of the flight engineer to close the fuel feed shut-off cock, one of several errors on his part, sustained the blaze despite the use of the engine fire-extinguishing system. Due to further crew errors, the No. 2 (centre) power plant was inadvertently shut down, leaving only the No. 1 operating. A loss of control apparently occurred during the attempted emergency landing, with the Tu-154 slamming to earth while in a right bank of about 50 degrees.

The break-up of the engine was attributed to the fatigue failure of the low pressure compressor's first-stage disc due to metallurgical and manufacturing defects. The resulting fire spread to the tail assembly of the aircraft, leading to the failure of the flight controls.

Date: 21 January 1985 (01:04)
Location: Reno, Nevada, US
Operator: Galaxy Airlines (US)
Aircraft type: Lockheed 188A Electra (N5532)

The four-engine turboprop took off from Runway 16R at Reno-Cannon International Airport on a domestic charter service to Minneapolis, Minnesota. Less than 30 seconds after becoming airborne, the first officer radioed the control tower requesting permission to land and reporting a 'heavy vibration'. Cleared by the controller for a return to the airport, the aircraft initiated a left turn, climbing to an estimated height of 200 to 250 ft (c. 60–75 m) above the ground.

Its undercarriage retracted, the Electra crashed approximately 1 mile (1.5 km) from the end of the runway and about half a mile (0.8 km) to the right of its extended centreline, bursting into flames on impact. All but a single passenger among the 71 persons aboard were killed, including the entire crew of six. Seven recreational vehicles parked in a dealership's lot were destroyed in the accident, which occurred in darkness and clear weather.

The circumstances surrounding the flight could best be described as 'hurried'. The crew were running on a tight deadline, with a departure for Seattle, Washington, slated less than 90 minutes after the aircraft's arrival at Minneapolis. Even though a change in the schedule had been reported to the captain, he and his two fellow flight crewmen may have been influenced by a sense of urgency to the degree that proper procedures were disregarded.

The flight engineer had instructed the baggage handlers to load all of the passengers' luggage in the transport's aft baggage compartment, since the forward bin contained the crew's bags and galley stores. In addition, testimony from the survivor indicated that the passengers themselves had not been properly distributed in the cabin, with the seats forward of row 18 not being filled first. As a result of these two factors, the aircraft's centre of gravity was probably aft of the allowable limit, and although this apparently did not contribute to the accident, it reflected a general lack of adequate planning by the crew.

An analysis of the cockpit voice recorder (CVR) tape also revealed the improper use of the 'before-start checklist', with certain items omitted or reversed.

After receiving clearance from the ground supervisor, the Electra started to taxi away from the gate with the air-start hose still attached to the fitting, located along the leading edge of the starboard wing inboard of the No. 3 power plant. The hose is used to pump air into an engine at a sufficient pressure to turn the turbine blades, thus facilitating its starting. When the aircraft began to move, the hose was pulled taut, preventing the ground handler from disconnecting it. Her supervisor, who had hand-signalled the crew to stop, removed it for her, but neither could remember closing the access door that encloses the fitting.

The noise heard on the CVR, coupled with the impact damage of the open latch of the door and statements from other pilots who had previous experiences with open air-start access doors, led the US National Transportation Safety Board (NTSB) to conclude that this was indeed the source of the vibration. Moreover, although it should not have significantly affected N5532 aerodynamically, the vibration generated by the open door caused a breakdown in crew coordination. The captain tried, unsuccessfully, to both establish the nature of the noise and fly the transport. Apparently believing that it was associated with engine trouble, he ordered that all four power levers be retarded.

A wiser course of action would have been to climb to a safe altitude, then check the engines individually, but the significant reduction of power resulted in a loss of air speed, which in turn led to a stall.

Besides the error by the pilot-in-command, the NTSB ruled that the first officer did not adequately monitor either the height or speed of the aircraft, shirking those more important responsibilities and instead responding immediately to the commands of the captain, who was considerably older and more experienced (factors that could have been a source of intimidation), and to the requests of the tower controller. His eventual call-out of 'a hundred knots' came too late to prevent the crash, despite the application of full power. The NTSB believed that the vibration may have masked the onset of the stall buffet, perhaps delaying corrective action. The failure of ground personnel to ensure that the air-start access door had been properly closed was considered contributory to the accident.

The board recommended that all Electra operators be notified of the potential danger of open access doors, and also criticised the US Federal Aviation Administration (FAA) for faulty surveillance of the airline's operations and maintenance, describing them as 'seriously deficient'. It further advised that smaller carriers such as Galaxy, which may lack the resources of the larger ones to implement programmes in the training of cockpit resource management, receive assistance in this area from the FAA.

Date: 19 February 1985 (09:27)
Location: Near Durango, Vizcaya, Spain
Operator: Lineas Aereas de Espana SA (Iberia) (Spain)
Aircraft type: Boeing Advanced 727-256 (*EC-DDU*)

Operating as Flight 610, the jetliner crashed while preparing to land at Sondica Airport, serving Bilbao, at the end of a domestic service from Madrid, and all 148 persons aboard (141 passengers and seven crew members) perished.

The accident took place some 20 miles (30 km) south-east of the airport during the intermediate

All 148 persons aboard perished when this Iberia Boeing 727 crashed on a mountain in northern Spain during an approach to land at Sondica Airport, serving Bilbao. *(CORBIS)*

phase of an approach to Runway 30, using very-high-frequency omnidirectional range/distance-measuring equipment (VOR/DME) and instrument landing system (ILS) procedures. Levelling off briefly at 7,000 ft (c. 2,000 m) and 5,000 ft (c. 1,500 m), as cleared by the control tower, the aircraft continued its descent and had been flying for nearly a minute below the minimum sector altitude of 4,354 ft (1,327 m) when it struck a television antenna rising about 100 ft (30 m) above Mt Oiz. Initial contact with the antenna mast occurred as the aircraft was on a heading of 96 degrees, turning right on to the final approach leg, and flying at an indicated air speed of 240 mph (385 kmh), with its undercarriage extended. Its left wing torn off by the force of the impact, the 727 then crashed inverted on the mountain at an approximate elevation of 3,400 ft (1,040 m), scattering wreckage down the sloping terrain. There was no general post-impact blaze but only small isolated fires from spilt fuel, primarily in the area of the empennage and the engines.

The airport weather around the time of the crash consisted of a broken overcast, with 2/8 stratocumulus clouds at 4,000 feet (c. 1,200 m) and 4/8 altocumulus at 8,000 ft (c. 2,500 m), and a visibility of around 2.5 miles (4 km) in mist. There was also a slight breeze from a south-south-easterly direction.

The descent was believed to have been made by the first officer, using the vertical guidance control of the autopilot, the captain apparently setting the various levels on the altitude alert system in lieu of providing 1,000-ft call-outs. The latter probably selected 4,300 ft (1,310 m) on the altitude alert, but the aircraft did not level off at that height as anticipated. This may have been due to his failure to press the 'ALT SEL' switch at all or in sufficient time to effect altitude capture, or from inadvertent disengagement by one of the pilots. However, a malfunction in the aircraft's automatic flight control system could not be ruled out, even though altitude capture had been accomplished twice before during the descent.

Though the flight had been cleared for a standard manoeuvre, the cockpit conversation indicated that the first officer had intended and desired a shorter procedure. Significantly, the shorter procedure required a minimum altitude of 7,000 feet at the same DME fix, 2,000 ft (c. 600 m)

higher than the standard manoeuvre. The rate of descent adopted seemed to indicate that he was starting the final approach from an altitude of higher than 5,000 ft.

Another factor that proved critical in this case was the use of 4,300 ft as the level-off height, rather than 4,400 ft, or the 100-ft increment above the minimum altitude. Also, the supervision provided by the captain was inadequate, though his apparent manipulation of the altitude alert system may have been his way of directing the operation without feeling it necessary to give audible instructions, even though, as noted in the investigative report, the use of the system still requires vigilance by the crew. There was an additional possibility of the misreading of the aircraft's drum-type altimeters, which are susceptible to such errors, especially at lower altitudes, when attention is divided among several activities.

In the final moments before impact the co-pilot may have misinterpreted the audible warning of the altitude alert system as being the approach to the selected minimum height.

Among other recommendations made by the Spanish investigative commission was a reiteration of the need for the pilot not at the controls to perform altitude call-outs. The report also urged the updating of aeronautical charts, as neither Mt Oiz or the antenna appeared on the chart used by the crew of Flight 610.

Date: 3 May 1985 (c. 12:00)
Location: Near L'vov, Ukraine, USSR
First aircraft
Operator: Aeroflot (USSR)
Type: Tupolev Tu-134A (SSSR-65856)
Second aircraft
Operator: Soviet Air Force
Type: Antonov An-26 (SSSR-26492)

The jet airliner and the twin-engine turboprop military transport collided in mid-air, and both crashed. A total of 94 persons perished in the disaster, 79 aboard SSSR-65856 (73 passengers and a crew of six) and 15 aboard SSSR-26492 (nine passengers and a crew of six). There were no survivors.

Operating on a scheduled domestic service from Tallinn, Estonia, to Kishinev, Moldavia, with an en

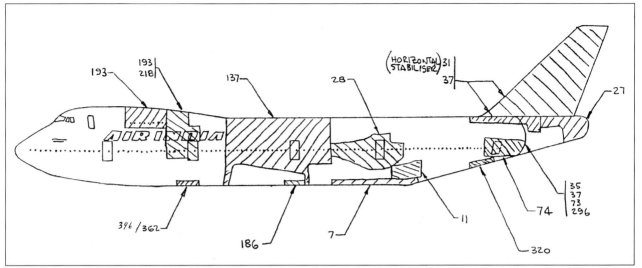

Diagram indicating the major parts of the Air-India Boeing 747 that were identified on the ocean floor.
(Canadian Aviation Safety Board)

route stop at L'vov, the Tu-134 was descending through clouds in preparation for landing at the city's airport, from where the An-26 had taken off shortly before, when the head-on collision occurred at approximately 13,000 ft (4,000 m), the altitude at which the latter had been cleared to fly.

The accident resulted from flagrant violations of air traffic control rules by the civil approach and the military controllers due to misidentification of the location of both aircraft in the area of the navigational station.

Date: 23 June 1985 (*c.* 07:15)
Location: North Atlantic Ocean
Operator: Air-India
Aircraft type: Boeing 747-237B (*VT-EFO*)

Originating at Toronto as Flight 181, the wide-bodied jet airliner had landed at Montreal International Airport, also in Canada. Redesignated as Flight 182, it then proceeded on towards London, its next scheduled stop during a service with an ultimate destination of Bombay, India. Its cargo included a 'fifth' engine, actually an in-operative one slated for repair that was being carried on the left wing between the fuselage and the No. 2 power plant.

Having nearly completed a transatlantic crossing, *VT-EFO* was flying on this Sunday morning in good weather conditions above a solid

overcast, with cloud tops at 15,000 ft (*c.* 5,000 m), when its target suddenly disappeared from the radarscope. The 747 crashed at sea some 110 miles (175 km) east of Cork, Ireland, killing all 329 persons aboard (307 passengers and a crew of 22). Subsequently, floating debris representing approximately 3 to 5 per cent of the aircraft's structure was recovered, as were 132 bodies. Many of the victims exhibited signs of hypoxia or decompression; a few had flail injuries, indicating that they may have been ejected from the cabin while the jet was still in the air.

The depth of the ocean where the aircraft had fallen was some 7,000 ft (2,000 m), dashing any hopes of raising the main wreckage. In lieu of such a recovery, a photographic and videographic map was made of the crash site. Distribution of the debris seemed to confirm that the 747 was not intact when it struck the water.

A significant find was that of the digital flight data (DFDR) and cockpit voice (CVR) recorders, which were fitted with submersible beacons. A read-out of the DFDR showed that *VT-EFO* had been cruising at flight level 310 and an indicated air speed of 340 mph (*c.* 550 kmh) when there was an abrupt cessation of electrical power to both recorders. Approximately half a second before, a loud noise was heard on the CVR tape, which, according to the British Air Accidents Investigation Branch, suggested an explosive decompression. A report by the Bhabha Atomic Research Centre, in India, further concluded that a series of audio bursts transcribed on the air traffic control centre recording were most probably generated by the in-flight break-up of the 747. It was considered likely that the section aft of the wings had separated from the rest of the fuselage.

In attempting to determine the reason for the disintegration of the aircraft, investigators could find no indication of structural failure, nor of any pre-existing defect. Though circumstantial, evidence pointed to an explosion in its forward cargo hold; this included small puncture holes in a section of skin panel located near the compartment, one of several larger pieces of wreckage that were retrieved from the ocean floor; tiny 'mooncraters' in a piece of alloy filled with plastic foam; and damage to the bottom of some recovered seat cushions.

The Indian investigative report ascribed the disaster to an act of sabotage, which had been widely suspected since the first few hours after the crash. It was believed that the detonation of an explosive device in the cargo hold had severely damaged the 747, causing an immediate depressurisation. The crew were believed to have taken some action, deploying the spoilers with the intention of initiating an emergency descent. But with the emergency oxygen system rendered inoperative, the pilots could have lost consciousness in only seconds, losing control of the aircraft, with a more general break-up occurring soon after.

The bomb theory was further buoyed by an event that took place about an hour before the Air-India disaster, wherein an explosive device had gone off in the transit area at Narita Airport, serving Tokyo, Japan. Two airport workers lost their lives in the blast and four were injured. The suitcase containing the bomb had been unloaded from Canadian Pacific (CP) Air Flight 003, having arrived from Vancouver, British Columbia, Canada, and was to have been placed aboard Air-India Flight 301, bound for Bangkok, Thailand.

Four days earlier, a man with an Indian accent had made bookings for two men with the same surname as his on two CP Air Flights, 003 and 60, with interconnections to, respectively, Air-India 301 and 181/182.

The day before the twin tragedies, a passenger booked on Toronto-bound CP 60 had requested his suitcase be interlined through to Flight 181/182. Since his seat on the latter was only standby and not reserved, the ticket agent explained that this would not be possible. The passenger persisted, and as the queues were long, the agent gave in to his demands. The same day, a passenger with the same last name, who was booked on Flight 003, checked in with one piece of luggage at the same counter. But there was no evidence that either man boarded the respective flights.

All checked-in baggage intended to be loaded on to *VT-EFO* at Toronto had to be screened with a hand 'sniffer', because the regular X-ray machine was inoperative at the time. It would later be revealed, however, that some of the employees who worked for the security firm providing services under contract to Air-India had not undergone refresher training. Shortcomings were also found in the equipment used to inspect the baggage. Furthermore, airline personnel at Toronto had deviated from prescribed company policy by not correlating checked-in luggage with boarding passengers. This allowed an unaccompanied suitcase, possibly containing a bomb, to go aboard the doomed 747. Recommendations made in the Indian report included hand searches of carry-on baggage and other items and the relocation of important avionics units away from aircraft cargo holds to reduce their vulnerability in case of such an in-flight explosion.

Several years later, a man belonging to India's Sikh religious sect was sentenced to 10 years imprisonment in Canada for involvement in the Narita Airport explosion. The bomb was to have destroyed Air-India 301 in apparent retaliation for the 1984 attack by the Indian Army on the Golden Temple, a Sikh shrine located in Amritsar, Punjab, which left hundreds dead. An incorrectly set timer probably accounted for its premature detonation.

In July 1992 the case surrounding the destruction of Flight 182 was finally broken when a 30-year-old suspected Sikh terrorist believed responsible for the crime was arrested in Bombay. Without elaboration, it was announced in June 1997 that the suspect had been killed while still in police custody in India. And in February 2003, a man who pleaded guilty to acquiring the materials used in the destruction of the aircraft was sentenced to five years' imprisonment by a court in British Columbia, Canada. But two other men were acquitted of murder and conspiracy charges in March 2005 in connection with the Air-India bombing.

Date: 10 July 1985 (*c.* 23:45)
Location: Near Uch Kuduk, Uzbek SSR, USSR
Operator: Aeroflot (USSR)
Aircraft type: Tupolev Tu-154B-2 (*SSSR-85311*)

Designated as Flight 7425, the jet airliner crashed and burned about 200 miles (320 km) north-north-west of Karshi, from where it had taken off earlier, on a domestic service to Leningrad (St Petersburg), RSFSR, with an en route stop at Ufa, Bashkir. All 200 persons aboard (191 passengers and a crew of nine) perished.

The aircraft had been cruising in darkness at an approximate height of 40,000 feet (12,000 m) and an indicated air speed of about 250 mph (400 kmh) when an abrupt change in the parameters was noted on its flight data recorder (FDR) read-out. These included elevator deflections and an increase in both pitch and angle of attack. After the Tu-154 had reached a critical angle of attack, thrust was reduced on all three engines. The FDR recorded a continued reduction in air speed, which ultimately fell to zero, while the angle of attack increased to or beyond the sensor limit of 45 degrees. During this period of time the jet deviated first to the left then to the right of the flight path. Following a stall and the beginning of a sharp descent, the crew radioed that the engines had shut down and the aircraft was moving 'in a strange way'. The descent continued for 143 seconds until impact.

Due to the destruction of the cockpit voice recorder (CVR), the analysis of the human factor aspect of the investigation had to be conducted by psychologists. This analysis revealed a high degree of fatigue on the part of the flight crew, who had spent 24 hours at the airport in high temperature conditions. Also identified in the final report were inadequate regulations for crews encountering abnormal conditions.

The weather at the time consisted of winds from a west-north-westerly direction of around 75 to 80 mph (120–130 kmh) at the approximate height at which *SSSR-85311* had been flying.

Date: 2 August 1985 (*c.* 18:05)
Location: Near Dallas, Texas, US
Operator: Delta Air Lines (US)
Aircraft type: Lockheed L-1011-1 TriStar (*N726DA*)

It had been more than 10 years since the New York City crash of the Eastern Airlines Boeing 727 (see separate entry, 24 June 1975), an accident that launched extensive research into the phenomenon of wind shear. Some progress had been made, from the development of detection systems, which had come into use at a number of airports, to the introduction of training programmes designed to teach pilots ways of dealing with this weather hazard. But as Delta Flight 191 began its final approach to land at Dallas/Fort Worth International Airport, an en route stop during a domestic transcontinental service from Fort Lauderdale, Florida, to Los Angeles, California, seemingly everything learned over that decade would be cast aside. Wind shear was about to claim another airliner.

Cleared for an instrument landing system (ILS) approach to Runway 17-Left, the L-1011 was believed to have entered a 'microburst' flowing from a thunderstorm at a height of between 850 and 550 ft (*c.* 260–165 m) above the ground. The outflow, which was estimated to have been approximately 2 miles (3 km) in diameter, contained divergent winds that had different effects on the aircraft. These effects were determined largely through the read-out of its digital flight data recorder (DFDR). Flying into the microburst, *N726DA* first encountered an increasing headwind, then a series of updraughts and down draughts, then an increasing tailwind, the latter reducing its indicated air speed by 50 mph (80 kmh). During this period of time it was also hit by a lateral gust of about 70 knots, causing a 20-degree roll to the right.

The first officer, who was flying the aircraft, had applied nose-up control inputs in accordance with normal wind shear penetration procedures. But after encountering an updraught, the aircraft's angle of attack increased dangerously close to the stall regime. The application of forward pressure to the control column coupled with a strong down draught then caused the TriStar to deviate below the proper glide path. Full power was then applied and the captain commanded 'Toga', or activation of a switch in order to provide flight director guidance for an optimum climb-out manoeuvre. The overshoot was initiated too late to prevent, but nevertheless could have softened, the initial impact with the ground.

Its flaps set at 33 degrees and leading-edge slats deployed, the wide-bodied jetliner was seen to emerge from a 'curtain' of rain before touching down on its extended main undercarriage in a ploughed field about 6,000 ft (1,800 m) short of the runway, and in approximate alignment with but some 360 ft (110 m) to the left of its extended centreline. After becoming airborne, it touched down once again, crushing a car as it traversed a highway. Having knocked down three light standards along the road, the aircraft grazed one large water tank, then slammed into a second located a little more than half a mile (0.8 km) from the point of initial ground contact, disintegrating in a fiery explosion. Only the rear fuselage/empennage section, which contained a majority of the survivors, remained relatively intact, sliding backwards out of the fireball.

The disaster claimed the lives of 137 persons, including eight crew members and the driver (and sole occupant) of the vehicle that was struck by the L-1011. Twenty-eight others aboard, including three cabin attendants, were injured, some seriously; a rescue worker was also hospitalised for chest and arm pains. Two passengers escaped unscathed.

The presence of the water tanks contributed to the severity of the accident, but in their absence the jetliner could well have struck two parked cargo jets, a DC-8 and a DC-10, with perhaps even more disastrous consequences. On the other hand, the quick response by the airport emergency personnel probably cut the death toll.

The US National Transportation Safety Board (NTSB) blamed the crash on the decision to initiate and continue the approach into the cumulonimbus cloud, ascribing the responsibility for such not just to the pilot-in-command but also to his two fellow flight crewmen; the absence of specific guidelines, procedures and training for avoiding and escaping from low-altitude wind shear; and the lack of definitive, real-time wind shear hazard information. The action by the crew was also contrary to the airline's thunderstorm-avoidance policy (which did

not, however, address the issue of what action was to be taken when operating in an airport terminal area). The decision may have been influenced by the fact that two aircraft had landed just before Flight 191 without reporting any difficulties. However, as noted in the investigative report, the captain had flown for many years in Delta's route structure and should have been aware of the volatility of convective-type storms.

The thunderstorm that had built up to the north of the airport on this Friday afternoon was rapid in development. No SIGMET or severe weather watch or warning had been issued. When the meteorologist assigned to the Fort Worth air traffic control centre went to dinner at around 17:25, there were no weather echoes within 10 miles (c. 15 km) of the airport. He returned some 45 minutes later to find a 'level 4' or 'very strong' intensity thunderstorm in progress. By then, the L-1011 had already crashed. Likewise, no warning was given by the airport's low-level wind shear alert system (LLWAS) until after the accident.

Several other crews had observed lightning in the vicinity of the airport, and one even reported seeing a funnel cloud; however, none of them communicated this information to the control tower. About 10 minutes before the crash, a message was broadcast from the ground to 'all aircraft listening', announcing 'There's a rain shower just north of the airport'. This transmission was received by Flight 191. A second message intended for another incoming aircraft, which reported 'a little bitty thunderstorm sitting right on final', was not.

Although the dissemination of information concerning the storm may have been lacking, the NTSB ruled that the Delta crew should have been able to assess adequately the meteorological conditions. During the approach the TriStar was flying directly towards the cumulonimbus build-up, which should have been observable on its weather radar and visible to the pilots. On the cockpit voice recorder (CVR) tape, the first officer was heard to say 'We're gonna get our airplane washed', indicating an awareness of the rain ahead. He also made reference to lightning, and the sound of rain hitting the aircraft could then be heard.

It was further concluded that the 'take-off/go-around' (TOGA) mode of the TriStar's flight director

Trailing fire from its damaged right wing, the Pacific Southwest Airlines Boeing 727 plunges to earth after collision with a light aircraft on 25 September 1978. *(Photo by Hans Wendt, courtesy National Transportation Safety Board)*

The relatively intact aft fuselage section of the Delta Air Lines L-1011, which contained most of the survivors of the crash at Dallas/Fort Worth International Airport on 2 August 1985. *(National Transportation Safety Board)*

The scene of devastation in the neighbourhood of a Los Angeles suburb where the Aeromexico DC-9 fell on 31 August 1986, resulting in 15 fatalities on the ground in addition to the occupants of the aircraft. *(AP Images)*

Relatively intact, the cockpit and front fuselage section of the Pan Am Boeing 747 lies in the Scottish countryside near Lockerbie after the disaster of 21 December 1988. *(AP Images)*

The crippled United Airlines DC-10, with visible damage to the right horizontal stabiliser, is photographed before crash-landing at Sioux City airport on 19 July 1989. *(National Transportation Safety Board)*

The crash of the Pakistan International Airlines A300 on 28 September 1992 was the second in two months involving an Airbus arriving at the Kathmandu airport. *(AP Images)*

An open field became a scene of death and destruction following the crash of the Simmons Airlines/American Eagle flight on 31 October 1994, in which 68 persons perished. *(AP Images)*

Still smouldering, the wreckage of the Korean Air Boeing 747 rests in hilly terrain after the disaster that claimed 229 lives on 6 August 1997. *(Los Angeles Times)*

Streaming flames, the Air France Concorde is photographed as it took off from Charles de Gaulle Airport on 25 July 2000 and moments before its fatal crash. *(AP Images)*

A portion of the empennage is the only recognisable part of the Vladivostok Air Tu-154M that crashed during landing approach to the Irkutsk airport, in Russia, on 4 July 2001. *(Associated Press/EMPICS)*

Salvage personnel hoist from Jamaica Bay a large section of the vertical stabiliser that came off the Airbus before its disastrous crash on 12 November 2001. *(National Transportation Safety Board)*

One frame from a videotape captures the hijacked United Airlines Boeing 767 an instant before it struck the No. 2 tower at the World Trade Center in Manhattan, New York, which was part of the terrorist attack on 11 September 2001. *(Evan Fairbanks)*

A fiery explosion marks the impact of the wide-bodied jetliner with the 110-storey skyscraper, as smoke continues to billow from the No. 1 tower, which had been struck by the same type of aircraft some 20 minutes earlier. *(Evan Fairbanks)*

The Helios Airways Boeing 737 crashed in Greece on 14 August 2005 after a freak accident that was believed to have been related to the depressurisation of the aircraft's cabin. *(AP Images)*

Most of the wreckage of the Kam Air Boeing 737 lay buried in snow after the crash in mountainous terrain in Afghanistan on 3 February 2005. *(AP Images)*

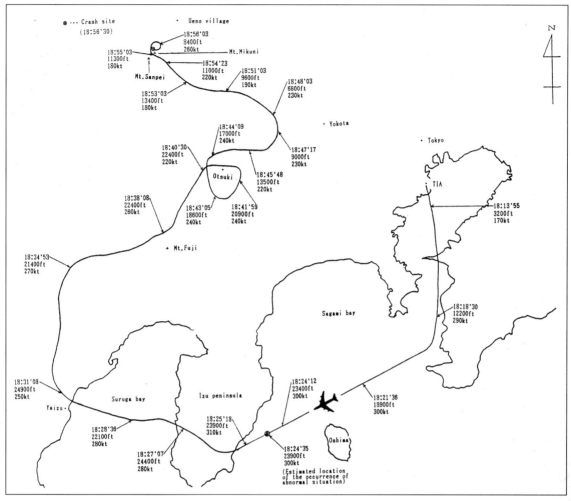

The estimated flight path of the Japan Air Lines Boeing 747 from take-off at Tokyo International Airport until its crash near Ueno village. *(Japanese Ministry of Transport)*

provided insufficient up or down guidance for penetrating wind shears. Additionally, the weather radar installed on *N726DA*, which had a minimum range setting of 50 nautical miles (*c.* 90 km), may not have presented an accurate depiction of the thunderstorm.

Subsequent to this accident, a more sophisticated LLWAS, one employing more sensors, came into use. Among the first airports in the US to receive the new system were Dallas/Fort Worth and Stapleton International, serving Denver, Colorado, where in 1989 it was credited with saving a commercial jet from a powerful microburst. This refined LLWAS has proved to be even more effective when combined with another technological development, Terminal Doppler weather radar.

Date: 12 August 1985 (18:56)
Location: Near Ueno village, Gumma, Japan
Operator: Japan Air Lines (JAL)
Aircraft type: Boeing 747SR-46 (*JA8119*)

Operating as Flight 123, the wide-bodied jetliner took off from Tokyo International (Haneda) Airport on a domestic service to Osaka. Some 10 minutes later a loud noise was heard in the cabin, which then experienced a sudden loss of pressurisation. The flight crew immediately squawked the emergency code 7700 on the aircraft's transponder and the captain requested, and was granted, permission to return to its point of departure.

Assigned by the Tokyo air traffic control centre to maintain a magnetic heading of 90 degrees, the

The remains of the 747, its left wing still identifiable, lie on a mountain slope after history's worst single-aircraft accident, which killed 520 persons. *(AP Images)*

747 strayed from that path. It also began oscillating in longitudinal (phugoid) and later ('Dutch roll') motions, which would continue for the rest of the flight. At one point the controller asked the crew 'What is the nature of the emergency?' There was no response. The controller then radioed the heading instructions once again, receiving in return the terse statement 'Now uncontrollable'.

Unbeknown to the crew, the aircraft's aft pressure bulkhead had ruptured, sending an airflow from the cabin into the unpressurised empennage. The auxiliary power unit wall was then broken, and air rushed up into the vertical tail fin. The pressure within the fin destroyed the fixture between the stringer and the rib chord in the upper portion of the aft torque box, and within seconds the internal damage led to the separation of a large section of the vertical stabiliser/rudder assembly. All four lines of the corresponding hydraulic systems were severed, and in less than 2 minutes the 747's power-assisted flying controls had been rendered useless.

Traversing Suruga Bay, *JA8119* turned northwards, passing to the west of Mt Fuji. The aircraft had descended to flight level 170 before the crew reported 'Aircraft uncontrollable', repeating 'uncontrollable' twice over the next several minutes. Acknowledgement that both Tokyo and Yokota airports were available for use was the last message received from the flight.

Its undercarriage having been lowered and flaps partially extended, the jetliner executed a 360-degree right turn and was observed in a slight nose-up attitude before it brushed against one tree-covered ridge, then crashed into another at an approximate elevation of 5,000 ft (1,500 m) and some 70 miles (110 km) north-west of the capital city, disintegrating and bursting into flames on impact. All but four passengers among the 524 persons aboard were killed, including the crew of 15, making it the highest death toll ever in a single-aircraft accident. The seriously injured survivors, among them an off-duty JAL cabin attendant, had all been seated in row 54, in the aft part of the cabin. The crash took place in twilight, and the weather, which was not considered a contributing factor, consisted of rain showers and a broken overcast in the general area.

The structural failure that befell *JA8119* was linked to repairs made after a mishap that occurred in June 1978, in which the aircraft dragged its rear fuselage while landing at Osaka, Japan. The manufacturer carried out the repairs, replacing the aft bulkhead, which had been deformed in the non-fatal accident.

After the new bulkhead was installed, the margins around the rivet holes at the splice of the upper and lower webs were found to be less than those specified. As a corrective measure, a splice joint was to have been fitted between the webs of the upper and lower halves of the bulkhead, in order to reinforce the structure. However, the work was not completed as planned. One of the doubler plates was narrower than required, and Boeing engineers left a gap between the top rivets. And instead of the necessary two, only one row of rivets had been used in the splicing. The result was a reduction of about 30 per cent in the strength of the bulkhead compared with its strength had the procedure been carried out properly, increasing its susceptibility to fatigue-cracking. A number of cracks had propagated, primarily at the one-row rivet connection points, in the 12,319 flights of the 747 since the repairs. They were not detected prior to the crash despite half a dozen inspections, which the investigative commission ruled were inadequate.

Flight 123 was the fifth trip for JA8119 on the day of the accident. The failure of the bulkhead took place at a height of about 24,000 ft (7,300 m) due to the difference in pressure between the cabin and the air outside. The rupture left a hole some 6 ft by 10 ft (2–3 m) in diameter in the structure. The subsequent failure of the 747's multiply-redundant hydraulic system and the absence of any manual back-up left the thrust levers as the only means of controlling the aircraft. Pitch control could have been accomplished through the increase and decrease of power and directional control through the application of asymmetrical thrust, but the process would be delicate and severely tax the resources and training of the crew.

Possibly due to preoccupation with maintaining control, the pilots did not initiate an immediate emergency descent, and proceeded on for nearly 20 minutes above 20,000 ft (6,000 m). Apparently failing to use their oxygen masks, they may also have suffered from hypoxia, which would cause a deterioration in judgement and thus affect their ability to cope with the emergency.

The extension of the undercarriage did help reduce the phugoid motions, but after the jetliner had descended to a lower altitude, the crew were faced with another frightening dilemma – the mountains looming ahead in its flight path. In the final moments before the 747 slammed into the first ridge, the captain, as transcribed on the cockpit voice recorder (CVR) tape, was heard to say 'Nose up', and asked for a reduction in flap angle, repeating both orders several times. He then commanded 'Power', which was repeated twice. About 10 seconds after the activation of the ground-proximity warning system (GPWS), which gave the alert to 'Pull up', a crashing sound was heard and the recording then ended. At the time of the initial impact, the aircraft was in a 60-degree right bank, on a westerly heading

and flying at an indicated air speed of around 300 mph (480 kmh).

Nightfall and the inaccessibility of the terrain prevented members of the Japan Self-Defence Force from reaching the crash site until the following morning, some 15 hours after the accident. A section of the rudder was later recovered from Sagami Bay, as a further indication of structural failure.

As a result of the tragedy, the US Federal Aviation Administration (FAA) ordered the instal-lation on 747s in service of a cover for the opening to the vertical fin, to prevent internal damage in the event of an increase in pressure within the structure. It later instituted a requirement for the securing of the hydraulic system on the aircraft type to preclude a total loss of fluid were its four lines to be severed, as was the case with JA8119.

Understandably, the disaster generated severe repercussions at JAL, a carrier that had built up a reputation for safety throughout the world. The president of the company, Yasumoto Takagi, later resigned, accepting full responsibility for what had happened, and even visited families of the victims to apologise in person. Guilt over his involvement led one JAL maintenance manager to commit suicide. The airline also experienced a drastic reduction in both passenger traffic and revenues, which was directly attributable to the crash. In 1987, and concurrent with its move towards privatisation, the firm adopted a new logo in an attempt to bolster its fallen image.

Date: 22 August 1985 (c. 07:15)
Location: Near Manchester, England
Operator: British Airtours
Aircraft type: Boeing Advanced 737-236 (G-BGJL)

The jet airliner was nearly loaded to capacity, with all but one of its 130 passenger seats filled and also carrying two infants plus six crew members, as it began its take-off from Runway 24 at Manchester International Airport on a non-scheduled service to Corfu, in the Ionian Islands of Greece.

After the 737 had accelerated to about 140 mph (225 kmh), and before reaching the decision speed, the outer casing of its No. 1 engine's compression chamber ruptured. The case had split along an axial line adjacent to the No. 9 combustor can and then 'petalled' apart, with the domed portion and a

The gutted hulk of the British Airtours Boeing 737 sits on the exit ramp after the blaze precipitated by uncontained engine failure. *(AP Images)*

panel section of the fan case striking and puncturing a fuel tank access panel on the underside of the left wing. Escaping fuel then ignited after coming into contact with the flames and hot material emanating from the damaged power plant. The crew immediately rejected the take-off when a 'thump' or 'thud' was heard, but because the captain considered the possibility of a tyre failure, he advised the first officer against excessive braking.

Despite the rapid deployment of emergency vehicles and personnel and the fact that none of the aircraft's occupants were harmed in the engine explosion, 55 persons aboard lost their lives, including the two rear cabin attendants, the fatalities attributed to the effects of the fire. An additional 15 passengers were seriously hurt and dozens of others, including a fire fighter, suffered lesser injuries.

Investigation revealed that a circular crack had formed around the circumference of the No. 9 can, in the area of the third and fourth liner joint. The dome portion, experiencing air loads on its face and having lost the support provided by the aft section

of the can, had then begun to cant outwards by bending the mounting lug and pin. Eventually the dome became canted from its normal axis, and hot combustion gases started to consume the aft portion of the can and to heat the inner surface of the combustion chamber, a process that progressed until the final rupture.

The British Air Accidents Investigation Branch (AAIB) could not determine the amount of time that had elapsed between the full development of the crack and the ultimate failure; available evidence showed that it was not simultaneous.

A metallurgical examination indicated that the source of the crack was thermal fatigue. Evidence of localised 'hot spots', which could signify the early stages of such damage, was found in other combustor cans in the power plant that failed and in other engines of the same type used by the carrier and its parent company, British Airways. The possible causes of heat-related blistering and/or cracking could have ranged from a distorted fuel nozzle flow pattern to disruption of the flow of cooling air attributed to repairs or faulty design or manufacture.

The No. 1 engine of *G-BGJL*, a Pratt & Whitney JT8D-15, had been repaired previously for two separate cracks in the same can. According to the power plant manual, no restriction had been placed on the length of a crack that could be repaired. However, a survey revealed that a number of other operators of the same engine had voluntarily imposed their own limits. British Airways was a relatively new user of the JT8D-15, not obtaining the type until after the manufacturer had deleted a limit of 3 in (*c.* 8 cm) to a repairable crack. In addition, the actual welding carried out on the can was faulty.

Prior to the disaster, only three cases of ruptures in the combustion chamber outer casing had been recorded in some 300 million flying hours with the JT8D, but numerous failures without external damage or cases of bulging or overheating had been, enough to indicate that a problem with the engine existed. Difficulties with this particular power plant, including slow acceleration, had been reported on 20 different occasions from the time of its installation in February 1984 until its catastrophic failure. Slow acceleration was in fact a symptom of a disrupted can, but this information had not been communicated to the operator by Pratt & Whitney. The airline apparently felt that it was immune from such a failure because its fleet of 737s were fitted with 'improved durability' cans, none of which had been in use for an exceptionally long time, and because its inspection programme was considered more conservative than other carriers. Examination of other JT8D engines used by different British air carriers revealed similar cracking, leading to the grounding of numerous 737s until inspections could be completed.

Following the explosion of the engine, there were several factors that contributed to the seriousness of the accident. The captain's decision not to use maximum braking was understandable under the circumstances, especially considering that the engine fire warning bell did not activate immediately. However, the delay in bringing the jet to a full stop as soon as possible cost some precious seconds in evacuation time. Another factor was the use of reverse thrust to stop the aircraft. Though in accordance with prescribed procedures, the deployment of the reverser buckets created a turbulent wake that helped mix fuel flowing from the ruptured wing tank with the air, thus intensifying the blaze that had already started.

Even more critical was the decision of the captain to turn off the runway and stop on an exit ramp. Again, while the action was in line with the operations manual, it resulted in the placement of the fuselage downwind of the burning engine and the blazing fuel that had formed a pool on the left side of the aircraft. The wind, which was a relatively light 5 to 7 knots, blew the flames towards the 737 and also created a pressure field around the stationary aircraft that must have allowed entry of the fire into its cabin when the doors on the right side were opened. The blaze also penetrated the skin of the transport from the outside within 20 seconds of its stopping, resulting in the collapse to the ground of the rear fuselage section in less than a minute.

Difficulties were also experienced in the emergency evacuation, with the front door jamming momentarily, an escape hatch falling inward due to improper operation and briefly trapping a passenger, and a narrow space between the seats disrupting egress from the same exit. Portable oxygen bottles and even the presence of spirits and aerosol spray cans could have increased the fire.

Other important contributing factors were the vulnerability of the wing tank access panels to impact damage, a lack of any effective provision for fighting major fires inside the cabin, and the extremely toxic nature of the emissions from the burning cabin materials. Survivors reported that after the 737 had stopped, the aft cabin suddenly filled with thick black smoke, inducing panic among the passengers, causing many to collapse in the aisle and forcing others to clamber over the seats in order to escape.

The UK Civil Aviation Authority (CAA), which even before this accident had implemented a requirement for the use of flame-retardant upholstery in British airliners (becoming effective in 1987), subsequently took further action to enhance occupant survivability. These included the mandated removal or re-arrangement of seats in some cases to improve access to emergency exits, and floor-level lighting to assist in the egress from a dark or smoke-filled cabin. And British Airways, the parent company of British Airtours, subsequently altered its emergency procedures, instructing its flight crews to immediately bring the aircraft to a stop in the event of such an occurrence, instead of taxiing clear of the runway.

Date: 12 December 1985 (06:46)
Location: Near Gander, Newfoundland, Canada
Operator: Arrow Air Inc (US)
Aircraft type: McDonnell Douglas DC-8 Super 63PF (*N950JW*)

Chartered by the Multinational Force and Observers (MFO) to carry American service personnel home from the Middle East, the jetliner took off from Runway 22 at Gander International Airport, an en route stop during a service originating at Cairo, Egypt, with an ultimate destination of Fort Campbell, Kentucky, US. Reaching a maximum height of about 125 ft (40 m), the aircraft then began to descend, passing over the Trans-Canada Highway at an unusually low altitude. The DC-8 then crashed in a wooded area approximately half a mile (0.8 km) from the end of the runway and some 700 ft (200 m) to the right of its extended centreline, bursting into flames on impact. All 256 persons aboard, including a civilian crew of eight Americans, were killed.

The investigation of the accident was hampered by the condition of the wreckage and irregularities in the operation of the aircraft's flight data recorder (FDR). Largely for these reasons the Canadian Aviation Safety Board (CASB) was unable to hypothesise on the probable sequence of events leading up to the crash. Available evidence supported the conclusion that shortly after becoming airborne the DC-8 experienced an increase in drag and reduction in lift, resulting in a stall from which recovery was not possible.

The most probable cause of the stall was ice contamination on the leading edge and upper surface of the transport's wings. The weather would have been conducive to the accumulation of ice, with a freezing drizzle and/or light snow falling during much of the time that *N950JW* was on the ground, and freezing temperatures throughout; however, before departure the crew had not requested that the jetliner be de-iced. A light snow was still falling when it took off, with a solid overcast at 2,500 ft (*c.* 750 m), scattered clouds down to 700 ft (*c.* 200 m) and a visibility of 12 miles (*c.* 20 km). It was still dark at the time.

As past research had demonstrated, a film of ice only .03 in (*c.* 1 mm) thick – about the roughness

The estimated flight profile of the Arrow Air Super DC-8 that crashed soon after take-off from Gander International Airport. *(Canadian Aviation Safety Board)*

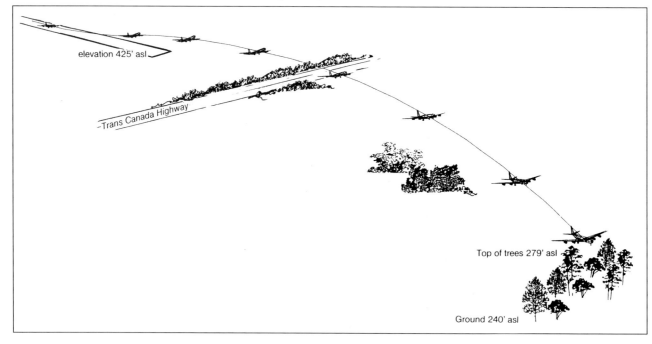

elevation 425' asl

Trans Canada Highway

Top of trees 279' asl

Ground 240' asl

Charred wreckage and levelled trees mark the scene of the troop transport disaster in Newfoundland. *(Canadian Aviation Safety Board)*

of a piece of sandpaper – will adversely affect an aircraft's performance by decreasing lift and increasing drag and its minimum stalling speed. The absence on the DC-8 of wing leading-edge high-lift devices would have increased its susceptibility to the effects of icing.

Another significant operational factor revealed in the inquiry was that the load sheet did not correspond to the actual weight of the aircraft at the time of the take-off, with the amount being underestimated by some 14,000 lb (6,400 kg). This could be explained by the fact that the crew did not take into account the nature of the passenger load, especially when considering that with personal supplies and (unloaded) weapons, the weight of each soldier would have been more than the 170 lb (77 kg) allotted to each passenger when carrying civilians. Though N950JW was neither overloaded nor improperly loaded, this underestimation of weight would have been a factor in the determination of the correct take-off reference speeds and the setting of the aircraft's horizontal

stabiliser, with a heavier load requiring both higher velocities and a higher nose-up setting. Other evidence suggested that the crew may have inadvertently used reference speeds for a take-off weight that was approximately 35,000 lb (16,000 kg) less than the actual load.

Although there were no indications of any major pre-impact mechanical failures, the damage sustained by the aircraft's No. 4 engine was consistent with a lower rotational speed, perhaps as little as about 50 per cent of the norm. The power plant had been running at a higher temperature than the others during the flight to Cairo, prompting the crew to throttle it back slightly, and the same procedure was probably being used in the take-off from Gander.

The investigative report concluded that rotation had been initiated at around 5 mph (10 kmh), and possibly as much as 10 mph (c. 15 kmh), below the appropriate speed. After the DC-8 became airborne, and as it flew over the rough, down-sloping terrain, the benefits of the ground effect decreased, and its degraded aerodynamic performance would have become apparent to the pilots. At that time the pitch attitude was probably increased to counter the lower than normal rate of climb, but simultaneously the drag effects of the icing would have reduced its rate of acceleration, which was followed rapidly by a loss of air speed. Further performance degradation could have resulted from a compressor surge in the No. 4 engine. Due to a higher speed and lower angle of attack than that normally expected in a stalled condition, there was probably little or no warning from the stall-alert system.

Its undercarriage still down and flaps partially extended, the DC-8 initially struck the trees while in a slightly nose-high attitude and banked a few degrees to the right, and the jetliner then yawed to starboard as it began to disintegrate. The duration of the flight was approximately 20 seconds.

The final report was not unanimously endorsed. In a dissenting opinion, four of the nine CASB members wrote that the findings of the investigation did not totally support the conclusions. They noted that the ground handlers had not observed any ice on the aircraft before its departure, and contended that its attitude after the take-off was not consistent with a stall. The minority opinion was that the four thrust reversers may have been deployed prior to impact and that the deceleration experienced after the take-off more likely resulted from a substantial loss of power plant thrust than from icing.

The dissenters also raised the possibility of an in-flight fire. They noted that eyewitnesses had reported an orange or yellow glow somewhere on the aircraft before it crashed (which the majority suspected may have been confused either with the effects of engine compressor stalls and surges associated with a reduction in air intake due to its pitch angle, or with its external lighting), and that medical findings also pointed to a pre-impact blaze. Toxicological tests disclosed evidence of carbon monoxide and hydrogen cyanide in many of the victims, suggesting smoke inhalation before death. Though the majority report concluded that more than half of the occupants may not have been killed immediately, the dissenters expressed the belief that the impact was non-survivable and that the victims had been exposed to toxic fumes beforehand.

Although the manifest did not list any ordnance or explosives being carried aboard the DC-8, the minority report suggested this as a possibility.

Moreover, the nature of the flight, its point of origin and the state of world affairs at the time also fuelled speculation that N950JW had been sabotaged by pro-Iranian terrorists. Considering all these factors, the dissenting report held that explosive detonations in a cargo hold had caused catastrophic systems failures in the aircraft.

One of the safety recommendations made by the CASB was to use actual rather than standard average weights in calculations when the passenger load differs from the norm in air carrier operations.

Though not directly related to this crash, the US Federal Aviation Administration (FAA) subsequently uncovered numerous shortcomings in the maintenance and operating practices of Arrow Air.

Date: 18 January 1986 (*c.* 08:00)
Location: Near San Andres, Peten, Guatemala
Operator: Aerovias de Guatemala SA
Aircraft type: Sud-Aviation Caravelle VI-N (*HC-BAE*)

All 88 persons aboard (82 passengers and a crew of six) perished when the jetliner, which had been leased from the Ecuadorean carrier SAETA and was on a scheduled domestic service from the city of Guatemala, crashed and exploded while attempting to land at Santa Elena, located some 150 miles (250 km) north-north-east of the national capital, the accident occurring during a fog and low overcast.

Having already abandoned an approach due to the poor visibility conditions, the Caravelle began a second landing attempt, but this time slammed into the hilly, jungle-covered terrain approximately 8 miles (13 km) west of the Santa Elena airport. The flight crew had proceeded with the approach despite the fact that the weather was below the prescribed minima. Considered as contributing factors were inadequate assistance from the air traffic controller and possible defects in the aircraft's instruments.

Date: 31 March 1986 (*c.* 09:15)
Location: Near Maravatio, Michoacan, Mexico
Operator: Compania Mexicana de Aviacion SA (Mexico)
Aircraft type: Boeing Advanced 727-264 (*XA-MEM*)

Operating as Flight 940, the jet airliner crashed and burned about 15 minutes after taking off from Benito Juarez International Airport, serving Mexico

City, bound for Puerto Vallarta, Jalisco, the first segment of a service with an ultimate destination of Los Angeles, California, US. All 167 persons aboard (159 passengers and eight crew members) perished.

The 727 had reached flight level 310 before the crew declared an emergency and requested descent clearance. Subsequently, the aircraft plummeted into mountainous terrain some 100 miles (150 km) north-west of the capital city.

It was determined that a left main gear tyre had burst, possibly due to drag and resultant over-heating of the corresponding brake during the take-off ground run, the blast shattering a portion of the port wing, rupturing fuel and hydraulic lines, severing electrical cables and causing cabin decompression. Spilt fuel then must have ignited, starting a fire, with a resultant loss of control and in-flight break-up. It was also reported that the failed tyre had not been filled with nitrogen gas, as recommended.

Date: 31 August 1986 (11:52)
Location: Cerritos, California, US
First aircraft
Operator: Aeronaves de Mexico SA de CV (Aeromexico)
Type: McDonnell Douglas DC-9 Series 32 (*XA-JED*)
Second aircraft
Operator: Private
Type: Piper PA-28-181 Archer II (*N4891F*)

The disaster that had been predicted and feared for many years – a collision between a commercial transport and one of the many light aircraft that fly over the Los Angeles basin – struck with a vengeance on this sunny Sunday.

Designated as Flight 498, which had last stopped at Tijuana, Mexico, during a service originating at Mexico City, the DC-9 was scheduled to land at Los Angeles International Airport, and was operating under instrument flight rules (IFR) and positive control.

Meanwhile the Archer, carrying a married couple and their daughter, took off from Torrance Municipal Airport, bound for Big Bear, a recreational community in the San Bernardino Mountains of Southern California; it was operating under visual flight rules (VFR). In accordance with these procedures, it was to have remained outside of the Los Angeles Terminal Control Area (TCA).

However, it did not do so, straying into the restricted airspace only 8 minutes into the flight as it proceeded eastward, on a crossing path with Flight 498, which was descending on a north-westerly heading. The weather was clear, with a visibility of about 15 miles (25 km).

The two aircraft collided at right angles and at an approximate height of 6,500 ft (1,980 m), with the horizontal stabiliser of *XA-JED* slicing into the upper cockpit section of *N4891F* and separating. The jetliner rolled over on to its back and plunged in a steep nose-down attitude into a residential area just north of the Artesia Freeway and some 20 miles (30 km) east-south-east of the airport, disintegrating in a ball of fire on impact, while the light aeroplane crashed in an open schoolyard about 1,500 ft (500 m) away. All 64 persons aboard the DC-9 (58 passengers and a crew of six), the three occupants of the Archer, who had been decapitated in the collision, and 15 others on the ground, all in the area where *XA-JED* fell, perished in the disaster. Eight persons were injured and 18 houses destroyed or damaged.

In its investigative report, the US National Transportation Safety Board (NTSB) attributed the

The Aeromexico DC-9 dives to earth in an inverted attitude following the collision with a light aircraft. *(Al Francis; Sygma)*

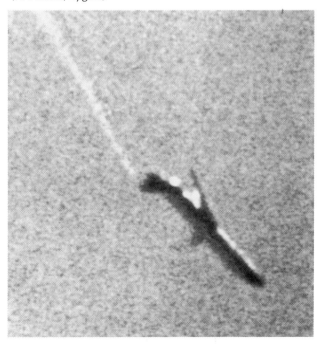

accident to limitations in the air traffic control system, in the areas of both procedures and automated redundancy. The major contributing element, and what in fact some observers in the aviation community regarded as the primary cause, was the unauthorised entry of N4891F into the TCA.

An autopsy performed on the body of the 53-year-old private pilot revealed moderate to severe coronary arteriosclerosis, triggering speculation that the intrusion had occurred after he had become incapacitated by a heart attack. However, a reconstruction of its flight path indicated that the aircraft was under control up until the collision. The pilot was described as methodical and professional in his approach to flying, with an awareness of the Los Angeles TCA and the regulations concerning its use and avoidance. As further proof of this, a TCA chart was found opened in the cockpit wreckage. Given the facts, the NTSB concluded that he had flown into the area inadvertently, probably after misidentifying his navigational checkpoints.

Also factoring in the accident were the limitations of the 'see and be seen' concept to ensure traffic separation. Tests demonstrated that each aircraft should have been visible to the other's crew in sufficent time to avoid the collision, especially in the case of the general aviation pilot; however, there was no evidence of any such prior sighting or evasive manoeuvres.

The Archer was equipped with a functioning non-encoding transponder, which would have made it observable on radar, and, indeed, a tape recording of the display did show the echo of N4891F. This evidence contradicted the approach controller's statement that its target 'was not displayed'.

One reason that the controller did not see the Archer was that he had been distracted by a second light aeroplane, a Grumman Tiger also operating under VFR, that had penetrated the TCA, its pilot requesting control assistance. Fearing a potential conflict with a commuter aircraft, he radioed the Tiger with a suggestion 'In the future you look to your TCA chart'. When he returned his attention to Flight 498, its target had disappeared from the radarscope. It was also considered possible that the controller had unintentionally discounted the radar return of the Archer, sans altitude information, believing it to be beneath the restricted airspace; that he had been distracted from his traffic monitoring duties when asked to relay to the DC-9 instructions for a change in landing runway; or that he may not have observed the target because the display had been weakened by the effects on the radar of an atmospheric temperature inversion. It could not be determined whether one or a combination of these factors prevented him from spotting the general aviation aeroplane and perhaps giving the Aeromexico crew a traffic advisory.

Subsequent to this disaster, the US Federal Aviation Administration (FAA) enacted a requirement that all aircraft flying within 30 nautical miles (55 km) of the primary airport in a TCA be fitted with altitude-encoding transponders. This collision also helped speed the installation on commercial transports of traffic alert and collision-avoidance system (TCAS) units, which, when used in conjunction with TCA procedures, would help greatly reduce the risk of mid-air crashes.

Date: 6 November 1986 (c. 11:30)
Location: Off Shetland Isles, Scotland
Operator: British International Helicopters Ltd
Aircraft type: Boeing/Vertol 234LR Commercial Chinook (G-BWFC)

In history's worst commercial helicopter accident, 45 persons aboard were killed when the twin-rotor, turbine-engine aircraft, on a non-scheduled service and carrying workers from the Brent oil field, plummeted into the North Sea approximately 3 miles (5 km) east of Sumburgh Airport, located some 20 miles (30 km) south of Lerwick, where it was to have landed.

One passenger and the captain, one of the three crew members assigned to G-BWFC, escaped with their lives. Though rescued by another helicopter only about 10 minutes after the crash, both survivors were seriously injured and suffered from hypothermia, with a considerable amount of water having entered their survival suits. The bodies of all but one of the victims were later found, and in every case death was due to trauma rather than drowning.

The local weather at the time was adverse, with rain, a visibility of around 12 miles (20 km), scattered cumulus clouds down to 1,500 ft (c. 500 m), and winds gusting up to almost 40 knots. The ocean was rough.

Approximately 90 per cent of the rotorcraft's wreckage, most of which had sunk in water some

A Boeing/Vertol 234LR Commercial Chinook, shown in the livery of British Airways Helicopters (the predecessor of British International Helicopters), which was the type involved in the North Sea disaster. *(Boeing)*

300 ft (100 m) deep, was subsequently recovered, and examination of the debris revealed the apparent cause of the accident, a fracture of the main spiral bevel ring gear in the forward transmission assembly that left a gap about ¾ in (2 cm) wide. Although the gap was equivalent to only two or three teeth, it had the effect of changing the ratio between the bevel ring gear and the pinion of the synchronising shaft, running from the rear engine transmission, part of the delicate mechanism designed to provide proper separation of the counter-rotating main blades. The resulting loss of separation may have occurred in less than 2 seconds and caused the aft rotors to overtake and clash with the forward ones. Damage to the blades would then have led to rotor imbalance, with the aft pylon structure ultimately breaking away, taking with it the transmission components. After the rotor assembly had been torn off, the helicopter fell in a tail-down attitude from an approximate height of 500 ft (150 m).

Evidence indicated that the gear failure originated from fatigue cracking associated with a groove formed by a combination of wear and corrosion in the bolted joint that attached it to the shaft. The corrosion appeared to have been aggravated by water in the aircraft's oil supply, which was possibly related to the marine environment in which *G-BWFC* had been operating.

The joint was of a modified design that had been recently introduced by the manufacturer, one that used larger bolts in the ring gear because those existing were found to work loose, with the requirement that operators check bolt torque between overhauls. It was ruled by the UK Air Accidents Investigation Branch (AAIB) that Boeing/Vertol and the agencies representing the nation of manufacture, the US Federal Aviation Administration (FAA), and of registry, the British Civil Aviation Authority (CAA), had failed to predict the different operational characteristics of the new design and detect its inherent weakness. Following the disaster, the entire fleet of Boeing/Vertol 234LR helicopters registered in the UK and the US was grounded pending replacement in every aircraft of the gear that failed on *G-BWFC*. Subsequently, the

British government announced a large monetary investment to improve rotorcraft safety, and even before the North Sea disaster, the CAA had begun working to develop a Health Usage and Monitoring System (HUMS) to detect wear and other anomalies.

Date: 9 May 1987 (11:12)
Location: Near Warsaw, Poland
Operator: LOT Polish Airlines
Aircraft type: Ilyushin Il-62MK (*SP-LBG*)

During a transatlantic service to New York City, the crew of Flight 5055 reported the failure of both port power plants, and that they were returning to Okecie Airport, serving Warsaw, from where the aircraft had taken off slightly less than half an hour earlier. With only two engines functioning, the return trip took longer, and as it was being vectored for landing on Runway 33, the jet airliner crashed in a wooded area and exploded. All 183 persons aboard (172 passengers and a crew of 11) perished.

The accident sequence began with the breaking loose of the low-pressure (LP) turbine shaft in the No. 2 power plant, which disrupted the mechanical link with the corresponding LP compressor assembly. Turbine speed then became critical until the rotor assembly broke up through centrifugal forces, hurling out fragments that struck and disabled the adjacent No. 1 engine and also pierced the aft fuselage section of the Il-62, leading to partial cabin depressurisation. Even greater damage was sustained internally, with engine debris destroying the aircraft's elevator control system and breaking its electric cables. Fire also erupted in the baggage compartment.

Following the uncontained power plant failure, the pilots initiated an immediate descent to about 13,000 ft (4,000 m), but could only maintain longitudinal control through movement of the entire horizontal stabiliser and by means of the elevator trim tabs. The crew could not complete the dumping of fuel, which had been initiated, due to the loss of electrical power. Broken electric wires had also rendered the fire warning system inoperative, and as a result, the blaze that had started in the baggage compartment continued to spread, the crew believing it to be extinguished.

Faced with a deteriorating situation, the crew first radioed their intention to land at the somewhat closer Modlin Airport, but owing to its superior rescue equipment, then elected to proceed to Okecie. The additional 8 minutes in the air proved critical, however, for during that time the fire consumed further components of the aircraft's airframe, control system and accessories, ultimately leading to a total loss of control. After a gradual loss of air speed, the Il-62 finally pitched down from an approximate height of 5,000 ft (1,500 m), then plunged to earth. Impact occurred about 3.5 miles (6 km) from the threshold of the runway, at a speed of around 290 mph (465 kmh), and with the aircraft banked slightly to the left. The weather in the area at the time was good and was not a factor in the crash.

The underlying cause of the engine failure proved to be a worn inter-shaft bearing, which led to an increasingly eccentric rotation of the low-pressure shaft. This in turn decreased the clearance between it and portions of the high-pressure turbine shaft. On this particular flight, the wear of the said bearing reached critical proportions, causing friction between the components. The heat produced by this friction eventually weakened the shaft, ultimately leading to its failure. The uncontained failure of the engine occurred without warning, not allowing the crew to shut it down in time to prevent the severe damage that its break-up inflicted.

Subsequent to this accident, a fuel tank located in the vertical stabiliser was removed from this particular model of the Il-62, and the time between overhauls on the aircraft's D-30KU engines was reduced by 1,000 hours.

Date: 16 August 1987 (20:45)
Location: Romulus, Michigan, US
Operator: Northwest Airlines (US)
Aircraft type: McDonnell Douglas DC-9 Super 82 (*N312RC*)

Operating as Flight 255, the jetliner took off from Runway 03C at Detroit Metropolitan Wayne County Airport, bound for Phoenix, Arizona, one segment of a domestic service originating at Saginaw, Michigan, with an ultimate destination of Orange County, in Southern California. Only 14 seconds after becoming airborne and while at an approximate height of 50 ft (15 m) above the ground, the aircraft struck, with its port wing, a lamp standard located about half a mile (0.8 km) beyond the end of the runway.

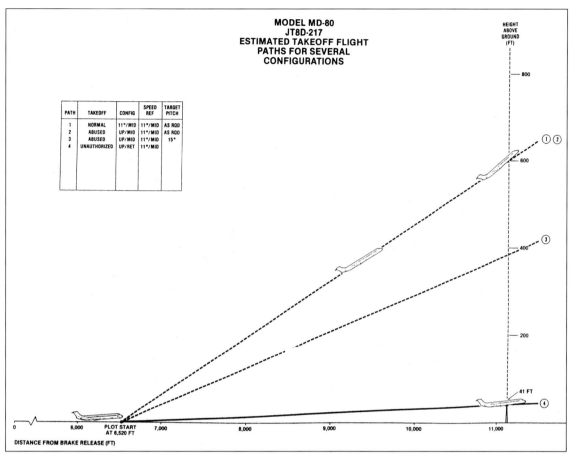

PATH	TAKEOFF	CONFIG	SPEED REF	TARGET PITCH
1	NORMAL	11°/MID	11°/MID	AS RQD
2	ABUSED	UP/MID	11°/MID	AS RQD
3	ABUSED	UP/MID	11°/MID	15°
4	UNAUTHORIZED	UP/RET	11°/MID	

MODEL MD-80
JT8D-217
ESTIMATED TAKEOFF FLIGHT
PATHS FOR SEVERAL
CONFIGURATIONS

Diagram illustrating the flight profiles of the DC-9 Super 80 series in different configurations, including the one (solid line) that led to the crash after take-off from the Detroit airport. *(National Transportation Safety Board)*

Its undercarriage still in the process of retracting, the DC-9 then clipped other lamp standards and the roof of a building and rolled to the left in excess of 90 degrees before it slammed to earth, disintegrated and burst into flames, scattering wreckage along a road and under a railroad and two highway overpasses. A total of 156 persons were killed in the disaster, including the aircraft's six crew members and two occupants of vehicles hit by the crashing jetliner. The sole surviving passenger was a four-year-old girl travelling with her parents and brother, who suffered severe burns, a fractured skull and other impact-related trauma. Five other persons on the ground were also injured, one seriously, and numerous vehicles, three on the road and the rest parked on a car-rental forecourt, destroyed.

Examination of the debris disclosed no evidence of a malfunction in the aircraft's engines, flight controls or avionics that could have directly contributed to the accident. One significant find was made, however: its flaps and leading-edge slats were determined to be retracted at the time of the crash. This was further corroborated by the position of the cockpit flap/slat handle and by the digital flight data recorder (DFDR) read-out, which includes these items among its transcribed parameters.

Playback of the cockpit voice recorder (CVR) tape also revealed that the two-man flight crew neither called for nor carried out the taxi checklist, on which the extension of the flaps and slats is the first item. In accordance with Northwest procedures, the first officer usually sets them after the start of the taxi, but at around the time that this should have been done, the co-pilot of *N312RC* was receiving information regarding a change of take-off runway. There was speculation that by the time he finished copying this automatic terminal information service (ATIS) message, the DC-9 had progressed beyond

Wreckage of the Northwest Airlines jetliner is scattered beneath road and railroad bridges after the disaster that claimed 156 lives. *(EMPICS)*

the point where the extension would normally be completed, which may have misled him to believe that the task had been accomplished.

The stated policy of the airline is that the captain is supposed to initiate the checklist routine. The captain of Flight 255 did not ask for the after-start, taxi or before-take-off checks, relegating this responsibility to his first officer, who did not follow suit. These and other factors, including confusion over the location of a particular taxiway despite the fact that the pilot had flown into this airport many times, led the US National Transportation Safety Board (NTSB) to conclude in its investigative report that the conduct of the crew did not conform to air carrier standards, even though both pilots had gained a reputation for competence and pro-fessionalism from their peers. The omission of the taxi checklist was, in fact, regarded by the Board as the primary cause of the disaster.

The Super DC-9 is equipped with a sophisticated control aural warning system (CAWS), which has an important component designed to recognise the conditions that could precipitate a stall, such as an improper flap/slat configuration, and is activated by movement of the thrust levers. No such aural warning (consisting of a voice stating 'flaps' and/or 'slats') was transcribed by the CVR, which the NTSB attributed to a loss of electrical power to the system. This may have resulted from intentional action by the crew or maintenance personnel; from a transient overload; or because the circuit breaker did not allow the current to flow to the CAWS power supply and did not annunciate the condition by tripping. The power loss was considered the principal contributing factor in the crash.

The absence of extended flaps and slats would have severely limited the climb capability and increased the aircraft's stalling speed. This accounted for its relatively long take-off ground run and the fact that *N312RC* assumed a higher than normal pitch angle after becoming airborne, while gaining little altitude. The stick-shaker stall-warning system was heard on the CVR tape to activate less than a second after lift-off. Once in the air the jetliner began rocking laterally, which the crew attempted to control by deploying the spoilers. The 'Dutch roll' motions and corrective action further degraded the performance of the DC-9.

A section of the left outer wing some 18 ft (5.5 m) long was torn off in the initial impact with the lamp standard, rupturing fuel tanks. Escaping fuel was then ingested into the aircraft's No. 1 power plant and ignited, thus explaining the in-flight fire reported by some witnesses.

The accident occurred at twilight; the weather at the time was fair, with a high overcast and scattered clouds down to 2,500 ft (*c.* 750 m), a visibility of around 5 miles (10 km) and a 12-knot wind out of the west. Wind shear advisories had been broadcast shortly before the departure of Flight 255, although there was no evidence from available information, including the DFDR read-out, that such a condition in any way contributed to the crash. Nevertheless, the alert may have influenced the actions of the crew, even to the point of reducing their ability to escape from the stall. The captain, who was flying the aircraft, apparently increased its pitch angle after the stall warning, indicating that he suspected an encounter with wind shear; stall recovery procedures normally involve lowering the nose and extending the flaps, which in this case would probably have prevented the disaster.

Subsequently, all operators of the Super DC-9 incorporated a crew checklist procedure to ensure that the CAWS was functional before take-off. The NTSB also recommended that the system's fail light be modified to compensate for one shortcoming, i.e. its inability to annunciate in the event of a power loss.

In May 1991 a US federal court rejected Northwest Airlines' contention that McDonnell Douglas share responsibility for the accident, ruling that the carrier was liable for all damages resulting therefrom.

Date: 31 August 1987 (15:36)
Location: Off Ko Phuket, Thailand
Operator: Thai Airways
Aircraft type: Boeing Advanced 737-2P5 (*HS-TBC*)

All 83 persons aboard (74 passengers and a crew of nine) perished when the jetliner plunged into the Andaman Sea about 10 miles (15 km) east of Phuket International Airport, where it was to have landed following a domestic service from Bangkok, as Flight 365.

The aircraft began its approach simultaneously with another 737, operated by the Hong Kong carrier Dragon Air, which was en route from Hong Kong. Both were utilising very-high-frequency omnidirectional range/distance-measuring equipment (VOR/DME) non-precision instrument procedures, and both were to have landed on Runway 27. Navigating along Radial 119 of the Phuket VOR station, the Thai transport had been approaching from the south-east, and the other aircraft, using Radial 025, from the north-east.

About 5 minutes before the crash of *HS-TBC*, the Dragon Air flight, then some 15 miles (25 km) from the navigational aid, was cleared for descent to 2,500 ft (750 m) and instructed to report when on final approach. Upon learning that it was 25 nautical miles (45 km) out, Phuket approach control assigned Flight 365 to be second to land, and shortly afterwards cleared it for descent to 3,000 ft (1,000 m). In a rapid series of events, *HS-TBC* passed the Dragon Air jet, with the latter's crew reporting the former 'ahead of us at one o'clock, about five miles at right'. After the Thai Airways captain transmitted the message, 'request visual', the aircraft was reassigned to land first. The

Dragon Air crew then cautioned the controller, 'The traffic ahead is above us and cannot descend through our level.' Less than a minute later, they reported the crash of the Thai aircraft.

Pitching down violently, *HS-TBC* disintegrated on impact with the water, which was approximately 60 ft (20 m) deep. At the time, the weather conditions were reportedly clear in the area of the accident and cloudy at the airport, with scattered cumulus at around 2,000 ft (600 m) and at 3,000 ft (1,000 m), stratocumulus at the latter height and broken cirrus at 30,000 ft (10,000 m), and a visibility of about 5 miles (10 km) in light mist. The wind was blowing from a west-north-westerly direction at 9 knots.

Searchers recovered the 'severely traumatised' bodies of the victims, a small amount of aircraft structure and both the flight data (FDR) and cockpit voice (CVR) recorders, and a transcription of the latter proved useful in determining the probable cause of the crash. An underlying factor was the apparent attempt by the Thai Airways crew to land ahead of the Dragon Air jet despite being behind it during the initial phase of the approach. An analysis of the cockpit conversation supported the assumption that they tried to accomplish this by increasing speed and requesting a visual landing.

After being assigned to be second to land, the captain of *HS-TBC* commented to the first officer that Dragon Air 'has to make an approach again'. From their conversation, the pilots seemed to believe that the other crew were trying to 'sneak in', or even make a false position report in order to get landing priority. After transmitting the message 'eight DME inbound' and requesting a visual approach, the latter of which the controller apparently did not hear because at the time he was communicating with the Dragon Air crew, Flight 365 received the reassigned landing priority based on the captain's misleading position report. The undercarriage of the 737 was then lowered, but its flaps were not extended nor its spoilers deployed, and the aircraft's speed remained about 70 mph (110 kmh) above the norm.

Despite the new clearance, the captain appeared to be concerned about his ability to land first, and after the Dragon Air warning, and in response to his first officer's remark, 'We'd better go', he was heard to say 'wait a minute, wait a minute'. He then asked the controller, 'Who is going to land first?' During this period of time, the speed of *HS-TBC* continued to decay, and when the stick-shaker stall-warning system activated, the captain asked for the retraction of the undercarriage. (The sound of an increase in engine power was also heard.) Its ground-proximity warning system (GPWS) then sounded, and at an indicated air speed of approximately 175 mph (280 kmh), the aircraft stalled. The violent pitching of the aircraft before impact may have resulted from the asymmetric application of thrust.

Although simulator tests showed that recovery could have been made from a stall at 3,000 ft, the pilot's preoccupation with the Dragon Air jet apparently delayed such action. It was also considered probable that because of his concentration on the conflicting traffic, the co-pilot failed to monitor his flight instruments. The investigative committee's report concluded that the approach controller should not have reassigned landing priorities, but instead instructed Flight 365 to have proceeded to its clearance limit and held. There had also been a violation by approach control in providing a vertical separation between the two aircraft of only 500 ft (150 m), which is half that of the minimum prescribed.

As a result of this accident, two air traffic controllers were reassigned and their supervisor faced a disciplinary hearing. Plans were also made to install radar at the Phuket airport, as recommended by the committee.

Date: 28 November 1987 (*c.* 04:00)
Location: Indian Ocean
Operator: South African Airways
Aircraft type: Boeing 747-244B Combi (*ZS-SAS*)

Everything was normal for the first 9 1/2 hours of Flight 295, which had originated at T'ai-pei, Taiwan, with an ultimate destination of Johannesburg, South Africa, and an en route stop planned on the island of Mauritius. The first hint of trouble was when the pilot-in-command reported smoke and that the 747 had initiated a descent to flight level 140. He then declared an emergency, and shortly afterwards radioed 'Now we have lost a lot of electrics. We haven't got anything on the . . . aircraft now.'

Approximately 3 minutes after the last message from the flight, the wide-bodied jetliner plunged into the sea some 150 miles (250 km) north-east of Sir Seewoosagur Ramgoolam-Plaisance International Airport, serving Mahebourg, Mauritius, which it was trying to reach, disintegrating into thousands of pieces on impact and leaving a trail of debris on the ocean floor in water about 15,000 ft (5,000 m) deep. All 159 persons aboard (140 passengers and 19 crew members) perished. The crash occurred in pre-dawn darkness, but the local weather was apparently good, with a visibility of at least 5 miles (10 km) and scattered cumulus and stratocumulus clouds.

Some wreckage, including articles of light cargo and cabin furnishings, was found floating in the ocean, some as far away as the coast of South Africa. Debris that washed ashore on the beaches of Madagascar could not be retrieved due to political animosity between that nation and South Africa. Of the three recording devices fitted to the aircraft, only the cockpit voice recorder (CVR) was recovered, providing useful information despite an incomplete transcript. The main wreckage was later photographed and videotaped on the seabed, and a few vital parts were raised. Human remains were also found, but only five victims could be identified.

There was sufficient evidence for the investigative board to conclude that fire had erupted before impact in the front pallet on the right side in the upper deck cargo hold of the 747. Numerous articles being carried in the compartment were found to have been burned, as was the structure itself. Some of the panels in the passenger cabin adjoining that section were also covered with soot.

The evidence was, however, insufficient for a determination of the source of ignition. The freight items consisted largely of computer components, some of which had been filled with nickel cadmium or lithium batteries, but these were not considered hazardous.

The cardboard and plastic packaging materials in the cargo hold were undoubtedly involved in the blaze, which could have developed rapidly, as in a 'flash' fire, even before the smoke sensors activated the alarm system. The burning of these materials would have produced the smoke mentioned by the captain, as well as carbon dioxide and carbon monoxide, noxious elements that must have penetrated the passenger compartment and possibly the flight deck. Autopsies revealed carbon monoxide poisoning in two of the victims, and it was considered a 'real possibility' that some, if not all, of the passengers and cabin staff had succumbed to the effects of the toxic fumes even before the crash.

The members of the flight crew, who were probably using their emergency oxygen masks, at least until the descent to a lower altitude, could also have been incapacitated, or at least suffered from the impairment of their physical or intellectual capacities. Disorientation consequent on reduced cockpit visibility due to the smoke or pilot distraction could also have led or contributed to an uncontrolled descent. One plausible scenario was that as the crew concentrated on the emergency, the jetliner continued to lose height until it hit the sea while in a tail-down attitude. Its fuselage then could have broken in two, with indication that the front section slammed into the water with its wings perpendicular to the surface of the ocean.

Another possibility, or additional causative factor, was that the blaze had affected the aircraft's structure or systems. Heat damage to the skin and flying controls, specifically the cable pulley clusters for the elevators, rudder, rudder trim and the manual operation of the horizontal stabiliser was, in fact, confirmed.

Had a crew member actually entered the cargo hold to fight the fire, the task would have been made difficult by the heat and limited visibility attributable to the smoke and/or loss of lighting caused by the damage to the electrical wiring. The use of the re-circulating fans, as required in the event of such an emergency, could have actually aggravated the situation by bringing smoke into the cabin. The blaze might have been contained or extinguished, but too late to prevent the crash.

Some two years after the disaster, the US Federal Aviation Administration (FAA) issued an airworthiness directive concerning Class B cargo compartments, i.e. those of a certain size and capacity that are easily accessible. Operators were given a choice of upgrading compartments to Class C, or self-contained, specifications; modifying them with fire detection, suppression and extinguishing features; or restricting the carriage of cargo to that placed in flame-resistant containers.

Date: 29 November 1987 (c. 11:00)
Location: Off Western Burma (Myanmar)
Operator: Korean Air (South Korea)
Aircraft type: Boeing 707-3B5C (HL-7406)

The jet airliner, which was operating as Flight 858 and carrying 115 persons (104 passengers and a crew of 11), crashed in the Andaman Sea while en route from Abu Dhabi, United Arab Emirates, to Bangkok, Thailand, one segment of a service that had originated at Baghdad, Iraq, and was ultimately destined for Seoul, South Korea. About two weeks later, a damaged and partially submerged liferaft identified as belonging to HL-7406 was recovered from the water approximately 30 miles (50 km) west of Heinz Bay, but no survivors or bodies were found.

At about the same time the aircraft was believed lost, two eyewitnesses in a fishing boat apparently saw the disaster, reportedly observing a bright flash in the sky followed by a trail of smoke falling into the sea, then black smoke rising from the same location, which was identified as being 75 miles (120 km) north-west of the city of Tavoy. The weather conditions in the area at the time consisted of high cirrus clouds and good visibility, with a 20-knot wind blowing from an east-south-easterly direction.

South Korean authorities, who suspected foul play soon after the flight was reported missing, began checking passengers who had disembarked at Abu Dhabi, and this led to the apprehension, two days after the disappearance of the aircraft, of a couple at the Bahrain airport. Both were found to be in possession of false Japanese passports. While being held under guard at the airport for interrogation, both swallowed poison capsules that had been hidden in cigarettes, and one of them, an elderly man, died. His young female accomplice, who survived the suicide attempt, subsequently confessed to carrying a bomb on to the aircraft when they boarded at Baghdad. The device was said to be C-4 plastic-type explosive hidden in a battery-operated portable transistor radio, and had been set to go off 9 hours later. Together with a liquor bottle containing the liquid explosive PLX, the bomb was placed in the overhead rack above Row 7 in the forward part of the economy class section, where they had been seated, and left there when they got off. The 707 had last been reported at an altitude of 37,000 ft (11,300 m), and it was considered possible that the detonation of the bomb and the consequent explosive decompression of the cabin and flash fire could have killed all of the occupants instantly.

South Korea claimed North Korean complicity in the mass murder, and the surviving saboteur was condemned to death for her own involvement.

However, she was pardoned by the President of South Korea in 1990.

Date: 18 January 1988 (*c.* 22:15)
Location: Near Chungking, Sichuan, China
Operator: Civil Aviation Administration of China (CAAC)
Aircraft type: Ilyushin Il-18D (*B-222*)

Designated as Flight 4146 and on a domestic service from Beijing, the turboprop transport crashed and burned approximately 5 miles (10 km) from Baishiyi Airport, located some 10 miles (15 km) from and serving Chungking, where it was scheduled to land, killing all 108 persons aboard (98 passengers and 10 crew members).

Before the disaster, the right starter in the aircraft's No. 4 power plant had become so hot that the tube supplying oil to the feathering mechanism was burned, rupturing when the crew tried to feather the corresponding propeller. The engine then caught fire and separated from the starboard wing. Severe shaking subsequently caused the No. 1 propeller to feather, and the Il-18 plunged into farmland after a loss of control. The crash occurred in darkness, but the weather was not a factor.

The accident was blamed on lax maintenance, and a subsequent safety check reportedly led to the grounding of the entire Chinese Il-18 fleet.

Date: 17 March 1988 (13:17)
Location: Near Cucuta, Norte de Santander, Colombia
Operator: Aerovias Nacionales de Colombia SA (AVIANCA)
Aircraft type: Boeing 727-21 (*HK-1716*)

All 143 persons aboard perished in the crash of the jetliner, which occurred less than 4 minutes after its departure from Camilo Daza Airport, serving Cucuta. The victims included a regular crew of six, and among the passengers was an off-duty pilot riding on the flight deck who had a significant role in the accident.

Operating as Flight 410, a domestic service originating at Bucaramanga, with an ultimate destination of Barranquilla, the 727 was delayed for 10 minutes on the ground due to three inbound aircraft. With mechanical failure having necessitated replacement in Bogota of the aircraft

orginally assigned to the service, which delayed initiation of the flight for 2½ hours, these extra few minutes only added to the pressure placed on the pilot. This may have been a factor in his request 'to climb on course', taking a more direct route than the one normally used. Bound for Cartegena, its next en route stop, *HK-1716* initiated a left turn after taking off from Runway 33. Subsequently, it slammed into the mountain El Espartillo at an approximate elevation of 6,000 ft (1,800 m), or abut 600 ft (180 m) below its summit, at an indicated air speed of around 320 mph (515 kmh), while on a heading of 310 degrees, and banked slightly to the right. The aircraft disintegrated on impact, and although small isolated fires erupted at the crash site, there was no generalised blaze. Thick fog blanketed the area at the time, while at the airport, the weather was overcast, with 3/8 cumulus clouds at 2,500 ft (750 m) and high cirrostratus, and a visibility of about 5 miles (10 km) in a smoky atmosphere. The wind was blowing from due north at 15 knots.

The absence of a crew briefing and the failure of the captain to provide any instructions for the visual flight rules (VFR) departure apparently led the first officer to initiate the left turn soon after the jetliner had become airborne. According to the investigative report, the cockpit voice recorder (CVR) transcript indicated the 'disorientation' that prevailed on the flight deck, and only after the flight engineer mentioned the fog did the captain instruct the co-pilot to 'start turning right'. Additionally, the presence of the off-duty pilot in the cockpit and 'his great talkativeness' contributed to the 'carelessness and disorientation' of the regular flight crew when monitoring the heading and air speed of the aircraft, which was necessary in avoiding the mountainous terrain as they proceeded towards the prescribed airway. It was inferred from their conversation that the pilots had given a greater priority to speed than altitude. The report also noted that the presence of the inbound traffic could have created even more pressure and a resultant desire to turn in order to avoid the descending aircraft.

The 'active' causes of the accident were considered to be the fact that the captain diverted his attention from the operation of the aircraft, failed to exercise adequate and constant supervision over the first officer, tolerated the inappropriate interference

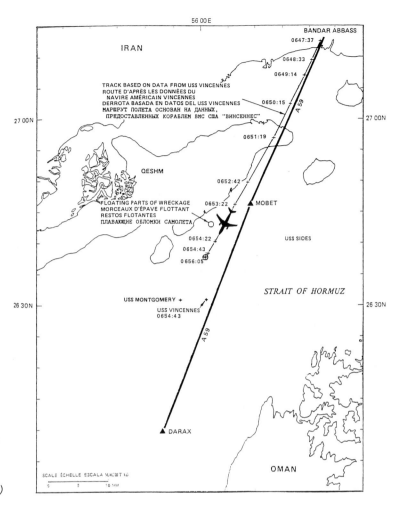

Diagram showing the route taken by the Iranian Airbus, which was shot down by a US Navy vessel, indicating a slight deviation from the prescribed airway. (*International Civil Aviation Organisation*)

of normal cockpit discipline by someone who had access to the flight deck, and continued under VFR into the instrument meteorological conditions. The very presence of the off-duty pilot and his interference with the crew was considered a 'primary' factor. Listed as 'passive' causative factors were the lack of teamwork displayed by the crew, which was reflected by their failure to coordinate the instructions needed to take off and climb out using a flight profile appropriate for the existing weather conditions, and delays resulting from the change of the original aircraft, which contributed to the captain's decision to place too much importance on company priorities and request to take off, rather than waiting, as had been suggested by the control tower.

It was subsequently recommended that instrument flight rules (IFR) procedures be used in all jet operations during departures and landings, and that strict controls be imposed limiting the access of anyone other than crew members to the cockpits of commercial aircraft.

Date: 3 July 1988 (*c.* 10:25)
Location: Persian Gulf
Operator: Iran Air
Aircraft type: Airbus Industrie A300B2-203 (*EP-IBU*)

The US government had committed naval forces to the convoying of Kuwaiti oil tankers sailing in the Persian Gulf in May 1987. This policy was implemented to counter attacks on commercial ships, which had become a part of the eight-year war between Iran and Iraq. The involvement had proved costly for the United States: only days into the operation, 37 American sailors lost their lives in a supposedly accidental missile attack on the frigate *Start* by an Iraqi Mirage jet fighter.

As a result of the *Stark* incident, US commanders were given a revised set of 'rules of engagement' that clarified their authority to take protective measures when faced with 'hostile intent'. Before 3 July 1988, American forces in the Gulf were alerted to the probability of significant Iranian

An Iran Air A300B2 of the type shot down over the Persian Gulf by a US Navy warship on 3 July 1988. *(Airbus Industrie)*

military activity, in retaliation for recent Iraqi military successes. This period covered the American Independence Day holiday weekend.

On this particular Sunday morning, the US Navy cruiser *Vincennes* was directed to an area in the Strait of Hormuz where a number of Iranian gunboats were reportedly threatening merchant vessels. Some 2 hours later, a helicopter assigned to the warship was fired upon by one of the small boats. A short surface battle ensued involving the *Vincennes* and an American frigate, the *Elmer Montgomery*.

During this period of time, Iran Air Flight 655 took off from the Bandar Abbas international airport, which also served military aircraft, including (American-built) F-14 jet fighters. Almost immediately, the target representing the A300 was spotted on radar by the crew of the *Vincennes*. Shortly afterwards, reports of Iranian F-14 activity were heard in the vessel's combat identification centre, and a Mode II identification of friend or foe (IFF) transponder indication, normally associated with a military aircraft, was detected. The target was identified by the crew to be an F-14.

As the wide-bodied jet airliner proceeded on towards the combat area, bound for Dubai, United Arab Emirates, and on an approximate heading of 200 degrees, it was given a number of warnings, one from another American warship, the frigate *John Sides*, and the rest from the *Vincennes*. The 11 challenges to the aircraft, which identified its course, speed, height and geographical coordinates,

were made on both the military air distress (MAD) and international air defence (IAD) radio frequencies and included the threat of defensive action.

At this point the crew of the *Vincennes* were faced with a multiplicity of ongoing events. Besides the potential threat of an air attack, they were still engaged in a sea battle. One of the vessel's guns had become fouled, necessitating constant manoeuvres in order to keep its remaining gun unmasked. Meanwhile, an Iranian P-3 Orion patrol aircraft was airborne some 70 miles (110 km) to the north-west of the scene, conceivably furnishing targeting information to the suspected fighter.

Under the pressure of the moment, the commanding officer of the *Vincennes*, Captain Will Rogers III, did what he felt he had to – defend his ship – and ordered the launch of two Standard surface-to-air missiles at the target. Both hit the aircraft a few seconds later, while still about 10 miles (15 km) away from the vessel and at an altitude of 13,500 ft (4,100 m). Losing its tail assembly and one wing, the A300 plummeted into the Strait some 5 miles (10 km) east of the island of Henqam. All 290 persons aboard (274 passengers and 16 crew members) perished. Floating debris, which included lightweight aircraft structure and furnishings, was later found in the water, as were victims' remains, with nearly 200 bodies being recovered subsequently.

The tragedy was investigated by both the US Navy and the International Civil Aviation Organisation (ICAO). The Navy report showed a divergence between the recollection of witnesses and tape recordings of the *Vincennes*'s AEGIS defence/radar system. Perhaps the most significant discrepancy was the identification of *EP-IBU* as belonging to the military despite the radar display clearly registering a Mode III transponder code, an indication (though not unequivocal evidence) of a civilian aircraft.

The misidentification apparently occurred after a temporary Mode II signal was detected by the ship around the time that the A300 became airborne. The Naval investigative board believed that the transmission had emanated from a military aircraft, perhaps an F-14 or even a C-130 transport, which was still on the ground. This would have been possible even though the airport was out of the line of sight of the vessel because the atmospheric conditions in the Gulf at the time, with a high level of evaporation, were conducive to radar ducting, or bouncing of the signal. As Flight 655 lifted off, the ship's identification supervisor locked on to its track. As the radar echo of *EP-IBU* moved towards the *Vincennes*, it retained the identification as a fighter. Interestingly, only one officer in the vessel's combat centre suggested the possbility that it was a commercial airliner.

Another important discrepancy was between the constant crew reports of the aircraft descending and the transcribed data showing it as ascending. Its ground speed, recorded as 440 mph (*c.* 710 kmh) at the moment of missile impact, had only increased slightly during the period that it was tracked. In the excitement of an impending engagement, the reports of descending altitude could have happened if the tactical information coordinator passed on only range values, which were interpreted as height, or if he misread his read-out and interchanged altitude and range.

In the final 1 minute 40 seconds before the missile launch, the anti-air warfare officer informed the captain that the radar target had veered from its flight path and was rapidly descending, while increasing in speed, as it approached the *Vincennes*, yet he made no attempt to confirm these reports on his own. Quick reference to the read-out on the console directly in front of him would have immediately shown the increasing height. Rather, he relied on the judgement of one or two second-class petty officers, buttressed by his own preconceived perception of the threat, and made an erroneous assessment to the commanding officer, according to the Navy report. The belief that the aircraft was rapidly descending directly towards the ship could have been pivotal in the decision to shoot it down.

It was further revealed that *EP-IBU* was operating within the established air corridor, A59, though off its centreline by approximately 3 or 4 miles (5–6.5 km). Its altitude was also below the norm for commercial air traffic, the route structure for which had been laid out on the large screen display (LSD) in the *Vincennes*'s combat centre.

Another factor was the failure of the Iran Air crew to heed the warnings. Although the A300 was not equipped to receive the MAD frequency, the pilots should have been aware of the company's instructions to monitor the IAD frequency when flying in the Gulf area. The absence of a response may indicate that they were not doing so, or perhaps did not identify theirs as the challenged aircraft.

Neither the *Vincennes* nor the *Elmer Montgomery* detected a weather radar emission from the target, which could have helped its identification as a commercial transport. However, as noted in the ICAO report, the meteorological conditions, consisting of an estimated 8–10-mile (*c.* 13–15 km) visibility and scattered clouds at around 200 ft (60 m), would not have warranted use of the radar. (The weather was such that the ship's crew never did make visual contact with the airliner.)

The violent manoeuvring of the vessel, which caused gear to fall in the combat centre, the noise of gunfire, the flickering of lights on the LSD and shouting voices heightened the tension as the aircraft was being scrutinised. Time compression also played a significant role in the incident. Only 3 minutes 40 seconds had elapsed from the time the captain became aware of the potential threat until he made the decision to engage.

In its report, the Navy defended the actions of Capt Rogers and his crew, referring to the destruction of Flight 655 as a 'tragic and regrettable accident'. It also placed considerable responsibility on Iran for allowing an airliner to operate in a 'war zone'.

Criticism, however, came from an unusual source, the captain of the *John Sides*. Writing in the magazine *Proceedings*, which is published by the US Naval Institute, Commander David R. Carlson claimed that the Airbus was shot down 'for no good reason'. He further wrote that the actions of the *Vincennes* 'appeared to be consistently aggressive', even before the day of the incident, and implied that the ship actually provoked the skirmish with the gunboats. The crew of the *John Sides* had also observed *EP-IBU* on radar, but Captain Carlson dismissed it as non-hostile. Iranian air traffic control units had been practising a 'red alert' procedure, wherein they were not to give clearances when military action posed a threat to civilian aircraft, but as they were not aware of any such activity, no alert had been issued on the day of the tragedy.

Citing a lack of such in the Gulf area, the ICAO recommended coordination between military and civil units in accordance with established procedures to prevent a recurrence of the tragedy.

The US Navy went further, suggesting that the ICAO change the commercial air route structure in this region and noting that an aircraft would only be considered as not a threat if it remained above 25,000 ft (*c.* 7,500 m).

In early 1996, the American government agreed to pay damages to the families of those who lost their lives in the downing of Flight 655, with awards reportedly totalling US $132 million.

Date: 19 October 1988 (*c.* 07:00)
Location: Near Ahmedabad, Gujarat, India
Operator: Indian Airlines
Aircraft type: Boeing Advanced 737-2A8 (*VT-EAH*)

Designated as Flight 113, the jetliner crashed during an attempted landing on Runway 23 at the city's airport, while on a domestic service originating at Bombay, killing 133 persons aboard, including the entire crew of six. Two passengers survived the accident with serious injuries.

Undershooting the runway, the 737 hit trees on the extended centreline of the runway but approximately 1.5 miles (2.5 km) short of its threshold, then slammed into a field and burned. At the time of the crash, the airport and the immediate vicinity were shrouded in haze, which reportedly reduced the visibility to only about 1 mile (1.5 km).

After levelling off briefly at the minimum descent altitude during the final phase of an approach using very-high-frequency omnidirectional range (VOR)

A crater and gutted houses mark the scene of devastation where a large portion of the Pan Am 747 fell in Lockerbie, Scotland. (© *Bryn Colton/ Assignments Photographers/CORBIS*)

procedures, with localiser guidance, the aircraft went below the normal glide path, with the deviation continuing until impact. It was considered possible that the crew had confused with the approach lights the lights at a construction site, and further suggested that the co-pilot's altimeter may have been in error by some 300 ft (100 m).

Date: 21 December 1988 (*c.* 19:00)
Location: Lockerbie, Dumfriesshire, Scotland
Operator: Pan American World Airways (US)
Aircraft type: Boeing 747-121 (*N739PA*)

It was doubtful that any of those boarding Flight 103 knew of the threat hanging over them. Only 16 days earlier an anonymous telephone message had been received at the US Embassy in Helsinki, Finland, warning that a sabotage attempt would be made some time over the succeeding two weeks against a Pan American aircraft flying between Frankfurt, (West) Germany, and the United States. Word of the threat was passed on from the US American embassies, presumably to give government employees a chance to make alternative travel arrangements if they chose, and to the carrier itself. But the general public was not made aware of the warning, on the rationale that such action would only serve to give the perpetrators publicity, and thus credibility, while potentially bringing financial harm to the airline industry. Besides, the threat had been dismissed as a hoax by some authorities.

A Boeing 727 was used on the initial leg of the transatlantic service. During a scheduled stop at London, the 49 continuing passengers were transferred to the larger 747 and joined by 194 others, making a total of 243 aboard the aircraft. In addition there were 16 crew members assigned to *N739PA*. Baggage, which had originally been screened at Frankfurt, was also transferred, without further scrutiny. Running almost half an hour late, the wide-bodied jetliner then took off from Heathrow Airport for New York City.

Not quite 40 minutes later, while cruising on an approximate heading of 320 degrees at flight level 310, in darkness and weather conditions consisting of broken clouds at lower altitudes and good visibility, the 747 disintegrated after a powerful explosion in a baggage container positioned on the left side of its forward cargo hold, scattering wreckage and victims over a wide area. Its wings and centre fuselage section then fell into the Sherwood Crescent residential district of Lockerbie, ploughing a crater some 150 ft (50 m) long and about 30 ft (10 m) deep and exploding in a ball of fire. All 259 persons aboard the aircraft and 11 on the ground perished. Five others were injured and more than 20 houses destroyed outright or damaged beyond repair.

A week after the disaster, the British Air Accidents Investigation Branch (AAIB) confirmed what many had already suspected, that Flight 103 had been sabotaged. The AAIB found evidence of a 'detonating high explosive', believed to have been the plastic Semtex. Some recovered items, identified as parts of baggage containers, exhibited damage consistent with such a blast. The bomb had apparently been hidden in the shell of a radio-cassette player that was being carried in a suitcase.

The direct effect of the explosion was to produce a high-intensity shock wave that ruptured the side and base of the container. As the wave expanded outward, it shattered and deformed the inner surface of the fuselage skin. A secondary high-pressure wave, which resulted somewhat from reflections off the baggage behind the immediate area of the blast but primarily from the chemical changes of the explosive itself after detonation, caused the skin to stretch and blister before bursting out in a star pattern, with fractures propagating in different directions.

The blast created a large hole, the approximate dimensions of which were 5 ft (1.5 m) wide and 15 ft (5 m) high, in the left belly area of the 747, forward of the wing, and also disrupted the main cabin floor. Within 3 seconds of the explosion, the forward fuselage section separated completely. Simultaneously, the rest of the jetliner entered a manoeuvre involving a marked nose-down and left-rolling attitude, which probably resulted from inputs applied to the control cables due to the disruption of the upper deck floor and main deck beams. The descent of the aircraft steepened throughout the break-up sequence, becoming vertical at a height of around 19,000 ft (5,800 m). All four engines broke away in the air, and the rear fuselage disintegrated during the vetical plunge.

A major proportion of the fuselage plummeted into a housing estate in the Rosebank Crescent district of Lockerbie, and the forward part, including the flight deck, was found in rolling terrain about 2.5 miles (4 km) east of the town. Carried by the westerly winds, lighter pieces of debris were scattered in two main paths stretching eastward past the town of Langholm and all the way to the eastern coast of England, a distance of some 80 miles (130 km).

A multinational inquiry into the bombing of Flight 103 was conducted, and a number of theories as to the motive were postulated. Given the most credibility initially was that the terrorist act had been carried out by the Popular Front for the Liberation of Palestine General Command, an organisation based in Syria with financial support from the Iranian government, in retaliation for the accidental downing of the Iran Air A300 by a US warship earlier in the year (see separate entry, 3 July 1988). Some 2½ years after the Lockerbie tragedy, a joint American/British investigation had shifted its focus towards Libya as perpetrator of the massacre, carried out to avenge the US bombing of its capital city in April 1986 (which was itself in retaliation for a terrorist attack).

In November 1991 the US Justice Department announced its indictment of two alleged Libyan intelligence agents wanted in connection with the Pan Am disaster. Reportedly they had planted the explosive device in a suitcase that was carried from Malta to Frankfurt on an Air Malta flight, then interlined on to 103. The primary clue in the criminal investigation was the minute portion of a timer, found embedded in a piece of the luggage container, which had been manufactured in Switzerland and sold to Libya in 1985. Were it not for the delayed departure from London, the 747 would have crashed in the Altantic Ocean, perhaps blotting out all evidence that it was destroyed by a bomb.

Pan American received harsh criticism for lax security in the wake of the tragedy, and both the airline and the US government for not announcing the prior warning. Slightly more than a year later a similar threat made against a Northwest Airlines transatlantic flight was made known to ticket-holders. Although the jetliner reached its intended destination without incident, this marked a change in American policy with regard to potential acts of terrorism.

For the families of the victims, some sense of justice was finally rendered in January 2001, when one of the two Libyan men, Ali Megrahi, was found guilty in connection with the crime by a panel of three Scottish judges and sentenced to life imprisonment. The second defendant, Lamen Khalifa, was acquitted by the same tribunal and returned to his country. The following year, Libya offered a payment of US $10 million compensation for each victim of the disaster.

One of the recommendations made by the AAIB in its investigative report was to explore ways of reducing the vulnerability of commercial aircraft to explosive damage.

Date: 8 February 1989 (13:08)
Location: Santa Maria, Azores, Portugal
Operator: Independent Air Inc (US)
Aircraft type: Boeing Advanced 707-331B (*N7231T*)

The jet airliner was on a transatlantic charter service, carrying as passengers mostly Italian tourists to the Dominican Republic from Bergamo, Italy, with an en route refuelling stop at Santa Maria Airport. During the intermediate phase of an attempted landing, the 707 slammed into a mountain about 5 miles (10 km) east of the airport, near the town of Santa Barbara. All 144 persons aboard, including a crew of seven Americans, perished in the disaster.

Cleared for descent to the minimum altitude of 3,000 ft (*c.* 1,000 m), the aircraft continued well below that height and ultimately crashed at an approximate height of 1,800 ft (550 m). Instrument meteorological conditions prevailed in the area at the time, with clouds obscuring the terrain.

The accident was attributed to a series of procedural errors by the flight crew, especially the first officer, and to a lesser degree the airport tower controller. The primary factor was a misunderstanding regarding the authorised descent altitude, largely attributable to a faulty communications technique on the part of the co-pilot.

During the final exchange between the tower and *N7231T*, and immediately after the crew reported passing through flight level 200, the controller radioed the aircraft 'You're cleared to . . . three thousand feet'. After a brief pause, she continued with runway instructions and a request to 'Report reaching three thousand feet'. Simultaneously, the first officer replied 'We're re-cleared to two thousand feet', and repeated the given above-sea-level pressure setting (QNH).

The overlapping of communications prevented the crew from receiving the last portion of the tower's instructions, and the controller from hearing the co-pilot's utterance of an incorrect altitude. Interestingly, one of the other two flight crewmen, believed to have been the captain, tried to correct the mistake, and was heard on the cockpit voice recorder (CVR) tape to say 'Make it three'. However, no further comments were made on this seemingly urgent matter.

Another serious error was the introduction of 2,000 ft into the aircraft's altitude alert by one of the pilots. This was contrary to the requirement that the setting be based on the minimum altitude published in the navigational chart, which in this case the crew apparently failed to consult. The ground-proximity warning system (GPWS) did activate 7 seconds before impact but, strangely, no verbal remarks were transcribed by the CVR and no corrective action was taken.

Initial impact was with a brick wall and trees on the west side of the mountain, at an indicated air speed of around 240 mph (390 kmh) and on a magnetic heading of 252 degrees, with the 707 apparently in a clean configuration. Several small post-crash fires were promptly extinguished.

Other contributing factors included the failure of the first officer to use standard terminology in his radio communications, an informal cockpit conversation, and the presence of what was believed to be a cabin attendant on the flight deck, whose voice could be heard on the CVR tape. This may have been an additional element of distraction and was in fact against prescribed policy when flying below 10,000 ft (*c.* 3,000 m).

Though within the limits of the airway, the jet had been operating somewhat off the authorised course, which was further to the north and passed over lower terrain. Such routeing was not uncommon for aircraft arriving at Santa Maria Airport, but combined with its unusually low altitude proved disastrous for *N7231T*.

Procedural errors were also ascribed to the tower controller, who was criticised in the investigative report for not requesting a read-back of her descent clearance and for giving insufficient attention to the 707. Perhaps even more significant was the relay to the crew of an incorrect QNH during the final radio exchange. The resulting mis-setting of the aircraft's altimeters placed the aircraft some 250 ft (75 m) lower than its indicated height. While this would not have been relevant had the 707 maintained 3,000 ft, its descent below the minimum altitude made the error the difference between a precariously low approach and a tragedy. The incorrect QNH may have been due to confusion by the controller with the indicated wind speed.

Among other recommendations, the Portuguese investigative commission responsible for investigating the accident proposed a revision of training programmes and manuals in order to ascertain that pilots have received practical experience in the execution of evasive manoeuvres following the activation of the GPWS. In the case of N7231T, insufficient crew training in this area was considered contributory to its crash.

Date: 7 June 1989 (c. 04:30)
Location: Near Paramaribo, Para, Suriname, South America
Operator: Surinnamse Luchtraart Maatschappij NC (Surinam Airways)
Aircraft type: McDonnell Douglas DC-8 Super 62 (N1809E)

Operating as Flight 764 on a non-stop transatlantic service from Amsterdam, The Netherlands, the jetliner crashed and burned while attempting to land at Zanderji International Airport, killing 178 persons aboard, including the entire crew of nine. Among the nine surviving passengers, only a child escaped injury.

The accident occurred in pre-dawn darkness and meteorological conditions consisting of fog and a low overcast, with layers of scattered stratus clouds down to about 400 ft (120 m). Visibility had dropped from approximately half a mile (0.8 km) some 20 minutes before the crash to around 1,500 ft (500 m) shortly afterwards. During the attempt to land on Runway 10, with its undercarriage down and flaps partially extended, the aircraft first struck a tree about 80 ft (25 m) above the ground some 2 miles (3 km) from its threshold and to the left of its extended centreline. Initial impact was with its No. 2 engine, and the DC-8 then slammed to earth and broke apart, coming to rest inverted.

According to an investigative commission, which received assistance from the US National Transportation Safety Board (NTSB), the accident resulted from a descent below the published

minimum altitude because of 'glaring carelessness and recklessness' on the part of the captain. Analysis of the cockpit voice recorder (CVR) tape revealed that while cleared for a very-high-frequency omnidirectional range/distance-measuring equipment (VOR/DME) approach, he had carried out the procedure in a different manner to that prescribed and had utilised information from the instrument landing system (ILS) despite knowledge that it was not fully operational, with an unreliable localiser. His statement that he had the field in sight and his repeated requests to increase the intensity of the runway lights further indicated his use of visual procedures during what should have been a non-precision instrument approach. The refraction of light through the fog could have created a distorted, inaccurate visual image and thus a false impression of the actual distance to the runway. Additionally, the weather was below the prescribed minima for a non-precision approach.

Nor did the pilot heed instrument indications of low altitude, including the activation of the ground-proximity warning system (GPWS). An attempt to level off at 200 ft (c. 60 m) was made, but the descent continued until impact. Coordination in the cockpit was found to be poor during the descent and approach phase, with the captain reacting slowly to accomplish certain required actions and executing a procedural turn at the wrong point. The first officer actually suggested to him that the aircraft had been too high despite a glide slope alarm that it was in fact too low.

Cited as an underlying factor in the accident was the failure of the airline's operational management to consider the relevant laws and the regulations contained in its operations manual pertaining to qualifications and proficiency when it recruited and employed the American flight crew from another agency. As he was six years past the normal retirement age for airline pilots (60), which violated Suriname aviation regulations, and because his last proficiency check flight had been given in a light, twin-engine aircraft instead of a DC-8, the captain did not have the authorisation to function in such a position.

The NTSB subsequently asked for tighter controls on agencies providing air carrier flight crews under contract. One of the other recommendations made in the investigative report was for improved

The main wreckage of the United jetliner came to rest in a cornfield after skidding off the runway. *(National Transportation Safety Board)*

emergency services at the Paramaribo airport with regard to both facilities and a plan of action.

Date: 19 July 1989 (16:00)
Location: Near Sioux City, Iowa, US
Operator: United Airlines (US)
Aircraft type: McDonnell Douglas DC-10 Series 10 (*N1819U*)

There was no hint of impending trouble as Flight 232 cruised at 37,000 ft (*c.* 11,300 m) over north-western Iowa, en route from Denver, Colorado, to Chicago, Illinois, the first segment of a domestic service with an ultimate destination of Philadelphia, Pennsylvania. Suddenly a noise resembling an explosion was heard and the wide-bodied jetliner shuddered.

In the cockpit, instrument indications confirmed the failure of the aircraft's No. 2 engine, mounted on the vertical stabiliser. But the situation was now more critical than the instruments could show, for the first-stage disc in the power plant had dis-

integrated. Fragments of the shattered rotor disc and fan that broke through the containment ring then severed the Nos 1 and 3 hydraulic systems lines, and forces associated with the engine failure fractured the No. 2 system; this loss of fluid soon rendered the flight control system of *N1819U* inoperative. This was first realised when the flight engineer observed the hydraulic pressure and quantity gauges reading zero. Use of the air-driven generator did not restore hydraulic pressure.

With no manual back-up available, the pilots had no way of operating the ailerons, elevators, rudder, flaps, slats or spoilers. Their only hope of controlling the DC-10 was the manipulation of thrust generated by the two remaining engines with the power levers. They were also faced with the uncontrolled pitch oscillation of the aircraft. Despite the best efforts of the crew, stabilised flight could not be maintained.

The transport, which had a tendency to turn right, made one wide circle and two similar ones before proceeding on a south-westerly heading in the direction of Sioux City. During this time the flight crew communicated with the carrier's maintenance facility, requesting any assistance it could give, and was also joined in the cockpit by a DC-10 training check pilot who happened to be aboard. Meanwhile, the cabin attendants prepared the other passengers for an emergency landing. The undercarriage was extended manually.

At the suggestion of the air traffic controller, the crew elected to continue on towards Sioux Gateway Airport and attempt to set the crippled jetliner down there. However, this would be no easy task; since it was not possible to control the phugoid motions with any measure of success, landing at a predetermined point and air speed would be a matter of chance.

The uncontrolled pitching and rolling continued until just before touchdown, when the aircraft's wing dropped, followed by its nose, the latter at an approximate height of 100 ft (30 m) above the ground. Striking the surface of Runway 22 slightly to the left of its centreline with its right wing-tip, followed by the right main gear, the DC-10 skidded to the right, rolled into an inverted position and burst into flames, breaking apart as it slid into a cornfield.

In the disaster, 112 persons aboard lost their lives, including a cabin attendant; one of the victims, a passenger, succumbed to his injuries about a month after the crash. Among the 184 survivors, who included the four men on the flight deck and the eight other members of the cabin crew, 171 persons were injured, many seriously; 13 passengers escaped unscathed. About a third of the fatalities resulted from smoke inhalation, the rest from trauma. The airport weather at the time, which was not considered a factor, consisted of a broken overcast and a visibility of 15 miles (c. 25 km). The wind was out of the north at around 15 knots.

Some three months after the accident the fan disc from the failed power plant was found in a rural area near Alta, Iowa, and about six months later farmers located the front flange of the engine's rotor shaft and a large section of the fan booster disc. Examination of the recovered parts revealed two principal fractures that caused approximately one-third of the rim to separate from the remainder of the disc.

It could be said that the failure sequence began 18 years earlier with the manufacture of the ingot from which the titanium disc would be forged by the Alcoa Company, and resulted from a defect associated with excessive nitrogen and/or oxygen introduced while the metal was still in a molten state. The anomaly led to a cavity that was most likely created during the final machining and/or shot peening process, with the latter probably causing minute cracking parallel to and just below the surface. This in turn initiated the fatigue cracking associated with stresses generated by the application of full engine thrust that grew to critical proportions culminating in the catastrophic break-up.

The disc components had undergone four inspections during their manufacture by General Electric Aircraft Engines (GEAE) before their installation in the CF6-6 power plant, including one using an ultrasonic method and one employing a two-step etching process. In its investigative report, the US National Transportation Safety Board (NTSB) concluded that the former technique may not have been capable of detecting the defect, and the latter was possibly improperly applied by GEAE personnel.

The accident itself was blamed by the NTSB on inadequate consideration given to human limitations in the inspection and quality control procedures used by United Airlines' engine overhaul facility, which also failed to detect the anomaly despite six detailed examinations in the service history of the disc. Faulty technique may have once again played a role in the omission, including one method that involved suspending a part by a cable (which could have obscured certain areas), as could the failure of the inspector to give the disc bore more than a cursory check, or a combination of these or other factors.

The manufacturer, operator and US Federal Aviation Administration (FAA) had considered the possibility of a total loss of the hydraulic-powered flight controls so remote as to negate any requirement for an appropriate procedure for dealing with such a situation. The NTSB concluded that the aircraft could not have been landed safely under the circumstances, and commended the actions of Capt Al Haynes and his fellow flight crewmen, who it said 'greatly exceeded reasonable expectations'. Cockpit resource management training, which the airline had implemented a decade earlier, proved useful in dealing with the emergency. Another fact that no doubt saved many lives was the time span of about 45 minutes between the power plant failure and the crash, which allowed agencies to prepare for what eventually happened.

Subsequent to the disaster, McDonnell Douglas introduced a modification in the hydraulic system of the DC-10 employing an electrically operated shut-off mechanism that would automatically activate if a drop in the hydraulic supply were to be detected, so a sufficient amount of the fluid would be retained to operate the empennage control surfaces.

The NTSB also called for child restraints in airline operations, noting that four infant passengers on Flight 232 were being carried on the laps of adults, one of whom was killed in the crash. However, the FAA later rejected this proposal, reasoning that families from lower-income levels could not afford the additional costs involved and would end up driving rather than flying to their destinations, resulting in even more children losing their lives in vehicular accidents.

Date: 27 July 1989 (*c.* 07:00)
Location: Near Tripoli, Libya
Operator: Korean Air (South Korea)
Aircraft type: McDonnell Douglas DC-10 Series 30 (*HL-7328*)

Designated as Flight 803, the wide-bodied jet airliner crashed and burned while attempting to land at the city's international airport, at the end of a service originating at Seoul, South Korea, which had last stopped at Jiddah, Saudi Arabia. The accident killed 72 of the 199 persons aboard the aircraft (68 passengers and four of its 18 crew members), plus six others on the ground. More than 100 persons suffered injuries and several houses and vehicles were destroyed.

The DC-10 had been on its final approach to Runway 27 when the accident occurred approximately 1 mile (1.5 km) from its threshold and some 500 ft (150 m) to one side of its extended centreline, and in conditions of heavy fog that had reduced the horizontal visibility to only about 150 ft (50 m). At the time, both the airport instrument landing system (ILS) and its very-high-frequency omnidirectional range (VOR) facility had been inoperative, information that was contained in a Notice to Airmen (NOTAM) released three months earlier.

Attributed to improper crew coordination likely to have been influenced by fatigue, the crash reportedly led to upgrades in the carrier's pilot training programme, including increased instrument flight time requirements and additional awareness in the use of the ground-proximity warning system (GPWS). The captain of *HL-7328* was later convicted of negligence in connection with the disaster and received a two-year prison sentence.

Date: 3 September 1989 (*c.* 19:00)
Location: Near Havana, Cuba
Operator: Empresa Consolidada Cubana de Aviacion (Cuba)
Aircraft type: Ilyushin Il-62MK (*CU-T1281*)

The jetliner, which was on a charter service to Milan, Italy, with an en route stop at Cologne, (West) Germany, crashed and exploded seconds after it had taken off from Jose Marti/Rancho Boyeros International Airport, serving Havana, killing all 126 persons aboard, including a crew of 11, and 45 on the ground. One of the passengers who was rescued alive succumbed to his injuries eight days later. About 50 others on the ground were injured and some three dozen houses destroyed. The accident occurred around dusk.

At the time of departure, heavy rain was falling and winds of around 20 knots were blowing across the runway, adversities associated with a nearby storm. The winds encountered by *CU-T1281* may have been even higher, perhaps in the vicinity of 25 to more than 40 knots.

Immediately after becoming airborne, the aircraft was caught in descending air currents, and the pilot retracted the flaps and apparently tried to accelerate while in a shallow climb, which would have reduced the possibility of gaining altitude. The jetliner reached an approximate height of 150 ft (50 m) before it started to descend on account of the down draughts and strong surface winds. It then struck navigational aerials and a hill, bounced and slammed into the populated area about 1 mile (1.5 km) beyond the end of the runway.

An investigative commission attributed the disaster to the captain's decision to fly after an abrupt deterioration in the meteorological conditions. Possessing nearly 30 years of flying experience and some 5,000 hours in the Il-62, he had actually been given an opportunity by the air traffic control unit to delay his departure, but elected to proceed over concern that the rain would get even heavier. He undoubtedly underestimated the risks of taking off and also misjudged the aircraft's bad weather performance.

Date: 19 September 1989 (*c.* 14:00)
Location: Near Sountellane, Zinder, Niger
Operator: Union de Transports Aeriens (UTA) (France)
Aircraft type: McDonnell Douglas DC-10 Series 30 (*N54629*)

All 170 persons aboard (156 passengers and a crew of 14) perished when the wide-bodied jet airliner, which was operating as Flight 772, crashed and burned some 400 miles (650 km) north-north-west of Ndjamena, Chad, from where it had taken off about 45 minutes earlier, bound for Paris, the final segment of a service that had originated at Brazzaville, in the Republic of the Congo.

The wreckage of the DC-10 was located the following morning, shortly after daybreak, strewn on a north-westerly heading across the Tenere Desert, over an approximate area 12 miles (20 km) long by 4.5 miles (7 km) wide. The cockpit and front fuselage section was found some 3 miles (5 km) south of where the main part of the transport, including two of its three engines, had fallen. About 90 per cent of the aircraft's structure was recovered,

and examination of the debris showed evidence of an internal explosion occurring before ground impact, including pieces of wood in which were embedded metal particles. A laboratory analysis found traces of the explosive penthrite, especially on a piece of luggage, confirming that *N54629* had been sabotaged. It was concluded that the blast had occurred in a cargo container positioned on the right side of the aircraft, and this had produced a high-pessure shock wave. After the explosion, the cockpit section had folded to the left, with aerodynamic forces subsequently leading to a more general break-up of the DC-10. The occupants not killed in the blast would have probably soon been rendered unconscious by the rapid depres-surisation of the cabin. According to the digital flight data recorder (DFDR) read-out, the jet had been in normal cruise at flight level 350 (*c.* 10,700 m) when the bomb detonated. The weather in the area was cloudy but otherwise good, with high cirrus at about 30,000 ft (10,000 m) over Lake Chad, located to the south of the crash site, and with scattered cumulus and altocumulus at lower altitudes. There was no evidence of significant turbulence or thunderstorm activity.

The container in which the blast occurred held only luggage loaded at Brazzaville, and there was no access to it during the short stopover at Ndjamena.

The front fuselage section of the UTA DC-10 rests in the Tenere Desert after an in-flight break-up attributed to a bomb blast. *(AP Images)*

For that reason, it was considered most likely that the explosive device had been put aboard at Maya Maya Airport, serving Brazzaville, where a French security expert found serious security lapses. The three most probable theories were that the suitcase containing the bomb had been placed on the luggage conveyor belt, to which there was easy access; it had been checked in under someone else's name, since passengers were not being matched to their luggage, or was brought aboard by one of the nine passengers who had disembarked at the Ndjamena airport, where security was also found to be inadequate.

In response to recommendations made in the investigative report on the catastrophe, security measures were later tightened at Brazzaville. In the specific case of Flight 772, six Libyans were convicted in absentia by a French court in 1999 for their involvement in the bombing, with plans established for compensation to be paid to the families of the victims by the Libyan government.

Date: 21 October 1989 (07:53)
Location: Near Tegucigalpa, Honduras
Operator: Transportes Aereos Nacionales SA (TAN Airlines) (Honduras)
Aircraft type: Boeing 727-224 (N88705)

Designated as Flight 414 and on a service originating at San José, Costa Rica, with an ultimate destination of Miami, Florida, US, the jetliner crashed some 7 miles (11 km) south of Toncontin Airport, serving Tegucigalpa, where it was scheduled to land, and 131 persons aboard (127 passengers and four crew members) were killed. Among the 15 survivors, who suffered varying degrees of injury, were the captain, first officer and two cabin attendants.

Cleared for a very-high-frequency omni-directional range/distance-measuring equipment (VOR/DME) instrument procedure approach to Runway 01, the aircraft was last reported descending out of 7,500 ft (c. 2,300 m). Less than a minute later, N88705 struck a mountain at an approximate elevation of 5,000 ft (1,500 m) and erupted into flames. The 727 had initially hit the ground with its starboard wing and while on a heading of around 18 degrees, and at the moment of impact its undercarriage was retracted and its flaps were near a setting of 25 degrees, but they

may have been in the process of moving. The airport weather about 5 minutes after the crash was overcast, with cumulus clouds at 1,800 ft (550 m) and 7/8 stratocumulus, the latter obscuring the terrain. Neither the wind, which at the surface was blowing at 12 knots from a direction of 130 degrees, nor the turbulence in the area was considered abnormal.

Despite the fact that the aircraft and most of its components were destroyed by fire, the investigative board found no evidence of in-flight malfunction in its engines or other vital systems, ruling that the accident apparently resulted from the failure of the crew to properly comply with the instrument descent procedure and the profile published in the approach chart with respect to the established altitudes and distances. As an indication of this error, at the point of impact, the 727 was more than 1,500 feet (500 m) below the minimum height over the VOR station that it had yet to reach. The board could not determine exactly why the flight had descended below the critical altitudes, but concluded that the adverse meteorological conditions must have contributed to the failure. The investigation also revealed that an improper flap configuration had aggravated the vertical descent rate of the aircraft. Additionally, the flight crew had not complied with rest requirements and may have been fatigued. There were no indications of any anomalies in the ground navigational aids.

Among the recommendations of the board were that the carrier scrutinise its training criteria with the intention of improving flight crew teamwork and discipline, one method being the use of cockpit resource management, and also that pilots receive proper training in the use of the ground-proximity warning system (GPWS), with instructions to take immediate action in response to warning alarms. Also recommended was greater attention to the scheduling of this flight, which could be very demanding for crews.

Date: 27 November 1989 (c. 07:20)
Location: Near Bogota, Colombia
Operator: Aerovias Nacionales de Colombia SA (AVIANCA)
Aircraft type: Boeing 727-21 (HK-1803)

Operating as Flight 203, the jetliner crashed about 5 minutes after taking off from the city's El Dorado

Airport, on a domestic service to Cali, Tolima. A total of 110 persons perished in the disaster, including a crew of six; three of the victims may have been passengers not on the manifest or persons killed on the ground. There were no survivors.

It was determined that a bomb apparently placed in a seat had detonated on the right-hand side of the aircraft's passenger cabin, with the blast rupturing and igniting the fuel/air vapours within the centre wing tank, and after the second explosion, the 727 fell in flames into hilly terrain.

The act of sabotage was believed to have been perpetrated by a drug cartel in order to eliminate police informants who were supposed to have been on the flight. A passenger who may have planted the device aboard the aircraft probably disembarked before its take-off.

The terrorist leader believed responsible for arranging the bombing was himself killed in a police raid three years later. A fellow conspirator was captured and brought to the US for trial, and in 1994 received a life prison term for this and other crimes.

THE 1990S

A s with the previous decade, aviation safety in the 1990s was marked by tremendous progress and some frustrating setbacks. During the first 11 months of 1995, for example, passenger fatalities remained remarkably low. But in December of that year there began a string of major disasters that would continue to the end of 1996. Among the more significant crashes during that time were the plunge of the ValuJet DC-9 into the Florida Everglades, the mid-air explosion involving TWA Flight 800 and the worst mid-air collision of the century, which occurred in India. Total fatalities in 1996 were in fact the third highest in the history of commercial aviation. However, with the airlines of the world carrying more than a billion passengers a year, the actual fatality rate remained very low.

After struggling through the 1994–96 period, which was marked by five major crashes claiming more than 500 lives, the US airline industry scored a major achievement in 1998 by not suffering a single fatality among the more than 600 million passengers it had carried during the year. Airlines flying under the British flag, which had always maintained an accident prevention record above the world average but had nevertheless lagged behind the safest nations, such as Australia and Scandinavia, firmly established themselves near the very top of the safety chart in January 1999, when they completed 10 years without a single fatal crash of a large passenger jet. Indeed, the airline safety records of these and such other noteworthy countries as Belgium, France, Germany, Japan, The Netherlands and Switzerland, had come to match or exceed those of any other form of mass public transport.

As it approached the new century and millennium, one of the most pressing issues facing commercial aviation became the complexity of new aircraft. Though greater automation can generally reduce pilot workload and decrease the chance of human error, it can aggravate the old 'man-versus-machine' controversy. This issue was brought to the forefront by accidents involving some highly automated Airbus and Boeing jetliners in the 1990s.

Another previously unknown threat realised during the decade was the phenomenon of airline pilots crashing passenger aircraft in acts of suicide. Three such incidents were suspected during the 1990s, the two most serious of which are discussed in this chapter.

Date: 25 January 1990 (c. 21:30)
Location: New York, New York, US
Operator: Aerovias Nacionales de Colombia SA (AVIANCA)
Aircraft type: Boeing Advanced 707-321B (*HK-2016*)

Among the aircraft 'stacked up' to await landing at John F. Kennedy International Airport (JFK) was Flight 52, on a service from Bogota and Medellin, Colombia. The delays were particularly long on this Thursday evening, with the deteriorating weather aggravating the usual heavy traffic.

During the 1 hour 17 minutes holding period, the 707 consumed its reserve fuel load, which was to have been used should the flight have been diverted to its alternative destination, designated as Boston, Massachusetts. When asked by the New York centre controller how much longer the aircraft could hold, its first officer responded 'about five minutes'. However, at that point such a diversion would have been out of the question. When asked to name its alternative, the co-pilot replied 'It was

The hulk of the AVIANCA 707 rests adjacent to a house after the fuel exhaustion accident that killed 73 aboard the aircraft. *(National Transportation Safety Board)*

Boston but we can't do it now . . . we run out of fuel.'

Finally *HK-2016* was cleared to proceed to JFK and, subsequently, for an instrument landing system (ILS) approach to Runway 22L. Beset by a strong headwind and wind shear, the aircraft descended below the glide slope during the attempted landing, forcing the crew to initiate a missed approach procedure. This action set the stage for the disaster, since the 707 did not have enough fuel to fly the circuit and complete a second approach.

Speaking in Spanish, the captain asked the first officer to inform the controller of the situation and the latter transmitted a message that included the advisory 'we're running out of fuel, sir'. Moments later the co-pilot again advised the controller, when

asked to ascend to a higher altitude, 'Negative, sir, we just running out of fuel'.

Only a few minutes afterwards the aircraft's No. 4 power plant failed from fuel exhaustion, followed in rapid succession by the other three engines. Subsequently, the jetliner crashed on a wooded hillside in the village of Cove Neck, located on the north side of Long Island some 15 miles (25 km) north of the airport, and while on a southerly heading. The accident killed 73 of the 158 persons aboard the 707 (65 passengers and eight members of its crew). All of the survivors, who included a cabin attendant, were injured, many seriously.

The aircraft's fuselage broke into three main sections on impact, although there was no post-crash fire. The rapid response by fire and rescue personnel, which included the use of helicopters to evacuate many of the survivors, probably kept the death toll down. It was dark at the time of the crash, and the airport weather consisted of fog, an overcast down to 300 ft (*c*. 100 m) and a visibility of approximately 1 mile (1.5 m).

In its investigative report, the US National Transportation Safety Board (NTSB) attributed the disaster to the failure of the AVIANCA flight crew to manage the aircraft's fuel load and to communicate the criticality of the situation to ground controllers.

The NTSB also revealed inadequacies in the carrier's dispatching of Flight 52 and in the planning by its crew. With regard to the former, it was learned that the dispatch service did not provide the pilots with the latest meteorological forecast for the New York area, nor with information about possible alternative airports. Among other deficiencies, the flight plan did not take into consideration air traffic control (ATC) or weather delays. Also there were no communications between *HK-2016* and the company's dispatcher, which normally take place in order to keep the crew informed on such issues as alternative landing sites and the amount of fuel needed to reach them.

The board concluded that the actions of ATC personnel were reasonable despite a lack of significance given to the co-pilot's request for 'priority' in landing. Under the circumstances the crew should have taken further steps to convey the sense of urgency of the situation. This was evident in the failure of the first officer to use the word 'emergency', as requested by the captain, when informing the JFK tower controller that the 707 was nearly out of fuel. (The New York centre controller later said that he did not hear a portion of the radio transmission from the flight that the aircraft could no longer reach its alternative airport and therefore did not notify the approach controller of such.)

Of course, had the crew been able to complete the first landing attempt successfully, the crash would have been averted. The NTSB believed that the approach had been made without the use of a properly functioning flight director, which would have added to the difficulties in maintaining the glide slope properly. Problems had also been reported with the aircraft's autopilot, leading to speculation by the NTSB that the crew may have flown manually on the long trip from Colombia.

Had this been the case, it could have added to the stress and fatigue generated by the other factors, including the concern about the fuel situation, and contributed to the unstabilised approach that ended in the overshoot manoeuvre.

The accident report criticised the air traffic management programme used at JFK by the US Federal Aviation Administration (FAA), which was blamed for the excessive landing delays.

Board member Jim Burnett dissented in the vote adopting the report, opting to place more responsibility for the disaster on inadequate ATC services, including their failure to provide the Colombian crew with the latest wind shear information. Similar criticism was expressed by Mayor Jorge Enrique Leal, chief of the Colombian Administrative Department of Civil Aeronautics' Flight Safety Division, who suggested improvements in the ATC system so as to better inform flight crews of anticipated delays. He further wrote that acceptance of the flight by New York approach control could have misled the crew of *HK-2016* into believing that clearance to land was imminent.

Date: 14 February 1990 (*c*. 13:00)
Location: Bangalore, Karnataka, India
Operator: Indian Airlines
Aircraft type: Airbus Industrie A320-231 (*VT-EPN*)

Designated as Flight 605 and on a domestic service from Bombay, the jetliner crashed while attempting to land at Bangalore Airport, killing 92 of the 146 persons aboard, including both pilots and three of its five cabin attendants. Most of the survivors were injured, 21 passengers and one crew member seriously.

During a combination visual/non-precision instrument approach to Runway 09, the aircraft was descending with its flight management and guidance system (FMGS) in the vertical speed mode, which is correct for landing, and with the autopilot disconnected. Inexplicably, the FMGS went into the open descent mode, automatically reducing engine power to the flight idle position and, in turn, resulting in an increased descent rate. Ultimately, and with its flaps and slats fully deployed, the twin-jet transport touched down on its lowered main undercarriage on a golf course some 2,300 ft (700 m) from the end of the runway and approximately 200 ft (60 m) to the right of its extended centreline.

The burned-out wreckage of the Indian Airlines Airbus A320 lies on flat terrain after the crash that occurred near Bangalore Airport. *(AP Images)*

Rolling along the ground for about 80 ft (25 m), it then became airborne again and finally slammed back to earth, and after its gear and both power plants were sheared off, the aircraft ploughed into an embankment, broke apart and burned. Most of the fatalities were attributed to the post-impact fire. The majority of the survivors had been seated in the rear cabin area. The weather conditions at the time were good, and about half an hour before the accident consisted of a broken overcast at 2,000 ft (600 m), with a visibility of around 5 miles (10 km) and variable winds of 5 knots.

The disaster was attributed to the failure of the flight crew to realise the gravity of the situation, even though they must have known the flight management and guidance computer (FMGC) had been in the incorrect mode. About 35 seconds before the initial impact, the A320 descended below the proper glide path and its velocity began to fall below the target speed. From that point there was no indication that the pilots monitored their air speed or altitude. Finally, and as transcribed on the cockpit voice recorder (CVR) tape, the captain was heard to say, 'Hey, we are going down!' The CVR had also recorded the synthetic voice of the radio altimeter call out above-ground altitudes in 100-ft increments between 400 and 100 ft

(120–30 m) and at 50 ft (15 m), which neither crewman apparently heard. At an approximate height of 130 ft (40 m) above the ground, the pilot apparently pulled back on his control stick in an attempt to arrest the high sink rate, and the increased angle of attack resulting from this action triggered the aircraft's 'Alpha Floor' protection system, designed to automatically increase thrust to take-off power. But due to the computer delay of approximately 1 second in the 'Alpha' system, of which the crew of *VT-EPN* were apparently unaware, the application of thrust came too late to prevent the crash.

The investigative report noted that while granting him type endorsement on the A320, the French Direction Generale de l'Aviation Civile (DGCA) had advised Indian Airlines that the pilot of the accident aircraft be 'positively monitored' in the operation of the FMGS and in the area of single-engine handling procedures and non-precision landings. Based on his overall performance during his training at Toulouse, France, the advisory required improvement on his part in these areas. The carrier intimated that this would be done during route checks, as was the case at the time of the crash, with his supervisory pilot serving as the first officer of *VT-EPN*.

Since neither the altitude selection nor the programming of the flight control unit (FCU) was among the parameters transcribed by the aircraft's digital flight data recorder (DFDR), the reason for the engagement of the FMGC into the open descent mode could not be determined. According to a source outside of the official inquiry, engagement occurred immediately after the crew had apparently selected a reference height, probably the minimum descent altitude of about 3,300 ft (1,005 m), which was slightly below the aircraft's actual height at the time.

It was concluded that the accident could have been prevented had the approach been continued with the FMGC in the vertical speed mode, if the flight directors had been switched off at the appropriate time, or had a member of the crew manually advanced the thrust levers to the take-off/go-around position up until 9 seconds before the initial impact. The Indian court of inquiry also observed that when the auto-thrust system was engaged, there would be no warning if engine power were to be reduced to idle for whatever reason during landing approach. Furthermore, the engine controls with which the A320 was equipped had removed thrust lever action when auto-thrust had been engaged, and the only way of determining the actual power setting was through the electronic centralised aircraft monitor (ECAM) display. As evidence that awareness of proper power settings among A320 flight crews may have been deficient, the report noted that even an Airbus Industrie test pilot was not aware of the power required during approach at a rate of descent of 1,000 ft/min (300 m/min).

An Indian government committee set up in the wake of the crash later accused Indian Airlines of rushing the A320 into operation when it was 'ill-equipped to handle this sophisticated aircraft in such large numbers'. The committee said that the company apparently did not appreciate the planning required in terms of training its pilots and engineering staff and arranging a suitable infrastructure to support the fleet. It also criticised Aeroformation, the Airbus training centre in France, for not meeting the specific requirements of the carrier and the environment in which the aircraft would be operating in India, which included limited navigational and landing aids. It was further noted in the accident report that the grave consequences of open descent mode engagement, either through inadvertent action by a pilot or due to a system malfunction, had not been part of the simulator training, indicating that such an occurrence could not have been visualised.

The grounding of Indian Airlines' entire A320 fleet only days after the crash was not lifted until late in the year, after the carrier had begun implementing recommendations of the afore-mentioned committee. With regard to this particular accident, the absence of a radio link with the control tower, which increased the response time of emergency personnel, and a poorly maintained airport road and a locked security gate, both of which hampered the ability of fire/rescue vehicles to reach the crash scene, probably contributed to the high death toll, and recommendations for improvements in these areas were also made in the report.

Date: 2 October 1990 (*c.* 09:15)
Location Near Canton, Kwangtung, China
First aircraft
Operator: Xiamen Airlines (China)
Type: Boeing Advanced 737-247 (*B-2510*)
Second aircraft
Operator: China Southern Airlines
Type: Boeing 757-21B (*B-2812*)
Third aircraft
Operator: China Southwest Airlines
Type: Boeing Advanced 707-3J6B (*B-2402*)

Operating as Flight 8301, the 737 was on a domestic service to Canton from Xiamen, Fujian, when it was hijacked by a young man who claimed to have explosives strapped to his body. He reportedly ordered the flight crew out of the cockpit with the exception of the pilot and demanded to be taken to Taiwan.

When the aircraft tried to land at Baiyun Airport, serving Canton, shouts and the sounds of a struggle were heard coming from the cockpit just before touchdown. Following a hard landing, the 737 veered off the runway and clipped the forward fuselage of the 707, which was parked, then the left wing and top fuselage of the 757, which was waiting to take off on a scheduled domestic service to Shanghai, Jiangsu. After hitting the latter, the Xiamen transport skidded to a stop upside-down in a grassy area.

A total of 132 persons were killed in the crash, all but 20 of the 104 aboard *B-2510* (77 passengers, including the hijacker, and seven members of its crew of nine), 47 of the 118 aboard *B-2182*, and the driver of an airport service vehicle. About 50 others suffered injuries, including the pilot (and sole occupant) of *B-2402*. Of the three jetliners involved, the 737 and 757 were destroyed by impact and fire, while the 707 sustained collision damage.

Reportedly, the air pirate had refused an offer by the Xiamen Airlines' captain to fly to Hong Kong, and the dispute continued until the aircraft's fuel supply was nearly exhausted, necessitating the landing.

Chinese authorities were said to have ordered managerial restructuring in the wake of the disaster, admitting procedural deficiencies that allowed the 757 to taxi in the midst of a hijacking.

Date: 2 October 1990 (time unknown)
Location: Near Kuwait City, Kuwait
Operator: Iraqi Airways
Aircraft type: Ilyushin Il-76

Approximately 130 persons were killed when the jet transport was hit by a surface-to-air missile fired by Kuwaiti resistance fighters shortly after it had taken off, then crashed. There were no survivors. The commercial aircraft was believed to have been carrying military personnel, its downing occurring during the occupation of Kuwait by Iraqi forces.

The China Southern Airlines Boeing 757 was broken in two after being struck by the hijacked Xiamen Boeing 737 at Canton airport. *(CORBIS)*

A Lauda Air Boeing 767-3Z9ER, sister to the aircraft that crashed in the Thai jungle after the uncommanded deployment of its left thrust reverser on 26 May 1991. *(Boeing)*

Date: 26 May 1991 (*c.* 23:15)
Location: Near Ban Thap Phung, Thailand
Operator: Lauda Air Luftfahrt Aktiengesellschaft (Austria)
Aircraft type: Boeing 767-3Z9ER (*OE-LAV*)

All 223 persons aboard (213 passengers and a crew of 10) perished when the wide-bodied jet airliner, designated as Flight 004, crashed and burned in a mountainous, jungle region some 110 miles (175 km) north-west of Bangkok, about 15 minutes after it had taken off from the city's Don Muang Airport, a scheduled stop during a service originating at Hong Kong, with an ultimate destination of Vienna, Austria.

Climbing in darkness to flight level 310, the aircraft had been proceeding at around 80 per cent the speed of sound and had reached an approximate height of 25,000 ft (7,500 m) before it plummeted to earth in flames. It was determined conclusively that extensive structural failure had occurred before its impact with the ground, and due to the relatively small wreckage 'scatter' area, the break-up must have taken place at a much lower altitude, i.e. probably under 10,000 ft (3,000 m), and with the 767 in a steep angle of descent. The accident occurred in visual meteorological conditions, with broken cumulus and stratocumulus clouds at 2,000 ft and 4,000 ft (600 m and 1,200 m), respectively, high cirrus and a slight breeze. No thunderstorm activity or precipitation was reported in the immediate area of the crash.

Prolonged exposure to the post-impact fire had rendered the digital flight data recorder (DFDR) tape unusable. However, investigation revealed the apparent unwanted deployment of the aircraft's left power plant thrust reverser as the cause of the disaster. This was confirmed by an analysis of the cockpit voice recorder (CVR) tape, on which the first officer was heard to say, 'reverser's deployed', which was followed by sounds similar to the airframe shuddering. Through physical examination of the wreckage, both reverser sleeves were found in the fully deployed position. An analysis of data developed from the non-volatile computer memory within the aircraft's electronic engine control (EEC) system indicated that deployment occurred at climb power, after which engine thrust was automatically throttled back to idle, and that within 10 seconds of these two events the fuel cut-off was selected by the crew. It further showed that before the crash an anomaly associated with the deployment had occurred between the channel 'A' and 'B' reverser sleeve position signals. However, since no specific component malfunction was identified, the cause of the uncommanded reverser deployment that led to the loss of control could not be positively established, and there was no evidence of either intentional or unintentional deployment by the crew. The absence of explosive residue or shrapnel in the wreckage allayed early concerns of hostile action, either internally with a bomb or through some outside attack on the aircraft.

On the 767 equipped with twin Pratt & Whitney PW4000 power plants, an electro-hydraulic thrust reverse system is used to redirect engine fan bypass airflow by means of left- and right-hand translating fan sleeves containing blocker doors. Normal operation of the reversers requires that the aircraft must be on the ground to close the air/ground switch when the main undercarriage moves out of its tilted position. Several levels of protection had been incorporated into the system to prevent uncommanded in-flight deployment. Nevertheless, the investigation of this accident disclosed that if certain anomalies existed in the circuitry of the auto-restow system, which was designed to provide for automatic restowing after sensing that the thrust reverser cowls are out of agreement with the

commanded position, the protection of these features could be circumvented. It was concluded that an auto-restow command in conjunction with an electrical system malfunction, such as a short circuit in the solenoid operating the directional control (DCV) pilot valve, could cause the reverser cowls to deploy. Contamination of the DCV could also result in an increase in pressure, leading to uncommanded deployment if the hydraulic isolation valve (HIV) was open to supply hydraulic pressure. Other potential system failures included vibration and the effects of internal leakage in the actuators (in this scenario, such leakage across the actuator piston was sufficient to deploy the actuators when the piston head seal and its bronze cap were missing and the HIV was open). The investigative report noted that contamination of the DCV, which could produce internal blockage, was a latent condition and might not have been detected until it began to affect thrust reverser operation. However, the DCV was not found until nine months after the crash, and had been tampered with, preventing an objective examination.

Playback of the CVR tape revealed that nearly 10 minutes before the actual deployment, the crew began to discuss the illumination of an instrument caution light, later determined to be the Reverser Isolation Valve (REV ISLN) indication, with the captain at one point stating, 'That keeps coming on'. (This indication appears when a fault has been detected in the reverser system, specifically, a disagreement between the HIV and the position of the associated reverser lever, or an anomaly in the air/ground mechanism.) It was also impossible they had been observing the cycling of the auto-restow system. No corrective actions were taken, or were required, although the pilots did consult the Quick Reference Handbook.

As certified, the application of reverse thrust on a 767 while in the air should not have jeopardised the flight. However, previous flight tests simulating such a condition had been conducted at relatively low air speeds, and with the engine at idle thrust when the reverser was deployed. It was assumed that at higher speeds there would be greater control surface authority, which would help maintain control effectiveness in the event of uncommanded deployment. This principle did not take into account the effects of reduced lift caused by the combination of the reverser plume and/or engine inlet spillage. Validation of this faulty assumption had come through cases of the in-flight application of reverse thrust in other jet transports, including four-engine Boeing 707 and 747 and three-engine DC-10 aircraft. However, differences in wing/engine geometry and reverser design were among the factors affecting aircraft experiencing reverse thrust. Evidence suggested that the farther the power plant is located from the wing, the less likely the reverse thrust plume would cause significant airflow disruption. And on jets with more than two engines, each power plant produces a smaller percentage of the total thrust, resulting in less thrust/drag asymmetry.

Wind tunnel tests and simulations indicated that the initial aerodynamic effects of the reverse thrust plume resulted in a 25 per cent loss of lift across the corresponding wing, which would have decreased as the engine spooled down to idle thrust. The result would be a rolling moment that would have to be promptly offset by coordinated flight control inputs, and a yawing effect that would require correction through rudder action. If corrective action were to be delayed, the roll and bank angle would increase, making recovery more difficult and less likely. (In a simulator, the chief 767 test pilot was unable to make a successful recover if corrective action were not taken within about 5 seconds of the initial upset.) Normal pilot training does not account for such a situation; furthermore, the fact that it was dark at the time of the accident, with few visible landmarks and possibly an indistinguishable horizon, would have adversely affected the attempted recovery from an unusual flight attitude. For these reasons, recovery by an unsuspecting flight crew would probably not have been possible.

The actions of this particular crew could not be assessed due to the destruction of the DFDR. Nor could the maximum velocity attained by OE-LAV during its uncontrolled descent be determined, but it was probably around 90 per cent the speed of sound, which was in excess of the aircraft's operating envelope. High structural loading probably occurred as the pilots tried to regain control, induced by strong control inputs. The parts of the aircraft that initially broke off from the effects of buffeting appear to have been pieces of the rudder and left elevator, which were followed by the separation of the starboard horizontal stabiliser, then the port horizontal and the entire vertical stabiliser. The excessive negative loading produced by the loss of the tail fins would have resulted in a sharp nose-over of the aircraft, which apparently led to downward wing failure. The next event in the sequence was the break-up of the fuselage, which must have occurred in a matter of seconds. Rupture of the fuel tanks and ignition of their contents accounted for the fire that was observed by eyewitnesses as the 767 plunged to earth.

An airworthiness directive (AD) issued by the US Federal Aviation Administration (FAA) about three months after the accident required the deactivation of electrically controlled reversers used on every 767 fitted with PW4000 engines. Results of inspections prompted by the AD showed that nearly half of the reversers checked had out-of-adjustment auto-restow position sensors.

No specific airline maintenance practice was identified as a factor in the crash, even though, over the previous nine months, 13 actions had been logged on the left engine thrust reverser of OE-LAV. Lauda Air personnel had been following proper procedures to resolve the recurring fault messages in the left engine propulsion interface monitoring unit (PIMU), which usually involved removing and replacing valves or actuators and making adjustments in the system. (Only the day before the crash, in Vienna, the reverser locking actuator had been replaced.) Although their continued troubleshooting efforts were unsuccessful, it was noted in the report that they had never sought assistance from the manufacturer.

As a result of testing and re-evaluation conducted in the wake of this disaster, Boeing proposed thrust reverser system design changes that were later mandated by a subsequent directive issued by the FAA concerning every PW4000-powered 767. These changes included replacement of the solenoid-type HIV with one operated by a motor; isolation and protective shielding of electric wiring from the electronics bay and flight deck to the engine strut, and the addition of a reverser system test as well as a system maintenance indicator unit and a thrust reverser deployment switch in the cockpit. These design changes, which had been completed by the following February, were to prevent in-flight deployment even after multiple failures. The FAA action also affected Boeing 747-400 and 757 jetliners using certain kings of power plants.

Date: 11 July 1991 (*c*. 08:40)
Location: Near Jiddah, Saudi Arabia
Operator: Nolisair International Inc (Nationair
Canada)
Aircraft type: McDonnell Douglas DC-8 Super 61
(*C-GMXQ*)

The jetliner had been leased to Nigeria Airways and
sub-leased to Holdtrade Services, another Nigerian
firm, and was on a charter service to Sokoto,
Nigeria. Its passengers were all Muslim pilgrims.

About 2 minutes after its departure from King
Abdulaziz International Airport, serving Jiddah, the
pilot reported a pressurisation problem, then
radioed that the aircraft was losing hydraulics and
would need to return. Turning back, the DC-8
proceeded southward in the airport circuit so it
could land in the same direction that it took off.
Control problems that made manoeuvring difficult
were reported during this time.

Cleared for a landing on any of the three parallel
runways, all numbered 34, *C-GMXQ* was observed by
one ground witness to descend in a nose-down
attitude, trailing smoke as it flew towards the north.
Its undercarriage extended, the jetliner moments
later plunged into the desert at an approximate speed
of 275 mph (440 kmh), some 2 miles (3 km) short of
the centre runway and around 150 ft (50 m) to the
right of its extended centreline, disintegrating in a
fiery explosion on impact. All 261 persons aboard,
including 14 crew members (all Canadians except for
one Frenchman), perished in the disaster. The
weather at the time was cloudless, with a visibility of
more than 5 miles (10 km).

Bodies of many victims, some of which had
suffered burns, were located along the flight path,
the first one about 11 miles (18 km) from the crash
site. Pieces of cabin furnishings were also found a
distance from the main wreckage.

Investigation confirmed that during the taxi to
the runway, the transfer of the load from the No. 2
tyre, which was not properly inflated, had caused
over-deflection, overheating and weakening of the
No. 1, also located on the left main gear, and both
then failed during the take-off ground run. Friction
generated when the No. 2 wheel stopped rotating,
for undetermined reasons, was sufficient to ignite
rubber remnants, which then came in close
proximity to hydraulic and electrical system
components when the undercarriage was retracted.

The remains of the Canadian Super DC-8 are strewn across the Saudi Arabian desert after the crash that claimed
261 lives. *(AP Images)*

Shown in Air Inter's earlier livery, this Airbus Industrie A320-111 is the type of aircraft that crashed near Strasbourg, France. *(Airbus Industrie)*

Subsequently, the hydraulic system ceased to function. Kerosene was probably introduced following a burn-through of the centre fuel tank, and the blaze ultimately disabled the aircraft's control systems. The fire had also consumed the cabin floor, which collapsed when the gear was re-extended, sending numerous occupants in their seats tumbling about 2,000 feet (600 m) to the ground. Witness statements seemed to confirm an in-flight break-up of the aircraft shortly before ground impact.

Low tyre pressures had been observed and measured on *C-GMXQ* four days before the accident. The lead mechanic had tried to rectify the problem, but the project manager allowed the aircraft to depart in this unairworthy condition. The cockpit voice recorder (CVR) tape indicated that the flight crew were aware of something amiss, with the first officer heard to ask during the take-off run 'We got a flat tyre, you figure?'. Given the information available and his training, which did not include procedures for tyre and wheel failures, the captain was not faulted for continuing the take-off.

Among other recommendations made in the Saudi Arabian investigative report on this accident were that commercial aircraft be equipped with wheel well fire detection and suppression systems

and that aviation regulatory authorities ensure adequate dissemination of information and proper crew training with regard to tyre failures during and after take-off as well as quality in all forms of maintenance work.

Date: 20 January 1992 (*c.* 19:20)
Location: Near Barr, Alsace, France
Operator: Air Inter (France)
Aircraft type: Airbus Industrie A320-111 (*F-GGED*)

Operating as Flight 148 and on a domestic service from Lyon, the jet airliner crashed and burned while attempting to land at Entzheim Airport, serving Strasbourg. The accident killed 87 persons aboard the aircraft, including five crew members; eight passengers and a cabin attendant, all but one of whom had been seated in the rear of the cabin, survived with various injuries.

Its undercarriage down, flaps set at 15 degrees and speed brakes deployed, the twin-engine jet ploughed into a wooded ridge near Mont Ste Odile during the very-high-frequency omnidirectional range/distance-measuring equipment (VOR/DME) instrument procedure approach to Runway 05. Impact occurred at an approximate elevation of

2,600 ft (800 m), some 10 miles (15 km) south-west of the airport and about half a mile (0.8 km) to the left of the runway axis, as the A320 was completing a left turn on to the final approach leg. It was dark at the time, and the local meteo-rological conditions consisted of a low overcast, with 3/8 stratocumulus clouds at around 1,000 ft (300 m) and 6/8 at approximately 2,500 ft (750 m), and a visibility of about 10 miles (15 km) in a freezing drizzle. The wind was out of the north-east, gusting up to 35 knots.

An investigation conducted by a 10-committee commission failed to determine the exact sequence of events leading up to the crash, but the primary factor was believed to have been improper use of the aircraft's flight control unit (FCU) due to selection of the wrong mode or the confusion between two different modes. This resulted in an excessive descent rate that was not stopped. With regard to the second theory, the FCU may have been inadvertently set in the heading/vertical speed instead of the track/flight path mode, with the crew then dialling '33' into the computer system, believing that they were putting in a 3.3-degree slope command (which is normally used in a VOR/DME approach at this airport). This would have led to a descent rate of 3,300 ft/minutes (1,005 m/min), or roughly that of the jet in the final moments before impact. The possibility of a malfunction in the computer system was not ruled out, but considered highly unlikely.

It could not be established why the rapid descent, more than four times the norm, was not detected, but this may have been related to the smooth flying qualities of the A320 noted by pilots.

Human factors that were identified as con-tributing to the accident were minor faults in the ground navigational aids and runway lighting; the comparative inexperience in the A320 by both the captain and first officer; poor crew coordination and cross-checking associated with ineffective intra-cockpit communications; and the pilots' involve-ment in a non-precision approach in less than ideal weather after initial plans for an instrument landing system (ILS) procedure. It was noted in the accident report that the crew had relaxed their attention during the radar guidance portion of the approach, leaving the 'vertical navigation' entirely to the autopilot. This behaviour could have been influenced by the short-haul routine of Air Inter's operations, wherein the many landings are usually carried out automatically.

Still another factor could have been the 'tense' working environment related to the controversy over giving the A320 a two- rather than three-member flight crew, which had reached the point whereby the carrier was controlling and restricting information released on minor technical difficulties with the transport.

A number of recommendations were made in the report, mostly pertaining to crew training and performance relative to the use of advanced technology aircraft.

Subsequent to this accident, the French Transport Ministry enacted a requirement that all commercial aircraft falling under its jurisdiction be fitted with a ground-proximity warning system (GPWS); under the voluntary arrangement existing before the disaster, the Air Inter fleet was not so equipped due to concern over false alarms. Changes were also recommended pertaining to the use of emergency locator beacons installed on aircraft; the post-crash failure of the unit installed on F-GGED hampered rescue workers in finding the accident site and probably cost the lives of half a dozen victims who had survived the impact.

Airbus Industrie had already introduced a modification in the FCU featuring a different instrument display designed to prevent confusion between the two modes, with plans to retrofit all the aircraft already in service.

Date: 31 July 1992 (12:45)
Location: Near Kistung Palung, Nepal
Operator: Thai Airways International
Aircraft type: Airbus Industrie A310-304 (*HS-TID*)

All 113 persons aboard (99 passengers and 14 crew members) perished when the wide-bodied, twin-engine jetliner, designated as Flight 311, crashed about 25 miles (40 km) north-north-east of Tribhuvan International Airport, serving Kathmandu, where it was to have landed at the end of a service from Bangkok, Thailand. Its wreckage was finally located two days later after a determination that the disaster had not occurred, as first thought, south of the airport.

The sequence of events leading up to the accident began after the aircraft had started its approach to Runway 02, using the very-high-

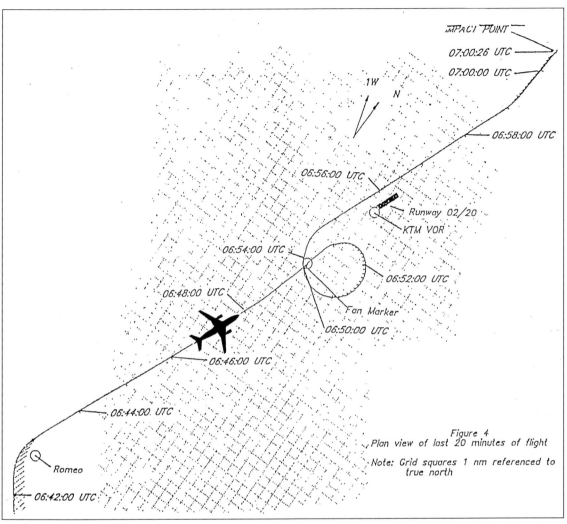

The track of the Thai Airways International A310, showing the 360-degree turn that led to an incorrect heading and the subsequent crash of the jetliner. *(Thai Department of Aviation)*

frequency omnidirectional range/distance-measuring equipment (VOR/DME) non-precision instrument technique, known at this airport as the 'Sierra' procedure. At a point about 25 miles (40 km) south of the airport, the crew experienced difficulty extending the flaps to the 15-degree position, prompting the captain to ask initially for clearance to proceed to Calcutta, India. The fault was rectified by retracting and then re-selecting the flaps. However, the A310 was by then too high and too near the airport to continue a straight-in approach, and so the crew abandoned the landing attempt completely, requesting clearance to proceed southward towards the Romeo navigational fix, a point located 41 nautical miles (75 km) out on the

202-degree radial, to begin another approach using the same procedure. After four requests to the Kathmandu tower controller for a left turn had gone unheeded, the aircraft finally turned right from its north-north-easterly heading and commenced a climb from 10,500 ft (3,200 m) to flight level (FL) 180.

Upon learning that it had begun to ascend, the tower controller instructed *HS-TID* to maintain 11,500 ft (3,500 m), due to the presence of a Royal Nepal Airlines aircraft inbound to Kathmandu. Instead of proceeding south, however, the A310 completed a 360-degree turn while descending from 14,000 ft (4,300 m) and continued on the same heading as its original approach course, but slightly to the left of the prescribed airway, passing through the 291-degree radial that was part of the missed approach procedure. Now approximately abeam of the airport, the captain reported correctly as being on a heading of 25 degrees and again asked to proceed back to the same fix. When he later reported 'We are five DME from Kathmandu', the aircraft was in fact north of the airport. It was determined from the cockpit voice recorder (CVR) tape that around this time the crew experienced difficulties when inserting the Romeo fix and other navigational information into the aircraft's flight management system (FMS), with the captain radioing, 'We got some technical problem concerned with the flight'.

Only about 5 minutes later, and after its course had turned slightly to the left to a heading of 5 degrees, the A310 struck the south-east ridge of a mountain in Langtang National Park on the 015-degree radial. Impact was at the approximate altitude to which it had been assigned, or some 4,500 ft (1,400 m) below the crest of the ridge, at a ground speed calculated to have been approximately 350 mph (560 kmh), upon which the cleanly configured aircraft disintegrated. Despite the apparent explosion occurring when the jetliner struck the deep rock face of the mountain, there was no major post-crash fire. The airport weather about 10 minutes before the accident was overcast, with broken cumulus clouds at 2,000 ft (600 m) above the ground, 4/8 stratocumulus at 3,000 ft (1,000 m) and high, broken altostratus, a visibility of 3 miles (5 km) in rain showers and a 5-knot wind from a south-easterly direction, while at the crash site, the meteorological conditions were also described as 'cloudy, with extensive rain'. Although the visibility at the airport had been below the operator's limit when the crew began the approach, continuing it until reaching the outer marker would have been permitted by the company flight operating manual.

The disaster apparently occurred through the pilots' mismanagement of their flight path, which resulted in the Airbus proceeding at too low a height, where the minimum altitude was FL 210, coupled with ineffective radio communications between them and the ground controllers, and in cockpit crew coordination with regard to their flight navigational duties. Among the contributing factors were the flap fault that necessitated abandonment

of the attempted landing, and what the investigative commission described as the 'misleading depiction' of the Romeo fix on the operator's approach chart at the start of the Sierra approach, which could have affected the actions of the crew.

No evidence was found of failure in the navigational or other major systems of the aircraft. The anomaly that had prevented the extension of the flaps beyond 15 degrees, which had occurred when the screw-jack torque limiter stopped, was possibly caused by friction in the system that had been aggravated by the momentary activation of the right wing spoilers. The accident report noted that the airline's emergency checklist did not provide much information on how to deal with a flap fault, and the captain's comments concerning the problem showed 'elements of frustration'. The malfunction was, however, transient in nature.

It was not determined why the A310 ended up on the wrong heading, flying past the airport to the point of impact, instead of returning to the beginning of the approach course. Though it may have been a deliberate attempt to intercept the missed approach track, which would have been followed by a turn back along the 022/202-degree radial, it was the opinion of the commission that the heading it assumed had been unintentional. It was considered possible that the pilots had lost track of time and the trajectory of the flight. The actions of the captain, which included a continued right turn that may have been related to the topography of the area, indicated that he believed he was south of the airport.

The Nepalese report noted that the crew, both members of which had flown into Kathmandu many times, had experienced a heavy workload during the turn due to ongoing communications with ground controllers that was related to a misunderstanding that the pilots did not have a valid clearance to carry out another Sierra approach. The captain's awareness of time would have been distorted by this workload. The crew's uncoordinated use of the flight management and guidance system (FMGS) for navigation may have led to confusing system outputs, reducing their ability to conduct effective problem-solving. The pilots had spent considerable time putting into the FMGS computer the codes for the Romeo fix and the Simara non-directional beacon (NDB), which are part of the Sierra procedure, the process likely to have begun around the start of the turn. However, the navigational points were apparently not displayed as expected because they were behind the aircraft and would therefore not have been on the Navigation Display (ND) when in the MAP mode. This could explain the first officer's comment, 'They are all gone . . . they have disappeared. We have to direct it again.'

Research studies and experience have shown that automation can present its own perils, including a loss of contact with the momentary progress of the flight, after which the crew may not revert to manual navigation methods. It can also deprive the crew of practice in manual modes, which can reduce proficiency, and can lead to less cross-checking by pilots of other instruments, including the compasses. In this case, instrument cues that the aircraft was proceeding towards the north would not have been very obvious to the crew. Both their VOR and automatic direction finder (ADF) presentations would have indicated that the airport was behind the aircraft had it been proceeding either way, and the DME values would have likewise increased regardless of heading. Nor would the course selector line been that obvious in providing direction information when the ND was in the ROSE VOR mode, and the compass rose displayed on the aircraft's radio magnetic indicator (RMI) units uses numerals and not letters to indicate cardinal points, such as 'N' and 'S'. The commission theorised that despite the fact that he read the correct heading to the controller, the captain could have still held an incorrect 'directional hypothesis' that was not altered by the compasses. Although the aircraft's weather radar system would normally have shown the high terrain towards which it was flying, the mountains on this day would have been masked by the heavy rain in the area.

It was likely that the co-pilot realised the potentially dangerous situation about 30 seconds before the crash, stating in a 'mitigated' or timid manner, 'Hey, we are going north, we are going north', to which the captain responded, 'We will turn back soon'. After the ground-proximity warning system (GPWS) had sounded, the first officer strongly suggested, 'Turn back, turn back!' Possibly influenced by erroneous warnings during previous flights into Kathmandu, the captain responded only by saying, 'It's false'. Following the instrument warning, he did announce 'Level change', and engine thrust was increasing at the

moment of impact, with the GPWS continuing to sound 'Terrain' for the last 16 seconds of the flight. Though the commission found that the crew's response to it had been 'slower than might be expected', it concluded that by the time it sounded, the accident could not have been prevented due to the steepness of the terrain and aircraft performance limitations even had they responded immediately to the warning. Additionally, the commission found that the operator's procedures did not provide sufficient guidance to the crew in dealing with GPWS alerts.

A possibly significant human factor was the captain's knowledge that the first officer had been eliminated from consideration for upgrade to captain because of his aptitude. During this particular flight, in fact, the latter had experienced difficulty in assessing the wind speed and had not provided the answers the captain had been seeking. However, the investigation found no evidence that the co-pilot had been unable to make the correct keystrokes to obtain the Romeo fix and Simara NDB, as on at least three occasions he correctly verbalised them. Although it was considered unlikely that the cockpit navigation displays had failed, the possibility that one FMGS computer ceased functioning because of simultaneous programming by both pilots could not be eliminated.

With regard to the communications factor, the commission concluded that the difficulties of both the crew and the controllers stemmed from radio clarity, the use of non-standard phraseology and the fact that they were speaking in other than their native languages. The communications did not clarify the situation, and the captain may have believed that the ground controllers could provide vectors, even though they were only able to offer procedural control without terrain clearance. The captain's comment 'Romeo radial . . . two zero two, 16 DME', which was recorded by the CVR, indicated that he indeed desired clearance to the initial point of the approach. Nevertheless, the commission labelled the request to return to the Romeo fix as 'unusual' and probably confusing to the controllers, because it was not part of the Sierra procedure and would have effectively involved the aircraft proceeding the wrong way along a prescribed airway. The failure of the controllers to respond or provide any further instructions could have been equally confusing to the crew. Thus, the pilots apparently did not perceive they had a valid clearance back to Romeo, but understood they were to continue in the same direction. Only after they had initiated the turn, and about the same time the aircraft was passing through the 202-degree radial, did the tower controller clear the flight to the navigational fix and also instruct the crew to contact the area control centre, which then issued them another clearance to the same point. Significantly, the centre controller was a trainee with nine months' experience, though his supervisor had also been fulfilling control duties.

The crew never mentioned the radial being used, and the controllers never solicited this information, only the distance from the VOR station. Thus, the position of the aircraft was never clarified at any time. The controllers later said they believed HS-TID had been south of the airport, heading towards the Romeo fix, and at a safe altitude. Also, the crew never made any reference using the term 'back to' Romeo, only 'proceed to' the fix. The centre controller apparently never heard the pilot's report that the aircraft was on a heading of 25 degrees. Although the airport tower did have a VHF direction finder capable of providing bearing information to an aircraft transmitting on usable frequencies, controllers reported a hesitation in operating it because it was not calibrated and no procedure had been published for its use. Because the direction finder could not detect frequencies used by the control centre, the bearing of the A310 would not have been indicated after the flight was transferred from the control tower.

During the 360-degree turn, the jetliner rolled out momentarily on headings of approximately 45 and 340 degrees, and the beginnings of a roll-out were noted at around 130 degrees and possibly near 290 to 300 degrees, before finally continuing in a direction close to that at the beginning of the manoeuvre. The commission noted, however, that a right turn was in conformity with proper missed approach procedures. Also, the fact that the pilot had elected to climb to a higher altitude indicated his concern for terrain clearance.

The final Nepalese report was considered 'not acceptable' to the Thai Department of Aviation (DOA), which said it contained 'far too many anomalies and assumptions we cannot support'. Thai officials believed that inadequate consideration had been placed on air traffic control services

provided to the aircraft, including the repeated requests by the crew to turn left, and in their rebuttal report said the Nepalese conclusions appeared 'biased in favour of the ATC and against the pilots'. The Thai report noted that many of the communications difficulties were related to the trainee controller, and even questioned his competence and supervision. Thailand objected that the Nepalese commission refused to discuss or include other possible causes submitted by the nation of the aircraft's registry. Thai authorities also questioned why the tower controller, whose jurisdiction was capped at 11,500 ft, had transferred the flight to the trainee centre controller when his clearance did not exceed that altitude. And the instructions to 'initially' maintain 11,500 ft implied that a follow-up clearance would be given, but never was, according to the Thai report, which also noted that the controller had broken communications with Flight 311 to speak with the Nepalese aircraft and did not afterwards request an acknowledgement from the former.

The Thai report noted that the post-accident search and rescue operation had been delayed because the controller could not remember the pilot's report concerning the aircraft's heading. Among other observations by the Thai agency were that the Romeo fix had been correctly depicted on the approach chart, rejecting the Nepalese contention that this had been a factor in the accident; that the roll-outs during the turn were consistent with use of the autopilot select mode, and not an indication of uncertainties on the part of the flight crew, and that the first officer's comment, 'We are going north' was in fact merely an advisory prompted by the slight change in course just before impact, and not really a warning to the captain. The Thai report also refuted the Nepalese contention that the crew had been unaware of their heading, and maintained that the crew had followed proper procedures following activation of the GPWS, noting the captain's 'Level change' request. Objections over the failure to consider other theories were also voiced by the nation of the aircraft's manufacture, France.

The commission noted that positive safety action had been taken by both the airline and Nepal's Department of Civil Aviation in the wake of the disaster. In response to recommendations made by the Thai DOA, the airline speeded up the implementation of cockpit resource management courses for pilots, which incorporated the facts of the crash. Procedural changes were also made in the Sierra approach, and simulator exercises and a visual programme developed for training crews flying into Kathmandu. In a dispute between Thai and Nepalese officials on the latter issue, the former claimed that Thai pilots had in fact received extensive training, countering a claim by the commission that the procedures used at Kathmandu had not previously been practised in simulator training sessions, which it said in this case increased the workload of the crew.

Date: 31 July 1992 (*c.* 15:00)
Location: Nanjing, Jiangsu, China
Operator: China General Aviation Corporation
Aircraft type: Yakovlev Yak-42D (*B-2755*)

Operating as Flight 7552, the jet airliner crashed on take-off from the city's Da Xiao Chang Airport, on a domestic service to Xiamen, Fujian, with a loss of 109 lives. Among the 116 passengers and crew of 10 aboard, 17 persons survived, all of whom were seriously injured.

Reportedly, the three-engine jet climbed to a height of approximately 200 ft (60 m) above the ground before it plunged into a shallow pond about half a mile (0.8 km) beyond the end of the runway and caught fire. An unofficial source attributed the accident to a power plant failure in combination with improper engine-out procedures on the part of the flight crew. Other factors may have been the high air temperature at the time and the possible overloading of the aircraft.

Date: 27 August 1992 (*c.* 22:45)
Location: Near Ivanovo, Russian Federation, Commonwealth of Independent States
Operator: Aeroflot (Russia)
Aircraft type: Tupolev Tu-134A (*SSSR-65058*)

Designated as Flight 2808 and on a domestic service originating at Mineral'nyye Vody, the jet airliner crashed about 1.5 miles (2.5 km) from the Ivanovo airport, where it was scheduled to land. All 84 persons aboard (77 passengers and seven crew members) were killed, and a woman on the ground was injured. The accident occurred in darkness, but the weather was not considered a factor.

Following an unstabilised initial approach, with the aircraft deviating considerably above and then slightly below the correct glide path, the Tu-134 struck the tops of trees some 2 miles (3 km) short of the threshold of the assigned runway, No. 29, and approximately 150 ft (50 m) to the left of its extended centreline. Initial impact was at an indicated air speed of about 230 mph (370 kmh), with its undercarriage still retracted and flaps not in the landing configuration, and after rolling to the right when its starboard wing disintegrated, the aircraft travelled more than 1,500 ft (500 m) until finally slamming to earth. There was no fire.

The accident was attributed to poor coordination on the part of the flight crew, who violated basic rules and whose members provided no assistance to the captain. Inadequate actions of the air traffic control service were an additional factor, with no notification of the flight despite its constant deviation from the proper track.

Date: 28 September 1992 (14:30)
Location: Near Bhadgaon, Nepal
Operator: Pakistan International Airlines
Aircraft type: Airbus Industrie A300B4-2C/103 (*AP-BCP*)

The second crash in less than two months of an aircraft arriving at Tribhuvan International Airport, serving Kathmandu, involved Flight 268. Though different in some ways from the disaster in July (see separate entry, 31 July 1992), this accident also occurred during an attempted landing on Runway 02, using the complex 'Sierra' very-high-frequency omnidirectional range/distance-measuring equipment (VOR/DME) non-precision instrument procedure that, again, was being conducted in conditions of poor visibility.

Having nearly completed a service from Karachi, Pakistan, *AP-BCP* was initially authorised by the control tower to begin the descent procedure, and shortly thereafter cleared for final approach, with instructions to report at the 'four DME' position, or when 4 nautical miles (*c.* 7.5 km) from touchdown. Acknowledgement of the clearance was the last radio transmission from the flight. Seconds later, the wide-bodied jetliner slammed into a mountainside at an approximate elevation of 7,300 ft (2,225 m), or some 150 ft (50 m) below its crest, and in alignment with the runway but approximately 10 miles (15 km) south of the airport. All 167 persons aboard (148 passengers and 19 crew members) perished; its four-member flight crew included a supervisory engineer.

Examination of the wreckage indicated that at the time of the crash, the A300 had been in a wings-level attitude, and that its flaps were fully extended and undercarriage apparently down. Its ground speed was determined to have been around 190 mph (300 kmh) at the moment of impact with the steep terrain, and the aircraft then must have exploded in a fireball. However, fires that erupted in the debris extinguished themselves. Five minutes after the accident, the airport weather was characterised by cloud layers at different altitudes, specifically, 3/8 cumulus at 2,000 ft (c. 600 m), 1/8 cumulonimbus at 2,500 ft (c. 750 m) and 6/8 stratocumulus at 3,000 ft (c. 1,000 m), with a visibility of more than 5 miles (10 km). The wind was from a south-south-westerly direction at 5 knots.

At the time and location of the disaster, the visibility had been reduced to only about 70 ft (20 m) in mist, but there was little or no wind and no reported rain or thunderstorm activity. The 'bumps' seen on the read-out of the aircraft's digital flight data recorder (DFDR) were symptomatic of light turbulence, indicating that AP-BCP had been in the clouds throughout the approach. But there was no evidence of severe weather in the area other than the scattered cumulonimbus.

There was no indication of in-flight fire, explosion, structural failure or major technical malfunction in the Airbus, including a significant altimeter error, or of unlawful interference with the crew, and the Nepalese government commission that investigated the crash considered the incapacitation of either pilot as extremely remote. Nor was there indication of any malfunction in the ground navigational aids. Evidence further indicated that AP-BCP had been under control at the moment of impact, in what appeared to be a classic controlled-flight-into-terrain (CFIT) accident. The balance of evidence suggested that the primary cause of the crash was related to the failure of one or both of the pilots to follow the approach procedure correctly, inadvertently adopting a profile that had the jetliner arriving at each DME fix one step ahead of the proper sequence, and thus below the specified minimum altitude. The mistake was clearly illustrated by its DFDR read-out, which the commission used in reconstructing its height and ground track during the final approach. After levelling off at 10,500 ft (c. 3,200 m), the aircraft reached the 16 DME point, where it should have been at 11,500 ft (c. 3,500 m), passed through 9,500 ft (2,900 m) at 13 DME, even though it should have been 1,000 ft (c. 300 m) higher at that location, and about the same time the first officer reported being at the 10 DME position, the Airbus descended through 8,200 ft (c. 2,500 m), which was the correct height for the 8 DME fix but below the minimum safe altitude for that portion of the approach. And at the moment of impact, AP-BCP was some 1,000 ft (300 m) below the minimum height at that location. Exactly how this error happened could not be determined with certainty because no part of the crew's interpersonal conversation had been transcribed by the aircraft's cockpit voice recorder (CVR). This was apparently related to a malfunction in the cockpit area microphone.

Given the minimal likelihood that a crew of this experience had attempted a visual approach or intentionally deviated below the minimum prescribed altitude while flying in clouds, it was considered probable that the pilots had mis-interpreted or somehow misread the approach chart. It appeared to the commission that initially, the chart had been interpreted in such a way so that the association between the 16 DME fix and the figure of 11,500 ft printed next to it was lost. Significantly, the Airbus had begun its descent from 11,500 ft (c. 3,500 m) at the 22 DME point, when the crew should have waited until 16 nautical miles (c. 30 km) from the transmitter. Perhaps also of some significance was the fact that the co-pilot had incorrectly reported the flight to be at 11,500 ft after interception of the final approach track. This error was apparently not noticed or corrected by the other flight crewmen. A possibly critical factor was that the minimum height at the 16 DME fix did not appear on the plan (overhead) view of the approach chart. It did appear on the elevation profile, but if the figure were to be obscured by the thumb of the person holding the chart, the starting altitude would have been less obvious.

The commission concluded that either both pilots had misinterpreted the approach procedure, or that the first officer had been incorrectly briefing the captain, who was actually doing the flying and may not have been checking his own chart, possibly due to his preoccupation with handling the rapidly descending aircraft, and with the mistake not being noticed by the third active member of the flight crew; relevant to the latter issue was that in accordance with company procedures, the flight engineer would not be directly involved in the approach. The investigative report noted that on the profile view of the approach chart, the printed data was unusually dense, there were far more than the usual number of step-down fixes, and the fan marker had been completely omitted. Nor had any descent profile advisory information been provided. And because the profile section was too cluttered to use for quick reference, other pilots had reported copying the information from the chart on to another piece of paper. This could open the possibility of a copying mistake, and thus an error in the information being transferred. Had the information been copied incorrectly by the crew of Flight 268, and with both pilots using the same erroneous data, cross-checking would not have revealed an earlier mistake by one of them.

Communications between the pilots may have been a factor had the captain misread the procedural altitude at the 16 DME point and decided to descend without asking or checking with the first officer as to whether it was correct. After beginning the final descent, the co-pilot would have briefed the captain on the minimum altitude at each DME fix, but may not have verbally correlated the height and the navigational checkpoint. But because of what the report referred to as 'his experience and unblemished training record', the commission considered it unlikely that the first officer had not adequately monitored the height of the aircraft during the approach.

With regard to the possibility of a malfunction in the aircraft's DME receiving equipment, the report observed that the 25 and 16 DME position reports were made at the correct ranges. It was possible that DME performance may have degraded during the latter stages of the approach, related to interruption of the signal by the terrain, as indicated by the fact that the 10 DME report had been issued early, but this would not have been a significant factor. One anomaly noted during the approach was the excessive speed of the A300, which was some 15 mph (25 kmh) above the norm after passage of the 10 DME point. This apparent

manual overriding by the handling pilot of the autopilot while in the 'command' mode may have been intentional on the part of the captain as a precaution against anticipated turbulence; been related to the misreading of the chart, or was due to a delay in configuring the Airbus for landing. Although the higher-than-usual velocity did not present a hazard to the flight, it did increase the workload of the captain. It also represented a deviation from the carrier's recommended technique for the final part of the approach, which commenced after the 10 DME point.

Although the aircraft's ground-proximity warning system (GPWS) should have been functioning properly, its aural alert was not transcribed on either the CVR or the air traffic control recordings, despite the fact that the first officer had been transmitting a message using a hand-held microphone at the time it should have activated. The possibility that the crew had intentionally disarmed the system in order to avoid nuisance warnings could not be completely discounted, but the absence of an alert was more likely related to the logic of the GPWS with which AP-BCP had been equipped, with activation being obstructed by the steepness of the terrain. In fact, only about 20 seconds before the accident, the A300 was almost 1 mile (1.5 km) from the mountain it struck and more than 500 ft (150 m) above the ground vertically. And it was unlikely that the aircraft's radio altimeter would have alerted the pilots, considering that the maximum decision height, to which one of the indicators had been set, would only have been around 500 ft (150 m). There was no evidence of an evasive manoeuvre beefore impact.

It was observed that the tower controller did not react when the first officer announced being at 8,200 ft 5 seconds after reporting the flight at the 10 DME point, although the former may have misconstrued this to mean that the jetliner had been descending to that height, which in turn may have been related to the delay between the position indication and the poorly phrased altitude report. Even had the controller challenged the co-pilot, it was doubtful that the accident could have been avoided, when considering that the latter's message ended only about half a minute before impact, with the disaster becoming unavoidable 15 seconds beforehand. Furthermore, terrain clearance was considered the responsibility of the crew, and some of the air traffic controllers who worked at Kathmandu reportedly had low self-esteem and were reluctant to intervene in piloting matters. Also significant, as in the case of the disaster in July, was the absence at Kathmandu of surveillance radar with an altitude interrogation capability. (A primary radar system would not have prevented this accident, since unlike the Thai Airways International Airbus involved in the earlier crash, this aircraft had been on the proper course.) The actions of the controller were not considered contributory to the sequence of events leading to the accident, but the commission nevertheless admitted that his failure to challenge the first officer with regard to the incorrect altitude report represented a 'missed opportunity' to perhaps prevent the disaster. The report cited no clearance errors by the air traffic control service, and noted that no other aircraft had been in the vicinity of the Airbus during its approach.

Considered as contributory to the accident was the complexity of the approach chart and of the Sierra procedure itself, which the report described as 'challenging to pilots', with a high workload and a descent gradient that in one segment of the course exceeded the recommended maximum for a VOR/DME procedure. The elevation profile on the Jeppesen chart could not even be followed by a jet aircraft, whose speed and inertia will not allow a high rate of descent and then a level-off in a relatively short distance. Also, altitude and temperature factors existing within the Kathmandu valley area can result in a true air speed some 15 per cent higher than that indicated. The investigation also found Pakistan International Airlines' route-checking and flight operations inspection procedures to be ineffective. And even though both pilots of *AP-BCP* had previously flown into Kathmandu several times, the Nepalese capital city was not a frequent destination for the carrier's A300 flight crews, and neither the captain nor the first officer had landed there within the previous two months. The captain had in fact never been route-checked into the airport. Noting that it was not in the database of the simulators used by the carrier, the commission recommended that the airline provide simulator practice in the Sierra procedure as part of qualifying pilots who operate into Tribhuvan International Airport, and that

such approaches be part of a line-oriented training session. The report further noted that the carrier had dismantled a route conversion unit that pilots could use for self-briefing and preparing for a landing at Kathmandu. Other factors identified in the investigation were the use by the carrier of hand-held microphones and the temptation of pilots to dispense with the accompanying headphones during approaches that involve a high workload, and the absence on *AP-BCP* of a clip on the control wheel, which could be used to hold the chart in place in front of the pilot. The report observed that the errors suspected in the crash of Flight 268 represented a breakdown in discipline on the part of the flight crew, something that could have been prevented through cockpit resource management training.

Subsequently, Nepalese aviation authorities implemented a new and permanent rule in which crews using either the Sierra or Echo approach procedures at Kathmandu would be required to state their flight level and DME position as instructed by controllers, with the latter alerting the former in the event of a discrepancy between the two pieces of information. Among other recommendations made by the commission were those pertaining to the establishment of a secondary radar facility and an instrument landing system (ILS) at the airport, and for improvements in the training and compensation of Nepalese airtraffic controllers and in GPWS technology.

Date: 24 November 1992 (*c.* 07:50)
Location: Near Liutang, Guangxi, China
Operator: China Southern Airlines
Aircraft type: Boeing 737-3YO (*B-2523*)

Designated as Flight 3943 and on a supplemental domestic service to Kweilin from Canton, Guandong, the jetliner crashed and exploded approximately 20 miles (30 km) south-east of its destination, while preparing to land. All 141 persons aboard (133 passengers and eight crew members) perished.

Its flight data recorder (FDR) read-out indicated that during the visual approach to Runway 36 at the city's airport and after levelling off at about 7,000 ft (2,000 m) with the autopilot and auto-throttle engaged, the left thrust lever advanced, while the right one remained at the idle position.

The resulting asymmetrical power condition was first corrected by the autopilot, but after the pilot manually centred the controls, the aircraft rolled to the right and plunged steeply to the ground. The fault in the throttle system could not be identified, although the problem had occurred earlier on the same flight and was corrected manually. The accident happened in cloudy weather conditions.

The following year, the Civil Aviation Administration of China (CAAC) announced new regulations to ensure minimum safety levels for the nation's independent airlines, which had begun appearing in the late 1980s.

Date: 22 December 1992 (*c.* 10:00)
Location: Near Tripoli, Libya
First aircraft
Operator: Jamahiriya Libyan Arab Airlines
Type: Boeing Advanced 727-2L5 (*5A-DIA*)
Second aircraft
Operator: Libyan Air Force
Type: Mikoyan MiG-23U

Operating as Flight 1103 and on a domestic service from Banghazi, the jetliner was attempting to land at Tripoli International Airport, from where the jet fighter had just taken off, when the two aircraft collided in mid-air and crashed some 30 miles (50 km) south-east of the capital city. All 157 persons aboard the 727 (147 passengers and a crew of 10) perished, while the two crewmen of the MiG reportedly parachuted to safety.

The collision occurred in clear weather conditions and at an altitude of about 3,000 ft (1,000 m), as the commercial transport was on the final phase of a visual approach to Runway 27.

Date: 8 February 1993 (*c.* 14:15)
Location: Near Karaj, Tehran, Iran
First aircraft
Operator: Iran Air Tours
Type: Tupolev Tu-154M (*EP-ITD*)
Second aircraft
Operator: Islamic Republic of Iran Air Force
Type: Sukhoi Su-24

Leased from the Russian carrier Aeroflot, the jet airliner had taken off shortly before from Mehrabad International Airport, serving the city of Tehran, and was on a non-scheduled domestic service to

Mashhad, Khorasan, when it collided with the combat jet, and both then plummeted into a military compound and exploded. All 132 persons aboard the commercial transport (119 passengers and 13 crew members, the latter including a Russian pilot) and both crewmen of the military aircraft perished in the disaster.

Departing from Runway 29-Right, the Tu-154 had reportedly crossed the path of the Su-24 and another military aircraft as the latter two were participating in an Air Force Day fly-past. The fighter then struck the tail of the airliner, the collision occurring at an estimated height of 1,300 ft (400 m) some 12 miles (20 km) north-west of the capital city.

Date: 5 March 1993 (*c.* 12:15)
Location: Near Petrovac, Macedonia
Operator: Palair Macedonian
Aircraft type: Fokker 100 (*PH-KXL*)

Designated as Flight 301 and bound for Zürich, Switzerland, the jet airliner crashed and exploded in a field immediately after its departure from the airport serving Skopje, killing 83 of the 97 persons aboard, including four members of its crew of five. The 13 passengers and one crew member who survived suffered various injuries.

Seconds after lifting off from Runway 34, the aircraft reportedly began to shudder violently, and while climbing through an approximate height of 50 ft (15 m) at an indicated air speed of around 170 mph (270 kmh) it rolled to the left, then to the right. After its starboard wing-tip struck the ground at a point some 1,300 ft (400 m) beyond the end of the runway, the transport cartwheeled and broke apart. The local weather was overcast, with a visibility of about half a mile (0.8 km) in moderate snow. The wind was blowing from a near-northerly direction at 5 knots.

The crash apparently resulted from a loss of control due to the accumulation of ice on the aircraft's wings. Having been on the ground for some 90 minutes, with snow falling during most of this time, the Fokker was not de-iced before take-off. Also before departure, it had been refuelled, which would have warmed the starboard wing and melted snow that had accumulated on its upper surface. After engine start-up, the operation of the fuel booster pump began to mix the recently added

A Palair Macedonian Fokker 100, identical to the aircraft that crashed on take-off from the Petrovac airport, in Macedonia. *(Fokker Aircraft)*

warm fuel with the existing, very cold kerosene, which then lowered the temperature of the wing surfaces, causing the melted snow to refreeze. And with more snow to stick to them, the wings rapidly became contaminated. Although the flight service engineer had conducted a cursory check of *PH-KXL* after refuelling was completed, there had been no examination of its outer-wing upper surfaces. Both pilots boarded the aircraft immediately upon their arrival at the airport, apparently having formed an erroneous conception of the meteorological conditions, and were not aware of the icing situation. Considered as a contributing factor in the accident was the lack of common background procedures of the crew, with the captain and first officer employed by different companies.

Subsequent to the accident, a reminder about de-icing was sent to all operators of the type.

Date: 19 May 1993 (15:06)
Location: Near Frontino, Antioquia, Colombia
Operator: Sociedad Aeronautica de Medellin Consolidada SA (SAM) (Colombia)
Aircraft type: Boeing 727-46 (*HK-2422X*)

All 132 persons aboard (125 passengers and a crew of seven) perished when the jet airliner, operating as Flight 501 and on a service orginating at Panama City, Panama, and ultimately bound for the Colombian capital of Bogota, crashed some 50 miles (80 km) north-west of Medellin, where it was to have landed.

Cleared for descent down to flight level 120 during the initial phase of the approach to Jose

Maria Cordova International Airport, the aircraft slammed into a mountain at an approximate elevation of 12,000 ft (3,700 m), the accident occurring during a thunderstorm. The crash was attributed to errors on the part of both the pilot-in-command and air traffic control personnel. Investigation revealed that while the crew reported as being over the Abejorral non-directional beacon (NDB), the aircraft was still some 60 miles (100 km) from that point, leading to a premature descent below the obstructing terrain.

Insufficient navigational aids in the area contributed to the disaster, with the replacement of a very-high-frequency omnidirectional range (VOR) station that had been vandalised in a guerrilla attack the previous year not being completed until after the crash. Additionally, the aircraft's automatic direction finder (ADF) may have been affected by the poor atmospheric conditions, which would have made it even more difficult for the crew to determine their exact position.

Date: 28 August 1993 (*c*. 10:45)
Location: Khorog, Tadzhikistan, Commonwealth of Independent States
Operator: Tajik Air (Tadzhikistan)
Aircraft type: Yakovlev Yak-40 (*SSSR-87995*)

This was classified as an operational loss that stemmed from a hostile act associated with the political and ethnic conflict in the area. Designed to hold about 30 passengers, the three-engine jetliner was loaded with some three times that number when armed men coerced its crew into taking off from the Khorog airport, in what should have been a scheduled domestic service to Dushanbe.

When considering the density altitude factor, with an airfield elevation of around 7,000 ft (2,000 m) and surrounding mountains, the aircraft was approximately 6,600 lb (3,000 kg) overweight, and the runway some 300 ft (100 m) too short.

The aircraft never got airborne on its take-off roll, and overran the end of the runway at high speed. Its left main gear first struck a low earthen embankment and about 200 ft (60 m) beyond that point its right gear hit a concrete pillbox, and the jetliner then fell down on a river bank and was destroyed. All but four passengers among the 86 persons aboard were killed, including the crew of five. There was no fire.

Under the circumstances, the crew undoubtedly believed that their odds for survival would be higher in obeying the demands of the armed men, as disobeying would probably have meant being shot. On the other hand, they were probably not completely aware of the hazard of performing such a take-off.

Date: 22 September 1993 (*c.* 18:30)
Location: Sukhumi, Georgia, Commonwealth of Independent States
Operator: Transair Georgia Airlines (Georgia)
Aircraft type: Tupolev Tu-154B (*SSSR-85163*)

The jetliner, which was on a Defence Ministry of Georgia charter service from Tiblisi and carrying mostly military personnel as passengers, received a hit by a missile apparently fired by Abkhazi separatists as it landed in twilight conditions at the Sukhumi airport. Struck during the landing flare, the transport then crash-landed on the airport runway, killing 106 of the 132 persons aboard, including half of its 12 crew members. All of the survivors were seriously injured.

Date: 20 November 1993 (*c.* 23:30)
Location: Near Ohrid, Macedonia
Operator: Aviaimpex Makedonija Airways (Macedonia)
Aircraft type: Yakovlev Yak-42D (*RA-42390*)

Operating as Flight 110, which had been on a service from Geneva, Switzerland, and was diverted by bad weather at Skopje, its original destination, the jet airliner crashed and exploded after abandoning a landing approach at the Ohrid airport. All 116 persons aboard were killed, including the crew of eight; one of the passengers was found alive at the accident site but succumbed later to his injuries. The disaster occurred in darkness and during a low overcast, with a cloud base of around 3,000 ft (1,000 m) and a visibility of more than 5 miles (10 km).

Cleared for a very-high-frequency omnidirectional range/distance-measuring equipment (VOR/DME) instrument approach to Runway 02, the three-engine jet was some 2,300 ft (700 m) too high to carry out a successful landing, necessitating the overshoot procedure. About a minute later, however, the crew radioed that they were not receiving the VOR signal. Due to a lack of equipment, the controller was unable to satisfy their request for a bearing, and when the crew advised that they could not see the runway lights, he actually went outside in an attempt to make visual contact with the aircraft. Around this time an explosion was observed; subsequently the wreckage was located at an approximate elevation of 4,000 ft (1,200 m) on Mt Trojani and about 1.2 miles (2 km) east of the airport.

The crash was attributed to a violation of the airport traffic pattern by the crew, who initiated a standard turn so as to head the aircraft towards the rising terrain. A contributing factor was their decision to proceed with the approach even though they were not receiving a navigational signal, being

Designed to carry about 30 passengers, the Yak-40 was loaded with more than 80 when it crashed during a coerced take-off. *(Aeroflot)*

A Yak-42, shown in an earlier livery of the Soviet airline Aeroflot, similar to the aircraft that crashed in Macedonia. *(Aviation Photo News)*

out of the range of the VOR station. After concluding that the flight was over Lake Ohrid, the captain elected to go around. Impact occurred 7 seconds after activation of the ground-proximity warning system (GPWS).

The Yak-42 had been leased by the Macedonian airline from a Russian Federation company.

Date: 3 January 1994 (*c.* 09:00)
Location: Near Irkutsk, Russian Federation, Commonwealth of Independent States
Operator: Baikal Air (Russia)
Aircraft type: Tupolev Tu-154M (*RA-85656*)

Operating as Flight 130, the jet airliner crashed and burned in snow-covered Siberian farmland approximately 7 miles (11 km) from the Irkutsk airport, from where it had taken off shortly before, on a domestic service to Moscow. All 124 persons aboard (115 passengers and nine crew members) and one person on the ground perished; a second person on the ground was seriously injured.

The crew had reported a fire in the aircraft's No. 2 (centre) power plant while climbing on a west-north-westerly heading and at an altitude of about 13,000 ft (4,000 m), requesting clearance to return

for an emergency landing, and shortly afterwards reported a loss of power in the other two engines and malfunctioning flight controls.

The underlying cause of the disaster was a faulty air-starter unit. Investigation revealed that while the transport was still on the ground, an instrument warning light had illuminated, indicating overspeeding of the air-starter. The flight engineer was heard to say that he could not switch it off by pressing the disconnect button. Although good operating procedures dictate an immediate shutdown of the engine, the crew continued with their pre-flight preparations and proceeded to take off despite the warning, the captain apparently confident that the starter was no longer running. Subsequently, the overspeeding starter turbine disc broke free and sawed through the No. 2 power plant, leading to the blaze. Damage produced by the uncontained starter failure rendered the engine fire-extinguishing system incapable of functioning properly. The subsequent loss of hydraulic pressure was attributed to mechanical and thermal damage to the links, which on this variant of the Tu-154 are located in the centre engine.

It was later determined that a piece of metal had become detached from the air cooling radiator of the starter, and had jammed open its air intake damper, leaving the starter running after engine start. Subsequent to the disaster, the Russian Air Transport Department (ATD) sent recommendations to operators of the Tu-154B and M models that their starter units be inspected.

The weather at the time, though not a factor in the accident, was cloudy, with a visibility of around 2.5 miles (4 km) in haze.

Date: 23 March 1994 (*c.* 01:00)
Location: Near Mezhdurechensk, Russian Federation, Commonwealth of Independent States
Operator: Aeroflot Russian International Airlines
Aircraft type: Airbus Industrie A310-308 (*F-OGQS*)

Designated as Flight 593, the wide-bodied jet airliner plummeted to earth in the Kuznetskiy Alatau region of Siberia, some 185 miles (300 km) south-east of Novosibirsk and about 2,000 miles (3,200 km) south-east of Moscow, from where it had taken off earlier, bound for Hong Kong. All 75 persons aboard (63 passengers and a crew of 12) perished.

Cruising in darkness and calm, clear weather conditions at an approximate height of 30,000 ft (10,000 m), the aircraft entered a steep right bank, which was followed by a stall and an uncontrolled spin. Ultimately, the A310 crashed and burned on a snow-covered hill at an elevation of about 1,300 ft (400 m), in a high rate of vertical descent, cleanly configured and with both engines operating.

Analysis of the cockpit voice recorder (CVR) tape indicated that the captain had allowed his two children to sit in the left-hand seat on the flight deck, his daughter first and then his son, and had demonstrated to both the operation of the autopilot. The boy requested, and was granted, permission to actually turn the control wheel. When his father, using the autopilot navigational control, attempted to bring the aircraft back to the correct heading, there occurred a conflict of inputs with the control wheel, which was being held in a slight right bank.

Although the autopilot remained engaged, this action activated the torque limiter and disconnected the autopilot servo from the aileron linkage. The right banking attitude gradually increased, reaching 45 degrees after 21 seconds. At this point the autopilot was no longer able to maintain altitude, and the Airbus started to descend. The three members of the flight crew appeared to pay no attention to what was happening until the bank exceeded 50 degrees and buffeting began. An attempt was then made to recover from the situation, but, apparently due to the extreme attitude the aircraft had reached, the delay in disconnecting the autopilot and autothrottle and some other factors, these attempts failed.

The autopilot disconnection apparently went unnoticed by the pilots due to the unavailability on the A310 of an instrument warning regarding such, which could have ensured its timely discovery and prevented the development of a dangerous situation; possible unawareness by the captain and first officer of the peculiarities regarding the actuation of the mechanism of disconnection and the conditions of such action because this information was not included in the operations manual and there is no such exercise in crew training programmes; complexity of identification of autopilot disconnection by the co-pilot only by physical sensations either due to laxity in the force applied to the control column, or because he took the change in the effort required as being due to the boy's actions, and the captain's absence from his seat and continued distraction caused by the presence of his daughter, who remained on the flight deck.

Contributing factors were the inadvertent and slight additional control inputs after disconnection of the autopilot servo; failure of the two pilots to discover the growth of the right bank beyond that allowed under normal operation, and their belated entry in the control loop due to distraction in finding out the cause of the roll; the entering of the buffeting and a high angle of attack even though the autopilot continued performing its functions of maintaining altitude and heading; and the failure of the first officer to disengage the autopilot in a timely manner and to apply forward pressure on his control column following onset of the buffeting. Also factoring in the loss of control could have been the working position of the co-pilot, whose seat was pulled back; the initiation, 2 seconds after the start of the buffeting, of an unintentional pitch-up of the aircraft, which led to an abrupt increase in its angle of attack and deterioration in its lateral control; lack of readiness of the crew in reacting to the situation due to shortcomings in flight training; and spatial disorientation in the night-time conditions.

Recommendations made in the investigative report dealt largely with improving state supervision of flight safety, with two specific proposals being the use of flight data recorders and CVRs to assure adherence to regulations and improvement in crew training in such areas as instrument flight and methods of recovering from unusual attitudes.

Date: 26 April 1994 (*c.* 20:15)
Location: Near Komaki, Aichi, Japan
Operator: China Airlines (Taiwan)
Aircraft type: Airbus Industrie A300B4-622R (*B-1816*)

Flight 140 had received clearance to land at Nagoya Airport, following a service from T'ai-pei, Taiwan. But as it continued its instrument landing system (ILS) approach to Runway 34, the co-pilot, who was actually flying the aircraft, committed a relatively minor error that would have catastrophic consequences.

After levelling off at an approximate height of 1,000 ft (300 m), the A300 began a steep climb. Reaching an altitude of about 1,700 ft (520 m), the wide-bodied jetliner nosed over and plummeted to earth, hitting the ground close to the taxiway and some 360 ft (110 m) to the right of the runway centreline and exploding in flames. All but seven

All but seven of the 271 persons aboard the China Airlines Airbus A300 were killed in the crash at Nagoya Airport. (*AP Images*)

passengers among the 264 persons aboard the aircraft were killed in the disaster, including its entire crew of 15. The survivors, all of whom had been seated above or forward of the wing, suffered serious injuries. The majority of the fatalities resulted from impact trauma.

It was determined that after the aircraft had flown over the outer marker beacon, the first officer inadvertently activated the 'GO' lever, which changed the flight director to the 'go-around' mode and automatically increased engine thrust. Though it was not exactly clear how this happened, he may have mistaken it for the autothrottle system (ATS) disconnect button while trying to change the ATS to manual, or when trying to move the thrust levers themselves. (Due to its position in the cockpit of the A300 below the thrust lever knob, the possibility existed of accidental activation of the 'GO' lever during normal operation of the power plant controls.)

As transcribed from the cockpit voice recorder (CVR) tape, the error was realised immediately by the crew. In response to the captain's comment, 'You triggered the lever', the co-pilot replied, 'Yes, yes, yes . . . I touched it a little'. The pilot then commanded him to 'disengage it'. It was at this point, some 3.5 miles (5.5 km) from the threshold of the runway, when the descending aircraft levelled off. As instructed by the captain, the first officer applied a nose-down elevator input with his control wheel and managed to re-align it successfully with the correct glide path. He also reduced engine thrust. Meanwhile, the flight director (FD) remained in the 'GO' mode, about which the co-pilot was twice cautioned by the captain. About 90 seconds before the crash, the Nos 1 and 2 autopilots were almost simultaneously engaged. At a height of about 500 ft (150 m), the captain himself took over the controls, and power was increased, then retarded. Power was again increased after the captain called out 'GO lever', and the A300 then began to climb. It was at that point that the first officer radioed the control tower, announcing 'going around'. As the jetliner continued its steep climb, with its air speed rapidly decreasing, its flaps and slats were partially retracted by the crew. The increase in thrust was presumably the automatic action of the 'Alpha Floor' function activated by the high angle of attack. In the final seconds before impact, the ground-proximity warning system

(GPWS) called out 'Glide Slope' and 'Terrain', and the stall warning sounded twice, the last time for approximately 5 seconds until impact. The A300 stalled and crashed after its velocity dropped to less than 90 mph (145 kmh); impact was in a somewhat left wing-down and nose-up but generally level attitude, with its undercarriage down. It was dark at the time, and the airport weather conditions shortly after the accident were generally good, with scattered cumulus clouds at 3,000 ft (1,000 m), a broken overcast at a higher altitude and visibility of more than 10 miles (15 km). The wind was blowing at 6 knots from a direction of 280 degrees.

The investigation of this crash revealed a disturbing lack of understanding on the part of the pilots of *B-1816* of the aircraft's automatic flight system (AFS). This was indicated by their actions despite their knowledge that the go-around mode was engaged. When the captain ordered the first officer to 'disengage it', he could have been referring to the ATS, but most likely meant the go-around mode to be disengaged. Although the captain probably intended the co-pilot to continue the approach, he apparently did not realise that the latter failed to do as instructed. He did follow the instructions of the captain in continuing to apply forward pressure to the control column. The potentially hazardous manipulation of the elevators with the control wheel while the autopilots are engaged was described in the flight crew operating manual (FCOM). Such action would cause an inverse movement of the elevators, being controlled by the pilot, and the horizontal stabiliser, which would still be receiving commands from the autopilot, and since the efficiency of the latter is greater, it could lead to an abnormal pitch-up angle. The crew's actions, which did indeed result in an out-of-trim condition, indicated that neither pilot properly understood the contents of this advisory. By the time the pilot took over the controls, he seemed to be unaware that the stabiliser was at the nose-up limit. He still apparently intended to land and reduced thrust. His confusion over the pitch-up of the aircraft, which was opposite to his control inputs, was reflected by his comment, 'How come like this?' The subsequent activation of the 'Alpha Floor' system generated a large pitch-up moment, but the captain tried to lower the nose and manually retarded the thrust

levers. Still unable to reduce the aircraft's pitch angle, it was only then that he elected to abandon the approach altogether with his 'GO' lever order, but he must have continued to struggle with the controls, apparently operating the pitch trim control switch intermittently until the stall. Even during the steep climb and with the pitch angle still increasing, he appeared not to have recognised the out-of-trim condition of the stabiliser, which could explain his intermittent activation of the switch.

It could not be determined whether both autopilots were engaged by the captain or by the first officer either acting on the instructions of the former or on his own, or why this was done. The crew may have engaged them with the intention of returning to the proper glide path and by selecting the 'Land' mode, but the latter was apparently not done by the co-pilot. (Complete disengagement of the go-around mode would have required the selection of another lateral mode, such

This diagram of the crash site indicates the impact of the China Airlines A300 adjacent to the runway at Nagoya Airport. *(Japanese Ministry of Transport)*

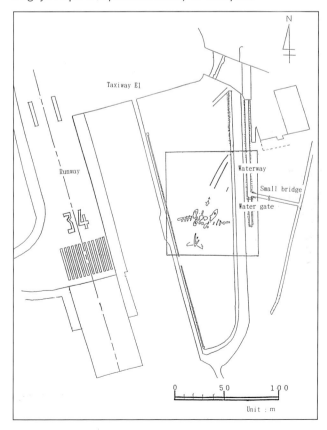

as Heading or Navigation.) It was possible that the captain had not realised that the autopilots were still engaged; may have thought they were engaged but that the co-pilot had disengaged the go-around mode, as instructed, or believed that the autopilot could be manually overridden. On the A300, a supervisory override function is available that only allows the pilot to assist the autopilot, through manipulation of the control wheel, in capturing the glide slope, localiser or very-high-frequency omnidirectional range (VOR) course. In this case, the crew may have incorrectly believed that the autopilot could be overridden at any phase of a landing approach. Subsequently, the autopilots were disengaged, but this failed to correct the out-of-trim condition because the go-around mode remained engaged. Even in abandoning the approach, the pilots used incorrect overshoot procedures, delaying activation of the slats/flaps lever and failing to retract the undercarriage.

Previous out-of-trim accidents associated with the improper use of the autopilot in Airbus aircraft had occurred, the first nearly a decade before the crash of Flight 140. The most recent event, involving an Airbus A310 near Moscow airport in 1991, was similar to the Nagoya Airport disaster, except that the crew recovered. The first incident resulted in a modification to allow for autopilot disengagement in every mode except 'land', when below 400 ft (120 m), and 'go-around'. Following two more incidents, the AFS was modified again so the autopilot could be disengaged in the two aforementioned modes. But whereas the first modification had been incorporated into B-1816, the second had not. Significantly, the latter service bulletin (SB) (A300-22-6021) had only been labelled 'Recommended', rather than 'Mandatory', and so China Airlines decided to carry out the modification only when the flight control computer (FCC) needed repair. But since none of the carrier's FCC units had been removed between the time it received the SB the previous July and the date of the crash, none of the aircraft in its A300 fleet were so modified.

The manufacturer was cited in the investigative report for not providing operators with sufficient technical information regarding the previous incidents, and the contents of the 'cautions' advisory added to the FCOM, the descriptions of the AFS modification and the proper disengagement procedures were considered hard to understand. Readers could have been misinformed as to the precise relationship between how the various modes were selected, displayed and actually worked. In addition, the FCOM did not outline clearly the primary purpose of the autopilot override function, the way to detect an out-of-trim condition or the procedure by which a crew could recover from such a situation. As Airbus Industrie had eliminated the aural 'whooler' that had been provided in its original design, the A300 was not equipped with a warning system to alert the crew of the onset of an abnormal out-of-trim condition.

Significantly, the two pilots involved in the accident had not attended the single training session conducted by the airline regarding the autopilot issue because, at that time, they had yet to be assigned to the A300. Inadequacies were also found in the dissemination of up-to-date training material provided by the manufacturer to the airline, and in the training of the carrier's pilots. Simulator training, for example, was being provided by Thai Airways International, but its simulator did not duplicate the autopilot overriding function while in the go-around mode in the A300. Whatever bearing this had on the accident could not be determined. In general, however, it was recognised that the training received by the pilots was not necessarily sufficient for them to understand the highly sophisticated AFS system.

Another possible contributing factor may have been in the design of the aircraft's pitch control system, which allowed a pilot to override the elevators while the stabiliser remained under the control of the autopilot when in the 'go-around' or 'land' modes. The report also noted that although it was designed as a safety feature, the 'Alpha Floor' function proved incompatible in dealing with an out-of-trim condition, instead generating the large pitch-up moment described earlier. This actually narrowed the range of action that could be taken by the crew and reduced the time available for recovery.

The investigative commission identified as an important human factor in the accident the poor coordination of the crew of B-1816. Although the first officer must have perceived the abnormally strong resistive force of the control wheel, he delayed reporting this to the captain, probably for a number of reasons, including his previous mistake in activating the 'GO' lever and possible confusion over being assigned the role as pilot flying the aircraft, then being given a series of instructions and cautions. Nor did he mention to the pilot that he could not change modes. The captain's judgement was also deemed inadequate, as indicated by his failure to verify whether the instructions and cautions he gave the first officer were being followed and to check the cockpit display properly to see if the mode had been changed. He also delayed taking over control and then failed to take appropriate actions. After the co-pilot had triggered the 'GO' lever, the captain seemed to disregard their duty assignment, and as a result the former lost his 'autonomy'.

Representatives from the nation of registry, the Civil Aviation Administration of Taiwan, and of the nation of manufacture, the French Bureau Enquetes Accidents (BEA), both responded to the Japanese Ministry of Transport accident report. Comments from the former included a challenge of the conclusions of the report that the actions of the accident crew were in any way uncoordinated. The Taiwanese rebuttal also stated that the design and location of the 'GO' lever was conducive to inadvertent activation, and thus a significant factor in the crash, and that the detection of the out-of-trim condition had been rendered 'highly improbable, if not impossible', due to the masking effect resulting from the increase in thrust associated with the 'Alpha Floor' function. The Taiwanese representative also noted that *B-1816* had encountered wake turbulence from another aircraft during its approach, and that this may have been a factor in the activation of the 'GO' lever. Comments from France included a refute of the Japanese contention that the manufacturer had not acted in response to earlier incidents, noting that a number of advisories had been issued regarding use of the A300 autopilot. The BEA also disagreed with the statement that the aircraft's auto-flight system is complicated, which it said 'was not supported by any of the facts established during the investigation'.

About a week after this disaster, the manufacturer notified all A300 operators, alerting them to the risks of moving the elevators when the autopilots were in 'GO' or 'land' modes. As additional preventative measures, Taiwanese aviation authorities ordered China Airlines to promptly complete modifications in accordance with the SB 22-6021, and a few days later to provide supplementary training to its A300-600R pilots, re-evaluate their proficiency and submit for review its pilot and re-evaluation plans.

Subsequently, the French Direction Generale de l'Aviation Civile (DGAC) issued its own air-worthiness directive, ordering revision of the flight manual and modification of the A300 and A310 transports so that a high control column force will automatically disconnect the autopilot to prevent an abnormal out-of-trim situation arising from a prolonged override while the AFS is engaged in the command mode. The modifications, previously issued in SB-22-6021, were re-categorised from 'Recommended' to 'Mandatory'. Similar air-worthiness directives were issued by aviation governing agencies to Airbus operators in their respective nations. Within four months of this accident, the airline involved had completed the modifications, re-checked the proficiency of all their pilots, particularly those flying the A300, and also carried out inspections of engines, flight control systems and autopilots on their aircraft.

The crash also affected the carrier's managerial structure, with two of its senior executives later resigning from the company.

Date: 6 June 1994 (*c.* 08:20)
Location: Near Xi'an, Shaanxi, China
Operator: China Northwest Airlines
Aircraft type: Tupolev Tu-154M (*B-2610*)

Operating as Flight 2303, the jetliner crashed about 10 minutes after it had taken off from Xi'an airport, on a domestic service to Canton, Guangdong. All 160 persons aboard (146 passengers and 14 crew members) were killed. The weather in the area at the time was poor, with a driving rain.

In its official report, a joint Chinese/Russian investigative commission blamed the disaster on 'errors of technical and flight personnel of the Chinese airline', specifically an autopilot mal-function resulting from faulty repair work the previous evening. This led to divergent oscillations producing in-flight loads that exceeded the aircraft's design limits, causing structural failure. The cross-wiring of the autopilot yaw and roll channels to the wrong control systems, which had been done 'in the field' and not at the workshop, was not detected because the required pre-flight ground check was not made.

An attempt to disconnect the autopilot by the captain, at the suggestion of the airport control tower operator who was also an experienced pilot, came too late to save the jetliner.

Date: 1 July 1994 (*c.* 08:30)
Location: Near Tidjikja, Mauretania
Operator: Air Mauretanie
Aircraft type: Fokker F.28 Fellowship Mark 6000 (*5T-CLF*)

The jet airliner crashed at the Tidjikja airport during a supplemental scheduled domestic service from the capital city of Nouakchott, located some 250 miles (400 km) to the west, killing 80 persons aboard, including the crew of four. The 13 surviving passengers were seriously injured.

Following a hard landing and the collapse of its undercarriage, the aircraft veered off the runway, then struck a rock outcrop and burst into flames. Visibility at the time had been reduced by blowing sand.

Date: 8 September 1994 (19:03)
Location: Near Aliquippa, Pennsylvania, US
Operator: US Air
Aircraft type: Boeing 737-3B7 (*N513AU*)

It would take a long and arduous investigation to determine the probable cause of the disaster that

Computer simulation shows the attitude of the US Air Boeing 737 near the end of its uncontrolled plunge to earth following uncommanded rudder deflection. *(National Transportation Safety Board)*

befell Flight 427, and the findings of the investigation would raise serious questions as to the safety of the world's most widely used commercial jet transport. Having nearly completed the first leg of a domestic service originating at Chicago, Illinois, with an ultimate destination of West Palm Beach, Florida, the 737 had been manoeuvring to land when it plummeted into hilly, wooded terrain some 5 miles (10 km) north-west of Greater Pittsburgh International Airport, itself located about 10 miles (15 km) north-west of the city it served and which was a scheduled en route stop. All 132 persons aboard (127 passengers and a crew of five) perished.

Following a descent from 11,000 ft (3,400 m), and after being instructed to turn left on to a heading of 100 degrees, the aircraft was levelling out at 6,000 ft (*c.* 1,800 m) when the accident sequence began. Its autopilot and autothrottle systems engaged, undercarriage retracted and leading-edge devices deployed, a configuration that slightly deflects the trailing-edge flaps, *N513AU* had yet to reach a wings-level attitude when it suddenly rolled back to the left. The 'Dutch roll' manoeuvre, in which the left-banking attitude decreased and then increased again, was accompanied by a yaw to the left, with the 737 ultimately rolling through inverted flight. Descending almost vertically from an above-ground height of around 3,600 ft (1,100 m), the aircraft's nose then began to rise until the twin-jet airliner slammed to earth in a nose-down attitude of approximately 80 degrees, in a left bank of nearly 60 degrees and at an indicated air speed of 300 mph (480 kmh), disintegrated and burned. Seconds before impact, the captain was able to transmit a distress message, 'Four-twenty-seven, emergency!' The airport weather around the time of the late afternoon accident was generally clear, with a few cirrocumulus clouds and a visibility of 5 miles (*c.* 10 km). At the surface level, the wind ranged from 6 to 8 knots from a west-south-westerly direction, and no turbulence in the area had been reported.

After months of investigation, the US National Transportation Safety Board (NTSB) was able to find no evidence of crew incapacitation, in-flight fire or explosion, including a bomb blast, structural failure, bird strike or encounter with clear-air turbulence, a major systems failure leading to asymmetrical spoiler or aileron activation, transient electronic signals causing uncommanded flight

The shattered remains of the US Air Boeing 737-300 lie in the woods near Pittsburgh after the disaster that took 132 lives. (Associated Press/EMPICS)

control movements, yaw damper malfunction or rudder cable pull or break. In a report released nearly five years after the crash, the NTSB concluded that the upset leading to the loss of control probably resulted from the uncommanded, dynamic and rapid deflection of the aircraft's rudder to the left, with the control surface shortly thereafter reaching its 'blow-down' limit, which occurs when the aerodynamic loads become equal to the force the power control unit (PCU) can apply to it. (Rudder deflection is then limited to less than its full mechanical range.) The rudder surface most likely deflected in a direction opposite to that commanded by the pilots, remaining in that position until impact.

Testing showed that when the secondary slide in the main rudder PCU was jammed to the servo valve housing at certain positions, the primary slide could travel beyond its intended stop point because of bending or twisting of the internal linkages within the unit. This deflection would then allow the primary slide to move to a position at which the PCU commanded the rudder in the opposite direction to that intended. The rudder reversal would occur when the slide was jammed at a point greater than 50 per cent beyond neutral towards the extended or retracted position and a full-rate command was applied to the PCU. Despite the absence of physical marks, it was considered possible that as a result of tight clearances within the servo valve, thermal effects, particulate matter in the hydraulic fluid or other unknown factors, such a jam could occur without leaving any such evidence. An analysis of a computer simulation, the cockpit voice recorder (CVR) tape and other data showed that the accident was consistent with such a scenario. With regard to one possible factor, tests indicated that when the temperature of the heated hydraulic fluid differed from the servo valve housing, the secondary slide jammed to the servo slide housing. A thermal system analysis by the manufacturer indicated that the failure of an engine-driven hydraulic pump could result in the overheating of the fluid in one of the aircraft's three hydraulic systems. It was further revealed that foreign material could lodge between the PCU servo valve primary and secondary slides or between the secondary slide and the valve housing, causing a jam in the mechanism. Also, the servo valve of N513AU may have been more susceptible to jamming because of its tighter clearances.

Occurring just before, but not related to the upset, was an encounter by the 737 with the wake turbulence of a Delta Air Lines Boeing 727-200 jet that had been flying about 4 miles (6.5 km) ahead of the former, also descending to 6,000 ft and assigned to the same heading, and which had passed through the same area about a minute earlier. This encounter generated perturbations in the read-out of the aircraft's flight data recorder (FDR), and it was later confirmed by radar and flight testing that N513AU had proceeded directly through the centre of the right core of the vortex. As a result of this encounter, about which both pilots were heard on the CVR tape to make verbal utterances of surprise, the 737 began to roll back to the left. It was as the crew attempted to return the aircraft back to level flight that the uncommanded rudder deflection took place. After the captain was heard to say, 'Whoa!', the rudder and the heading of the aircraft started to move significantly to the left. After the roll rate began to increase a second time, he was heard to exclaim for the first of three times, 'Hang on!' The rudder then reached the left blow-down limit, where it remained.

Subsequent flight tests using a Boeing 737 and a 727 showed that the wake encounter such as that experienced by Flight 427 was easily recoverable and would not have resulted in any pilot disorientation, especially considering the daylight and good meteorological conditions. There were no indications that the vortex or any other kind of atmospheric disturbance caused the rudder blow-down, nor were there any documented cases of such an event. It was ruled that while the crew recognised the initial upset in a timely manner and took immediate action, they could not have been expected to have assessed the flight control problem and then devised and carried out the appropriate recovery procedure, and therefore did not regain control of the 737. The CVR tape showed that the first officer had been flying the aircraft at the time, while the captain was apparently directing the recovery attempt. An analysis of the human performance data indicated that the co-pilot made the first physical response to the upset event and manipulated the flight controls during the early stages of the accident sequence. Although both crewmen probably operated them later, it was considered unlikely that the pilots manipulated them simultaneously, possibly opposing each other, during the critical period in which the aircraft yawed and rolled to the left. After the encounter with the turbulence generated by the 727, the control wheel must have been held in the full-right position until the aircraft hit the ground. It was

considered extremely unlikely, and the investigation found no supporting evidence indicating that the highly experienced crew of Flight 427 would have been so startled by a routine wake encounter as to hold a full-left rudder and full-right aileron as the aircraft spiralled to the ground. Even though the crew disconnected the autopilot, the wailing horn continued to sound, and was heard until the end of the recording. The roll to the left was arrested three times during the sequence and the control column was pulled essentially 'full-aft'. This control input led to the onset of a stall buffet, which was heard on the CVR tape, followed by the activation of the stick-shaker warning system, and ultimately the 737 stalled at an approximate above-ground height of 4,300 ft (1,300 m), and while in a left bank of around 70 degrees.

Although the aircraft had been maintaining the proper velocity, i.e. around 220 mph (355 kmh), at the beginning of the rudder anomaly, this was nevertheless, when considering its weight and configuration, slightly below the 'crossover' speed. This is the velocity at which the ailerons and spoilers would be able to overcome a roll induced by a fully deflected rudder; below it, recovery from such a condition is not possible. To regain control, the crew would therefore have needed to accelerate to this speed, which in this case would require placing the 737 in a descent. Under the circumstances, however, such a manoeuvre would be inconsistent with a pilot's training, instincts and expectations unless the crew had been aware of the crossover concept, which was based largely on knowledge gained through post-accident tests and analyses and of which the industry had been generally unaware at the time of the US Air crash. The failure of the manufacturer to advise operators of a speed at which the aircraft's lateral control authority could counteract a rudder deflection was in fact cited by the NTSB as a contributing factor in the disaster. The Board therefore concluded that the pilots of N513AU performed in a manner that was 'reasonable and correct' and adhered to the normal recovery procedures when they attempted to counteract the roll with lateral controls while trying to maintain altitude as they dealt with the situation, even though, unknown to them, their actions placed the aircraft in a position from which recovery was impossible. At the time of the accident, US Air pilot training included instructions on manoeuvring out of certain circumstances, but not from unusual attitudes or upsets. The carrier would subsequently implement selected events training, which did include recovery from inverted or other unusual attitudes. Other carriers followed suit. However, the NTSB concluded that such training may not have been beneficial in this case, one reason being that it assumed the proper functioning of the aircraft's flight controls.

The NTSB ruled that the dual-concentric servo valve used on 737 transports, which had been certified by the US Federal Aviation Administration (FAA), was not reliably redundant. Cited as reasons for this were that a pilot could not readily detect the presence of a jammed primary or secondary slide, and that the design allowed for failure modes in which one slide could directly affect the operation of the other one. Additionally, the valve was not capable of providing 'functional' redundancy, with the valve incapable of overcoming a jam. (During the certification process, the FAA had in fact expressed concern about these issues.) It was also noted in the Board's report that because of the engine placements on the wings, the rudder of the Boeing twin-jet had been designed to be sufficiently powerful to effectively counter an asymmetrical thrust condition in the event of a power plant failure occurring during a maximum gross weight take-off or at lower air speeds, especially in a crosswind. The result was a unique design that made the 737 the only large jet transport built in the West to have a single rudder panel and a single rudder actuator, while also lacking a mechanical/manual/trim tab actuation system.

Following an airworthiness directive (AD) issued by the FAA in 1996 requiring that the 737 flight manual be revised to include measures for maintaining control of an aircraft after an uncommanded yaw or roll or a jammed or restricted elevator, the manufacturer established procedures for dealing with most such conditions. Most airlines instituted minimum manoeuvring speeds in 737 operations to enhance recovery in the event of a rudder 'hard-over' or some other flight control malfunction. Pertaining to technical changes, the FAA initially issued an AD requiring the installation of a redesigned rudder PCU on the entire 737 fleet by the end of the decade, and another requiring a redesigned yaw damper in the type aircraft. Regular

inspections and testing would be required until the modifications were completed. Newer models of the jet would incorporate a hydraulic pressure limiter into the PCU. In October 2002, the FAA released an AD superseding those previously issued requiring an entirely new rudder system on the 737, with Boeing bearing the cost, reported to be nearly US $1 billion, of retrofitting every operational aircraft. With regard to the issue of flight recorders, the NTSB said the failure of the FAA to require enhanced FDR units on commercial transports, especially the 737, had 'significantly hampered investigators in the prompt identification of potentially critical flight safety conditions and in the development of recommendations to prevent future catastrophic accidents', which proved to be the case in the crash of Flight 427. Prompted by this criticism, the FAA went ahead with a directive for the installation of advanced recorders on every jet transport in the US fleet. But the FDR upgrade requirements were still considered inadequate by the NTSB because the newer units did not transcribe such parameters as pilots' flight control input forces and operation of the yaw damper.

Date: 31 October 1994 (*c.* 16:00)
Location: Near Roselawn, Indiana, US
Operator: Simmons Airlines (US)
Aircraft type: Avions de Transport Regional ATR 72-212 (*N401AM*)

Operating as American Eagle Flight 4184 and en route from Indianapolis, Indiana, the twin-engine turboprop crashed about 10 miles (15 km) east of the Illinois state border and some 65 miles south-south-east of Chicago's O'Hare International Airport, where it was to have landed, a scheduled stop during a domestic service with an ultimate destination of the Champaign/Urbana airport, also in Illinois. All 68 persons aboard (64 passengers and four crew members) perished.

Reconstruction of the events leading up to the disaster was made possible through the correlation of the digital flight data recorder (DFDR) read-out and the cockpit voice recorder (CVR) tape. Heavy air traffic and adverse weather conditions had postponed the arrival of *N401AM* at its intended destination, and so it was issued holding instructions, along with several other flights. More than half an hour before the accident, its captain

An American Eagle ATR 72, identical to the aircraft that plummeted to earth south of Chicago, Illinois. *(Avions de Transport Regional)*

reported 'entering the hold', with the ATR beginning a series of circuits in an area along the 157-degree radial of the Chicago Heights very-high-frequency omnidirectional range (VOR) station and at a height of 10,000 ft (c. 3,000 m). Subsequently, the aircraft's de-icing system, which had been switched on during the descent to the holding altitude, was deactivated.

About 20 minutes before the accident, the CVR recorded the sound of a single tone similar to a caution alert chime that could have been activated by any one of several aircraft systems, including the ice-detection advisory. Eight minutes later, one of the pilots was heard to say, 'I'm showing some ice now'. The captain then left the flight deck to use the lavatory, and when he returned, less than 5 minutes before the crash, the first officer was heard to advise him, 'We still got ice'.

Events began to move swiftly after the aircraft was cleared to descend to and maintain 8,000 ft (c. 2,500 m). The last radio transmission from the flight was a 'Thank you' from the co-pilot, in response to the air traffic controller's message that the aircraft would be 'cleared in' in about 10 minutes. During the descent, with the ATR proceeding on a south-westerly heading in the holding pattern at an indicated air speed of approximately 215 mph (345 kmh) and in a slight right-wing-down attitude, its autopilot engaged in

the vertical speed and heading modes, the sound of the flap overspeed warning was heard on the CVR tape. In response to this, the flaps were retracted by the crew, but then the angle of attack (AOA) and the pitch attitude began to increase. After a rapid aileron deflection and the sound of the autopilot automatically disconnecting (as it had been designed when aileron travel exceeds a pre-determined rate), the aircraft rolled rapidly to the right and the AOA started to decrease. It increased again, however, and the transport stopped rolling at an angle of 77 degrees right wing-down. As it rolled back towards a wings-level attitude, the aircraft's pitch stopped at approximately 15 degrees nose-down. In attempting to recover from the descent, the captain pulled back on his control column, but the aircraft again rolled to the right, through the inverted position. After one complete roll, the captain said 'alright man', but the ATR again rolled into a right-wing-down attitude, beyond the vertical, then back towards wings-level, but pitched down steeply. At an altitude of around 5,000 ft (1,500 m), the aircraft was descending in a nose-down angle in excess of 70 degrees, and the captain was heard to say 'Nice and easy'. A final but futile pull-up was tried after the ground-proximity warning system (GPWS) sounded 'Terrain', but at an approximate above-ground height of 1,700 ft (520 m), with the aircraft descending at a pitch attitude of nearly 40 degrees and an indicated air speed of about 430 mph (690 kmh), a loud 'crunching' sound was heard on the CVR tape. Subsequently, N401AM slammed into a soyabean field in a partially-inverted, nose and left-wing-down attitude, disintegrating on impact. The crash site was marked by three impact craters, and the outboard sections of both wings were determined to have separated some 10 ft (3 m) from their respective tips before the aircraft hit the ground. There was no fire.

The sudden autopilot disconnection, uncommanded aileron deflection and rapid roll experienced by the ATR, which apparently led to the loss of control, were consistent with airflow separation caused by a ridge of ice that had formed on the upper surface of the wing, aft of the de-icer boots. Data indicated that the ice ridge grew primarily after the flaps had been extended to 15 degrees. When the crew retracted the flaps in response to the aural overspeed warning, the autopilot increased the pitch attitude to maintain a preset vertical speed for the descent. As the nose of the aircraft pitched up and the AOA increased through 5 degrees, there was an increase in the airflow in the area of the right wing upper surface because of the ice ridge. As the AOA continued to increase, so did the airflow separation in the area of the right aileron, causing a reversal of the aileron hinge moment characteristics. This reversal action caused the ailerons to rapidly deflect to a right wing-down position. Unable to control the aileron deflection rate, it was then that the autopilot disconnected, and at that point the aircraft rolled to the right. As the crew tried to regain lateral control, the AOA began to increase and the airflow over the right aileron separated again, resulting in a second aileron hinge moment reversal and the second roll to the right. When airflow over the right aileron re-attached, the crew regained elevator control and had managed to raise the nose when the GPWS sounded. It was believed that after the aircraft descended through the lowest layer of clouds, the pilots saw the ground and attempted the last, desperation pull-up. The velocity of the ATR at that point was, however, some 130 mph (210 kmh) above its certified operating air speed, and the excessive aerodynamic loads associated with this recovery manoeuvre tore off the outer wing sections and the horizontal stabiliser.

In its investigative report, the US National Transportation Safety Board (NTSB) blamed the accident on the failure of the manufacturer to completely disclose to operators and incorporate into the ATR flight and flight crew operating manuals and training programmes adequate information concerning known effects of freezing precipitation on its stability and control characteristics, autopilot and related operational procedures when the type aircraft was flown in such conditions; inadequate oversight of the French Direction Generale de l'Aviation Civile (DGAC) of both the 72 and its smaller sister, the ATR 42, and its failure to take corrective action to ensure safe flight of the aircraft in icing conditions, and, in the area of safety communications, the failure of the DGAC to provide the US Federal Aviation Administration (FAA) with timely airworthiness information developed from a series of previous incidents and one fatal accident. Cited as contributing factors were the failure of the FAA to guarantee that aircraft certification and operational requirements for flight into icing conditions as well as FAA-published information on the subject adequately accounted for the hazards that can result from flying in freezing rain and other conditions conducive to icing not specified in the Code of Federal Aviation Regulations (FAR), Part 25, Appendix C, and also inadequate oversight on the part of the FAA to ensure continued airworthiness in icing conditions.

The report identified 13 previous roll control incidents, all involving ATR 42 aircraft, before the crash of Flight 4184. Aileron hinge moment reversals had, in fact, been experienced early in the flight testing of the airliner, prompting the manufacturer to develop and install vortex generators that were intended to raise the AOA at which ailerons would become unstable and reversals possibly occur. Following a non-fatal incident in the US in 1988, ATR issued an 'Operators' Information Message' and added to the aircraft an anti-icing advisory system. But according to the NTSB, the information contained in it did not clearly state the threat to the aircraft posed by icing. After two more incidents, ATR released its 'All Weather Operations' brochure, providing information about flight in freezing rain, which stated that 'Aileron forces are somewhat increased when ice accretion develops, but remain in the conventional sense.' But this was not consistent with the actual rapid and uncommanded aileron deflections and unusually high, unstable control wheel forces that were experienced by the crew of *N401AM*. Nor did the brochure explain that ice could accumulate a distance beyond the de-icer boots, and the manufacturer's warning that freezing rain could result in 'roll and axis anomalies' was considered vague, not explaining that it could result in autopilot disconnect or such rapid roll excursions and not providing explicit guidance on how to deal with aileron hinge moment reversals. With still another event occurring before the American Eagle disaster, the NTSB expressed the opinion that ATR had sufficient knowledge to conclude that the aircraft had a 'sufficient, recurring airworthiness problem' in icing conditions outside of its icing certification envelope, and that neither the vortex generators nor the operational information disseminated had corrected the problem.

The Board also ruled that following a non-fatal incident in early 1994, the DGAC should have required ATR to take further action to correct the ice-induced aileron instability, and that this inaction led directly to the crash later that year. The FAA had apparently misunderstood the function of the vortex generators when it approved their installation and rescinded the previously imposed flight restrictions, believing they would eliminate the hinge moment reversal problem rather than only delaying the onset of a greater AOA. Though neither ATR nor the DGAC provided the FAA with analyses of previous ATR incidents, or in one case sufficient information, the NTSB said that the FAA should have recognised the problems with the aircraft.

The ATR 42 and 72 had been certified under a Bilateral Airworthiness Agreement, but the role of the FAA in this compact was found to be inadequate by the NTSB, with insufficient monitoring of the process. The procedure was found to have been deficient in a previous case (contributing to two icing-related accidents involving the Spanish-built CASA 212). The US agency did not, for example, test the aircraft throughout a significant portion of the icing conditions specified in the Appendix C icing envelope, and the criteria did not include larger water drops, such as freezing drizzle and rain, conditions prevalent in much of the US during the winter months. Also, the manufacturer did not, nor was required, to explain to airworthiness authorities or operators the function of the stall protection system with which the ATR had been equipped to prevent, among other things, aileron hinge moment reversals in clean and iced configurations. The NTSB expressed the belief that the FAA should revise its certification regulations to guarantee proper testing of aircraft in all conditions in which they are authorised to fly.

In a related matter, the NTSB claimed that the FAA had 'not acted positively' on its previous recommendations pertaining to individual aircraft performance in icing conditions, and expressed the desire to expand the icing criteria to include both freezing drizzle and rain. It noted that the icing certification criteria had been developed in the 1940s and did not take into consideration technological changes. A review by the FAA of this issue was begun after the American Eagle crash.

The NTSB investigation included an assessment of the weather conditions that were closely linked to the crash. It was concluded that *N401AM* had encountered a mixture of rime and clear icing caused, respectively, by the instantaneous and slow freezing of large, super-cooled water droplets while circling in the holding pattern. There was also an indication of wind shear in the area, which could have resulted in larger drops; some of these drops were estimated to have been greater than 100 microns in diameter, some as large as 2,000 microns. These conditions contributed to the formation of the ice ridge on the aircraft's wing. Data from the DFDR revealed that, on two occasions in the circuit, there was evidence of small drag increases that were probably the result of ice accretions on the aircraft.

Although the NTSB ruled that the weather forecast was 'substantially correct', it expressed concern regarding the lack of meteorological information disseminated to the crew of Flight 4184. An AIRMET advisory, issued more than an hour before the disaster, had forecast 'light to occasional moderate rime icing in clouds and in precipitation; freezing level to 19,000 feet'. Although four such advisories were not included in a combined flight plan/weather package that had been provided to the pilots before their departure (nor was it the procedure of the carrier to do so), the NTSB expressed the opinion that their actions would not have been significantly different had they received them. The pilot of a light aeroplane had at 15:10 local time reported 'light icing' over the Boiler VOR, a waypoint of the ATR, but while the American Eagle crew was on the same frequency, it could not be determined whether the latter heard this radio message. The pilot of an A320 jetliner that had flown through the area around the same time reported icing conditions that he later said were probably 'light to moderate'.

Following the accident, a unique series of tests were conducted over Southern California, using an ATR 72 and an NKC-135A jet tanker that sprayed the airliner with cold water under conditions similar to those encountered by Flight 4184. Although previous testing by the manufacturer had demonstrated that the aircraft could fly safely in icing conditions for at least 45 minutes, meet FAA regulations and did not show any difficulties in conditions for which it was certified, the tanker tests indicated that a mechanism existed that could produce a ridge of ice behind the de-icer boots in both the flaps retracted and 15-degree extension configurations. Further tests confirmed that ice accretions caused by large, super-cooled water drops could extend beyond the active portion of the de-icer boots, and that trailing-edge airflow separations could occur at lower than normal angles of attack. It was also revealed that at near-freezing temperatures, these accretions could shed randomly, resulting in spanwise ice shape asymmetry. Analyses have shown that a sharp-edge ridge on a wing upper surface, in front of one aileron only, can cause an uncommanded deflection of the control surface. Tanker tests also resulted in aircraft behaviour consistent with autopilot disconnection, uncommanded aileron deflection and roll excursions similar to that experienced by N401AM. The NTSB report noted that the original certification test programme lacked evaluation of aircraft characteristics in conditions that it would expect to encounter.

Also studied by the Board were the actions of the crew of Flight 4184 and, specifically, their failure to make a successful recovery from the uncontrolled descent. The pilots' apparent lack of concern about their prolonged operation in icing conditions may have been influenced by their extensive experience of flying around the American Great Lakes region, with its notoriously cold winter weather. The ice

that had apparently been visible on the windscreen and other parts of the aircraft was probably not perceived as threatening. Also, they probably expected the hold to be of short duration, and had they seen the ice ridge, would probably have exited the area, the NTSB concluded.

It was noted in the report that in following procedures for flight in icing conditions, the crew had activated the aircraft's anti-icing and de-icing systems and set the propellers at 86 per cent of the maximum rotational speed. The system was then deactivated and the propeller speed reduced to 77 per cent, which the Board noted would have been appropriate for flying outside icing conditions. The latter actions were not considered a factor in the subsequent accident, however, because the system would not have prevented the formation of ice where it was believed to have occurred, nor affected airflow over the ailerons. After a second aural alert, about 7 minutes after the first, the Level III ice-protection system, which controls the de-icer boots on the wings, was again activated, and the propeller speed increased back to 86 per cent.

Based on information provided by the manu-facturer, holding with the flaps partially extended would have been considered a more desirable margin for stall protection, and the ATR brochure had in fact advised crews to extend the flaps as close to maximum flaps-extended speed (Vfe) when flying in freezing rain. Also, the pilots would have had no reason to believe that the extension of the flaps would result in an accumulation of ice in front of the ailerons. In addition, the only performance degradation they would have expected would have been a continuous loss of air speed until activation of the stick-shaker stall-warning device, and not a sudden aileron deflection. But in this case, the AOA was not sufficient to activate the stick-shaker prior to the deflection.

The NTSB noted that previous ATR aileron moment incidents occurred with the flaps retracted and involved large, long-term speed losses resulting from ice-induced drag that are normally recognised by pilots. And since the flaps had not been extended and therefore not retracted in these previous incidents, the aircraft were not trimmed for flight at angles of attack that were significantly higher than the aileron hinge moment reversal AOA, as was the case here. Therefore, in the previous upsets, a small increase in speed would have permitted the aircraft to maintain level flight at an AOA below that at which the aileron hinge moment would reverse. The crew of N401AM were thus faced with a more difficult situation. Aileron control would have been difficult and confusing due to multiple encounters with high control wheel forces and unusual oscillatory aileron behaviour. Also, at the time, the aircraft was probably in instrument meteorological conditions, which would have prevented the pilots from using outside visual cues for attitude reference. And due to the aircraft's 'Vfe lock-out' mechanism, they could not have re-extended the flaps to reduce the AOA. Since the ailerons of the ATR are not hydraulically activated, a pilot would have to overcome manually the rapid increase in the force produced by the aileron reversal action. Though the force required to regain control was within FAA regulations, the Board concluded that because the rapid, uncommanded rolls occurred without warning, and with the pilots lacking the proper training for such a situation, recovery would not have been possible. (The report noted that successful recoveries from previous upsets were partly attributable to rapid pilot action.)

By the time the pilots regained control of the ailerons, the ATR was in a near-inverted attitude and in a steep, high-speed descent that would have been unfamiliar to them, especially considering their lack of unusual attitude recovery training in the type aircraft. The crew could have believed the control difficulties were due to autopilot, structural or mechanical failure, and under the circumstances, conventional unusual-attitude recovery techniques may have been ineffective. The crew had levelled the wings and were bringing up the nose of the aircraft when the structural failure occurred.

In accordance with NTSB recommendations made a week after the accident, the FAA, about a month later, banned operation of both the ATR 42 and 72 into known or reported icing conditions and use of its autopilot if icing were to be inadvertently encountered, pending a review of the aircraft. As an additional preventative measure, air traffic control (ATC) personnel were directed to provide priority handling to an ATR whenever the pilots requested deviations to avoid icing conditions.

This accident led to a redesign of the aircraft's wing de-icing boots so they would cover a larger area, and subsequent tanker tests proved the modification as successful in preventing the accretion of ice aft of them. Within seven months of the crash, all US-registered ATR 42/72 aircraft had been so modified, and the NTSB said the addition of the extended boots coupled with improved operational procedures and heightened awareness by pilots had reduced the risk of a similar accident involving the type. In its report on the crash of Flight 4184, the Board suggested the revision of FAR icing criteria for aircraft, with greater emphasis on such specific issues as liquid water content, temperature and drop-size distribution, which the FAA had previously rejected on the grounds that it would be 'excessively penalizing and economically prohibitive', and the NTSB also reiterated the need for training of pilots in recovering from unusual attitudes, which it had first called for in an accident report published in 1972, but without action by the FAA. Other recommendations included a requirement that Hazardous In-flight Weather Advisory Service (HIWAS) broadcasts consistently include all pertinent information contained in meteorological reports and forecasts.

The NTSB received a stunning rebuke from the Bureau Enquetes Accidents (BEA) for its report on the American Eagle disaster. The French agency expressed 'disappointment' at not being asked to participate in the investigation into the crash in the areas of analysis, findings and safety recommendations, and further said it 'strongly disagreed' with all but one section of the report, including the conclusions and probable cause, which it labelled as 'incomplete, inaccurate and unbalanced'. Instead, the BEA listed as the probable cause of the accident the loss of control by the flight crew caused by an accretion of the aforementioned ridge of ice due to the prolonged operation of the aircraft in conditions of freezing drizzle, well beyond its certification envelope, close to the Vfe and utilising a 15-degree flap configuration that had not been authorised in the Aircraft Operating Manual, which led to a sudden roll upset following an unexpected aileron hinge moment reversal when the pilots retracted the flaps during the descent. Contributing to what it called a 'highly unusual chain of events' were the failure of the crew to comply with basic procedures, to exercise situational awareness, crew resource management and 'sterile' cockpit procedures in a known icing environment, which prevented them from exiting these conditions before the roll event, and their lack of appropriate control inputs to recover after the upset had occurred; the insufficient recognition by airworthiness authorities and the worldwide aviation industry of the potential threat to aircraft performance and controllability posed by freezing drizzle; failure of Western airworthiness authorities to ensure that aircraft icing certification adequately accounted for the hazards that can result from flight in conditions outside FAR Part 25, Appendix C, and to adequately account for such hazards in their published icing information; the lack of anticipation by the manufacturer as well as aeronautical authorities in Europe and the US prior to the tanker tests that the ice-induced aileron reversal phenomenon could occur, and the improper release, control and monitoring of Flight 4184 by ATC personnel.

In its own report, the BEA said the NTSB investigation clearly showed that the crew had entered icing conditions, yet failed to comply with published requirements. It noted that despite the forecast of freezing temperatures, the crew had turned off the de-icing system, initially failing to activate it even after the first warning chime indicating the possibility of ice, and selected a propeller speed that was not to be used in icing conditions. It also emphasised that higher air speeds would have prevented the use of flaps, which was contrary to both the manufacturer's and the carrier's operating manuals stating that holding should be accomplished in a clean configuration. The BEA refuted the claim by the NTSB, stating that ATR did disseminate to its operators, including American Eagle, extensive information and warnings reminding them that prolonged exposure to conditions of freezing rain was to be avoided and that icing could affect performance and controllability in such a way as to cause autopilot disconnect and subsequent roll excursions. Regarding the aileron hinge moment reversal problem, it noted that four previous incidents were stall departures following ice accumulation that resulted from the failure of the flight crew to select airframe de-icing and to maintain minimum air speeds or proper propeller settings. The BEA maintained that a specific warning about the aileron reversal would not therefore have been needed to prevent this accident had the crew followed proper procedures. According to the DGAC, testing of the ATR was 'comprehensive' and

included simulated icing, using the most critical shapes, and tests in natural icing conditions, and its ice-protection systems have demonstrated 'acceptable performance'. It was noted in the French report that while some minor uncommanded aileron activity had been noted during icing tests, this was considered normal, and that neither the manufacturer nor the airworthiness agencies representing either nation had specifically identified the aileron hinge moment reversal phenomenon.

With regard to the actions of the crew, the BEA referred to what even the NTSB described as 'some potentially distracting events' taking place aboard N401AM, notably, about 15 minutes of personal conversation between the captain and the junior flight attendant, the playing of music on an automatic direction finder (ADF) frequency that began shortly after the aircraft entered the holding pattern and lasted nearly 20 minutes, and the departure of the captain from the flight deck for around 5 minutes. It was the opinion of the BEA that the cockpit atmosphere 'lacked the conservative and attentive nature to detail that is required when operating a commercial aircraft'. Specifically, the BEA noted the absence of a response from the crew to the single caution chime, which may have been from the anti-icing advisory system, and that at the time the captain had been explaining the GPWS to the attendant; the departure of the captain from the flight deck without providing the first officer with any instructions only seconds after the comment from one of the pilots, 'I'm showing some ice now', and at least two separate intercom conversations between the co-pilot, then alone in the cockpit, with the cabin attendants and the captain. And even considering his 'biological' needs, the BEA said there was no evidence that the captain had used his trip to the lavatory at the back of the aircraft to check for airframe ice. When he returned to the cockpit, he did not acknowledge the comment of the first officer, 'We still got ice'. Nor was the controlling ATC agency notified of the situation. This crew inactivity was further illustrated by their failure to comment on a traffic alert and collision-avoidance system (TCAS) warning of possible conflicting air traffic less than 5 minutes before the crash, according to the BEA. The French agency also criticised the CVR transcript that appeared in the NTSB report, which it said was 'highly edited' and left out what the former classified as 'non-pertinent conversations' that it considered 'highly pertinent'.

The BEA stated that holding at 10,000 ft in icing conditions constituted a 'critical' phase of flight, and that the 'sterile cockpit' rule should have applied. This differed from the NTSB findings, which found the actions of the crew as not contributing to the accident (specifically noting that the captain's departure from the flight deck occurred during a relatively low workload, and that the traffic that triggered the TCAS alert had been several miles away and would therefore only have been 'advisory' in nature). Regarding the actions of ATC personnel, the BEA report noted that the Indianapolis controller released the flight following a 42-minute hold on the ground despite having been informed that an in-flight hold would also be required. Also, the failure of controllers to solicit a pilot report from N401AM, which was required when they became aware of light-to-moderate icing conditions, violated FAA regulations and contributed to the accident. And since the ATR had been the only aircraft in the area, clearance to another altitude would have been possible, or the crew could have exited the area altogether after encountering the icing.

It was further observed in the French report that following the upset, the pilots did not discuss what was occurring or how they should respond to the situation. Data from the DFDR also showed that their recovery actions were not coordinated, and involved them pulling on their respective control columns at different times. During the uncontrolled flight deviations the rudder deflection was found to have been 'erratic', and never exceeded 2 degrees, even though the maximum available deflection was 3.5 degrees. With regard to the crew's background and experience, the BEA noted that the captain had previously failed to competently demonstrate proficiency in a single-engine non-precision approach in an ATR 42, and that the first officer was neither type-rated nor a licensed airline transport pilot, only possessing a commercial certificate and no 'aircraft type' rating.

In its own analysis of the American Eagle crash, the BEA said the initial roll resulted from both the local asymmetrical lift loss and the roll moment created by aileron suction, both directly related to airflow separation. But it insisted that aerodynamic

'efficiency' was maintained despite this condition, and that recovery would have been possible.

The BEA generally agreed with the recommendations of the NTSB, but one of the areas in which it differed pertained to the 'sterile' cockpit rule, which the former said should apply to all operations in icing conditions.

Date: 8 December 1995 (*c.* 04:20)
Location: Near Sovetskaya Gavan, Russian Federation, Commonwealth of Independent States
Operator: Far East Aviation (Russia)
Aircraft type: Tupolev Tu-154B (*RA-85164*)

All 98 persons aboard (90 passengers and a crew of eight) perished when the jet airliner, operating as Flight 3949, crashed some 200 miles (320 km) north-east of Khabarovsk, which was an en route stop during a domestic service originating at Yuzhnosakhalinsk, on Sakhalin, with an ultimate destination of Novosibirsk. The wreckage of the aircraft was located in a forested, mountainous region 11 days after its sudden disappearance.

Last reported cruising in early morning darkness at an approximate height of 35,000 ft (10,050 m), with its autopilot engaged, the Tu-154 had plunged to earth at a high rate of speed and in a near-vertical angle of descent, disintegrating on impact. There was no fire. The crash could have resulted from a combination of the following factors: deviations in the aileron control system, which, while under automatic flight control, decreased the available lateral control moment and in turn caused an increase of the tendency to bank to the right that went unnoticed by the crew; excessive banking of the aircraft, which the crew attempted to correct by means of asymmetric fuel transfer from the wing tanks, a method that had not been prescribed by the operations manual but was nevertheless not forbidden; fuel imbalance occurring during normal transfer associated with a lack of distinctive deviations from the prescribed parameters of fuel asymmetry in the wing tanks coupled with insufficient information about the abilities of lateral automatic trimming of the transport, which prevented the crew recognising the abnormal situation; insufficient control of the aircraft's right-banking tendency because the crew were distracted by a landing briefing, combined with the

An American Airlines Boeing 757–200 of the type involved in the controlled-flight-into-terrain accident near Cali, Colombia. *(Author)*

deactivation of the 'high bank' alarm in the Tu-154 model transport, and as a result the pilots had been too late in recognising the situation; or belated action on the part of the crew in recovering from the progressive banking condition that was related to the absence of unusual attitude recovery training of pilots, and in this case led to spatial disorientation and their inability to prevent the accident. The weather was not considered a factor.

Technical and operational recommendations stemming from the investigation of this crash included a check of the flight control systems in the entire Tu-154 fleet, and a proposed reactivation of the type aircraft's excessive bank alert and a revision of its operations manual to clarify fuel transfer procedures, and the implementation of pilot training programmes for the recognition of and recovery from unusual attitudes.

Date: 18 December 1995 (time unknown)
Location: Near Caungula, Lunda Norte, Angola
Operator: Trans Service Airlift (Zaire)
Aircraft type: Lockheed 188C Electra (9Q-CRR)

In the highest death toll ever in a disaster involving a propeller-driven airliner on a passenger flight, 141 persons aboard lost their lives when the four-engine turboprop crashed and burned as it was taking off from the Jamba airport. Among the three injured survivors was the co-pilot, one of five crew members assigned to the aircraft.

The Electra, which had been chartered by the National Union for the Total Independence of Angola (UNITA), was returning refugees to northern Angola, and 83 of its passengers were children. There were reports that the rearward movement of unsecured baggage may have shifted the aircraft's centre of gravity, resulting in a stall and a consequent loss of control.

Date: 20 December 1995 (21:41)
Location: Near Buga, Valle del Cauca, Colombia
Operator: American Airlines (US)
Aircraft type: Boeing 757-223 (N651AA)

Having nearly completed an international service from Miami, Florida, US, Flight 965 was cleared for a very-high-frequency omnidirectional range/distance-measuring equipment (VOR/DME) procedure approach to Runway 19 at Alfonso Bonilla Aragon International Airport, serving Cali. Over the next few minutes, a period marked by confusion on its flight deck, the jetliner strayed from the proper course, descended below the minimum altitude and ultimately crashed in the Andes some 25 miles (40 km) north-north-east of its destination. All but four passengers among the 163 persons aboard the aircraft were killed in the disaster, including the entire crew of eight. The survivors, who included a man and his 6-year-old daughter, two members of a family of four on the flight, suffered serious injuries.

In accordance with its original flight plan, the aircraft was to have used Runway 01, but in an apparent attempt to expedite the landing, the crew decided to approach from the opposite direction. After the aircraft was granted clearance for descent down to flight level 200, and in response to the approach controller's query as to its position, the captain responded, 'The DME is six three'. Following passage of the Tulua VOR station (ULQ), which was the initial approach fix, the 757 turned to the left of the cleared course and proceeded in an easterly direction for about a minute. It then turned right back towards the airport, after which the pilot reported his position as 38 miles north of Cali and asked, 'You want us to go to Tulua and then do the Rozo . . . to runway one nine?' Subsequently, and while on a magnetic heading of 223 degrees and at a position about 10 miles (15 km) east of the prescribed airway, the jetliner struck trees on the east side of a mountain, just below its crest, at an approximate elevation of 9,000 ft (2,700 m), its undercarriage and flaps retracted at the moment of the crash. After the initial impact, the aircraft continued over the top of the ridge and came to rest on the west side of the mountain, where the wreckage burned. It was dark at the time, but the meteorological conditions in the area were good, with scattered clouds at 1,700 ft (c. 520 m) and a broken overcast at 8,000 ft (c. 2,500 m), and a visibility of around 5 miles (10 km). The winds were from a south-south-easterly direction at 4 knots, and rain showers had been reported in the vicinity.

Aeronautica Civil of Colombia, which investigated the accident, was able to identify a series of operational errors committed by the two pilots that led to the crash when the mistakes interacted, and which began with their acceptance of the controller's offer to land on Runway 19, even though 01 had normally been used in American Airlines' operations. As the cockpit voice recorder (CVR) only transcribed the last 30 minutes of the flight crew's conversation, it did not contain details of whatever approach briefing had taken place beforehand, or whether there had been one at all. However, the evidence indicated that the aircraft had continued on the appropriate flight path until it entered the Cali approach airspace. The accident report cited as the probable cause of the disaster the failure of the crew to adequately plan and execute the approach and to use the aircraft's automation properly; their failure to discontinue the approach despite numerous cues indicating the inadvisability of continuing it, and a lack of situational awareness by the pilots with regard to the terrain and location of critical navigational aids. Concerning the planning issue, there was no evidence that the crew had

reviewed the approach chart earlier in the flight, or referred at all to the Cali area chart. They then failed to revert to basic radio navigational guidance when the computer-assisted navigation became confusing and demanded an excessive workload in a critical phase of the flight.

Listed as contributing factors were the crew's ongoing efforts to expedite the approach and landing in order to avoid potential delays, as well as their execution of an escape manoeuvre with the aircraft's speed brakes (spoilers) deployed; the flight management computer (FMC) logic which erased all the intermediate fixes from the displays during an attempted direct routeing, and the system of symbolising radio aids in the FMC that differed from those appearing on the navigational charts being used by the crew.

The crew's decision to expedite the landing by changing the approach pattern, which was made after a brief exchange between the pilots, had undoubtedly been related to a 2-hour delay in the departure of the flight from Miami. This change made it necessary to, among other things, locate the correct approach chart, review it while engaged in other critical tasks, change the flight management system (FMS) computers, recalculate air speeds, altitudes and configurations and hasten the descent because of the shorter distance involved. According to the report, the 'hurried nature' of the tasks that needed to be performed and the inadequate review of critical information between the offer to land on Runway 19 and their passage of ULQ indicated that insufficient time was available to effectively accomplish these actions. Consequently, several necessary steps were carried out improperly or not at all, and the pilots failed to recognise they were heading towards the high terrain until just before impact.

A significant factor in the accident was the improper use of the aircraft's FMS. Although such specific FMS information as heading, altitude and selected navigational aids were not among the parameters transcribed by the flight data recorder (FDR), it was believed that one of the pilots had entered into the system the incorrect identifying code for the Rozo non-directional beacon (NDB), which was located near the end of the runway, apparently using only the letter 'R'. This simple error would have resulted in the display of 12 such beacons, and choosing the first one in the list would have been a logical assumption by a pilot. However, to retrieve the identifier for the Rozo beacon, the entire name would have been required. The letter 'R' actually represented the Romeo beacon, located near Bogota, some 130 miles (210 km) east-north-east of Cali. This programming of the FMS was done without verification that it had been the correct selection and without the approval of the other pilot, which was contrary to American Airlines' procedures. Simulations indicated that when 'R' was inserted into the control display unit (CDU) keyboard, the autopilot would turn the aircraft in the direction taken by N651AA.

The confusion on the flight deck at this point was illustrated by the comments of the two pilots, which were transcribed by the CVR. Less than 3 minutes before the crash, the first officer asked, 'Where are we?' Seconds later, he asked, 'Where are we headed?' The captain then responded, 'I don't know . . . what happened here?' This disorientation was related to their inability to locate the Tulua VOR on the FMS displays. The deviation was finally realised by the crew, who tried to return to the extended centreline of the runway by turning right. But since the 757 had been proceeding on an easterly heading and was to the left of the direct track to the Rozo NDB, the turn took the aircraft on a south-westerly heading in the direction of the mountainous terrain that lay in between. It was then that the captain requested clearance to proceed directly to the Rozo beacon. But as he had previously altered the FMS in order to proceed directly to the Cali VOR station, he removed the fixes between it and the aircraft, including Tulua, towards which the crew was to have proceeded. At that point, the 757 had already passed the initial approach fix, and from the CVR transcript, there was no evidence that the crew recognised either this or the fact that ULQ had been deleted from the display. In what was referred to in the report as 'cognitive tunnel vision', the pilots never reconsidered and in fact 'doggedly pursued' their decision to land on Runway 19. After the descent had begun, neither of them made an attempt to terminate it despite their deviation from the published approach course and into a valley between two mountain ridges. The descent from flight level 230 was in fact continued until just before impact.

The captain had previously flown 13 times into Cali, and his experience may have lured both crewmen into believing they could rapidly employ a modified, deviated approach. The first officer had no previous experience there, and in the darkness he may have relied upon the former's experience and relaxed his vigilance. His inexperience may also have reduced what should have been a more assertive role as the pilot flying. And the fact that Cali had not been considered a 'high-altitude' facility, as are other South American airports, both crewmen may not have exercised the same level of caution. In the final seconds before impact, the CVR recorded the activation of the ground-proximity warning system (GPWS), and the captain was heard to say, 'Pull up, baby'. Although the first officer initiated a go-around manoeuvre in accordance with prescribed procedures, neither pilot had recognised that the spoilers remained deployed, and no attempt was made to retract them. It could not be determined with certainty whether the escape manoeuvre would have been successful with them retracted, though an initial performance study showed that had they been a second after the initiation of the overshoot, the 757 may have cleared the trees at the top of the ridge. Significantly, the airline did not include speed brake retraction as part of a GPWS escape manoeuvre, and the spoiler annunciator was only activated when in the landing configuration and/or below 800 ft (c. 250 m). And due to the limited aerodynamic effects of them, flight crews may not be aware of their deployment. Before the crash, full engine thrust was applied, and the stick-shaker stall-warning system activated when the nose of the aircraft started to rise. The FDR revealed that the pilots then relaxed their control column back pressure. And even though the weather was not considered a factor in the accident, the night-time conditions would have prevented the crew from seeing the terrain in time.

This accident also highlighted the inter-relationship between pilots and so-called 'glass cockpit' transports, such as the 757, equipped with highly sophisticated FMS systems using computerised cathode ray tube navigational displays. In its report, Aeronautica Civil said the crash indicated the need to revise procedures in the operation of such aircraft. Noting that American Airlines' superior crew resource management training had advised pilots to use charts and partially or completely disengage the FMS when they believed the system was exacerbating and not alleviating a difficult situation, the report stated that the crash of Flight 965 also demonstrated that merely informing crews of the hazards of over-reliance on automation may be inadequate. The FMS graphically portrays the aircraft's position and, using a magenta-coloured line, its future flight path, as well as available navaids. It is so accurate that pilots may come to rely on it as the primary means of navigation. However, it does not indicate terrain relief, nor navaids that are behind the aircraft. Also noting that technological advances have made it possible to present terrain information on FMS displays, the investigative agency recommended that the US Federal Aviation Administration (FAA) encourage the development and implementation of the new technology. Furthermore, considerable differences existed in the presentation of identical navigational information between that on the approach chart and that in the FMS database, such as a different labelling of DME fixes, even though it had been provided by the same map company. And despite its prominent display as 'R' on the approach chart, the crew were evidently not aware of the fact that the letter did not correspond to the Rozo beacon. Nor had the airline begun using new navigational charts that employ colour-enhanced graphics to indicate surface features instead of the dots that appeared on the chart that was this crew's primary source of information pertaining to terrain elevation.

Still another factor was the relationship between the crew and the Cali approach controller, whom the report exonerated of all responsibility in the crash. It was noted that the captain had established the erroneous flight path initially by misin-terpreting the controller's instructions to proceed to Cali as a direct routeing, as indicated by his read-back of the message, 'Cleared direct to Cali VOR . . . report Tulua'. He received an 'affirmative' from the controller, because the statement indicated he would report crossing the fix first. Limited in the English language and not trained to solicit information from the pilots to determine the extent of the difficulty they were experiencing, the controller said the pilot's request to fly direct to ULQ when the aircraft was 38 nautical miles (70 km) north of the Cali VOR, and obviously past the former navaid, made no sense to him, but he added that he believed the pilot merely forgot to report passing the station. And although the controller said there were no language difficulties between him and the crew, he later admitted that he

would have asked the pilots more detailed questions regarding the routeing and approach had they spoken in his native Spanish. Also, with the airspace not having radar coverage or the computer software to provide an alert that an aircraft is deviating from a safe altitude, the controller was entirely dependent on information from the crew to determine its position, height and heading. Despite his experience in South America, the captain's actions indicated that his expectations of the controller's capabilities were influenced by his experience in the US, where surveillance radar is usually available, along with terrain clearance advisory service. Warnings regarding the hazards to operations in less developed nations such as Colombia had been posted in American Airlines' training manual.

The report noted that while the wreckage of the downed jetliner was not located until the following morning, nearly 9 hours after the accident, and that five passengers initially survived the crash, with one succumbing later in hospital, the search and rescue effort had been 'timely and effective' when considering the remote, mountainous terrain.

Since the initial certification of the FMS on the 757 and its wide-bodied sister, the Boeing 767, the system had been modified to allow such fixes to be retained in the display, but this modification had yet to be incorporated into N651AA. Such an improvement was one of the recommendations made in the report, as was the development and implementation of an enhanced GPWS. With regard to the latter, American and other carriers subsequently announced plans to equip their aircraft with such units. Aeronautica Civil also recommended that the International Civil Aviation Organisation (ICAO) establish a single, worldwide standard to provide unified criteria for electronic navigational databases used in FMS systems. Meanwhile, the FAA issued a bulletin in the wake of this crash that listed inconsistencies between FMS databases and aeronautical charts.

Date: 8 January 1996 (*c.* 13:00)
Location: Near Kinshasa, Congo
Operator: African Air (Congo)
Aircraft type: Antonov An-32B (*RA-26222*)

Though not occurring on a true passenger service, this crash is noteworthy because of the extra-ordinarily large number of fatalities on the ground, which in fact made it the worst 'third party' accident in the history of commercial aviation.

Leased from the Russian carrier Moscow Airways and on a non-scheduled domestic cargo flight to Kahemba, Bandundu, carrying food and consumer goods, the twin-engine turboprop began its take-off at Ndolo Airport, serving Kinshasa, its flaps having been extended to 25 degrees. The aircraft accelerated to about 120 mph (195 kmh), which corresponded to the rotation velocity (Vr) at the declared maximum take-off weight (MTOW) of 26 tonnes (58 MT), but while the load on it lightened slightly, the nose wheel never became airborne. Nearly 50 seconds into the ground run, and after having reached an approximate speed of 125 mph (200 kmh), the crew aborted the take-off but could not bring the aircraft to a safe stop. (No traces of braking were found on the pavement.) Overrunning the runway, the An-32 crossed a drainage ditch and a road before it finally ploughed into an open air market and caught fire. A total of 298 persons lost their lives in the accident, including one crew member; among the 258 injured were the five survivors from the aircraft, i.e. the three other members of the crew and two non-revenue passengers. The weather at the time was clear, with a visibility of around 5 miles (10 km) and a 6-knot wind from a west-south-westerly direction.

It was determined that the MTOW of the An-32 had exceeded the maximum allowed by 1,000 to 3,000 pounds (2,200–7,000 kg). There had also been inadequate supervision of the loading of the aircraft, which was accomplished by personnel of the Congolese airline without the crew being present. An operational factor in the disaster was the belated recognition of the situation on the part of the pilots, which led to the delay in abandoning the take-off. Contributing to the high death toll was the proximity to the airport of the heavily congested market.

Date: 6 February 1996 (*c*. 23:50)
Location: North Atlantic Ocean
Operator: Alas Nacionales (Dominican Republic)
Aircraft type: Boeing 757-225 (*TC-GEN*)

Leased from the Turkish carrier Birgenair Charter Group, Inc, and on a non-scheduled transatlantic service with an ultimate destination of Frankfurt, Germany, the jet airliner had taken off from the airport serving Puerto Plata, Dominican Republic, bound for Gander, Newfoundland, Canada, the first of two en route stops. Only about 5 minutes later, the 757 plunged into the sea approximately 15 miles (25 km) north-east of the city, in water some 7,000 ft (2,000 m) deep. All 189 persons aboard, including a crew of 13, perished in the crash. Nearly all of the passengers were German tourists returning home. Searchers subsequently recovered the remains of around 80 victims but virtually none of the aircraft's wreckage. However, both its digital flight data (DFDR) and cockpit voice (CVR) recorders were retrieved by the US Navy, and, following analysis by the US National Transportation Safety Board (NTSB) in Washington, DC, provided considerable evidence for a determination of the probable cause of the disaster.

A significant event in the accident sequence was the removal from service, due to a 'technical defect', of the Boeing 767 jet that was originally supposed to make the trip. This necessitated bringing in *TC-GEN* and a new crew. During the take-off roll of the 757, the captain was heard to say that his air speed indicator was not working properly. This prompted him to ask the first officer to refer to his own instrument, which was functioning, and the take-off proceeded. After becoming airborne, the pilot said that his indicator was operating. The autopilot and autothrottle were then engaged, with the former placed in the vertical and lateral navigation modes. Subsequently, the engine indicating and crew alerting system (EICS) activated, displaying 'Rudder Ratio' and 'Mach/Speed Trim' advisory messages. After the crew realised something was wrong, the co-pilot noticed his air speed indicator to be showing 200 knots – and falling. At that point, the captain's indicated air speed was about 145 mph (230 kmh) above the reading of the first officer's instrument, and the height about 5,300 ft (1,600 m). Concerning the different readings, the captain asked, 'What can we do?' As the aircraft continued to climb, the overspeed warning sounded, but the captain ordered it switched off. Moments later, and after the stick-shaker stall-warning system had activated, the autothrottle was also switched off. When engine output started to drop, the pilot asked, 'We are not climbing . . . What should I do?' The co-pilot replied that the descent had to be stopped and said he would turn on the altitude hold function of the autopilot. Thrust remained low until the captain ordered the application of full power, but the output of the left engine then went down as the right one remained at the maximum rate. Its bank angle increasing and power remaining approximately constant, the aircraft was at a height of about 2,370 ft (720 m) and in a nose-down pitch attitude when the ground-proximity warning system (GPWS) sounded, seconds before impact. It was dark at the time of the accident, and the meteorological conditions in the area, which were not considered a factor, consisted of good visibility, with scattered clouds below 1,800 ft (550 m) and up to 7/8 coverage at 7,000 ft (c. 2,000 m), and east to south-westerly winds of 10 knots.

The great divergence between the aircraft's indicated air speed, whose values were not considered accurate, and its actual ground speed – at one point, while at an approximate altitude of 7,000 ft (2,000 m), the former was recorded by the FDR to have been around 400 mph (650 kmh), or more than 200 mph (320 kmh) above the latter, which was calculated from radar data – and this divergence corresponded to a total loss of the static system for the captain's air speed indicator. A blocked pitot tube would account for such an erroneously high reading. Tests by the manufacturer showed that such blockage would cause a lower static pressure in the system, making the indicated velocity increase at the same rate as the increase in the altitude of the aircraft. There was no evidence of any other technical failures, nor of a pre-impact fire or explosion, and even the failure of the pitot system should not have jeopardised the flight.

The primary factor in the accident was determined to have been the uncoordinated actions of the pilots in response to the different air speed indications, and their failure to effectively carry out the proper recovery technique following the activation of the stick-shaker. The initial failure was that of the captain, who was remiss in not giving enough importance to the divergent readings and who should have discontinued the take-off upon observing the anomaly. (Calculations proved that the aircraft could have been stopped on the remaining runway at that point.) Although both he and the first officer seemed to realise that the standby air speed indicator was showing the correct velocity, neither seemed to realise the significance of this reading. In fact, none of the three flight crewmen, who included a relief pilot, proposed any cross-checking or changing to the first officer's system. The crew were equally negligent in recognising the aircraft's unusual pitch attitude, which continued to increase as the 757 ascended. The increase in pitch was related to the engagement by the crew of the vertical speed mode of the autopilot; the switching off of the autothrottle led to the power reduction. The pitch of the aircraft had reached nearly 20 per cent when the stick-shaker activated, and at that point the autopilot automatically disengaged. And because it was disconnected, the attempt to switch to the altitude hold function had no effect on arresting the descent after TC-GEN had begun to lose height.

Simulations showed that recovery could have been possible by reducing pitch, but by the time the GPWS activated, the 757 was already out of control as a result of the crew's poor discipline, lack of knowledge of the aircraft's systems, inadequate basic piloting skills and their failure to follow the operating handbook regarding an erroneous air speed indication. Still another factor was believed to have been pilot fatigue, since the crew involved in the accident had to be brought in to replace the one originally slated to make the flight, and were thus out of their planned work routine. At 62, the Turkish captain was two years past the retirement age for airline pilots in many countries. Nearly 10 per cent of his 24,000 flying hours were in the 757, though his first officer had only 71 hours in the type.

The left pitot tube, which provided the information for the pilot's air speed indicator, was not recovered, preventing the investigative commission from determining the cause of its failure. The most likely reason was dirt and/or insects in the tube. Significantly, the aircraft had not been flown for 20 days before the date of the crash. Engine tests were conducted on the ground during this time, but maintenance personnel apparently did not cover the tubes. A check of the static pressure system, which was recommended before a flight, would probably have revealed the suspected blockage.

In its report, the Dominican Republic's Directorate General of Civil Aviation proposed that the Boeing 757/767 handbook be revised to remind crews that simultaneous 'Rudder Ratio' and 'Mach/Speed Trim' warnings signified erroneous air speed indications, and that Boeing incorporate a caution alert to warn of such incorrect readings. Noting that Birgenair lacked such pilot training, it also recommended the greater use by airlines of crew resource management.

Date: 29 February 1996 (20:26)
Location: Near Yura, Arequipa, Peru
Operator: Compania de Aviacion Faucett SA (Peru)
Aircraft type: Boeing 737-222 (*OB-1451*)

Designated as Flight 251, the jet airliner crashed in the Andes Mountains while attempting to land at Rodriguez Ballon Airport, serving the city of Arequipa, which was a scheduled intermediate stop during a service originating at Lima, with an ultimate destination of Tacna. All 123 persons aboard (117 passengers and six crew members) were killed.

The aircraft had been authorised for a landing approach to Runway 09, using very-high-frequency omnidirectional range/distance-measuring equipment (VOR/DME) non-precision instrument procedures. After being instructed to report when the runway was in sight, the crew asked whether the airport lights were at their maximum intensity, to which the control tower replied to the affirmative. Less than 20 seconds after that last communication, *OB-1451* struck a hill at an approximate elevation of 8,000 ft (2,500 m) and while on a near-southerly heading, i.e. in alignment with the runway but some 4.5 miles (7 km) short of its threshold. Its undercarriage extended and flaps set at 30 degrees, the 737 was in almost level flight at the time of the initial impact, and it then broke apart and caught fire, coming to rest on the opposite side of the ridge. It was dark at the time, and the weather in the area about half an hour before the accident consisted of a low overcast, with the clouds scattered at 1,000 ft (*c.* 300 m) and broken at 3,000 ft (*c.* 1,000 m), and the visibility having been reduced by a low, dense fog to less than 1.5 miles (2.5 km). Another pilot reported being able to see the runway from a distance of 2 miles (*c.* 3 km).

Although most of the aircraft's instruments were destroyed, the pilot's air speed indicator showed a reading of around 150 mph (250 kmh), and his corresponding altimeter indicated the correct elevation. A height of 8,500 ft (*c.* 2,600 m) had been selected on the altitude alert system. Apparently not having been serviced in more than

six years, the cockpit voice recorder (CVR) had not transcribed anything on this particular flight and thus proved of no use in the investigation of the crash. Examination of the wreckage revealed no evidence of pre-impact malfunction in the engines or other vital components of the 737.

The principal cause of the accident was determined to have been error by the crew, specifically, their descent below the minimum altitude during the final approach phase. When the flight reported being at 9,500 ft (*c.* 2,900 m), it had actually been some 1,500 ft (500 m) below that height. And after going below the minimum descent altitude, the pilots apparently tried to make visual contact with the runway. The crew were thus proceeding under visual flight rules (VFR) procedures in the instrument meteorological conditions (IMC), and during this time *OB-1451* lost an additional 130 ft (*c.* 40 m), leading to the impact with rising terrain at a point approximately 250 ft (75 m) below the elevation of the airport. Significantly, the ground-proximity warning system (GPWS) would have been deactivated when the aircraft was in the landing configuration, providing its descent rate had not been excessive.

It was recommended in the investigative report for airlines to take action to ensure that their flight crews adhere to minimum prescribed altitudes, and also avoid the use of VFR procedures when flying in IMC.

Date: 11 May 1996 (*c.* 14:15)
Location: Near Miami, Florida, US
Operator: ValuJet Airlines (US)
Aircraft type: McDonnell Douglas DC-9 Series 32 (*N904VJ*)

All 110 persons aboard perished when the jet airliner, operating as Flight 592, crashed approximately 17 miles (27 km) north-west of Miami International Airport, from where it had taken off about 10 minutes earlier, on a domestic service to Atlanta, Georgia. The victims included a crew of five and a 4-year-old riding on an adult's lap who had not been listed on the passenger manifest.

The scene of this particularly grisly tragedy was in a swamp of the Everglades region, where the water ranged up to 7 ft (2 m) deep. Cleanly configured, the aircraft was in a nose and left-wing-

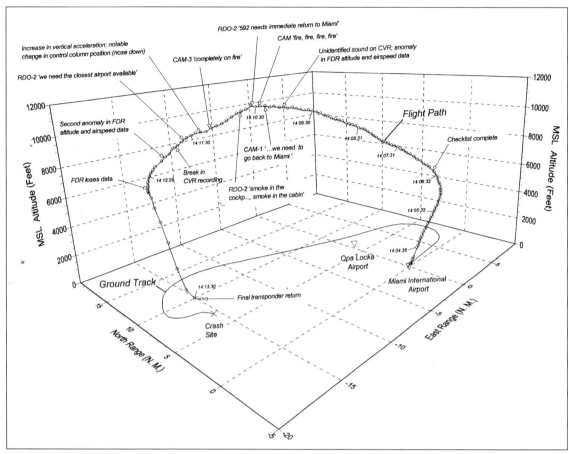

Three-dimensional diagram showing the path of the ValuJet DC-9 which crashed in the Florida Everglades due to uncontrollable fire in the cargo hold. *(National Transportation Safety Board)*

down attitude at the moment of impact, upon which it disintegrated, leaving a crater in the mud and sawgrass. Although its flight data recorder (FDR) had stopped functioning about a minute before the crash, computations made from radar data indicated that at impact the velocity of the DC-9 had been more than 450 mph (740 kmh). The airport weather shortly after the accident on this Saturday afternoon was generally good, with scattered clouds at 4,000 ft (*c.* 1,200 m) and a broken overcast at 8,000 ft (*c.* 2,500 m), a visibility of 10 miles (*c.* 15 km) and a 10-knot wind blowing from a south-easterly direction. Among the human remains retrieved from the scene of the crash, 68 of the victims were identified.

Despite the difficult conditions, recovery operations yielded nearly 80 per cent of the aircraft's structure, and examination of the forward cargo compartment, which was reassembled into a full-scale, three-dimensional mock-up, exhibited soot and heat damage, confirming that an in-flight fire had occurred aboard *N904VJ*. Pieces of a number of chemical oxygen generators were also found at the accident site. These were part of a shipment of about 150 such units contained in five boxes that had been loaded aboard the aircraft, along with three DC-9 tyres, and classified as company-owned material (COMAT). The oxygen generators, which were beyond or approaching their expiry dates, had been removed from two MD-80 jet transports recently purchased by ValuJet, with the work being done for the airline on a contractual basis by the firm SabreTech.

The generators are part of the emergency oxygen system in a passenger aircraft, designed for use in the event of a cabin depressurisation. Each unit is activated by a percussion cap, and when its core is heated to its 'decomposition' temperature, oxygen is liberated as a gas through a chemical reaction. Through this process, the exterior of the generator becomes very hot, typically 450 to 500 degrees Fahrenheit (c. 230–260 Celsius). Given this hazard, generators are supposed to be actuated before they are transported; unexpended, they are regarded as hazardous material. However, only about half a dozen of the units placed on Flight 592 had apparently been deactivated.

It was concluded by the US National Transportation Safety Board (NTSB) that the blaze that led to this disaster had been initiated by the activation of one or more of the generators in the forward cargo compartment of N904VJ. This must have occurred at some point after the loading process began, but possibly as late as during the take-off roll. The subsequent uncontrolled descent occurring as the aircraft was returning to the airport most likely resulted from flight control failure due to both the extreme heat and structural collapse.

The final desperate minutes aboard Flight 592 were captured by the aircraft's cockpit voice recorder (CVR). About 5 minutes after take-off, the captain was heard to say 'We got some electrical problem'. Seconds later she said, 'We're losing everything'. Shouts in the background were also heard, and a male voice exclaimed, 'We're on fire . . . we're on fire!' After the first officer had radioed a request for an immediate return to Miami, the aircraft was cleared on to a due-westerly heading and for descent to 7,000 ft (2,000 m), the maximum height it had reached during the climb-out being just under 11,000 ft (3,400 m). The departure controller continued to provide vectors to the crew and advised them, as requested, of their position and distance to Opa Locka Airport, a possible landing site. One of the last comments recorded on the CVR, some 2½ minutes before impact, was a remark from a flight attendant, 'Completely on fire!' Even though only light sooting on the cockpit area was indicated on the recovered wreckage, and only a small amount of smoke had apparently entered the flight deck before the crew's last recorded verbalisation, heard only seconds after the attendant's remark, it could not be completely ruled out that the pilots were incapacitated by the heat or smoke in the final 7 seconds of the flight. (None of the occupants' remains were suitable for determining carbon dioxide and hydrogen cyanide

levels.) The NTSB concluded that because of the absence of smoke in the cockpit and/or their heavy workload, the crew did not use or delayed using their oxygen masks and goggles, and noted that there are no requirements for use of the latter equipment. And although the Board concluded that it would probably not have prevented the accident, the fact that many airlines place the goggles in sealed plastic wrapping can hamper the donning process.

That the improper carriage of the generators aboard a commercial flight had been allowed in the first place was blamed by the Board on the failure of SabreTech to properly prepare, package and identify the units before presenting them to ValuJet, without the airline's authorisation, for transport back to the latter's main hub at Atlanta. The lack of a formal system in the contractor's shipping and receiving department, including procedures for tracking the handling and disposition of hazardous materials, contributed to this failure.

The mechanics who removed the units from the other aircraft were not made fully aware, by reading only the corresponding work card, of their hazardous nature or of the existence of an approved, uncomplicated procedure for expending the generators that required no unusual equipment. Because there was no requirement for an inspector's sign-off of the work card at the completion of each task, there may have been no inspection of the maintenance work related to the removal of the units. The NTSB investigation revealed that one of the mechanics who was aware of the need for safety caps on the generators, which would have prevented an accidental activation, later carried the open boxes containing the units to the shipping and stores area without informing anyone there what they were, or of their hazardous nature. And one of the SabreTech inspectors who also knew they needed safety caps signed the 'final inspection' block on the work card anyway, with the understanding that the issue would be taken care of 'in stores' of that department, but never verified this as having been done. Plans were then made to ship the five cardboard boxes containing the generators; however, the canisters were labelled as 'empty' when placed in the No. 1 and No. 2 cargo compartments of N904VJ after its arrival from Atlanta and minutes before its departure on the return flight that would end in disaster. The Board

The outline of the doomed ValuJet DC-9 and fragments of debris are all that is visible in the swamp following the disaster that claimed the lives of all 110 persons aboard the aircraft. *(www.popperfoto.com)*

concluded that had a warning label or emblem clearly indicating their danger been affixed to each generator, it might have alerted the personnel handling them and prompted the acquisition of safety caps. (Although the use of the wrong tags on the oxygen units was identified by the NTSB as another procedural shortcoming of SabreTech, it probably did not contribute to the mishandling of the generators that led to their placement aboard the aircraft.) Also cited as a factor in the accident was inadequate oversight by the airline of its subcontractor, specifically, its failure to ensure compliance with maintenance and hazardous materials requirements and practices, this despite the fact that it had conducted an initial inspection and an audit of SabreTech and assigned three technical representatives to its facility.

The disaster could not have come at a less opportune time for ValuJet, an upstart airline that had begun operations only about 2½ years earlier. Two previous non-fatal accidents and 46 regulatory

violations occurring since its inauguration of services had in fact prompted a 120-day surveillance of the carrier, starting on 22 February 1996, by the US Federal Aviation Administration (FAA). By the first day of May, more than 300 inspections of the airline's operations and airworthiness activities had been conducted; however, none of these had taken place at SabreTech or any of the carrier's other heavy maintenance contractors. The surveillance programme continued after the accident, and on 18 June, after finding ValuJet in violation of Federal Aviation Regulations, the FAA suspended its operating certificate. After paying US $2 million for 'administrative' costs incurred during the review and submitting to an FAA requirement to revise its organisational structure as well as its maintenance programme and procedures, which included the retraining of personnel, the airline resumed operations on 30 September. An FAA inspection of SabreTech, which was launched after the crash, revealed numerous deficiencies there, including the lack of a formal mechanic training programme and syllabus. SabreTech ceased operations of its Miami repair station and, in January 1997, closed its other station in Orlando, Florida.

The repercussions of the crash of Flight 592 went well beyond the airline and its contractors, however. On the same day it grounded ValuJet, the FAA announced a 90-day review of itself, emphasising ways to strengthen its oversight of airlines that rely on contract maintenance and training and enacting additional requirements for new entrant airlines. The failure of the FAA to adequately monitor SabreTech's repair station certificate and ValuJet's heavy maintenance programmes and responsibilities, including the airline's oversight of its contractors, had in fact been cited as contributory to the disaster. Additionally, the lack of an explicit requirement for the designated principal inspector to survey Part 145 repair stations that had been performing such maintenance was considered by the NTSB as a 'significant deficiency' in the oversight function of the FAA. In part because he was responsible for so many operators, the principal maintenance inspector assigned to oversee SabreTech in Miami had been unable to provide effective supervision of the operations conducted at that facility.

In its investigative report, the NTSB pointed to other lapses in the regulatory authority of the FAA as contributing factors. The former ruled that had the latter responded to prior oxygen generator fires by allocating sufficient resources and initiating programmes to address the potential hazards of these units, including the issuance of follow-up warnings and the inspection of shipping departments and aircraft maintenance facilities, the shipment that led to this tragedy might have been stopped. According to the Board, the FAA had in fact known of five previous non-fatal incidents in which such generators had initiated fires, the first of these, occurring nearly 10 years before the ValuJet crash, having destroyed a wide-bodied DC-10 that was on the ground. Following that blaze, the FAA did issue a warning to all airlines concerning this hazard, but no further action was taken despite the fires occurring thereafter. It was noted in the NTSB report that while the FAA had one, its hazardous materials programme had previously been shifted to its security division, and

that most of the time of the inspectors assigned to it was in fact spent on security issues.

Also identified by the NTSB as an omission on the part of the FAA was the latter's failure to require fire- and smoke-detection and fire-extinguishing systems in Class 'D' aircraft cargo compartments despite a number of blazes and several related safety recommendations by the former. In accordance with Code of Federal Regulations (CFR) requirements, a fire occurring in either of the two Class 'D' compartments located in the underside of the DC-9 should have been completely confined without endangering the aircraft or its occupants, and not have been able to progress beyond safe limits. In response to recommendations made following a non-fatal blaze aboard an MD-83 in February 1988 for fire/smoke detection and extinguishing systems in Class 'D' compartments, the FAA claimed that liner and container requirements already in effect were sufficient. The Board noted that in the case of Flight 592, even had the blaze not started until after the jet was airborne, a warning device would have alerted the pilots more quickly and allowed them more time to return to the airport. And had the DC-9 been equipped with a fire-suppression system, it may have checked, or at least delayed, the spread of the blaze, and in conjunction with an early warning, would likely have given the crew enough time to land safely. Though admitting that the intensity of the fire aboard N904VJ may have been so great that a suppression system might not have fully extinguished it, the NTSB concluded that an FAA requirement for one would probably have prevented the crash.

Not quite 13 months after the ValuJet disaster, the FAA issued a directive requiring the retrofitting with both smoke detection and fire-suppression systems in Class 'D' cargo compartments of airliners registered in the US. The industry would have three years from the time the rule became effective to meet the new standards. About six months before the FAA announced these plans, the US Airline Transport Association, representing carriers throughout the nation, announced that its members would voluntarily retrofit existing Class 'D' compartments with smoke detectors.

With regard to the movement of hazardous materials by air, the FAA announced about two months after the crash a realignment of US $14 million to improve its oversight in this area, and the following year began a series of inspections at major air transportation hubs in direct response to the issue. The NTSB noted that in hiring a programme manager and increasing its staff by more than 100, the FAA 'should provide the leadership and personnel necessary to oversee an effective hazardous materials programme.' The Board nevertheless expressed concern over the transportation of undisclosed hazardous materials in regular US mail shipments carried aboard commercial aircraft. The continued transport of oxygen generators on passenger aircraft had been prohibited in a rule issued by the US Research and Special Programs Administration about two weeks after the ValuJet disaster, though the NTSB noted that the prohibition in effect even before the crash had 'not been completely effective'. (ValuJet may in fact have been previously carrying hazardous aircraft equipment on its passenger flights, even though it went contrary to company policy.)

Just over three years after the disaster, and in an action considered unprecedented in US commercial aviation history, SabreTech was charged in a 24-count criminal indictment in connection with the crash. In December 1999, a federal jury found the firm guilty on nine counts, but two years later, all but one of the convictions were quashed by an appeals court. The one count that was upheld

A still from a video simulation showing the initial break-up of the TWA Boeing 747 following explosion in the aircraft's centre wing fuel tank. *(Central Intelligence Agency)*

blamed SabreTech for failing to conduct hazardous materials training. Meanwhile, the carrier ValuJet has vanished into history, having merged in 1997 with AirWays Corporation and changed its name to AirTran Airways.

Date: 17 July 1996 (*c.* 20:30)
Location: Off Long Island, New York, US
Operator: Trans World Airlines (TWA) (US)
Aircraft type: Boeing 747-131 (*N93119*)

No airline disaster in US history has generated more rumours, speculation, misguided theories and outright misinformation than the crash of Flight 800.

Having arrived at John F. Kennedy International Airport following a service from Athens, Greece, *N93119* was on the ground for slightly under 4 hours as maintenance personnel refuelled and readied it for its next international trip, to Paris, France. Its scheduled departure had been delayed for about an hour because of a disabled piece of ground equipment, combined with concerns about a suspected passenger/baggage mismatch. It then took off from Runway 22R, after which the 747 turned eastward, roughly paralleling the southern coast of Long Island as it climbed towards its cruising altitude. The last radio transmission from the aircraft was acknowledgement of authorisation for ascent to 15,000 ft (*c.* 5,000 m). Less than a minute later, or some 12 minutes into the flight, radio and radar contact with *N93119* was lost. Around this time, hundreds of witnesses reported hearing an explosion and seeing a large fireball in the sky.

The wide-bodied jetliner had exploded at a position approximately 10 miles (15 km) south of the town of East Moriches and about 60 miles (100 km) east of New York City, then fell in pieces into the Atlantic Ocean. All 230 persons aboard were killed, including a regular crew of 18 and 17 off-duty crew members riding as passengers. Among its four flight crewmen was a check engineer riding in the cockpit jump-seat. The disaster occurred just after sunset on this Wednesday evening, and the weather about 15 minutes later at the nearest meteorological reporting point, some 15 miles (25 km) north of the crash site, consisted of scattered clouds at 6,000 ft (*c.* 1,800 m), a visibility of around 5 miles (10 km) in haze and a surface wind of 4 knots from a direction of 240 degrees. There

A virtual 'sea of fire' was produced by burning fuel atop the ocean surface where TWA Flight 800 crashed off Long Island, New York. *(Newsday Inc. © 1996. Reprinted with permission)*

was no evidence of any significant weather conditions in the immediate area of the crash.

The catastrophic nature of the disaster, a rarity in modern commercial aviation, pointed to the strong possibility that the destruction of Flight 800 was no accident but a criminal act. Media reports and the almost immediate entry into the investigation of the US Federal Bureau of Investigation (FBI) only fuelled speculation that *N93119* had either been sabotaged by an explosive device planted aboard or brought down by a missile, possibly a shoulder-mounted type. The suddeness of the event was reflected by the simultaneous stoppage, at 20:31:12 local time, of both the aircraft's digital flight data (DFDR) and cockpit voice (CVR) recorders. A review of the data and the intra-cockpit conversation of the crew indicated that the performance of the aircraft had been normal throughout the flight until the instant the recorders ceased functioning. A few minor anomalies were noted, one of which was difficulty experienced on at least one occasion in trimming the 747 by the pilot flying it, who apparently had limited time in the type. There were also 'drop-outs' on one CVR channel and the captain's comments about a 'crazy' No. 4 fuel flow indicator, and these electrical anomalies would prove significant in the subsequent investigation. At the end of the recorded

data, the cleanly configured transport was determined to have been at an approximate height of 13,800 ft (4,200 m), in a slight nose-up attitude and proceeding on a true course of about 70 degrees at a speed of 437 mph (703 kmh). What the report of the US National Transportation Safety Board (NTSB) described as a 'very loud sound', obviously the first fraction of a second of the explosion, was heard on the CVR tape before that recording ended. The noise transcribed was compared to recordings from other aircraft disasters, two resulting from bombs. However, the sounds from the TWA crash more closely resembled that of a fuel tank explosion in a Boeing 737 that was on the ground and from another 747 that had suffered an explosive decompression after the loss of its forward cargo door at high altitude.

The truth of what had apparently happened to Flight 800 would come to light after a lengthy investigation by the NTSB, which involved considerable related research and testing. With conflicting eyewitness reports and neither the DFDR nor the CVR yielding much information, solving the mystery of what caused the disaster would have to be found in the wreckage of *N93119*, which itself lay strewn across the ocean floor, distributed in three main debris fields along a north-easterly path about 4 miles (6.5 km) long and approximately 3.5

miles (5.5 km) wide, in water some 120 ft (40 m) deep. A small amount of debris was found on the surface of the water, but most had to be lifted from the seabed in a massive operation, which itself got disrupted by a hurricane that swept over the area in September 1996. This was a two-pronged effort that also involved the retrieval of victims. A total of 99 bodies were taken from the surface within 24 hours of the crash; the rest were found on the bottom of the ocean, some intermingled with the debris. The recovery was accomplished by US Navy and local police divers, working in extremely hazardous conditions due to the depth of the water and the condition of the wreckage. The last of the human remains were found more than 10 months after the disaster. Most of the identifications were through fingerprints and dental records, though in 29 cases, DNA or radiographic techniques were employed. Based on pathological examinations, the NTSB concluded that while the crash was non-survivable, some of the occupants may not have been killed in the initial explosion.

More than 95 per cent of the aircraft's wreckage was ultimately recovered, and significant parts of N93119 were then painstakingly reassembled on the floor of a hangar at Calverton, on Long Island, including a section of the fuselage 93 ft (28 m) long. One area of unrecovered or unidentified fuselage structure, measuring approximately 1 sq ft (0.3 sq m), was in the vicinity of the centre wing fuel tank (CWT). Outward bulging or deformation of its upper and lower surfaces indicated what the report described as an 'over-pressure event' occurring within the centre tank. The evidence of an in-flight fire included blackened structure, melted wiring and aluminium materials and burned composite materials from the fuel tank areas.

In its investigation, the NTSB examined various theories and possible factors in its attempt to determine the underlying cause of the disaster. The evidence discounted the two hypotheses receiving the most attention early in the investigation, i.e. the destruction of the 747 by a bomb or missile. This evidence was the absence in the wreckage of the characteristics typically associated with a high-energy explosion, such as pitting, cratering or petalling in the aircraft's structure. And none of the missing pieces of fuselage were large enough to have encompassed the damage that would have resulted from such a detonation. Nor did any of the victims show signs of exposure to a high-energy blast. Though identified in one press account as 'rocket fuel', a reddish-brown substance found on several passenger seats proved consistent with an adhesive material used in their construction. Trace amounts of explosive residue found in three separate locations in the wreckage were first thought to have been deposited during an explosives-detection dog-training exercise the previous month, or perhaps when N93119 was used to transport military troops to the Persian Gulf five years earlier. But since such residues would be expected to dissipate after only two days of water immersion, and because very little wreckage was recovered in such time, the material more likely came from the many military ships and personnel that participated in the search and recovery operation. And in any case, the trace amounts were not linked to an actual explosion.

The NTSB even examined the possibility of the nearby detonation, rather than a direct hit, which sent a single fragment into the CWT without peppering the 747 with holes. But since this would have required a detonation sufficiently far from the aircraft not to leave any other damage but close enough to provide the fragment with enough velocity to penetrate the tank, this theory was considered 'highly improbable'. In further exploring the missile hypothesis, the NTSB reviewed data from ground radar stations in four states, including long-range installations in Massachusetts, New York and Pennsylvania, and also from the US Air Force. The radar targets of three aircraft were observed in the immediate area of N93119, but all were identified. Four uni-dentified primary returns were believed to have been boats on the surface of the ocean. Several other echoes were believed to have been radar 'reflections' off the ground or buildings, or primary returns of aircraft causing false primary targets in another geographic area. The absence of physical and radar evidence also put to rest the theory that Flight 800 had been the victim of 'friendly fire', shot down accidentally by a US Navy ship; besides, records showed there had been no military surface vessels within about 15 miles (25 km) of the crash site at the time. There were no indications of pre-existing fatigue, corrosion or mechanical damage that could have contributed to the in-flight disintegration of the jetliner, nor that the crash had been precipitated by the separation of the aircraft's forward cargo door.

On the basis of evidence, the Board concluded that the break-up of *N93119* had been initiated by an explosion in the centre wing tank. The largest of seven fuel tanks in the 747 and the only one not in the wings, the CWT could hold nearly 13,000 gallons (5,000 dkl). But since the tank had not been refilled before take-off, it was believed to have contained only 50 to 100 gallons (*c.* 20–35 dl) of kerosene-type Jet-A fuel at the time of the explosion. The tank was thus filled with a highly volatile fuel/air mixture, which had ignited. A ground test performed in England involving the detonation of explosive charges in a retired 747 confirmed that a fuel/air explosion in the CWT could lead to the destruction of the aircraft. No determination could be made with certainty as to the energy release mechanism, nor exactly where in the tank the ignition had occurred, but the NTSB concluded that the blast was most likely caused by a short circuit producing excess voltage that had been transferred to the centre tank by the wiring of the fuel quantity indicator system (FQIS). (This system uses probes and compensators to measure the amount of fuel in each tank, and this information is then relayed electronically to the flight deck.) Significantly, the only electrical wiring components in the CWT of a 747 are those associated with the FQIS. Among other possible ignition sources examined were a lightning strike, an uncontained power plant failure, a turbine burst in the aircraft's air-conditioning packs, or a malfunctioning fuel system jettison/override pump, but all of these were considered 'very unlikely'. The NTSB could not totally rule out a malfunction in the scavenge pump in the CWT, even though the unit, designed to remove the last amount of usable fuel from the tank, was believed to have been switched off at the time. A hot surface ignition, such as a fire in a wheel well, would almost certainly have left significant evidence of thermal damage, and due to the design of the fuel tank vent system, there would be little chance of a fire originating in another fuel tank and then migrating to the CWT.

Although there was no clear indication of any arcing in any of the components connected to the centre tank FQIS, the investigative report noted that the evidence could have been obscured by the extensive fire damage in the area or by the complexities in these wiring and circuit assemblies. Also, a lower-power short or one resulting from moisture could have occurred without leaving any evidence of arcing. There was evidence of possible arcing of other FQIS wires and wires adjacent to them, and of possible arcing or heat damage on two wires routed in the same raceway as the centre tank FQIS. The latter two were found near numerous floor and structural repairs made after the bursting of a portable water tank. (This area was near the 'C' galley, which was the site of reported leaks in the two weeks preceding the disaster.) Such leakage could have dripped on to electrical wiring beneath the galley floor and caused a short circuit that in turn affected the FQIS wiring in the centre tank. Repairs to the area around the upper deck flight attendant lighting panel, carried out about a month before the crash, could also have created a situation conducive to short-circuiting when considering that the repaired wire was part of a bundle that contained CWT and port wing FQIS wires that led to the upper deck airborne integrated data system (AIDS) unit and also contained high-voltage wiring. The lighting wires were also bundled with wires attached to the CVR and the No. 4 fuel-flow wires along some portions of their path, and a short circuit in any of them could have manifested itself in the electrical anomalies indicated on the CVR recording and the No. 4 fuel-flow indicator about 2 minutes before the explosion. It was noted in the NTSB report that the manipulation of wires occurring during repairs could have resulted in their displacement and consequent cracking.

Much of the insulation on the wiring recovered from the 747 was cracked or otherwise damaged, often exposing the inner conductor, which when powered would have been vulnerable to short-circuiting. Although some of this damage probably occurred as a result of the accident or during the recovery operation, the degraded condition of the wiring found in other commercial jets of approximately the same age suggested that at least some of it did not. In fact, some 20 per cent of the wiring in these aircraft failed dielectric testing, an indication of the loss of integrity of their insulation. But since only about 4 ft (1.2 m) of the centre tank FQIS wiring from *N93119* was recovered, the degree of the pre-existing damage could not be assessed. According to TWA, the fuel quantity probes and compensators used in the FQIS as well as most other electrical and system components are 'conditioned-monitored' items, which would only have been replaced when inoperative and only inspected during the major 'D' check, which had last been carried out on the aircraft nearly four years earlier. These were in fact the original probes and compensators installed on N93119, which was 25 years old and had some 93,300 flying hours.

Examination of the recovered FQIS wires revealed repairs to them before the crash, as well as repairs that did not comply with either the manufacturer's or the carrier's standards. These findings included an oversized strain relief clamp on the terminal block of the compensator in the No. 1 fuel tank, through which passed a cable harness that had not been firmly secured, and with chafing observed on some wires; numerous wire splices whose ends were left open at a number of locations throughout the aircraft, and wire bundles containing splices that were not spaced as recommended. Additionally, the connector pins in the recovered fuel totaliser gauge were found to contain excessive soldering, which itself had cracked between them, and appeared to have been inadvertently joined to the connecting pins and wires from the right main and centre wing tank FQIS.

Such improper soldering could have created a mechanism by which a short circuit from a higher-voltage wire in the right wing FQIS wiring could have carried excessive voltage to the CWT. Another way to transfer excess energy to the CWT would be a short circuit from a higher-voltage wire to the left wing FQIS wiring. Also, the presence of a conducive material, such as metal drill shavings or safety wire, could have provided a mechanism leading to the arcing of FQIS components. Shavings could have been introduced during the extensive structural repairs carried out on the aircraft, or when its cabin was altered. Testing revealed that the Teflon-cushioned wire clamps found in the CWT and inboard main fuel tanks were particularly susceptible to electrostatic charging. There was no proof of this being capable of producing enough voltage to ignite Jet-A fuel, but in view of previous fuel tank explosions, the possibility of static electricity as the ignition source could not be completely ruled out.

Research and testing conducted during the investigation of the crash found that silver-coated copper parts inside fuel tanks, such as those used in the FQIS, can develop sulphide deposits that are semi-conductive and thus capable of reducing the resistance between electrical connections, and this could in turn permit arcing. Such deposits were in one case found in a Boeing 757 jetliner with only 750 flying hours. (Newer aircraft use nickel instead of silver plating to avoid this problem.) Resistance heating could have been in itself a potential source of ignition, occurring when a thin filament became heated through contact with a wire, probe or compensator exposed to excess voltage. Evidence of such could also have been lost or at least obscured by fire damage. The NTSB explored the possibility that the ignition had been precipitated by electromagnetic interference (EMI) from radio frequency sources external to the aircraft, or possibly even from a personal electronic device. However, its study found neither capable of producing a sufficient electrical signal needed to ignite the vapour, and this theory was therefore considered unlikely.

Reconstruction of the probable break-up sequence after the explosion in the CWT indicated that after the failure of the front spar, the combined load of normal cabin pressurisation and vented over-pressure from the tank and centre wing section ultimately fractured the keel beam. The belly structure then separated, followed some 3 to 5 seconds after the initial blast by the forward fuselage section. Computer simulations based on radar data, trajectory calculations and simulated aircraft performance indicated that after the separation of the nose section, N93119 ascended to a height of around 15,000 ft (5,000 m), then rolled into a descending right turn. During the descent, and after about half a minute of crippled flight, the outboard sections of both wings separated simultaneously, resulting in the release of fuel from the main wing tanks that precipitated fuel-fed fires. The rest of the port wing then tore away, which explained what some witnesses described as the 'splitting' of the fireball. The break-up sequence was confirmed by the distribution of the wreckage, with the aft portion having been found further along the flight path than the forward fuselage section. It was concluded that the 'streak of light' observed by numerous witnesses before the appearance of the fireball had actually been the aft part of the 747 still climbing after the initial CWT explosion. It was possible the crippled aircraft might have appeared to have been rising vertically, especially to those in a position to see it coming directly towards them. But there was no evidence that anyone saw a missile streaking towards the jetliner before the first explosion. The entire break-up sequence until impact with the water was believed to have occurred in slightly less than a minute.

A major reason for the flammability of the fuel/air mixture in the CWT was the design of the 747, in which the aircraft's three air-conditioning packs were located in the bay directly below the tank. (On two other American jumbo jets, the DC-10 and the L-1011, the packs were located in the aircraft's nose section.) The design in Boeing's wide-bodied transport allowed heat generated by the packs to be transferred through the bottom of the tank, causing temperatures in the CWT to rise above the flammability limit. It was noted in the report that in the case of Flight 800, two of the aircraft's air-conditioning packs had remained in operation for about 2½ hours before its departure. And in a simulated flight using a 747 that almost exactly duplicated the conditions encountered by *N93119* on that summer evening, sensors indicated the ullage temperature in the tank to have reached 145 degrees Fahrenheit (*c.* 60 degrees Celsius). This was well above the 96 degrees Fahrenheit (*c.* 35 degrees Celsius) at which one study found the Jet-A vapours could be ignited. Under the circumstances, therefore, a single ignition source such as one previously mentioned could cause an explosion. The NTSB in fact cited this design as a contributing factor in the crash of Flight 800, and recommended industry action in this area to reduce the threat of fuel tank explosions.

Even before the release of the final report, several immediate measures were taken as a safety precaution. One of these was an airworthiness directive (AD) issued in January 1997 by the US Federal Aviation Administration (FAA) requiring the removal of wires from conduits in the Nos 1 and 4 fuel tanks of every Boeing 747 in service and inspections and replacement of damaged sleeving or wires. The AD was subsequently modified to include the inspection in the 747 fleet of auxiliary fuel tank jettison pumps, and a subsequent directive required similar inspections on another Boeing transport, the twin-jet 737. The manufacturer itself issued a service bulletin

requiring the inspection, modification and possible replacement of the scavenge pump.

In its report, the Board concluded that the existing standards may not provide adequate protection against damage from short-circuiting. Noting that no special separation was required for FQIS and other fuel system wiring, including that to probes and gauges, the NTSB recommended that the FAA review the design specifications for aircraft wiring systems to ensure that adequate separation is provided, and also identify the systems most critical to safety. The report further noted that a design and certification philosophy relying solely on the elimination of all ignition sources while accepting the existence of fuel tank flammability is 'fundamentally flawed', concluding that operating transport-category aircraft with flammable mixtures in their fuel tanks presented 'an avoidable risk of explosion'. The Board also expressed concern about the effort by the FAA in 'minimizing, rather than eliminating' fuel tank flammability. The FAA would later announce that it was undertaking a 'parallel effort' to address the threat of fuel tank explosions by eliminating or significantly reducing the presence of fuel/air mixtures in new designs, those in production and in the current fleet of aircraft. One technique recommended by the NTSB was the use of nitrogen-inerting systems and insulation. In December 2002, the agency announced the development of such an inerting system, one that reduces the percentage of oxygen in a fuel tank while increasing the amount of inert gases. Additionally, the FAA began to examine the possible use of ground sources in providing air-conditioning to aircraft. And in following the recommendations of a US Presidential commission on aviation safety formed only about a week after the crash of TWA Flight 800, the FAA established the Ageing Transport Systems Rulemaking Advisory Committee in order to address the issue of older aircraft in the American commercial fleet.

Date: 29 August 1996 (10:22)
Location: Spitsbergen (Svalbard), Norway
Operator: Vnukovo Airlines (Russia)
Aircraft type: Tupolev Tu-154M (*RA-85621*)

The jetliner crashed in the Advantdal Valley region on the island of Nordenskiold some 10 miles (15 km) east of Svalbard Airport, located near Longyearbyen,

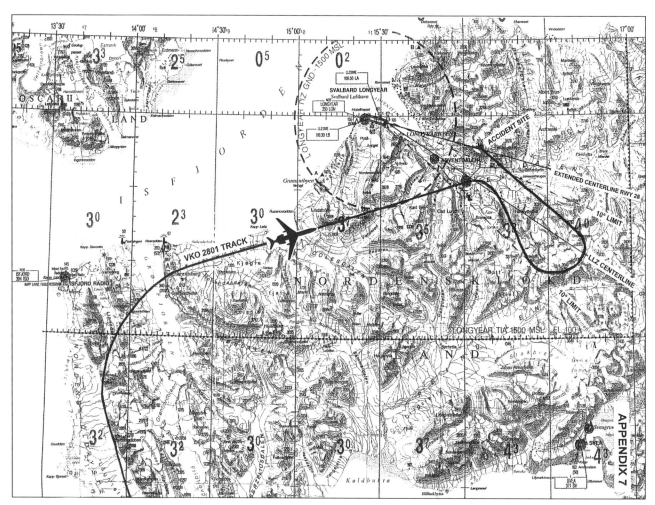

The approach path of the Vnukovo Airlines Tu-154, indicating the deviation from the localiser centreline that led to the crash on Spitsbergen. *(Norwegian Aircraft Accident Investigation Board)*

where it was to have landed at the end of an international charter service from Moscow, Russia. All 141 persons aboard perished. Included among the 11 crew members were two technicians; both of the pilots were captains, one of whom had previously landed at Svalbard. The passengers consisted of workers and their families on their way to the coal-mining towns of Barentsburg and Pyramiden, both also on Nordenskiold.

Although the crew had intended to carry out an approach from the west, over water, the Aerodrome Information Service (AFIS) officer informed them that the runway 'in use' was 28. A landing from the east would involve a localiser-only procedure, with the localiser transmitter slightly offset from the runway centreline. In following the approach

pattern, *RA-85621* initially turned on to the downwind leg of the airport circuit, without intercepting the outbound course from the non-directional beacon (NDB) designated 'ADV'. During this time, a malfunction occurred in the aircraft's electric trimming mechanism, which would have moved the control columns back to a nose-up attitude. This problem was corrected by the crew, and the Tu-154 then turned back towards the north-west in order to assume the magnetic heading of 300 degrees prescribed on the approach chart. After passing through the localiser centreline and when the turn was completed, the jetliner rolled out on to a magnetic heading of 290 degrees. But instead of intercepting it, the aircraft proceeded on the right side of the centreline, more or less paralleling the localiser course with some minor heading changes. Subsequently, *RA-85621* hit the edge of the mountain Operafjellet at an approximate elevation of 3,000 ft (1,000 m) and some 2.5 miles (4 km) to the right of the localiser centreline, leaving a wreckage trail in a direction of around 330 degrees. There was no fire. At the moment of impact, the aircraft's flaps were set at 15 degrees and its undercarriage was transitioning to the extended position. As given to the crew, the airport weather some 20 minutes before the crash was overcast, with the clouds broken at 4,000 ft (*c.* 1,200 m), scattered at 2,000 ft (*c.* 600 m), and a few of them down to 1,500 ft (*c.* 500 m), and a visibility of more than 5 miles (10 km) in rain showers. The wind was blowing at 16 knots from a direction of 230 degrees.

A joint Norwegian/Russian inquiry revealed a number of factors as leading up to the disaster. Significant to the accident sequence was the change of direction in the approach to the runway to the opposite of that originally planned, and the acceptance of the new clearance by the crew without challenge. (This may have been partially due to a misunderstanding between the AFIS officer and the navigator, who was handling the radio communications, related to the latter's difficulty with the English language in which both were speaking, coupled with the philosophy of Russian flight crews, who are accustomed to giving more authority to ground and air traffic control personnel than those in the West.) In accordance with the carrier's procedures, the navigator had been responsible for lateral control of the aircraft, using the autopilot control knob, while the co-pilot was controlling vertical navigation. The simultaneous handling of the radio by the navigator was, however, contrary to normal procedures. It was concluded that the navigator had in fact performed 70 to 75 duties of varying difficulty and duration, apparently including the resetting of the aircraft's instruments for the new approach, which demanded his attention for some 20 minutes during the procedure. With this workload, he had little time to recheck his tasks, which would have set the stage for uncorrected mistakes. Two such errors by the navigator were a poor execution of the turn on to the outbound track, and his misidentification of the NDB for the localiser.

After turning outbound from ADV, the crew made the proper correction to compensate for the south-easterly wind, but not the substantial heading change required to intercept the correct 155-degree track. As a result, *RA-85621* assumed a heading of 160 degrees, or to the west of the proper course. Just correcting for drift would explain why the aircraft overflew the final approach course after it turned inbound back towards the airport, and the situation would have been aggravated by the tailwind component encountered in the turn. The intra-cockpit conversation indicated that the crew were aware of being out of alignment with the proper course. However, the fact that the navigator had the Jeppesen approach chart in front of him made it difficult for the pilots to maintain awareness of the situation. There was also disagreement between both pilots and the navigator, with the latter heard on the cockpit voice recorder (CVR) tape to ask for a corrective turn to the right and the captain stating, 'No! Turn to the left!' Probably taking the distance-measuring equipment (DME) reading, the navigator was then heard to command, 'It's thirteen. Let's descend.' The final error by the crew was the initiation of the descent over the hazardous terrain and in the instrument meteorological conditions without a firm and positive control of the lateral navigation of the aircraft. And despite their uncertainty as to whether the approach was being conducted properly, they proceeded with the landing attempt instead of climbing to a safe altitude. After the Tu-154 started turning to the left, it apparently entered an area of strong turbulence created by its proximity to the mountainous terrain, as indicated by the course corrections made by the autopilot and manually by the first officer. A heading of around 290 degrees was maintained in the last 5 seconds until impact.

Just under 10 minutes before the crash, the first of six radio altimeter warnings was heard on the CVR tape. The initial terrain alerts should not have been of concern to the crew, because at that point the aircraft was maintaining a safe altitude, even after the turn on to the final approach leg. Nine seconds before impact, the ground-proximity warning system (GPWS) activated, and although its warning horn apparently failed to function, a second aural alert and a red light annunciator were available to warn the crew. However, the fact that the warning horn was not working could have affected the crew's reaction time. And when the radio altimeter sounded a sixth time, they were probably unsure as to the urgency of the situation, leading to a somewhat slower than ideal reaction. Also, by the time the GPWS activated, there would most likely not have been enough time to apply full power and the maximum control input needed to clear the terrain, even though the flight data recorder (FDR) read-out did indicate an increase in engine thrust seconds before impact.

Although the correct approach track was 300 degrees, a course of 283 degrees, which corresponded to the runway heading, had been selected on both of the aircraft's horizon situation indicator (HSI) units and on the course deviation indicator (COI) located in the centre of each instrument, and the direction towards which the latter would have been pointing could have created the impression of drift, prompting the crew to initially turn to the right. Confusing HSI indications could have created uncertainty on the part of the crew as to their position relative to the runway centreline, and the position of the CDI pointing 17 degrees to the left of the runway heading must during the final approach have convinced the captain and perhaps the first officer that they were to the right of centreline, necessitating a corrective turn to the left. Considered as a 'latent failure mechanism laying dormant in the system' was the rule requiring the landing course to be set on the HSI and the lack of a Russian procedure for an 'offset' localiser approach that modified the requirement of setting the landing course on the HSI. A reassessment of this policy was one of the recommendations made in the accident report.

Other factors identified in the investigation were the failure of the crew to make full use of the available navigational aids, including the aircraft's No. 1 automatic direction finder (ADF) unit, and their over-reliance of the on-board global positioning system (GPS), which the accident report noted was not permitted as a primary approach aid, and whose display should always be confirmed by another source. (The GPS unit installed on *RA-85621* was not recovered, apparently having been removed from the wreckage sometime during the salvage operation.) Significantly, the crew did not conduct a new approach briefing after switching from Runway 10 to 28, and they demonstrated neither satisfactory crew resource management nor situational awareness. Neither investigating board was aware of a procedure that used the radio altimeter as a ground-proximity indicator, nor of one that dealt with the elimination of nuisance warnings. No evidence was found of any anomalies in the ground navigational aids, and atmospheric interference with their signals was considered unlikely. And despite their errors, the crew had selected the correct localiser frequency after changing runways.

The airport had no VOR or ground radar, and the latter could possibly have averted the accident.

Date: 31 October 1996 (08:27)
Location: São Paulo, Brazil
Operator: Transportes Aereos Regionais SA (TAM) (Brazil)
Aircraft type: Fokker 100 (*PK-MRK*)

Designated as Flight 402 and on a domestic service to Rio de Janeiro, the jet airliner crashed and burned approximately half a minute after its departure from Congonhas Airport, located within the city. A total of 99 persons lost their lives in the disaster, including four on the ground; there were no survivors among the 95 aboard the aircraft (89 passengers and a crew of six). A number of houses and buildings were destroyed or damaged as a consequence of both the impact and fire.

This was an accident resulting from a complex sequence of events related to both material failure and the actions of the flight crew, one member of which, the first officer, had limited experience on the Fokker 100. The primary factor was believed to have been the unwanted deployment of the aircraft's starboard engine thrust-reverser. Evidence indicated that the aircraft's electrical system was contributory to the in-flight deployment of the reverser. According to a report prepared by Fokker technicians, high resistance was found on the S-1 switch of the actuator, which could have adversely affected the functioning of the 'Stow Limit' relay, sending spurious signals to the stow solenoid of the selector valve. The Brazilian Centro de Investigacao e Prevencao de Acidentes Aeronautics (CENIPA) investigative agency accepted the possibility that a simple failure of the K-1266A relay unit, characterised by the fusing of any one of its three contacts, could cause a continuous command from the deploy system. This could also have led to the malfunctioning of the secondary lock relay of the

No. 2 engine, which itself depends upon the closure of contacts that in this case did not occur, thus inhibiting the cockpit warning that the reverser was deployed. There was in fact no evidence from the cockpit voice recorder (CVR) transcript that the crew had received either a master caution alert or a 'reverser unlocked' warning. This malfunction, which would have been dormant and thus gone unnoticed, could have been related to a drop in voltage in the electrical system or to other electrical anomalies occurring at the moment of lift-off. When the starboard reverser was examined, the protection cap separated with much greater ease than expected, the apparent result of extended exposure to heat. Also, the surfaces of both contacts in the unit were found to have been contaminated with silica originating from the degradation of organic silicon. Completely foreign to the components, the source of this material was unknown. The manufacturer had not considered the possibility of such a fusion of the contacts in the secondary lock relay system. Also underestimated by the manufacturer, because of the protections in the system, was the probability of the in-flight deployment of a thrust reverser, the chance of which had been placed at only one in 100 billion. So remote was the probability that the training of pilots for such an event had not been considered necessary. Accordingly, and in consultation with Fokker, the carrier discontinued simulator training for reverser unlock during the take-off phase, a decision that would prove significant in the crash of Flight 402.

The investigation revealed that the performance of the crew until the time of the emergency had generally been in accordance with prescribed procedures, except for the fact that the before-start checklist had been carried out only by the first officer, without the presence of the captain on the flight deck, although this did not factor in the subsequent accident. There had apparently been no evidence of the secondary lock being open before departure, and no visual confirmation of any anomaly in the reverser system that was known to have been made during the pre-flight external inspection of the Fokker. There were, however, indications of problems with the aircraft's autothrottle system (ATS), the first of these being the double beep of a caution alert that was heard on the CVR tape before beginning the take-off.

Subsequent warnings were heard during the ground run, at a velocity of around 90 mph (145 kmh), although they were cancelled, and the captain on three occasions made reference to the apparent ATS malfunction. Such a failure should not have jeopardised the safety of the flight, but would have necessitated the manual manipulation of the thrust levers.

Commencing rotation at 150 mph (c. 250 kmh), PK-MRK lifted off from Runway 17-Right, and it was at this time that the No. 2 engine thrust reverser deployed. The only indication on the flight deck of this would have been the automatic retardation of the corresponding thrust lever. The voice recorder transcript indicated that the crew initially misinterpreted the anomaly as a malfunction in the ATS. A pounding sound also recorded by the CVR could have been the crashing of the reverser clamshell doors, and at least two complete reversion cycles were observed by a witness. In response to its retardation, one of the pilots, probably the first officer, forced the lever to its forward limit, apparently taking along with it the No. 1 lever. When the cycle was repeated, the levers snapped back, overcoming the strength of the crew. Quite probably, reference was being made to the inability to move the power plant control in the comment by the co-pilot, also transcribed by the CVR, 'It's locked'. The captain's request to the first officer to switch off the ATS was a further indication that the crew had misidentified the reason for the malfunction of the power plant controls. The co-pilot, apparently confirming his disconnection of the ATS, was then heard to say, 'It is off'.

Three times the No. 2 thrust lever was retarded and then advanced, and that these interventions provoked a retardation of the No. 1 lever had a detrimental effect on the performance of the aircraft. The fact that the No. 1 lever was not returned immediately to take-off power, the delay lasting more than 4 seconds, reduced the ability of the Fokker to climb. Eventually, the velocity of PK-MRK fell to about 145 mph (235 kmh), or just below the safety speed, and consistent with the reduction in speed, its above-ground height never exceeded 120 ft (c. 40 m). The fact that the lever was held forward in combination with the ricochet force produced by the opening of the reverser doors ultimately led to the separation of the feedback cable, which advanced the power plant to higher thrust. With the engines accelerating, the crew would have been unable to identify the reason for the deterioration in the performance of the aircraft and the subsequent loss of control. After the stick-shaker stall-warning system activated, the captain was heard to exclaim, 'Oh my God!' Turning uncontrollably, the jet initially struck, with its starboard wing-tip, the roof of a two-storey building. Its right banking attitude had increased to 108 degrees when the aircraft finally hit the ground. The local weather at the time was good and not considered to have been a factor in the accident, with a visibility of more than 5 miles (10 km) and the wind at 6 knots from a direction of 60 degrees.

When the Fokker 100 was certified in Brazil, its electrical system had been configured so that the 'Stow' solenoid of the thrust reverser selector valve always remained energised, ensuring that the calmshell doors mounted at the rear of the engines would remain closed except when commanded. This was changed, however, through the introduction of the manufacturer-approved 'Stow Limit' relay. The reverser actuators were designed to be isolated from the aircraft's flight controls by 'touchdown' switches, supposedly to prevent their inadvertent, in-flight deployment. But testing revealed that the reverser's secondary lock actuators presented a performance that proved much inferior to guarantee a minimum level of safety and reliability. Tests showed that the thrust selector valve could be moved with less than 2 per cent of the normal pressure when in the de-energised condition that existed at the time of the accident. And since the reverser remained de-energised during the period when there was no command from the crew, this created what the investigative report described as an 'unstable and dangerous' situation. It was also determined that power could be applied beyond the idle thrust position with the reverser doors partially deployed, a fact that did not satisfy Federal Aviation Regulation (FAR) requirements.

Although the specific intentions of the pilots could not be determined, their lack of awareness as to the nature of the abnormality had apparently caused them to abandon the normal procedural sequence, including the retraction of the under-carriage and the activation of the autopilot. Simulator tests showed that even with the gear extended, the adversity could have been overcome

by applying full power on the unaffected engine. Nevertheless, the report noted that the circumstances the crew faced were unusual, with an asymmetrical power condition at a very low altitude, when normally an attempt to manage an emergency situation is not advisable below a height of 400 ft (c. 120 m). Also, the change of thrust had demanded various corrections, which distracted the captain. The absence of cockpit warnings reinforced the belief of the crew as to the nature of the abnormality, just as the lack of information and specific training contributed in their inability to recognise and cope with the situation. Considered as an additional factor was the limited experience in the type aircraft on the part of the first officer, which limited the information and help he could give to the captain. Because of the unique circumstances of the abnormality, however, the effect of this was difficult to determine.

Subsequent to the accident, an airworthiness directive requiring pre-flight testing of the thrust-reversers was sent to operators of the twin-jet transport. Also, take-offs were prohibited when the aircraft's autothrottle was unserviceable. Among the recommendations made by CENIPA in its report on the crash were modifications in the reverser selector valves to prevent any instability from increasing the likelihood of an unwanted deployment, and in the wiring of the alarm system.

Date: 7 November 1996 (c. 17:00)
Location: Near Epe, Lagos, Nigeria
Operator: Aviation Development Corporation (ADC Airlines) (Nigeria)
Aircraft type: Boeing 727-231 (5N-BBG)

Operating as Flight 86, the jetliner had been on a domestic service from Port Harcourt to the city of Lagos, and was to have landed at Murtala Muhammed Airport. It was from there that another 727, flown by Triax Airlines, had taken off. Also in the vicinity at the time was a third aircraft, owned by ELF Petroleum. Following a near-collision between the two jet transports, 5N-BBG plunged into a lagoon some 25 miles (40 km) east-north-east of the capital city, disintegrating on impact, and all 143 persons aboard (134 passengers and nine crew members) perished.

The ground controller had prematurely terminated radar service to the Triax aircraft, allowing it to continue under its own navigation as it proceeded on an easterly course at a height of 16,000 ft (c. 5,000 m). He then delayed a descent request by the ADC 727, which was flying in a westerly direction at 24,000 ft (c. 7,300 m), to allow for safe passage of the corporate aircraft, which had been proceeding on the same heading, but 3,000 ft (c. 1,000 m) lower. However, the controller reportedly 'forgot' about the delay, and when he finally cleared 5N-BBG for descent to 5,000 ft (c. 1,500 m), he must have assumed it was already down to 10,000 ft (c. 3,000 m), or below the other 727.

The traffic alert and collision-avoidance system (TCAS) with which 5N-BBG was equipped activated, and the pilot took evasive action, rolling the aircraft to an excessive bank angle, apparently losing control in the process. During its descent, the 727 rapidly accelerated from about 320 mph (515 kmh) to almost 600 mph (965 kmh), and had nearly reached the speed of sound before its impact, at which time it was in an inverted attitude. The accident occurred shortly before sunset.

The following May, aviation authorities from 55 nations proposed a number of recommendations to improve air safety throughout Africa, which included greater coordination between civilian and military operations in dealing with airspace management.

Date: 12 November 1996 (c. 18:40)
Location: Near Charkhi Dadri, Haryana, India
First aircraft
Operator: Saudi Arabian Airlines (Saudia)
Type: Boeing 747-168B (*HZ-AIII*)
Second aircraft
Operator: Air Kazakhstan
Type: Ilyushin Il-76TD (*UN-76435*)

The worst accident in aviation history was the collision between two commercial jets, which occurred on the ground in the Canary Islands in 1977 (see separate entry, 27 March 1977). This tragedy, occurring some 50 miles (80 km) west of the Indian capital of New Delhi, resulted in the highest death toll in the slightly different category of mid-air collision.

Designated as Flight 763 and bound for Dhahran and Jiddah, Saudi Arabia, the wide-bodied 747 had taken off less than 10 minutes earlier from Indira

Gandhi International Airport, serving Delhi; this was the intended destination of the Il-76, which had nearly completed a non-scheduled cargo/ passenger service from Chimkent, Kazakhstan, Commonwealth of Independent States. At an altitude of 14,000 ft (c. 4,300 m), in darkness and overcast weather conditions, the two jet transports struck head-on, the left wing of *UN-76435* striking the engines of *HZ-AIH*. Following an explosion that was witnessed by the crew of a US Air Force C-141 flying in the area, the two aircraft crashed and burned in open terrain about 5 miles (10 km) apart. A total of 349 persons perished in the disaster, 312 aboard the 747 (289 passengers and 23 crew members) and 37 aboard the Il-76 (27 passengers and a crew of 10). There were no survivors.

While descending, the Air Kazakhstan crew informed the New Delhi centre air traffic controller of their location as 74 nautical miles (137 km) from the airport, and passing through 23,000 ft (c. 7,000 m). The controller then cleared the aircraft to descend to flight level (FL) 150 and to report when at that height, which the crew did, while at a distance of 46 nautical miles (85 km) and on a due-easterly heading. The crew were also advised of the Saudi Arabian transport, on a directly reciprocal heading and at a distance of 14 miles (22 km), and asked to report when making visual contact with the 747. Meanwhile, *HZ-AIH* had itself been instructed to maintain FL 140; its height was relayed to the crew of *UN-76435*. As transcribed on the aircraft's cockpit voice recorder (CVR), the

A Russian-registered Ilyushin Il-76 jet transport, similar to the Air Kazakhstan aircraft involved in the mid-air collision over India with a Saudia Boeing 747. *(Philip Jarrett)*

The smouldering remains of the Saudi Arabian Airlines 747 that crashed after colliding with an Air Kazakhstan transport, with a loss of 349 lives. *(AP Images)*

captain of the Il-76 had, only seconds before the accident, asked the first officer what was their assigned altitude, which indicated that the crew did not understand the controller's instructions and were not sure of the correct flight level. The radio operator, who had been relaying communications, then answered the captain, 'Maintain 150 . . . are not descending . . . this one in at 140.' The Il-76 had actually descended through 14,000 ft and was in a slight ascent when it collided with the 747.

The failure of the Air Kazakhstan transport to maintain its assigned height was attributed to poor command of the English language by its pilots, which caused a misunderstanding between them and the controller, coupled with what the investigative report described as the crew's 'lack of professionalism' and their poor cockpit discipline. Contributing factors in the disaster were the absence of a secondary radar system covering the area, which would have provided the controller with the height of both aircraft; the use of the same airway for arriving and departing flights, and the fact that neither the 747 nor the Il-76 had been equipped with a collision-avoidance system.

A secondary radar system was in fact in the process of being installed at the time of the accident, but had yet to become operational. Arrival and departure procedures were subsequently changed in the New Delhi terminal area, with a new corridor being established in what had previously been military airspace in order to provide for lateral separation of inbound and outbound aircraft.

Date: 23 November 1996 (*c.* 15:20)
Location: Comores
Operator: Ethiopian Airlines
Aircraft type: Boeing 767-260ER (*ET-AIZ*)

Operating as Flight 961, the wide-bodied jetliner had taken off from Addis Ababa, Ethiopia, bound for Nairobi, Kenya, the first segment of an international service with an ultimate destination of Abidjan, Ivory Coast. Some 20 minutes after its departure, the aircraft was seized by three passengers, all of them Ethiopians, who got up from their seats and stormed into the cockpit. They then beat the first officer and forced him out of the flight deck.

Despite the claim by one of them to have a bomb, the hijackers were in fact unarmed at the beginning of the seizure, but they grabbed an axe and a fire extinguisher from their respective stowages in the cockpit for use as weapons, and ordered the pilot to fly them to Australia. Saying they had read in a magazine article that the 767 could remain airborne for 11 hours, the assailants rejected the request of Capt Leul Abate to land for refuelling at Mombasa, Kenya, due to the inability of *ET-AIZ* to make the trip non-stop. Nor did they allow the pilot to send any radio transmissions after informing the Addis Ababa control centre of the unlawful interference with the flight.

After passing Mombasa, and as the jetliner proceeded further along the south-easterly coast of Africa, the pilot again tried to convince the hijackers of the need to stop for refuelling, but apparently not understanding the danger of the situation, they again refused. During this time, the leader of the group was reportedly fiddling with the controls from the first officer's seat while drinking whiskey. Even after the low fuel caution light had illuminated, the hijackers warned Capt

Abate not to descend below the cruising altitude of 39,000 ft (*c.* 12,000 m). Once the starboard engine had failed due to fuel exhaustion, one of the assailants began manipulating the controls, which caused the flight path of the 767 to become erratic. After completing three irregular circles, the aircraft assumed a near-northerly course, and during this time the second power plant flamed out. After the cabin staff began preparing the passengers for a ditching, the first officer forced his way back into the flight deck to help the captain. Finally, the hijackers stopped harassing the pilots, but *ET-AIZ* was already doomed.

With both engines having failed, only the RAM air turbine would be available to power the standby instruments, and both the cockpit voice recorder (CVR) and the digital flight data recorder (DFDR) stopped functioning, which prevented a determination of the performance of the aircraft in the final moments of the flight. As it glided low over the Indian Ocean, the pilots tried to turn the 767 in order to land parallel to the waves, but at that moment it struck the surface of the water while in a left wing-low attitude. Its undercarriage and flaps

The initial impact with the surface of the water is captured on videotape an instant before the hijacked Ethiopian Airlines Boeing 767 crashed in the Indian Ocean. *(Paris Match)*

still retracted, the aircraft then slammed into the ocean off the northern end of Grand Comore Island and close to Galawa Beach, breaking into four main sections. The crash occurred on this Saturday afternoon in full view of beach-goers and rescue personnel, who rushed to the scene some 1,500 ft (500 m) offshore, and probably because of their efforts, 50 of the 175 persons aboard *ET-AIZ* escaped with their lives, including its three flight crewmen and three of the nine members of its cabin staff. Among the survivors, many suffered serious injuries and only four passengers reported no physical harm. The three hijackers were among the 125 persons killed in the disaster. All of the victims' bodies were subsequently recovered, and although no post-mortem examinations were performed on them, most of their deaths were believed to have resulted from impact trauma, with some of them having drowned. The weather conditions were good in the area at the time, with a north-easterly wind of 8 to 10 knots and towering cumulus clouds reported over Moroni International Airport, located some 12 miles (20 km) south of where the jetliner had gone down.

The report of the investigative committee noted that the security procedures in effect at Bole International Airport, serving Addis Ababa, had been successful in preventing the assailants from smuggling weapons on to the 767. The committee further observed that while not employed here, the use of security personnel aboard the aircraft might have been beneficial in this case. Additionally, the carrier's security training procedures dealing with hijackings and other unusual situations were found not to have been conducted in a formal or well-structured manner. It was noted that an opportunity to perhaps prevent the disaster was lost at one point, while all the assailants were in the cabin, when the captain asked over the public address system for the other passengers to 'react to the hijackers'. Though intended to encourage the passengers to overpower the three men, his message was given only in English, and perhaps as a result, the others did not understand his plea for help and took no action.

Among the recommendations made in the report were for a back-up power supply to be available to ensure continued operation of flight and voice recorders on commercial transports, and also that the fire axe stored in an aircraft be secured so as to be inaccessible to anyone other than the members of the flight crew.

Date: 6 August 1997 (01:42)
Location: Near Agana, Guam
Operator: Korean Air (South Korea)
Aircraft type: Boeing 747-3B5B (*HL-7468*)

Flight 801 had been in the final stages of its approach when authorised to land on Runway 06-Left at Guam International Airport, its intended destination at the end of a service from Seoul, South Korea.

The last radio transmission from the 747 was acknowledgement of its landing clearance; slightly more than a minute later the wide-bodied jet airliner struck Nimitz Hill approximately 3.5 miles (5.5 km) south-west of the airport. The crash claimed the lives of 229 persons aboard the aircraft, including 14 members of the crew; three of those killed died within 30 days of the accident and a fourth succumbed two months later. Three cabin attendants and 22 passengers survived, all of whom were seriously injured.

Since Guam is an American territorial island, the investigation was conducted by the US National Transportation Safety Board (NTSB), which concluded that the disaster had resulted from improper in-flight decisions and planning by the pilot-in-command, coupled with a poorly executed instrument landing system (ILS) approach on his part, and from the failure of his two fellow flight crewmen to monitor and cross-check him. Considered as contributory were the fatigued state of the captain, inadequate training by the carrier of its pilots and the fact that the minimum safe altitude warning (MSAW) system incorporated into the airport surveillance radar (ASR) system had been intentionally inhibited.

With the glide slope transmitter inoperative, the crew would be making a localiser-only ILS approach. Vertical navigation would be accomplished using the Nimitz very-high-frequency omni-directional range (VOR) station as a 'step-down' fix between the final approach fix (FAF) and the runway and distance-measuring equipment (DME) to identify the step-down points. Significantly, the DME facility was 3.5 miles (5.5 km) south-west of the airport, which would require the crew to identify the distance past the navigational aid in

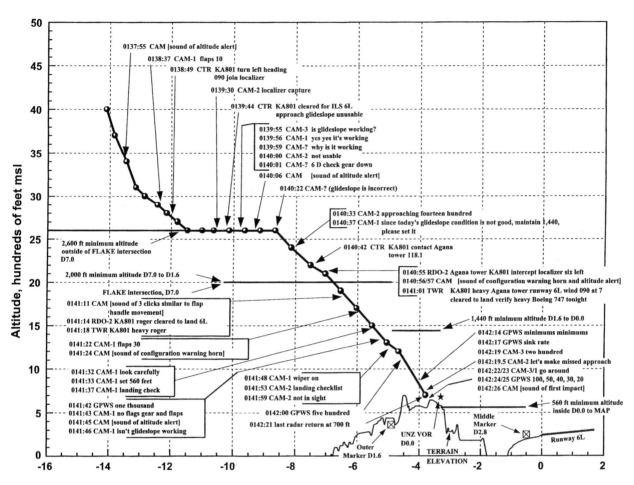

A condensed plot illustrates the descent profile of Flight 801 leading up to the crash on Guam. *(National Transportation Safety Board)*

order to determine the distance to the runway. An analysis of the aircraft's cockpit voice recorder (CVR) tape indicated that the pilots had initially seen Guam in the early morning darkness. Although *HL-7468* would subsequently enter instrument meteorological conditions, the captain probably had a continuing expectation of a visual approach, using the ILS as a back-up. There was evidence that the crew had not been aware of the status of the glide slope, as indicated by conflicting statements made by all three of its members. In response to a question from the flight engineer with regard to it, the captain was initially heard to say, 'Yes, yes, it's working'. Shortly thereafter, however, the first officer stated that it was 'not usable'. Less than a minute before impact, the captain asked, 'Isn't the glide slope working?' This time, there was

no response from either of his fellow crewmen. In its report, the NTSB noted that although an aircraft's ILS receiver could momentarily be affected by a spurious signal, resulting in the movement of the glide slope indicator needle, a continuous indication that also caused the retraction of the glide slope off-flag on the horizon situation indicator (HSI) would have been unlikely. But especially with the Combined Centre/Radar Approach (CERAP) controller having announced the fact, the NTSB concluded that the crew had sufficient information to be aware that the glide slope had been inoperative.

Shortly after the captain appeared to become preoccupied with the status of the glide slope, he allowed the 747 to descend below the respective intermediate altitudes of 2,000 ft (*c.* 600 m) over the FAF and 1,440 ft (*c.* 400 m) over the VOR. Using the autopilot, he twice commanded the entry of a lower height into its altitude selector before the aircraft had reached the step-down fix. These actions further indicated that the pilot was not aware of his position. There could also have been confusion on the part of the crew as to the location of the DME transmitter. Had they believed it to be situated at the airport, they might have assumed the aircraft had been closer to the runway than was actually the case (this could also explain the incorrect altitudes at the step-down points). However, the NTSB noted that the navigational fixes were clearly shown in DME values on the approach chart. Whether he was confused with regard to the DME, preoccupied with the glide slope or because he believed he would return to visual flight conditions, the captain conducted the approach without properly cross-referencing the fixes with his height and lost awareness of his position along the localiser course, leading to the premature descent into the terrain.

Equally improper was the captain's response to the alerts of the aircraft's ground-proximity warning system (GPWS), which were heard on the CVR tape to first sound 'one thousand' and then 'five hundred'. Twelve seconds before impact, the system sounded a 'minimums' annunciation, alerting the crew as to their height, which was followed by a sink rate warning. The first officer replied, 'Sink rate okay'. After the flight engineer called out 'two hundred', the co-pilot was heard to say, 'Let's make a missed approach'. Seconds later, the captain stated, 'Go-around' and the aircraft's digital flight data recorder (DFDR) indicated an increase in the engine power and indicated air speed. About the same time as the thrust increased, a slight nose-up control input was noted. The recorded altitude values continued to decline, however, while the CVR transcribed the height warnings of the GPWS at 100 ft and then at 10 ft intervals starting at 50 ft above the ground. Its undercarriage extended and flaps set at approximately 25 degrees, the 747 was proceeding on a magnetic heading of 63 degrees when it slammed to earth about half a mile (0.8 km) south-west of the Nimitz VOR and at an above sea-level elevation of around 700 ft (200 m). Initially striking the terrain with its No. 1 engine, left wing and main gear, the 747 then broke apart and caught fire. The

airport weather about 5 minutes after the accident was overcast, with cumulonimbus at 4,000 feet (*c.* 1,200 m), scattered clouds at 2,500 ft (*c.* 750 m) and a few of them down to 1,500 ft (*c.* 500 m), and a visibility of 5 miles (*c.* 10 km) in light rain. The wind was variable at 4 knots. According to a hunter who had been at Nimitz Hill, it was not raining in the immediate area at the time of the crash. However, radar data indicated the flight had encountered heavy precipitation during the approach, and even though it exited the rain, the crew would probably not have been able to see the airport.

The briefing conducted by the captain before beginning the final approach was considered inadequate in that it did not include certain vital information, including the definitions of the FAF and the step-down fixes and their associated crossing altitudes. Nor did he discuss what descent technique would be employed, i.e. one flown at a continuous angle or one that involved descending to and then levelling off at each fix. Due to the faulty briefing, the pilot-in-command missed the opportunity to prepare himself and his fellow crewmen for the relatively complex non-precision landing, and also made it more difficult for the co-pilot and flight engineer to monitor the approach and challenge any errors made by him. The likelihood that the first officer had been using an out-of-date approach chart could also have hindered his ability to properly assess the actions of the captain. As the designated non-flying pilot, the first officer would have been responsible for monitoring and providing guidance to the captain, and although he did correctly call for a missed approach 6 seconds before the crash, he failed to challenge the latter's errors, as required by Korean Air procedures. The application of power was delayed, and the first control inputs were not initiated until just before impact. An analysis of the DFDR data indicated that had the overshoot been initiated immediately after the GPWS 'minimums' call-out, the jet would have safely cleared the terrain.

Despite the errors by the crew, the disaster might still have been averted had the MSAW not been inhibited. This action was taken 2½ years earlier by the US Federal Aviation Administration (FAA) in response to nuisance warnings that had been reported by air traffic controllers and involved the installation of new hardware, and had the effect of eliminating visual and aural alerts when aircraft descended below minimum altitudes within 54 nautical miles (100 km) of the ASR-8 radar site, which included the area where the crash occurred. A simulation showed that with the system in use, *HL-7468* would have generated such an alert more than a minute before impact, which would have been sufficient time for the CERAP controller to notify the tower and for the latter to then relay the alert to the crew. The NTSB in fact described the performance of the CERAP controller as 'substandard', in that he failed to provide the flight with a position advisory relative to a fix along the localiser course, and also did not inform the crew or the tower of a rain shower he had observed on the final approach path. Nor did he monitor the 747 after its transfer to the tower radio frequency, and as a result, did not immediately recognise that the flight was overdue. Had he been monitoring the aircraft on the terminal radar display, which would have been clearly visible to his immediate right, and made easier by the fact he had no other immediate duties at the time, he might have seen its target descend prematurely and alerted the crew.

With regard to the fatigue issue, the captain was heard on the CVR tape, some 20 minutes before the accident, to complain of being 'really . . . sleepy'. According to one study referred to in the report, the early morning hours after midnight have been associated with degraded performance and a higher probability of errors and accidents. The NTSB also noted that non-precision approaches are generally more complicated than full instrument landings, and that the incidence of controlled-flight-into-terrain accidents occurring during them is five times greater.

Not pertaining to the cause but factoring in the issue of occupant survival was an emergency response that 'lacked coordination', according to a Guam Department of Public Health physician. Due to a lapse partially blamed on the delayed discovery of the accident by air-traffic control personnel, the first emergency equipment did not arrive on the scene of the disaster until almost an hour after it had happened, despite the presence of a fire station only about 1 mile (1.5 km) away. There were also equipment problems, and additional difficulties attributed to the blockage of an access road by an oil pipe that was 1 ft (*c.* 5 cm) in diameter and had

been severed by the crashing aircraft. This delay in the timely evacuation of survivors may have cost the life of at least one passenger. For those who did not survive, death was due to a combination of trauma, burns and carbon monoxide inhalation.

For the South Korean flag carrier, the crash of Flight 801 was only the latest in a series of mishaps, including several high-profile disasters, dating back nearly 20 years. The number of its aircraft destroyed in accidents during the 10-year period 1988–98 represented a hull loss some 15 times that of the two major US carriers, American and United. This time, drastic action was deemed necessary, and to serve as a 'warning', the South Korean Ministry of Construction and Transport (MOCT) ordered the airline to suspend some 140 flights per week on 10 of its domestic routes for half a year. Subsequent to the accident, Korean Air announced plans to spend more than US $100 million (£68 million) over a period of two years on safety initiatives. Administrative and technical changes included increased qualification requirements for captains flying large aircraft, more simulator training for pilots and revisions in the carrier's flight operations and other manuals. A new airport familiarisation programme using audio-visual presentations was also implemented, and perhaps most needed for pilots flying into Guam, since the videotape previously shown to them fostered the expectation of a visual approach there, and did not emphasise the 'offset' DME. Additionally, the airline announced, nearly two years after the crash, plans to equip its entire fleet of jetliners with enhanced GPWS, which a simulation revealed would have warned the crew of *HL-7468* about a minute before impact. On the government level, the Korean Civil Aviation Board, which the NTSB claimed had been ineffective in its oversight of the company's operations and pilot training programmes, took action to bolster its surveillance capabilities, even hiring more inspection personnel to carry out the task.

Nine days after the disaster, the FAA announced that as a 'routine precaution' it had ordered the testing of nearly 200 MSAW facilities throughout its jurisdiction, all but two of which were found to be working properly, and made several internal recommendations for improvement in its use. The system on Guam was reconfigured to once again provide low-altitude alerts, and in a manner so that such warnings would be received in both the CERAP and the Agana tower. The agency also frequency-paired and co-located the DME and the localiser, and changed the Jeppesen chart for the ILS Runway 6L approach at the Guam airport.

Noting that Nimitz Hill was not depicted on the approach chart being used by the crew of Flight 801, the NTSB suggested in its accident report that the FAA evaluate the issue of improving the depiction of terrain on aeronautical charts, and also recommended that the same agency shorten the time for requiring the installation on commercial aircraft of enhanced GPWS systems. In a dissenting opinion, Member Bob Francis asked the Board to issue a recommendation urging the timely installation of such equipment. It was also noted in the report that on-board vertical guidance systems that indicate a constant rate of descent during a non-precision landing procedure could provide the safety advantages of a precision approach, and accordingly, the NTSB made two recommendations regarding the installation and use of such navigational equipment.

Date: 26 September 1997 (13:31)
Location: Near Pancurbatu, Sumatera Utara, Indonesia
Operator: Garuda Indonesia
Aircraft type: Airbus Industrie A300B4-220 (*PK-GAI*)

A thick haze produced by hundreds of fires burning throughout Indonesia, most of them intentionally set as part of a vegetation-clearing project, hung over the area as Flight 152 began its approach to land at Polonia International Airport, serving Medan, on the island of Sumatera, following a domestic service from Jakarta. The airport visibility had in fact been reduced to less than half a mile (0.8 km), which was nevertheless above the landing minimum.

All 234 persons aboard perished in the crash of Garuda Airbus A300 near Medan, on the Indonesian island of Sumatera, which occurred during the initial approach to land. *(AP Images)*

As part of the instrument landing system (ILS) procedure approach to Runway 05, the aircraft was receiving vectors from an air traffic controller that involved two turns, the first of which placed it on a heading of 215 degrees. A second turn to a heading of 46 degrees was then needed to effect runway alignment. During this time, the flight was also cleared for descent to 2,000 ft (600 m), or 500 ft (150 m) below the normal initial approach altitude. Cleanly configured, the A300 had been proceeding in the same general south-westerly direction to which it had been previously assigned when it initially struck the ground while in a left wing-low attitude and at an indicated air speed of approximately 240 mph (385) kmh). The wide-bodied jetliner then crashed in a narrow valley some 25 miles (40 km) south-south-east of the airport, disintegrated and burst into flames. All 234 persons aboard (222 passengers and 12 crew members) perished in the disaster.

An analysis of air/ground communications indicated confusion between the controller and the crew of *PK-GAI*. After turning left and then being instructed to turn right, back towards the airport, the pilot queried, '. . . confirm turning left or turning right, heading 046'. The controller replied, 'Turning right, sir', which was acknowledged by the aircraft. Concerned that the jetliner had begun turning left, the controller asked, '. . . confirm you're making a left turn now?' When the pilot reported turning right, the controller replied, 'OK, you continue turning left now.' The pilot then stated, 'Confirm turning left? We are starting to turn right now.' The crash occurred about 10 seconds later, at an approximate elevation of 1,100 ft (335 m). Significantly, the primary radar system in use at Medan was not capable of providing controllers with the altitude information of a given target.

The accident prompted a safety audit of the carrier by Indonesian aeronautical authorities.

Date: 15 December 1997 (*c.* 18:30)
Location: Near Sharjah, United Arab Emirates
Operator: Tajik Air (Tadzhikistan)
Aircraft type: Tupolev Tu-154B-1 (*EY-85281*)

The jet airliner crashed and burned about 10 miles (15 km) from the Sharjah airport, where it was to have landed following a non-scheduled service from Dushanbe, Tajikistan, Commonwealth of Independent States. All but one of the 86 persons aboard (77 passengers and eight crew members) lost their lives in the accident; the navigator survived but was seriously injured.

During an approach being conducted in darkness and unlimited visibility conditions, but over terrain that offered no visual cues, the aircraft was vectored to the base leg of the airport circuit, on to a heading of 190 degrees, to effect alignment with the signals of the instrument landing system (ILS). When the Tu-154 neared the extended centreline of the runway, the ground controller cleared it to descend to 1,475 ft (450 m) and instructed it to turn right on to a due westerly heading. The crew acknowledged these instructions, but failed to report at the required point, and in fact continued descending during the turn. Lacking proper coordination, the crew failed to arrest the descent after reaching the minimum assigned height. The descent continued until reaching an altitude of 200 ft (60 m), when the 'decision height' alert came on, with the crew still not arresting the descent. Ultimately, and shortly after its undercarriage had been lowered, *EY-85281* struck the ground at an approximate speed of 230 mph (370 kmh).

The captain had apparently failed to recognise the continued descent of the aircraft, despite two verbal warnings from the navigator. Contributing to the accident was the failure of the navigator to confirm that the captain understood the controller's instructions, and the failure of both he and the first officer to warn the captain of the descent below the minimum assigned altitude; insufficient cockpit discipline, which led to these misunderstandings, and poor command of the English language on the part of the pilots. None of the aircraft's flight crew members had previously flown into this airport.

During the descent of the Tu-154, the controller, who was stationed at nearby Dubai because Sharjah did not have its own radar system, had been distracted by communicating with another aircraft. When he returned his attention to the radar screen, the target representing *EY-85281* had disappeared.

Date: 19 December 1997 (*c.* 16:15)
Location: Near Sungsang, Selatan, Indonesia
Operator: SilkAir Pte Ltd (Singapore)
Aircraft type: Boeing 737-36N (*9V-TRF*)

The crash of Flight 185 was shrouded in mystery from the moment it occurred, and could not be explained after a lengthy investigation. However, information attained during the inquiry coupled with the absence of evidence of any other possible cause pointed to the disturbing possibility that this was no accident, but rather resulted from an intentional act of suicide by the pilot.

Having taken off about half an hour earlier from Soekarno Hatta International Airport, serving Jakarta, and bound for Singapore, the jet airliner was last observed on radar cruising at 35,000 ft (c. 1,050 m) before it entered a rapid descent and plunged into the River Musi some 30 miles (50 km) north-north-east of Palembang, on the island of Sumatera, and about 250 miles (400 km) north-north-west of the Indonesian capital. All 104 persons aboard (97 passengers and seven crew members) perished.

As a result of the high-speed impact, the 737 was severely fragmented and had in fact penetrated the riverbed, beneath some 30 ft (10 m) of water. Few human remains were found, and only six victims could be identified, although nearly three-quarters of the wreckage, based on weight, was ultimately recovered. Additionally, parts of the aircraft's empennage, including sections of both horizontal stabilisers and the corresponding elevators measuring approximately 3 ft (1 m) long, were located on land, one piece about 2.5 miles (4 km) from the main impact site.

The Indonesian National Transportation Safety Committee (NTSC) found no evidence of in-flight fire or explosion, pre-existing corrosion or fatigue, or of pre-impact malfunction in the aircraft's electrical system, flight controls, leading- or trailing-edge flaps, engines or thrust reversers, the latter of which were determined to have been in the stowed position. Suspected problems with the Boeing 737 and certain similarities with the 1994 US Air crash (see separate entry, 8 September 1994) raised concern that this disaster may also have resulted from an uncontrolled rudder deflection. There was, however, no indication of technical failure in the main power control unit, yaw damper modulating piston or other components of the rudder assembly of 9V-TRF. Distribution of the wreckage indicated that the structural failure of the control surfaces had taken place between 12,000 and 5,000 ft (c. 3,700–1,500 m). The meteorological conditions in the area at the time were good, with scattered altocumulus, cumulus, stratocumulus and cirrus clouds and no reported turbulence in the area.

One highly significant finding was the stoppage of both the aircraft's cockpit voice (CVR) and flight data (FDR) recorders prior to impact, with the former ceasing less than 10 minutes before the crash and the latter approximately 6 minutes later. The stoppage of the CVR could have resulted from a technical failure, such as an interruption in its power supply or a short circuit, or from the intentional pulling of its circuit breaker, while the stoppage of the FDR could have been attributable to a loss of its power supply or to a malfunction in the unit itself. There was no explanation as to why they ceased at different times. Shortly before the CVR tape ended, the captain was heard to voice his intention to exit the flight deck, but there was no indication he did in fact leave. Seconds later, the CVR recorded a metallic snap, which could have been the sound of a seat belt buckle hitting against something.

According to the report of the NTSC, this was 'a very extensive, exhaustive and complex investigation' made extremely difficult by the degree of destruction of the aircraft, the difficulties presented by the location of the crash and the lack of information from the recorders during the final moments of the flight. The agency was unable to determine the reason for the stoppage of the FDR and CVR, nor for the departure of the 737 from its cruising level. The NTSC emphasised that there was no evidence to establish positively that the final descent had been intentional. However, the report noted that according to simulations, such a descent resulting from any single failure of the autopilot or flight control system would not have matched the trajectory taken from radar data.

And based on the same simulations, one possible explanation for the dive could have been the combination of lateral and longitudinal control inputs together with its horizontal stabiliser being moved to its forward manual and electrical limit of 2.5 degrees nose-down.

At the centre of the mystery was the 41-year-old pilot of Flight 185, Capt Tsu Way Ming. The report noted that at the time of his death, he was operating a securities-trading account in Singapore, which had accrued increasing losses over a period of four years, starting in 1993. There was, however, no evidence that his business activities had affected his performance as a pilot, nor any indication that a mortgage policy taken out by him in connection with a housing loan had any relevance to the crash that claimed his life. And based on interviews with his superiors, colleagues, friends and family, there had been no change in the personal behaviour of Capt Tsu in the days preceding the disaster, and no difficulties were known to have existed between him and the first officer of the aircraft. It was noted in the report that Capt Tsu had experienced several operational-related events, one of which resulted in his removal as a line instructor pilot.

Understandably, there was a variance in opinion as to what caused the disaster between the other principal parties involved, with the nation of registry down-playing the theory that the crash had been intentional and the nation of manufacture highlighting this possibility. Singaporean authorities stressed that the condition of the wreckage affected the efforts to establish the cause, and also raised the issue of a possible weather factor by noting that another flight had reported thunderstorm activity about 10 miles (15 km) east of the track of 9V-TRF. They further observed that Capt Tsu was well regarded by other pilots and had a reputation for competence, and that the overweight landing for which he had been demoted was made necessary by a power plant malfunction occurring after a take-off. With regard to his reported financial difficulties, they noted that his realisable assets were greater than his loans and debts. The Singaporean view-point was solidified through legal authority when, in October 2001, a court on the island nation dismissed a lawsuit against the airline brought by families of some of the victims, ruling that there was no evidence the pilot had intent-ionally crashed the aircraft.

A different point of view was expressed by the US National Transportation Safety Board (NTSB), which emphasised the lack of evidence of failure in the aircraft's flight controls or related components, noting that the separation of parts of its empennage resulted directly from the high velocity, above the speed of sound, which 9V-TRF attained during the descent. Other observations made by American authorities were the belief that the 737 had been responding to flight control inputs from the cockpit, with the nose-down trim condition, which they noted could have been overcome with appropriate flight control inputs, resulting from a sustained

manual manipulation, and that according to a separate report, there were some indications that Capt Tsu had been quieter than normal in the days before the disaster. And finally, the NTSB discounted the possibility of the CVR and FDR failing from separate technical faults only minutes apart, noting that the breaker panel for both recorders was located directly behind the captain's seat.

The NTSB did agree with the Indonesian agency's recommendations to identify and rectify factors associated with the stoppage of an aircraft's recorders before a primary occurrence. And although the structural break-up of 9V-TRF had resulted from overstressing during and did not precipitate the descent, the US Federal Aviation Administration (FAA) issued an airworthiness directive three weeks after the crash of Flight 185 requiring operators of newer models of the 737 to inspect the horizontal stabilisers within 24 hours or five flights to ascertain that all fasteners and elevator attachment bolts in those structures were properly in place.

Date: 2 February 1998 (c. 10:50)
Location: Near Claveria, Misamis Oriental, The Philippines
Operator: Cebu Pacific Air (The Philippines)
Aircraft type: McDonnell Douglas DC-9 Series 32 (RP-C1507)

Designated as Flight 387 and on a domestic service originating at Manila, the jet airliner crashed on the island of Mindanao some 30 miles (50 km) north-east of Cagayan de Oro, where it was to have landed. All 104 persons aboard (99 passengers and a crew of five) perished.

With the approval of the captain, the carrier had modified the flight plan of RP-C1507 to include a stop at Tacloban, on the island of Leyte, with the intention of delivering personnel and parts needed to service another company aircraft stranded there by mechanical trouble. This unscheduled landing would factor in the subsequent accident by significantly altering the route normally taken by the flight. After its departure from Tacloban, the DC-9 climbed to a height of 25,000 ft (c. 7,500 m), and it subsequently left the prescribed airway and proceeded directly towards its destination. In their last message, the crew reported descending out of 11,500 ft (c. 3,500 m) during the very-high-frequency omnidirectional range (VOR) instrument procedure approach to Lumbia Airport, serving Cagayan do Oro. Shortly thereafter, the jet plowed into a ridge of Mount Lumot, in the Sumagaya range, at an approximate elevation of 7,000 ft (2,000 m) and while in a slight left wing-low attitude. The impact occurred in a densely wooded area some 500 ft (150 m) below the summit of the mountain, whereupon the DC-9 disintegrated. There was no fire.

The weather between Tacloban and Cagayan de Oro was overcast, with a ceiling of around 10,000 ft (3,000 m) and the clouds lowering to about 1,500 ft (500 m) or less and obscuring the mountains within the areas of scattered rain showers. Visibility ranged from more than 5 miles (10 km) in light precipitation and haze down to only about 2 miles (3 km) within areas of heavy rain, and the surface wind at the airport was from an east to a north-easterly direction and varied from approximately 5 to more than 20 knots. There was also thunder-storm activity in the vicinity, in which the wind gusts exceeded 30 knots. Based on the transcript of the aircraft's cockpit voice recorder (CVR), in which the pilots made no mention of the hazardous terrain ahead of them, the descent leg was believed to have been carried out in instrument meteo-rological conditions (IMC). The CVR also indicated that during this time the ground-proximity warning system (GPWS) sounded a 'Pull-up' warning, but there was no evidence of the crew initiating evasive action.

There was no indication of technical failure in the aircraft, and the investigative board determined that the crash apparently resulted from the lack of familiarity of the crew with the selected route and their continuation into the IMC under visual flight rules (VFR) procedures, which led to the controlled-flight-into-terrain impact. Records showed that neither of the pilots were familiar with off-route flying, especially the track taken by Flight 387.

In a safety review of Cebu Pacific Air, whose operations were suspended by the Philippine government in the wake of the disaster, the carrier was cited for 'poor operational control as well as inadequate and unacceptable training standards and practices, particularly nonconformity with prescribed training requirements relative to pilots and aircraft dispatchers.' Among the recom-mendations made in the accident report were a re-evaluation of the airline before its resumption of revenue operations and an expansion of the safety programme used in the assessment of this and other carriers in the Philippines.

Date: 16 February 1998 (c. 20:05)
Location: T'ao-yuan, Taiwan
Operator: China Airlines (Taiwan)
Aircraft type: Airbus Industrie A300B4-622R (B-1814)

Less than four years after its disaster at Nagoya Airport, in Japan (see separate entry, 26 April 1994), China Airlines was struck by this remarkably similar crash, which involved the same type of aircraft and also occurred after a stall and subsequent loss of control.

Following a service from Denpasar, Bali, Indonesia, Flight 676 had been cleared for an approach to Runway 05-Left at Chang Kai Shek International Airport, serving T'ai-pei, using distance-measuring equipment (DME) and instru-ment landing system (ILS) procedures. At a position approximately 1.5 miles (2.5 km) short of the runway threshold, the A300 was at a height of about 1,500 ft (500 m), or some 1,000 ft (300 m) above the glide slope. About 20 seconds later, when over the threshold, go-around power was applied. Its undercarriage in the retracted position and flaps having been raised to 20 degrees, the aircraft ascended to just over 1,700 ft (520 m), while in a pitch attitude of 35 degrees. Climbing to nearly 2,800 ft (850 m) above the ground, its pitch attitude increased to more than 40 degrees and its indicated air speed decreased to only about 50 mph (80 kmh) until the wide-bodied jetliner finally stalled. It then crashed tail-first approximately 2 miles (3 km) beyond the threshold and some 200 ft (60 m) to the left of the runway, skidded across a highway central reservation and into a residential area and exploded in flames.

A total of 202 persons perished in the disaster, all 196 aboard the aircraft (182 passengers and 14 crew members) and the rest on the ground. It was dark at the time of the crash, and the airport meteorological conditions consisted of a low ceiling, with broken clouds at 300 ft (100 m) and an overcast of 3,000 ft (1,000 m), a visibility of approximately half a mile (0.8 km) in light drizzle and fog, and a runway visual range of around 4,000 ft (1,200 m).

Having failed to achieve the correct descent profile during the approach, the pilot subsequently did not monitor the aircraft's pitch angle and did not apply the proper control input after applying full power during the manually flown go-around. This error led to the loss of speed and consequent loss of control.

In the wake of the accident, and with the assistance of the German carrier Lufthansa, China Airlines instituted a rigorous pilot retraining programme and also established a task force to improve safety.

Date: 29 August 1998 (*c.* 13:00)
Location: Near Cotocollao, Pichincha, Ecuador
Operator: Empres Consolidada Cubana de Aviacion (Cuba)
Aircraft type: Tupolev Tu-154M (*CU-T1264*)

Operating as Flight 389, the jet airliner crashed and burst into flames after an aborted take-off at Mariscal Sucre International Airport, serving Quito. A total of 79 persons lost their lives in the disaster, including the 14 members of the aircraft's crew and 10 others on the ground, some of them children who had been playing in a soccer field where the Tu-154 came to rest; 25 others were injured, most of them surviving passengers.

Bound for Guayaquil, also in Ecuador, one segment of an international service with an ultimate destination of Havana, Cuba, and carrying 91 persons, *CU-T1264* began its take-off on Runway 07, but apparently never became airborne. Overrunning the runway, the jet then smashed through a wall and struck a repair shop, narrowly missing a residential neighbourhood. The weather at the time consisted of scattered clouds at 4,000 ft (*c.* 1,200 m) and a broken cloud layer at high altitude. The wind was blowing from the south at 10 knots.

The accident was attributed to the delayed connection or failure to connect the aircraft's elevator hydraulic boost system. This omission was probably related to mechanical trouble encountered before departure, with two of its engines being started by ground power and the third by the crew after the Tu-154 had begun to taxi. During this delay of nearly 40 minutes, the crew failed to complete the checklist and also apparently did not switch on the hydraulic valves of the flight control

system. A significant contributing factor in the subsequent crash may have been the delay of the pilot in abandoning the take-off when the aircraft could not be successfully rotated.

Date: 2 September 1998 (22:31)
Location: Near Halifax, Nova Scotia, Canada
Operator: Swissair AG
Aircraft type: McDonnell Douglas MD-11 (*HB-IWF*)

Occurring just two days short of the 35th anniversary of the carrier's worst previous disaster, the crash of Swissair Flight 111 was similar in other ways to that fiery Caravelle accident in 1963 (see separate entry, 4 September 1963). It too resulted from an intense in-flight fire in the aircraft's fuselage, leading to an uncontrolled descent and a high-speed, non-survivable impact.

Having departed from John F. Kennedy International Airport, serving New York City, *HB-IWF* was not quite one hour into a non-stop, transatlantic service to Geneva, Switzerland, when there occurred the first hint of trouble, the detection by the crew of an unusual odour and seconds later of smoke in the cockpit. A few minutes later, and after a discussion between the two pilots and a cabin attendant who had been summoned to the flight deck, the latter of whom also detected the odour, the crew sent to the air traffic control (ATC) centre at Moncton, Canada, a 'Pan Pan Pan' message, an indication of trouble, but not something that necessarily requires urgent attention, accompanied by a request for an immediate diversion to a 'convenient place'. Initially cleared to return to Boston, Massachusetts, US, which at the time was nearly 350 miles (560 km) behind the aircraft, the crew subsequently accepted a suggestion by the ATC controller instead to divert to Halifax, located only about 65 miles (105 km) ahead of the flight.

The MD-11 had descended from its cruising height of 33,000 ft (*c.* 10,050 m) and was still at flight level 210 (6,400 m) when instructed to turn left on to a heading of 30 degrees in preparation for landing on Runway 06 at Halifax International Airport, located some 15 miles (25 km) north-north-east of the provincial capital. At the time, the airport was some 35 miles (55 km) away, a distance the pilots believed to be insufficient to complete a

A Swissair McDonnell Douglas MD-11, identical to the aircraft that crashed in the Atlantic Ocean off Nova Scotia, Canada. *(Douglas Green)*

successful final descent and landing. The flight was then instructed to turn on to a northerly heading, giving more track distance for the crew to lose altitude. Based on the limited cues available to them initially, the pilots believed that although a diversion was necessary, the threat was not sufficient to warrant the declaration of an emergency or initiate an immediate descent. The crew did specify the need to dump fuel, accepting an offer by the controller to instead turn southward, remaining within no more than about 40 miles (65 km) from the airport in case they needed to get down in a hurry. Less than a minute later, both pilots simultaneously declared an emergency, while announcing they were starting to dump fuel and also had to land immediately. The crew were cleared to dump fuel following a second emergency declaration, but there were no further communications with the flight. Approximately 5 minutes after the last transmission from the crew, observers in the area of St Margaret Bay saw what was believed to have been *HB-IWF* fly over.

Around 20 minutes after the initial detection of smoke on the flight deck, the wide-bodied jet airliner crashed in the North Atlantic Ocean about 5 miles (10 km) south-west of the coastal town of Peggy's Cove, itself located some 20 miles (30 km) south-west of Halifax, and in water that was around 180 ft (55 m) deep. All 229 persons aboard (215 passengers and 14 crew members) perished. The accident occurred in darkness, and the weather in the area consisted of a broken overcast, accompanied by rain showers; the visibility was described as 'good' over the land, but had been reduced by mist out to sea, and the winds were around 10 knots. A sufficient amount of human remains was found to allow, through various methods, the identification of all of the victims. One of the passengers, an off-duty pilot, was wearing a life vest. With regard to the aircraft's wreckage, approximately 98 per cent of its structure was recovered by various means, including dredging and remotely operated submersible vehicles.

Conducted by the Transportation Safety Board (TSB) of Canada, the investigation was complex, and besides the prolonged recovery operation involved a detailed examination of the debris and an assessment of the many pertinent technical issues. Hampering the investigation was the fact that both the aircraft's digital flight data (DFDR) and cockpit voice (CVR) recorders had stopped almost simultaneously more than 5 minutes before impact. Additionally, the extensive damage resulting from the in-flight fire that was known to have occurred aboard the MD-11 and the high-energy forces imposed when it struck the water either obscured or obliterated vital evidence and precluded a complete and detailed inventory of the aircraft's structure and components.

Examination of the front section of the transport that was some 30 ft (10 m) in length and had been fabricated in mock-up form helped delineate the boundaries of the pre-impact fire damage, which were primarily centred in the attic above the cockpit ceiling liner and forward cabin drop-ceiling area. Many of the ducts from the front attic area had been heat-damaged. Numerous power cables and wires were present in this part of the aircraft, running to or from the avionics compartment or the cockpit circuit breaker (CB) overhead switch panels. This section also contained numerous other electrical components, such as ground studs, light fixtures, battery packs, two electrically powered galleys and two lavatories. Of all the potential locations analysed, the right side close to the cut-out in the top of the cockpit rear wall was found to have been the area where the blaze began. From there, smoke and fumes could migrate into the flight deck at a location where it could be interpreted as coming from the air-conditioning system via the right overhead diffuser outlet. It was also possible to assess the direction of the propagation of the fire as from forward to aft. And based on known flammability characteristics and airflow patterns, a fire propagating rearward from this area could return to the cockpit with more intensity and after a time delay.

Among the approximately 3,000 wire and cable segments that were recovered, 20 exhibited signs of arcing. The definitive location of nearly half of those 20 could not be identified, but the rest were determined to have been portions of the aircraft's in-flight entertainment network (IFEN) power supply (PSU) cables. Most of the arcing damage on these could be attributed to the effects of the fire, but this was not the case with one of the recovered segments. Although it was unable to identify the specific circumstances of ignition, or which of the segments were involved, the TSB ruled that an electrical arcing event involving breached wire insulation must have been the initiating factor in the fire. It appeared that at least two wires were involved in this event. The Board further concluded that the arcing most likely ignited the nearby thermal acoustic insulation blanket material that was encapsulated by a protective cover made of metallised polyethylene terephthlalate (MPET). There was no evidence of sabotage with either an explosive or an incendiary device as factoring in the crash of Flight 111. And although the possibility was examined, the TSB found no evidence that the fire had stemmed from anything external to the aircraft, including high-intensity radiation fields produced by lightning or powerful radar transmitters.

The burning of large quantities of MPET-covered insulation material in the vicinity of the riser duct assembly would have created a significant heat release. After the blaze had begun in the attic area above and on the right side of the flight deck, the rearward direction by which it propagated meant that the amount of smoke initially entering the cockpit itself would likely have been small and intermittent in nature. Additionally, the smoke would have been significantly diluted when mixed with diffuser air. Based on their comments transcribed on the CVR, the pilots did indeed initially assess the smoke to be emanating from the air-conditioning system. And since it has been generally accepted that such a condition does not pose an imminent threat to an aircraft, the crew saw no need to accept the additional hazard of attempting an emergency landing. There were several other factors that could have affected the decision of the flight crew, one being that the weight of the aircraft would have exceeded the maximum authorised for landing, and that at the time meal service to the passengers had been under way. Also, the back-course instrument procedure had not been pre-programmed into the aircraft's flight management system (FMS), and the approach charts required for the landing at Halifax were not readily available to them, and, being located beneath the right

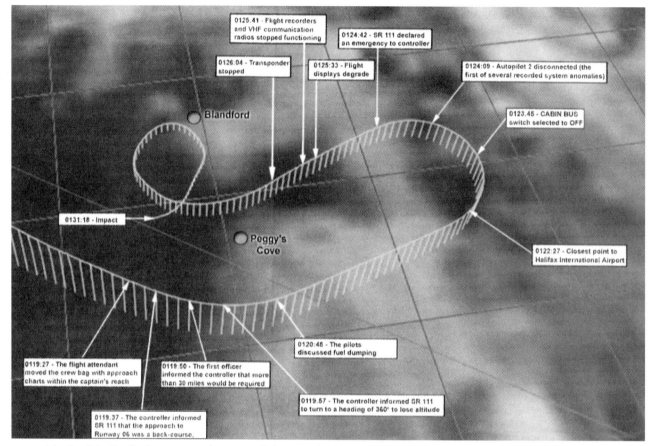

0125.41 - Flight recorders and VHF communication radios stopped functioning

0126:04 - Transponder stopped

0125:33 - Flight displays degrade

0124:42 - SR 111 declared an emergency to controller

0124:09 - Autopilot 2 disconnected (the first of several recorded system anomalies)

0123.45 - CABIN BUS switch selected to OFF

Blandford

0131:18 - Impact

Peggy's Cove

0122:27 - Closest point to Halifax International Airport

0120:46 - The pilots discussed fuel dumping

0119:27 - The flight attendant moved the crew bag with approach charts within the captain's reach

0119:50 - The first officer informed the controller that more than 30 miles would be required

0119.57 - The controller informed SR 111 to turn to a heading of 360° to lose altitude

0119.37 - The controller informed SR 111 that the approach to Runway 06 was a back-course.

The track in the final moments of Swissair Flight 111 after the start of the in-flight fire and consequent loss of control. *(Transportation Safety Board of Canada)*

observer's station, had to be retrieved by a cabin attendant. The TSB concluded that even had the crew immediately initiated the smoke/fumes of unknown origin checklist, the read-back of which could have taken 20 to 30 minutes to complete, it was unlikely to have affected the eventual outcome, as the fire was believed to have been self-propagating even before it was noticed.

Slightly less than 6 minutes before impact, and over a period of some 90 seconds, the DFDR recorded a number of technical failures that were associated with the malfunction of certain aircraft systems and which possibly or apparently resulted from heat and fire damage. The first of these was the disconnection of the No. 2 autopilot, with the sound of its aural warning clearly recorded on the CVR tape. Other failures included primary power to the No. 1 flight control computer and the air data computer (ADC-1). The aircraft was at an approximate height of 10,000 ft (3,000 m) when

almost simultaneously the DFDR and the CVR stopped functioning, apparently due to fire-related power interruptions. (Neither recorder had an independent power supply.) Less than 30 seconds later, the aircraft's transponder also ceased transmitting. Only about half a minute after the beginning of these failures, the captain declared an emergency, the transmission coming just after the cabin staff indicated that electrical power had been lost in the passenger compartment, necessitating the use of flashlights as the crew made preparations for landing. Shortly thereafter, the first officer advised the captain that he was flying the MD-11, and that his instrument displays were dark. Under the circumstances, attitude and heading could probably be ascertained through the primary flight displays, but the crew would have to rely on a standby instrument for altitude and air speed information. And due to their smaller size and location, it would have been difficult for the pilots to transition to these instruments, especially considering the deteriorating cockpit environment.

Since it was not heard on the CVR tape, the TSB considered it doubtful whether the authorisation by the Moncton centre to dump fuel had been heard in the cockpit. The dumping of fuel had not started before the stoppage of the flight recorders, and there was no evidence it was under way at the moment of impact. It was established that due to fire damage to the corresponding cable, the left emergency electrical bus had lost power shortly before the recorders stopped functioning. This would have rendered inoperable numerous warning lights, including the master warning. Due to the proximity of their cables, and despite the use of protective sleeving to maintain separation, the remaining emergency or battery buses would have been exposed to the same fire threat, although it could not be determined whether they were affected the same way as the left emergency bus. (The Board found that the manner by which the power bus cables were routed together near the overhead switch panel would have increased the opportunity for the services provided by them to be lost as a result of a single-point failure.) Examination of them disclosed that at the time of the crash, both wing engines had been producing thrust, with the No. 1 in fact operating at high speed. The No. 2 (centre) power plant was producing no thrust, apparently having been intentionally shut down by the crew. The reason for this could not be determined with certainty, but the action may have been prompted by a false fire warning related to damage from the in-flight blaze. Under the circumstances, power control would still have been available, but alert status information pertaining to the engines would not have been. It was noted in the investigative report that since witnesses had observed aircraft lights, some of the electrical systems of *HB-IWF* must have remained powered. The TSB concluded that primary electrical power must have been available up until the moment of impact. Also, since the primary flight controls on the MD-11 were hydraulically and not electrically powered, the crew should have been able to maintain control of the aircraft.

Radar data indicated that despite the need to land, *HB-IWF* continued on a southerly track, away from the airport and out to sea, suggesting that the pilots were unable effectively to navigate the aircraft. Although the reading of the instrument may not have been accurate due to the loss of electrical power, the aircraft's standby attitude indicator showed a right bank of around 110 degrees and a nose-down pitch of 20 degrees when the jet struck the surface of the ocean. Based on its standby air speed indicator, the velocity of the MD-11 at the moment of impact was around 350 mph (560 kmh). At the same time, its undercarriage was retracted and flaps were set at 15 degrees; its slats were not deployed, as would be expected with flap extension, but their operation had probably been affected by fire damage. There was no evidence of structural failure occurring before the crash, or that the fire had burned completely through the skin of the aircraft.

Significant to the disaster was the presence of flammable materials in *HB-IWF* that allowed both the ignition and the spread of the fire. Although the aforementioned MPET cover material probably ignited initially and must have been the main source of fuel in the fire, other items contributed to the propagation and intensity of the blaze, including silicone elastomeric end caps, hook-and-loop fasteners and thermal acoustic insulation splicing tapes. Even though they met regulatory standards for flammability, these materials were found to be combustible even when not contaminated with dust and lint. One of the conclusions of the TSB was that standards for material flammability in aircraft were inadequate. The report noted that had the Swissair crew been aware that flammable materials were present in the attic space of the MD-11, this knowledge might have affected their evaluation of the situation.

The ability of the crew to deal with the emergency was significantly hampered by the lack of built-in detection and suppression equipment in the area of the fire. Lacking the proper equipment, the pilots were at a notable disadvantage in their attempt to reach the smoke and fumes. Also, they would probably not even have anticipated a serious fire threat from the attic or any other hidden area in the aircraft. Even had the flight crew known the source of the fire early in the accident sequence, the report described as a 'significant challenge' for one of the pilots to gain access to the area where the blaze continued to burn. And by the time the location of the fire aboard *HB-IWF* became known in the final minutes of the flight, it was considered unlikely that anyone could have accessed the attic and brought it under control using the available hand-held extinguishers. All but one of the eight portable fire extinguishers carried aboard the MD-11 were recovered, but because of the lack of individual features and the damage sustained in the crash, it could not be determined whether one of them was the single Halon unit mounted in the cockpit, or whether any of them had been used.

Thus, the fire-fighting efforts of the crew, if any, remained unknown. However, it was established that the two pilots had donned their emergency oxygen masks some 15 minutes before the crash.

Another significant factor in the disaster was the absence of a requirement for any built-in flame suppression features in the attic of the MD-11, the reason for this being that it was not considered either a designated fire area, such as the engines, or a potential fire area, such as the cargo compartment or lavatories. It was ruled by the TSB that before this accident, regulators, manufacturers and operators had perceived as minimal the threat of in-flight fire in areas other than those designated as such and in the cabin. In fact, the US Federal Aviation Administration (FAA) had placed a low priority to fire threats in these other areas. The TSB further ruled that certification standards did not account for the potential consequences of a fire-related breach or failure of an aircraft system in such a location as the attic, which in turn allowed for the construction of components whose failure could exacerbate the blaze.

The report noted that before this disaster, there was an expectation within the industry that crews could distinguish with a high degree of certainty between smoke emanating from an air-conditioning source and that generated by an electrical malfunction. However, the assumption that human sensory perception is capable of making such a differentiation was considered 'invalid' by the TSB. In this case, human detection methods certainly proved to be inadequate, as the location and extent of the smoke and fire were not discerned until the blaze had become unmanageable with available means. The report further observed that the decision to land in the event of an unsuppressed in-flight blaze must be made quickly. Perhaps significant was the fact that the checklists of neither the airline nor the manufacturer emphasised the need to immediately start preparations for a

landing. Instead, the reference to landing was the last item on both versions. The first item in the carrier's smoke/fumes of unknown origin checklist was to select off the cabin bus, and as confirmed by the report of the loss of electrical power in the cabin, this must have been done. (The Swissair check-list did not require activation of the emergency cabin lighting before deactivation of the cabin bus.) The cabin bus switch was designed to cut off electrical power from the aircraft's cabin services, and the Board noted it reasonable to assume that Swissair flight crews would believe its use would also de-power the IFEN. But it would also turn off the re-circulation fans, which would change the airflow above the forward cabin drop-ceiling to a direction towards the cockpit. With hot combustion by-products being drawn in that direction, the cockpit smoke barrier must have ultimately failed, and the rapid heating of the air spaces and electrical components behind the CB panels would in turn have caused various aircraft systems to malfunction. The TSB further determined that the aluminium cap assembly used on the stainless steel oxygen line above the cockpit ceiling was susceptible to leaking or fracturing when exposed to the temperatures experienced, which could potentially affect the crew oxygen supply. If it occurred, an oxygen leak would also have exacerbated the situation, as would have the fire-related failure of the elastomeric cap situated on the end of the conditioned air branch duct located immediately aft and overhead of the cockpit door, with the latter leading to a continuous release of conditioned air.

With regard to their specific actions, the Board concluded that the pilots were initially unaware that smoke had been present in the hidden areas above the cockpit ceiling and cabin attic space, and likewise that a fire was propagating in the aircraft. Consistent with other carriers, Swissair provided no specific training in fighting fires in hidden or inaccessible sections. Nor was there training with regard to the location of potentially inflammable material in these areas. According to the TSB, this reflected a lack of knowledge within the industry about the presence of such materials. And with simulator training generally reinforcing a positive outcome to smoke-related events, crews did not come to appreciate how rapidly in-flight fires can develop into uncontrollable situations. Among the environmental factors affecting the crew were the increasing concentration of smoke and heat in the cockpit, and the dripping of molten aluminium from the ceiling of the flight deck. The pilot's position on the left side of the flight deck would have been more directly in line with the area of the cockpit ceiling liner that was first breached, although it could not be ascertained whether the captain had remained in his seat throughout the accident sequence. (His seat was in fact found in the egress position, and the corresponding seat belt unfastened, while at the moment of impact the first officer's seat remained occupied.) During the descent, *HB-IWF* would have encountered layers of clouds, the bottom of which had a base of no lower than 1,500 ft (*c.* 500 m). And once through the lowest cloud layer, it would have been dark over the sea because of the clouds, mist and lack of surface lights, thus providing the crew with no outside visual references. The failure shortly before the crash of the aircraft's electronic navigational equipment and communications radios would have left the pilots with no accurate means of establishing their geographic position, speaking with ATC personnel or even locating the airport. They would also have had to deal with a barrage of fault messages, cues and alerts, which would have been distracting and difficult to cope with. In the final moments of the flight, the crew may have contemplated landing in the water, even though the ditching mode button on the overhead switch panel had not been activated. When considering the absence of outside visual cues, the lack of instrumentation and the fact that they had not received specific training in flying the aircraft using only the standby indicators, there being no regulatory requirement for such, the pilots may have lost orientation with the horizon. Or they may simply have become incapacitated from the effects of the blaze. However, there was no way of determining this, since none of the toxicological specimens submitted for testing proved suitable in providing a meaningful analysis of carbon monoxide inhalation. In any case, the MD-11 was not in controlled flight at the moment of impact.

When the crew reported starting to dump fuel and that the aircraft had to land immediately, the ATC controller was partly occupied by coordination activities, and he apparently did not fully comprehend the entire radio transmission. He therefore did not offer further information, such as a vector towards the airport in the few seconds before the aircraft's radios failed, ending all air/ground communications. Nevertheless, the actions of the controller were not considered to have been a factor in the outcome of the flight, and were found to have conformed to standard practices. In fact, calculations confirmed that because of the rapid deterioration of aircraft systems, the pilots would not have been in a position to complete a safe landing at Halifax from any point along the flight path after *HB-IWF* started to descend.

Even before the Swissair disaster, and in the wake of ground fires involving its MD-11 and MD-80 aircraft, McDonnell Douglas had recommended that operators discontinue the use of insulation blankets and reference tapes using the aforementioned metallised Mylar material. After the crash, the FAA announced it would develop a new test specification for insulation materials; the previous method, which involved suspending a strip over a Bunsen burner for a selected time period, was considered inadequate. Later, the US agency issued airworthiness directives calling for the removal of MPET-covered insulation blankets. Although the investigation found no evidence that it was directly contributory to the initiation or propagation of the fire, the TSB did identify a significant design flaw in the IFEN system used in the Swissair MD-11 fleet, which had been installed by an independent firm. The configuration in which the IFEN had been certified was not compatible with the emergency electrical load-shedding design philosophy employed in the aircraft, and could not be deactivated when the cabin bus was switched off. This in the opinion of the Board constituted a 'latent unsafe condition'. Due to the condition of its wreckage, no determination could be made as to whether any specific deficiencies existed in *HB-IWF* before the accident. However, an examination conducted after the crash of Flight 111 revealed such wiring discrepancies as cracking, chafing and improper routing in other MD-11 jets, some of which belonged to Swissair, prompting a recommendation by the US National Transportation Safety Board (NTSB) and a subsequent series of directives by the FAA requiring more thorough inspections and corrective action. Perhaps the most aggressive safety action was taken by Swissair, which elected to remove the IFEN systems in the aircraft in which they had been installed. A number of other changes were also enacted by the carrier, among them the adoption of new emergency checklists and the installation in its fleet of an additional standby flight instrument, new wiring and additional smoke detection equipment, the latter including video cameras in certain hidden areas. But the precautionary actions taken by the carrier would do little to alter the economic difficulties of Swissair, which industry observers attributed to an unsuccessful attempt to expand its European service network combined with a downturn in business beginning in 2001. The carrier ceased operations in March 2002 and was replaced by the new national airline, Swiss.

Date: 11 December 1998 (*c.* 19:00)
Location: Near Surat Thani, Thailand
Operator: Thai Airways International
Aircraft type: Airbus Industrie A310-204 (*HS-TIA*)

The second major Airbus accident in the Far East during the year involved Flight 261, which had been on a domestic Thai service from Bangkok and was scheduled to land at the Surat Thani airport.

Due to the removal of the airport's instrument landing system (ILS), which was part of a construction project intended to lengthen the runway, a precision approach would not have been possible, necessitating the use by the crew of non-precision very-high-frequency omnidirectional range/ distance-measuring equipment (VOR/DME) procedures. Compounding the night-time and adverse meteorological conditions, with a visibility of approximately 1 mile (1.5 km) in heavy rain and a cloud base of around 1,000 ft (300 m), was the fact that some of the runway lights were also inoperative. Following two unsuccessful attempts to land, *HS-TIA* began a third, but during its approach to Runway 22 the A300 suddenly pitched up sharply and entered a steep climb. The wide-bodied jetliner then plunged into a rubber plantation about half a mile (0.8 km) south-west of the airport and to the left of the runway centreline, bursting into flames on impact. The crash killed 102 persons aboard the Airbus, including both pilots and nine other crew members. Three cabin attendants and 41 passengers survived with various injuries.

No evidence was found of any malfunction in the aircraft's engines, flight control or navigational systems, and the accident apparently occurred after

the pilot had experienced spatial disorientation, resulting in the pitch-up and consequent stall. Before the crash, a member of the flight crew reported being unable to see the runway, and the stall-warning alarm was heard on the cockpit voice recorder (CVR) tape just before impact.

Date: 31 October 1999 (*c.* 01:50)
Location: North Atlantic Ocean
Operator: EgyptAir
Aircraft type: Boeing 767-366ER (*SU-GAP*)

Flight 990 had arrived late the previous evening from Los Angeles, California, and was on the ground for about 90 minutes at John F. Kennedy International Airport before taking off on the second leg of an international service to Cairo, Egypt. During its stop in New York, there was a change of flight crew, one of its members being 59-year-old Relief First Officer Gameel el-Batouty, whose name would play a prominent role in the investigation of the ensuing disaster.

Less than half an hour after departure, the 767 had reached its assigned cruising altitude of 33,000 ft (*c.* 10,050 m). Minutes later, the wide-bodied jet airliner plunged into the sea some 60 miles (100 km) south-south-east of Nantucket Island, Massachusetts, US. All 217 persons aboard (203 passengers and 14 crew members) perished; the remains of more than two-thirds of the victims would be identified within a year. No distress message was heard from the aircraft and there were no known witnesses to the crash, which occurred in early morning darkness and visual meteorological conditions.

Although the scene of the disaster was in international waters, the investigation into it would be undertaken, at the request of the Egyptian government, by the US National Transportation Safety Board (NTSB). At first, the task of the Board seemed as formidable as its investigation into the crash of TWA Flight 800 (see separate entry, 17 July 1996), which occurred three years earlier about 150 miles (250 km) to the west and took nearly six years to complete. The wreckage of *SU-GAP* was found in two main debris fields some 1,200 ft (350 m) apart, at an approximate depth of 230 ft (70 m). Within two months of the disaster, about 70 per cent of the aircraft was recovered, with the subsequent retrieval of additional debris, including the left power plant. Examination of both

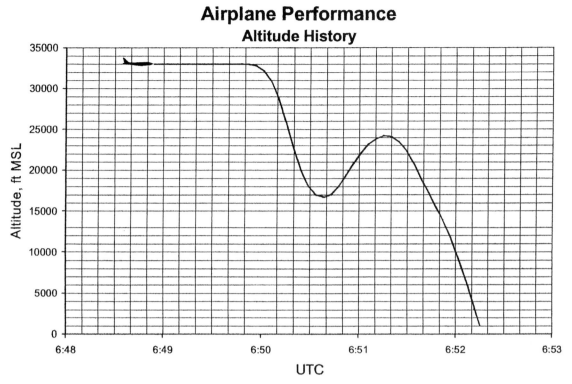

The 'roller coaster' flight path of the EgyptAir Boeing 767, indicating the pull-up manoeuvre before the final dive into the Atlantic Ocean. *(National Transportation Safety Board)*

engines revealed little evidence of rotation, if any. Early in the search, the aircraft's flight data (FDR) and cockpit voice (CVR) recorders were found, and unlike the case of TWA 800, both yielded useful information before they had stopped almost simultaneously. Information about the remainder of the flight would come from the wreckage and recorded primary data from three radar sites in New York and Massachusetts, which indicated that after an initial descent that was arrested at around 15,000 ft (5,000 m), the 767 climbed to around 25,000 ft (7,500 m), and its heading changed from 80 degrees to 140 degrees before the final plunge into the ocean. Information provided by the CVR was particularly enlightening, if not disturbing.

About 20 minutes after take-off, as the aircraft was still climbing to its cruising altitude, Relief First Officer el-Batouty suggested he relieve the command co-pilot, indicating he wanted to fly this portion of the trip, even though this changeover would normally have taken place 3 to 4 hours into the flight. After some initial resistance, the regular co-pilot agreed to relinquish his seat, and would subsequently leave the flight deck. Minutes later, after *SU-GAP* had levelled off, the pilot, Capt Ahmed al-Habashy, left the flight deck to use the lavatory. It was then that First Officer el-Batouty was heard on the CVR to say to himself, 'I rely on God'. This phrase would be repeated by him another 10 times over a period of approximately 2 minutes. During this time the disconnection of the autopilot was recorded by the FDR, and less than 10 seconds later, the thrust levers were retarded from cruise power to the idle setting. Almost simultaneous with the reduction in thrust, the jet pitched down and began to descend. Shortly thereafter, Capt al-Habashy returned to the flight deck, asking several times, 'What's happening?' His queries elicited no response from the co-pilot, who continued to repeat, 'I rely on God'. At an approximate height of 30,000 ft (*c.* 10,000 m), the 767 exceeded its maximum operating velocity of nearly 90 per cent the speed of sound, as indicated by the activation of the master warning alarm in the cockpit. Just above 27,000 ft (8,200 m), and with the aircraft descending at a nose-down angle of around 40 degrees, the elevator surfaces began moving to reduced nose-down deflections, and subsequently the FDR recorded a 'split' elevator condition, with the left control surface in a nose-up position and the right one nose-down. In a rapid sequence of events, the engine start lever switches were moved to the cut-off position and the thrust levers from the idle position to full power, and the aircraft's speed brakes were then deployed. The switching off of the power plants prompted the captain to ask, 'What is this? What is this?' In the final seconds of the recording, the captain said, 'Get away in the engines,' followed by 'Shut the engines'. This order evoked the only response from the co-pilot during the entire sequence, 'It's shut'. Until the recording ended, the captain was repeatedly heard to say to the first officer, 'Pull with me!'

The NTSB attempted to determine whether any mechanical failures could have caused the elevator movements that precipitated the dive. Virtually every possibility was ruled out, including autopilot malfunction, which the Board's report noted would not have resulted in any elevator movements. Four elevator malfunction scenarios, each of which involved two failures, warranted further study because they could potentially cause nose-down elevator movements or a split elevator condition similar to that shown by the FDR of the EgyptAir jet. These were as follows: (1) The disconnection of the input linkages to two of the three power control actuator (PCA) units on the right elevator, which could have resulted from the failure of any of the components that encompass the actuator input linkage system, including the bell-crank; (2) A jam of the input linkages or servo valves in two of the three PCA units on the same control surface involving the internal slides of the affected servo valve that would first have to be moved either manually or by autopilot input to an offset position and then to jam in a nose-down setting; (3) A jam of the input linkage or servo valve in one PCA and the disconnection of the input linkage to another actuator, also on the right elevator, or (4) A jam in the elevator flight control cable connecting the right control column to the right aft quadrant assembly in combination with a break in the same cable. However, the NTSB ruled that none of the four scenarios was consistent with the elevator movements recorded after the initial upset. Evidence against such a malfunction included the

continued functioning of the elevator surfaces throughout the descent.

The contention of the NTSB that none of the failure sequences could have been a precipitating factor was also confirmed through simulations, which showed that the pilots were consistently able to regain control of the aircraft using normal recovery techniques. The investigative report further noted that the redundant elevator system of the 767 had been designed so that pilots could overcome such dual failures by allowing the non-failed surface to respond to any nose-up flight control input. Furthermore, the Board's testing and evaluation of the system showed that none of the failure modes examined would have resulted in control column movements without concurrent identifiable movements of the elevators, which would have been observed in the FDR read-out. Another interesting factor was the behaviour exhibited by the relief first officer, which the Board considered inconsistent with a pilot encountering an unexpected or uncommanded flight condition. As confirmed by the CVR, he neither exhibited any audible expression of surprise, nor called for help, and did not respond to the captain's repeated questions as to what was happening. Based on the assumption that another pilot would have said something regarding the sudden transition of the aircraft into a steep descent, the NTSB further concluded that First Officer el-Batouty had been alone in the flight deck at the beginning of the sequence.

From the considerable amount of available factual evidence, the NTSB came to the determination that the relief first officer had initiated the descent, ruling that all of the manual control inputs were made by him. And the absence of a disconnect warning tone on the CVR tape was consistent with the autopilot being manually disconnected by rapidly double-clicking the switch mounted on the yoke. There were no indications of any major systems malfunction, conflicting air traffic or other event that might have prompted him to do this, nor was there any logical operational reason at that point to disconnect the autopilot. It was similarly concluded that the thrust lever movements from the cruise power setting to idle did not result from autothrottle commands but rather from deliberate manipulation by the co-pilot. And since they occurred after the power was reduced to idle, the control column movements must not have been in response to any movements of the elevators.

Because of the override mechanisms, the two control columns had the authority to independently command the aircraft's elevators. Testing confirmed in fact that the left and right elevator surfaces could be moved in opposite directions by differential control column inputs. The 'split' elevator condition noted during the descent thus must have resulted from the two men on the flight deck applying opposing control inputs, the first officer nose-down and the captain nose-up. Although there should have been sufficient time to effect recovery had they been working together, the NTSB found 'no evidence of co-operative effort by the pilots'. It was considered unlikely that under the circumstances Captain al-Habashy would have suspected upon his return to the cockpit that the actions of the co-pilot were directly contributing to the dive. The Board also concluded that the efforts by the former to prevent the crash could have been complicated by a loss of electrically powered cockpit displays after the engines were shut down. The NTSB was unable to explain the intention or motivation of First Officer el-Batouty for apparently sending the jet into its fatal plunge. However, it was noted in a press report that he had been disciplined by the airline for alleged 'sexual misconduct' in the US six months earlier, and according to a former EgyptAir pilot, the executive responsible for that reprimand had been a passenger on Flight 990 when it crashed.

Understandably, the airline argued against the contention that one of its pilots could have intentionally crashed an aircraft. In a rebuttal to the NTSB report, EgyptAir provided several reasons for this, most significantly that First Officer el-Batouty had no motive to commit suicide and mass homicide, pointing to the possibility that this was an accident resulting from an elevator system malfunction. As further evidence of this, the company claimed that the recovered wreckage indicated damage before impact, pointing to a sheared pin and an improperly positioned bias spring in the right outboard PCA and the failure in opposite directions of the right elevator bell-crank shear rivets. The airline also maintained that the elevator 'split' observed in the FDR data could have been a manifestation of the loss of the starboard elevator. Its dissenting opinion brought the operator in direct dispute with the manufacturer, which had conducted simulator tests and could find no mechanical failure mode consistent with the data obtained from the FDR. Asking for additional testing, EgyptAir said Boeing's technical analysis submitted to the NTSB contained 'many inaccuracies, omissions and selective use of evidence'. The airline claimed that ground tests and simulations conducted during the investigation 'did not reflect the actual operation of the airplane'.

According to EgyptAir, an analysis of the facts and of the design of the aircraft's elevator control system indicated that malfunctions in two PCA units on the starboard elevator may have precipitated the dive. The airline's contention was that this dual malfunction could have involved a failure that had been totally or nearly latent and may have existed for a period of time, coupled with the jam of the second PCA occurring shortly before the crash. The carrier noted that a pilot flying *SU-GAP* the day before the disaster had disconnected the autopilot after noticing some unusual movement in the control column, and said this could have been further evidence of something wrong with the elevator. (Anomalies with the autopilot had indeed been uncovered by NTSB, but according to its report, examination of the aircraft's maintenance logbooks had revealed no related write-ups.)

Coming less than two years after the crash of SilkAir Flight 185 (see separate entry, 19 December 1997), which some believed resulted from an act of suicide by its captain, the EgyptAir disaster would raise the issue of improving means in detecting personal or psychological difficulties among air carrier pilots.

2000 AND BEYOND

From the first eight months of 2001, it appeared that in the first year of the new millennium the airlines of the world would attain a new record of achievement in the area of safety. Then came September 11. Within 2 hours on that Tuesday morning, four commercial jets on domestic US flights would be hijacked and turned into weapons of mass destruction. One never reached its intended target. The other three struck with a vengeance, destroying the World Trade Center complex in New York City and badly damaging the Pentagon building, located outside Washington DC. Nearly 3,000 lives were lost in the carefully coordinated terrorist attack, most of whom were on the ground.

Despite its quest to protect itself from some of the most formidable threats – bad weather, air traffic congestion, engineering flaws – commercial aviation had become a victim of the world's most destructive force, human conflict. Not only was this the greatest tragedy in the history of airline travel in terms of casualties, but the attack proved damaging to the industry economically, especially in the US but also in the rest of the world. Recovery was not expected to take place for years, and for some carriers, never did.

One notable loss not related to terrorism during this period was the Concorde disaster in July 2000. The crash near Paris ended a stretch of nearly a quarter of a century of supersonic passenger operations without a fatality, and combined with a downturn in business related to the 9/11 attacks, ultimately led to the end of service of the Anglo-French aircraft. The early twenty-first century also witnessed a rare major disaster involving the Scandinavian airline industry, which had attained a reputation for being one of the world's safest. On the positive side, the airlines of Great Britain increased to more than a decade and a half the period of operations without a fatal crash involving a large fixed-wing aircraft. A pattern that always existed has become even more pronounced in the new century, with Third World countries, particularly in Africa and Latin America, accounting for most serious accidents. In the industrialised world, where the air traffic is the heaviest, major airline disasters have become extremely rare events. As one aviation publication best phrased it, when it comes to air travel, there indeed appears to be 'safety in riches'.

This short chapter contains accounts, of major commercial aviation disasters some of them based on preliminary information, beginning in 2000.

Date: 30 January 2000 (*c.* 21:09)
Location: Near Abidjan, Ivory Coast
Operator: Kenya Airways
Aircraft type: Airbus Industrie A310-304 (*5Y-BEN*)

Operating on a scheduled international service originating at Nairobi, Kenya, the aircraft had landed at Felix Houphouet-Boigny International Airport, serving Abidjan, having flown past Lagos, Nigeria, where it was to have stopped earlier but could not due to the effects of the Harmattan, a seasonal wind that blows westwards from the Sahara Desert, carrying with it large amounts of dust.

Redesignated as Flight 431, it then departed for Lagos, but less than a minute after lifting off from Runway 21, the wide-bodied jetliner crashed in the Gulf of Guinea, killing 169 persons aboard, including the 10 members of its crew. Ten passengers survived, most of whom escaped serious injury.

Less than 2 seconds after the 'gear up' command was given, the aircraft's stick-shaker stall-warning

A Kenya Airways Airbus A310, the type aircraft that crashed at sea after taking off from Abidjan, Ivory Coast. *(Philip Jarrett)*

system activated, and continued as *5Y-BEN* transitioned from a climb to a descent with its undercarriage still extended. Subsequently, the A310 slammed into the sea about half a mile (0.8 km) offshore, in water that was around 150 ft (50 m) deep and in an area where the waves were some 3 ft (1 m) high. The accident occurred in darkness but the weather was good, with the sky clear and the air virtually calm. Within a week of the crash, the bodies of about half of the victims had been recovered. Incidental to the accident was the death of a diver, who lost his life during wreckage recovery operations.

The disaster was attributed to the incorrect application by the flight crew of the prescribed procedures in response to the stick-shaker warning, which had apparently been false. In accordance with the Airbus flight crew operating manual, the pilots should have responded to a low-altitude stall indication by applying take-off/go-around (TOGA) power, reducing the angle-of-attack of the aircraft and levelling its wings, and verifying that the speed brakes were fully retracted. The investigation revealed that while the pilot flying the A310 did reduce its pitch angle, there had been no application of TOGA power. It was not possible to determine whether the other prescribed actions had

been taken. Also, the pilot apparently lowered the nose too far, which placed the jetliner in a descending attitude, leading to the activation of the ground-proximity warning system (GPWS). This should have alerted the crew as to the proximity of the aircraft to the ocean, but in this case the GPWS alert must have been obscured by the flaps/slats overspeed indication. Another contributing factor in the accident was that the take-off had been made towards the sea, which at night afforded the pilots no outside visual references.

Date: 31 January 2000 (*c.* 16:20)
Location: Near Oxnard, California, US
Operator: Alaska Airlines (US)
Aircraft type: McDonnell Douglas MD-83 (*N963AS*)

All 88 persons aboard (83 passengers and a crew of five) perished when the jetliner crashed in the Pacific Ocean some 60 miles (100 km) north-west of Los Angeles and in the vicinity of the Channel Islands. A sufficient amount of human remains was found to allow for the identification, through various means, of the victims of the tragedy.

Operating as Flight 261, the aircraft had departed from Puerto Vallarta, Jalisco, Mexico,

Floating debris marks the crash site of the Alaska Airlines MD-83 that plunged into the Pacific Ocean off Southern California. *(US Coast Guard)*

bound for San Francisco, California, the first segment of an international service with an ultimate destination of Seattle, Washington, US. About 1 hour 40 minutes into the trip, the crew contacted the airline's dispatch and maintenance control facilities at Seattle, reporting that the aircraft's horizontal stabiliser was jammed. After a period of troubleshooting by the two pilots, the captain radioed the Los Angeles air traffic control centre, 'We've lost vertical control of our airplane'. Passing to the west of Los Angeles International Airport (LAX), *N963AS* initially descended from its cruising height of flight level 310 (*c*. 10,000 m). Over a period of around 10 minutes, the MD-83 continued in a north-westerly heading in what the report of the US National Transportation Safety Board (NTSB) described as 'unstabilised flight'. After the crew reported being able to maintain altitude 'with difficulty', the flight was cleared to proceed to LAX, where a landing would be attempted. It was also authorised to turn on to a heading of 280 degrees and descend to 17,000 ft (*c*. 5,200 m). But over the next few minutes, the situation grew from critical to

catastrophic. Entering the final descent from an approximate height of 18,000 ft (5,500 m), the MD-83 plummeted into the sea about 3 miles (5 km) north of Anacapa Island, and some 15 miles (25 km) offshore from the mainland, striking the surface of the ocean in a nearly inverted, steep nose-down and left wing-low attitude. The accident occurred in visual meteorological conditions, with scattered clouds at 1,200 ft (*c*. 350 m) reported in the area of LAX at the time.

The depth of the water in the area was around 700 ft (200 m), which precluded human diving activity, but through dragging operations and the use of remotely operated submersible vehicles, about 90 per cent of the aircraft's wreckage was ultimately recovered, including both its universal flight data (FDR) and cockpit voice (CVR) recorders. There was no evidence of in-flight fire, explosion or foreign impact damage occurring before the crash, nor of malfunction in either engine; the lack of rotation of the right power plant indicated a flame-out related to airflow disturbances or fuel unporting, either of which could have been caused by the extreme descent angle before the impact with the ocean surface. Among the components recovered were the jack-screw assembly, which serves as the actuating mechanism of the horizontal stabiliser on the MD-83. Electrically powered, this mechanical unit raises or lowers the leading edge of the control surface, while the trailing-edge pivots about its hinge points, thus changing the pitch of the aircraft. It is activated either automatically when the autopilot is engaged, or manually by the pilots using switches on either control wheel or separate pairs of handles and switches located on the centre control console.

A closer examination disclosed metallic filaments wrapped around the central part of the acme screw, which were themselves identified as severely worn and sheared remnants of the accompanying nut. The NTSB ruled that this damage had occurred before, and was directly related to, the disaster.

Specifically, the Board concluded that the threads inside the acme nut on *N963AS* had been incrementally worn down by the screw over a period of time, and during the accident flight were completely sheared off, leading to the jamming of the assembly. It was also determined that approximately 90 per cent of the thread thickness had worn away before the remainder of the threads were sheared off. An analysis further revealed only small flakes of dried and hardened grease attached to the aforementioned nut remnants, which would not have been capable of providing sufficient lubrication of the assembly. Although the parts had been immersed in salt water for the one week before their recovery, tests showed that this would not have significantly altered or removed grease had it been present. The NTSB concluded that there had been insufficient lubrication of the acme screw and nut interface, leading to the excessive and accelerated wear that was directly causal to the crash of Flight 261.

No determination could be made as to the reason for the jamming of the screw to the nut, though possible causes included the bending of the worn threads before or during the shearing, distortion of the remnants after they were sheared off, or loads resulting from the screw threads pulling upwards across the ridges that remained on the nut. The read-out of its FDR indicated that the aircraft's longitudinal trim control system had functioned normally during the flight from San Francisco to Puerto Vallarta, and that the assembly became jammed during the outbound trip, about 15 minutes after take-off and as the MD-83 was climbing through 23,400 ft (7,100 m) at an indicated air speed of 380 mph (*c.* 610 kmh). Under the circumstances, the autopilot would have attempted to achieve trim by continuing to add elevator input to compensate for the lack of movement of the stabiliser.

Approximately 3 minutes after the last movement of the control surface, the autopilot was disconnected, probably by the crew in response to the trim annunciator warning light. Although their actions were not transcribed due to time limitations in the recording ability of the CVR, the crew must have noticed that the aircraft was mistrimmed and it is likely they would have tried to correct the problem by manually activating the primary or alternate trim systems in order to move the horizontal stabiliser. The aircraft ultimately reached its cruising height through the pilots' activation of the elevators. Manual control of the jetliner was continued for a period of around 2 hours, whereupon the crew briefly engaged the autopilot, then disengaged it minutes later. It was then re-engaged and disengaged just before the initial descent. The deployment of the speed brakes about half a minute after the final disconnect of the autopilot was most likely an attempt by the crew to reduce the rapidly increasing air speed of the MD-83. The FDR would record no movement of the stabiliser until the beginning of the period of unstabilised flight, which began when the jam was apparently overcome as a result of the operation of the primary trim motor. Just before the final descent, the aircraft's slats and flaps were deployed and shortly thereafter retracted, both times at the request of the captain. Approximately 1 minute later, these units were again deployed, at which time an extremely loud noise was heard. Immediately thereafter, N963AS went into its final dive, during which it reached a nose-down pitch angle of at least 70 degrees.

The release of the jam must have involved the acme screw being pulled upwards through the nut by aerodynamic forces, which would have caused the upwards movement of the horizontal stabiliser and, in turn, greater nose-down motion of the aircraft. This upwards pulling motion would have continued until the lower mechanical stop on the screw came in contact with the lower surface of the nut, preventing further upwards movement of the stabiliser. Loads imposed during the period of unstabilised flight weakened and ultimately fractured the torque tube inside the screw, with the strength of the component apparently having been greatly reduced already by low-cycle fatigue cracking. Immediately afterwards, the tip fairing brackets of the vertical stabiliser also failed, allowing the leading edge of the horizontal stabiliser to move upwards to a position significantly beyond what was permitted by a normally functioning jack-screw. The loud bang recorded by the CVR less than 90 seconds before the crash was probably caused by the failure of the brackets, leading to the loss of the tip fairing and structural deformation of the assembly, which would have resulted in local aerodynamic disturbances. The upwards movement of the leading edge of the stabiliser also created an excessive aerodynamic tail load, causing the uncontrollable downwards pitching of the jetliner, from which recovery was not possible. Although the position of the horizontal stabiliser leading to the final pitch-over could not be determined due to limitations in the recording capability of the FDR, engineering studies indicated that the horizontal tail fin would contact the vertical stabiliser tip brackets at an angle of 3.6 degrees nose-down.

The single jack-screw assembly used on the MD-80 series transport and on its forerunner, the smaller Douglas DC-9, was originally expected to have a service life of 30,000 flying hours. But a subsequent sampling programme revealed a wear rate considerably above that predicted. After wear was discovered in the aluminium/bronze acme nut units on some aircraft in the DC-9 fleet, the manufacturer developed a procedure enabling operators to determine the amount of movement, or end-play, between the nut and screw threads, which would not require removal of the jack-screw. And initially, the manufacturer recommended lubrication of the jack-screw assembly at intervals of 600 to 900 flying hours. This was later increased to 3,600 hours or 15 months, whichever came first. The NTSB ruled that these extensions, which had been approved by the US Federal Aviation Administration (FAA), increased the likelihood that a missed or inadequate lubrication would have resulted in excessive wear of the nut threads. The Board further concluded that although the time interval eventually adopted by the airline was still less than that required by the manufacturer, the extensions directly factored in the excessive wear of the jack-screw assembly in N963AS and thus contributed to the disaster. Significantly, Alaska was at the time the only US carrier that had a calendar-based lubrication interval, with no 'whichever comes first' specification. At the time of the accident, only four months had elapsed since what should have been the last jack-screw assembly lubrication performed on the MD-83. But the condition of the assembly indicated that at least that lubrication had either been missed or been inadequate. The adequacy of lubrication procedures by operators of the type aircraft was also brought into question by the NTSB. An interview with the Alaska Airlines' mechanic responsible for the lubrication of the jack-screw assembly of N963AS revealed a lack of knowledge as to how the procedure should have been performed. Laboratory demonstrations established that applying grease only through the acme nut grease fitting would result in insufficient lubrication of the nut/screw assembly. Also, the removal of degraded grease would increase the effectiveness of the lubrication procedure.

Alaska Airlines had consistently required end-play examinations at the time of every other 'C-class' maintenance check. But when the C-check interval was extended to 15 months, end-play checks would only be required every 2½ years. And with the carrier's utilisation of its aircraft also having increased, the time interval of the check nearly doubled the period of 5,000 flying hours initially employed. The NTSB determined that the extension of the end-play check interval, which had also been approved by the FAA but was not supported by technical data, allowed the acme nut threads in the accident aircraft to wear to the point of failure without being detected and thus contributed to the crash. It was noted in the investigative report that the steps required to conduct the end-play check procedure properly were not well described in the manufacturer's overhaul/maintenance manual. Investigators who observed checks being performed by maintenance personnel from several MD-80 operators identified numerous potential sources for inaccurate measurements. Also, the restraining fixtures being used by Alaska Airlines to determine end-play did not meet the engineering drawing requirements of the manufacturer. The Board concluded that as it was being practised, the procedure had 'not been validated', and had 'low reliability'.

With regard to the human factors issue, the NTSB considered as 'understandable' the decision of the crew not to return to Puerto Vallarta immediately after recognising the horizontal stabiliser malfunction. Neither of the carrier's checklists pertaining to either an 'inoperative' or a 'runaway' stabiliser required a landing at the nearest suitable airport if corrective actions were not successful. And the report noted that as the MD-83 lacked an inflight dumping system, it would have had to remain airborne for some 45 minutes in order to burn off enough fuel to avert an overweight landing, which would only have been appropriate had the pilots realised the potentially catastrophic nature of the trim anomaly. Based on the handling characteristics of the aircraft, they would not have been aware of the seriousness of the situation. Furthermore, the positive aerodynamic effects of the higher cruise speed would have reduced the necessary flight control pressures and made the jetliner easier to control. The Board did, however, criticise other actions of the crew, concluding that their use of the autopilot was not appropriate and went contrary to company procedures. Besides masking the true condition of the aircraft, had it disengaged without one of the pilots holding the control wheel and making immediate corrective inputs, the out-of-trim situation would have led to a severe downward-pitching manoeuvre after the disconnect. Also, the NTSB ruled that the repeated attempts to activate the primary trim system 'went well beyond' what was called for in the airline's procedural checklist, especially when considering that the electrical load meter would have registered spikes during these attempts, which should have alerted the pilots that the system had been jammed beyond the capability of the activating motor. The report noted that while the use of the trim motor as part of the troubleshooting efforts did not in itself release the jam, the torque created by its operation apparently provided enough force ultimately to do so. Over the next few seconds, the increasing angle of attack of the horizontal stabiliser and the increased elevator deflections would in turn have increased the tension loads on the screw, contributing to its upwards motion through the nut. It was observed in the

report that the severity of the initial dive changed the situation to an emergency, which required 'a more deliberate and cautious approach' by the crew.

Nor did the captain brief the first officer as to what to expect when the slat and flap configuration was changed or what to do if this action affected the flying characteristics of the jetliner. Comments transcribed on the CVR indicated that the captain considered retrying the primary system after the initial descent, but abandoned the plan after the first officer suggested they land. It was not clear from the CVR why only seconds later, and after stating that the aircraft was 'pretty stable', the captain ordered the retraction of the flaps and slats. It was then that the velocity of the jetliner began to increase. The final descent came after the flaps were again extended, transitioning from 7 to 11 degrees. The Board recognised that from an operational perspective, the flight crew could not have known the extent of the damage to the aircraft. It further noted that the disengagement of the acme nut and screw exceeded any event anticipated in emergency training scenarios, and that the pilots therefore lacked the ability to devise and execute the appropriate procedures. And since it was not known how many times the crew had activated the primary trim before the release of the jam, the NTSB could not determine with certainty whether its use caused or contributed to the accident. The Board concluded that the decision to land at LAX was probably based on several factors, including a more favourable crosswind condition, even though the carrier's dispatch personnel appeared to have attempted to influence the crew to continue on to San Francisco.

Less than two weeks after the disaster, and after metal shavings were found in the jack-screw assemblies of two other transports of the same type flown by Alaska Airlines, the FAA issued an airworthiness directive (AD) requiring the inspection of every operational DC-9, MD-80 and sister Boeing 717. However, few anomalies were found in the aircraft examined. And a special inspection of carrier, conducted in April of the same year, revealed serious deficiencies in the operations of the company pertaining to such issues as record-keeping in its maintenance programme and vacancies in its management staff. The NTSB even discovered a work card made up after the last end-play check of *N963AS*, more than three years before the accident, recommending the replacement of its jack-screw assembly due to excessive wear. But after a second check, another mechanic overruled the plan. So serious were some of the accusations that criminal charges against the airline were initially contemplated, but none were actually filed. More ominously, certain irregularites pertaining to the compliance with FAA regulations that had been identified in the airline some years before the crash of Flight 261 had apparently not been corrected. Five months after the disaster, Alaska announced an 'airworthiness and operations action plan' with the intention of meeting or exceeding FAA regulations pertaining to maintenance activity. Although it was not a direct factor in the crash, the carrier had switched to a different type of grease in lubricating the jack-screw assemblies of its aircraft than that originally specified. Subsequently, it reverted back to the use of the prescribed grease. Another significant change was a reduction in its lubrication intervals to 650 flight hours. Despite these changes, one member of the Board, writing in the report, expressed concern that some deficiencies continued to exist in the carrier and suggested a follow-up inspection by the FAA.

Pertaining to engineering factors, the NTSB concluded that despite its critical importance to flight safety, the design of the jack-screw assembly used in the DC-9 and its derivatives had not taken into account the loss of acme nut threads as a single-point failure mode. It further noted that neither the manufacturer nor the FAA had accounted for the catastrophic effects of such a failure during the design and certification process, and that the consequences of excessive wear in the horizontal stabiliser trim system were not adequately considered and addressed. Ruling that the dual-thread design did not provide sufficient redundancy with regard to wear, the Board also concluded that the absence of a fail-safe mechanism to prevent the catastrophic effects of total acme nut thread loss contributed to the disaster, and recommended a modification of the trim system. The week after the accident, the manufacturer Boeing, which in 1997 had merged with McDonnell Douglas, issued a flight operations bulletin concerning procedures to be used in the event of a stabiliser trim malfunction, which advised against actions beyond those contained in the appropriate checklist. Reacting to concern expressed by the

NTSB over inadequate surveillance of Alaska Airlines, the certificate management office of the FAA increased its staff. The FAA also issued an AD that reduced the end-play check to 2,000 flight hours. After the NTSB expressed further concern that excessive wear could occur in even less time, and that the check could still be missed or not performed properly, Boeing agreed to revise the end-play procedure.

Date: 19 April 2000 (*c.* 07:00)
Location: Near Samal, Davao Oriental, the Philippines
Operator: Air Philippines
Aircraft type: Boeing Advanced 737-2H4 (*RP-C3010*)

Designated as Flight 541 and on a domestic service from Manila, the jet airliner crashed and burned on Samal Island, located in the Davao Gulf just off the southern coast of Mindanao. All 131 persons aboard (124 passengers and seven crew members) perished.

After being instructed to discontinue its approach to Runway 05 at the airport serving the city of Davao, due to conflicting traffic, the crew of *RP-C3010* requested clearance to land on the runway from the opposite direction. During the very-high-frequency omnidirectional range/distance measuring equipment (VOR/DME) procedure approach, the 737 slammed into a hill at an approximate elevation of 600 ft (180 m) and while properly aligned with the runway but some 4 miles (6.5 km) short of its threshold. Its altitude at the moment of impact was about 1,000 ft (300 m) below the proper glide path. The weather in the area at the time consisted of a low overcast.

Date: 25 July 2000 (16:44)
Location: Near Gonesse, Ile-de-France, France
Operator: Air France
Aircraft type: Aerospatiale/British Aircraft Corporation Concorde (*F-BTSC*)

After nearly a quarter of a century of providing the only sustained supersonic passenger service, the Concorde suffered its first fatal accident in this fiery crash some 10 miles (15 km) north-north-east of Paris, which occurred following its departure from Charles de Gaulle Airport, on a non-scheduled service to New York City.

The remains of Concorde and the hotel it destroyed near Paris after the accident that brought to an end the fatality-free safety record of the supersonic transport. *(AP Images)*

Chartered by the German tour company Peter Deilman Reederei GmbH and carrying passengers who were to cap their transatlantic trip with a Caribbean cruise, *F-BTSC* began its take-off from Runway 26-Right. After it had reached a recorded speed of around 200 mph (320 kmh), and approximately 1 mile (1.5 km) from the start of the runway, the front-right tyre of the left main undercarriage ran over a strip of metal lying on the pavement. Flying debris then touched off a chain of events leading to a massive fire on the left side of the aircraft. Lifting off, the jetliner was airborne for a little more than a minute, unable to maintain either speed or altitude, before it struck a hotel and exploded in a fireball some 3.5 miles (5.5 km) from the end of the runway, its undercarriage extended and nose/visor in the down position at the moment of impact. All 109 persons aboard, including the nine members of its crew, plus four others on the ground perished in the disaster. An additional six persons suffered injuries, and the building was demolished. The airport weather at the time was partly cloudy, with scattered cumulus at around 1,800 ft (550 m) and at approximately 2,300 ft (700 m) and 5/8 coverage at about 3,000 ft (1,000 m), and a visibility of some 10 miles (15 km). The average wind was 4 knots from due east.

When it struck the metal strip, the tyre was immediately destroyed. The impact against the wing by one piece of tyre weighing about 10 lb (4.5 kg) that had been tossed into the air resulted in the rupture of the No. 5 fuel tank. One of 13 fuel tanks in Concorde, the No. 5 was located in the port wing, and at the time contained 94 per cent of its total volume, which would be considered full. Along with various other debris, a structural part of the tank measuring about 1 sq ft (32 x 32 cm) was later found on the runway, an indication of the force of the rupture. Through a combination of the effects associated with rotation and of its bursting, the velocity of the chunk of rubber could have been around 300 mph (480 kmh). The impact with the object occurred only seconds after attainment of the decision speed (V1) had been announced by the first officer, as transcribed by the cockpit voice recorder (CVR), and he was then heard to say, 'Watch out!' Based on the stain of unburned kerosene on the runway, a large quantity of fuel must have leaked out before the fire erupted. Following the stain were soot deposits on the pavement, and a wheat field located approximately 1.5 miles (2.5 km) beyond the end of the runway was also damaged by fire. As the aircraft commenced rotation, the ground controller notified the crew, 'you have flames behind you'. Several witnesses described the conflagration as occurring in two phases, with a small or blowtorch-like flame appearing suddenly before it grew much wider as it enveloped the two power plants on the port side. The forward propagation of the flames led to the intense blaze under the wing. During this time, both of the engines directly affected by the fire experienced a loss of thrust, which was severe for the No. 2 and slight for the No. 1. This loss of power caused a pronounced yaw to the left, which was countered by the application of right rudder. Also, when the No. 2 tyre burst, the load that it was bearing got redistributed to the left outer wheels, changing the equilibrium of the gear. Thus, holding the track became difficult and the control inputs required to maintain it were greater than those normally used during training for an engine failure. The marks on the pavement were evidence of the jetliner drifting to the left of the runway centreline. After becoming airborne, the aircraft attained a maximum above-ground height of around 200 ft (60 m), and its airspeed reached about 240 mph (385 kmh) before it began to fall. As the crew struggled with the emergency, the first officer radioed in the final seconds of the flight that the aircraft was headed for nearby Le Bourget Airport. However, the crew had no way of either assessing or extinguishing the blaze. In the final seconds of the flight, Concorde's angle of attack increased to more than 25 degrees, its left bank to 113 degrees and its magnetic heading changed from 270 to 115 degrees.

Examination of the piece found on the runway allowed investigators to exclude the possibility that the breach of the tank resulted from a direct puncture by a large piece of debris or by the tearing off of the structure through the same process. The

rupture was believed to have resulted from a complex process of the transmission of energy produced by the impact on the exterior but at another point on the tank, producing a shock wave that propagated outwards at the speed of sound and caused the deformation of the tank skin and the movement of fuel, with perhaps the contributory effects of other less serious shocks and/or the phenomenon of a hydrodynamic surge. The mechanism leading to the rupture had never before been seen on a civilian aircraft and its process could not be determined precisely. Tests were in fact not able to reproduce the breakage sequence. Nevertheless, studies did demonstrate the possibility of such a pressure surge as causing damage to the rib connection areas on the lower side of the tank. The French Bureau Enquetes Accidents (BEA) was unable to exclude the possibility that the rupture of the tank panel resulted from an accumulation of phenomena, such as the combination of several impacts and punctures caused by small, heavy objects travelling at high velocity. A loss of fuel in tanks 2 and 6, located aft of No. 5, could not be readily explained, but probably resulted from the fire after the break-up of the latter.

As to the cause of the consequent fire, various potential sources of ignition of the fuel leaking from the tank were identified, two of which were considered possible. The first of these was arcing resulting from damage to a 115-volt electrical harness in the area of the main gear. However, modifications made after a take-off incident in the US in 1979 made this less likely than ignition resulting from contact with hot sections of the engine and/or hot gases. With regard to the latter theory, the ingestion of kerosene from the ruptured tank could have occurred through the auxiliary air intake and/or the ventilation door, and the fuel could then have ignited on contact with the hot walls of the power plant or with the gas coming from the reheat cut-out, at the level of the thrust nozzle. In this area, many obstacles allow the development of what the investigative report described as 'recirculation zones', and ensure the retention of the flame in the rear part of the engine. This hypothesis was also consistent with the evidence found on the pavement. The report noted that there were, however, no traces of fire actually discovered during the examination of the engines. Following a separate analysis, a British accredited representative and his advisers concluded that the blaze had resulted from arcing of the damaged wheel-brake fan power supply cables in the left undercarriage bay.

Tests could not reproduce the forward propagation of the fire and its subsequent retention in the slipstream of the undercarriage. But though unusual, the phenomenon was known to exist, having occurred under somewhat different circumstances in a business-type jet crash in France more than three decades earlier, and would have been possible despite the rushing airflow through the complex geometry of Concorde's wing. Although none of the aircraft's four power plants had apparently sustained any damage in the initial tyre failure, both the No. 1 and No. 2 experienced surging, and the resulting loss of thrust was similar to a double engine failure. The initial surging of the No. 1 was most likely caused by the ingestion of hot gases or solid debris, and the No. 2 apparently due to the ingestion of hot gases emanating from the fire. After the aircraft had become airborne, the rudder was automatically switched to mechanical mode, apparently due to the failure of the 'Green' electrical system, which led to the loss of yaw auto-stabilisation.

After its nose gear lifted off at approximately 210 mph (340 kmh), or more than 15 mph (25 kmh) below the normal rotation velocity (VR), the aircraft got airborne at 235 mph (c. 380 kmh). The rate of rotation appeared to confirm that the captain, who was the pilot flying, had been aware of his taking off below the normal VR. The No. 1 engine had regained almost normal power before suffering, at the moment of take-off, a second surge that led to a severe loss of thrust, while at the same time the No. 2, which had been in a slight recovery phase, also surged for a second time. This time and in both cases, the surging was apparently attributable to the ingestion of hot gases and/or kerosene. The loss of thrust of the No. 2 resulted in the automatic switching to the contingency mode, which would allow the use of power greater than take-off thrust on the remaining engines. Immediately after the aircraft got airborne, the fire alarm for the No. 2 power plant activated, and the crew instituted appropriate procedures, the flight engineer announcing 'Shut down engine two' and the corresponding thrust lever being positioned to idle. After a third surge due to the ingestion of aircraft

structure, of hot gases and/or of kerosene, the No. 1 experienced a final loss of thrust, as indicated by the flight data recorder (FDR). It was at this point that the left banking attitude of the jetliner and its angle of attack increased sharply.

Another dilemma facing the crew was their inability to retract the aircraft's undercarriage. They were aware of this, as indicated by the first officer's comment, 'The gear isn't retracting'. This technical failure could only be explained by the partial opening of an undercarriage door, probably the left one, which could have suffered damage linked to the destruction of the tyre as well as the fire.

The retraction problem was not believed to have resulted from a hydraulic system failure, since the gear on Concorde is independently powered, and there were no indications of undercarriage asymmetry. Because of the reduction in thrust and the fact that its gear remained extended, the aircraft was unable to either ascend or accelerate. Also, the inability to retract the undercarriage probably contributed to the retention and stabilisation of the flames throughout the flight. An additional factor would have been structural damage caused by the fire, since extreme heat would have led to a rapid deterioration of the mechanical characteristics of the alloy used in a majority of Concorde's structure, causing a six fold reduction in them at about 580 degrees Fahrenheit (300 degrees Celsius).

Both starboard power plants continued to operate normally until less than 15 seconds before impact, when they too experienced a significant loss of thrust that was probably partially attributable to action by the crew. This was determined through a spectral analysis of the CVR recording, which indicated that their thrust levers had been moved to the idle stop position, probably with the intention of decreasing the steep bank caused by the significant thrust asymmetry and through the destruction by the fire of vital control surfaces. The decrease in thrust on the two starboard engines must also have been accentuated by surging due to airflow disruption caused by the angle of attack and level of the yaw reached at that moment. In these extreme conditions, i.e. with the combination of lateral and thrust asymmetry and the major thrust/drag imbalance, and for which there was no way of compensating through the initiation of a descent because of the low altitude of the aircraft, a loss of control occurred. The inability of the crew to maintain control was probably accelerated by the structural damage. The BEA concluded that even with all four power plants functioning properly, the damage to the wing structure and some of the flight controls would have made the crash inevitable.

No attempt was made by the pilot to bring the aircraft to a halt despite the comment of the flight engineer, after noticing the initial loss of thrust, to 'Stop!' However, simulations showed that to abandon the take-off at that point would have led to a runway excursion at such a speed as to cause the collapse of the undercarriage, and with the blaze raging under the wing, the aircraft would have immediately burst into flames and the results would probably have been catastrophic for the occupants. Based on Air France procedures, the decision to abort a take-off must only be made in the case of a significant loss of thrust, a power plant fire or with certainty that the aircraft would be unable to fly. And having passed the decision speed before noticing any anomalies and then being faced with what appeared to be an imminent lateral excursion from the runway, the crew were mentally prepared for rotation.

It was determined that the object Concorde struck had fallen from a DC-10 Series 30 wide-bodied jetliner, operated by the US airline Continental, which had taken off about 5 minutes earlier. Approximately 17 inches (44 cm) long and made of mostly titanium, the piece was identified as the lower left wear strip from the aircraft's No. 3 power plant. Maintenance documents showed that the wear strips had been replaced some six weeks earlier, although the replacement part had neither been constructed nor installed in accordance with procedures approved by the manufacturer. The BEA report noted that the absence of the strip would not have been easily noticed when the cowl doors were closed.

Although the sequence that led to the destruction of F-BTSC was not predictable, it should not have been totally unforeseen. There had in fact been 57 previous cases of tyre bursts and deflations in Concorde operations, a third of which were caused by foreign objects. Six of these had resulted in the penetration of fuel tanks, including the event more than 20 years earlier that had led to the aforementioned modifications. A study conducted after this accident by Aerospatiale concluded that the risks and consequences of tyre bursts were greater than those that had been taken into account at the time of certification. However, as was noted in the report, the small size of the Concorde fleet had impeded the treatment of problems encountered in the operation of the jetliner.

Besides the safety of Concorde itself, the crash highlighted the importance relative to aviation safety of the condition of airport runways. It was noted that runway surveillance had been the initiative of each airport in France, which at the time had no national regulations pertaining to the issue. At Charles de Gaulle, the daily average number of inspections had been limited to two, one fewer than specified, but after the accident was increased to three. However, the report emphasised that inasmuch as the metal strip responsible for the disaster had been on the ground for only a matter of minutes, it would be 'inconceivable' to base a policy of preventing risks from such debris on inspections alone.

The investigation also revealed deficiencies in Concorde flight operations and maintenance practices. One of the latter apparently led to the omission of the spacer on the left front under-carriage bogie, which had been replaced about a week before the crash, an error that was nevertheless not considered a factor in the catastrophe. Also on the accident flight an operational error was made by the crew, who had not taken into account the fuel not consumed while taxiing. As a result, the take-off weight of F-BTSC had under the conditions exceeded its authorised maximum by about 5 tonnes (5 MT), although any effect on take-off performance resulting from this condition would have been negligible. Nevertheless, because of these discrepancies, the BEA recommended that the French Direction Generale de l'Aviation Civile (DGAC) undertake an audit of the Air France Concorde programme. Noting that the parameters that determine engine speed were incomplete, it was recommended that Air France adopt the use of the same type of flight recorders as those used on the British Airways' Concorde fleet. And since the loss of the strip from the DC-10 resulted from inadequate maintenance practices, the BEA recommended an audit of Continental Airlines by the US Federal Aviation Administration (FAA).

As a consequence of the disaster, both the French DGAC and the British Civil Aviation Authority (CAA) revoked Concorde's certificate of airworthiness. As recommended in the report, significant safety measures later implemented were the installation on the remaining aircraft of flexible linings in certain tanks, reinforcement of electrical harnesses in the main undercarriage bay and new tyres designed to resist blow-outs. The modifications were completed before re-entry of the Concorde into regular service in November 2001.

The improvements would enhance Concorde's safety but in the end would not be able to save the aircraft from an inevitable fate. In the spring of 2003, the only two operators of the SST, Air France and British Airways, announced that due to low passenger loads, high maintenance costs and the general slowdown in the airline industry, they would terminate Concorde service by the end of the year, withdrawing from use the rest of the aircraft in their small fleets. The technological pioneer would thus, early in the twenty-first century, become an aeronautical relic, depriving passengers access to supersonic travel for perhaps years to come.

Date: 23 August 2000 (*c*. 19:30)
Location: Near El Manama, Bahrain
Operator: Gulf Air Ltd (Bahrain, Oman, Qatar, United Arab Emirates)
Aircraft type: Airbus Industrie A320-212 (*A40-EK*)

Operating as Flight 072, the jet airliner crashed in the Persian Gulf about 3 miles (5 km) north-east of Bahrain International Airport, located on the northern tip of the island nation and where it was scheduled to land at the end of an international service from Cairo, Egypt. All 143 persons aboard (135 passengers and a crew of eight) were killed.

Cleared for a very-high-frequency omni-directional range/distance-measuring equipment (VOR/DME) instrument procedure approach to Runway 12, *A40-EK* was approximately 1 mile (1.5 km) from touchdown and at a height of around 600 ft (180 m) when the crew requested and received authorisation

A portion of the aircraft's fuselage is visible above the waterline after the crash of the Gulf Air Airbus A320 in the Persian Gulf off Bahrain. (© GNA/BAHR/CORBIS SYGMA)

from the air traffic controller for a left-hand orbit. After completing about three-quarters of the circling manoeuvre, the aircraft rolled out on to a south-south-westerly heading. It was then that the first officer reported the flight was 'going around'. About a minute later, the A320 plunged into the sea in a slight nose-down attitude and at a recorded air speed of about 320 mph (515 kmh), its wreckage coming to rest in water some 10 ft (3 m) deep. At the moment of impact, the aircraft's undercarriage was up, its flaps were within 2 degrees of full retraction and its slats extended to the 12-degree position. The accident occurred in darkness, but the meteorological conditions in the area were good, with a visibility of more than 5 miles (10 km). The wind was at 8 knots from due east.

The investigation found no evidence of engine, structural or any other technical failure in A40-EK that could have caused the crash, nor of in-flight or post-impact fire. As disclosed by both the flight data (FDR) and cockpit voice (CVR) recorders, a number of what the Bahrain Civil Aviation Affair's report described as 'individual and systemic issues' were identified in the investigation, the combination of which led to a descent from a low altitude that went unnoticed by the two pilots until it was too late. Some of the actions of the crew represented serious deviations from standard operating procedures.

A significant deviation by the captain was his failure to achieve a stabilised approach in order to accomplish a successful landing. At the final approach fix (FAF), the velocity of the A320 was 256 mph (412 kmh), or 100 mph (c. 150 kmh) above the target speed, this despite the use of the speed brakes, and its height some 150 ft (50 m) above the prescribed altitude of 1,500 ft (c. 500 m). Additionally, the aircraft was not properly configured, its flaps not having been lowered to the fully extended position. The excessive speed of the jet could perhaps be attributable to the planning of the descent, or of the clearance not being properly integrated into the descent profile. (There was in fact no evidence of an approach briefing by the captain heard on the CVR, which recorded the last 30 minutes of the flight.) Perhaps important to the sequence of events was the absence of a speed limit below 10,000 ft (c. 3,000 m) within the airspace that included the descent path of Flight 072. Simulation and flight tests demonstrated that based

on aircraft configuration, velocity and altitude at the FAF, a successful landing could have been made, especially had the speed brakes been continuously deployed, although this would have involved manoeuvring at a steep angle of approach and rapid deceleration producing 'severe discomfort' for the passengers.

After he remarked to the co-pilot, 'Visual with the airfield', indicating he had transitioned from instrument procedures, the captain apparently realised his predicament, stating out loud, 'We're not going to make it'. At this point, he elected to carry out the 360-degree turn, the apparent objective of which was to lose speed and altitude, thereby avoiding the execution of a missed approach procedure, which would have been the correct course of action. During the orbit, which was hand-flown by the captain, the first officer applied full flaps at the request of the former. This also went contrary to good operating procedures when considering that full flaps are intended for use only during the final approach phase and can otherwise increase drag and degrade the manoeuvrability of an aircraft. This would have been an appropriate time to abandon the approach altogether, but again the crew requested and were granted clearance to land on Runway 12. It was not known why the captain did not complete the 360-degree turn, although the level-off may have been an attempt by him to regain orientation. In the process, however, the A320 flew through the extended centreline of the runway. After the co-pilot stated 'Runway in sight', he was heard to say, 'We overshot it'. Being completely out of alignment with the runway, the crew then announced their intention to initiate a go-around and also accepted radar vectors from the tower controller in order to begin another approach. A further error occurred at this point, when the pilot continued turning even though the correct missed approach procedure would have been to maintain the runway heading.

After the pilot called for undercarriage retraction, take-off/go-around (TOGA) thrust was applied and the jet then crossed over the runway, climbing to about 1,000 ft (300 m) while on a north-easterly heading, pitching up slightly as it rapidly accelerated. Shortly thereafter, the maximum flap extension velocity (Vfe) aural warning chime sounded and the co-pilot alerted the captain, 'Speed, overspeed limit'. Seconds later, the aircraft's ground-proximity warning system (GPWS) sounded, initially alerting the crew of 'sink rate', followed by a 'pull up' command, and it was at this time that the pilot ordered 'Flaps up', indicating his desire for them to be fully retracted. Considering his low altitude, the proper way of dealing with the flap overspeed warning would have been to increase pitch attitude. However, and as indicated by the FDR read-out, the captain actually applied a nose-down pitch input to his side-stick control unit, the most likely reason for this being his false physical sensation that the aircraft was pitching up. (This so-called somatogravic illusion is a form of spatial disorientation involving the absence of visual cues combined with rapid forward acceleration, which in turn creates a powerful pitch-up sensation.) Few outside visual references would have been available for determining attitude during the orbit until the coastline came back into view, with the night being moonless, only a few scattered stars capable of being seen through the haze, no lights visible over the water and the horizon probably not distinguishable. His totally inconsistent action indicated that the pilot had been relying primarily upon visual reference, since the aircraft's instruments would have been indicating something completely opposite. After the nose-down pitch input, the A320 began to descend.

Holding the side-stick in the forward position for about 10 seconds, the pilot finally did apply a nose-up input, but FDR data indicated the command was not maintained and that subsequent inputs never exceeded 50 per cent of the full-aft capability, and as a result A40-EK continued to descend. Having not immediately responded to the 'sink rate' warning, as required, the crew were equally remiss when the GPWS began to sound 'pull up', indicating the pilots did not realise the dangerous situation facing them. The 'pull up' alert continued until impact, some 10 seconds after it began.

Among the violations of standard procedures were the excessive speed during and the failure to stabilise the approach. The 360-degree turn was considered in the report as an 'exceptional' violation and an 'unsafe act', and Gulf Air would subsequently issue instructions against such manoeuvres by its pilots. According to the report, his actions indicated the captain had experienced an 'information overload', which can have a number of consequences, including the ignoring of

some signals or responsibilities, delayed responses and the 'channelling' of conscious attention on one element of a particular task to the exclusion of others. As evidence of this, he concentrated on the flap overspeed warning, despite the fact that the GPWS alert was of greater urgency. High levels of stress and anxiety, such as those occurring when the approach did not go as planned for him, could increase these psychological effects. It was further revealed that the first officer, who had considerably less experience than the captain, had not played an effective part in the flight management and decision-making process in his role as the non-flying pilot. According to his training records, he was 'shy' and 'unassertive', and his operational performance was described as 'marginal'. The first officer did not mention the numerous deviations by the captain, including those in attitude and height occurring during the circling manoeuvre that resulted in a steeper-than-prescribed bank. Also, the FDR read-out indicated no control-stick inputs by the co-pilot throughout the accident sequence. It could not be determined what extent fatigue could have affected the performance of either pilot, but there was no evidence that it had played a role.

One reason the pilot did not carry out a missed approach procedure when the landing seemed unattainable was that such an action would have required him to submit an air safety report, which he might have believed would have been regarded unfavourably by the airline. Although it was already company policy, the airline reiterated after the accident the fact that a pilot executing a missed approach would not be subject to disciplinary action. And even though there had been no conflicting air traffic, the authorisation of the orbit by the controller, which was considered a non-standard manoeuvre, did not conform to prescribed procedures. However, the report noted that when he granted approval of the manoeuvre, the controller was unaware the crew had already made visual contact with the airport.

The investigation also revealed inadequacies in the Gulf Air A320 training programme in such areas as GPWS response and in the carrier's flight safety department, and its flight data analysis system was found not to have been functioning in a satisfactory manner. Some of these inadequacies had been identified in a safety review of the airline three years before the disaster, but Oman's

Directorate General of Civil Aviation and Meteorology (DGCAM) had been unable to make the company comply with some critical regulatory requirements.

A lack of crew resource management training probably contributed to the lack of effective team-work by the flight crew indicated by the CVR, and the implementation of such a programme, which had already been under development, was one of several safety measures taken by the airline after the crash. Other changes included the issuance of new A320 fleet instructions pertaining to such items as speed control at lower altitudes, modifications in the type aircraft's flight system to automatically reinstate the flight director bars when an overshoot manoeuvre is initiated, and the introduction of enhanced training in go-around procedures for pilots flying the twin-engine jet and new screening tests used in upgrading pilots. Additionally, Gulf Air suspended all instructor appointments in September 2000 to allow for a review of the system, with the intention of enhancing procedures as well as the selection criteria.

Date: 31 October 2000 (*c.* 23:20)
Location: T'ao-yüan, Taiwan
Operator: Singapore Airlines
Aircraft type: Boeing 747-412B (*9V-SPK*)

Designated as Flight 006, the wide-bodied jetliner crashed at Chiang Kai-shek International Airport, serving T'ai-pei, which was an en route stop during an transpacific service that had originated at Singapore, with an ultimate destination of Los Angeles, California, US. The disaster killed 83 of the 179 persons aboard the aircraft, including four cabin attendants. Among the survivors, 57 passengers and 13 crew members suffered injuries and 25 other persons escaped unscathed, the latter including two of the three flight crewmen.

Authorised to use Runway 05-Left, the aircraft inexplicably began its take-off on the adjacent 05-Right, which was partially closed due to work in progress. Slightly more than half a minute after commencing its ground run, the 747 struck several 'jersey' barriers, some construction equipment, including a bulldozer, and a pile of metal rein-forcement bars that were on the runway, between

Taxiways N4 and 5. The aircraft then broke into several large pieces and caught fire. The accident occurred in darkness and adverse meteorological conditions that were associated with Typhoon 'Xangsane', which at the time was located some 200 miles (320 km) to the south. Just after the crash, the airport weather consisted of broken clouds at 200 ft (*c.* 60 m) and an overcast of 500 ft (*c.* 50 m). Heavy rain had reduced the prevailing visibility to less than half a mile (0.8 km), but at slightly less than 1,500 ft (500 m), the runway visual range value (RVR) for 05L was above the minimum requirement. The wind was blowing from a north-north-easterly direction at 30 knots, with gusts of more than twice that velocity.

Two months earlier, a Notice to Airmen (NOTAM) had been issued concerning the closure of the runway, and this warning was also contained in an automatic terminal information service (ATIS) transmission that was being broadcast on the night of the accident. The three members of the flight crew, who included a relief pilot, later stated that they were fully aware of the status of the runway. In following the route indicated on the airport navigation chart, *9V-SPK* should have turned on to Taxiway N1 and proceeded in a straight line some 1,000 ft (300 m) in order to reach the start of Runway 05L. A second turn would then be required in order to effect line-up with the correct take-off heading. Instead, the 747 continued turning right after leaving Taxiway NP, completing a half-turn until aligned with 05R. The information that was available to the crew to determine their presence on 05L included the airport chart, the runway sign and threshold marking on the pavement and the configuration of the runway lights. Among the more obvious visual incon-gruities were the absence of touchdown zone lights and the fact that Runway 05L was wider than 05R. Also available to the crew were the aircraft's primary flight display (PFD) and para-visual display (PVD) systems, both which would have provided heading information using the 05L instrument landing system (ILS) localiser beam. The cockpit voice recorder (CVR) tape indicated that after completing the turn on to 05R, the first officer had in fact informed the captain that the PVD indicator had not 'unshuttered', confirming alignment with the correct runway. The latter expressed no concern over the PVD indication because at this point, relying only on visual cues, he seemed confident of being on 05L.

There were also some factors that could have confused the pilots and contributed to their error. Significantly, the airport was not at the time in conformity with the standards of the International Civil Aviation Organisation (ICAO) in that it lacked both flashing yellow guard lights, designed to demarcate an active runway, and stop bar lights, which were intended to hold an aircraft until clearance is provided. Additionally, signs identifying the runway were not properly located at the corresponding holding position. Located just before the construction site, the concrete 'jersey' barriers were themselves approximately 30 in (0.8 m) high and 3 ft (1 m) long, painted yellow and orange and had flashing red lights atop them. No barriers had been placed at the start of the runway, although there was no requirement for such. The investigative report further noted that barriers at that location would have interfered with the use of 05R as a taxiway, and the use of mobile signs would not have been practical, at least on the night of the crash, because they could have been blown over in the high winds and become a threat to aircraft. As observed in the report, permanent barriers would nevertheless have provided a potential 'last defence' to prevent the inadvertent use of the runway. Also contrary to ICAO standards enacted in 1995, the airport at the time lacked a lighting interlocking system, which would have allowed for the independent operation of the lights on the adjacent runways. As a result, the centreline lights of Runway 05R were on at the time. The absence of a centreline marking on Taxiway N1 leading to 05L, combined with the gaps in the centreline lighting marking the route to the correct runway and the fact that at least one of the lights had been inoperative at the time, created a clear path for the crew of Flight 006 to the beginning of 05R. The captain later said that he felt compelled to immediately turn on to 05R because it was brightly illuminated with centreline and edge lights, and that he could not see the barriers further down the runway. But whereas the centreline lights on 05L were white, the designation of an active runway, the green lights on 05R should have been an indication of its use as a taxiway. Apparently preoccupied with the weather and related poor visibility, the pilots must not have noticed the colour discrepancy.

(Following the green taxiway lights was the normal procedure at Changi Airport, serving Singapore, and the home base of the airline, and their familiarity with the configuration could have further misled the crew.) According to an analysis of the CVR transcript, at the time the 747 was turning on to the runway the captain had been engaged in the before take-off checklist, while at the same time monitoring the taxiway centreline lights and also his ground speed to ensure the maintenance of control on the slippery pavement. The attention of the first officer and the relief pilot were at the time directed inside the cockpit, and both later said that they had been unable to see outside clearly through the area not swept by the windscreen wipers. And when they saw the painted 'piano keys' at the threshold of the runway, the crew believed they were in the correct position for take-off.

The Taiwanese Aviation Safety Council (ASC) concluded that the pilots 'lost situational awareness' in entering and commencing take-off on 05R, and this proved to be the underlying cause of the disaster. It further ruled that the poor weather and wet runway conditions must have, in a subtle manner, influenced the decision-making ability of the flight crew to maintain situational awareness. The CVR indicated they made no oral confirmation that they had entered the correct runway, although at the time there was no such requirement. The report further noted that their concern over the approaching typhoon may have enticed the pilots to hasten their departure without giving enough attention to details that would have confirmed they were on 05L. And despite the testimony of the captain, the ASC pointed to evidence that included videotapes from airport security cameras and the statement of one of the four controllers in the tower at the time that the 05R edge lights had been off throughout the accident sequence. Though adverse, the meteorological conditions were not considered sufficiently bad to warrant cancelling the flight. The airport surface detection equipment (ASDE), with which ground personnel might have noticed the deviation, had yet to become operational at T'ai-pei, and the airport had no specific plan for low-visibility operations. And although 9V-SPK was the only aircraft moving on the ground there at the time, none of the controllers in the tower observed it line up with the wrong runway. The report noted that while the local controller did not issue progressive taxi instructions or utilise phraseology relative to low-visibility operations, the information and clearance that had been provided to the crew was not considered misleading. The absence of safety oversight by the Taiwanese government, of operations and practices at Chiang Kai-shek International Airport was also considered a factor in the ASC report.

The jetliner had reached the decision velocity (V1) and was travelling at a ground speed of approximately 150 mph (250 kmh) at the moment of initial contact with the first barrier. During the break-up sequence, the 747 made one complete revolution, during which time the aft portion separated from the rest of its fuselage. The wreckage scattered along the runway included the aft end and the front portion, the latter coming to rest to the left of the centreline. The weather also hampered the post-accident rescue operation and the medical assistance of the victims. With regard to the survival issue, the ASC found that the airline's emergency evacuation training, though generally meeting industry standards, did not include methods of dealing with exposure to adverse meteorological elements, fire and smoke. The investigation revealed that most members of the cabin staff had waited for a command rather than initiating an evacuation on their own after *9V-SPK* had come to a stop, and two of them did not open their designated emergency exits. Probably affecting the actions of the cabin crew was the failure of the aircraft's public address system, especially considering that the airline did not have a back-up plan for such a contingency. However, the effect of this failure on the survivability of the crash could not be determined. Additionally, some of the survivors reported they could hardly see the cabin emergency lights, making it difficult for them to escape. (This fact raised the question of the effectiveness of emergency lighting systems in aircraft under certain circumstances.) Inadequacies in staffing in the airport fire service were also identified, as was improper coordination in handling the injured survivors.

A Singaporean team ruled that the ASC draft final report had presented an 'unbalanced account' of the accident, which minimised the significance of the many systemic factors they considered as contributory, including deficiencies in runway lighting, signage and markings at the airport. The team's rebuttal also said the ASC report contained 'factual inaccuracies, internal contradictions and hypothetical statements' that were not supported by empirical evidence. Authorities representing the nation of registry viewed the cause of the disaster as 'a failure of the aviation system', citing the absence of warning signs, markings and barriers at the beginning of the runway as the most important contributing factor. And with the small number of lights along N1, they said the continuous line of green taxiway lights leading to 05R presented the crew 'with the picture of a brightly-lit active runway'. The Singaporean team said the ASC report placed too much emphasis on the error of the crew, noting that subsequent changes made at the airport, which included the removal of the 05R threshold and designator markings, essentially represented an acknowledgement by Taiwanese authorities that many of the deficiencies were major contributing factors, even though none appeared in the ASC report. The rebuttal report also challenged many of the Taiwanese findings, among them that the crew did not verify their taxi route, felt a sense of urgency to take off, and that the captain lacked proper training in low-visibility taxiing techniques. With regard to the status of the runway edge lights, the Singaporean team said that metallurgical tests conducted on the corresponding wires indicated that they were probably on at the time of the accident. Singapore was also critical of the fact that its accredited representative and his advisers were not permitted to participate in the deliberations of the ASC related to analysis, findings, causes and safety recommendations, in accordance with ICAO provisions.

The airport chart that was dated before the crash and became effective the day afterwards redesignated Runway 05R/23L as Taxiway NC. Additionally, the runway edge lights were disconnected, and elsewhere at the airport lighting and markings were altered to conform with ICAO guidelines.

Other safety measures enacted after the disaster included the development by the Taiwanese Civil Aeronautics Administration (CAA) of new airport design and operational regulations and the implementation by the airline of a new crew resource management programme and a revised check list designed to confirm the presence of an aircraft on the correct runway. Two of the three pilots on the flight deck of *9V-SPK* when it crashed were subsequently dismissed by the carrier.

Date: 4 July 2001 (02:08)
Location: Near Budyonnovka, Russian Federation, Commonwealth of Independent States
Operator: Vladivostok Air (Russia)
Aircraft type: Tupolev Tu-154M (*RA-85845*)

Operating as Flight 352 and on a domestic service from Yekaterinburg (Sverdlovsk) to Vladivostok, the jet airliner crashed and burned approximately 13.5 miles (22 km) south-east of the Irkutsk airport, which was a scheduled en route stop. All 145 persons aboard (136 passengers and a crew of nine) perished.

During the initial phase of the landing approach, and at a height of around 7,000 ft (2,000 m), the captain reported establishing visual contact with the runway, and the crew extended the spoilers in order to reduce the speed of the aircraft. The crew were then cleared to turn on to the base leg of the circuit and to descend to 2,800 ft (850 m). After it had initiated a left turn, with a bank angle of up to 20 degrees and with the autopilot operating in the height stabilisation mode, its angle of attack increased to 12 degrees. Because of the decreasing velocity, engine thrust was increased, but the Tu-154 would not accelerate due to the pitch-up of its elevators as the autopilot tried to maintain altitude. More than once during this time the captain warned the first officer, who was flying the aircraft, about the decrease in speed. A 'critical angle of attack' warning was activated after it increased to more than 16 degrees. After the pitch of *RA-85845* had diminished through a manual input, the crew turned the control wheel to the left and this action disengaged the autopilot, first in its pitch and then in its bank mode. An increase in the left-banking attitude to 44 degrees prompted a 'high bank' alert, and after a momentary turn to the right, the left bank increased to nearly 50 degrees. At this point the speed of the jet had increased to about 250 mph (400 kmh), while its height was approximately 2,500 ft (750 m) and decreasing.

In view of the deteriorating altitude, the crew pulled back on the control wheel some 20 seconds before impact, and with the high angle of attack combined with the high bank angle, the forward speed of the aircraft decreased, eventually to zero.

At that point, *RA-85845* went into a flat spin, with the pilots being unable to effect recovery through a forward pitch control input. Its undercarriage extended, the Tu-154 hit the ground at a vertical descent rate of around 105 mph (170 kmh), in an angle of attack of 45 degrees and while on a south-westerly heading. It was dark at the time, and the local meteorological conditions were overcast, with the cloud base at about 3,600 ft (1,100 m) and the visibility some 5 miles (10 km). The wind was blowing from a direction of 280 degrees at around 10 knots.

There were no indications of any in-flight malfunctioning in the aircraft's power plants, flight control system or other components, and the disaster was wholly attributable to the improper handling by the crew which led to the unusual attitudes and consequent stall.

Date: 11 September 2001 (*c*. 09:00)
Location: New York, New York, US
First aircraft
Operator: American Airlines (US)
Aircraft type: Boeing 767-223ER (*N334AA*)
Second aircraft
Operator: United Airlines (US)
Type: Boeing 767-222 (*N612UA*)

The darkest single day in the history of commercial aviation began with two routine departures from Logan International Airport, serving Boston, Massachusetts, with both wide-bodied jetliners making the same trip, a non-stop domestic transcontinental service destined for Los Angeles, California.

First to take off, shortly before 08:00 local time on this Tuesday morning, was American Flight 11, which was carrying 92 persons, including a crew of 11. It was followed 15 minutes later by United Flight 175, which carried 65 persons, nine of them crew members. Among the passengers, as subsequently identified by US federal government authorities, were 10 suspected members of the infamous al-Qaida terrorist organisation, divided into two groups of five men on each aircraft, on a suicide mission. One member of each group had taken flying lessons in the US and elsewhere studied to enable them to steer a jet transport. Their intention was to hijack the aircraft and turn them into weapons of mass destruction. All of the suspects were able to board the flights after being subjected to the normal screening procedures then in effect at airports in the US.

As neither cockpit voice recorder (CVR) would survive the subsequent catastrophe, the exact sequence of events could not be determined with certainty. But telephone messages sent by passengers and cabin attendants indicated that the two pilots of each aircraft had been killed or otherwise physically incapacitated by the assailants. In both cases, the hijackers reportedly used knives or some kind of cutting tools; Mace, pepper spray or some other aerosol irritant, and claimed to have a bomb. Since the rules of the US Federal Aviation Administration (FAA) required cockpit doors to be closed and locked while airborne, the manner by which the assailants gained entry to the flight decks of both aircraft remains a mystery. It was possible that on at least one of them, one of the pilots had been lured out of the cockpit by attacks on passengers or other crew members; on the American Airlines 767, two cabin attendants were reportedly stabbed.

Based on radio communications and other evidence, Flight 11 was seized approximately 15 minutes after its departure, and after it had received instructions from the Boston air traffic control centre to climb to its cruising height of 35,000 ft (c. 10,700 m). Flight 175 was believed to have been commandeered about half an hour into the trip. In both cases, the hijackers switched off or changed the code of the aircraft's transponders, which would have reduced their respective radar targets to only a primary return. The courses of both were turned to the south, towards New York City. The target of the terrorists would be the World Trade Center, a complex of buildings located on lower Manhattan Island highlighted by twin towers that had for some three decades served as perhaps the most recognis-able symbol of American economic power. Both rising more than 1,000 ft (300 m) above the street, the two skyscrapers would have been visible from a great distance considering the good meteo-rological conditions, with the weather at La Guardia Airport, located some 10 miles (15 km) to the north-east, consisting of only a few clouds at 25,000 ft (c. 7,500 m) and a visibility of 10 miles (c. 15 km).

The final few moments of Flight 11 were described by stewardess Amy Sweeney, speaking via telephone to an American Airlines flight services manager at Boston. 'We are in a rapid descent . . . we are all over the place,' she said. The message ended with, 'Oh my God, we are way too low!' At 08:46 local time, N334AA was deliberately flown into the north or No. 1 tower, by the hijacker-pilot. Approaching from the north at an estimated speed of approximately 430 mph (690 kmh), the jetliner struck the north side and near the top of the 110-storey building, setting off a huge explosion. Emergency personnel immediately rushed to the scene of what first seemed to be an unimaginable accident, on a mission that for many of them would prove fatal. Less than 20 minutes after the first strike, at 09:03 local time, N612UA was crashed by its hijacker-pilot into the south side of the south or No. 2 tower. After going into a rapid descent as it proceeded in a north-easterly direction, and while flying at a velocity estimated to have been in excess of 500 mph (800 kmh), the 767 slammed into the building at around the 80th floor. Again, a huge explosion ensued, with parts of the aircraft actually coming out from the other side of the skyscraper. Damaged by the force of the impact and by the fire, which was fuelled by the load of kerosene carried aboard the jetliner, the South Tower collapsed just before 10:00 local time, with its floors 'pancaking' on top of one another in a mass of smoke and dust. About half an hour later, and in a remarkably similar manner, the North Tower fell. Later that same day, a 47-storey building that was part of the complex also collapsed. Although early casualty reports proved to be greatly exaggerated, the toll was nevertheless staggering. Among the 2,759 persons who perished in the attack were all 157 aboard the two aircraft and 343 members of the New York City fire department. More than 6,000 others on the ground suffered injuries. Damage estimates exceeded US $90 billion.

Although the death and destruction was by far the worst in New York City, the hijacking and intentional crashing of the American and United flights there represented just part of a concerted terrorist attack carried out on this day against the US, which would also involve two more aircraft.

Date: 11 September 2001 (09:37)
Location: Near Arlington, Virginia, US
Operator: American Airlines (US)
Aircraft type: Boeing 757-223 (N644AA)

Coordinated with the attacks in New York City was this hijacking of Flight 77, which had departed

The impact of the American Airlines 757 against the Pentagon resulted in severe fire damage and the partial collapse of the huge complex in the terrorist attack outside Washington, DC. (© Reuters/CORBIS)

from Dulles International Airport, serving Washington, DC, at 08:20 local time. It was on a non-stop domestic service to Los Angeles, California, and carried 64 persons, including a crew of six. Five of the passengers were identified by federal authorities as al-Qaida terrorist suspects, one of whom had acquired flying skills in the US. Although two of them required additional screening with hand-held electronic devices, all five were able to board the aircraft, thus eluding the security procedures then in effect at American airports.

The hijacking began between 30 and 35 minutes into the trip, and after N644AA had reached its assigned cruising height of 35,000 ft (c. 10,700 m), whereupon the transport started to deviate from its assigned course, turning southwards and initiating a descent. It was believed that the aircraft had been commandeered in the same manner as the two flights out of Boston, i.e. through the murder or incapacitation of its two pilots. Speaking via telephone, a passenger and a cabin attendant reported the assailants using knives and/or box

cutters. Since its transponder had been switched off, the target representing the 757 would have been difficult to discern on ground radar. At one point, in fact, even primary radar contact with the aircraft was lost as it proceeded in an easterly direction, towards the nation's capital.

Considering the clear weather conditions, the many landmarks in the District of Columbia would have been visible and thus an easy prey for the terrorists. In this case, however, their target was the symbol of the American military complex, the Pentagon building, located across the Potomac River from Washington. After completing a 330-degree right turn, the hijacker-pilot increased power and descended towards the mammoth, five-storey structure, hitting its north-west side at an approximate speed of 530 mph (850 kmh). The impact of the jetliner and consequent fiery explosion resulted in the collapse of a portion of the building. Including all of those aboard the aircraft, a total of 189 persons perished in the attack, while more than 100 others suffered injuries. Among those killed on the ground, more than half were civilians, the rest US service personnel.

Within a year of the attack, the damaged portion of the building would be completely repaired, but long before the work was finished, the Pentagon would resume its vital function, this time with a new role, coordinating the war on terrorism.

Date: 11 September 2001 (10:03)
Location: Near Shanksville, Pennsylvania, US
Operator: United Airlines (US)
Aircraft type: Boeing 757-222 (*N591UA*)

The fourth aircraft hijacked on this day of terror was Flight 93, which had taken off from Newark, New Jersey, on a non-stop domestic transcontinental service to San Francisco, California. Its passengers apparently included four members of the al-Qaida terrorist group, who were among the 19 assailants identified by the US government as participating in what has become known in America as the '9/11' attack. (The operative likely to have been a fifth hijacker was a Saudi Arabian who had been refused entry into the US by a suspicious immigration inspector.)

Scheduled to depart at 08:00 local time, *N591UA* took off from Newark International Airport some 40 minutes late. Only about 5 minutes after the flight crew had received a warning from a United Airlines' dispatcher regarding cockpit intrusions associated with the other hijackings occurring that morning, or shortly before 09:30 local time, and as the 757 was cruising at 35,000 ft (*c.* 10,700 m) over northeastern Ohio, the assailants attacked. One of the flight crewmen at that point declared a 'Mayday' distress message, while a radio transmission containing unintelligible sounds of possible screaming or a struggle was also heard at the Cleveland air traffic control centre. Both pilots must have been killed or physically incapacitated, as apparently was a stewardess. Within minutes of the takeover, the transport climbed above 40,000 ft (*c.* 12,000 m) as it turned left, ultimately assuming a south-easterly heading, towards Washington, DC. And again, the hijackers must have manipulated the aircraft's transponder, resulting in the loss of its secondary radar return.

The cockpit voice recorder (CVR) from *N591UA* was the only unit to survive from the four aircraft commandeered on this day, and although the initial phase of the hijacking had been erased due to transcription capacity limitations, it helped to provide details of what transpired during the final half hour of the flight. Also revealing were the telephone messages sent by passengers and two of the cabin attendants, who reported that the assailants claimed to have a bomb, which was probably not real. In telephone conversations with family members or other persons on the ground, the occupants of Flight 93 learned about the other attacks, and were thus given a unique perspective of their own fate, which undoubtedly motivated them to take action. In the end, they would be unable to save themselves, but in preventing the aircraft from reaching its target, which was probably either the Capitol building or the Presidential White House in the District of Columbia, they probably saved countless lives.

After some of the passengers announced via telephone that they were going to assault the flight deck, the pilot-hijacker began to roll the 757 to the left and right in an apparent attempt to knock them off balance. The terrorists remained at the controls, but must have judged that the others were only seconds from getting into the cockpit and overcoming them when they elected to crash the aircraft short of its intended target, with one of the assailants at this time being heard to twice shout, 'Allah is the greatest!' Having rolled over on to its back while descending, the jetliner slammed to earth at 580 mph (*c.* 930 kmh). Including the hijackers and its crew of seven, all 44 persons aboard the aircraft perished. A smouldering crater in a field marked the impact site, some 80 miles (130 km) south-east of Pittsburgh and no more than 20 minutes flying time from the nation's capital. Although US military forces had been alerted about the hijackings, and two Air Force F-16 jet fighters were airborne in the area, no official authorisation to shoot down Flight 93 was given until after the aircraft had crashed. (The question as to whether the 757 would have reached its target had those aboard not taken action on their own remained disturbingly unanswered in the report issued by a federal commission established to investigate the terrorist attack.)

The crash of Flight 93 brought the combined death toll in the worst act of terrorism in history to 2,992, including the 19 identified hijackers. But the attack had other implications as well. One was an

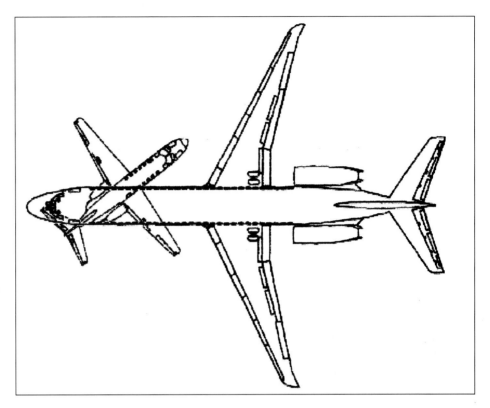

Drawing shows how the Cessna Citation was literally 'run over' by the jet transport after entering the active runway on which the latter was taking off. *(Agenzia Nazionale per la Sicurezza del Volo)*

unprecedented, two-day grounding of all civilian aircraft in US airspace. The resulting slowdown in air travel would also bring about great financial harm to the airline industry, not only in the US but throughout the world. One positive aspect was the introduction of new and more rigid security procedures by American carriers, resembling those practices of the Israeli airline El Al, which, had they been in effect at the time, might well have averted the atrocity.

Date: 4 October 2001 (*c.* 13:45)
Location: Black Sea
Operator: Sibir Airlines (Russia)
Aircraft type: Tupolev Tu-154M (*RA-85693*)

Designated as Flight 1812 and en route from Tel Aviv, Israel, to Novosibirsk, Russia, the jetliner crashed some 120 miles (190 km) south-west of Sochi, Russia. All 78 persons aboard (66 passengers and a crew of 12) were killed.

The bodies of 16 victims were recovered, and examination of wreckage that was retrieved from the water revealed shrapnel holes. It was later determined that the Tu-154 had been accidentally shot down from its cruising height of 36,000 ft (*c.* 11,000 m) by an S-200 surface-to-air missile fired at a target drone by Ukrainian defence forces during a training exercise.

Date: 8 October 2001 (08:10)
Location: Linate, Lombardy, Italy
First aircraft
Operator: Scandinavian Airlines System (SAS) (Denmark/Norway/Sweden)
Type: McDonnell Douglas MD-87 (*SE-DMA*)
Second aircraft
Operator: Air Evex Gmbh (Germany)
Type: Cessna 525A CitationJet CJ2 (*D-IEVX*)

The two jet aircraft were involved in a collision at Linate Airport, serving Milan, and the commercial transport then crashed into a building used for baggage handling. A total of 118 persons lost their lives in the disaster, including four workers in the structure; there were no survivors among the occupants of either aircraft. Four others on the ground were injured, one seriously.

Having arrived earlier in the morning from Cologne, Germany, the CitationJet, which was privately owned but registered to Air Evex, departed from the West apron, used for general aviation operations, in preparation for taking off on a demonstration flight with an ultimate destination of Paris, France. It was carrying two passengers in addition to its two pilots. The twin-engine jet had been cleared by the ground controller to taxi 'north via Romeo five' and was also instructed to 'call me back at the stop bar of the . . . main runway extension'. Though instructed to proceed in a northerly direction along the taxiway designated as R5 and essentially circle the airport near its perimeter, the aircraft headed towards the south-east and entered Taxiway R6. Subsequently, the controller instructed *D-IEVX* to continue taxiing, but used the word 'main' instead of 'north' in reference to the apron located in the north-east sector of the airport, near the main terminal, through which it would have to pass in order to reach the beginning of the active runway, 36-Right. The last transmission from the Cessna was, 'I'll call you back on the main taxiway.' As instructed, *D-IEVX* should have proceeded to the end of the runway via the taxiway located on its east side, but instead it taxied from the north-west across 36R, on which *SE-DMA* had just been cleared to take off. Operating as Flight 686, the MD-87 was bound for Copenhagen, Denmark, with 104 passengers and a crew of six aboard.

The read-out of its digital flight data recorder (DFDR) indicated that the commercial transport was some 40 seconds into its take-off run and had just commenced rotation while maintaining the correct runway heading at an indicated air speed of around 170 mph (270 kmh) when it collided with the general aviation aircraft, which had crossed the path of the former diagonally as it continued to taxi in a direction estimated at 135 degrees. Approximately 1 second before impact, a large elevator nose-up command was registered by the DFDR of the MD-87, and this combined with an unintelligible exclamation transcribed by its cockpit voice recorder (CVR) indicated that at least one of its two pilots had seen *D-IEVX* before the collision. Evidence indicated that at the time of impact, the nose gear of the airliner was in the air, while its main undercarriage remained on the pavement. Initially, the nose gear probably struck the horizontal stabiliser of the smaller jet, after which the MD-87 literally 'ran over' the Citation, the

former's left and right main gear assembly hitting the leading edge of the latter's starboard wing. The forces associated with the collision caused the separation of the transport's right main gear wheels and brake units, and sheared off its starboard power plant from the corresponding pylon. After hitting the slow-moving Citation, the pilot of *SE-DMA* increased power and the aircraft climbed to an approximate above-ground elevation of 30 ft (10 m). It remained airborne for about 10 seconds but was unable to sustain flight due to the ingestion of debris and the consequent loss of thrust in the remaining engine, touching down again on the pavement, near the end of the runway. In view of the truncated right main gear leg, the aircraft's starboard wing-tip made contact with the ground, and the transport then slid sideways across a grassy area, its longitudinal axis some 45 degrees to the right of the runway heading. The left power lever of the MD-87 was found in the maximum reverse position, indicating such action had been taken by the crew, but this and the application of brakes were only partially successful due to the altered geometry and balance of the aircraft and the limited effectiveness of the flight controls in combination with the wing-tip dragging across the ground. Slamming into the building at a calculated speed of around 160 mph (260 kmh), the transport then broke apart and some of its wreckage burned. Fire likewise swept through the structure, which was also destroyed. The Cessna was split into three major sections in the collision, two of which were consumed by flames. It was concluded through medical investigation that the passengers and crew members of the MD-87 died of traumatic injury, while the occupants of the Citation succumbed to both impact trauma and the effects of the fire. Based on an automatic terminal information service (ATIS) report issued within 2 minutes of the accident, the airport weather was characterised by a low overcast, with a ceiling of only 100 ft (c. 30 m) and a visibility of around 300 ft (100 m). The measured runway visual range (RVR) at the time was less than 700 ft (200 m), but could have been even lower, perhaps less than half that amount at certain points within the airport boundaries. There was no wind.

It was apparent that the disaster stemmed directly from the fact that the general aviation aircraft had entered the active runway at the wrong

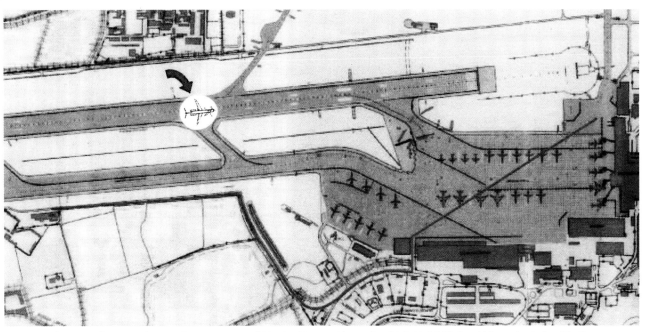

A diagram showing the North apron area of Linate Airport, through which D-IEVX should have taxied, with the arrow marking the point where the aircraft collided with the SAS MD-87. *(Agenzia Nationale per la Sicurezza del Volo)*

point. The precise intentions of the Air Evex pilots could not be established with certainty due to the absence on the aircraft of a CVR unit. One plausible reason for the mistake was a navigational error that could be explained by the crew simply getting lost in the dense fog and taxiing the wrong way, i.e. to the south-east rather than to the north. However, the Italian investigative organisation Agenzia Nazionale per la Sicurezza del Volo (ANSV) considered it more likely that despite the correct read-back of the instructions to utilise the Romeo five (R5) taxiway, the pilots followed the path to which they believed they had been cleared, i.e. along Taxiway R6. It was further concluded by the ANSV that the Cessna crew had not been aided properly with the cues needed to enhance the awareness of their position by airport signage, markings and lighting facilities. These shortcomings included a lack of directional, instructional and 'no entry' signs, and those existing were partially hidden in grass or were difficult to read. Nor were there any holding position markings at the extension of Runway 36R. Additionally, the white flashing lights at the intersection of R6 and Runway 18L/36R, which were described on official charts, had been deactivated a decade earlier and

substituted with unidirectional alternate green and yellow lead lights to guide aircraft on to the taxiway, while the green lights guiding them the other way remained unchanged. It could also be assumed that the crew may have been confused by the runway stop bar, which consisted of uni-directional red lights and did not conform to international standards. The facilities at Linate did not in many cases satisfy International Civil Aviation Organisation (ICAO) guidelines, and the failure of the airport to comply with requirements in this area was considered to have been contributory to the accident.

When the Citation commenced taxiing, albeit in the wrong direction, position and direction signs were missing all the way up to the final and only Category (CAT) III instrument landing system (ILS) sign before it entered Runway 36. And the fact that the first of the green centreline lights of Taxiway R6 would have been closer and more easily seen in the poor visibility conditions than the first light demarcing R5 could have induced the pilots to take the former. Their action could also have been influenced by the fact that the centreline lights were switched on upon the entry by the aircraft on to R6, and by both the absence of a sign and the poor condition of the markings visible on the tarmac. Furthermore, there could have been an expectation of them that they would follow the same path, in the opposite direction, of the one taken on arrival, with the location of R6 being clear in their minds. However, the ANSV report noted that a careful review by the Air Evex crew of the Jeppesen charts should have made it apparent that reaching R5 would have required taxiing to the north and through the entire length of the West apron, in accordance with the clearance; also the distance travelled would be considerably greater. Additionally, designates showing 'R6' along the taxi route should have served as a 'trigger' to remind the Cessna crew of the route being taken, as would a 'runway vacated' sign some 500 ft (150 m) from the centreline of the main runway. As D-IEVX continued taxiing on R6, it would have crossed a white 'Stop' and a yellow runway holding marking, both painted on the asphalt, the red light bar, the above-ground CAT III sign and then a second holding marking on the pavement before entering 36R, following the taxiway lights leading towards the runway centreline. The presence of the centreline lights beyond the light bar and the characteristic sideline lights should have confirmed its entry on to the runway. In view of these facts, the ANSV concluded that the pilots believed they were on the correct path and cleared to enter the runway. The report also noted that controllers had no way of switching on and off the light bar, and that pilots were accustomed to overrunning it after receiving clearance.

The ANSV further identified potentially misleading instructions in the Aeronautical Information Publication (AIP) of Italy that aircraft utilising 'Linate West' were to be stopped at the signal on R6, which could be interpreted as an obligation for all traffic to and from the general aviation apron to follow that taxiway in conditions of low visibility. Another instruction in the same paragraph forbidding the use of Taxiways 2 or 3, both of which connected with 18/36, could also be interpreted as an explicit order to backtrack on the runway from R6 for the purpose of reaching the end of 36R, perhaps to avoid conflict with traffic occupying the main taxiway.

Although the original taxi clearance issued by the ground controller contained the necessary instructions to correctly identify the route to be

followed, the read-back did not reflect the message accurately, with the pilot of the Citation stating, 'Roger, via Romeo five . . . and call you back before reaching the main runway'. However, his omission of 'north' in reference to the apron, to 'the stop bar' and the 'extension', or end of the runway, went unchallenged by the controller, who may not have noticed the difference between the clearance and the read-back, perhaps considering it sufficient or possibly tempered by complacency acquired in dealing with general aviation pilots thought to have been sufficiently familiar with taxi procedures and the layout of the airport. The investigative report further noted that when spoken by someone whose first language is Italian, 'north' is a short word, and within a sentence may not have been perceived adequately by the German crewmen. Subsequently, the pilot of the Cessna issued an unsolicited position report, 'approaching Sierra Four'. (This would have been in reference to the yellow marking visible on Taxiway R6.) The fact that the controller asked for a confirmation of the position indicated the message was not clear to him. The pilot then replied with a somewhat different message, 'Approaching the runway . . . Sierra Four'. This transmission elicited no warnings from the controller, who might have interpreted it to mean that D-IEVX was nearing the extension of 18L, or the opposite end of the active runway, and he merely responded, 'Roger, maintain the stop bar . . . I'll call you back'.

It was noted in the report that the presence of the (Sierra) S1 and 2 runway-holding position markings on Taxiway R5 and S4 and 5 on R6 were unknown to controllers, making it difficult for them to assess the position of taxiing aircraft.

Approximately 1 minute before the collision, and after its pilot reported being at the 'Hold' position, the Cessna was cleared to 'continue your taxi on the main apron . . . follow the Alpha line'. It was evident that the controller believed the Citation at that time to be at the bar of lights across Taxiway R5, located north of the runway. However, the crew apparently did not realise the inconsistency between the clearance and the actual position of the aircraft, which could be attributable to superficial listening; the immediate read-back of the clearance, which reflected the transmission accurately, was considered typical of pilots in a busy traffic situation, implying partial understanding of a message, often with the intention of obtaining later clarification. Moreover, the next instruction by the controller to call him back upon entering the 'main taxiway' may have created the impression in the pilot that he had to rapidly cross the runway in order to reach the Alpha line, which actually ran through the parking area on the North apron. The use by the controller of 'main taxiway' instead of 'main apron' could have been interpreted by the pilot as a simple misuse of terms. Furthermore, the Alpha line was not depicted on any AIP documentation.

With regard to the issue of communications, an analysis of a transcript of radio transmissions involving West apron traffic revealed that terms used by both controllers and pilots in identifying the general aviation area, as well as positions and taxiways, did not conform to the information in AIP Italy. These included such terms as 'main apron' and 'main runway'. Additionally, the message 'report at the stop bar' was found to be used alternatively in conjunction with clearances involving both Taxiways R5 and R6 without any further clarification or identification for the route to be followed, and that the word 'main' had been used in conjunction with clearances referring to both Runway 36 and the North apron. Nor did pilot read-backs conform to the stated taxi clearances, and during the time span analysed, controllers seldom acknowledged the accuracy of the read-backs. Moreover, there was no numeral designation of the taxiway that ran parallel to Runway 18L/36R in the charts being used by either the Air Evex or the SAS crews. And the monitoring of air/ground radio transmissions would have been no advantage in this case, as even before D-IEVX had received taxi clearance, the pilots of SE-DMA had switched to the frequency of the control tower, with the former remaining in contact with the ground controller throughout. As a result, neither crew would have heard the instructions to the other's aircraft. At the time of the accident, the ground and tower controllers were busy handling traffic calls, which would have inhibited their ability to monitor and cross-check each other as well.

About 30 seconds after the Cessna had been authorised to taxi, the same clearance was issued to another aircraft, LX-PRA, parked on the West apron. However, the message was given in Italian and probably could not have been understood by the German crew, even had they been listening. Though instructed to follow the Citation, LX-PRA did not begin to taxi and its pilot reported being unable to see the former, later asking where it was. Based on his response that D-IEVX was on the 'Main apron', the controller must have been convinced as to its position. Even after the collision, when asked by LX-PRA about the location of the German jet, the controller again replied, 'He is on the Main apron'.

An analysis of the facts gathered by the ANSV pointed to the conclusion that Linate Airport did not meet the requirements for a low visibility operation under CAT-IIIB ILS conditions. Significantly, the airport had no functional safety management system, and the investigation into the accident revealed a 'lack of coordinated efforts' between the three principal organisations responsible for its oversight with regard to safety matters. Among other shortcomings, the airport had no operations manual, no recurrent pro-gramme for air traffic control personnel, and no deviation reporting system. That it did not meet with specified flight safety requirements was seen as 'remarkable' by the ANSV when considering Linate was a major international airport. Furthermore, neither the Citation nor its crew were certified to operate in the visibility conditions existing at the time of its arrival or subsequent to take-off, which should have alerted airport authorities to the potential risks of making the flight. However, the report noted that under the regulations in effect at the time, D-IEVX would have been allowed to taxi out in preparation for departure, but not actually to take off, a procedure sometimes employed by crews when a rapid improvement in the weather is anticipated. (In response to a recommendation made by the ANSV, the regulations pertaining to low visibility operations were subsequently extended to all aircraft.) It was further observed in the report that in this particular situation, the nature of the operation may have exerted a 'certain pressure' on the Air Evex crew to commence the flight despite the conditions.

Recommendations that were part of an interim report issued by the ANSV emphasised the need for the use of the English language in air/ground radio communications, and, in accordance with an ICAO-recommended procedure, for explicit clearance when crossing a runway. The English-language requirement later became compulsory at Linate. At the time of the collision, nearly two years had

A scene of devastation is left in the neighbourhood of Belle Harbor, New York, located on Long Island, by the crash of the American Airlines Airbus A300 . *(AP Images)*

passed since the airport had a functioning surface movement monitoring radar system, which, as noted in the report, was one means of ensuring safe operations in conditions of poor visibility. The need for having such 'anti-incursion' facilities was mentioned in the final report.

Those deemed responsible for the Linate tragedy paid a heavy price for their actions or inactions. In April 2004, judges handed down eight-year prison sentences for both the director of Linate Airport and the ground controller on duty at the time of the accident; the former head of Italy's air traffic control agency Ente Nazionale di Assistenza al Volo SpA (ENAV) was sentenced to six years and the overseer of Milan's two main airports got six months. On the other hand, the airline was exonerated of any responsibility. Indeed, the report commended the 'professional performance' of the SAS crew in their efforts to maintain control of the damaged transport after the collision, and in the process perhaps preventing a greater disaster by avoiding the main airport building and nearby aircraft parked on the North apron. This fact may have helped to lessen the pain suffered by an airline renowned for its

safety record, one of the best in the world, having suffered only two previous accidents involving passenger deaths since its formation in 1946, the last one occurring nearly 33 years before the Linate collision.

Date: 12 November 2001 (09:16)
Location: New York, New York, US
Operator: American Airlines (US)
Aircraft type: Airbus Industrie A300B4-605R (*N14053*)

Still reeling from the terrorist attack two months earlier, New York City was the scene of this horrific crash, the worst aviation accident to occur in the US in more than 20 years and the worst ever in terms of passenger fatalities involving an American commercial aircraft on a scheduled international service.

Designated as Flight 587, the A300 had departed from John F. Kennedy International Airport on this Monday morning, bound for Santo Domingo, in the Dominican Republic. Lifting off from Runway 31-Left, the aircraft almost immediately initiated a left turn towards the south while continuing to climb. The last radio transmission from the flight was acknowledgement of instructions to proceed to the WAVEY navigational intersection, located some 30 miles (50 km) south-east of the airport. Less than 2 minutes after becoming airborne, the wide-bodied jetliner plunged into the Belle Harbor neighbourhood, located on the Rockaway Peninsula of Long Island, and exploded in flames, its main wreckage coming to rest in the intersection of Newport Avenue and Beach 135th Street approximately 4 miles (6.5 km) south-west of the airport. All 260 persons aboard the aircraft (251 passengers and nine crew members) and five others on the ground perished in the disaster. In addition to the casualties, four houses were destroyed and seven damaged.

Witnesses reported seeing *N14053* spurting flames, trailing smoke and shedding parts before its impact with the ground. Both engines were found at different locations about 800 ft (250 m) from the main wreckage area, obviously having separated while the A300 was still in the air. The aircraft's vertical stabiliser, minus the rudder and portions of the spar structure that attached the control surface to the tail fin, was recovered from Jamaica Bay, not quite 1 mile (1.5 km) from the crash site; the assembly must have also been sheared off from the aft fuselage while in flight. Additionally, the six main attachment fittings and the three pairs of transverse load fittings had been fractured. Along with the attachment fittings that failed, the vertical stabiliser and rudder were constructed of composite materials consisting primarily of long fibres of carbon or glass manufactured as sheets, or plies, held together by an epoxy polymer. The fact that this was the first major air carrier accident involving an in-flight failure of a major structural component made of such materials initially raised questions about their strength and durability. But in its investigation, the US National Transportation Safety Board (NTSB) observed no micro-cracking or any evidence of fatigue or a pre-existing defect in the stabiliser.

The read-out of its flight data recorder (FDR) indicated that approximately 1 minute after it became airborne, *N14053* had encountered the wake turbulence generated by another aircraft, presumably a Japan Airlines Boeing 747-400

jetliner that had taken off about 1 minute 40 seconds before the Airbus. Seconds after registering excursions that were consistent with a wake encounter, the FDR transcribed a series of movements of the aircraft's flight controls. Besides nose up and down control wheel inputs, there was alternating activation of the rudder pedals, with corresponding deflections in the control surface itself. After an initial wake turbulence encounter, occurring while the aircraft was at a height of around 1,700 ft (520 m) and in an approximately wings-level attitude, the A300 again flew into the vortices apparently generated by the 747, this time while in a left bank of 23 degrees. In response to the second encounter, the aircraft's control wheel was moved rapidly to the right and its right rudder pedal depressed. Seconds later, there were five subsequent, alternating, full-rudder pedal inputs, which continued until the separation of the stabiliser. Such abrupt rudder inputs can result in an 'over-swing' of the aircraft, leading to considerable yaw and side-slip angles, as well as an amplified roll rate. In this case, the activation of the pedals led to increasing side-slip angles that, in combination with the continued rudder deflections, produced extremely high aerodynamic loads on the fin. The rudder and side-slip angles became so large that portions of the stabiliser began to exhibit stall behaviour, i.e. regions of separated airflow.

In its report on the disaster, the NTSB concluded that the cyclic motions of the rudder pedal were directly the result of rudder pedal inputs by the co-pilot, 34-year-old Sten Molin, who had been flying the aircraft throughout the accident sequence. The investigation found no evidence of any mechanical failure that could have caused the rudder deflections, nor of any unusual atmospheric condition as factoring in the accident, with the airport weather about 10 minutes after the crash consisting of a few clouds at around 5,000 ft (1,500 m) and a visibility of 10 miles (*c.* 15 km); the wind was blowing at 8 knots from due west. The Board further ruled that the high loads leading to the structural break-up were not in any way associated with the effects of the wake turbulence. The NTSB concluded that both the performance of the vertical fin and the manner by which it separated were consistent with its design and certification. But at the time of its separation, the stabiliser was experiencing aerodynamic loads that were approximately twice the certified design limit. As indicated by a structural analysis utilising computational models, the right rear attachment lug had failed initially, after which all of the remaining lugs fractured sequentially. This process initiated a nearly instantaneous separation of the vertical tail fin. At that moment, the CVR recorded a loud bang and the FDR registered a lateral acceleration, both apparently associated with the structural failure. When the right rear attachment fitting failed, the Airbus was in a right side-slip, with its rudder deflected about 10 degrees to the right. The stabiliser separated less than 20 seconds before the impact with the ground, while the cleanly configured aircraft was flying at an approximate altitude of 2,500 ft (750 m) and at an indicated air speed of around 290 mph (465 kmh). Both power plants then tore away from the wings, with a flash fire possibly occurring at the time of their separation and resulting from the ignition of fuel. Also, the disruption of airflow during the descent of the jetliner before their loss, which would have caused compressor surges, most likely accounted for the flames seen emanating from the engines.

The NTSB report noted that structural certification requirements for transport aircraft did not take into account such 'extreme' manoeuvres as those related to alternating full rudder movements, which could produce loads that are higher than those required for certification and may exceed structural capabilities even when the rudder limiter is in effect. Furthermore, it was found that aerodynamic loading on the vertical stabiliser would increase if the rudder were returned to its neutral position at the point of the over-swing side-slip. The manufacturer indicated that either this motion or a full-rudder deflection followed by a movement in the opposite direction would result in external loads that were slightly higher than those under prescribed regulations.

Since the second wake encounter did not place N14053 in an upset condition, the NTSB concluded that the actions of the co-pilot were 'too aggressive' and 'unnecessary'. A review of his flying record revealed a tendency for him to react aggressively to wake encounters, one such incident occurring four years earlier while he was serving as the co-pilot of a Boeing 727 jet. According to the captain of that particular flight, First Officer Molin mentioned how he had been taught to use the rudder in such a manner during his advanced aircraft manoeuvring programme (AAMP) training, which he had initially received in 1997. The Board determined that the upset recovery programmes of American and other carriers encouraged pilots to use the rudder to assist the ailerons and spoilers with roll control during the recovery from upsets under certain circumstances, including wake turbulence encounters. But the NTSB report noted that since the rudder was not designed and certified for roll control, it might not be well suited for such use. Two of the five Board members gave greater attribution to the American pilot training programme as a contributing factor in the crash of Flight 587.

Tests conducted by the NTSB found that the rudder motion in the American Airlines A300-600 simulator produced by normal and high pilot input forces resulted in different pedal displacements than experienced in the aircraft itself, attributed to the inaccurate software representation of the elastic cable stretch in the former. And the airline's excessive bank angle recovery simulator exercise may have contributed to a misunderstanding of the need for, or the effects of, rudder use in response to wake turbulence. The exercise was somewhat similar to the circumstances of Flight 587, i.e. a take-off behind a Boeing 747, with the simulator indicating an initial disturbance and a slight rolling movement, after which it unrealistically rolled in the opposite direction beyond 90 degrees. The misleading nature of the exercise could have contributed to an inaccurate expectation that a wake turbulence encounter in an A300 could be a potentially catastrophic event, requiring an immediate and forceful pilot response. The simulator had been programmed in such a way to suggest that the wake was overpowering the controls, depriving the pilot of an opportunity to experience the actual aircraft response to such inputs, including the side-load accelerations, creating a misconception of their real effects. The NTSB learned that in order to ensure that the simulator reached a 90-degree angle during the aforementioned exercise, the airline inhibited the effectiveness of the control wheel and the rudder pedals during the initial phase of the roll, a fact about which pilots were unaware, even though they had been briefed by instructors to react quickly to the upset. This would have promoted an inaccurate understanding as to the proper use and the effectiveness of the flight controls. And since no input could prevent the simulator from rolling to or beyond the vertical, a pilot might learn to position the controls at their full deflections in order to minimise the recovery time, even though the situation may not require such action. Due to these issues, the simulator employed in the company's AAMP training could have had the unintended consequences of providing pilots with improper training in responding to wake turbulence, even to the point of being potentially dangerous in real aircraft. (Even before the accident, Airbus had been concerned about the types of manoeuvres being practised in simulators and the conclusions that were being drawn from them, with the manufacturer expressing the belief that upset training should be confined to the normal flight envelope and stop at the point of stall-warning activation.) In its report, the NTSB noted that the use of non-motion simulators or simple computer screen displays may be more appropriate in providing the necessary awareness training.

Unlike the simulator, the A300 being flown by First Officer Molin responded to the initial right turn of the control wheel with a large and immediate right rolling moment, and to the initial rudder pedal input with a yawing moment to starboard, which caused the aforementioned left side-slip, and an additional rolling moment to the right. He was thus faced with an abrupt and aggravated rolling moment to starboard, while at the same time the aircraft continued to develop a substantial yaw and a heading change, both also to the right. And even had he intended to command a partial rudder deflection, he was likely to be surprised and confused at the response of the jetliner to his control inputs. His subsequent rudder pedal inputs ultimately led to the hazardous build-up in the side-slip angle and, in turn, to the high loads that resulted in the separation of the vertical stabiliser. Also, if he believed the sudden acceleration of the Airbus to the right was the result of the wake encounter and not of the control inputs, it could have prompted his full and immediate turn of the control wheel to the left and his application of the left rudder pedal. It was noted in the report that a pilot who uses the rudder pedals to roll a transport-category aeroplane will experience a significant phase lag between the input and the

development of the roll. This is because the roll response is a secondary effect of the yawing moment generated by the deflection of the control surface and does not result from the input directly. Consequently, the aircraft can continue to develop a rolling moment in one direction, even though the rudder is subsequently deflected in the opposite direction. If the motion becomes highly dynamic, the relationship between the pedal inputs and the roll response of the aircraft can become confusing. Significantly, most airline pilots lack sufficient awareness and understanding to correctly anticipate the response of an aeroplane to large rudder inputs. In this case, the initial over-control and lack of an appropriate understanding regarding the response of the Airbus on the part of First Officer Molin may have combined to serve as a trigger to an adverse aircraft–pilot coupling (APC) event, which has been described as 'rare, unexpected excursions' resulting from 'anomalous interactions' between the aircraft and the person at the controls.

Still another pertinent issue identified in the investigation was the variable stop design of the rudder travel limiter system with which the A300-600 was equipped. This design limits both rudder pedal travel and deflection of the control surface as air speed increases, while at the same time pedal sensitivity increases at greater velocities. Although the variable stop design provides a consistent ratio between the pedal and rudder deflection at any air speed, the response of the aircraft to a given pedal input increases with increased velocity, resulting in significantly different performance characteristics at opposite ends of the design envelope. The characteristics of the system might in this case have contributed to the large magnitude of the rudder movement even had the co-pilot intended only a partial deflection. The NTSB expressed the opinion that the rudder system may increase its susceptibility to an APC event, and recommended a 'review of the options' by Airbus for possible modification of the A300 and its close relative, the A310, to provide increased protection from potentially hazardous rudder inputs at high speeds. Before this crash, A300-600 pilots, including those of American Airlines, were not trained to understand how the aircraft's rudder travel limiter system operated, and also seemed to believe that it would prevent an overload of the vertical stabiliser. The NTSB observed in its report that rudder control systems with a variable ratio limiter might provide better protection against excessive loads from sustained rudder pedal inputs at higher velocities than those with a variable stop limiter because the former require more physical effort from a pilot to produce cyclic full-rudder inputs. Certification standards pertaining to rudder pedal sensitivity were in fact suggested by the Board in order to minimise the potential for the type of event that led to this disaster. Nor in this case did the aircraft's yaw damper system prevent the development of the side-slip angle resulting from the alternating full-rudder pedal inputs. And although *N14053* had been flying more than 20 mph (30 kmh) below its design manoeuvring velocity (Va) at the time of stabiliser separation, the investigation revealed that pilots seemed to have an incorrect understanding of the extent of structural protection afforded when the aircraft is operated below this speed. (The American Airlines' operating manual in fact had only one reference to the Va.)

With regard to the actions of the pilot-in-command, 42-year-old Capt Edward States, the report noted that based on his comments, he recognised the initial wake encounter correctly, but then appeared to believe that the subsequent motion of the aircraft, even after the loss of the stabiliser, was also caused by the wake vortices. He did not intervene or assume control of the Airbus, which would have been within his authority, but considering his limited knowledge of the circumstances and the short duration of the accident sequence, his response was considered 'understandable' by the NTSB. Nor were there any irregularities in the procedures of air traffic control personnel handling both the A300 and the 747, who complied with wake turbulence spacing requirements.

Subsequent to the crash of Flight 587, changes were made in the American Airlines training programme, including a revision in the upset recovery exercise, wherein the simulation could be stopped and discussed by the instructor. The carrier also took steps to inform pilots about the use of rudders, operation of rudder travel limiters, and such issues as side-slip angle and vertical stabiliser loading. Similar action but on a larger scale was also taken by the manufacturer and the US Federal Aviation Administration (FAA) to inform operators about the risks of opposite rudder inputs, and an

airworthiness directive was issued by the latter requiring the inspection of vertical stabiliser and rudder attachment points on A300-600 and A310 jet transports, even though structural defects were not a factor in the disaster involving *N14053*. And noting that vital flight control surface position information during the accident flight had not been recorded by the aircraft's FDR due to filtering by the system data analogue computer, the NTSB recommended corrective action by the FAA, which the latter agreed to make through new rules and design changes.

Date: 28 January 2002 (10:24)
Location: Near Guachucal, Narino, Colombia
Operator: Transportes Aereos Militares Ecuatorianos (TAME) (Ecuador)
Aircraft type: Boeing 727-134 (*HC-BLF*)

All 94 persons aboard (87 passengers and a crew of seven) perished when the jet airliner crashed and burned on the El Cumbal volcano, some 15 miles (25 km) north-west of Tulcán, in Ecuador, where it was scheduled to land.

Operating as Flight 120, which originated at the Ecuadorean capital of Quito and was ultimately bound for Cali, Colombia, *HC-BLF* had received authorisation to descend from its cruising altitude to 14,000 ft (*c*. 4,300 m) during the initial phase of the approach to the airport serving Tulcán. Subsequently, the 727 slammed into the mountain at an approximate elevation of 15,000 ft (5,000 m), or some 1,500 ft (500 m) below the summit. As given to the flight, the weather at Tulcán and at nearby Ipiales, Colombia, consisted of broken clouds at around 700 ft (200 m), an overcast of approximately 1,500 ft (500 m) and a visibility of about 5 miles (10 km). The winds in the area constituted no more than a slight breeze.

The underlying cause of the accident was the decision of the crew to continue the approach in meteorological conditions that were below the minima prescribed by the company. Other factors identified in the investigation were inadequate navigational procedures and improper operation of the aircraft, the latter including the entrance into the holding pattern at an indicated air speed that was some 60 mph (100 kmh) above the specified velocity, which caused *HC-BLF* to stray out of the lateral limits of the area of protection.

Date: 12 February 2002 (c. 08:00)
Location: Near Khorramabad, Lorestan, Iran
Operator: Iran Air Tours
Aircraft type: Tupolev Tu-154M (*EP-MBS*)

Designated as Flight 956 and on a domestic service from Tehran, the jetliner crashed and burned some 200 miles (320 km) south-west of the capital city as it was preparing to land at the Khorramabad airport. All 117 persons aboard (108 passengers and nine crew members) perished.

The aircraft had been on its approach to Runway 11 when it struck a mountain in conditions of poor visibility due to heavy fog and rain mixed with snow. Impact was at an elevation of around 9,000 ft (2,700 m), some 10 miles (15 km) from the threshold of the runway and approximately 3 miles (5 km) to the left of its extended centreline. The Iranian Civil Aviation Organisation attributed the accident to 'pilot error,' but offered no specific details.

Date: 15 April 2002 (11:21)
Location: Near Kimhae, Kyongsang-Namdo, South Korea
Operator: Air China
Aircraft type: Boeing 767-2J6ER (*B-2552*)

Operating as Flight 129, the wide-bodied jet airliner crashed and burned some 3 miles (5 km) north of Kimhae International Airport, serving the city of Pusan, where it was scheduled to land at the end of a service from Beijing, China. Including the two designated co-pilots and two other victims who succumbed within three weeks of the accident, 129 persons aboard the 767 lost their lives; the captain, two of the aircraft's eight cabin attendants and 34 passengers survived with various injuries. Most of the fatalities resulted from impact trauma, but as many as 16 deaths may also have been related to the effects of the fire.

Although they had been initially informed to expect a straight-in approach for a landing on Runway 36-Left, the flight crew were notified by the air traffic controller minutes later that they were to land in the opposite direction, i.e. on 18-Right. (The switch was made after a slight change in the direction of the wind and an increase in its velocity.) An arrival from the north would involve a circling manoeuvre carried out visually and based on timing

after an initial approach to Runway 36, using instrument landing system/distance-measuring equipment (ILS/DME) procedures, with the crew then reporting 'field in sight'. This procedure did not have a prescribed track using visual references on the ground, which could cause difficulties in conditions of poor visibility. After passing to the west of the airport and then initiating a 180-degree right turn back towards the south, *B-2552* struck Mt Dotdae at an elevation of around 700 ft (200 m). Its undercarriage extended and flaps set at 30 degrees, the 767 was, at the moment of impact, proceeding on a heading of 149 degrees at a ground speed of approximately 150 mph (250 kmh) and in a right bank of about 25 degrees, initially striking trees with its starboard wing before it slammed into the hill and broke apart. The airport weather some 10 minutes before the accident was overcast, with the cloud coverage 3/8 at 500 ft (c. 150 m), 6/8 at 1,000 ft (c. 300 m) and 8/8 at 2,500 ft (c. 750 m), and the visibility 2.5 miles (c. 4 km) in fog and rain. The wind was blowing from a south-south-westerly direction at 10 knots.

In its investigation into the disaster, the Korea Aviation Accident Investigation Board (KAIB) found no evidence of prior technical failure in the aircraft structure or its systems, ruling that the crew had apparently experienced a loss of 'situational awareness' regarding their position relative to the high terrain to the north of the airport as they transitioned from ILS guidance to the circling manoeuvre, and after the captain reported seeing the runway. In its report, the KAIB expressed the belief that this error had been precipitated by the lack of a proper approach briefing by the crewmen after the landing runway was changed. (The initial briefing for a landing on Runway 36 had been conducted in accordance with the applicable procedures.) The evidence further indicated a breakdown in crew coordination, which was also related to the inadequate briefing. Additionally, the aircraft was not properly configured for the circling approach, which increased the workload of the pilots and led to a poorly executed turn on to the downwind leg of the airport circuit. And while the crew had notified the appoach controller that they were flying a category 'C' aircraft, the air speed of B-2552 when it passed abeam of the threshold of Runway 18 was some 20 mph (30 kmh) more than the maximum velocity prescribed for that type of operation, which could have extended the downwind leg. (The Boeing 767 can fit into two different categories, depending upon its landing weight, but in accordance with the carrier's operating manual, this particular procedure would have been considered a category 'D' approach.) During their briefing for the circling manoeuvre, neither the captain nor the first officer mentioned anything of such important issues as the weather minima, the procedures to be used or the precise assignment of crew duties. These omissions may have been related to their failure to conduct the briefing in a systematic manner. Furthermore, and apparently due to a lack of understanding about them, the crewmen failed to make the standard call-outs during the manoeuvre. There was also evidence that the three members of the flight crew had not been communicating properly among themselves or with air traffic control personnel. A review of the cockpit voice recorder (CVR) transcript revealed virtually no discussion among themselves in order to verify the different aspects of the circling procedure, and they did not point out errors made by their fellow crewmen. Evidence indicated that the crew did not appreciate the seriousness of the situation or the danger in continuing the approach until it was too late, having failed to maintain an awareness of the flight path of the 767 and its proximity to the terrain.

The initial phase of the circling approach was being flown manually by the first officer, and based on the read-out of the aircraft's flight data recorder (FDR), he did not employ the standard rate turn at the beginning of the manoeuvre. The shallow bank resulted in a delay in the turn on to the correct north-westerly heading and, in combination with the wind direction and velocity, led to a deviation from the normal circling pattern. Perhaps in consideration of the visibility and the effects of the tail-wind, and after the co-pilot stated that it was 'very difficult to fly', the captain assumed manual control of the 767, disconnecting the autopilot less than a minute after it had been re-engaged. Initially, he turned the aircraft to the left, apparently intending to widen the pattern. Presumably having been distracted by the landing clearance from the control tower, the captain then delayed starting the turn on to the base leg and at that point was advised by the first officer to 'Turn quickly, not too late'. Also, there was no adequate

compensation for the prevailing tailwind. As the aircraft continued turning right, the captain concentrated his attention on monitoring his attitude indicator, trying to keep external references and the runway in sight, and at the same time listening to the landing clearance. These actions did not comply with the correct procedure of initiating the base turn first, then listening to air/ground communications. And since the pilot-in-command was seated on the left side of the flight deck, it would have been difficult for him to maintain visual contact with the runway during the right-hand turn. It was during this turn that the 767 entered some low clouds, but the captain did not at that point comply with the requirement to execute an immediate missed approach when visual or ground references are lost. (The pilot-in-command later stated that he intended to abandon the landing when the aircraft entered the clouds, but wanted to wait until after it had rolled out on to the final approach course.) In the final seconds before the crash, the captain asked, 'Have the runway in sight?' The first officer initially replied, 'No, I cannot see out', and immediately afterwards stated, 'Must go around'. He was then heard to say, 'Pull up! Pull up!' The captain neither reacted to the command of the first officer, nor abandoned the approach himself, and this failure was considered by the KAIB an important factor leading to the crash. Before impact, the pitch attitude of B-2552 increased slightly, but there was no change in engine thrust.

The Board ruled that in the exercise of his command authority, the captain failed to take into account the overall situation, and to make timely decisions. Never having carried out a circling approach into Kimhae, he did not have adequate knowledge of the procedure and failed to clearly assign duties to his fellow flight crewmen. The KAIB also identified inadequacies in the performance of the two co-pilots assigned to the flight. Specifically, the first officer demonstrated a 'less than aggressive attitude' towards his duties, and he further neglected his responsibility of providing immediate advice to the captain as to whether the runway was visible, especially when considering he had been seated on the right side of the flight deck and would have been in a better position to see. Meanwhile, the second officer, who had been riding in the cockpit jump-seat and was primarily responsible for handling radio transmissions, did not properly communicate with air traffic control personnel. Among other 'inappropriate' comments cited by the Board were his improper response to the controller's question, 'Can you landing?' Nor did he advise the captain of any procedural deviations, such as the entry into the clouds, which could indicate what the report described as a 'lack of knowledge, experience and positive attitude' towards his duties.

The fact that the aircraft had been proceeding in or near level flight while in the landing configuration would have inhibited the operation of the Honeywell Mark II ground-proximity warning system (GPWS) unit with which it was equipped, and as a result, there were no terrain warnings before impact. Relevant to this issue was that Air China had not implemented a service bulletin issued by Boeing 16 years earlier for an enhanced GPWS. Also perhaps significant was the fact that the airline had provided only one set of Jeppesen manuals to the flight crew, which made cross-checking difficult, and that the available chart did not depict the high terrain to the north of the airport. Another factor related to risk was that the training of the crew had been conducted in a flight simulator only for Beijing airport, with the pilots never having been trained for a circling approach to Runway 18 at Kimhae. Additionally, the carrier's crew resource management was found to be inadequate for a three-member complement.

The investigative report noted that when the tower controllers lost sight of the 767 as it proceeded on the downwind leg, they tried to reacquire it visually but did not use the available BRITE observation aid, which is an enhanced radarscope. It further noted that neither Korean standard nor Kimhae local procedures specified radar monitoring of an aircraft conducting a circling approach by either the minimum safe altitude warning (MSAW) system or by BRITE, despite their availability to controllers at the airport. Also, the MSAW used in the Kimhae control tower had only a visual low-altitude warning alert and not an aural one, which had been recommended by the International Civil Aviation Organisation (ICAO), and would therefore not have been noticed in a timely manner without close monitoring. And since the circling approach area and the terrain within it were not depicted on the airport radar video map, it would have been difficult for the tower controller to assess accurately the position of the aircraft and the hazards in its path.

A Chinese investigative team generally agreed with the findings of the KAIB, concluding that the crew of B-2552 'mishandled' the circling manoeuvre and failed to abandon the approach after losing sight of the runway. But in their separate report, the Chinese team also cited as factors the failure of the controller to provide a warning after receiving a visual MSAW alert, as well as an 'unintelligible' radio frequency transfer instruction by the local controller and frequent communications with the crew, which it said had an 'impact' on the performance of the latter during the base turn and the final approach. They further claimed that the automatic terminal information service broadcast was 'hard to comprehend', and noted that although the meteorological conditions existing at the time were actually below the minima required for a category 'D' circling approach, the controller did not communicate this to the flight.

Among the recommendations made by the KAIB were for Air China and for the General Administration of Civil Aviation of China to review the carrier's training programme for circling approaches to ensure proper understanding of an adherence to the prescribed procedures, and also examine the need for enhanced GPWS units on commercial aircraft. Other recommendations were made to the Korea Ministry of Construction and Transportation, including one to establish a method of depicting either the circling approach area or at least a 'safety line' on the radar video map at Kimhae airport.

Date: 4 May 2002 (c. 13:30)
Location: Kano, Nigeria
Operator: EAS Airlines (Nigeria)
Aircraft type: BAC One-Eleven 525FT (5N-ESF)

Designated as Flight 4226 and on a domestic service from Jos to Lagos, the jetliner crashed in a heavily populated suburban area approximately 1.5 miles (2.5 km) from Kano Malam Aminu International Airport, which was a scheduled en route stop and from where it had taken off shortly before. A total of 153 persons lost their lives in the disaster, more than half of whom were on the ground; among the 79 aboard the aircraft, three passengers and one of its eight crew members survived.

Due to construction at the airport, *5N-ESF* had used a shorter runway, and the aircraft reportedly overran the pavement during its ground run before becoming airborne, after which it struck some approach lights. The One-Eleven reached a height of 300 to 400 ft (*c.* 100–120 m) above the ground before it began to descend, then struck houses and a mosque, broke apart and burst into flames. Some two dozen structures on the ground were destroyed, including the mosque and a school. The weather at the time was good, but the air temperature of more than 100 degrees (40 degrees Celsius) may have been a factor in the disaster.

Five days after the accident, every One-Eleven registered in the country was grounded, and the Nigerian Federal Ministry of Aviation also announced that it would no longer register aircraft that were more than 22 years old. Operators would have five years to phase them out of service.

Date: 7 May 2002 (*c.* 21:30)
Location: Near Dalian, Liaoning, China
Operator: China Northern Airlines
Aircraft type: Shanghai Aircraft Manufacturing Factory/McDonnell Douglas MD-82 (*B-2138*)

All 112 persons aboard (103 passengers and a crew of nine) were killed when the jetliner, which was operating as Flight 6163, crashed in the Bohai Haixa (channel) some 10 miles (15 km) south-west of Zhoushuizi Airport, serving Dalian, where it had been scheduled to land at the end of a domestic service from Beijing. By the following day, the bodies of more than 60 of the victims had been recovered from the water, and the aircraft's flight data (FDR) and cockpit voice (CVR) recorders were later found.

The MD-82 plummeted into the sea in darkness shortly after the pilot had reported a fire in its cabin, traces of which were found on recovered wreckage. There was also evidence of the use of an accelerant, possibly gasoline. A passenger who had purchased seven insurance policies before boarding the flight was seated in the area where the blaze apparently started, and Chinese authorities suspected sabotage as the cause of the disaster. Neither the weather nor crew error were considered to have been factors in the crash.

Date: 25 May 2002 (*c.* 15:30)
Location: Taiwan Strait
Operator: China Airlines (Taiwan)
Aircraft type: Boeing 747-209B (*B-18255*)

Designated as Flight 611 and bound for Hong Kong, the wide-bodied jetliner broke up at high altitude about 20 minutes after its departure from Chiang Kai-shek International Airport, serving T'ai-pei, then plummeted into the sea some 25 miles (40 km) north-east of Makung, in the (Taiwanese) P'enghu Ch'untou (Pescadores) island group. All 225 persons aboard the aircraft (206 passengers and 19 crew members) were killed. Subsequently, the bodies of 175 victims were recovered, along with approximately 1,500 pieces of wreckage representing some 75 per cent of the aircraft's structure, including all four engines, most of its two wings, the cockpit section and both the flight data (FDR) and cockpit voice (CVR) recorders; some of the debris was found floating on the surface of the water, the rest at a depth of between 150 and 230 ft (50–70 m) in a four-month salvage operation that included trawling and the use of a remotely controlled submersible vehicle.

Based on several factors, among them radar data and wreckage distribution and examination, the Aviation Safety Council (ASC) of Taiwan considered it 'highly likely' that the disaster had resulted from structural failure in the aft lower lobe section of the aircraft's fuselage. The break-up presumably occurred approximately 100 ft (30 m) below and just before *B-18255* had reached its cruising height of 35,000 ft (*c.* 10,700 m), and as it was proceeding on a south-westerly heading at an indicated air speed of around 345 mph (*c.* 555 kmh). Both its FDR and CVR had stopped recording simultaneously, and a sound signature of the last 130 milliseconds of the latter's tape transcript revealed that the initial structural break-up was in the aircraft's pressurised area. The investigation found no evidence of in-flight power plant failure or opening of the cargo door, a hazardous cargo situation, ignition in a fuel tank or any other type of on-board fire or sabotage with an explosive device. Nor were adverse meteorological conditions a factor, with the weather at Makung Airport at the time consisting of broken clouds at 8,000 ft (*c.* 2,500 m), a few of them at 1,800 ft (*c.* 550 m), a visibility of around 5 miles (10 km) and a 16-knot

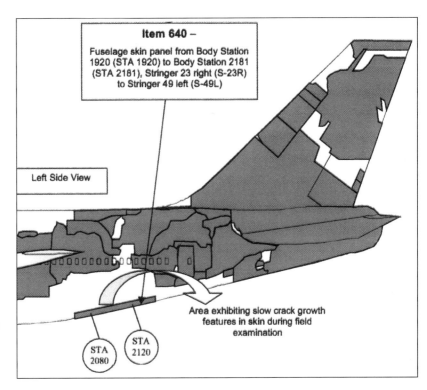

Item 640 –

Fuselage skin panel from Body Station 1920 (STA 1920) to Body Station 2181 (STA 2181), Stringer 23 right (S-23R) to Stringer 49 left (S-49L)

Left Side View

Area exhibiting slow crack growth features in skin during field examination

STA 2080

STA 2120

A diagram of the aft fuselage of the China Airlines Boeing 747, showing the area affected by cracking, which led to the in-flight break-up of the jetliner. *(Taiwanese Aviation Safety Council)*

wind blowing from a north-north-easterly direction; there was no indication of any precipitation in the area of the crash.

Acquired by China Airlines nearly 23 years earlier, *B-18255* had been involved in a tail-strike while landing about six months after its delivery to the carrier. The subsequent repair of the affected area on the underside of its fuselage must not have been in accordance with the Boeing structural repair manual. Specifically, the section of damaged skin was not trimmed, and the repair doubler sheet used did not extend sufficiently beyond the aforementioned area in order to restore structural strength. Evidence of fatigue existing before the accident was found near the edge of the doubler and outside the outer row of the securing rivets. Examination of the wreckage also confirmed multiple-site damage (MSD), consisting of a through-thickness main fatigue crack some 15 in (6 cm) long as well as some small cracks, and the ASC concluded that the large crack and most of the smaller ones had initiated from scratching damage existing on the faying surface of the skin and associated with the 1980 accident. The fatigue crack pattern pointed to an increasing growth rate that propagated inward, which was attributed to the

MSD growing from many origins on the skin surface at the scratch locations. A residual strength analysis indicated that the main crack in combination with the other damage were of sufficient magnitude and distribution to facilitate their local linking, so as to produce a continuous crack about 40 in (100 cm) in length within a two-bay region. The ASC could not determine the amount of time over which the fatigue cracks propagated through the skin thickness, nor the length of the cracking in the 747 before its final flight. However, the extent of hoop-wise fretting marks that were found on the doubler and the regularly spaced marks and deformed metal cladding on the fracture surface suggested that a continuous crack that could have been no less than about 6 ft (2 m) long was present before the in-flight disintegration of the aircraft. The analysis further indicated that during the application of normal operational loads, the residual strength of the fuselage would be compromised with a continuous crack of approximately 5 ft (1.5 m); the one existing in *B-18255* would therefore be large enough to cause the suspected rupture of the fuselage.

As the aircraft approached its cruising altitude, the increasing pressure enabled the pre-existing cracks centred around station 2100, between stringers S-48L and S-49L, to reach the length that reduced the residual strength to its operating limits, resulting in an 'unstable separation' combined with a rapid loss of cabin pressure. Also, the progression of the fracture towards the upper skin severed the power wiring to the FDR and CVR, accounting for their sudden stoppage. Pieces of wreckage that had begun separating on either side of the fuselage must have struck the vertical fin, and once the structural integrity of the remaining portion of it could no longer support the loads, the entire empennage tore away. During the break-up sequence, all of the aircraft's power plants separated from the wings, probably at an altitude of just under 30,000 ft (10,000 m) and apparently almost simultaneously; the forward fuselage section with the wings still attached must have been intact and hit the water in a relatively flat attitude. Papers and light materials from the aft fuselage area were found in central Taiwan, having drifted more than 60 miles (100 km).

Considered as a factor 'related to risk' was the failure of the China Airlines' Engineering and Maintenance Division personnel to detect in B-18255 the ineffective structural repair of the damage suffered in the tail-strike incident and the fatigue cracks that were developing under the doubler. The 747 had been inspected for the first time in conjunction with the Corrosion Prevention and Control Programme (CPCP) in November 1993; however, the second CPCP inspection of the lower lobe fuselage area took place 13 months later than at the required four-year interval. Reduced aircraft utilisation had led to the regular flight hour inspections being postponed, and thus the corresponding CPCP inspections were deferred beyond the required date. Maintenance records showed that as of November 1997, a total of 29 CPCP inspection items had not been accomplished in accordance with the carrier's Aircraft Maintenance Programme and the Boeing 747 Ageing Airplane Corrosion Prevention and Control Programme. The ASC investigative report noted that the examination of photographs taken six months before the disaster, during the carrier's Repair Assessment Programme (RAP) structural patch survey, revealed traces of staining on the aft lower lobe fuselage that were an indication of possible hidden structural damage beneath the doubler. It

was also learned that before the first mid-period visit structural inspection in 1998, the bilge area of B-18255 had not been cleaned, something that should have been done to ensure a closer examination of the area. These failures had led to the aircraft being operated with unresolved safety deficiencies for more than four years.

Whereas China Airlines' oversight and surveillance programmes did not detect the missed inspections, and most of the documents pertaining to the tail-strike occurrence were not even available due to poor record-keeping, the shortcomings of the company's maintenance practices had not been identified in audits conducted by the Civil Aeronautical Administration (CAA) of Taiwan. Nor were there good communications between the airline and the manufacturer concerning the work done on the jetliner. In fact, there were no records showing that the Boeing field service representative had a role in providing advice on the permanent repair of the damage suffered in the 1980 accident. It was further observed in the ASC report that before the manufacturer's RAP, which was introduced to the carrier in 2000, the deter-mination of the implementation of the maximum flight cycles had been based primarily on the testing for fatigue of a production aircraft structure, and did not take into account variations in the standards of repair, maintenance, workmanship and follow-up inspections existing among different air carriers.

Subsequent to the crash of Flight 611, China Airlines grounded the four remaining 747-200 transports in its fleet. It also conducted inspections and re-examined all patch repairs on the rest of its aircraft; changed its record-keeping; revised its 'philosophy' with regard to planned maintenance tasks, including the adoption of a computerised system to store relevant data, and scheduled an early implementation of CPCP tasks on its affected fleet of newer 400-series 747 jetliners. Having previously issued a service bulletin recommending the inspection of aircraft that had undergone similar repairs to B-18255, Boeing announced continuing efforts to improve inspection methods. With regard to the latter issue, the report noted that a high-frequency eddy current inspection would not have detected cracks in a repair doubler, and that a more effective non-destructive method should be developed to improve the detection of hidden structural defects.

Date: 1 July 2002 (23:35)
Location: Near Überlingen, Baden-Württemberg, Germany
First aircraft
Operator: Bashkirian Airlines (Russia)
Type: Tupolev Tu-154M (*RA-85816*)
Second aircraft
Operator: DHL Aviation (Bahrain)
Type: Boeing 757-23APF (*A9C-DHL*)

Introduced in the early 1990s, the traffic alert and collision-avoidance system (TCAS) and its European counterpart, the airborne collision-avoidance system (ACAS), have probably been more important in preventing mid-air crashes involving commercial aircraft than any technological innovation since radar came into use as a tool in air traffic control. But any system designed and utilised by humans is fallible, as was proved by this, the first fatal in-flight collision between two civilian jet transports to occur in the Western world.

Having last stopped at Moscow, *RA-85816* had been on an international charter service originating at Ufa, in the Russian Bashkirian (Bashkortostan) Republic, with an ultimate destination of Barcelona, Spain. It was carrying 69 persons, including a crew

A computer diagram of the collision over Germany between the Bashkirian Airlines Tu-154 and the DHL Boeing 757 cargo transport. *(Federal Bureau of Accident Investigation)*

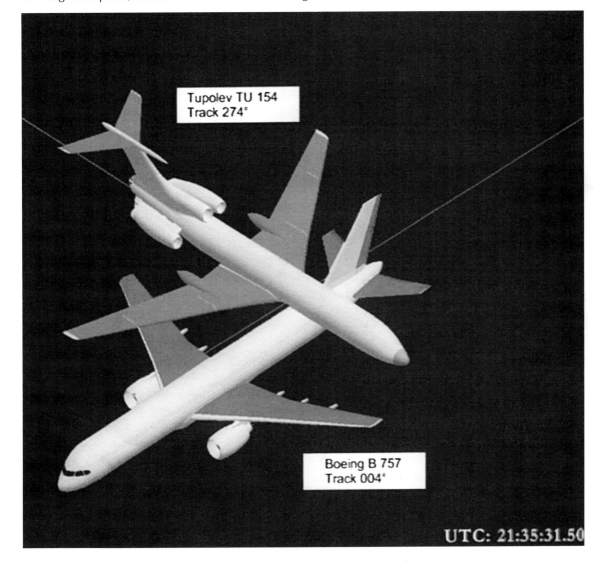

of nine; most of the passengers were children and adolescents on their way to a vacation on the Mediterranean. Designated as Flight 611 and on an international freight service from Bahrain to Brussels, Belgium, *A9C-DHL* had last stopped at Bergamo, Italy. Both aircraft were operating under instrument flight rules (IFR).

Minutes after the two jets came under the jurisdiction of the Zürich air traffic control (ATC) centre, both crews began to receive advisories regarding the opposing aircraft from their respective TCAS units. During this period of time, the Russian transport was also provided with traffic guidance from the Zürich centre. Inexplicably, the two jets collided at a height of just under 35,000 ft (10,700 m) some 70 miles (110 km) south of Frankfurt, and both then crashed. Including the two flight crewmen (and only occupants) of the cargo jet, a total of 71 persons perished in the disaster. There were no casualties on the ground in the impact area of both aircraft, which was in a sparsely populated region north of Bodensee (Lake Constance), located on the German/Swiss border. The accident occurred in darkness, and the collision itself took place above the highest cloud layers, where the visibility was no less than 5 miles (10 km).

Cited by the German Federal Bureau of Accident Investigation (BFU) as the two principal causes of the collision were the failure of the Zürich centre to notice in time the imminent separation infringement of the two transports, in combination with the failure of the Russian crew to follow proper procedures in response to the resolution advisory (RA), or alert, issued by their aircraft's TCAS unit. The first event leading to the accident was the attainment by *A9C-DHL* of flight level (FL) 360, its cruising altitude; although the crew did not report levelling off at that height, there was no requirement to do so. Some 20 seconds later, the crew of *RA-85816* made contact with the centre, also reporting to be at 36,000 ft (*c.* 11,000 m). At that point, the aircraft were some 75 miles (120 km) apart, but the conflict had been set in motion, as both had been cleared for a direct approach to two different very-high-frequency omnidirectional range (VOR) stations at the same flight level, a fact not immediately noticed by the lone ATC controller who at the time would have been responsible for traffic control within the Zürich sector. (This would have involved him covering two adjacent work

stations comprised of two radar monitors and different radio frequencies.) A significant event in the sequence was an advisory from the controller to the Russian crew, reporting traffic at their '2 o'clock position'. This advisory was incorrect, as at the time the 757 would have been to the left of the Tu-154. A subsequent order for *RA-85816* to descend would probably have been more effective had the controller used the word 'immediately', instead of prefacing it with 'expedite'. Also, his comment 'I have crossing traffic' did not emphasise the urgency of the situation. The BFU report noted that under the circumstances, he should have alerted the Russian crew to expedite the descent a minute earlier. The instruction to descend was given when the prescribed separation with the DHL transport could no longer be ensured, and the Bureau considered this to be an immediate causative factor in the disaster.

At the same time as he would have been responsible for monitoring the two aircraft involved in the collision, the controller was concentrating his attention on a third jetliner, an Airbus A320, which was approaching to land at Friedrichshafen, Germany. This involved him moving to another work station, and he also experienced difficulty contacting the Friedrichshafen airport due to a defect in the bypass telephone system occurring during a critical period of around 10 minutes and ending less than 1 minute before the accident. Significantly, the optical portion of the short-term conflict alert (STCA) at the Zürich centre was not available at the time as a safety aid. Although the aural STCA sounded more than 30 seconds before the collision, it went unnoticed. The optical alert would have warned the controller approximately 2½ minutes before the accident, but the system did not automatically indicate that it was not available, and its inoperative status must have been forgotten by the controller. However, it was noted in the investigative report that the loss of this feature should not necessarily have degraded the safety of the system so long as procedural changes had been introduced to compensate for its absence. Also during the night, sectorisation work, or rearrangement of the sectors, was being carried out at the Zürich centre, with the radar system being operated in the 'fall back' mode. Accordingly, the separation minimum had been increased to 8 statute miles (*c.* 13 km), or approximately 2.5 miles (4 km) more than the normal requirement. Once this criterion was infringed, the Tu-154 should have been instructed to descend to flight level 350 in order to ensure a vertical separation of 1,000 ft (c. 300 m). It was observed by the BFU that compliance with this requirement would have prevented the collision.

After sectorisation work began and air traffic volume had decreased, one of the two controllers on duty retired to rest in the lounge. The remaining controller thus had to assume the tasks of two personnel and if necessary the role of the supervisor. One of these individuals, the radar planning controller, would have had the responsibility to compare the flight data on the control strips with the actual position of the aircraft as displayed on the radar monitor. Had this task been properly executed, the controller could have recognised the conflict between the two jets involved in the accident. But since the prepared control strips no longer corresponded to their actual flight paths, the conflict would only have been detectable in conjunction with a radar display. Although the lone controller believed he could handle the conflicting traffic as well as the A320, and for that reason did not ask for assistance from his colleague in the lounge, the BFU expressed the opinion that he was not in a position to assume the additional tasks. Once he realised the problem with the inoperative telephone system, it was too late for him to alert the other controller. (Two assistants were at the disposal of the two regular controllers to provide support with routine coordination duties, but they had no authorisation to assume any air-traffic control functions). The BFU concluded that the staffing level had eroded the defences of the system, particularly during a time of degraded technical capability. It further ruled that the insufficient number of personnel working the nightshift had resulted from a duty schedule that did not ensure a continuous staffing of each work station when one of the two assigned controllers took a prescribed break. This policy, which had been practised unofficially at the Zürich centre for many years and been tolerated by the air navigation service company, did not provide redundancy so that a loss of attention or procedural errors or omissions might not be noticed, leading to hazardous situations. Nor had any compensation been made on the night of the accident for the inoperative status of the STCA through heightened awareness or human back-up. Additionally, controllers in the Zürich centre control room were not provided with clear guidance in the handling of unusual events and system degradations. These deficiencies were considered by the BFU as 'systemic causal factors' in the disaster. The report noted that the Karlsruhe upper area centre radar controller had been alerted by his STCA of the potential conflict between RA-85816 and A9C-DHL, but his attempts to warn the Zürich controller were not successful as a telephone connection could not be established between the two facilities due to the aforementioned breakdown. It was therefore the opinion of the BFU that the Karlsruhe centre controller would not have been able to prevent the collision.

With regard to the actions of the two flight crews, the Bureau concluded that the DHL pilots had reacted correctly to the situation. The aircraft's TCAS initially activated just after the first officer got up to use the lavatory, and while returning to the flight deck he was heard on the cockpit voice recorder (CVR) to say, 'Traffic, right there'. The captain, who was the pilot flying, acknowledged this remark and, having switched off the autopilot, he reduced engine thrust and transitioned from an ascent to a descent within 5 seconds of the advisory, reaching the required rate within an adequate period of time. As the 757 continued down, the crew radioed 'TCAS descent' to the Zürich centre, although the controller apparently did not hear or at least comprehend the message. Two direct orders were then given by the first officer to the pilot-in-command, the last of which was 'descend hard'. A full nose-down control input was applied 2 seconds before the collision.

A review of the CVR recovered from the wreckage of RA-85816 revealed a somewhat different reaction to that aircraft's TCAS on the part of the Russian crew, which was comprised of five members, including a captain under supervision and a second co-pilot who had no flight duties. Approximately 2½ minutes before the accident, the crewmen began a discussion concerning an aircraft approaching from the left, A9C-DHL, which was displayed on their TCAS. Except for the flight engineer, the crew were involved in this discussion. Seven seconds after the TCAS generated a 'traffic, traffic' warning, the Tu-154 was instructed by the

Zürich centre to descend to FL 350. Almost at the same time the crew initiated a descent, the TCAS commanded 'climb, climb', and the message was repeated by the non-active co-pilot. Although the instructor mentioned the fact that the controller was 'guiding us down', the pilot flying initially pulled back on the control wheel, momentarily arresting the descent. Also during this time, engine thrust was twice reduced. The discussion among the crewmen was then interrupted by the controller's instructions to 'expedite' the descent to 35,000 ft. During this transmission, the navigator was heard on the CVR tape to say, 'It is going to pass beneath us'. Ultimately, the descent rate of the Tupolev increased to more than 2,000 ft/min (c. 600 m/min). Meanwhile, the TCAS issued an order to 'increase climb', after which the afore-mentioned co-pilot exclaimed, 'It says climb!' An instant before impact, the control column was abruptly pulled back and the thrust levers were advanced.

At the time they hit, the Tu-154 was banked 10 degrees to the right and proceeding on a near-westerly heading, having turned to the left just before the collision, while the 757 had been level laterally, in a slight nose-down attitude and flying in an almost due-northerly direction. Initial impact was with the vertical tail fin of the latter and the port wing, then the left fuselage section, in the area of the emergency exits, of the former. This resulted in an explosive decompression in the Tu-154, which then broke into several pieces and fell in flames; the 757, which lost most of its stabiliser in the collision, slammed into a forest in a steep nose-down angle and also burned. Based on the angle and velocity of both aircraft, their closure rate was determined to have between approximately 805 and 825 mph (1,295–1,330 kmh). An analysis of the approach showed that at the time the Russian transport was receiving conflicting instructions from the TCAS and the controller, neither crew could have known what avoidance manoeuvre should be taken because the flight path of the opposing aircraft and thus the collision risk could not have been determined visually with sufficient accuracy.

There was no evidence of technical failure in either aircraft's TCAS unit, which in both cases had been integrated into their respective vertical speed indicators. Based on the logic of the system, the one in the Tu-154 had issued instructions to ascend because that transport was initially slightly above

the 757. Although the Russian crew undoubtedly believed that their decision to follow the instructions of the controller was correct, the BFU considered the descent by the Tu-154, which went contrary to the TCAS, as one of the immediate causative factors in the disaster. The Bureau assumed that the Russian crew would have followed the TCAS had the controller not earlier given the instructions to initiate a descent. But the fact that the TCAS avoidance manoeuvre instructions were not discussed by the two pilots of RA-85816 led the BFU to conclude that the decision to descend was never questioned. And although this particular version of the TCAS had the capability of generating a reverse command, it would have done so only under certain circumstances, one of them being that the altitude difference between the conflicting aircraft must have already exceeded 100 ft (c. 30 m) in the direction of the alternate manoeuvre. The report further noted that the incorrect position report concerning the 757 during the controller's second descent order 'temporarily unsettled' the Russian crew.

Identified by the Bureau as one of the principal 'systemic causes' leading to the accident was what it described as the 'insufficient' integration into the civil aviation industry of the ACAS/TCAS II systems. Specifically, the regulations concerning the system published by the International Civil Aviation Organisation (ICAO) and, as a result, the regulations adopted by national aeronautical authorities as well as the operational and procedural instructions of the TCAS manufacturer and of operators were found to be incomplete, somewhat contradictory and not standardised. There were, for example, no clear directives in ICAO documents as to what actions a flight crew should take if there is a contradiction between a controller's instructions and a TCAS RA. However, they did include a clear statement that manoeuvres contrary to an RA are prohibited. On the other hand, the flight operations manual of Bashkirian Airlines stated that ATC guidance was to be the 'main and major condition of collision avoidance', but did not consider the priority of a TCAS RA. The BFU considered this wording as 'not sufficiently unambiguous'. Furthermore, practical TCAS training of the Russian crew would not have been possible because the carrier's flight simulators were not appropriately equipped. This would have been 'disadvantageous' to the crew, according to the Bureau. The report noted that at the time of the

A Turkish Airlines Auro RJ100, identical to the aircraft that crashed during an attempted landing at the airport serving the city of Diyarbakir, in Turkey. *(Douglas Green)*

collision the TCAS system worked only semi-automatically, and that an automatic down-link integrated into the TCAS equipment and conveying RA information issued to respective ATC units had yet to be introduced on a worldwide basis.

Six weeks after the disaster, an industry alert bulletin was issued, emphasising 'immediate and correct' crew response to TCAS advisories, and that a crew should always respond 'in the direction and to the degree' that has been indicated. The bulletin also noted that while pilots should communicate with ATC personnel 'as soon as practicable' after a TCAS RA is issued, a manoeuvre contrary to the advisory that is based solely on ATC instructions should not be attempted. Controllers were also asked not to knowingly issue instructions that are contrary to RA guidance when a TCAS manoeuvre is in progress. In its report, the BFU recommended that the ICAO should change its published guidelines so that pilots are required to obey and follow TCAS resolution advisories regardless of whether they are contrary to ATC instructions. Also recommended were improvements in the Zürich centre, including a requirement that at least two controllers be on active duty at all times, and ACAS training for flight crews of operators based in the Russian Federation.

An additional fatality resulted indirectly from the accident, when, in February 2004, the Swiss controller whose errors contributed to the collision was stabbed to death in his Zurich home. A Russian man whose wife and two children had been aboard the Tu-154 was convicted of the murder in October 2005 and sentenced to eight years' imprisonment.

Date: 8 January 2003 (*c.* 20:20)
Location: Near Bagivar, Diyarbakir, Turkey
Operator: Turk Hava Yollari AO (Turkish Airlines)
Aircraft type: Avro RJ100 (*TC-THG*)

Operating as Flight 634 and on a domestic service from Istanbul, the jetliner crashed while attempting to land at the airport serving the city of Diyarbakir, killing 75 persons aboard, including its entire crew of five. The five surviving passengers were seriously injured.

The accident occurred in darkness as *TC-THG* was on its approach to Runway 34, using very-high-frequency omnidirectional range/distance-measuring equipment (VOR/DME) non-precision instrument procedures. About half an hour earlier, the airport weather was characterised by a broken overcast, with the clouds scattered at 1,000 ft (*c.* 300 m) and a few of them at 400 ft (*c.* 120 m), and the visibility having been reduced by fog in the immediate area of the crash. The wind was calm.

After it hit the ground half a mile (0.8 km) short of the runway, the RJ100 broke apart and burst into flames. Reportedly, the pilots had reached the minimum descent altitude without having established visual contact with the runway.

Date: 6 March 2003 (15:15)
Location: Near Outoul, Tamanrasset, Algeria
Operator: Air Algerie (Algeria)
Aircraft type: Boeing Advanced 737-2T4 (*7T-VEZ*)

Designated as Flight 6289 and on a domestic service with an ultimate destination of Algiers, and a scheduled en route stop at Ghardaia, the jet airliner crashed and burst into flames immediately after its departure from Tamanrasset-Aguenar Airport, serving the provincial capital. All but one of the 103 persons aboard the 737 were killed in the accident, including the six members of its crew. The surviving passenger, who had been seated in the last row of its cabin, was seriously injured.

Lifting off from Runway 02, *7T-VEZ* initially veered to the left, then pitched up, reaching an approximate height of 400 ft (120 m) before it began to descend. Its undercarriage extended, the jet was banked slightly to the right when it slammed to earth some 4 miles (6.5 km) from the take-off point and to the left of the extended centreline of the runway. Around the time of the crash, the airport weather consisted of 6/8 cloud coverage above 20,000 ft (6,000 m), a visibility of around 25 miles (40 km) and no wind.

The underlying factor in the accident was determined to have been the failure of the aircraft's port engine, with the fault originating in the high-pressure (HP) turbine, just aft of the combustion chamber. This rupture also caused damage to the low-pressure turbine. Examination of the power plant revealed cracks on the leading edge of the two blades of the nozzle guide vanes that must have existed before the crash. Partially hidden by coke deposits, these cracks had stemmed from thermal fatigue and were related to what was described as the 'very high' operating time of the HP turbine blades. The malfunction would have resulted in a sharp reduction of thrust, causing the 737 to yaw to the left.

Occurring during a critical phase of flight, i.e. about 5 seconds after rotation, the power plant malfunction led to the crash in conjunction with errors by the flight crew, specifically, their failure to retract the gear, which would have significantly increased drag, and the action of the captain in taking over the controls from the first officer, who had been the pilot flying at the time, before having clearly identified the problem. Apparently significant to the first error, and as indicated by the cockpit voice recorder (CVR), the failure of the turbine occurred almost simultaneously with the request by the co-pilot to retract the gear. Subsequently, the 737 progressively lost speed, then stalled, with the activation of the stick-shaker alert system and the sound of the 'Don't Sink' aural warning being heard on the CVR tape just before impact.

Probable contributing factors were the rapidity of the power plant failure sequence, which gave the pilots little time to react to and recover from the situation; the action of the crew in maintaining the normal rate of climb, which would not have been appropriate under the circumstances; a lack of teamwork between the captain and first officer, and the take-off weight of *7T-VEZ* being close to, though not in excess of, the authorised maximum, especially when considering the elevation of the airport, which was around 4,500 ft (1,400 m), and the prevailing temperature of about 75 degrees Fahrenheit (25 degrees Celsius). Additionally, the CVR revealed what the investigative report described as 'perfunctory' flight preparation by the crew, wherein the pre-start-up and before-take-off checklists were not completed, and emergency procedures not even mentioned. (The initial phase of the flight preparations was accomplished alone by the first officer, with the captain arriving late, and subsequently the latter conversed with the chief steward, who was present in the cockpit throughout the take-off.) As a result of these failings, the pilots would not have been adequately equipped to deal with the situation they encountered. After the engine malfunction, there were no formalised actions by the pilots, leading to the aforementioned omissions pertaining to the aircraft's configuration, velocity and flight path, and no coordination in the handling of the emergency situation, with the captain more than once asking the first officer to 'let go' of the controls and the latter, though apparently following this request, seeming unsure of what role she was supposed to play. Also, the uneven desert terrain around the airport was unsuitable for an emergency landing.

The accident brought to light shortcomings in pilot task-sharing, joint control of an aircraft and handing over the controls from one to another, and one of the recommendations made in the report was that Air Algerie and other airlines ensure that their cockpit resource management training programmes heighten crew awareness effectively in these critical areas.

Date: 8 July 2003 (*c.* 04:15)
Location: Near Port Sudan, Red Sea, Sudan
Operator: Sudan Airways
Aircraft type: Boeing 737-2J8C (*ST-AFK*)

Operating as Flight 319, the jetliner crashed and burned in open terrain some 3 miles (5 km) east of the Port Sudan airport, from where it had taken off shortly before, on a domestic service to Khartoum. All but one passenger among the 117 persons aboard the 737 were killed, including its entire crew of 11. The survivor, a 3-year-old boy, was seriously injured.

The crew had initially reported a power plant malfunction, shutting down the engine and turning back in an attempt to return to the airport. Subsequently, an instrument landing system (ILS) approach to Runway 35 was abandoned due to improper alignment with its centreline, with the pilots increasing power and retracting the aircraft's undercarriage. The accident occurred as *ST-AFK* was positioning for a second approach, and after an apparent loss of control, with its wreckage being strewn over a distance of approximately 600 ft (180 m) and oriented along a south-south-easterly track. It was dark at the time of the crash, being before dawn, with a reported visibility of around 2.5 miles (4 km) in blowing sand.

Date: 25 December 2003 (*c.* 15:00)
Location: Near Cotonou, Atlantique, Benin
Operator: Union des Transports Africains de Guinee SARL (Guinea)
Aircraft type: Boeing Advanced 727-223 (*3X-GDM*)

Commercial aviation's stellar safety record does have some notable weak spots, with the perform-ance of carriers in less developed nations generally lagging behind that of carriers in the Western world. Symbolic of the haphazard practices found far too often among operators based on the African continent was this disastrous and totally preventable accident involving an overloaded aircraft.

Flight 141 had originated at Conakry, Guinea, with an ultimate destination of Dubai, United Arab Emirates, and three scheduled en route stops, the first of these at Cotonou. As it was taking off from Cotonou/Cadjehoun International Airport, the jet airliner struck the instrument landing system (ILS) localiser facility building immediately after becoming airborne, then crashed on a beach along the Gulf of Guinea and broke apart, coming to rest in the Atlantic Ocean some 500 ft (150 m) offshore. A total of 141 persons lost their lives in the disaster, including the co-pilot of the 727 and four other members of its crew of 10; three of those killed could not be positively identified as having been aboard the aircraft, and although they were probably passengers, they could have been on the ground. Among the 22 survivors of the accident, all of whom suffered injuries, were the four others on the flight deck, including two representatives of the carrier; the occupant of the small building was also injured.

The boarding of passengers on to *3X-GDM* and the loading of their baggage had been accomplished without adequate supervision and 'with great confusion', according to the Bureau Enquetes Accidents (BEA) of France, which conducted the technical investigation of the crash and released the final report. Whereas some of the passengers had checked in at the terminal counter, at least 10 others boarded the 727 directly from an incoming flight. Boarding passes had no seat assignments, and some of those arriving at the last minute may have purchased their passes from other passengers. Due to insufficient documentation, the exact number of passengers could not be established, but upon completion of the boarding process, every seat was occupied, plus there were six infants being carried in the laps of adult passengers. Although the airline normally allowed 165 lb (75 kg) per adult in determining passenger weight, there was no evidence that this had been done before the departure of *3X-GDM*. Also, the travelling-bags of those boarding had not been weighed, despite reports of a large amount of personal luggage, and the front cargo hold of the 727 was reportedly fully loaded. The weight of the aircraft was estimated to have been approximately 190,000 lb (86 MT). Lacking precise information, the crew must have realised that the jet was very heavy. Additionally, it was probably in an excessively 'nose heavy'

The cockpit section of the Union des Transports Africains de Guinee Boeing 727 was recovered after the Christmas Day 2003 crash in Benin, on the Atlantic coast of the African continent. *(AP Images)*

condition. As a further indication of the disorder experienced by Flight 141, some of the passengers were still standing as the 727 began to taxi, sitting down only after being asked to do so by cabin attendants.

In view of the situation, the crew elected to employ a 'full power/on brakes' departure procedure, throttling up the engines while holding back the aircraft, using thrust instead of speed to gain acceleration. A flap setting of 25 degrees was selected before *3X-GDM* began its take-off on Runway 24. About 45 seconds into the ground run, the captain announced almost simultaneously 'V1, VR', which corresponded to the respective decision and rotation velocities. He then stated 'Rotate, rotate'. It was only then that the weight and balance factors that had not been properly calculated became fully realised by the crew. The first officer, who was actually flying the 727, apparently did not get the normal aircraft reaction upon initiation of the rotation manoeuvre, and after a hesitation, pulled back a second time on the control wheel, with the wheels of the transport lifting off some 7,000 ft (2,000 m) from the point of brake release, at 170 mph (c. 270 kmh). It was then that the captain was heard on the cockpit voice recorder (CVR) tape to exclaim, 'Pull! Pull! Pull!' With the end of the pavement rapidly approaching, the take-off at that point could not be abandoned, but once airborne, *3X-GDM* climbed at too shallow an angle

to avoid hitting, with its extended main undercarriage, the localiser structure, which was just under 10 ft (3 m) high and located approximately 400 ft (120 m) beyond the end of the runway. The jet then smashed through a concrete airport boundary fence before its crash on the beach. There was no fire. The survivors were seated in the front and rear sections of its cabin, near where the aircraft's fuselage had ruptured. The local meteorological conditions were described as 'dry and stable', with scattered to broken stratocumulus clouds, the lowest at 1,500 ft (c. 500 m), high cirrus, a visibility of more than 5 miles (c. 10 km) and a 6-knot wind blowing from the south. One possibly significant weather factor affecting aircraft performance was the high air temperature of around 90 degrees Fahrenheit (32 degrees Celsius).

In its report, the BEA observed that the safety of the flight would ultimately have been the responsibility of the captain. In this case, the pilot-in-command elected to proceed with the take-off in the excessively loaded transport, and the crew essentially ignored its centre of gravity, with these factors relating directly in their inability to execute a successful climb-out. However, the agency further noted that there had been 'commercial and operational' pressures to complete the flight, and that this was a 'stressful' situation for the crew, who did not have much experience with the airline. (An analysis by Boeing in fact revealed that under the circumstances the jet could have safely taken off through an immediate and vigorous pull-back of the control wheel, although the manufacturer recommended against commencing a flight that violated safety margins.) Considered as 'structural' causative factors in the disaster were what the report referred to as a 'grave insufficience' in the areas of competence, organisation, documentation and adherence to regulations on the part of the carrier and its subcontractors, combined with improper oversight by the regulatory authorities of the nation of registry. One obvious shortcoming identified in the investigation pertained to the carrier's flight manual, which was incomplete, had not been adapted to the Boeing 727, and made no reference to the loading of an aircraft or to weight and balance factors. Among the possible contributing factors cited were the relative shortness of the runway at Cotonou and the need for, and the pressures associated with, the maintaining of an air link between West Africa and the Middle East. Although it was not a factor in the crash, the report noted that the cabin crew members had exceeded their flight time limits.

Among the recommendations of the BEA were for Guinea and other nations to immediately implement regulations to ensure adherence by the airline industry to proper procedures, and also develop means of examining the safety practices of individual operators.

Date: 3 January 2004 (04:45)
Location: Near Sharm el Sheikh, Janub Sina, Egypt
Operator: Flash Airlines (Egypt)
Aircraft type: Boeing 737-3Q8 (*SU-ZCF*)

The jetliner crashed in the Red Sea off the southern tip of the Sinai Peninsula and approximately 5 miles (10 km) south-west of Sharm el Sheikh International Airport, from where it had taken off some 3 minutes earlier, on a charter service to Paris, France, with a planned en route stop at Cairo, Egypt. All 148 persons aboard perished, the victims including six off-duty crew members, four regular cabin attendants and an observer accompanying the two pilots on the flight deck; except for two of them, the passengers were French tourists. The depth of the water in the area, which was about 3,000 ft (1,000 m), precluded the recovery of significant human remains, but with the aid of remotely controlled submersible vehicle

operations, both the flight data (FDR) and cockpit voice (CVR) recorders were retrieved, as was some of the aircraft's wreckage, including portions of its control surfaces and of its elevator control system.

Lifting off from Runway 22R, *SU-ZCF* began a climbing left turn, and after levelling off briefly, it rolled into a right bank. During this time, the aircraft's autopilot was momentarily engaged, then disconnected. The 737 reached a maximum height of just under 5,500 ft (1,700 m) before it started to descend. Simultaneously, its right banking angle continued to increase, reaching an attitude well beyond 90 degrees. As transcribed by the CVR, the first officer on several occasions in the final minute of the flight was heard to say 'Overbank', while the captain once called out 'Autopilot'. However, there was no evidence of autopilot re-engagement. The FDR indicated a reduction of power in both engines to idle thrust, and also of the continued recovery from the steep right bank and nose-down attitude seconds before the jetliner slammed into the water at an indicated air speed of around 480 mph (770 kmh). At the moment of impact, the right-banking and nose-down attitudes of the aircraft were both approximately 25 degrees. The accident occurred in pre-dawn darkness, with no moon, and in good weather, with the ceiling and visibility unlimited and no adverse wind or other atmospheric conditions reported.

Although no specific technical or human factors were identified in the investigation, a combination thereof was considered possible as the cause of the disaster.

Date: 3 February 2005 (*c.* 15:15)
Location: Near Sarowbi, Kabul, Afghanistan
Operator: Kam Air (Kyrgyzstan)
Aircraft type: Boeing Advanced 737-242 (*EX-037*)

Operating as Flight 904 and on an internal Afghanistani service from Herat to the city of Kabul, the jet airliner crashed in mountainous terrain some 20 miles (30 km) east-south-east of its destination. All 104 persons aboard (98 passengers and six crew members) were killed in the accident.

The aircraft had been scheduled to land at Kabul International Airport before radio and radar contact with it were lost. Before the crash, no technical failures or any other concerns had been reported by the crew. The wreckage of *EX-037* was located two days later, at an approximate elevation of 11,000 ft (3,400 m) and only about 50 ft (15 m) from the top of a ridge, with the 737 having struck the mountain while proceeding on an easterly heading. Conditions of extremely low visibility had been reported at the time in the area surrounding the airport, with falling snow. Although the aircraft's flight data recorder (FDR) was recovered, it yielded no useful information.

Date: 14 August 2005 (*c.* 12:00)
Location: Near Avlida, Attiki, Greece
Operator: Helios Airways (Cyprus)
Aircraft type: Boeing 737-31S (*5B-DBY*)

Occasionally, aircraft disasters have causes so implausible that it becomes difficult to understand how they ever occurred. Such was the case of Flight 522, which had been on an international service originating at Larnaca, Cyprus, with an ultimate destination of Prague, Czechoslovakia, and a scheduled en route stop at Athens, Greece.

Shortly after it had taken off from Larnaca airport, and at a height of 14,000 ft (*c.* 4,300 m), the cabin oxygen masks automatically deployed and a master caution light illuminated in the cockpit. Subsequently, radio contact with *5B-DBY* was lost. The pilots of two Greek Air Force F-16 jet fighters scrambled to investigate reported the first officer of the transport was slumped over the controls, while the captain could not be seen and two unidentified individuals were in its flight deck. About half an hour later, the jetliner crashed and burned some 20 miles (30 km) north of Athens. All 121 persons aboard (115 passengers and a crew of six) perished.

The previous night, the 737 had undergone maintenance, but after completion of the testing, the pressurisation mode selector (PMS) was reportedly left in the 'manual' position, rather than in the 'auto' mode. As a result, the crew would have to manually open or close the outflow valves, but in this case, the pilots apparently failed to notice the status of the PMS in their pre-departure checks.

After the initial cabin pressure problem, the crew received an avionics bay temperature alarm, which was apparently attributed to a loss of cooling in the compartment. During radio communications with a company engineer, the German captain and Cypriot first officer were informed that the alarm could be turned off by pulling the circuit breaker located in the cabinet to the rear of the cockpit. The captain was apparently doing this when both he and the co-pilot were affected by hypoxia as the aircraft continued to climb to its cruising height. Incredibly, as neither of them seemed to realise that the problems they were experiencing were related to a loss of cabin pressure, neither pilot had donned their emergency oxygen masks.

In accordance with the programming of its autopilot, *5B-DBY* levelled off at 34,000 ft (*c.* 10,400 m) until it eventually ran out of fuel, resulting in double engine failure and an uncontrolled descent into the hilly terrain.

Date: 16 August 2005 (*c.* 03:00)
Location: Near Machiques, Zulia, Venezuela
Operator: West Caribbean Airways (Colombia)
Aircraft type: McDonnell Douglas MD-82 (*HK-4374X*)

The jetliner crashed and burned in a cattle-ranching area approximately 70 miles (110 km) south-west of Maracaibo. All 160 persons aboard perished in the accident, including its crew of eight; the passengers were all tourists from the West Indian island of Martinique.

Having taken off earlier from Panama, *HK-4374X* was on a non-scheduled international service to Martinique. Based on information obtained from its flight data (FDR) and cockpit voice (CVR) recorders, the MD-82 had been cruising at 33,000 ft (*c.* 10,050 m) when the flight crew began to express concern about the weather, including possible icing. The pilots also discussed turning on the aircraft's power plant and airfoil anti-ice systems. Shortly thereafter, the crew requested and were granted authorisation to descend to flight level 310. Seconds after the autopilot was disengaged and the jetliner began its descent, the CVR transcribed an audio warning similar to an altitude alert, followed by a sound similar to a stick-shaker stall indication and then an aural stall alert. These warnings continued until the end of the recording. During this time, the crew requested lower altitudes, the last of which was 14,000 ft (*c.* 4,300 m), and about 1 minute after what was believed to have been the start of the activation of the stick-shaker, reported a double engine flame-out.

Approximately 3 minutes after the audio warning was first heard, the jetliner hit the ground in a nose-up and slight right-wing-down attitude, its horizontal stabiliser in the full nose-up position at the time of impact. The crash had occurred in pre-dawn darkness.

Date: 5 September 2005 (*c*. 10:00)
Location: Near Medan, Sumatera Utara, Indonesia
Operator: Mandala Airlines (Indonesia)
Aircraft type: Boeing Advanced 737-230 (*PK-RIM*)

Designated as Flight 91 and on a domestic service to Jakarta, the jetliner crashed and burst into flames in an urban residential area immediately after its departure from Polonia International Airport, serving Medan. The disaster claimed the lives of 101 persons aboard the aircraft, including its entire crew of five, plus 44 others on the ground. The 16 passengers who survived with various injuries had been seated in the rear of the cabin. At least 20 houses were destroyed.

The 737 had lifted off from Runway 05/23 before it slammed into a street, the accident occurring in good meteorological conditions, with scattered clouds at 1,500 ft (*c*. 500 m) and at 5,000 ft (*c*. 1,500 m), and a 6-knot wind from a south-south-easterly direction.

Date: 22 October 2005 (*c*. 20:40)
Location: Near Lissa, Ogun, Nigeria
Operator: Bellview Airlines (Nigeria)
Aircraft type: Boeing Advanced 737-2L9 (*5N-BFN*)

Operating as Flight 210 and on a domestic service to the capital city of Abuja, the jetliner plunged to earth some 20 miles (30 km) north of Lagos. All 117 persons aboard the aircraft (111 passengers and a crew of six) perished.

The accident occurred less than 5 minutes after *5N-BFN* had taken off from Mohammed Murtala International Airport, serving Lagos. It was dark at the time, and the airport weather consisted of scattered to broken clouds, with some thunderstorm activity reported in the area. A crater in the marshy terrain marked the scene of impact; however, there was no post-crash fire.

Date: 10 December 2005 (*c*. 14:10)
Location: Near Port Harcourt, Rivers, Nigeria
Operator: Sosoliso Airlines (Nigeria)
Aircraft type: McDonnell Douglas DC-9 Series 32 (*5N-BFD*)

All but one of the 109 persons aboard lost their lives when the jetliner crashed at the Port Harcourt airport. Those killed included the aircraft's entire crew of seven; most of the passengers were school children returning home for the holidays.

Designated as Flight 1145 and on a domestic service from the Nigerian capital of Aruja, *5N-BFD* was initially cleared to land on Runway 21. Subsequently, the DC-9 slammed to the ground, broke in two and burst into flames, skidding off the runway before coming to rest. There was thunderstorm activity in the area at the time, with broken clouds at 1,300 ft (400 m), and a visibility of 5 miles (10 km). The wind was blowing from a direction of 220 degrees at 9 knots.

A preliminary investigation indicated that the aircraft had encountered a wind shear condition, which could have resulted in a loss of control or sudden descent.

Date: 3 May 2006 (*c*. 02:15)
Location: Near Adler, Russian Federation, Commonwealth of Independent States
Operator: Armavia (Armenia)
Aircraft type: Airbus Industrie A320-211 (*EK-32009*)

Operating as Flight 967 and on an international service from Yerevan, Armenia, the jet airliner plunged into the Black Sea approximately 4 miles (6.5 km) south-west of the Adler airport, which also serves Sochi and where it was scheduled to land. All 113 persons aboard (105 passengers and a crew of eight) perished. Both the flight data (FDR) and cockpit voice (CVR) recorders were recovered from a depth of around 1,500 ft (500 m), as was some wreckage and victims' remains.

The aircraft was instructed to abandon an approach to Runway 06, and it then began a right-hand climbing turn before it crashed while flying away from the airport. It was dark at the time of the accident, and the weather consisted of a low overcast, with a visibility of 2½ miles (4 km) in light rain and thunderstorm activity in the area.

GLOSSARY

AIRMET – General weather advisory to pilots.

Airway – Designated air route, usually defined by ground-based navigational aids.

Angle of attack – The angle between the centre of a wing and the direction of the relative wind.

Attitude director indicator (ADI) – Three-dimensional cockpit display that provides the pilot with a reference to the horizon.

Automatic Direction Finder (ADF) – Basic navigational instrument, used in conjunction with a ground-based radio beacon.

Back course – Course flown along an ILS beam in the reverse direction of the signal.

Circuit – Landing pattern of an airport, consisting of a downwind leg, which is parallel but in the opposite direction to the landing runway; base leg, which is at right-angles to the runway; and final approach leg.

Clean configuration – Denotes the retracted position of an aircraft's undercarriage and lifting surfaces.

Climb gradient – Vertical height gained in relationship to the distance travelled horizontally.

Cockpit voice recorder (CVR) – Tape recording device that transcribes comments and audible actions of the flight crew.

Combustion chamber – Area in a gas turbine engine in which the combustion of fuel takes place.

Combustor can – Tube in a gas turbine engine used for the mixing of fuel and air.

Decision height – Specified altitude at which the crew must decide either to continue or abandon a landing approach.

Decision speed – Velocity at which the crew must decide to continue or abandon a take-off.

Density altitude – Density or lifting ability of the air, which declines with increasing altitude and/or temperature.

Design manoeuvring speed (Va) – The maximum velocity that an aircraft structure can safely sustain loads while manoeuvring in the air.

Distance-measuring equipment (DME) – Airborne radar system used in conjunction with a ground-based facility to determine an aircraft's position along a given route.

Droops – High-lift devices that are hinged to the leading edge of an aircraft's wings.

'Dutch roll' – Lateral oscillation of an aircraft involving both a rolling and yawing action.

Echo – Image of an aircraft or other airborne object appearing on a radarscope.

Empennage – Tail section of an aircraft, including both the horizontal and vertical stabiliser assemblies.

Engine number – Position of a power plant on an aircraft, from left to right when looking forward.

Feather – Adjustment of an aircraft's propeller so as to reduce drag following the stoppage of an engine.

Fix – Geographical position determined by one or more ground navigational aids.

Flight – An aircraft on a scheduled service.

Flight data recorder (FDR) – Device that transcribes the vital flight performance information of an aircraft. A digital flight data recorder (DFDR) is a refined version with greater recording capability.

Flight director – Instrument providing the pilot with pitch, roll and associated flight information.

Flight level – Above-sea-level height of an aircraft, expressed in hundreds of feet.

Flight profile – Vertical path of an aircraft in relationship to the ground track.

General aviation – All civil air traffic operations except scheduled and non-scheduled air carriers; includes private and corporate flying, air-taxi services and commuter airlines.

Glide path – Vertical track of an aircraft during its landing approach.

Ground-controlled approach (GCA) – Ground-based radar system by which the controller provides the pilot with vertical and horizontal guidance during landing.

Ground effect – Cushion of air providing lift to an aircraft flying at a very low altitude.

Holding pattern – 'Racetrack' pattern in which an aircraft can circle to await landing clearance.

Inertial navigation system (INS) – Sophisticated navigational equipment capable of pinpointing an aircraft's position without reliance upon ground-based radio aids.

International Civil Aviation Organisation (ICAO) – Worldwide association based in Montreal, Canada, established to promote aviation safety through dissemination of accident reports and other information.

Instrument flight rules (IFR) – Guidelines used during a flight along an airway or specific route, usually while in radio contact with an air traffic control facility.

Instrument landing system (ILS) – Standard landing aid comprising a glide slope beam for vertical and a localiser beam for lateral guidance.

Manufacturing station – A particular location, either along the fuselage or the wings, on an aircraft.

Marker beacon – Electronic navigational aid designed to provide position information along a specific course.

Missed approach – Abandonment of a landing approach, also termed overshoot. A 'go-around' is another attempt to land following such a manoeuvre.

Moment – The turning of an object, including an entire aircraft, about an axis.

Navigational aid, or navaid – A ground-based electronic device, including NDB and VOR.

Non-directional beacon (NDB) – Basic ground-based radio facility, normally used in conjunction with airborne ADF.

Non-precision approach – Landing without use of ILS.

Octa – Unit of measurement of cloud coverage expressed in eighths, often preceding the type of cloud.

Outflow valve – A regulating valve through which air is allowed to vent from an aircraft into the atmosphere.

Phugoid motion – Pitch oscillation of an aircraft.

Pilot flying – The crew member actually handling or flying the aircraft.

Pitch trim compensator (PTC) – Mechanism designed to correct automatically an aircraft's pitch attitude at higher air speeds.

Pod – Aerodynamic structure containing an aircraft's power plant.

Positive control – Operation of an aircraft in a radar environment, with identification and tracking by an air traffic control facility.

Radio range – Early navigational aid, consisting of a transmitter broadcasting continuous coded signals to identify a specific airway.

Rotation – Raising of an aircraft's nose gear off the ground during take-off.

Rotor disc – Disc-shaped structure that holds the compressor or turbine rotor blades in an engine.

Runway number – Figure at the start of a runway that denotes its compass heading when multiplied by 10.

Runway visual range (RVR) – Horizontal distance visible when looking down a runway centreline.

SIGMET – Weather advisory to pilots concerning significant, specifically hazardous, meteorological conditions.

Slat – Movable portion of the leading edge providing additional lift to an aircraft's wings.

Spar – Internal structure providing strength to a wing or control surface.

Spoiler – Hinged surface on the upper side of a wing designed to reduce lift.

Squawk – Manipulation of a transponder to assist in identifying an aircraft.

Stall – Breakdown in the airflow around an airfoil, leading to a loss of lift. Deep stall is a condition caused by the loss of effectiveness of an aircraft's horizontal stabiliser resulting from an extreme nose-high attitude.

Sterile cockpit – Rule wherein pilots are to maintain strict concentration on the operation of the aircraft and adherence to prescribed procedures.

Stick-shaker – Mechanism designed to literally shake the control stick or wheel to warn of an impending stall.

Stringer – The manufactured member of the fuselage, wings or tail surface that gives shape to the airframe and supports the outer skin.

Tactical air navigation (TACAN) – Ground-based navigational aid providing bearing and distance information to an aircraft relative to a facility.

Target – Radar echo of an aircraft or airborne object.

Transponder – Transmitter designed to increase the intensity of an aircraft's echo on radar. An encoding transponder has the capability of providing additional information, such as altitude and aircraft identification.

Trim tab – Small hinged section located on the trailing edge designed to hold a control surface, such as an aileron or elevator, in a desired position.

Turbine disc – The centre portion of a turbine power plant on which the individual blades are mounted. A turbine stator is a 'ring' of fixed blades.

Undercarriage – Wheels or supporting gear of an aircraft used for take-off, landing or taxiing on the ground.

Vector – Issuance of heading instructions to an aircraft by an air traffic controller.

Very-high-frequency omnidirectional range (VOR) – Facility emitting radio beams, known as radials, in specific directions to provide navigational guidance to aircraft.

Visual approach slope indicator (VASI) –Airport lighting system designed to provide visual guidance to a landing aircraft.

Visual aural range – Obsolete navigational system in which the airway is identified by both instrument indications and coded radio signals.

Visual flight rules (VFR) – Guidance of an aircraft by the pilot involving traffic separation by sight, usually independent of an air traffic control facility.

Wide-bodied aircraft – A large transport with a double-aisle seating arrangement in the passenger cabin.

Windmilling – Turning of a propeller that is not under power by the force of the rushing air.

Wind shear – Currents representing a significant change, in terms of direction or speed, from the general airflow. A 'microburst' is a particular type of wind shear consisting of a comparatively small but powerful downward gust that flows outward in all directions upon reaching the ground.

Yaw damper – A mechanism designed to sense the onset of and automatically adjust an aircraft rudder in response to a yaw.

Yoke – The control wheel or handle used by the pilot.

INDEX

AIRCRAFT TYPE

INDEX BY TYPE OF INCIDENT

Controlled-flight-into-terrain, cruise phase